*EARLY EDUCATION
OF AT-RISK AND
HANDICAPPED
INFANTS,
TODDLERS, AND
PRESCHOOL CHILDREN*

Scott, Foresman Series in Special Education
Series Editor: Richard Morris, University of Arizona

EARLY EDUCATION OF AT-RISK AND HANDICAPPED INFANTS, TODDLERS, AND PRESCHOOL CHILDREN

DIANE D. BRICKER
University of Oregon

Scott, Foresman and Company   Glenview, Illinois London, England

To my parents.

Library of Congress Cataloging-in-Publication Data
Bricker, Diane D.
  Early education of at-risk and handicapped infants, toddlers, and preschool children.
    (Scott, Foresman series in special education)
    Includes bibliographies and indexes.
    1. Handicapped children—Education (Preschool)—United States. 2. Handicapped children—United States—Testing. 3. Home and school—United States. I. Title. II. Series.
LC4031.B695   1986   371.9   86-3872
ISBN 0-673-18007-7

Copyright © 1986 Scott, Foresman and Company.
All Rights Reserved.
Printed in the United States of America.

1 2 3 4 5 6—KPF—91 90 89 88 87 86

PREFACE

This book is intended as a textbook for early childhood/special education (ECH/SE) courses. It offers students a contemporary view of the field with concrete intervention strategies. Practicing professionals who are currently delivering services to populations of at-risk or handicapped infants and children will also find the book useful. It will assist them in keeping abreast of new information and practice.

Part One of the book presents the theoretical foundations needed to understand Part Two, which treats program development and implementation. A comprehensive overview of the field of ECH/SE, with factual information as well as speculative, is presented. The reader will discover that the speculative far outweighs the factual. Nonetheless, ample information exists to allow the field to support "best practice," with the clear understanding that best practice may be replaced by more effective approaches and content. Such an understanding will enable students, trainees, and field personnel to evaluate outmoded practices and replace them with more effective ideas and approaches.

Early Education of At-Risk and Handicapped Infants, Toddlers, and Preschool Children demonstrates how theory can and, indeed, must serve as the foundation for the development and implementation of early-intervention practice. The book's presentation of an integrated approach to theory and practice is designed to offer several distinct pedagogic advantages. First, the reader can in a single volume study both the conceptual framework and the how-to materials and thus determine the relationship between the two. Second, the integrated approach, by showing how principles underlie procedure, enhances our understanding of how to replace or alter ineffective procedure. Third, the book's explanation of how to apply theory helps the interventionist translate a theoretical position into daily programming activities. Finally, there is no danger in the reader being offered only one of many possible approaches for delivering services because the book presents theory and practice in a manner that allows for their incorporation into a number of intervention formats.

The growing field of ECH/SE demands programs and professionals that reflect and deliver relevant content and procedures. The purpose of this book is to provide students and professionals with a resource that will help them meet these demands.

Acknowledgments This book reflects the synthesis of many years of involvement in early childhood/special education. The book is based on written and spoken interactions with colleagues and parents and observations of children in a variety of intervention programs, experiences that have directed my thinking. The flaws in the book come from my limitations in learning all that I should have from these experiences.

More recently, a number of individuals have been of considerable help in the development of this book. E. J. Bailey, Susan Janko, Kris Slentz, and Sarah Gumerlock have been enthusiastic supporters of this project and have provided helpful editorial suggestions. I wish to thank Sarah Gumerlock especially for her valuable assistance in the preparation of Chapter 15. Karen Reed has done an outstanding job of assisting in the preparation of the manuscript. I am grateful to all these individuals for their time, effort, and support.

CONTENTS

Part One: Theory and Foundation

Chapter 1
Overview of the Book *2*

Chapter 2
Early Experience *16*

Chapter 3
History and Rationale for Early-Intervention Programs *34*

Chapter 4
The Impact of Early-Intervention Programs on Children and Families *62*

Chapter 5
Legal and Legislative Decisions *103*

Chapter 6
Population Description *127*

Chapter 7
Parents and Families *155*

Chapter 8
Approaches to Intervention and Common Elements *186*

Part Two: Practical Application

Chapter 9
Program Overview and Operation *206*

Chapter 10
Deployment and Training of Program Personnel and Family Members *228*

Chapter 11
Program Preliminaries: Intake Procedures and Development of Individual Education Plan and Family Program Agreement *249*

Chapter 12
The Intervention Process *273*

Chapter 13
Curricular Approaches and Content *297*

Chapter 14
Environmental Engineering *315*

Chapter 15
A Linked Assessment-Intervention-Evaluation Approach *335*

Chapter 16
Major Themes and Future Directions *368*

Appendix A   Approximate Age Range for Selected Developmental Skills   379

Appendix B   Early-Intervention Programs   389

Appendix C   Intake Forms   402

Appendix D   Family Impact Measures   413

Name Index   *425*

Subject Index   *430*

*EARLY EDUCATION
OF AT-RISK AND
HANDICAPPED
INFANTS,
TODDLERS, AND
PRESCHOOL CHILDREN*

PART ONE

THEORY AND FOUNDATION

CHAPTER 1

OVERVIEW OF THE BOOK

THE NEED

I am often alarmed at the apparent lack of understanding by the layman and the professional community about intervention efforts with the at-risk and handicapped infant and young child. This statement is not meant to be critical, but rather it is meant to underline the need for analysis and reanalysis of the field of early childhood/special education (ECH/SE). My observations of programs and of comments by those who operate these programs, those who are consumers, and those who support these programs through their tax dollars lead me to believe that the ECH/SE enterprise is poorly understood, both as a science and as a therapeutic venture.

To the observer, whether legislator, community agency personnel, or interested citizen, early-intervention programs for at-risk and handicapped infants and preschool-age children seem to be thought of as exceptional caregiving facilities. The enrolled children and their families are obviously valued, and the program personnel are dedicated to assisting the participating children and families in a number of areas. Staff members of these programs are often referred to as "angels of mercy." Rarely does one hear comments that suggest the observer appreciates the rigor and structure that is necessary for an effective program. Perhaps the comments are not forthcoming because, in fact, the rigor and structure are not present. If the profession of ECH/SE is to be viewed by the outside world as a sound educational enterprise based on objective findings, then we must begin to demonstrate, through our actions and words, that such an evaluation is warranted.

Much of the current appeal of ECH/SE, at least to the outside observer, appears to be our concern for young children and their families. It may be fair to say that informed citizens, allied health professionals, and others associated with the development of social policy see our efforts as mainly in the category of *cannot hurt and might help;* other people are indiscriminately supportive of all ECH/SE efforts whether valid or not. That is, how can providing services for at-risk and handicapped children be bad? All too often we, as professionals in the field, do not make effective moves to counter such opinions whether internally or externally held. If the ECH/SE enterprise expects to become respected as a sound educational and scientifically rigorous undertaking, then a first step is for the ECH/SE professional to adopt a position that will lead to the systematic development of effective procedures and content based on sound theoretical premises. We cannot hope to change and shape outside opinion if we do not have our own house in order.

We face a challenging decision. We can pursue the path of many ventures that are a part of public education in which the administrative and teaching staffs have side-stepped their responsibility to America's children and fostered mediocrity rather than excellence. The alternative is to accept that responsibility and move forward in the development of effective early-intervention programs for at-risk and handicapped infants and children. The field of ECH/SE is new and thus not yet laden with tradition and folklore. This reality provides us with an exceptional opportunity to build a field that responds to fact, not fancy; sound theory, not whimsey; and structure, not fad. We have the excitement and the opportunity, and now we must continue to garner the necessary financial and personnel resources to develop a field that does, indeed, maximize the growth and learning potential of at-risk and handicapped children.

PERSPECTIVES

Before we proceed into the "meat" of the book this initial chapter will highlight the predominate perspectives that are the hallmark of this approach and that reflect, as well, many of the major perspectives of the field.

Developmental Perspective

All but perhaps the most radical positions accept the perspective that learning for most children follows developmental guidelines or at least logical progressions that move the child to increasingly complex response repertoires. That is, infants learn to roll over before they can sit up, sit up before they stand, stand before they walk, and walk before they run or climb stairs. Development can be visualized as an inverse pyramid with the basic building blocks acquired by the infant being gradually differentiated into increasingly more and higher-level responses.

Figure 1–1 presents an example of the potential sequence of development for early communication taken from norms found in the literature. As illustrated in Figure 1–1, infants are first able to produce sounds that indicate

Overview of the Book

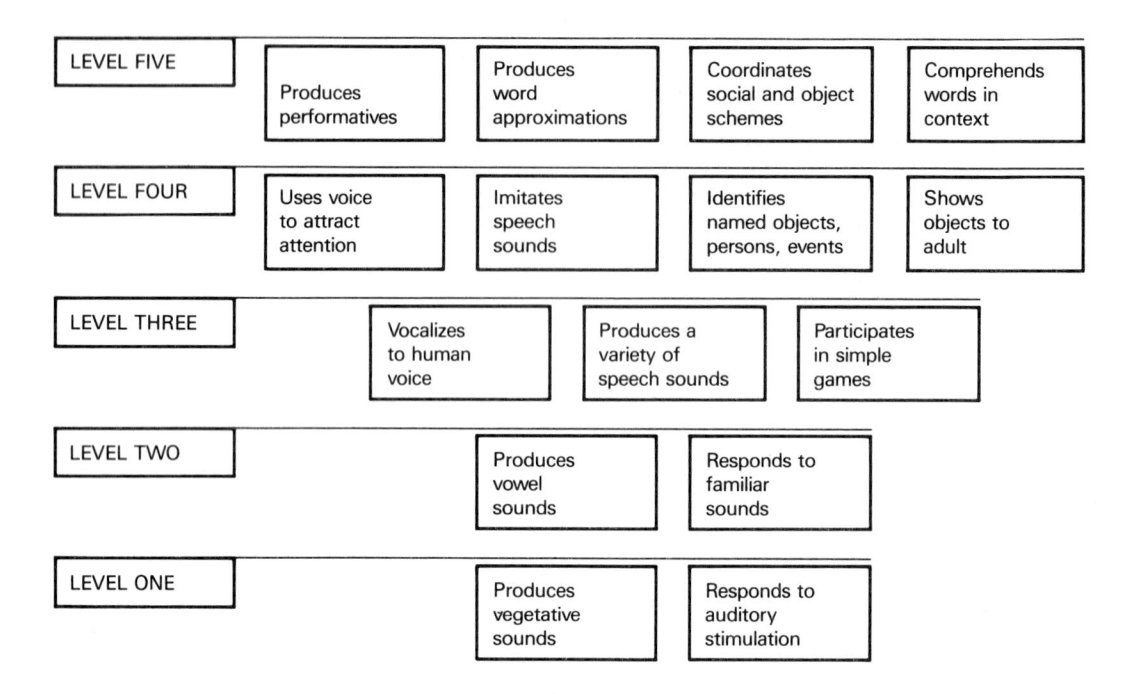

LEVEL FIVE	Produces performatives	Produces word approximations	Coordinates social and object schemes	Comprehends words in context
LEVEL FOUR	Uses voice to attract attention	Imitates speech sounds	Identifies named objects, persons, events	Shows objects to adult
LEVEL THREE	Vocalizes to human voice	Produces a variety of speech sounds	Participates in simple games	
LEVEL TWO		Produces vowel sounds	Responds to familiar sounds	
LEVEL ONE		Produces vegetative sounds	Responds to auditory stimulation	

FIGURE 1-1. *Developmental hierarchy for language.*

pleasure or discomfort. At this level, infants can also respond to environmentally produced sounds; however, responses may vary from increasing activity to becoming still and attempting to locate the sound source. Entry into the second level is indexed by the production of vowel sounds and ability to respond to familiar sounds by infants. At the next level, infants can vocalize to the human voice, produce a variety of speech sounds, and play simple games (e.g., peek-a-boo) with caregivers. By the next level, infants have learned to use their voice to attract attention; imitate a variety of sounds; correctly identify familiar objects, people, and events when named; and use objects to attract caregivers' attention. These responses, in turn, evolve into the production and comprehension of words and familiar phrases.

The model presented in Figure 1-1 probably does not accurately reflect developmental change in children. Rather, as Kagan, Kearsley, and Zelazo (1978) point out, a better analogy is to view early development as a canvas upon which certain impressions are made. As the artist works on the canvas, these initial strokes are blended into increasingly more complex images that often do not reflect any vestiges of the initial form. The building-block model presented in Figure 1-1 should be viewed likewise in that early response forms are blended and modified into behaviors that may not reflect their origin. Even with this caveat, a variety of criticism has been directed toward the use of the developmental model.

Perspectives

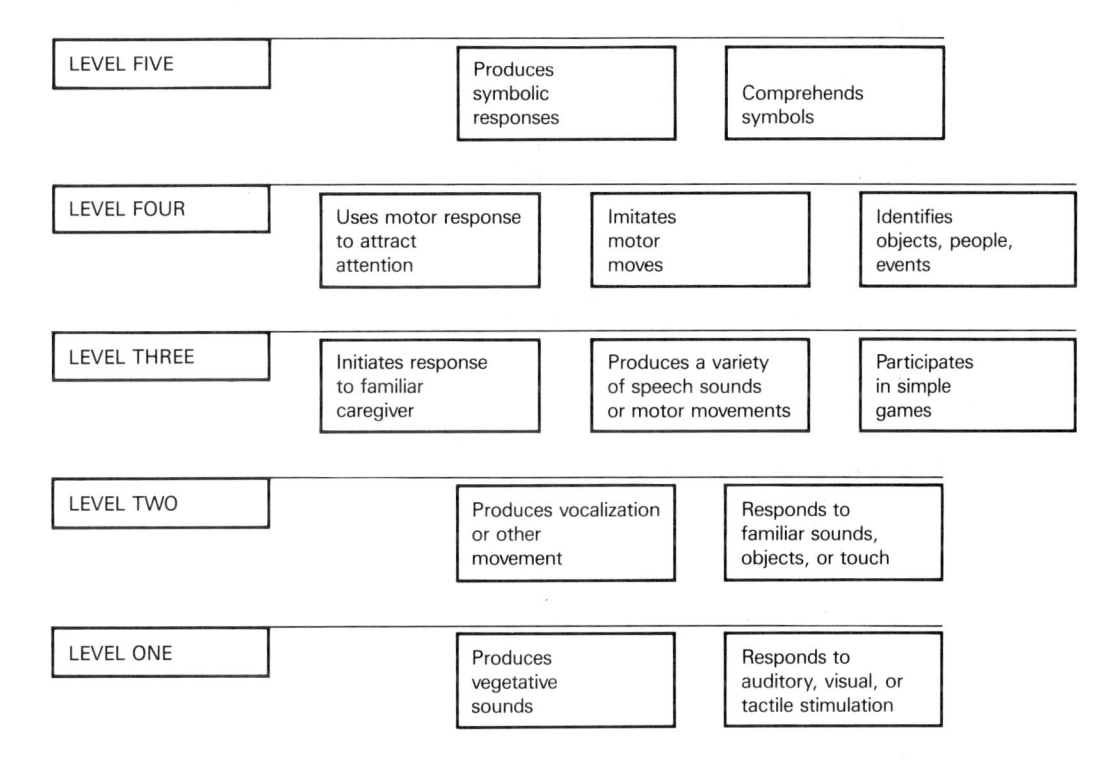

LEVEL FIVE		Produces symbolic responses	Comprehends symbols
LEVEL FOUR	Uses motor response to attract attention	Imitates motor moves	Identifies objects, people, events
LEVEL THREE	Initiates response to familiar caregiver	Produces a variety of speech sounds or motor movements	Participates in simple games
LEVEL TWO		Produces vocalization or other movement	Responds to familiar sounds, objects, or touch
LEVEL ONE		Produces vegetative sounds	Responds to auditory, visual, or tactile stimulation

FIGURE 1-2. Generic developmental hierarchy for language development.

Many critics will be quick to indicate that although an outlined sequence, such as the one in Figure 1-1, is appropriate for nonhandicapped children, rarely do such hierarchies reflect the sequence of development seen in disabled populations—particularly those with motor and/or sensory impairments. Some authorities suggest that the presence of specific pathologies may impact emergent response forms in ways that produce significant deviations in the developmental path followed by an infant or child. The validity of this criticism depends upon the specificity with which one defines the hierarchical sequences. If at each level the development of specific responses is indicated, then such criticism is valid. If, however, the response classes in Figure 1-1 are rewritten to be more generic, as shown in Figure 1-2, then the developmental hierarchies would seem appropriate for most handicapped infants or children. These hierarchies, although general, can still provide a useful set of guidelines for the interventionist.

Critics of using a developmental perspective with handicapped infants and children also question whether using developmental hierarchies leads to the most efficient training sequence. Indeed, the question is asked, in particular for more severely disabled children, whether sufficient time is available to move a child systematically through so many levels of learning or instruction.

There are a few studies that indirectly address this issue. In general, these studies involved teaching the subjects word-object associations and then examined the generalization of the training (see, e.g., Bricker & Bricker, 1970). If training was successful, and it was not always, then the generalization of the responses was usually disappointing. That is, the children learned to use the label only under specific conditions and did not use the acquired words in a communicative sense (e.g., to make wants known).

Although these investigations were not designed to yield causal data, one tenable hypothesis is that to develop labeling skills without the necessary communicative underpinnings will result in the child learning a rote response elicited only under specific training conditions. Time spent in assisting handicapped children in acquiring skills thought to be prerequisite for communication may eventually produce children with more elaborate and useful language behavior.

A final word in defense of using developmental hierarchies with disabled populations is concerned with the rigidity with which such models of development are followed. Looking at a road map to find a route from city A to city B (given each is of adequate size) generally reveals the availability of several different routes between the two destinations. One route may be more direct and thus the one most commonly followed between the two cities. However, for a variety of reasons, people may choose to substitute one of the less traveled routes. Using a set of developmental hierarchies should be viewed in a like manner. That is, most children follow the specified route, but that does not mean that the interventionist cannot or should not consider variations when a child has a disability that appears to preclude moving along the common route. The developmental model is useful only when viewed and applied with a fundamental understanding of individual differences. Its value comes from providing a general overview of how development proceeds in important behavioral domains. That value can be neutralized unless the interventionist acknowledges the need for individual tailoring of instruction that is often necessary when dealing with at-risk and handicapped infants and young children.

Transactional Perspective

The transactional perspective that underlies the approach to ECH/SE described in this book is based on the important chapter published in 1975 by Sameroff and Chandler. In that chapter, Sameroff and Chandler's review of pertinent literature leads to the inescapable conclusion that the outcome for infants and children is directly dependent upon their organismic integrity and the quality of their caregiving environment. These authors propose viewing the infant along two continua of risk: one called *reproductive risk* and one called *caregiver risk*. The continuum of reproductive risk refers to the genetic and biological constitution of the infant. Infants with Down syndrome have a genetic condition that renders their development at serious risk. So, too, infants who suffer severe asphyxia at birth are at considerable risk for the development of serious problems. The continuum of caregiver risk refers to the social and physical environment experienced by infants. If the environment is appropriate, the chances of infants prospering are increased, while caregiving environments that are abusive or neglectful of infants increase the chances that infants will not develop without problem.

Thus, where these two continua of risk bisect for each infant determines the quality of life that can be expected. In a general sense, the more biologically competent the infant, the more the infant can compensate for the effects of a poor caregiving environment. The child that survives an abusive home and becomes an outstanding student at Harvard most likely had the biological competence to compensate for a poor caregiving environment. The brother or sister of this individual may have been born several weeks premature and thus developed associated problems that precluded offsetting the negative impact of an inadequate caregiving environment; thus, this individual may spend time in special education classes and never become fully self-sufficient. There are infants and children with biological insults so great that no amount of appropriate environmental caregiving can completely compensate. Effective environmental stimulation may reduce the impact of the disability; but for the moderately to severely handicapped individual, the effects of major biological insults, such as cerebral palsy, hydrocephalus, or Down syndrome, cannot be completely erased. On the other hand, even the most biologically competent child may suffer from the effects of particularly abusive homes, if only in the sense that whatever potential the child had will never be fully realized.

The transactional perspective just described is focused on the on-going exchanges between the continua of reproductive and caregiving risk. An equally important aspect of the transactional model to be considered by ECH/SE personnel is the daily transactions that occur between infants or children and their environments. These transactions form the substance of the educational intervention provided to the at-risk and handicapped child. Understanding this perspective and incorporating it into the interventionist's philosophical approach to intervention are essential.

Several years ago, the predominant theoretical position on the environment-child interaction was unidirectional—that is, investigators primarily examined the effect the environment had on the infant or young child and not the children's effect on their environment (Bell, 1974). For example, in a series of influential investigations (e.g., Bowlby, 1973; Dennis, 1963), findings suggested the depressive effects of institutional environments on young children. This research was unidimensional because the focus was on the effects of inconsistent caregiving or mothering on the young child. These studies did not examine the impact of the child on the environment.

In the 1960s, another group of investigators began examining the social environment's impact on the infant. For example, Rheingold, Gerwirtz, and Ross (1959) found that responses like vocalization were affected by social consequences provided by caregivers. Although such investigations demonstrated that environmental manipulations could control affective forms of behavior, the focus remained unilateral because the investigators examined only the effect of the caregiver's behavior on the infant's behavior.

In spite of Piagetian theory, the interactionist model did not come into vogue until the early 1970s. During this period, many investigators (see, e.g., Lewis & Rosenblum, 1974) began considering the child-caregiver relationship as one in which both participants affected the behavior of the other. Reciprocal exchanges governed by each participant's response became the focus of attention and study. Patterns of social interaction governed by the partner's response to each other formed a circular feedback system, which initially was pictured as a rather simplistic system. Lewis and Lee-Painter (1974) have discussed the problems associated with the position that child-caregiver interactions form a simple interactive network, and these investigators have offered a more complex model in which both the child and caregiver are actively involved and "significantly influence each other."

The daily transactions that occur between the at-risk and handicapped infant and young child and the caregiver serve as the basic unit in the kind of educational intervention that is the focus of the approach described in this volume. The reciprocal exchanges between the child and environment serve as the foundation of the intervention strategy. The intervention procedures and content are formulated around the basic unit of the reciprocal interaction between the child and the environment; therefore, inherent in the approach is concern not only for the child's behavioral repertoire but also for how that repertoire impacts the environment over time. Adopting such an approach requires attention both to the reciprocal exchanges between the caregivers and the child and to the larger social context in which the child and caregiver reside. In effect, one is required to examine the transactions that occur between the child-caregiver, caregiver-family, and family-community.

Family Systems Perspective

Although caregivers and families will be discussed in detail in Chapter 7, it seems important to provide the reader with the basic philosophy toward families adopted in this book. To be effective in intervention efforts with infants and young children, ECH/SE personnel must begin to formulate their input on the basis of the larger social context in which the family resides. Sameroff (1982) and Schell (1981) have articulated the need to take into account the resources, stresses, values, and desires of family members before developing elaborate intervention plans that the family finds unsuit-

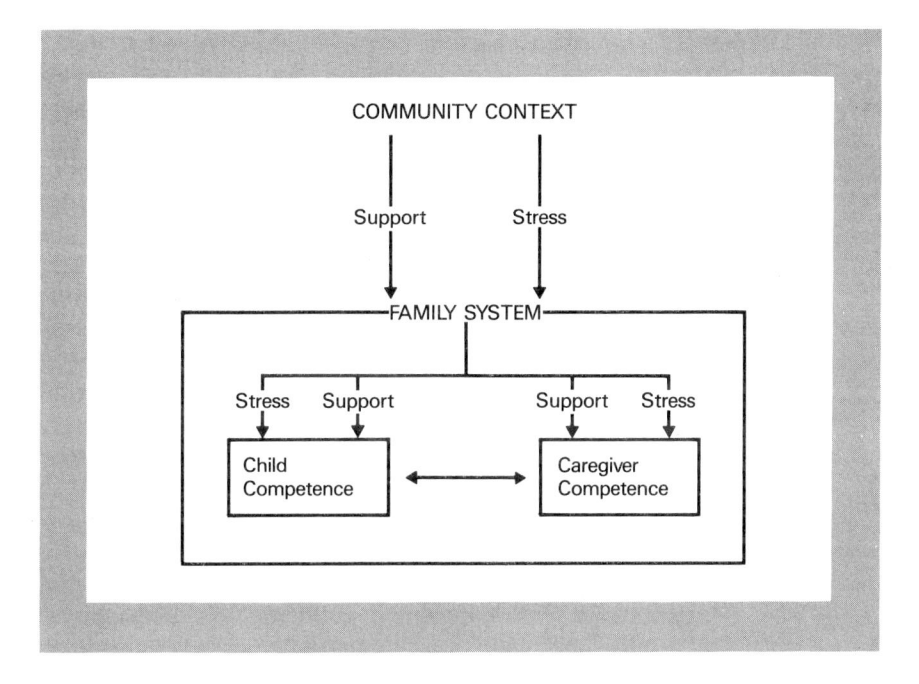

FIGURE 1-3. Transactional model in environmental context.

able or even distasteful. In a review chapter, Parke and Tinsley (1982) have assembled evidence that strongly suggests intervention efforts with at-risk and handicapped infants are significantly enhanced when the primary caregiver (generally the mother) receives adequate support from her spouse and when both parents, in turn, receive adequate community support, whether from the extended family members, organizations (e.g., church), or friends.

Thus, it seems imperative that the transactions that occur between the caregiver/interventionist and the infant/child should be, in turn, placed in the larger social context of the family. The approach described in this book reflects this position, and thus, the interactional model presented in Figure 1-3 has been expanded to include this perspective. Figure 1-3 presents a view of the transactional exchanges between the child and caregiver embedded in the family's larger social context.

Educational Perspective

Another important perspective underlying the approach presented in this book is its educational orientation. The approach is designed to permit the interventionist to focus on arranging environmental contingencies to produce change in the infant or child. The key concept is taking action to produce change in the child and family. This perspective requires that education be defined in its broadest sense and does not refer exclusively to programming of skills more traditionally thought of as educational (e.g., reading and writing). Rather, in the present approach, education refers to any skill or behavior that can be acquired through some form of environmental manipulation.

The previous definition of education provides the interventionist with a broad array of domains to consider as potential intervention targets. Working in tandem with an orthopedist and physical therapist to assist a child in learning to properly use a prosthetic device would be considered an educational goal. So, too, assisting a mother in acquiring more effective intervention strategies would be considered within the purview of education. Even assisting the family in acquiring social services that might indirectly impact on the care of the handicapped child would be considered educational and thus an appropriate target within the present approach.

During the past few years, there has been a major reinterpretation of the importance of play for the young child (see Chance, 1979), and a number of investigators have suggested the importance of play for the handicapped child as well (McHale & Olley, 1982). Thus, the area of play that may have been previously thought of as recreation for young children is coming to be viewed as activity essential to their growth and development. This reevaluation of the merits of play suggests that these activities be considered within the educational enterprise as well. Consequently, the approach here considers acquiring skills such as manipulation of toys, interactional skills with peers, imitation, and imaginary play behaviors to be important to the development of the young child whether handicapped or not and thus legitimate training targets.

The only areas not dealt with directly in this approach would be techniques that attempt to alter the basic anatomy of the child, for example, surgery to repair a structural deficit. However, even in cases in which medical intervention is required, it may be necessary to work on some corollary behavior that is considered educational. The child with hydrocephalus may require the surgical implant of a shunt to drain off excess spinal fluid; but if that child has suffered some neurological damage associated with the hydrocephalus, then some form of educational intervention may be required to assist the child in functioning as normally as possible.

The point to be emphasized is that the approach described is comprehensive and is focused on educational endeavors. The term *educational* is defined in its broadest sense to include any intervention efforts in which change can be produced by the systematic arrangement of environmental contingencies.

From Research to Application

This book has been written primarily for ECH/SE personnel in training or currently delivering services to at-risk and handicapped children; thus, a section on research issues might seem somewhat off target. However, I do not share this position and feel strongly that interventionists, program developers, therapists, and any others associated with delivering quality services to young children and their families should be concerned with information developed by the research community and how to apply such information, when appropriate, to service delivery.

Many researchers and practitioners assume that information flows unilaterally from the laboratory to field application for the enhancement of general knowledge or for the implementation of specific rehabilitative procedures for the benefit of specific populations. Some writers have questioned whether the unilateral flow from researcher to practitioner produces the greatest positive clinical change. In fact, several writers have emphasized that the practitioner need not play the role of an empty vessel waiting to be filled with selected information provided by the research community (Butterfield, 1978). Rather, the interventionist or educator should actively seek and apply a variety of therapies and procedures as they appear useful and relevant to the problems at hand—even if such procedures lack a strong empirical or scientific base. The generation of ideas, information, and strategies that may enhance the quality of life for individuals and groups comes from both the practitioner and the researcher.

Communication is a second source of difficulty leading to the long-standing gap between knowledge and practice. Researchers and practitioners, with rare exceptions, form camps within which inhabitants talk and write predominately for each other. As Baumeister (1981) commented, communication among colleagues tends to be horizontal rather than vertical. Rather than crossing borders into the other camp, conversations tend to occur among individuals with similar thoughts and modes of operation.

Although it is probably safe to surmise that barriers to the flow of information and communication have hindered the research-practice exchange, the literature does contain examples of productive reciprocity between researcher and practitioner. For example, Tyler and Kogan (1977) conducted an investigation in which eighteen preschool cerebral palsied children were used and the focus was on providing the participating mothers with a special training program to enhance mother-child interactions. The content of the training program was derived from previous clinical observations of increasing negative behavior by the child and decreasing positive interactions between mother and child over time. By implementing an intervention program under controlled conditions, these investigators were able to produce a positive impact on behaviors that have clinical importance to young cerebral palsied children and their mothers. Conversely, procedures developed under controlled conditions have found relevant and useful clinical application. For example, Eilers, Wilson, and Moore (1977) developed a procedure to examine speech discrimination in infants. This operant procedure, termed *visually reinforced infant speech discrimination* (VRISD), has subsequently been adopted for hearing evaluations of young children in clinical settings (Northern & Downs, 1978). Work underway in the area of infant perception has evolved into a potentially useful strategy for assessing the intellectual capacity of handicapped infants (Fagan & Shepherd, 1982). The early work was conducted to study the ability of infants to discriminate and remember visually presented information. Fagan and his colleagues have reported that using laboratory-developed visual discrimination procedures has produced better predictive validity concerning developmental outcomes for infants than have standardized intelligence tests. If such work is replicated, clinicians and interventionists will have an added valuable assessment tool.

A third major barrier to effective transactions between the research and practitioner communities is the lack of articulate and credible individuals to function as translators of research and clinical findings. Most professionals working in the area of early childhood consider themselves to be either researchers or practitioners and not both. The research community is interested in the controlled and systematic manipulation of selected variables, while the practitioner community is interested in producing verifiable change in their target population. Neither group accepts as a primary role the description of research outcomes to the applied community or the description of practical problems to the research community.

Even if people were available to discuss research findings and barriers to clinical practice, few mechanisms exist to facilitate the systematic movement of useful research outcomes into the practitioner's realm or the reverse. The advent of journals such as *Topics in Early Childhood Special Education* and the *Journal of the Division of Early Childhood* has been helpful in addressing this problem because they do provide vehicles for establishing a researcher-practitioner dialogue. The availability of these journals and conferences specifically focused on early childhood special education helps considerably in bridging the research-to-practice chasm; however, the literature on child development, intervention, and relevant environmental factors remains vast and scattered (Hayden, 1978), requiring considerable effort by researcher and practitioner alike to maintain currency with the array of information that may be potentially relevant and useful to their respective activities.

The perspective of this book is that, first, interventionists are capable of digesting and understanding information generated by the research community. Second, that interventionists are interested in any information, whatever the source, that will enhance intervention efforts with at-risk and handicapped infants and children. Third, that interventionists recognize that one way to increase the effectiveness of the field is to apply state-of-the-art knowledge and then collect systematic information on the effectiveness of the approach or content with specified populations of infants and children. We can do no less if we are to become a respected profession built on fact, not fancy.

Given this perspective, this book has blended relevant research outcomes into a comprehensive and cohesive intervention approach for at-risk and handicapped infants and young children. An attempt has been made to present the major theoretical underpinnings that direct our current intervention efforts and to use those conceptual underpinnings as the basis for formulating the practical knowledge contained in this book.

SUMMARY

Historically, in education there has been a schism between theory and application and between research and practice. Over the years, these areas have at times moved into proximity then synchrony; but as often there have been periods when research/theory and practice/application appear to be on disparate courses. I believe we are currently moving into an era when a variety of professionals see value in drawing together theory, research, and application. However, collaborative efforts between theoreticians and practitioners face significant barriers because of the different philosophical orientations and different goals of these professionals and the different demands they face. These differences produce at the very least uneasiness and, more likely, hostility. Few of us feel comfortable in ranging between the two camps. Nonetheless, it is time to develop or enhance the rapprochement between theory and practice. That is the goal of this text.

The first part of this book addresses two critical areas: (1) selected major theoretical issues facing early interventionists and (2) selected research findings on general efficacy and more specific intervention parameters. Part 2 discusses the application of the theory and research presented in Part 1. There is nothing to preclude the reader from reading one part without the other or reading selected chapters; however, the book has been constructed to present a unified approach.

Some readers may be expecting that this volume will present and contrast the major approaches to early intervention. They will be disappointed. Rather, this book presents a description of one general approach that is comprehensive. An attempt has been made to present the approach in a balanced manner, but no attempt has been made to describe the many competing and complementary procedures or content currently available.

The history of the early-intervention enterprise has been short and eventful. The future appears full of opportunity to advance our knowledge and practice.

References

Baumeister, A. (1981). Mental retardation policy and research: The unfulfilled promise. *American Journal of Mental Deficiency, 85,* 449–456.

Bell, R. (1974). Contributions of human infants to caregiving and social interaction. In M. Lewis & L. Rosenblum (Eds.), *The effect of the infant on its caregiver.* New York: Wiley & Sons.

Bowlby, J. (1973). *Attachment and loss: Separation, anxiety, and anger.* New York: Basic Books.

Bricker, D., Seibert, J., & Casuso, V. (1980). Early intervention. In J. Hogg & P. Mittler (Eds.), *Advances in mental handicap research.* London: Wiley & Sons.

Bricker, W., & Bricker, D. (1970). Development of receptive vocabulary in severely retarded children. *American Journal of Mental Deficiency, 74,* 599–607.

Butterfield, E. (1978). Behavioral assessment of infants: From research to practice. In F. Minifie & L. Lloyd (Eds.), *Communicative and cognitive abilities: Early behavioral assessment.* Baltimore, MD: University Park Press.

Chance, P. (1979). *Learning through play.* New York: Gardner Press.

Dennis, W. (1963). Environmental influences upon motor development. In W. Dennis (Ed.), *Readings in child psychology* (2nd ed.). Englewood Cliffs, NJ: Prentice-Hall.

Eilers, R., Wilson, W., & Moore, J. (1977). Developmental changes in speech discrimination in infants. *Journal of Speech and Hearing Research, 20,* 766–780.

Fagan, J., & Shepherd, P. (1982). Theoretical issues in the early development of visual perception. In M. Lewis & L. Taft (Eds.), *Developmental disabilities: Theory, assessment, and intervention.* New York: Spectrum.

Filler, J. (1983). Service models for handicapped infants. In G. Garwood & R. Fewell (Eds.), *Educating handicapped infants.* Rockville, MD: Aspen Publications.

Fischer, K. (1980). A theory of cognitive development: The control and construction of hierarchies of skills. *Psychological Review, 87,* 477–531.

Fischer, K., & Corrigan, R. (1981). A skill approach to language development. In R. Stark (Ed.), *Language behavior in infancy and early childhood.* New York: Elsevier.

Garwood, G. (1983). The role of theory in studying infant behavior. In G. Garwood (Ed.), *Educating handicapped infants.* Rockville, MD: Aspen Press.

Hayden, A. (1978). The implications of infant intervention research. *Allied Health and Behavioral Sciences, 1,* 583–599.

Kagan, J., Kearsley, R., & Zelazo, P. (1978). *Infancy: Its place in human development.* Cambridge, MA: Harvard University Press.

Kopp, C. (1982). The role of theoretical frameworks in the study of at-risk and handicapped young children. In D. Bricker (Ed.), *Handicapped and at-risk infants: From research to application.* Baltimore, MD: University Park Press.

References

Lewis, M., & Lee-Painter, S. (1974). An interactional approach to the mother-infant dyad. In M. Lewis & L. Rosenblum (Eds.), *The effect of the infant on its caregiver.* New York: Wiley & Sons.

Lewis, M., & Rosenblum, L. (Eds.) (1974). *The effects of the infant on its caregiver.* New York: Wiley & Sons.

McHale, S., & Olley, G. (1982). Using play to facilitate the social development of handicapped children. *Topics in Early Childhood Special Education, 2,* 76–86.

Northern, J., & Downs, M. (1978). *Hearing in children.* Baltimore, MD: Williams & Wilkins.

Parke, R., & Tinsley, B. (1982). The early environment of the at-risk infant. In D. Bricker (Ed.), *Intervention with at-risk and handicapped infants: From research to application.* Baltimore, MD: University Park Press.

Rheingold, H., Gerwirtz, J., & Ross, H. (1959). Social conditioning of vocalizations in the infant. *Journal of Comparative Physiological Psychology, 52,* 68–73.

Sameroff, A. (1982). The environmental context of developmental disabilities. In D. Bricker (Ed.), *Intervention with at-risk and handicapped infants: From research to application.* Baltimore, MD: University Park Press.

Sameroff, A., & Chandler, M. (1975). Reproductive risk and the continuum of caretaking casualty. In F. Horowitz, M. Hetherington, S. Scarr-Salapatek, & G. Siegel (Eds.), *Review of child development research* (Vol. 4). Chicago: University of Chicago Press.

Schell, G. (1981). The young handicapped child: A family perspective. *Topics in Early Childhood Special Education, 1,* 21–27.

Tyler, N., & Kogan, K. (1977). Reduction of stress between mothers and their handicapped children. *The American Journal of Occupational Therapy, 31,* 151–155.

CHAPTER 2

EARLY EXPERIENCE

Before discussing the approach to early intervention proffered in this book, it will be useful to discuss in some detail the essential philosophical premises on which the early-intervention enterprise has been built. Too often those of us working in this area take for granted the importance of early experience for the developing child. We often suggest that if the infant or young child gets off to the right start, future success is assured. The discussion that follows calls into question that assumption and offers a more comprehensive and perhaps thoughtful perspective on early experience.

Early intervention with infants and children who are either at-risk or handicapped as a result of medical or environmental factors has become big business in the twentieth century. Considerable resources have been captured and deployed to support a variety of programs to enhance the growth and development of infants and children suffering from biological or environmental conditions that predispose them to contemporary or future problems. What have been the evolutionary paths which have moved our thinking from a philosophy of predeterminism and a belief in the constancy of the IQ from the early years throughout the life span to the general acknowledgment of the importance of early experience and the plasticity of the infant and young child?

Early intervention is predicated on the belief that early experience is instrumental in the child's future development. Even theorists who do not view development as a continuous process admit that "There is no question that early experience seriously affects kittens, monkeys, and children" (Kagan & Klein, 1973, p. 960). The importance of early experience for the infant and child seems to be based on a widely held premise: Early experience is essential to later development because continuity exists between early behavior and subsequent behavior. It is "as the

16

twig is bent so grows the tree" philosophy. Prior to exploring the historical roots of the importance of early experience, a discussion of the concept of continuity will be useful.

CONTINUITY

As Anne Pick notes:

> We assume and believe that there is continuity of development, but, as both Horowitz and Scott document, our present measures provide meager evidence for our assumptions. Nevertheless, a belief in continuity is the basis for attempting to carry out early assessment for problem remediation and prevention in the first place. (Pick, 1978, p. 107)

As indicated in the quote, the notion of continuity is fundamental to prevention and early-intervention. Continuity suggests some basic consistency to intellectual and personality variables in the development of the child into an adult. The infant who begins as a placid, easygoing baby is thought to develop most likely into a relaxed adult. It is not uncommon to hear an individual's parents comment, "John has been that way since he was a baby." So, too, we tend to believe, given a normal environment, that the bright, active toddler will grow into a capable, productive adult. Most people seem to hold the belief that there is a strong relationship between personality and intellectual functioning of the child and the type of adult the child becomes. How often when an adult performs some particularly outstanding or unpleasant event (e.g., appears to murder without provocation) do we look for the roots of such behavior in the person's early experiences? In fact, Freud's theory of the cause of the adult's maladaptive behavior can be traced to some early traumatic event that the child/adult has repressed. Through psychoanalysis this event is brought into the person's consciousness to be confronted and thus eliminated or put into perspective (Freud, 1978).

The belief in continuity—that is, behavioral repertoires evolve in consistent ways set by the early experiences of the child—underlies the early-intervention effort. If infants and young children who are handicapped or at-risk for developing a problem can be set on a positive developmental path, then the outcome for the child should be enhanced. However, if deviations from normal patterns go unchecked or become too pronounced, then subsequent outcomes are more likely to be negative (e.g., the child remains or becomes maladaptive). Keeping the concept of continuity in mind will help the reader understand the historical basis for the contemporary view of the impact of early experience. The final section of this chapter presents a reinterpretation of early experience.

HISTORICAL PERSPECTIVE

Ramey and Baker-Ward (1982) have indicated that since World War II the belief in the primacy of early experience has been the pervasive model for viewing and interpreting normal and atypical development. These investigators argue that until recently the early experience model has colored and influenced both "educational practices and social policy" to the exclusion of most other paradigms. How did this occur? To understand, let us look first at the development of the concept of predeterminism.

The concept of predeterminism is based on the belief that development is genetically determined. Developmental outcomes and rate are seen to be exclusively controlled by maturation. This position became popular in the 1900s and, according to Hunt (1961), had its modern roots in the Darwinian theory of natural selection. An early advocate of predeterminism was Francis Galton, whose writing argues that physical traits and mental abilities are largely inherited. In an edited volume on the topic of individual differences (Jenkins & Peterson, 1961), Galton's article entitled "Classification of Men According to Their Natural Gifts" argued that men come with mental abilities that are normally distributed and that are relatively resistant to training. Some men are born with great gifts, while others, who Galton labeled as "idiots and imbeciles," have little ability (1961). This view was consonant with the notion of the constancy of the IQ held by a number of influential educators and psychologists at the turn of the century (Hunt, 1961).

A corollary of the position of the heritability of mental abilities is that the environment has little impact on the developing child. Those who believed in predeterminism argued that the infant came genetically well-equipped or poorly equipped, and thus the environment could do little to counter or enhance the youngster's developmental outcome. Interestingly, investigators supporting the predeterminism position during this early period failed to recognize, or perhaps refused to acknowledge, that those children that tended to perform well came from adequate homes while those children who did poorly tended to reside in circumstances of poverty. The view that environmental stimulation produces minimal change provided little hope that intervention during the early years could affect the ultimate path of the child:

> There is a definite limit to the muscular powers of every man, which he cannot by any education or exertion overpass. This is precisely analogous to the experience that every student has had of the working of his mental powers. (Galton, 1961, p. 2)

Thus, no reason existed for providing early schooling (for that matter any schooling) to the intellectually or otherwise handicapped person. Rather, the most appropriate solution was to remove these individuals from society and provide them with custodial care (Wolfensberger, 1969).

Given the apparent strength of the predeterminism position, what factors were responsible for the shift from the position that the primary determiner of the individual is the genetic contribution to a belief in the primacy of the environment? In approximately four decades we have witnessed a dramatic change in the view of environmental influences and the primacy of early experience.

THE PENDULUM SWINGS: MORE CONTEMPORARY VIEWS

A number of factors appear to be responsible for the shifting view of the importance of environmental impact on a child's welfare and the primacy of early experience. These factors include: (1) environmental influences; (2) psychoanalytical influences; (3) animal research on the impact of early experience; and (4) reanalysis of environmental impact on humans.

Environmental Influences

The philosophy of John Locke is frequently cited as antithetical to the position of predeterminism. Locke believed that all men were free to set their own developmental paths and destinies (Kagan, Kearsley, & Zelazo, 1978). Perhaps because this position is more consonant with many of the ideals reflected in the democratic philosophy of this nation, it gradually increased in popularity. The predominate view became "nurture" over "nature." That is, the child begins as a neutral being and the environment determines the direction and rate of the child's future growth. Thus, the better the child's start during the early years, the greater the probability of future success. Children experiencing poor beginnings might never be able to compensate for lost time or experience. Adoption of such a philosophy provides pervasive support for the impact and importance of early experience.

Psychoanalytical Influences

Based on the work of Freud and others sharing his psychoanalytical orientation, a view that emotional or mental disturbance often had its roots in some traumatic experience of infancy or early childhood evolved. The psychoanalytical perspective has been characterized by Anderson (1963):

1. The child is passive and responds to all the stimulation to which he is exposed without action or selection on his part;
2. The child is so delicate and tender that he must be protected at all

costs, and must have exceptional amounts of love, affection, and security;

3. The child carries forward all his memories and experiences to later behavior, and is particularly affected by so-called "traumatic" episodes or single intense experiences. (Anderson, 1963, p. 312)

According to Anderson (1963), analytic writings are filled with examples of supposed traumatic events, often sexual in nature, that affect later development. This position presupposes the importance of the child's early environmental experiences. If raised in a loving home, the child would develop into a well-adjusted adult, while children raised in settings where they experienced some intensely unpleasant events are marred for life. For example, the work of Spitz, as reviewed by Hunt (1961), attributes decreases in the developmental quotients of institutionalized infants to the lack of consistent mothering. Depriving these infants of the necessary early emotional relationship with their mothers produces a traumatic reaction that affects all aspects of the infant's development.

The psychoanalytical position can be seen represented in the more contemporary work of Kennell and Klaus. These investigators have assembled findings that they interpret as showing "the importance of the first few minutes and hours of human maternal-infant contact..." (Kennell, Voos, & Klaus, 1979). Mothers who were allowed immediate and extended contact with their infants were reported to have developed better bonding with their infants than did mothers not given this experience. Initial differences between control and experimental mother-infant dyads are reported to have been maintained over several years (Kennell et al., 1979).

Thus, the psychoanalytical position has had and continues to have an impact on how the early developmental period is viewed. This position holds that, although the individual's biological proclivities are important, the early experiences of infants and young children are critical to the development of balanced, well-adjusted adults.

Animal Research

A variety of investigations conducted on young animals during the 1940s and 1950s has also lent support to the view of the primacy of early experience. Although criticized for the extrapolation from animal to human (see Clarke & Clarke, 1976), a number of writers have employed animal research findings to build a circumstantial case for the importance of early experience for the developing child. For example, when Mason (1970) wrote, "Radical deprivation can thus lead not merely to developmental arrest but to functional disintegration of established systems" (pp. 35–36), he was basing this conclusion on research conducted with animals. The implications of this statement for human infants seemed clear in a climate that emphasized the primacy of early experience.

The impact of social isolation on young animals was illustrated in a series of important studies conducted by Thompson and Melzack (1956). Scotty puppies were divided into two groups: one group was raised normally in a home setting while the other group was isolated in small cages, one puppy per cage. The isolated puppies never saw their keepers. A series of experiments was conducted with both groups of puppies between the ages of seven and ten months. In every experiment the isolate-reared puppies behaved differently from the home-reared puppies. Thompson and Melzack characterized the isolate-reared puppies as immature, and in situations that required learning or problem solving, their performances were significantly inferior to those of the home-reared dogs. For example, in learning to avoid a toy mechanical car that delivered a shock when touched, the home-reared puppies learned to avoid the car after receiving an average of six shocks, while it took the isolate-reared puppies an average of twenty-five shocks to learn to avoid the car. Based on their work, Thompson and Melzack's conclusion was "that a rich and stimulating environment in early life is an important condition for normal development. Restriction of experience during this crucial period can result in enduring retardation . . ." (p. 6).

Deprivation studies conducted with other animal species often produced comparable outcomes. Depriving kittens of the opportunity to move freely in the environment results in deficient motor behavior (Held, 1965).[1] The classic work of the Harlows with rhesus monkeys is well known. The Harlows reported that rearing infant monkeys in situations in which the mother or peers are inaccessible results in aberrant adolescent and adult animals (Harlow & Harlow, 1966). However, except for the animals that experienced long-term social deprivation (e.g., six to twelve months), placement with other monkeys produces a rehabilitative effect over time. Nonetheless, the Harlows concluded:

> Both normal mothering and normal infant-infant affectional development are extremely important variables in the socialization of rhesus monkeys and presumably of the higher primates. (p. 272)

The impact of early environments has also been demonstrated with animals who are provided enriched early experiences. Rats, dogs, cats, and primates raised in enriched environments outperform control animals when confronted with problem-solving tasks. For example, rats exposed to a variety of playthings during the early developmental periods are better at running mazes than rats who have not experienced such a variety of objects in their cages. "A recent study with chimpanzees suggests that early experience may have an enduring effect on problem-solving skills . . ." (Mason, 1970).

---

[1] Campos, Svejda, Campos, and Bertenthal (1982) report that independent ambulation affects a human infant's perception as well.

Early Experience

In 1949, Donald Hebb published a detailed description of his theory on the neuropsychological basis of thought. An important aspect of Hebb's theory was the postulate that the more of the brain's cortex that is used for associative functioning (that is, those responses that are acquired through learning), the more adaptive the animal. Thus, the human has a larger associative area than the dog. A second postulate was that the size of the associative area is directly influenced by early experience (Hunt, 1961). According to Hebb, the associative areas are made up of "cell assemblies" that are the primary neurological linkage that permit intelligent behavior. Early sensory experience was thought to be particularly significant for the formation of cell assemblies (Ramey & Baker-Ward, 1982). Thus, Hebb's theory provided a rich and plausible explanation of the effects of early experience on young animals. When young animals or infants were deprived of appropriate environmental stimulation, the organism was unable to develop the necessary underlying neurophysiological basis for maximum adaptive behavior.

Human Research: Reanalysis of Environmental Impact

In 1961, the book *Intelligence and Experience* was published, in which Hunt reevaluated and reinterpreted the data on the concept of predeterminism, the constancy of the IQ, and the impact of early experience on the developing child. This reinterpretation focused, in part, on earlier work using animals. This earlier work had purported to show that experience had little impact on development. Hunt's analysis led him to conclude the opposite. In addition, he reviewed works such as the Kirk (1958) study that involved children. This study examined the impact of early intervention on a group of community-based and institutionalized preschool retarded children. Hunt reported the Kirk findings to be positive in terms both of immediate impact after the conclusion of intervention and upon follow-up. (This conclusion was not supported by everyone; see Clarke and Clarke, 1977.) Such studies taken in concert with other findings, such as those on the relationship between environments and the performance of twins, led Hunt to suggest a reinterpretation of the impact of early experience. This reinterpretation was dramatically different from views held by those who believed that heredity was the overriding variable in determining a child's outcome.

Other important investigations that purported to demonstrate the impact of early experience on the infant and young child were conducted by Wayne Dennis and his colleagues. One of the more pertinent studies involved 174 children whose ages ranged from one to four years and who lived in three Iranian institutions. The children were generally found to be significantly retarded in the onset of motor milestones (Dennis, 1963). The more impoverished the institution, the greater the children's retardation. Dennis concluded:

> The data here reported also show that behavioral development cannot be fully accounted for in terms of the maturation hypothesis. The important contributions of experience to the development of infant behavior must be acknowledged. (Dennis, 1963, p. 94)

In another intriguing study, Dennis and Dennis (1951) reared two fraternal female twins from the age of two to fourteen months. The experimenters provided all the care, and the twins saw no other children and few other adults.[2] The infants were not rewarded or punished for any response nor were they provided any instruction. Finally, the environment, although healthy, was relatively sterile. The Dennises took extensive notes and tested the infants periodically. They reported that the twins acquired most of the early motor responses (e.g., smiles, vocalizes, reaches, sits) gradually over time; however, many more advanced behaviors such as rolling, kneeling, creeping, and standing were significantly delayed in their onset. In addition, one twin never acquired several important behaviors, such as standing and stepping alone, during the duration of the study. These findings led the Dennises to conclude that many motor responses that develop after the first months require stimulation and practice if such responses are to appear in the infant's repertoire at the expected time.

Another interesting finding that stimulated evaluation of environmental impact on test performance was the study of the army recruits who failed to perform satisfactorily on the Army General Classification Test during World War II. All prospective recruits for military service during World War II were required to take a general intelligence test called the Army General Classification Test. Ginzberg and Bray (1953) found that 716,000 men between the ages of eighteen and thirty-seven years were rejected from the service on the grounds of mental deficiency determined by their test performance (Masland, Sarason, & Galdwin, 1958). This figure was astounding given that these men were not recruited from institutional settings but were presumably functioning appropriately within society. The poor performance of these recruits appeared to reflect, in part, a mismatch between information required to survive in their environment and information requested on the standardized intelligence test.

A forerunner to this important study was conducted by Alper and Boring (1961), who compared intelligence test scores of Northern and Southern whites with those of black recruits in 1918. The findings led Alper

---

[2]Conduct of such a study today would be prohibited by research ethics governed by institutional research boards.

and Boring to conclude that "it is the Negro's educational disadvantage and not actually his color which handicaps him in these tests" (p. 550). Following this same line of inquiry, Masland et al. (1958) reported that the rejection rates were significantly different for varying geographical sections of the country. For example, ninety-seven recruits were rejected per one thousand from the South, while only ten per one thousand were rejected from the West. Such outcomes convinced Masland et al. (1958) that cultural and educational influences were clearly at work. Their primary concern was to stimulate research that could prevent and attenuate cultural-familial mental retardation.

> Regardless of theoretical bent, no responsible investigator has denied that the level and quality of the functioning of the mentally retarded reflects social and cultural factors. What has not been systematically studied is how these kinds of factors operate so as to have an interfering effect on development. The question of the degree of influence of these factors cannot be answered until we understand how and when they exert their influence. (Masland et al., 1958, p. 392)

By the late 1950s and early 1960s, the weight of the various pieces of evidence had moved the pendulum from viewing nature as the dominant force to viewing nurture as the deciding factor. The popular view became the overriding importance of the environment, the reduced influence of hereditary factors, and thus the primacy of early experience. It was this perspective that served to motivate two powerful movements. First, the war on poverty was begun and with it the development of the Head Start programs that were designed to provide children in circumstances of poverty with an enriched environment (Zigler & Cascione, 1977). The second major move was the application of the experimental analysis of behavior to institutionalized populations (Bricker & Bricker, 1975).

A REINTERPRETATION OF THE PRIMACY OF EARLY EXPERIENCE

During the 1970s, several questions emerged that suggested that a reinterpretation of the primacy of early experience might be needed. First, a number of investigators had found essentially no correlation between the scores infants obtained on intelligence tests before age two years and scores obtained in later developmental periods. For a group of 252 children who were tested periodically between twenty-one months and eighteen years, Honzik, MacFarlane, and Allen (1963) reported that predictions became increasingly poor as the time interval between tests increased, the correlation between test scores at twenty-one months and eighteen years being .07. The lack of predictive validity between performance on intelligence tests before age two and performance of adolescence called into question the continuity between early and late forms of behavior and further suggested that the infant's early environment, whether adaptive or maladaptive, can be offset by subsequent intervening variables (McCall, 1979).

The animal and human research that appeared to provide evidence of the impact of early environmental enrichment or deprivation was reexamined. In a number of instances, it was found that what appeared to be permanent effects of early experience could be eliminated with subsequent intervention. As mentioned earlier, many of the monkeys undergoing social deprivation—if the deprivation were not too extreme—came to develop normal adult behaviors after spending time with nonisolate monkeys (Harlow & Harlow, 1966). In a cross-cultural study, Kagan and Klein (1973) reported that infants raised in a remote Indian village in Guatemala appear listless, fearful, and quiet. When the performances of such infants were compared with those of American infants along a number of dimensions, three months' retardation was generally evidenced by the Guatemalan infants. Yet by eleven years of age the children of the village conducted themselves in responsible ways meeting the demands of their society in a competent and acceptable manner. Further, these children were able to perform a number of cognitive tasks in ways similar to patterns shown by middle-class American children. Thus, Kagan and Klein concluded:

> If the first environment does not permit the full actualization of psychological competence, the child will function below his ability as long as he remains in that context. But if he is transferred to an environment that presents greater variety and requires more accommodations, he seems more capable of exploiting that experience and repairing the damage wrought by the first environment than some theorists have implied. (1973, p. 960)

Even in situations in which great deprivation is experienced, many reports exist that suggest the resiliency of children and the reversibility of early effects. Marie Mason (1963) described the changes she observed in a young child who had been raised in isolation by her handicapped, uneducated mother for six and one-half years. When admitted to the hospital, the child could not talk or walk and had few socialized behaviors. After two years of habilitative efforts, both educational and medical, the child made a "striking social adjustment" and was considered to be of normal intelligence (Mason, 1963). In the Clarke and Clarke book, *Early Experience: Myth and Evidence* (1976), a number of remarkable case studies are presented in which children make near-miraculous recoveries from situations in which they experienced extreme forms of deprivation. Also, Dennis and Najarian (1963) found that significant retardation during the first year of life in institutionalized infants did not necessarily predict that these children would perform poorly at age six. These investigators concluded that their findings did not support the "permanency of early environmental effects."

A final source of information causing questioning of the primacy of early experience came from early-intervention efforts. In some notable cases, the experimental children who participated in early-intervention programs did not show performances superior to those of controls (Blatt & Garfunkel, 1969), or initial differences in favor of the experimental children dissipated over time. According to Clarke and Clarke (1977), Kirk's work was one such project in which the initial superior performances of the children attending a preschool program were lost after the control children completed one year of school. The Clarkes contended that the outcome of the Kirk study (1958) accurately predicted the "washout" effects reported for the Head Start programs (Ramey & Baker-Ward, 1982). And thus, for many "experts," the Head Start programs became the target of arguments against short-term and nonecological approaches (e.g., failure to include family members, failure to examine other relevant environmental variables such as living conditions, subsequent school expectations) to the war on poverty (Bronfenbrenner, 1975). Thus, as the evidence accumulates, the need increases for yet another reevaluation of the early-experience model.

A REINTERPRETATION OF EARLY EXPERIENCE AND CONTINUITY FOR THE 1980s

The previous discussion has reflected the shifting views of early experience since the late 1800s. Through the arguments presented in the previous discussion, the reader should have gained a sense of the changing perspectives on early experience. These historical perspectives serve as an important foundation for understanding today's view of early experience held by a number of theoreticians, researchers, and interventionists (see, e.g., Ramey & Baker-Ward, 1982; Pick, 1978; McCall, 1979, 1981; Clarke & Clarke, 1976; and Kagan et al., 1978).

Reading and analyzing contemporary writings on early experience leads to the following assumptions:

1. early experience is important;
2. subsequent experience is also important;
3. an enriched early experience does not protect the child from subsequent poor environments; and
4. a deprived early environment does not have to doom the child to retardation or maladaptive functioning *if* corrective action is taken (e.g., child's environment changes in positive ways).

This set of assumptions, if correct, provides early interventionists with a useful model in which early experience is seen as but one link in the chain of growth and development. However, given the assurance of a reasonable environment, the better an infant or young child's beginnings, the more likely is future success. This caveat may be particularly pertinent for handicapped children for whom a good start may assist in attenuating the impact of the handicapping condition. Parents, early interventionists, program developers, and policymakers should respect the early developmental periods and create effective programs for handicapped and at-risk infants and young children. However, we must not forget that our efforts can be eliminated or diminished if subsequent programs fail to measure up to the quality of the early services.

So what of continuity of behavioral development? Although the concept of continuity appears to have weak empirical support, it is important to recognize that support for discontinuity is based primarily on the inability to make long-term predictions from early to later behavior. In addition, to view development as discontinuous is, as Lewis and Starr (1979) note, unattractive for two reasons. First, the level of analysis may tend to make development appear to be either continuous or discontinuous. To view superficially the evolution of the caterpillar into a butterfly, the impression would be that development is discontinuous. However, studying cellular changes would lead to the conclusion of developmental continuity. The second reason derives from logic. "Speaking of a given behavior pattern as being without developmental antecedents gives us little in the way of useful knowledge" (Lewis & Starr, 1979, p. 655). Studying a completely baked cake will provide useful information about its structure and contents, but to fully understand the process would require awareness of the initial ingredients and the composition of the batter prior to the baking. Thus, it seems that in the case of the child there is intuitive logic to the notion that at least some continuity exists over time. But what is the nature of that continuity? What variables affect it? Finally, of what relevancy is continuity for early interventionists?

The relationship between behavioral continuity and early intervention is important. If early behavioral repertoires are directly linked to future motor and conceptual development, logic would argue for the importance of early experience for the child's subsequent development. If, however, behavior is discontinuous, then early experience may be of less importance to the child's future, as Clarke and Clarke have suggested (1976). The continuity dilemma hinges, in part, on the length of time one would expect to be able to predict behavioral continuity. Further, it would seem that some amount of predictability is predicated on the relative continuity of the individual's environment. Even those strongly committed to the continuity position recognize that dramatic changes in an environment would tend to produce significant changes in a child's behavior.

The continuity issue will no doubt remain a controversy for many years; however, for present purposes a reasonable resolution might be to accept the

Early Experience

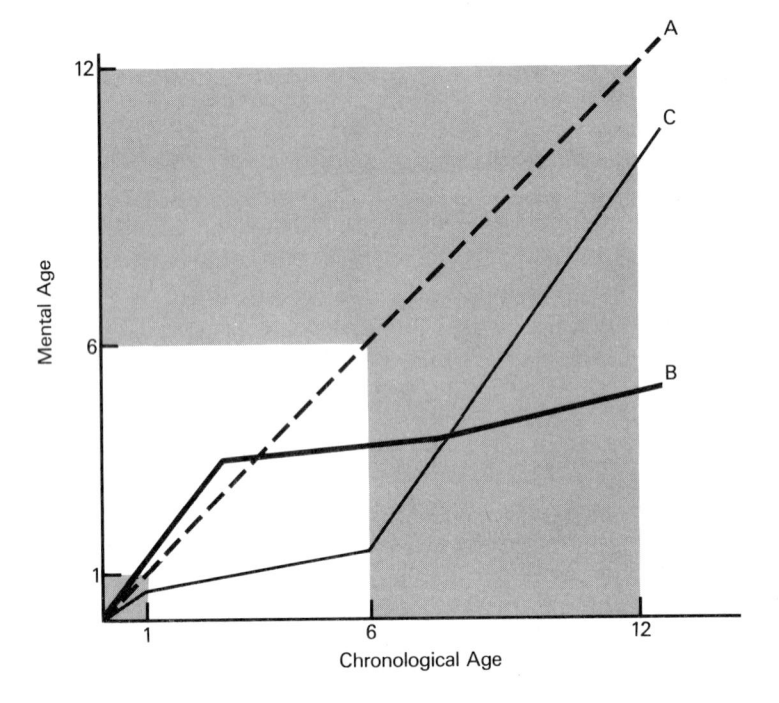

FIGURE 2-1. Hypothetical growth curves.

notion of contiguous continuity. That is, the current behavioral repertoire provides the foundation for the development of the next succeeding stage, which, in turn, directly affects the next subsequent stage or level of development. This perspective is not new; see, for example, Honzik et al. (1963). The developmental curves presented in Figure 2-1 illustrate the notion of contiguous continuity.

Curve A represents a normal growth curve in which there is a direct correspondence between mental age and chronological age. The dotted lines indicate the expected convergencies between these two variables. Such a curve permits accurate predictions from adjacent periods (e.g., age one to two years) as well as nonadjacent periods (e.g., age two to twelve years). Curve B illustrates growth that began slightly better than expected then gradually tapered off. Reasonable predictions can be made to adjacent periods (e.g., age one to two *or* six to seven years), but predicting across several periods would not be accurate (e.g., from age two to six *or* age three to twelve years). Curve B might represent the growth reported for many Down syndrome children whose behavior moves further from the norm as they grow older (see Ludlow & Allen, 1979). Curve C again demonstrates the possibility of correctly predicting from adjacent periods but the inability to make accurate predictions across nonadjacent periods.

The knowledge that prediction diminishes over time, especially for young children, is certainly not new (see, e.g., McCall, 1979). However, little apparent thought has been given to the relationship between longevity of program impact and the diminishing capability to predict later development from earlier performance. Without adequate recognition of the variables that may impact and change growth, disappointment, or worse, is voiced when children do not maintain initial headstarts.

Whether behavior acquired earlier in the child's life is reflected much later is a moot point for now. What is obvious is the immediate impact of the child's current behavioral repertoire on the acquisition of subsequent new response forms. Perhaps the more reasonable hope should be to demonstrate successive impact over time rather than attempting to predict much later behavior based on the preschool years. It seems rather remarkable that investigations have been able to report long-term effects such as those described by Lazar, Darlington, Murray, Royce, and Snipper (1982). These outcomes suggest the importance of attempting to study the environments of the children to determine what aspects have maintained the original gain or what changes have occurred to reduce or dilute the initial experimental and control differences.

The collection of such information will no doubt reflect the interactive nature of development, as has been proposed by a number of major theorists (Piaget, 1970; Uzgiris, 1981; Sameroff & Chandler, 1975; Lewis & Rosenblum, 1974). Development is systematically shaped by the transactions between the organism and the environment. An intricate web of reciprocal transactions occurs that leads to the transformation of the child's behavioral repertoire. Unless the child's biology and environment remain relatively constant, one would be correct to predict variable outcomes for individual children. When investigations report that experimental groups maintain their superiority over time, one might speculate that the early intervention has impacted not only the child but also influenced other important environmental factors as well (e.g., the parent).

What then is a reasonable expectation for program impact? A simple answer seems unlikely. Rather, program impact is most likely determined by a number of variables. The length, quality, and content of an early-intervention effort will doubtlessly affect the longevity of the impact. The Early Training Project developed by Gray and Klaus (Gray, Ramsey, & Klaus, 1982) documented the change of the experimental and control children enrolled in this project over a period of eighteen years in tandem with attempting to examine changes in the environments of the children and their families. The outcomes of this investigation accurately reflect the issues raised in the preceding discussion. That is, one cannot reasonably hope to evaluate the long-term impact of early-intervention efforts in a vacuum. Rather, the continuity or discontinuity of development mirrors environmental change. Early-intervention programs cannot protect at-risk or handicapped children from the future. Such programs may be able to enhance the child's development, but these enhancements are surely not automatically retained. Rather, the child's progress will depend upon his or her current repertoire and the transactions that occur with subsequent environments.

SUMMARY

Early experience is important, but to leave that statement unqualified leads to the somewhat misleading conclusion of the primacy of early development. There is ample evidence that even children who experience severely neglecting and abusive environments can recover normal functions when placed in a positive and supportive environment. However, it is not clear how well these children may have developed if they had not experienced such negative early environments. These children may have recovered because of particularly powerful innate endowments and had they been placed in a reasonable early home might have developed outstanding capabilities. We simply do not know.

Although children with apparently normal capabilities can compensate for early deprivation, it is less clear how adverse environments affect handicapped children. As a group, the handicapped infant and young child by definition have fewer resources with which to compensate for poor environmental input. It may be appropriate to assume that neglecting and abusive parents may have a greater and more enduring impact on handicapped children. Children who begin with a disadvantage, whether physical, sensory, or intellectual, are less well equipped to compensate for yet further deficits produced by uncaring or ill-informed adults.

Until the field of early intervention is able to generate more definite findings on the impact of early environments on at-risk and handicapped infants and young children, it seems wise to assume that quality early intervention is necessary to assist these children in the acquisition of adaptive responses that lead to independent functioning. Further, there appears to be a direct relationship between behavioral repertoires sampled at adjacent periods that provides support to the concept of contiguous continuity. These beliefs form a basis for intervening early and continuing some form of intervention until the child provides clear evidence of being able to cope effectively with environmental demands without special support.

References

Alper, T., & Boring, E. (1961). Intelligence-test scores of northern and southern White and Negro recruits in 1918. In J. Jenkins & D. Paterson (Eds.), *Studies in individual differences*. New York: Appleton-Century-Crofts.

Anderson, J. (1963). Personality organization in children. In W. Dennis (Ed.), *Readings in child psychology*. Englewood Cliffs, NJ: Prentice-Hall.

References

Blatt, B., & Garfunkel, F. (1969). *The educability of intelligence.* Washington, DC: The Council for Exceptional Children.

Bricker, W., & Bricker, D. (1975). Mental retardation and complex human behavior. In J. Kauffman & J. Payne (Eds.), *Mental retardation: Introduction and personal perspectives.* Columbus, OH: Charles E. Merrill.

Bronfenbrenner, U. (1975). Is early intervention effective? In B. Friedlander, G. Sterritt, & G. Kirk (Eds.), *Exceptional infant: Assessment and intervention* (Vol. 3). New York: Brunner/Mazel.

Campos, J., Svejda, M., Campos, R., & Bertenthal, B. (1982). The emergence of self-produced locomotion: Its importance for psychological development. In D. Bricker (Ed.), *Intervention with at-risk and handicapped infants.* Baltimore, MD: University Park Press.

Clarke, A., & Clarke, A. (1976). *Early experience: Myth and evidence.* New York: The Free Press.

Clarke, A., & Clarke, A. (1977). Prospects for prevention and amelioration of mental retardation: A guest editorial. *American Journal of Mental Deficiency, 81,* 523–533.

Dennis, W. (1963). Environmental influences upon motor development. In W. Dennis (Ed.), *Readings in child psychology* (2nd ed.). Englewood Cliffs, NJ: Prentice-Hall.

Dennis, W., & Dennis, M. (1951). Development under controlled environmental conditions. In W. Dennis (Ed.), *Readings in child psychology.* New York: Prentice-Hall.

Dennis, W., & Najarian, P. (1963). Development under environmental handicap. In W. Dennis (Ed.), *Readings in child psychology* (2nd ed.). Englewood Cliffs, NJ: Prentice-Hall.

Freud, S. (1978). The origins and development of psychoanalysis. In R. Corsiri (Ed.), *Readings in current personality theory.* Itasca, IL: Peacock Publishers.

Galton, F. (1961). Classification of men according to their natural gifts. In J. Jenkins & D. Paterson (Eds.), *Studies in individual differences.* New York: Appleton-Century Crofts.

Ginzberg, A., & Bray, D. (1953). *The uneducated.* New York: Columbia University Press.

Gray, S., Ramsey, B., & Klaus, R. (1982). *From 3 to 20: The early training project.* Baltimore, MD: University Park Press.

Harlow, H., & Harlow, M. (1966). Learning to love. *American Scientist, 54,* 244–272.

Hebb, D. (1949). *The organization of behavior: A neuropsychological theory.* New York: Wiley & Sons.

Held, R. (1965). Plasticity in sensory-motor systems. *Scientific American, 213,* 84–94.

Honzik, M., MacFarlane, J., & Allen, L. (1963). The stability of mental test performance. In W. Dennis (Ed.), *Readings in child psychology.* Englewood Cliffs, NJ: Prentice-Hall.

Hunt, J. McV. (1961). *Intelligence and experience.* New York: Ronald Press.

Kagan, J., Kearsley, R., & Zelazo, P. (1978). *Infancy: Its place in human development.* Cambridge, MA: Harvard University Press.

Kagan, J., & Klein, R. (1973). Cross-cultural perspectives on early development. *American Psychologists, 28,* 947–961.

Kennell, J., Voos, D., & Klaus, M. (1979). Parent-infant bonding. In J. Osofsky (Ed.), *Handbook of infant development.* New York: John Wiley.

Kirk, S. (1958). *Early education of the mentally retarded.* Urbana: University of Illinois Press.

Lazar, I., Darlington, R., Murray, H., Royce, J., & Snipper, A. (1982). Lasting effects of early education: A report from the consortium for longitudinal studies. *Monographs of the Society for Research in Child Development, 47* (Serial No. 195).

Lewis, M., & Rosenblum, L. (1974). *The effect of the infant on the caregiver.* New York: Wiley & Sons.

Lewis, M., & Starr, M. (1979). Developmental continuity. In J. Osofsky (Ed.), *Handbook of infant development.* New York: John Wiley.

Ludlow, J., & Allen, L. (1979). The effect of early intervention and preschool stimulus on the development of the Down's syndrome child. *Journal of Mental Deficiency Research, 23,* 29–44.

Masland, R., Sarason, S., & Gladwin, T. (1958). *Mental subnormality.* New York: Basic Books.

Mason, M. (1963). Learning to speak after years of silence. In W. Dennis (Ed.), *Readings in child psychology* (2nd ed.). Englewood Cliffs, NJ: Prentice-Hall.

Mason, W. (1970). Early deprivation in biological perspectives. In V. Denenberg (Ed.), *Education of the infant and young child.* New York: Academic Press.

McCall, R. (1979). The development of intellectual functioning in infancy and the prediction of later IQ. In J. Osofsky (Ed.), *Handbook of infant development.* New York: John Wiley.

McCall, R. (1981). Nature-nurture and the two realms of development: A proposed integration with respect to mental development. *Child Development, 52*(1), 1–12.

Piaget, J. (1970). Piaget's theory. In P. Mussen (Ed.), *Carmichael's manual of child psychology* (Vol. 1). New York: Wiley & Sons.

References

Pick, A. (1978). Discussion summary: Early assessment. In F. Minifie & L. Lloyd (Eds.), *Communicative and cognitive abilities: Early behavioral assessment*. Baltimore, MD: University Park Press.

Ramey, C., & Baker-Ward, L. (1982). Psychosocial retardation and the early experience paradigm. In D. Bricker (Ed.), *Intervention with at-risk and handicapped infants: From research to application*. Baltimore, MD: University Park Press.

Sameroff, A., & Chandler, M. (1975). Reproductive risk and the continuum of caretaking casualty. In F. Horowitz, M. Hetherington, S. Scarr-Salapatek, & G. Siegel (Eds.), *Review of child development research* (Vol. 4). Chicago: University of Chicago Press.

Thompson, W., & Melzack, R. (1956, January). Early environment. *Scientific American* (reprint), 1–6.

Uzgiris, I. (1981). Experience in the social context. In R. Schiefelbusch & D. Bricker (Eds.), *Early language: Acquisition and intervention*. Baltimore, MD: University Park Press.

Wolfensberger, W. (1969). The origin and nature of our institutional models. In R. Kugel & W. Wolfensberger (Eds.), *Changing patterns in residential services for the mentally retarded*. President's Committee on Mental Retardation, Washington, DC.

Zigler, E., & Cascione, R. (1977). Head Start has little to do with mental retardation: A reply to Clarke and Clarke. *American Journal of Mental Deficiency, 82,* 246–249.

CHAPTER 3

HISTORY AND RATIONALE FOR EARLY-INTERVENTION PROGRAMS

In this chapter, three major areas are addressed: (1) the historical development of early-intervention programs for environmentally at-risk children, handicapped children, and medically at-risk children; (2) a rationale for the provision of early-intervention programs for at-risk and handicapped populations; and (3) the philosophy that provides the foundation for the intervention procedures described subsequently in this volume.

A BRIEF HISTORY OF PROGRAM DEVELOPMENT

Programs for the handicapped child appear to have evolved, in part, from a more general set of programs for young children who suffered primarily from conditions stemming from poverty. When preschool programs were initiated in the late 1800s, the primary strategy for dealing with those handicapped children that survived was institutionalization in a large residential facility generally located in remote rural areas (Wolfensberger, 1969). The historical philosophy and concern that led to the development of programs for young children is important to appreciate because a similar philosophy and concern seems to continue to undergird the expansion of social and educational services for the youth of this country today (for a detailed review of early treatment of the handicapped, see Hewett & Forness, 1977). An appreciation of the evolution of services for the young children of this nation assists in understanding current legal mandates, such as P.L. 94–142, that exist in the United States. Examining the historical context should help convince the reader that such legal and legislative precedents are based on a firm commitment to assist those who, through poverty or organic defects, need protection and additional support to assure equal access to societal benefits.

A Brief History of Program Development

According to Lazerson (1972), the historical roots of early childhood education in this country have evolved around three major themes. The first is that early schooling can be instrumental in social change. Thus, much of the historical and current emphasis in education has been focused on social reform for the poor. Second is that the early developmental period is unique and important. Third is that early childhood programs have been viewed by some as a means to reform rigid and narrow educational approaches often found in the public schools.

A philosophical basis for the importance of the early childhood period existed before the 1900s; however, the actual catalyst for the development of early educational programs appears to have been the concern for children growing up in the squalid conditions of poverty. According to Maxim (1980), important educational reforms for young children were stimulated by a number of concerned individuals living in different countries. For example, programs for young children living in poverty were initiated in the late 1800s–early 1900s by Robert Owen in Scotland, Friedrich Frobel in Germany, Margaret McMillan in England, and Montessori in Italy and appear to have borne some interesting similarities. Owen, McMillan, and Montessori, in particular, began programs because of their concern for the health and abuse of young children living in poverty. These programs were developed to offer poor children the opportunity to thrive physically and intellectually.

Inspired in particular by the work of Frobel, kindergarten programs were introduced in the United States in the mid-1800s, and by 1900, public school kindergartens were well established (Maxim, 1980). In Lazerson's view (1972), the growth of kindergarten programs in this country was intimately tied to social reform. That is, workers such as Jane Addams, Robert Woods, and Kate Wiggin saw the need to assist city children who were growing up in conditions of extreme poverty. An underlying philosophy appeared to be that to develop a sense of middle class values, the child of poverty must be apprehended and educated early. A second goal of these initial kindergarten programs was to influence the family life of slum dwellers through education of the parent (Lazerson, 1972), a theme that gained support once again in the 1960s.

Although the nursery school movement in this country also had European roots and its development was subject to many of the same forces, nursery school programs developed separately from the kindergarten movement (Maxim, 1980). As with kindergartens, nursery schools were originally developed to serve children living in poverty. During the 1920s, few nursery school programs were available; but following the great depression, a significant growth in programs occurred largely because of support from the federal government to create jobs. The operation of nursery schools provided jobs for unemployed teachers and also provided facilities where working mothers could leave their children.

Following on the heels of the great depression came World War II, which produced a need for child-care facilities so women could join the war effort. However, these day-care programs were custodial in the sense that little attention was given to the children's educational needs (Maxim, 1980). After the war, federal support for day care was discontinued, while support for programs from private agencies began to grow. This shift meant that many of the programs for young children began serving privileged rather than underprivileged children. During the postwar era, little was done in the way of program development for poor or handicapped young children.

In the 1960s, two important moves began: a new view of young children and a renewed attack to mitigate the impact of poverty on young children. A burgeoning area of research on infants and young children began to suggest that the young human was a more capable learner than was generally believed. Researchers began to report that infants could perform sophisticated discrimination and memory feats (see Schaffer, 1977). Such data provided strong support for the view that learning could begin early in the child's life. Further, in 1964 Bloom published his influential work that indicated much of the child's cognitive growth occurred during the first four years of life. Of course, many authorities question the validity of this position today.

Paralleling these findings, a number of writers were beginning to argue in favor of the plasticity of a child's intellectual growth and the enormous impact of the environment on the child (Hunt, 1961). In addition, influential work by Bowlby (1973) and Spitz (1946) pointed to the catastrophic effects of placing infants in nonstimulating environments, which added fuel to the argument of the importance of early experience and the long-term impact of early environments.[1] These two positions—the ability of the young child to learn and the impact of the environment—along with political motivation provided the foundation for the development of a massive social program labeled "The War on Poverty," which was designed to salvage the young child being raised in poverty (Beller, 1979).

Precursors to Contemporary Programs

Wayne Dennis (1976) and his colleagues were able to observe the effects of what he termed a "natural experiment." Before 1956, a Lebanese social agency called the Creche had kept foundling children assigned to their care from birth to 16 years. A new policy, which required placement of foundlings in adoptive homes within a few years (preferably before two), was instituted. A comparison of children who had remained in the Creche for an extended period with those that were placed in adoptive homes before age two was made:

---

[1] As discusseed in Chapter 2, not until sometime later was the impact of early experience placed in perspective to the child's longitudinal growth.

> It was found that, as a group, children adopted from the Creche within the first two years of life overcame their initial retardation and soon reached a mean I.Q. of approximately 100, which was maintained. (p. 123)

However, children adopted after the age of two did not overcome this preadoption retardation. Further, Dennis's findings indicated that the longer the child remained in the institutional environment, the greater the retardation.

A similar and more widely known study conducted by Skeels and his colleagues reported findings similar to those of Dennis. This longitudinal study focused on two groups of infants who grew up in extremely different environments. Initially, both groups of infants were residents of an orphanage and were comparable and generally functioning in the retarded or low-normal range (Skeels, 1966).

Thirteen of these infants were placed in an institution for the retarded as "house guests" of a group of retarded females and the ward staff. These thirteen children came to constitute the experimental group who, because of marked improvement, were placed in adoptive homes. The contrast group was composed of those children who remained wards of the state and resided in an institutional environment. The initial differences reported between the experimental and control groups were subject to violent attack by a number of prominent psychologists (see Goodenough & Maurer, 1961). These critics were inclined to defend the relative constancy of the IQ and asserted that "the differential patterns of gains and losses upon retest shown by children whose initial IQs fell at the extremes of the distribution is a statistical rather than an educational phenomenon" (Goodenough & Maurer, 1961). After a considerable hiatus, Skeels and his coworkers began to track the progress of the experimental and contrast groups (Kirk, 1977). In a thirty-year follow-up study, Skeels (1966) reported:

> All 13 children in the experimental group were self supporting and none was a ward of an institution, public or private. In the contrast group of 12 children, one had died in adolescence following continued residence in a state institution for the mentally retarded, and four were still wards of institutions, one in a mental hospital, and the other three in institutions for the mentally retarded. In education, the disparity between the two groups was striking. The contrast group completed a median of less than the third grade. The experimental group completed a median of the twelfth grade (p. 55).

The early work of Dennis, Skeels, and their colleagues has had a significant impact on the field of early intervention. These "natural" experiments suggested two important possibilities. First, that young children's growth and development is dependent, in part, upon their early environment, thus making the context and arrangement of events of importance during the formative years. Second, that early repertoires are susceptible to changing environmental conditions that can eliminate early deficiencies or deficits.

Children who have problems or the strong potential for developing problems can be conveniently divided into three groups: those who are at-risk for environmental reasons, those who are at-risk for medical reasons, and those who are handicapped. Contemporary programs for these three groups have evolved from different philosophies and consequently can be usefully separated in terms of their recent program development. The separation of children into these different programs serves us well in terms of discussion, but it should be remembered that many infants or children can be appropriately classified into more than one of these categories. For example, the premature infant from a low-income family is often medically and environmentally at-risk.

Programs for Environmentally At-Risk Children

Without doubt the major early-intervention effort in this country for the environmentally at-risk child has been Head Start; yet, according to Zigler and Cascione (1977), "Since its inception, Head Start has been a program shrouded in confusion and misunderstanding" (p. 248). Thus, it may be useful to review the goals of this important social-educational program for young children. In 1964, President Johnson's administration created the Office of Economic Opportunity. A major program developed by this federal agency was Operation Head Start. Head Start funds were deployed to local community action groups throughout the country to develop preschool programs for children living in poverty, and the specific goals included the following:

1. Improve the child's physical health and physical abilities.
2. Help the emotional and social development of the child by encouraging self-confidence, spontaneity, curiosity, and self-discipline.
3. Improve the child's mental processes and skills with particular attention to conceptual and verbal skills.
4. Establish patterns of expectations of success for the child which will create a climate of confidence for his future learning efforts.
(Maxim, 1980, p. 22)

Summarily, Zigler and Cascione (1977) emphasized that the goal of the Head Start programs "should be the enhancement of the participants' social competence..."

Not only have the goals of Head Start been poorly understood but the outcomes or impact of this massive federal program have been hotly debated (see, e.g., Clarke & Clarke, 1977; Zigler & Cascione, 1977; Cicerelli, Evans, & Schiller, 1969). A source of this conflict must be, in part, the variety of programs subsumed by the Head Start umbrella. Approaches vary in terms of curricular focus, staffing patterns, structure, and service delivery models. Attempting to arrive at some meaningful consensus given such a variety of programs is probably not realistic. It is rather more likely that some Head Start programs are effective in meeting the established goals while others are not.

In 1972, the Head Start legislation was amended to ensure that 10 percent of the Head Start enrollment be handicapped (Ackerman & Moore, 1976). Since 1973, it has been reported that the Head Start programs have served approximately 30,000 handicapped children per year. This legislative change has provided an extraordinarily rich opportunity for many handicapped children to participate in a mainstreamed program during their preschool years.

Studies investigating the impact of early-intervention programs have produced mixed results. For example, the results of a study undertaken approximately at the same time the Head Start program was initiated were published in 1969 by Blatt and Garfunkel. A group of fifty-nine preschool-age children from low-income homes were randomly assigned to experimental and nonexperimental groups. The experimental group attended a structured intervention program, while the nonexperimental group did not. Extensive evaluation of the children's performances found that:

> Disadvantaged children are influenced more by the home setting than by the external manipulation of their school environment. In light of what we believe to have been the face validity of an enriched preschool program, the inability of this program to produce measurable differences between experimental and nonexperimental children causes us to suggest that it is not enough to provide preschool disadvantaged children with an enriched educational opportunity. (Blatt & Garfunkel, 1969, p. 119–120)

This conclusion suggests that other factors present in children's homes can outweigh the impact of even sound school-based intervention. More attention to elements within the home environment appear essential to ensure maximum impact of early intervention.

A number of other early-intervention efforts developed during the early phases of Head Start report more positive outcomes than those of Blatt and Garfunkel (1969). For example, Gray and Klaus's (1976) Early Training Project reported a seven-year follow-up of eighty-eight black children from low-income homes in rural Tennessee. These children were assigned to two experimental groups that differed in length of intervention. In addition, there were local and distal control groups who received no intervention. Comparisons of performances for these four groups are reported for 1962 to

1968 when these children completed the fourth grade. In Gray and Klaus's words:

> Intervention caused a rise in intelligence which was fairly sharp at first, then leveled off, and finally began to show decline once intervention ceased. The control groups on the other hand tended to show a slight but consistent decline with the single exception of a jump between entrance into public school and the end of first grade.

As noted by Gray and Klaus, the remarkable feature of the project may be the sustaining impact on the experimental children over a considerable time given the relative brevity of early intervention, rather than the fact that the differences between experimental and control children diminished over time. A subsequent follow-up of this project has been recently published (Gray, Ramsey, & Klaus, 1982).

The results reported from this seventeen-year follow-up are complicated and difficult to summarize. Gray et al. (1982) report that initial differences between experimental and control groups on school performance measures did not maintain over time, but some other differences were retained (e.g., better social adjustment). Although these data may appear to indicate lack of success of the early-intervention efforts, Gray et al. (1982) take an alternative position. They argue that any difference that can be retained for such extended time periods reflects the potential powerful effect of early experiences.

Undoubtedly the most impressive contemporary longitudinal study of children from low-income environments is the consortium effort coordinated by Irving Lazar. "In 1976, 12 investigators who had independently designed and implemented infant and preschool programs in the 1960's pooled their original data and conducted a collaborative follow-up of the original subjects..." (Lazar, Darlington, Murray, Royce, & Snipper, 1982). This collaborative effort permitted assessment of program effects across a number of projects and follow-up of a substantial group of children through high school. The population enrolled in these twelve projects were infants and young children from low-income homes. The individual projects varied in philosophy and approach; however, adequate similarity existed to pool findings on four dependent variables: school competence, developed abilities (as measured by achievement and intelligence tests), children's attitudes, and impact on family.

A recent monograph (Lazar et al., 1982) describes the procedures, analysis, and results in detail;[2] primary outcomes will be highlighted here.

---

[2]This monograph is highly recommended to those readers interested in an in-depth description of the consortium activities. A recent comprehensive description of another consortium project is provided by Karnes et al. (1981) as well. This report is particularly relevant because the intervention group contained handicapped children. Beller (1979) also presents a comprehensive review of programs for environmentally at-risk children.

The most salient outcome was that significantly fewer children who participated in preschool programs were assigned to special education classes and retained in a grade than children who did not participate in preschool programs. Other findings are less supportive of program impact except that mothers of experimental children were more satisfied with their children's school performance and had higher expectations for the children than mothers of control children.

Summary

The past intervention work that has been conducted with environmentally at-risk populations is encouraging and discouraging. If society is willing to make the economic investment in what Bronfenbrenner (1975) and others have termed long-term ecological intervention, then the results of studies by Lazar et al. (1982) and others suggest that the majority of young children in poverty can be given the necessary boost to function well within the public schools and subsequently as productive, contributing citizens. Without comprehensive intervention efforts that include the family, outcomes appear considerably less optimistic.

Programs for Biologically At-Risk Children

Infants and children assigned to the category of biologically at-risk can display a broad range of problems that develop during the prenatal, perinatal, or neonatal periods. These problems can stem from a variety of causes (e.g., genetics, trauma, infection, prematurity), can be manifest in numerous ways, and can impact the infants' respiratory system, size, weight, or tone (Werthmann, 1981). However, the condition most often associated with biological at-risk infants is a preterm birth, a shortened gestation period usually associated with a low birth weight. The more premature the infant, the lower the birth weight and increased frequency of other associated problems.

As Kopp (1983) points out, the infant mortality rate has dropped dramatically during the past 100 years, although as recently as 1983–84, the Public Health Service has indicated no change in the infant mortality rate. However, as medical science becomes more sophisticated, smaller and sicker infants are surviving, creating other dilemmas, such as deciding upon optimal care for these often tiny, fragile newborns.

Initially, early care of the biologically at-risk infant (most often the preterm infant) was provided by obstetricians. Gradually, care for the preterm and sick infant was shifted to the new speciality area of pediatrics. Today, care of the biologically at-risk infant is primarily handled by neonatalogists who are trained specifically to care for distressed newborns. Most major medical facilities have neonatal intensive care units (NICU), which are designed to provide special medical care and contain sophisticated equipment to monitor and maintain distressed newborns. NICUs are generally staffed with a cadre of neonatalogists and specially trained nurses. Hospitals that do not have NICUs refer newborns with serious problems to a metropolitan or regional medical facility that has an NICU.

With the advent of NICUs and increased medical knowledge that permits successful handling of smaller and sicker newborns, two issues have taken on growing attention. The first issue concerns the ethics involved in the saving and maintenance of severely damaged newborns, and the second issue concerns the type of care or stimulation that will maximize biological or psychological growth in the biologically at-risk infant.

The first issue requires serious consideration by medical and educational personnel as well as by society in general. At least two factors need to be confronted. First, what is the quality of life for those infants saved through heroic efforts of the medical community? Second, what is the cost of such care? The future quality of life is currently difficult to predict. In many cases, there appears to be little relationship between the state of the infant during the early months and subsequent developmental outcomes. As Sigman, Cohen, and Forsythe (1981) note, the "prediction from early medical complications to later mental performance is poor" (p. 313). As these investigators suggest, the great plasticity in the early stages of development taken in conjunction with the significant impact possible from the caregiving environment can lead to considerable fluidity in the subsequent repertoires displayed by biologically at-risk infants. Thus, we are currently in a poor position to make sound judgments about the developmental outcomes of biologically at-risk infants.

The cost of care and of the increasing survival rate of the biologically at-risk infant are growing concerns. A report published by the U.S. Congress's Office of Technology Assessment (Budetti, Barrand, McManus, & Heinen, 1981) found that in 1978 the cost ranged from $1,800.00 to $40,000.00 per patient. An analysis examining cost by birthweight indicated that the average cost for infants less than one thousand grams (under three pounds) was $22,508.00, and the cost per survivor was $46,340.00. As the weight increases, the cost decreases. As significant as these costs appear, they probably do not reflect the cost of similar care in an NICU today. Thus, we are clearly saving more infants, but the cost is reaching astronomical proportions.

The second major issue that has been raised by increasing the survival rate of the biologically at-risk infant concerns the form of care or stimulation provided the infant once the baby's medical status becomes stable. During the 1960s and 1970s, a variety of intervention strategies were undertaken. Cornell and Gottfried (1976) have classified these as two basic types. One strategy entailed designing interventions to make up for presumed sensory deficits, for example, providing additional auditory stimulation (e.g., heart beat) or movement (e.g., rocking). The other strategy was to provide the preterm infant with "extraordinary" stimulation, for example, extra handling, talking, and auditory or visual stimulation. In an analysis of the impact of these various intervention strategies on the biologically at-risk infant, Cornell and Gottfried (1976) concluded: "In summary, the most pervasive trend involves what may be generally described as motor development. The performance of stimulated or experimental-group infants tended to exceed that of control-group infants on measures of sensorimotor and motor skills, as well as muscle tonus" (p. 37). However, these authors caution about drawing generalizations because of the diversity of the populations, treatments, and measures employed in the investigations.

From the original work that focused on stimulation of the preterm or at-risk infant evolved a perspective that changed the focus from the infant to the infant-caregiver relationship (Barnard, 1976), or what many writers refer to as bonding or attachment. As researchers studied the interactions that occurred between caregivers (primarily mothers) and their infants, it became clear that caregivers are the primary presenters and interpreters of environmental input to their young infants. As the importance of the early environment provided by the caregiver became increasingly clear to researchers and practitioners, programs to encourage and enhance the attachment of the parent to the infant increased (Barnard, 1976).

Much of the underlying rationale for the increased attention to attachment and bonding was stimulated by the work of Klaus and Kennell and their colleagues (1976). These investigators argued that shortly after birth there was a critical and heightened period for establishing maternal attachment. Delivering a preterm or sick infant who was subsequently removed to an NICU separated mother and infant during this period, thus affecting maternal-infant bonding. Many intervention programs conducted in NICUs attempted to attenuate the disruption by encouraging parents to be present as often as possible and to assist in the care of the infant; thus affecting maternal-infant bonding less significantly. Studies of early maternal-infant separation have generally not focused on the possible negative or long-term impact on maternal-child relationships (Kopp, 1983). This is not to indicate, as Ramey, Zeskind, and Hunter (1981) remark, that having a premature or sick infant is not a significant event; rather, it suggests that when separation occurs, the outcomes are not uniformly predictable.

Influenced in large part by the maternal-bonding research, a number of investigators became interested in studying caregiver-infant interactions. Models were proffered that attempted to better explain outcomes of the at-risk population. In particular, the transactional model described by Sameroff and Chandler (1975) has received considerable attention. Based on transactional or interactional theory, a series of studies were conducted that attempted to examine mother-infant interaction of term and preterm and/or sick infants (Kopp, 1983, reviews a number of these investigations). In particular, investigators compared the behavior of at-risk infant-mother dyads with "normal" infant-mother dyads to isolate differences in the interactional patterns as well as to look at selected factors (e.g., amount of maternal verbal responding) as predictor variables. As Kopp (1983) notes, "difference between term and pre-terms emerged but many of the differences were of low magnitude and some could have been accounted for by other variables" (p. 105).

A number of longitudinal studies of at-risk infants (primarily pre-terms) have been conducted. Four of the more ambitious are the San Francisco study (Hunt, 1981), Springfield study (Field, Dempsey, & Shuman, 1981), Staten Island study (Caputo, Goldstein, & Taub, 1981) and Los Angeles study (Sigman, Cohen, & Forsythe, 1981). The outcomes to date have been analyzed by Sameroff (1981), who reports that in three of these four longitudinal studies "The single most potent factor influencing developmental outcome turns out to be the cultural environment of the child, as expressed in socioeconomic status and parental educational level" (p. 392). Further, Sameroff notes that "No single factor, either birth weight alone or accompanying physical problems, clearly predict a specific developmental outcome" (p. 392).

Nonetheless, when taking preterm infants or infants having other conditions placing them at-risk as a group, the outcomes are less positive than for well, term infants. This finding has served as a basic rationale for continuing to develop early-intervention programs to use with at-risk infants, both during their stay in the NICU and after discharge.

In spite of our inability to predict which at-risk infants will thrive and those that will not and the equivocal outcomes of intervention efforts (Cornell & Gottfried, 1976; Kopp, 1983; Gibson & Fields, 1984), a number of researchers and clinicians see value in offering early-intervention programs to infants at-risk. Taft (1981) indicates two reasons he favors intervention programs: First, the considerable plasticity of the nervous system during the early developmental periods and, second, that many of the positive outcomes of intervention have not yet been measured (e.g., family comfort and satisfaction with the child).

Contemporary intervention approaches for at-risk infants are designed to be conducted in the NICU, after discharge of the infant, or both. Current NICU intervention programs differ in target populations, period of intervention, staffing, service-delivery systems, and intervention goals (Sweet, 1982).

Most NICUs have established criteria for determining the population to be served or for isolating selected subgroups of infants (e.g., those at extreme risk). Programs also vary in when or how long they intervene with the target population. Some states, such as Florida and California, provide developmental assessment during the first year for infants meeting certain risk criteria (Sweet, 1982).

Some intervention programs are conducted by the nursing staff, some by social workers, and some by specially trained educators (Cole & Gilkerson, 1982). Those conducted in the NICU are largely in the form of assisting the parent when possible to provide the infant with appropriate stimulation. In addition, support groups for parents are often available. Once the infant is discharged, the program may provide home visitation, a center where the family can bring the infant, or both. These programs generally assist parents in coping with infants, many of whom may be irritable and difficult during the first weeks at home. Many intervention programs initially focus on helping the parents feel comfortable with their infants and on developing the assurance that they can satisfactorily manage and meet the infant's needs (Bromwich, 1981). Once the parent feels comfortable and in control, strategies for enrichment of the infant's environment are often suggested. For those readers interested in reading about specific intervention programs for at-risk infants, see Field, Sostek, Goldberg, and Shuman, 1979; Kopp, 1983; Tjossem, 1976; Badger, 1977.

This section has provided a global review of the changing perspectives on at-risk infants. In a brief period, these babies have become an important target for research in the development of better medical and educational information and technology. Today, smaller and sicker infants are surviving. This reality requires thoughtful consideration by the medical, educational, and general population of the care to be provided and the associated responsibility for that care.

The intervention approaches for at-risk infants have changed from focusing exclusively on the infant to a general concern for the infant's ecology. Intervention efforts today are designed to account for medical and environmental factors to maximize the infant's growth and the family's adjustment.

Programs for the Handicapped Child

Concerns for the child coming from circumstances of poverty have been paralleled by concerns for the handicapped child. There has been increasing focus on the rights of children and recognition by legislators, courts, and program implementers of the need to eliminate discriminatory practices against the handicapped individual (Hayden, 1974). Kirk (1978) suggested that two major events following World War II acted as triggers for the development of educational programs for the handicapped child:

> First, a number of states that previously had not supported programs of special education in the public schools passed laws to subsidize such programs . . . The second major impetus was the parent movement. (Kirk, 1978, p. 6)

The historical roots of educational programs for the handicapped were perhaps initiated in part by the work of Alfred Binet. As Kirk has noted (1977), contrary to popular belief, Binet did not believe in the fixed nature of intelligence nor did he construct his original test to measure a fixed entity.

Rather, Binet was interested in differentiating among children who would benefit from special instruction. He began classes for the mentally retarded in Paris in 1909; thus, Kirk has dubbed Binet the father of "modern special education" (Kirk, 1977).

Before Binet's work, Itard conducted an experiment with a young adolescent boy found unattended in the woods. Victor, as this child came to be known, was originally unable to speak and had no socialized behaviors. Leading authorities declared Victor an incurable idiot, but Itard believed the boy could be trained. During a four-year period, a highly structured sensory training program was developed and implemented with Victor. Because Victor failed to acquire many of the skills Itard had set out to teach, he considered the "experiment" a failure; however, a more realistic view of changes in Victor's repertoire has lead others to conclude that the intervention devised by Itard was clearly successful (Ball, 1971). A remarkable aspect of Itard's work is the sophistication of the training offered to Victor at a time when few research or educational resources existed.

An early attempt at ameliorating mental retardation through early education was conducted by Kirk. Kirk indicated he had become interested in such a venture because of his long-time association with Harold Skeels and because "In 1946, I read a number of articles published in the *Reader's Digest*, in *The Ladies Home Journal*, and in a psychological monograph that intimated that feeblemindedness could be cured" (Kirk, 1977, p. 6). In 1948, Kirk received support to begin an experiment that was originally developed to replicate the Skeels study.

The Kirk investigation included eighty-one mentally retarded preschool children between the ages of three to six years with IQs that ranged from 45 to 80. The subjects were from four different groups: a community experimental group in which the children attended a community-based preschool program; a community contrast group that attended no preschool program; an institutional experimental group that attended an institutional preschool program; and an institutional contrast group that attended no preschool program. Upon completion of the preschool experience, the experimental subjects in both the community and the institutional preschool groups outperformed the contrast subjects. A follow-up after the first year of elementary school found that the initial differences between contrast and experimental community subjects tended to "wash out" through either an acceleration in the contrast subjects or limited change in experimental subjects, or both. Nevertheless, according to Kirk (1977), "The conclusion we drew from this experiment was that intervention at the preschool level accelerates the rate of mental and social development, while no intervention at that age level tends to allow the rate of mental and social development to slow" (p. 7).

In 1969, an extremely interesting monograph was published by the State of California's Department of Mental Hygiene (Rhodes, Gooch, Siegelman, Behrns, & Metzger, 1970). The study reported was a follow-up to some work completed by Stedman and Eichorn (1964), which compared the development of a group of ten home-reared Down syndrome children with that of ten institutionalized Down syndrome children. Most comparisons favored the home-reared children and, thus, a further experiment was formulated to see if changes in the institutional program and environment could produce changes in the Down syndrome children.

Changes were made in the children's physical setting, staff were trained, and a comprehensive training program was initiated. Language training was the focus of the training. The reported results indicated that positive changes were seen in language behavior, intellectual growth, and social skills of a population previously thought by many to be uneducable (Rhodes et al., 1970).

In 1968, the United States Congress enacted the Handicapped Children's Early Education Program (HCEEP). The purpose of this federal program for preschool-age handicapped children was "to demonstrate the feasibility of early education to the American public" (Ackerman & Moore, 1976, p. 669).

> The Act provided monies for demonstration programs, insisted that such programs be geographically dispersed, mandated the involvement of parents, and ordered dissemination of the results to the communities that surrounded the preschool programs. Furthermore, the Act insisted that programs be coordinated with other existing programs and that they be evaluated in order to show others their worth. (Ackerman & Moore, 1976, pp. 669–670)

Until recently, the appropriations for the HCEEP have steadily increased, resulting in an increased number of programs and children being served. An article by Swan (1980) indicates the success of this federal program in terms of the number of programs that have been continued in communities using local or state funds. In addition, a recent evaluation report issued by the Littlejohn Associates for Special Education Programs indicates the enormously positive impact of these programs. To highlight a few outcomes noted by the Littlejohn report:

- Projects have been active in every state and in several territories . . .
- Fifty-five percent of the children who leave HCEEP demonstration projects are placed in integrated settings with non-handicapped children which is less expensive than more specialized placements.
- Eighty percent of the 280 projects (studied by this report) are still continuing to serve children independent of HCEEP funding.
- More than 30,600 children have been served in continuation projects at no cost to the HCEEP.

- Replication programs are known to have served 107,850 children.
- More than 3,000 products have been developed by HCEEP projects . . .
- Twenty-one HCEEP projects have been approved for dissemination by the Joint Dissemination Review Panel of the Department of Education on the basis of evidence of effective programming and in cost of replication. (Roy Littlejohn Associates, 1982, p. 146–147)

The Roy Littlejohn Associates report concludes that "The accomplishments of the HCEEP projects as shown by the survey results are greater and more varied than for any other documented education program we have been able to identify" (p. 149). Others may not share the enthusiasm for the HCEEP found in the Littlejohn report, but there seems little doubt that from both a historical and a contemporary perspective, the impact of this federal program on the development of early intervention programs for handicapped infants and preschool-age children has been significant.

Toward the end of the 1960s and in the early 1970s, other events occurred that encouraged the development of early-intervention programs for handicapped preschool children. A few states began passing legislation that mandated community services for selected preschool handicapped populations, and P.L. 94-142 was signed into law in 1975.

The final link to contemporary programs can be found in a number of exemplary programs developed in the 1970s—many of which were supported by HCEEP funds. Descriptions of many of the notable programs that lay the groundwork for what we do today can be found in the influential volume edited by Friedlander, Sterritt, and Kirk (1975) and in Tjossem (1976). This latter volume was the product of an important conference held in Chapel Hill, North Carolina, in May 1974. This conference and the book have been of great importance because, for many of us working with young handicapped children, this was the first opportunity to learn about other professionals working in the area and to share ideas and ideals. I was a young investigator attending this conference and can still remember the excitement of talking with other researchers and interventionists working toward the same goals. This conference was a significant force in the move to develop early-intervention programs for at-risk and biologically impaired infants and young children in the United States.

Summary

A comparison of the historical background of programs for handicapped infants and children with programs for environmentally and biologically at-risk shows considerable philosophical and pragmatic overlap. The major difference may be in the area of impact. Given appropriate and long-term programs, the prognosis for the environmentally and biologically at-risk child seems excellent; to date such optimism for the handicapped child should be tempered with the real constraints of technology and knowledge facing interventionists dealing with infants or children who have sensory, motor, or cognitive impairments. Our history indicates genuine progress in learning how and what to offer handicapped children and their families; nonetheless, too often information and technological limitations find us falling short of the goal of independent functioning for handicapped populations.

THE RATIONALE FOR EARLY INTERVENTION

Certainly since the introduction of J. McV. Hunt's book, *Intelligence and Experience* (1961), contemporary psychologists and educators have come to acknowledge the importance of the environment on the development of the human organism. For a number of years, many investigators placed such an emphasis on environmental variables that the genetic or organic contribution from the individual was overlooked or, at least, undervalued. Fortunately, the work of investigators such as Sameroff and Chandler (1975) has rekindled interest in the organism-environment interaction. Acknowledgment of genetic limitations with the acceptance that the organism's potential for development can be reduced or enhanced by environmental variables appears the preferred position now, and this position generates a number of potent theoretical arguments to support early intervention (Sameroff, 1982).

The following rationale for early intervention is composed of four major arguments. These arguments for early intervention include: (1) maximizing the infant/child's developmental outcomes; (2) preventing the development of secondary disabilities; (3) providing support/instruction for families; and (4) cost-effectiveness. These arguments tend to be formulated using logic rather than empirical support because of the limited objective data available on the impact of early intervention.

The first basic argument for early intervention is derived from the premise of environment-and-genetics interaction and suggests that early learning lays the foundation for subsequent development of more complex behavior (Bricker, Seibert, & Casuso, 1980). Piaget's (1970) theory of early development supports such a position with the belief that the systematic interaction of early responses with the environment produces increasingly more complex behavior. A logical underlying assumption of this position is that without the early simple response forms, a child does not have the building blocks from which to evolve more complex understanding or knowledge of his or her world. Without systematic early intervention, many handicapped children may not acquire even simple sensorimotor behavior albeit more complex response forms. A few examples may serve to make this point.

The infant who has difficulty coordinating basic schemes, such as movement of the arm/hand to retrieve a visually located object, will generally most likely be delayed in exploring and manipulating the environment. For the systematic retrieval of interesting or desired objects, coordination of the visual or auditory system with reaching is generally required, except when the infant makes contact by happenstance. Reduced physical exploration of the environment generally depresses the onset of these important behaviors. For example, the blind infant's understanding of the concept of objects appears to be acquired more slowly than for nonvisually impaired children (Fewell, 1983). Unless at some future point the infant can make up such deficits, a gradually increasing gap between the expected and the actual repertoire occurs.

The absence or significant delay in the onset of critical responses appears generally to have cumulative effects over time. Consequently, to minimize these deficits, intervention should be offered to the infant or child when such deficits are identified. ECH/SE professionals believe that in most cases, to wait or to delay treatment produces more pervasive and complex problems that are more difficult and costly to remedy.

This argument in no way suggests the primacy of early experience or a continuing overpowering effect on subsequent development. Rather, in agreement with Clarke and Clarke (1976), this argument sees early experiences as one segment in the life of the developing organism and their importance determined, in part, by the child's constitution and subsequent environmental experiences.

Many handicapped or at-risk infants and children are inclined, without proper handling, to develop a variety of undesirable behaviors (Risley & Wolf, 1966; Baumeister & Forehand, 1973) or to fail to respond in a manner that is reinforcing or satisfying to the caregiver. Such behaviors are not inevitable accompaniments of a handicapping condition but appear rather as the result of inappropriate handling.

Thus, a second argument for intervening early with at-risk and handicapped children can be labeled as preventative. That is, parents or families can attenuate or inhibit the development of secondary or associated disabilities in their at-risk or handicapped infant or child *if* they are provided the necessary information and instruction to acquire effective coping strategies.

The reciprocal nature of parent-child interactions assumes an underlying time-sequence frame. That is, one partner's response generally precedes the other's. The timing, or synchrony, of the mother's or the caregiver's response to the baby appears to have the potential of seriously affecting the quality of their relationship even during the very early phases of development (Osofsky, 1976). Synchrony of responding refers to the parents' ability (and to a lesser extent, the child's capacity) to monitor the state, mood, or needs of the child and to respond in a facilitating manner according to the child's needs. For example, if a baby is thrashing and crying vigorously, a synchronous move on the part of the parent is to respond with behaviors that are soothing to the infant; for example, the parent might lift the child, rock him, and talk quietly to him. If the baby were awake and alert, an appropriate response might be to offer some form of stimulation the baby might find interesting, for example, showing the baby a bright-colored toy, tickling her toes, or returning her coos and gurgles.

Such synchronous responding to infants and young children takes the form of "doing what comes naturally" to most parents. Fortunately, most babies and their parents arrive at a reasonable synchrony of their reciprocal responses; however, a number of investigators (Brazelton, Koslowski, & Main, 1974; Bell, 1974; Denenberg & Thoman, 1976) have noted that some babies exceed the ability of their caregivers to cope or respond in a synchronous manner. The development of an asynchronous relationship can result from having a difficult-to-manage child (e.g., autistic child) or a caregiver with little sensitivity to the state or needs of the child. In examining the caregiver's sensitivity, Brazelton et al. (1974) reported the differential effects produced by mothers on two similarly tense, overreactive infants. The mother who was able to modulate or synchronize her behavior to the infant helped the baby become more responsive, while in the other case, the infant learned to escape his mother's increased stimulation by tuning her out. These two parallel cases demonstrate that a mother's behavior "must not only be reinforcing and contingent upon the infant's behavior, but that it must meet more basic 'needs' of the infant in being aware of his capacity to receive and utilize stimuli" (Brazelton, Koslowski, & Main, 1974).

Although the quality of the early parent-child interaction is probably more dependent upon the sensitivity of the adult, asynchrony in the relationship can be produced by the infant as well. Denenberg and Thoman (1976) discuss a case in which the infant's irritable and unresponsive behavior apparently made it extremely difficult for the mother to respond appropriately. An investigation of the state or mood changes of this infant revealed that this baby shifted states significantly more often than other infants of comparable age. The erratic behavior of this infant made it difficult for the mother to modulate her responses appropriately, and the amount of time the mother spent with her infant was observed to gradually decrease over time. Decreasing the amount of interaction between the child and his or her parent may eventually lead to an even more ineffectual relationship.

A second facet of the prevention argument is the apparent irreversibility of some disabilities if steps are not taken for correction during the formative years. For example, without proper exercising and positioning, the child with severe spasticity may develop contractures that are permanent. A hearing-impaired child may not learn to use his or her residual hearing unless trained to do so early in life (Horton, 1976). Children with major disabilities may never function completely within the normal range across a number of behavioral domains, but there are data to suggest that such disabled children can be assisted in becoming more adaptive and independent (Bricker, Bailey, & Bruder, 1984; Simeonsson, Cooper, & Scheiner, 1982).

The third argument for early intervention focuses on the needs of families who have a handicapped child and appear to undergo considerable stress (Roos, 1978; Gallagher, Beckman, & Cross, 1983). Early intervention may be a valuable resource for parents and siblings in three areas. Early-intervention programs can be instrumental in helping parents or family to adjust and cope with their at-risk or handicapped infant or child. First, programs can assist families in adjusting to the handicapped infant or child. There seems little question that the advent of an at-risk or handicapped infant—particularly the latter—produces trauma, fear, and stress for most parents or families. Descriptions of the phases or cycles that parents move through in the adjustment process abound in the literature (Gabel, McDowell, & Cerreto, 1983). Accompanying reflections offered by many parents facing such adjustment processes was the dismay they felt toward professionals, friends, or family who could not or did not offer constructive help or support and the gratitude they felt toward those who were supportive and helpful (Turnbull & Turnbull, 1978).

A second aspect of this argument for the potential value of early intervention for parents or families is that these programs can assist caregivers in acquiring the necessary skills for managing and instructing their children. Most infants and young children tend to spend more time with family members than with other people—even early interventionists. Thus, if the child's learning opportunities are to be maximized and are to generalize across environments, then family members must have the management and instructional skills that will make them able to cope with and teach their children.

A third aspect of this particular argument for early intervention indicates that programs can assist families in obtaining support such as counseling, social services (e.g., food stamps), appropriate medical assistance, or child care. Not all families require such assistance, but many do. In our own experience with parents, we have noted the frequency with which parents ask staff and other parents for help in solving a specific problem with their child. For example, do you know a dentist who is willing to work with a difficult-to-manage child? Parents who may be feeling unusually stressed can be assisted by a staff member in locating a counseling service that is appropriate and affordable. Without such essential supports for the families, the probability of alienation from the child is increased, with the effect that neither child nor family members make or maintain an adequate adjustment to each other. Early-intervention programs may be pivotal for many families in the evolution of an acceptable relationship with their handicapped member. Such acceptance should lead to maintaining the handicapped individual in the community and obviate institutionalization.

A fourth argument some early interventionists cite as a rationale for early intervention is cost (see, e.g., the Colorado Department of Education report entitled, "Effectiveness of Early Special Education for Handicapped Children"). The cost of providing special education exceeds the cost for regular education. The average annual cost per child for regular education has been reported to range from $1,148 to $2,060.[3] Based on the lowest reported cost figure, the average cost per child for regular education to age 18 (for years 1978–79) is $13,776 and $16,072, including two years of preschool. The average cost per child for special education to age 18, when beginning intervention at birth, age two, and age six, is $37,273, $37,600, and $46,816 respectively (Interact, 1981).

The cost of special education varies according to the type and severity of the handicapping condition and the type of service offered (Rossmiller, Hale, & Frohreich, 1970). The cost of special education also varies as the age of beginning special education is postponed. For example, based on 940 children ranging from mild to severely handicapped, the median cost of special education (per child per year) was reported to be $2,021 for infants, $2,310 for preschoolers, and $4,445 for elementary and secondary students (Interact, 1981). These figures are no doubt confounded by such factors as length and intensity of various programs and type and severity of handicapping conditions.

In some cases, early special education services enable school-age children to attend regular education classes. For example, many graduates from the Mama Lere Parent Teaching Home (Horton, 1976), an early-intervention program for hearing-impaired children from birth to six years, were enrolled in elementary school classes. The average cost for hearing-impaired children attending regular classes was $847 per child per year as compared with the average cost for special education classes for the hearing impaired, which was $1,710 per child per year. A considerable savings was realized when handicapped children are able to attend regular classes.

The cost to operate an early-intervention program is far less than the cost of residential (or institutional) services. For example, the Child Development Units Program (Texas) provided classroom programs for ninety-seven preschool handicapped children. The cost of operating this ten-month program was $3,908 per child. Had this program not been available, many of the children would have qualified for enrollment in a state residential school. The average cost for residential school services ranged from $12,888 to $29,868 per child per year (Liberman, Barnes, Ho, Cuellar, & Little, 1979).[4] The cost of institutional care was also greater than the cost for special education programs in public school settings. As mentioned earlier, the average cost for special education classes for hearing-impaired children was

---

[3] Information in this section came from a variety of sources, and cost data were aggregated to estimate average cost of special and regular education and cost savings of early intervention. For an explanation of data sources, procedures for calculating costs, assumptions, and limitations for these figures, see Interact (1981).

[4] These figures are outdated but nonetheless reflect the comparative costs of regular and special education and community versus residential care.

$1,710 per child per year. The average cost per child per year at the State School for the Deaf was $5,107 (Horton, 1976).[5] Compared with the costs of regular education for one year in Ypsilanti, Michigan, a special education self-contained classroom increases the cost of schooling by 143 percent. Institutional care increases the cost of schooling (school district contribution) by 187 percent (Schweinhart & Weikart, 1980).

In addition to direct savings when children are placed in regular education programs and maintained in the community, other economic advantages have been reported. The economic analysis of the Perry Preschool Project (Weber, Foster, & Weikart, 1978) suggests that the benefits of early intervention outweighed the costs. The total economic benefit for two years of preschool was estimated to be $14,819 per child, a 248 percent return on the original investment of $5,984 per child. Three sources contributed to the derived economic benefit calculations: decreased education costs (fewer children needing special education services); increased lifetime earnings and the value of parents' released time while their children attended preschool (Schweinhart & Weikart, 1980).

A follow-up study of children who had participated in the INREAL program for three-to-five-year-old language-impaired and bilingual (Spanish) children indicated that early intervention is cost effective. Three years after completing the program, children required fewer special education services (e.g., speech and language therapy, special education classes) than did children who had not been in the program. The need for later special education services resulted in considerable savings of educational costs. A savings of $1,283.76 per child was realized for language-impaired children, and a savings of $3,076.16 per child was realized for bilingual children (Weiss, 1981). The cost data discussed here are summarized in Table 3-1.

TABLE 3-1 Summary of cost benefits analyses for Early-Intervention Programs

Source	Cost of Early Education Per Child Per Year ($)	Range of Cost of Alternatives Per Child Per Year ($)
Weberman et al.	3,908	12,888 to 29,868
Horton	1,710	5,107
Schweinhart & Weikart	2,992	6,345*
Weiss	1,283	3,076

*Projected as a reduced need for special education services.

[5] Again these figures are dated but still provide useful comparisons between public school and residential costs.

The more traditional rationale of maximizing developmental outcomes, preventing associated disabilities, and supporting and instructing families becomes more persuasive when economic benefits are considered. At the very least, significant savings can be realized if early intervention only prevents the need for residential or institutional care. However, reducing the probability of custodial care is only one economic advantage of providing early-intervention services to handicapped infants or children and their parents. There is considerable savings in educational costs if early intervention increases the likelihood of regular educational placement. A savings is also realized for children who need long-term special education services if intervention begins before school age. In some cases, early intervention enables parents of handicapped children to become more self-sufficient. In general, the accrued economic benefits appear to outweigh, or at least to justify, the expenditures required to ensure the availability of services for young handicapped children and their parents.

SUMMARY

As a prelude to the approach to early intervention advocated in this volume, this chapter has offered a brief history of the early-education movement that was begun in the 1800s. Discussion of selected contemporary programs targeting environmentally and medically at-risk and handicapped children served to illuminate the issues that continue to require attention and innovative solutions. Finally, a multifaceted rationale that has been garnered from the available literature and clinical experience was discussed in some detail. In large measure, the arguments favoring the establishment of early-intervention programs are relative to the weight given to such variables as long-term versus short-term investments, selected criteria to determine success or adequate progress, and the importance attached to every human being regardless of the potential for normalcy.

References

Ackerman, P., & Moore, M. (1976). Delivery of educational services to preschool handicapped children. In T. Tjossem (Ed.), *Intervention strategies for high risk infants and young children.* Baltimore, MD: University Park Press.

Badger, E. (1977). The infant stimulation/mother training project. In B. M. Caldwell & D. J. Stedman (Eds.), *Infant education: A guide for helping handicapped children in the first three years.* New York: Walker & Company.

Ball, T. A. (1971). *Itard, Sequin & Kephart: Sensory education—A learning interpretation.* Columbus, OH: Charles E. Merrill.

Barnard, K. (1976). Nursing: High-risk infants. In T. Tjossem (Ed.), *Intervention strategies for high risk infants and young children.* Baltimore, MD: University Park Press.

Baumeister, A., & Forehand, R. (1973). Stereotyped acts. In N. Ellis (Ed.), *International review of research in mental retardation* (Vol. 6). New York: Academic Press.

Bell, R. (1974). Contributions of human infants to caregiving and social interaction. In M. Lewis & L. Rosenblum (Eds.), *The effect of the infant on its caregiver.* New York: Wiley & Sons.

Beller, E. (1979). Early intervention programs. In J. Osofsky (Ed.), *Handbook of infant development.* New York: Wiley & Sons.

Blatt, B., & Garfunkel, F. (1969). *The educability of intelligence.* Washington, DC: The Council for Exceptional Children.

Bloom, B. (1964). *Stability and change in human characteristics.* London: John Wiley.

Bowlby, J. (1973). *Attachment and loss: Separation, anxiety, and anger.* New York: Basic Books.

Brazelton, B., Koslowski, B., & Main, M. (1974). The origins of reciprocity: The early mother-infant interaction. In M. Lewis & L. Rosenblum (Eds.), *The effect of the infant on its caregiver.* New York: Wiley & Sons.

Bricker, D., Bailey, E., & Bruder, M. (1984). The efficacy of early intervention and the handicapped infant: A wise or wasted resource? In Wolraich & Routh (Eds.), *Advances in Developmental and Behavioral Pediatrics* (Vol. 5).

Bricker, D., Seibert, J., & Casuso, V. (1980). Early intervention. In J. Hogg & P. Mittler (Eds.), *Advances in mental handicap research.* London: Wiley & Sons.

Bromwich, R. (1981). *Working with parents and infants: An interactional approach.* Baltimore, MD: University Park Press.

Bronfenbrenner, U. (1975). Is early intervention effective? In B. Z. Friedlander, G. M. Sterritt, & G. E. Kirk (Eds.), *Exceptional infant* (Vol. 3). New York: Brunner/Mazel.

Budetti, P., Barrand, N., McManus, P., & Heinen, L. (1981, August). *The implications of cost-effectiveness analysis of medical technology. Case Study No. 10: The cost and effectiveness of neonatal intensive care.* Office of Technology Assessment, Washington, DC.

Caputo, D., Goldstein, K., & Taub, H. (1981). Neonatal compromise and later psychological development: A 10-year longitudinal study. In S. Friedman & M. Sigman (Eds.), *Preterm birth and psychological development.* New York: Academic Press.

Cicerelli, V., Evans, J., & Schiller, J. (1969). *The impact of Head Start on*

References

children's cognitive and affective development: Preliminary report. Washington, DC: Office of Economic Opportunity.

Clarke, A., & Clarke, A. (1976). *Early experience: Myth and evidence.* New York: The Free Press.

Clarke, A. D. B., & Clarke, A. M. (1977). Prospects for prevention and amelioration of mental retardation: A guest editorial. *American Journal of Mental Deficiency, 81,* 523–533.

Cole, J., & Gilkerson, L. (1982). Developmental consultation: The role of the parent/infant education in a hospital/community coordinated program for high risk premature infants. In A. Waldstein (Ed.), *Issues in neonatal care.* WESTAR/TADS.

Colorado Department of Education (no date). *Effectiveness of early special education for handicapped children.* (Report commissioned by the Colorado General Assembly.)

Cornell, E., & Gottfried, A. (1976). Intervention with premature human infants. *Child Development, 47,* 32–39.

Denenberg, V., & Thoman, E. (1976). From animal to infant research. In T. Tjossem (Ed.), *Intervention strategies for high risk infants and young children.* Baltimore, MD: University Park Press.

Dennis, W. (1976). Children of the Creche: Conclusions and implications. In A. Clarke & A. Clarke (Eds.), *Early experience: Myth and evidence.* New York: The Free Press.

Fewell, R. (1983). Working with sensorily impaired children. In G. Garwood (Ed.), *Educating young handicapped children.* Rockville, MD: Aspen Publications.

Field, T., Dempsey, J., & Shuman, H. (1981). Developmental follow-up of pre- and postterm infants. In S. Friedman & M. Sigman (Eds.), *Preterm birth and psychological development.* New York: Academic Press.

Field, T., Sostek, A., Goldberg, S., & Shuman, H. (Eds.) (1979). *Infants born at risk.* New York: Spectrum.

Friedlander, B. Z., Sterritt, G. M., & Kirk, G. E. (Eds.) (1975). *Exceptional infant: Assessment and intervention.* New York: Brunner/Mazel.

Gabel, H., McDowell, J., & Cerreto, M. (1983). Family adaptation to the handicapped infant. In G. Garwood & R. Fewell (Eds.), *Educating handicapped infants.* Rockville, MD: Aspen Publications.

Gallagher, J., Beckman, P., & Cross, A. (1983). Families of handicapped children: Sources of stress and its amelioration. *Exceptional Children, 50,* 10–19.

Gibson, D., & Fields, D. (1984). Early stimulation programs for Down's Syndrome: An effectiveness inventory. In M. Wolraich (Ed.), *Advances in behavioral and developmental pediatrics* (Vol. 5). Greenwich, CN: JAI Press.

Goodenough, F., & Maurer, K. (1961). The relative potency of the nursery school and the statistical laboratory in boosting I.Q. In J. Jenkins & D. Paterson (Eds.), *Studies in individual differences.* New York: Appleton-Century-Crofts.

Gray, S., & Klaus, R. (1976). The early training project: A seventh-year report. In A. Clarke & A. Clarke (Eds.), *Early experience: Myth and evidence.* New York: The Free Press.

Gray, S., Ramsey, B., & Klaus, R. (1982). *From 3 to 20: The early training project.* Baltimore, MD: University Park Press.

Hayden, A. (1974). Perspectives of early childhood education in special education. In N. Haring (Ed.), *Behavior of exceptional children.* Columbus, OH: Charles E. Merrill.

Hewett, F., & Forness, S. (1977). *Education of exceptional children.* Boston, MA: Allyn & Bacon.

Horton, K. (1976). Early intervention for hearing-impaired infants and young children. In T. Tjossem (Ed.), *Intervention strategies for high risk infants and young children.* Baltimore, MD: University Park Press.

Hunt, J. (1981). Predicting intellectual disorders in childhood for preterm infants with birthweights below 1501 gm. In S. Friedman & M. Sigman (Eds.), *Preterm birth and psychological development.* New York: Academic Press.

Hunt, J. McV. (1961). *Intelligence and experience.* New York: Ronald Press Co.

Interact (1981). *Early intervention for children with special needs and their families.* Manuscript prepared by Interact: The national committee for services to very young children with special needs and their families. Monmouth, OR: WESTAR.

Karnes, M., Schwedel, A., Lewis, G., Ratts, D., & Esry, D. (1981). Impact of early programming for the handicapped: A follow-up study into the elementary school. *Journal of the Division for Early Childhood, 4,* 62–79.

Kirk, S. (1977). General and historical rationale for early education of the handicapped. In N. Ellis & L. Cross (Eds.), *Planning programs for early education of the handicapped.* New York: Walker & Co.

Kirk, S. (1978). The federal role in special education: Historical perspectives. *UCLA Education, 20,* 5–11.

Klaus, M., & Kennell, J. (Eds.) (1976). *Maternal-infant bonding.* St. Louis: Mosby.

Kopp, C. (1983). Risk factors in development. In M. Haith & J. Campos (Eds.), *Infancy and the biology of development,* Vol. 2. From P. Mussen (Ed.), *Manual of child psychology.* New York: Wiley & Sons.

References

Lazar, I., Darlington, R., Murray, H., Royce, J., & Snipper, A. (1982). Lasting effects of early education: A report from the consortium for longitudinal studies. *Monographs of the Society for Research in Child Development, 47* (Serial No. 195).

Lazerson, M. (1972). The historical antecedents of early childhood education. *Education Digest, 38,* 20–23.

Liberman, A., Barnes, M., Ho, E., Cuellar, I., & Little, T. (1979). The economic impact of child development services on families of retarded children. *Mental Retardation, 17,* 158–159.

Maxim, G. (1980). *The very young: Guiding children from infancy through the early years.* Belmont, CA: Wadsworth.

Osofsky, J. (1976). Neonatal characteristics and mother-infant interaction in two observational situations. *Child Development, 47,* 1138–1147.

Piaget, J. (1970). Piaget's theory. In P. Mussen (Ed.), *Carmichael's manual of child psychology* (Vol. 1). New York: Wiley & Sons.

Ramey, C., Zeskind, P., & Hunter, R. (1981). Biomedical and psychosocial intervention for preterm infants. In S. Friedman & M. Sigman (Eds.), *Preterm birth and psychological development.* New York: Academic Press.

Rhodes, L., Gooch, B., Siegelman, E., Behrns, C., & Metzger, R. (1970). A language stimulation and reading program for severely retarded mongoloid children. *California Mental Health Research Monograph,* No. 11, State of California.

Risely, T., & Wolf, M. (1966). Experimental manipulation of autistic behaviors and generalization in the home. In R. Ulrich, T. Stachnick, & J. Mabry (Eds.), *Control of human behavior.* Glenview, IL: Scott, Foresman & Co.

Roos, P. (1978). Parents of mentally retarded children—Misunderstood and mistreated. In A. Turnbull & H. Turnbull (Eds.), *Parents speak out.* Columbus, OH: Charles E. Merrill.

Rossmiller, R., Hale, J., & Frohreich, L. (1970). *Educational programs for exceptional children: Resource configurations and costs.* (National Education Finance Project, Special Study No. 2). Wisconsin: Department of Educational Administration.

Roy Littlejohn Assoc., Inc. (1982, November). *An analysis of the impact of the Handicapped Children's Early Education Program.* Prepared for Special Education Programs, U.S. Dept. of Education.

Sameroff, A. (1981). Longitudinal studies of preterm infants: A review of chapters 17–20. In S. Friedman & M. Sigman (Eds.), *Preterm birth and psychological development.* New York: Academic Press.

Sameroff, A. (1982). The environmental context of developmental disabilities. In D. Bricker (Ed.), *Intervention with at-risk and handicapped infants: From research to application.* Baltimore, MD: University Park Press.

Sameroff, A., & Chandler, M. (1975). Reproductive risk and the continuum of caretaking casualty. In F. Horowitz, M. Hetherington, S. Scarr-Salapatek, & G. Siegel (Eds.), *Review of child development research* (Vol. 4). Chicago: University of Chicago Press.

Schaffer, H. (Ed.) (1977). *Studies in mother-infant interaction.* New York: Academic Press.

Schweinhart, L., & Weikart, D. (1980). Young children grow up: The effects of the Perry preschool program on youths through age 15. *Monographs of the High/Scope Educational Research Foundation,* No. 7.

Sigman, M., Cohen, S., & Forsythe, A. (1981). The relation of early infant measures to later development. In S. Friedman & M. Sigman (Eds.), *Preterm birth and psychological development.* New York: Academic Press.

Simeonsson, R., Cooper, D., & Scheiner, A. (1982). A review and analysis of the effectiveness of early intervention programs. *Pediatrics, 69,* 635–641.

Skeels, H. M. (1966). Adult status of children with contrasting early life experiences. *Monographs of the Society for Research in Child Development, 31*(3, Serial No. 105).

Spitz, R. (1946). Hospitalism: A follow-up report. *Psychoanalytic Study of the Child, 2,* 313–342.

Stedman, D. J., & Eichorn, D. H. (1964). A comparative study of the growth and development trends of institutionalized and noninstitutionalized mongoloid children. *American Journal of Mental Deficiency, 69,* 391–401.

Swan, W. (1980). The handicapped children's early education program. *Exceptional Children, 47,* 12–16.

Sweet, N. (1982). New faces and approaches in the intensive care nursery: The roles of the developmental/education specialist. In A. Waldstein (Ed.), *Issues in neonatal care.* WESTAR/TADS.

Taft, L. (1981). Intervention programs for infants with cerebral palsy: A clinician's view. In C. Brown (Ed.), *Infants at risk.* Johnson & Johnson Baby Products Company Pediatric Round Table Series, 5.

Tjossem, T. (Ed.) (1976). *Intervention strategies for high risk infants and young children.* Baltimore, MD: University Park Press.

Turnbull, A., & Turnbull, R. (Eds.) (1978). *Parents speak out.* Columbus, OH: Charles E. Merrill.

Weber, C., Foster, P., & Weikart, D. (1978). An economic analysis of the Ypsilanti Perry Preschool Project. *Monographs of the High/Scope Educational Research Foundation,* No. 5.

Weiss, R. (1981). INREAL intervention for language handicapped and bilingual children. *Journal of the Division for Early Childhood. 4,* 40–51.

Werthmann, M. (1981). Medical constraints to optimal psychological development of the preterm infant. In S. Friedman & M. Sigman (Eds.), *Preterm birth and psychological development.* New York: Academic Press.

Wolfensberger, W. (1969). The origin and nature of our institutional models. In R. Kugel & W. Wolfensberger (Eds.), *Changing patterns in residential services for the mentally retarded.* President's Committee on Mental Retardation, Washington, DC.

Zigler, E., & Cascione, R. (1977). Headstart has little to do with mental retardation: A reply to Clarke and Clarke. *American Journal of Mental Deficiency, 82,* 246–249.

CHAPTER 4

THE IMPACT OF EARLY-INTERVENTION PROGRAMS ON CHILDREN AND FAMILIES

Those of us working with at-risk and handicapped children should take seriously the role of advocate. Often, those intimately associated with an area tend to forget that others may not share their enthusiasm for an endeavor to which they are professionally committed. An individual who knows little about the devastating effects of physical, mental, and behavioral impairments cannot be expected to understand the need for intervening early when a child with such a defect is identified. Further, uninformed people do not automatically understand or accept that infants and young children can benefit from intelligently designed intervention programs.

Obviously, professionals working in early-education programs have a responsibility to provide services to children and families; they have a secondary responsibility, perhaps not so obvious, to inform the community about the importance of providing these services to young at-risk and handicapped populations. As well-informed spokespersons, we may be able to assist the larger community in gaining an understanding of and appreciation for the needs of young at-risk and handicapped children and their families.

To be an effective spokesperson, one should be armed with logical arguments and relevant information about the effectiveness of early-intervention programs. In Chapter 3, a rationale for early intervention was presented; in this chapter, selected outcome data on the impact of early programming for at-risk and handicapped infants/children and their families is discussed. The intent is to provide the reader with a rich source of information for becoming an effective advocate for programs that serve at-risk and handicapped young children.

THE ISSUE: IS EARLY INTERVENTION EFFECTIVE?

Many interventionists hold that the value of early intervention is obvious and has been demonstrated (Hayden & McGinness, 1977); critics, even those predisposed philosophically toward the benefits of early intervention, argue that the efficacy of early-intervention efforts still awaits objective verification (Clarke & Clarke, 1976; Gibson & Fields, 1984). In all probability, however, the supporters are too easily convinced of the value and the critics too harsh in their judgment, given current knowledge and resources available for studying program impact.

In addition to the polarization of views about the benefit of early intervention, the field has been crippled by imprecise language. Claims and criticisms tend to be articulated in broad pronouncements that elicit defensive reactions rather than assist in clarifying issues, positions, and evaluation outcomes. For example, statements by Jensen (1969) indicating that compensatory education has been tried and apparently failed has led to vigorous counterattacks. Although some responses are carefully reasoned and valuable (e.g., Zigler & Cascione, 1977), counterarguments often have a similar lack of logic and precision.

A complex array of variables affects the development of young children. Evidence that will enhance our understanding of biological growth factors is needed and salient environmental variables that may significantly affect developmental outcomes must be determined. For example, in the Down syndrome population, the precise impact that oral-motor problems (e.g., mouth cavity is small, motor coordination of lips and tongue is poor) have on language acquisition and production is still not known. Nutrition of pregnant women is important, but the impact of certain dietary deficiencies during the fetal growth period on a child's subsequent learning is poorly understood. How much a responsive environment can offset neurological damage experienced by asphyxiated infants is yet to be determined. Understanding the genetic-environment interplay can be compared to weaving a tapestry in which threads emanating from a variety of sources are woven into a pattern. The pattern is influenced by the quality of thread and the weaver's ability to create the conceptualized design. So with children, the outcome is determined by the quality of genetic-biological constitution and by salient environmental determinants (Sameroff & Chandler, 1975). This point has been discussed in detail in Chapter 2 and will be addressed again later in this chapter.

As indicated before, the purpose of this chapter is to reflect on the state of the art of early intervention with the recognition of the complexity and multiplicity of variables impinging on the young child. The goal is to analyze outcome data from early-intervention programs in terms of the impact on enrolled children and their families.

EARLY-INTERVENTION PROGRAMS

Major developments in early-intervention programs have occurred since the early 1970s and have been directed toward two populations: biologically impaired children and children at-risk for medical or environmental reasons.[1] The distinctions between these two populations are important. The biologically impaired child shows clear evidence of some significant structural or behavioral deficit or deficiency usually identifiable early in life. This group includes children with genetic abnormalities (e.g., Down syndrome), metabolic disorders (e.g., phenylketonuria), neurological disorders (e.g., cerebral palsy), and sensory impairments (e.g., visual or hearing impairments). The children classified as at-risk for medical or environmental reasons, or both, include those who are born premature or suffer some medical difficulty early in life (e.g., respiratory distress syndrome), who have caregivers with questionable competencies (e.g., teenage mothers), or who are in abusive or neglecting environments. The reader should acknowledge the distinctions between these populations in terms of etiology, homogeneity (e.g., similarities and dissimilarities), incidence, prognosis, and the possible need for differing intervention approaches. Chapter 6 discusses these differences in detail.

The programs reviewed in this chapter were selected because the authors presented objective outcome data on program impact; because the results were published in generally accessible sources (e.g., journals or books as opposed to unpublished or inhouse reports); and because intervention efforts were formalized approaches used with more than one child. The review of the intervention efforts that were focused on children medically and environmentally at-risk includes only representative studies and is not comprehensive.

Programs for Down Syndrome Children

The biologically impaired population receiving considerable attention by intervention researchers is the Down syndrome child. This population holds appeal because the majority of these children (1) are identifiable at birth; (2) have a common genetic aberration (trisomy 21); and (3) constitute the largest population with a specific genetic abnormality (Hayden & Beck, 1982). These commonalities have led to the conclusion that Down syndrome individuals are a homogeneous population, and consequently, treatment effects on individuals or population subgroups have been largely ignored. This tendency probably has masked a wide range of variability in this

---

[1]This distinction is admittedly arbitrary. Children with medical difficulties could be classified as biologically impaired; however, the present text has not chosen to do so for two reasons. First, many medically at-risk infants recover without enduring problems. Second, the efficacy literature makes a distinction between the organically handicapped and the medically at-risk infant.

population (LaVeck & Brehm, 1978). Data on the Down syndrome infant have indicated ranges in intellectual impairment from mild to severe (Bricker & Carlson, 1982; Bricker & Sheehan, 1981), emotional and social interactional differences (Cicchetti & Sroufe, 1976), and differences in motor development and tone (Harris, 1981). In addition, many of these youngsters have heart defects, hearing impairments, and other serious difficulties that interfere with development. Such defects and population variability affect treatment outcomes; however, as we shall see, intervention researchers appear to have given little attention to these important variables.

Early in the 1970s, Alice Hayden and her colleagues began a project that has produced a decade of information and material on the Down syndrome child (Hayden & Dmitriev, 1975; Hayden & Haring, 1976; Dmitriev, 1979; Hayden & Haring, 1977). In 1977, Hayden and Haring reported program impact data on three groups of Down syndrome children: those involved in the Model Preschool Project (N = 53); those who formerly attended the program but were now in public schools (N = 13); and those who did not participate in the early-intervention project (N = 28). Demographics for the three groups were similar; however, the age ranges for the three groups differed: model preschool group ranged from 20 to 78 months (median = 42 months); graduates ranged from 72 to 118 months (median = 96 months); and nonparticipants, 70 to 162 months (median = 118 months). Unfortunately, the analysis of outcome data is difficult to interpret because of the age discrepancies in the three groups. A comparison of the performances on the Down Syndrome Performance Inventory of model program children with performances of nonparticipating age matches using a cross-sectional analysis suggests that the model program children initially functioned higher and maintained this advantage. Further, analysis in which comparisons were made on rates of development suggests that the developmental rate declines for the model program children and increases for the nonparticipating children, as shown in Figure 4-1. Final analyses conducted between performance level and rates of progress are interpreted by Hayden and Haring to indicate the value of early intervention.

Alternative interpretations of the analyses conducted by Hayden and Haring are less favorable. First, the rate of growth reported for the model population on the Down Syndrome Performance Inventory often exceed those of a normal population. This rate renders the Down Syndrome Performance Inventory suspect because a group of Down syndrome children exceeding the projected normal rate of development seems highly unlikely. Second, the most interpretable data indicate, as the authors themselves note, "... that the model preschool program is not changing the basic developmental patterns of its children, but simply maintains the same developmental patterns at a higher overall rate" (p. 134). It seems plausible that a selection factor was operating. That is, more concerned caregivers sought early programming for their children—and this early advantage was maintained over time. Whether the model program was instrumental in creating and maintaining the early advantage is unanswerable with the available data.

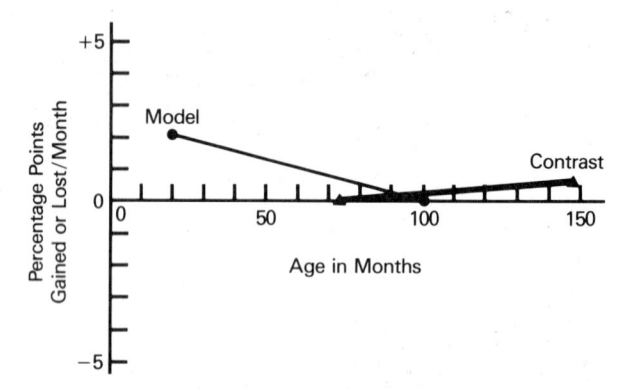

FIGURE 4-1. Relationship between gain or loss in developmental level and age for all children in each group during the assessments conducted in school years 1974-75 and 1975-76. Reprinted from Hayden and Haring (1977), p. 138. Used by permission.

An investigation conducted by Ludlow and Allen (1979) reflects a similar phenomenon. In this study, the progress of three groups of Down syndrome children was compared over a ten-year period. Group A (N = 72) was composed of children living at home who attended at least two years of preschool before their fifth birthday and whose parents received counseling. Group B (N = 79) was composed of children living at home who had no preschool experience and whose families received no counseling. Group C (N = 33) was composed of Down syndrome children placed in a residential placement before their second birthday. With the Griffiths Scales, the children's development was compared from birth to ten years. Testing the children at the same age was not possible, and thus, interpretation of scores was required.

As shown in Figure 4-2, a rapid decline in development for all groups during the first three years was reported. For Group A, development continued to decline slightly until age ten. For Group B, development declined until age five and then stabilized until age ten. For Group C, the initial sharp decline was modified, but the downward trend occurred until age ten. Although the shape of the curves for the groups are similar, Group A scored approximately 10 IQ points higher initially and maintained this superiority over Group B until approximately age eight. The mean difference in Group C's performance dropped from 10 IQ points initially to approximately 23 IQ points by age ten when compared with Group A. Similar though less dramatic differences are reported on the Stanford-Binet. A measure of personal-social development and speech development found Group A functioning significantly better than Groups B and C. Perhaps the most significant finding reported was that the percentage of Group A children attending public schools at ages five and ten was much higher than for Group B children.

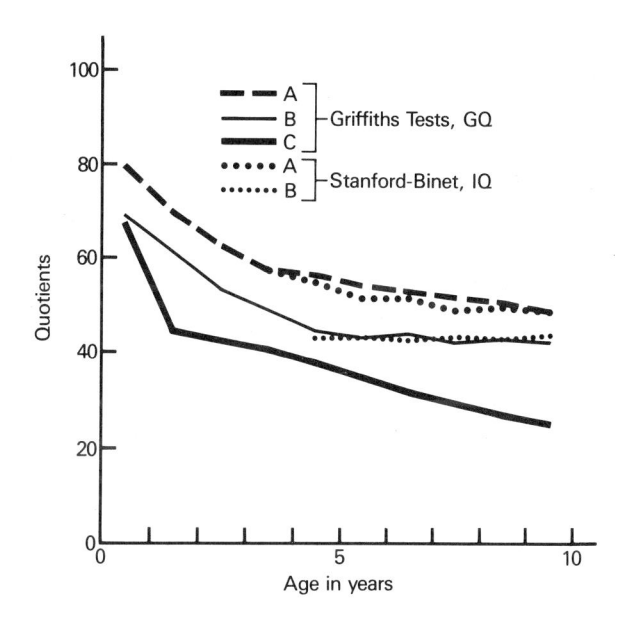

FIGURE 4–2. Comparison of Developmental (Griffiths Scales) and Intelligence (Revised Stanford-Binet) Quotients in Groups A, B, and C from nought to ten years. Reprinted from Ludlow and Allen (1979), p. 34. Used by permission.

These optimistic outcomes should be tempered by several factors. First, the initial superior performance of Group A (in the range of 10+ IQ points) strongly suggests these children may have come from a more concerned, responsive home environment. Ludlow and Allen suggest this may not be so because no selection was made in terms of family/children included in the early intervention and counseling. Second, Groups A, B, and C "... showed remarkable homogeneity on the variables examined (e.g., social class, parent education)." The investigators' explanation of the early difference is the probable impact of the early programming and counseling. Nonetheless, although the program did not discriminate or select, the parents themselves may have. Another potential contaminant recognized again by the investigators was the possibility of biased testing because the investigators did a significant portion of the assessments.

Addressing the same issue of the effects of early training on Down syndrome children, Aronson and Fallstrom (1977) conducted a less global, better controlled investigation. Sixteen Down syndrome children ranging in age from twenty-one to sixty-nine months living in a small residential home were matched for CA (chronological age) and sex and divided into training and no training groups. Although the investigators were unable to match individual children for MA (mental age), the mean MA for each group was 20.6 months. All children participated in a preschool program, and the training group received an additional fifteen minutes to one hour of specialized training twice a week for eighteen months. The children were given tests every six months during this period plus a follow-up test twelve months after training was completed. The Griffiths Scale revealed an average increase in MA of 10.5 months for the trained group and 3.5 months for the controls, a reliable difference. The twelve-month follow-up found no statistically significant differences between groups; however, this comparison was marred somewhat because one pair was not included because of the death of a child and because eight of the children had moved to other institutions. Determining the effect of subject attrition is impossible. However, when the performances of the remaining matched pairs were compared at follow-up, the children receiving the training outperformed the control children in six out of seven pairs.

Clunies-Ross (1979) assessed the impact of a structured intervention program on three groups of Down syndrome infants. The three groups were composed of children from successive yearly intakes into the program (in 1976, N = 16, mean CA = 16.2 months; in 1977, N = 13, mean CA = 15.5 months; in 1978, N = 7, mean CA = 11.2 months). In addition to the structured classroom program for the infants, parents were required to attend a ten-week course focused on child development and management. The children were assessed at four-month intervals using the Early Intervention Development Profile (Rogers, D'Eugenio, Brown, Donovan, & Lynch, 1977); other measures were used periodically. Data were reported for six test points for the 1976 group, four test points for the 1977 group, and two test points for the 1978 group. A review of these data indicate steady progress for each group in similar increments over test periods. The 1978 group for which training was begun earliest show the highest developmental index (DI).

To illuminate this finding, Clunies-Ross (1979) performed a second analysis. Eight children from each successive enrollment year with at least four completed test periods were assigned to a birth-to-eleven-months, twelve-to-twenty-three-months, or over-twenty-four-months group depending upon their age at enrollment. The performances of the eight children in each of these age groups was then compared as shown in Figure 4–3. This comparison revealed that the DI of the youngest group was initially highest. Perhaps the most important aspect of these data is the consistent report of accelerating development. This result, as the investigator notes, is in direct conflict with much of the previous reported data on the Down syndrome child, which previously had shown a decelerating rate of development.

Hanson (1976, 1977) conducted an intervention program similar to that of Clunies-Ross. The intervention was structured, directed toward building specific skills, and parents were included as an integral part of the program; however, the Hanson project delivered services in the home. The interventionist also kept systematic data on the infant's acquisition of developmental milestones. The data were then compared with developmental data on normal infants and home-reared Down syndrome infants not

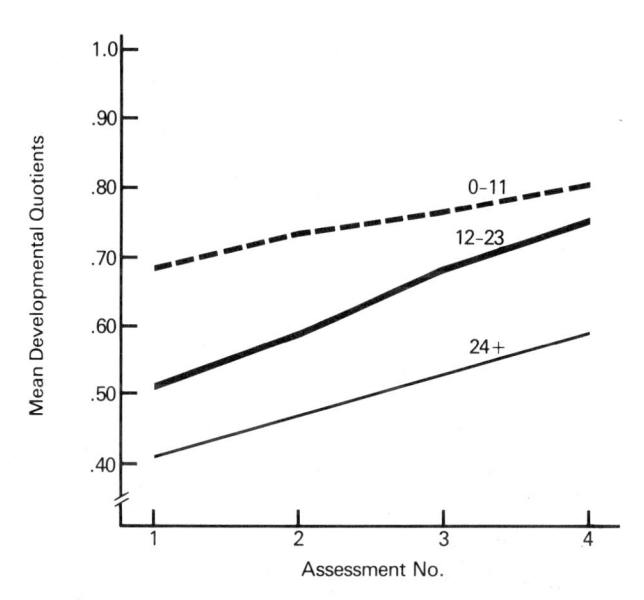

FIGURE 4-3. Mean developmental quotients on four assessments for children in three enrollment-age categories: 0–11 months, 12–23 months, 24 months and over. Reprinted from Clunies-Ross (1979), p. 174. Used by permission.

enrolled in early-intervention programs. "These comparisons show that, in general, infants in the intervention program achieved developmental milestones at a slightly later age than the norms (i.e., normal infants) but consistently earlier than the Down syndrome infants not involved in an intervention program" (Hanson & Schwarz, 1978). The differences reported for the intervention infants and the nonintervention Down syndrome infants are quite dramatic. For example, a mean difference of ten months was reported when 50 percent of the intervention infants could drink unassisted from a cup; a mean difference of seven months for independent walking was reported. In other areas, differences were minimal. Direct comparisons between investigations conducted in different settings must be made carefully, as done by Hanson and Schwarz (1978). The use of differential criteria for attainment of the milestone behaviors could significantly affect the comparisons.

Two recent intervention studies with Down syndrome infants have yielded less optimistic outcomes. Piper and Pless (1980) recruited thirty-seven Down syndrome infants under the age of twenty-four months. Twenty-one infants were assigned to the experimental group, while the remaining sixteen infants composed the control group. Assignment to groups was made on the basis of referral dates. The experimental infants received center-based, biweekly, one-hour therapy sessions. Stimulation activities were demonstrated to the parents. At the initiation of the intervention program, the Griffiths Scales and the Home Observation for Measurement of the Environment Inventory (Caldwell, 1978) were administered and again in six months, at the program's termination. A discriminant analysis found the experimental and control groups reliably different only on one subscale of the Home Inventory. Change scores from pretest to posttest were not significantly different for the experimental and control groups; however, although mean developmental quotients declined for both groups over the six-month period, the control group declined less.

Piper and Pless acknowledged that this investigation has some limitation. For example, the experimental and control subjects were assessed at different times of the year, which may have produced a bias. In addition, the length of intervention, the intensity, and the location may have affected the outcome. Finally, Piper and Pless indicated an inability to determine the frequency or fidelity with which the parents conducted the prescribed therapy.

This investigation has a number of problems; for example, as noted by Bricker, Carlson, and Schwarz (1981), an infant may have received as little as twelve hours of training during a six-month period. Furthermore, the concordance between the intervention and the chosen outcome measure seems questionable. In the Clunies-Ross (1979) and Hanson (1977) investigations, the length of intervention was considerably longer, the content more comprehensive, and the measurement instruments more relevant to the focus of training. Finally, Piper and Pless did not specify the genetic pedigrees (e.g., trisomy, translocation, or mosaic) for their Down syndrome infants, which may have had an influence on the outcomes.

A more focused intervention project was conducted and reported by Harris (1981), in which twenty Down syndrome infants ranging in age from 2.7 to 21.5 months were provided neurodevelopmental therapy. The Bayley Scales of Infant Development (Bayley, 1969) and the Peabody Developmental Motor Scales (Folio & DuBose, 1974) were administered before and after treatment. Based on the initial assessment, individual neurodevelopmental treatment plans were developed for each infant. Equivalent groups of infants were formed, then randomly assigned to a treatment or no-treatment group. Forty-minute therapy sessions were conducted three times per week in the infant's home (except for one child) for a period of nine weeks. The no-treatment infants were enrolled in early-intervention programs. There was a statistically reliable difference between groups on the attainment of the treatment objectives. However, a t-test comparison found no differences between groups on the Bayley and the Peabody Developmental Motor Scales. At first glance, these findings may seem inconsistent, but probably are not because treatment was focused on specific objectives and only a few items on the Bayley or Peabody tests reflected the treatment emphasis.

An extensive report on an early-intervention program has been provided by Kysela and his colleagues (Kysela, Hillyard, McDonald, & Ahlster-Taylor, 1981). This program had a home-based component which provided educational services for twenty-two infants who had a mean age of 13.5 months at the initiation of the program. Nineteen of these infants had Down syndrome. The center-based component served eight Down syndrome toddlers whose mean age was 28.4 months upon entry into the program. Parents involved in the home-based component were required to complete a formal training program, followed by visits to the families by a home specialist on a weekly or biweekly basis. The toddlers attended a half-day session four or five days per week. The investigators provided a detailed description of the conceptual and programmatic aspects of the program.

Results for the home-trained infants and center-based toddlers are reported in terms of progress in the expressive and receptive language program (a primary training target for all infants). These data are difficult to summarize; however, Kysela et al. (1981) suggest that the results indicate that the children from both groups ". . . acquire[d] complex language skills with a rapid rate of learning and very few errors" (p. 370).

A second form of evaluation included administering the Bayley Scales of Infant Development, the Stanford-Binet (for older children), and the Reynell Developmental Language Scales (Reynell, 1969). These measures were administered three times over the first fourteen months of the project with test intervals of approximately six to nine months. The children's scores on these instruments were converted to developmental ratios because many of the children scored below the available test norms. The mental ages and developmental ratios increased for both the home and center groups across the three-test period; however, the changes were statistically significant for only the home group between Test 1 and Test 2. The overall test trend for the center group approached significance ($p < 10$). Results from the Reynell Language Scales were reported separately for the expressive and comprehension sections. On the expressive section, the home group showed no significant change over test periods, while a significant effect was found for the center group. However, the expressive ratios for the home children were initially significantly higher, and no decline in these ratios occurred, while the center group showed a gain in expressive ratios over the three-test period. In the area of comprehension, both groups showed reliable changes from the first test to later tests. Again, the comprehension ratios for the home group exceeded those of the center group. On the whole, these data indicate that the program had a positive effect on the participating children even though, as the investigators note, controls were unavailable for comparison purposes.

In 1968, Rynders and Horrobin (1975, 1980) initiated a family-center early-intervention project for Down syndrome infants. From the point of referral until thirty months, the instruction was conducted in the infant's home with daily structured play sessions. When the infant reached thirty months of age he or she was enrolled in a preschool program. The focus of this program was on concept utilization and communication by the child. At age five years, the children moved into a public school program.

To assess the impact of the program, Rynders and Horrobin (1980) created a distal control group from another city. There were eighteen control and seventeen experimental children; all were diagnosed as having trisomy 21 and were matched on several demographic and physical variables. Comparisons were made at sixty months using the Boehm Test of Basic Concepts, an experimental language sampling instrument, the Stanford-Binet, and an adapted version of the Bruininks-Oseretsky Motor Test.

Interestingly, these investigators reported no differences between the control and experimental subjects on the language measure and the Boehm test but found reliable differences favoring the experimental subjects on the Binet and Bruininks-Oseretsky test. These findings were somewhat unexpected because the focus of the experimental program had been on concept formation and communication. The measure chosen to sample these areas did not reflect superiority of performance by the experimental subjects. Rather, the experimental subjects outperformed the controls on the more global measures of intelligence and motor behavior.

This investigation is one of the better controlled investigations of early intervention. Although random assignment of control and experimental subjects was not possible, an effort was made to recruit a group of distal controls who looked similar to the intervention subjects on a number of important variables. What is important, these infants did not perform differently on the Bayley Scales at twelve months of age but did diverge on an IQ measure at sixty months. Similar results were reported by Connolly, Morgan, Russell, and Richardson (1980), who compared two groups of Down syndrome children matched on CA and parental education. The group participating in an early-intervention program outperformed the nonintervention group on measures of IQ and SQ.

A description of an early-intervention program was published in 1975 by Bidder, Bryant, and Gray. The approach used was to train mothers of Down syndrome infants whose mean CA was twenty-four months and mean MA was approximately fifteen months. The mothers were divided into an experimental (N = 8) and control group (N = 8). The eight mothers in the experimental group received twelve two-hour training sessions during a six-month period. The training focused on teaching the mothers to employ behavior modification principles to assist the child in gaining desired behaviors. The experimental mothers were able to attend a discussion counseling group. The Griffiths Scales were administered before and after. Significant differences were reported for the experimental children for the language and performance scales; however, no differences were found for the other scales or overall scores. In addition, the experimental mothers reported increased knowledge about their children and improved morale.

A recent study nicely summarizes the findings of the research just discussed. Berry, Gunn, and Andrews (1984) evaluated the development of thirty-nine Down syndrome children using the Bayley Scales of Infant Development and the Merrill-Palmer Scale. These children attended a variety of private and public early-intervention programs throughout Australia. Berry, Gunn, and Andrews' independent longitudinal assessment of the children's performance indicated "... that development in these children is consistently proportional to their chronological age and there is no evidence of plateaus during this period" (p. 167). The authors attribute consistent proportional mental growth observed in this population to their attendance in early-intervention programs.

Summary

Many studies have focused on determining the impact of early intervention on the Down syndrome population; however, only those with objective evaluative outcomes were reviewed. This review leads to several general conclusions:

1. Significant variability exists in the length and nature of proffered intervention services for the children and their families. These variances make drawing general and valid conclusions difficult. That is, do programs with different emphases and intervention time produce different effects? For specification and comparison of this variability, see Guralnick and Bricker (in press) and Bailey and Bricker (1985) as well as Chapter 8.
2. Analyses have examined total program impact, thus the relative importance of specific elements (e.g., family participation, curricula employed, staff) is unknown.
3. A variety of instruments have been employed to assess program impact. Attempting to compare children's performances across measures is questionable because of differences in content and administration.
4. The most common measures employed have been standardized intelligence tests. Use of these tools presents problems. First, the measures have not been standardized on nonhandicapped populations, and second, the test content may not reflect the instructional objectives emphasized by the program.
5. Intervention researchers are faced with a number of changing variables that are difficult to control (e.g., child's health, family participation, child attrition, fidelity of treatment). Most experimental designs are not adequate to manage the uncontrolled and shifting variables facing intervention researchers.
6. The uniformly positive effects reported across children and programs suggest that early intervention with young Down syndrome populations does have an impact.
7. Instruments, designs, and methods of analyses are improving for evaluating the impact of early intervention; however, further work in these areas is needed.

Programs for Biologically Impaired Non-Down Syndrome Children

Shifting from intervention projects focused exclusively on the Down syndrome child, we find a sizeable descriptive literature available. Most of these reports tend to be descriptive and provide little material for objective evaluation of program impact. However, a few studies are available that provide, if not totally satisfactory, at least limited objective information on aspects of program impact.

In 1975, an early-intervention program was begun at the University of Miami (Bricker & Dow, 1980). The focus of this program was on the severely and profoundly handicapped child, birth to five years of age. During the three years of this program, fifty children met the criteria for inclusion in the evaluation analysis. Of these fifty children, thirty-five were classified as severely/profoundly retarded, thirteen as moderately retarded, and two as mild or not retarded (but with severe motoric disabilities). These children attended a daily, full-day, center-based program. The program was structured to assist each child in acquiring critical skills in motor, communication, social, self-help, and cognitive areas. Daily/weekly probe data were gathered on individual children's progress toward specific objectives. For an overall assessment of program impact, the Uniform Performance Assessment System (White, Edgar, Haring, Affleck, Hayden, & Bendersky, 1980) was administered. A correlated t-test comparison of pretest and posttest performance indicated a significant improvement ($p < .001$) for each of the four developmental domains and for the overall score in terms of the percent of items passed.

Given the serious problems of this population, these findings were encouraging, even though adequate controls were lacking. In addition, upon graduation from this program, 88 percent of these children were placed in the public school at a time before P.L. 94-142 was being systematically enforced.

Bricker (1981) and Bricker and Sheehan (1981) reported findings from a project located at the University of Oregon. This program, offered to children and families, operated a half day, four days per week. Children were assessed and then IEPs developed to address cognitive, motor, communication, and social deficiencies. A small-group training approach was used, the children's educational objectives being embedded in daily group activities. Child-initiated behavior and parental involvement were major goals for all participants.

During Years 2 and 3 of the project, the Bayley Scales of Infant Development were administered to eighteen (mean CA = 20.0 months) and seventeen (mean CA = 15.7 months) infants, respectively, in the fall and again in the spring. The analysis revealed a reliable difference from pretest to posttest for the entire group as well as for subgroup analyses of infants classified as mildly, moderately, and severely handicapped (with the exception of two subgroups). The McCarthy Scales for Children's Abilities (McCarthy, 1972) were used with children whose CA exceeded thirty months. Twenty-four children (mean CA = 46.8 months) were included in the Year 2 analysis, while thirty-two children (mean CA = 45.9 months) were included in the Year 3 analysis. The pre/post comparison made with the General Cognitive Index and mental age showed a significant difference. In addition, the subgroup analyses for Years 2 and 3 were generally significant. Two criterion-referenced instruments were used: the Uniform Performance Assessment System (White et al., 1980) and the Student Progress Record (Oregon State Mental Health Division, 1977). All pre/post comparisons using these two measures for Years 2 and 3 were significant.

Using a similar approach, but with an increased emphasis on parental involvement and on the programming of functional skills by daily activities, Bricker, Bailey, and McDonnell (undated) report data from a three-year early-intervention program supported by the Handicapped Children's Early Education Program, U.S. Department of Education. The outcome data for Years 2 and 3 were reported for two groups of children: toddlers served in center-based classes and infants served at home. During Year 2, thirty-six children were enrolled with a mean age of one-year-six-months, while during Year 3, forty-six children were enrolled with the same mean age. Pre/post-test five-month interval comparisons were conducted using a standardized test (the Gesell) and a programmatic assessment (Comprehensive Early Evaluation and Programming System). Because the program was developmentally integrated, a total group and subgroup analysis for the normal, at-risk, mild, moderate, and severe groups was conducted when an adequate N was available. For the Gesell, the pre/post comparisons using the MA scores were significant for Years 2 and 3 for the total groups. The subgroup analysis found reliable differences for the nonhandicapped, mild, and moderate groups for Years 2 and 3. The pre/post difference was significant for the at-risk and severe groups for Year 3 (the small N during Year 2 did not permit a comparison). The pre/posttest comparisons on the programmatic measure for total groups and subgroups, where adequate N permitted calculation, were all significant.

These investigations can be criticized because they lack adequate controls, however, the uniformity of results across years and across instruments suggests the reported change was a real phenomenon. That such change would have occurred without the benefit of an early-intervention program seems remote but must remain a plausible possibility.

A project described by Rosen-Morris and Sitkei (1981) is similar in many ways to the Bricker and Dow (1980) investigation in that a highly structured classroom program was developed for severely handicapped infants and young children. Subjects in the Rosen-Morris project ranged in age from eighteen months to six years. Approximately 50 percent had cerebral palsy, while the remainder had a combination of sensory impairments, Down syndrome, and epilepsy. Three measures were used to assess program impact: the Bayley Scales of Infant Development, the Student Progress Record, and the Preschool Attainment Record. Testing was done in the fall and then nine months later. Bayley mental- and motor-age equivalency scores were reported on eleven children. A t-test on the raw score indicated a reliable change. Thirty students were included in the pre/post analysis of the Student Progress Record and Preschool Attainment Record.

The results indicated a significant change on both measures. Given the nature of the target population, i.e., severely handicapped, the uniformly positive outcomes are encouraging. However, qualification of these results is necessary. First, the investigators indicated the need to adapt presentation of the Bayley items. Although this undoubtedly was necessary, it is unclear how such modifications of the testing instrument affected the results. Also, the t-test appears to have been computed on the raw scores rather than the age equivalencies. Finally, although the differences were reported as significant, the actual change in scores or age equivalencies is minimal. This small percentage change was true for the Bricker and Dow (1980) investigation as well. A relevant question then becomes, How much change is necessary for the effect to be considered educationally significant?

In a program with a center-based approach, sixteen multiply handicapped children between sixteen and sixty months of age received concentrated training in language, social skills, motor skills, and problem solving. To evaluate the program impact, Bagnato and Neisworth (1980) employed a variety of measures using a pre/post design. Multiple assessments were conducted every twelve weeks from four to twenty-four months (depending on child's length of enrollment). An intervention-efficiency index was calculated for each child and showed an average developmental gain of 1.11 months for each month of participation. Bagnato and Neisworth (1980) reported that nine of the children showed a monthly gain in excess of one month.

The Portage Project (Shearer & Shearer, 1976) was similar to the Bricker (1981) project, but some important differences existed. Perhaps the most salient difference was the delivery of educational services in the home rather than in a center. A home teacher visited participating families for 1.5 hours per week. An individual program was developed, and the teacher instructed the parents in its implementation. Child progress was monitored through the use of activity charts and progress reports that parents completed weekly. Unfortunately, general evaluation results were only summarized. Shearer and Shearer (1976) reported results from the Cattell Infant Test and the Stanford-Binet that indicated that "The average child in the Project gained fifteen months in an eight-month period, as measured by these pre-post assessment tools." A second analysis entailed a comparison between a group of children enrolled in the Portage Project and a group of randomly selected children from a program for low-income children. The Binet, Cattell, Alpern-Boll Developmental Profile and the Gesell Developmental Schedules were administered before and after to both groups. "A multiple analysis of covariance was used to control for IQ, practice effect, and age." Portage project children were reported to have made significantly greater gains in mental age, IQ, language, and in academic and socialization skills.

In another article, Shearer and Shearer (1972) reported significant mean IQ gains on the Binet and Alpern-Boll Tests when "...children served as their own control." The lack of specificity in the reported results makes evaluation difficult. The number of children for whom the evaluation data are presented is not specified nor is the time interval for test administration. The nature of the analysis is described in only the most global fashion. However, Revill and Blunden (1979) also reported positive outcomes when employing the Portage model with a diverse group of nineteen handicapped children and their families. The subjects served as their own control, and the intervention began after a two-month baseline period. Although outcomes were variable, children's performances on the Griffiths Scale improved after intervention.

A group of investigations employing a combination home- and center-based approach have reported similar outcomes of early-intervention programs on enrolled children. Barrera et al. (1976) included seven moderately to severely impaired children; Nielsen et al. (1975) included nineteen children with a variety of etiologies and functioning levels; and Jew (1974) included twenty-four children with a variety of disabilities. These investigators indicated that the enrolled children made significant progress during the duration of their respective programs.

Safford, Gregg, Schneider, and Sewell (1976) and Shapiro, Gordon, and Neiditch (1977), employing center-based approaches, measured program impact using the children's developmental progress in specific areas, such as motor skills and communication. Safford et al. (1976) measured the gains of the six participating severely handicapped children using functional age equivalents. Shapiro et al. (1977) used systematic anecdotal records to examine developmental growth in their population of sixty multiply handicapped children.

Soboloff (1981) reported a project in which fifty cerebral-palsied children seen in a clinic setting from 1952 to 1965 but who were not enrolled in any early-intervention program were compared with fifty cerebral-palsied children seen between 1965 and 1978 who were enrolled in an early-intervention program. No systematic attempt was made to match these two groups; rather, individuals with complete clinic records were included in the comparison. Records of the one-hundred children were evaluated independently by an orthopedic surgeon, a physical therapist, a nursery school teacher, and a speech therapist.

A number of comparisons were made. First, the percentage of children having some form of corrective surgery was examined, and the results indicated that in the group who had early intervention, 19 percent had surgery, while only 9 percent of the nonintervention group had surgery.

Second, the records indicated that the early-intervention group developed mobility and ambulation earlier. Comparison of family reactions also favored the early-intervention group. Finally, the number of individuals from the two groups functioning in normal social settings (mainstreamed) was not different.

These findings led Soboloff (1981) to conclude, "In the present study there was no question that early stimulation was effective . . ." (p. 265). However, this conclusion warrants caution for several reasons. A number of significant changes in treatment variables could have occurred between the times that the two samples were drawn. In addition, the type of cerebral palsy in the two groups differed. Finally, the study was confounded by age because therapy was begun for the early-intervention group considerably earlier than for the comparison groups. This difference alone could have accounted for the discrepancies reported between the groups. Nonetheless, this investigation is one of the few attempts to evaluate the impact of early intervention on a population of motorically impaired children.

Preschool programs for sensory impaired children can be found in most public schools, and yet objective documentation of program impact is limited. Simmons-Martin (1981) reported outcome data on forty-four deaf children who entered an early-intervention program at an average age of twenty-six months. The Scales of Early Communication Skills were used to evaluate child progress. The children were given the measure twice a year, and all children were tested over a two-and-one-half year span, receiving five separate communication skill ratings. Simmons-Martin reported that across these five ratings, the children's performance reliably improved. Unfortunately, one has no way to link this change directly to program impact rather than to maturation or other environmental variables.

Horton (1976) described two projects developed at the Mama Lere Home that were also focused on a hearing impaired population. In the first study, she reported that three groups of children were compared on a language competence measure while in the second grade. Group 1 included six hearing impaired children and their parents, who had participated in the Mama Lere Home intervention program. These children had been fitted with a hearing aid before age three. The five hearing impaired children included in Group 2 had not participated in the Mama Lere Home program, had hearing aids fitted after age three, and had parents who received no formal instruction. Group 3 included six hearing second grade children. The results indicated language competence for Group 1 was similar to that for Group 3, while the performance of Group 2 was significantly different between Groups 1 and 3. Although the severity of hearing loss for Groups 1 and 2 was similar, other differences make the cautious interpretation of these results necessary. First, no mention is made of initial selection factors that may have been operable in the composition of Groups 1 and 2. Further, how particular children were chosen for inclusion in the comparison was not explained.

The second study described by Horton (1976) entailed comparing the mean percentile ranks on the Metropolitan Achievement Test of six hearing impaired children who attended the Mama Lere program with those of fifty-three normal-hearing second grade children. There was a difference in the mean percentile ranks for math scores of approximately twenty-five points, favoring the normal hearing children; however, the mean percentile ranks for reading skills "were virtually equivalent" for the two populations.

A longitudinal study of ten blind infants provides limited comparative data on this population (Fraiberg, 1975). The intervention focused on providing support and guidance for parents as well as techniques for assisting the infant in acquiring adaptive behavior. Homes were visited twice per month and narrative records kept on the infants' progress. These records of behavioral progress were compared with norms in a previous study of sixty-six blind infants on select items in which the criteria used to determine successful acquisition were similar (Adelson & Fraiberg, 1975). On these items, which represent important benchmarks (e.g., sits, stands, walks), the early-intervention group reached criteria ahead of the comparison group. For early-occurring responses, a difference of two months was reported, but this difference increased over time until a seven to thirteen month difference separated the groups. As the investigators noted, such a comparison must be carefully qualified; however, the differences in the acquisition of later motor skills were so dramatic as to strongly suggest a program impact.

Summary

Many of the conclusions presented after the section on efficacy studies with Down syndrome children can be reiterated for the present group of studies:

1. Again, diversity is the rule because program length, instructional content, and approach vary considerably across programs. For specification and comparison of this variability, see Guralnick and Bricker (in press), Bailey and Bricker (1984), and Chapter 8.

2. Again, design problems exist because researchers were often required to make comparisons without adequate controls. Few children per cell as well as violations of assumptions of homogeneity make the use of some statistical procedures questionable.

3. In addition to using the more common methods for assessing program impact (e.g., standardized tests), some investigators used strategies designed to measure more qualitative outcomes (e.g., anecdotal accounts of program impact, family reactions, placement in regular education programs).

4. Finally, at least one research group conducted analyses of subgroups of the total population to determine if program impact was differential for at-risk, mildly, moderately, or severely impaired children.

Programs for At-Risk Children

Better controlled intervention studies have been conducted on populations of at-risk children than on biologically impaired children for several reasons: First, larger numbers of at-risk children exist; second, less heterogeneity is found in this population; third, the formulation of nonintervention controls raises fewer ethical concerns than in populations of biologically impaired children.

Four of these programs have been selected for discussion. Each of these programs was chosen because it represented a specific population (e.g., premature, low-income), was a well-controlled study, and offered a different perspective on the effects of early intervention.

Scarr-Salapatek and Williams (1973) randomly assigned thirty premature (mean gestation age = thirty-two weeks), low-birth-weight infants (1,300 to 1,800 grams) born to young Black mothers living in poverty to an experimental ($N = 16$) and control group ($N = 15$). The experimental infants were placed in a special nursery and were provided designed stimulation activities (mobiles in the isolettes, extra handling). The controls received standard care for low-birth-weight infants. After discharge, a visitor made weekly visits to the homes of the experimental infants. Systematic input on handling and stimulation were provided to the mother. A follow-up at one year tested nine control (four children were lost and two refused to bring the infant in for testing) and fifteen experimental subjects with the Cattell Infant Intelligence Scale.

The results indicated that the experimental group's performance was near normal levels and significantly different from that of the control infants. The random assignment and independent assessment leave little doubt, as the authors conclude, that this early-intervention program produced a significant advantage in the behavioral functioning of the participating infants. An obvious concern with this investigation is the attrition in the control group.

The Scarr-Salapatek and Williams (1973) investigation confounded the variables of poverty and low birth weight. An investigation by Leib, Benfield, and Guidabaldi (1980) evaluated a special neonatal treatment using a population of preterm infants from white middle class homes. Twenty-eight preterm infants (mean gestation age = 32 weeks) were assigned to a control or experimental group. No significant differences were found between the groups prior to treatment. Treatment consisted of placing a mobile in the isolette, tactile/kinesthetic stimulation during feedings, and auditory stimulation (playing a music box). The control group received standard nursery care. The Brazelton Scales were administered prior to treatment and prior to discharge. The experimental infants performed significantly better on items reflecting interactive processes (e.g., responses to social stimuli such as cuddliness and consolability) but were not different from the controls on motor and organizational processes. In addition, no significant differences between groups in weight gain were found. At six months, the Bayley Scales of Infant Development were administered. The treated infants' developmental status on the mental and motor scale was significantly higher than that of the untreated infants. The authors suggest that this prescribed intervention program for high-risk preterm infants appeared to have enhanced the quality of development in the experimental group.

A sizeable number of early-intervention programs for infants or children from low-income families have been reported in the literature (e.g., Madden, Levenstein, & Levenstein, 1976; Heber & Garber, 1975; Fowler, 1975; Gray, Ramsey, & Klaus, 1982; Karnes et al., 1981). A number of excellent reviews of these programs exist (Bronfenbrenner, 1975; Beller, 1979) and, thus, only one representative program will be discussed here.

Perhaps the most thoroughly researched project on the effects of early intervention on infants from poverty has been conducted by Ramey and his colleagues (Ramey & Campbell, 1979; Ramey, Farran, & Campbell, 1979). Four yearly cohorts of 121 biologically normal infants from low-income homes were randomly assigned to experimental or control groups. The experimental infants attended a day-care program with a comprehensive curriculum. Attendance in the program began by three months of age, and the infants attended full-time, five days per week, fifty weeks per year. The Bayley Scales were used until the infants were eighteen months old, then the Stanford-Binet, McCarthy Scales, and Wechsler Preschool Scale were used from twenty-four to sixty months. The major goal of this project "... has been the prevention of a decline in intellectual development in the experimental group of high-risk children" (Ramey & Campbell, 1979, p. 14).

At twelve months, no differences between groups were found on the Bayley, but from then on significant differences in the range of 10 to 15 IQ points were reported between control and experimental groups. These investigators also reported differences in language development and in social confidence in favor of the experimental children (Ramey, MacPhee, & Yeates, 1983).

Hunt (1980) provides a fascinating description of an early-intervention project conducted in an orphanage in Tehran. For ethical reasons, this project had no simultaneous controls but rather looked at the effect of social and environmental changes by noting the ages the infants acquired selected behaviors. The foundling infants were studied in groups or "waves" from successive years. The first wave ($N = 15$) received the usual institutional care and were tested routinely until age three. The second wave ($N = 10$) received auditory and visual enrichment through tape recorders and mobiles which the infant could activate. The third wave ($N = 10$) received "human enrichment" in which the infant-caregiver ratio was reduced and the staff responded to the infants as they deemed appropriate. The fourth wave ($N = 20$) replicated the second wave but was implemented with more care. Wave five ($N = 11$) received human enrichment, but the staff was trained to deliver systematic intervention. Testing with the Uzgiris-Hunt Scales (1975) indicated that each successive intervention subsequent to wave two hastened development of the infants, the wave five intervention producing the greatest effect. Hunt also noted qualitative differences in language and social-responsiveness in favor of the wave five infants.

Summary

For several reasons, some of the previously discussed methodological and design problems facing the researcher using handicapped populations are absent when examining program effects with at-risk groups. First, control groups are easier to establish because there are no ethical constraints similar to those associated with withholding treatment from handicapped populations. Second, the availability of controls and larger numbers of infants make possible employing more traditional designs and analyses. Third, standardized instruments can be more appropriately used because the at-risk group does not deviate as far from norms as handicapped groups. Fourth, because the at-risk population does not generally suffer from significant chronic organic impairments, growth and development may occur more rapidly, permitting assessment of short-term intervention efforts. This constellation of variables permits the conduct of better controlled studies with at-risk populations. The consistent findings suggest early intervention can have a major and sustaining impact on at-risk groups, particularly the environmentally at-risk.

Follow-up of Contemporary Programs

Evaluations of long-term effects of early-intervention programs with handicapped children are limited. There are probably two explanations. First, the conduct of longitudinal research is difficult and costly. Second, if one accepts the perspective that the developing child is affected at each stage in life and that hundreds of variables intercede between childhood and later life, there might be little reason to expect an early advantage to be maintained over time.

Descriptions of follow-up studies by Field, Dempsey, and Shuman; Sigman, Cohen, and Forsythe; Hunt; and Caputo, Goldstein, and Taub in an edited volume by Friedman and Sigman (1981) provide a rich source of longitudinal data on the sick, premature, and low-birth-weight child. Sameroff (1981) has summarized the findings of these four investigations. First, by entry into school, many at-risk children have developed problems. Second, "The single most potent factor influencing developmental outcome turns out to be the cultural environment of the child, as expressed in socioeconomic status and parental educational level" (Sameroff, 1981, p. 342). This latter finding provides powerful support for early-intervention efforts to (1) reinforce families already providing an enriching environment for the infant and

(2) assist parents who provide unsatisfactory physical and social environments in acquiring more facilitative strategies for interacting with their infants.

Apart from the Skeels (1966) report, the most impressive contemporary longitudinal study of children is the consortium effort directed by Irving Lazar. "In 1976, 12 investigators who had independently designed and implemented infant and preschool programs in the 1960's, pooled their original data and conducted a collaborative follow-up of the original subjects ..." (Lazar, Darlington, Murray, Royce, & Snipper, 1982). This collaborative effort, which included the work of Beller, the Deutschs, Gordon, Gray, Karnes, Levenstein, Miller, Palmer, Weikart, Woolman, and Zigler (Lazar et al., 1982), permitted assessment of program effects across a number of projects and follow-up of a substantial group of children through high school. The population enrolled in these twelve projects were infants and young children from low-income homes. The individual projects varied in philosophy and approach; however, enough similarity existed for them to pool their results.

A recent monograph (Lazar et al., 1982) describes the procedures, analysis, and results of the consortium effort in detail. The most salient outcome was that significantly fewer children who participated in an early program were assigned to special education classes, and fewer were retained in a grade than the control children. No significant differences between experimental and control children on measures of achievement and intelligence were found.

Two notable investigations initiated in the late 1960s and early 1970s also focused on children from low-income families and have produced outcome data that supplement the consortium finding. Long-term differences in IQ and other academic and achievement measures in favor of the experimental groups were reported (Heber & Garber, 1975; Garber & Heber, 1977; Ramey & Campbell, 1979).

A follow-up study conducted by Moore, Fredericks, and Baldwin (1981) focused on nine-, ten-, and eleven-year-old moderately to severely handicapped children enrolled in trainable mentally retarded public school classes. This group of children differed in that some ($N = 68$) had no preschool experience, some ($N = 35$) had one year of preschool experience, and some ($N = 48$) had two years of preschool experience. A statewide assessment instrument, the Student Progress Record, was used to compare performances in language, academics, self-help, and motor skills of these three groups of children. The results indicated that those children enrolled in preschools for two years performed significantly better on the language, academic, self-help, and motor scales. The performance of the group with one year's preschool experience was not reliably different from that of the group with no experience. Such results must be considered tentative because this was retrospective investigation with all the problems inherent in such an approach. Furthermore, a selection factor may have been operating because concerned families may be more apt to seek a preschool placement for their handicapped children; thus, the differences may stem not so much from the preschool experience as from the family's handling of the child.

The Bureau for the Education of the Handicapped (now Office of Special Education Programs) issued a contract to the Battelle Institute to collect follow-up data on a sample of Handicapped Children's Early Education Programs (Stock, Wnek, Newborg, Schenck, Gabel, Spurgeon, & Ray, 1976). Thirty-two Handicapped Children's Early Education Programs (HCEEP) were selected to participate in this investigation with a total of 160 handicapped children. Using a developmental instrument, the Children's Early Education Developmental Inventory, pre- and posttest performance of the selected children indicated that these programs had a positive impact on the children above what could be expected through maturation. In addition, 82.7 percent of the parents surveyed reported their child's participation in the project as very successful, while 11 percent indicated somewhat successful (Stock et al., 1976). The Battelle study also examined school placement of ninety-five graduates from HCEEP. Ninety percent of these children were in special education placements, the remaining 10 percent in regular education programs. Finally, on cognitive and social skills measures, teachers rated HCEEP graduates more advanced than similarly handicapped peers who had no HCEEP experience.

This investigation can be seen as a parallel endeavor to the Lazar et al. (1982) consortium project, except that the focus was biologically impaired children. Two major differences exist, however. First, the HCEEP did not have control groups for comparison. Second, this follow-up study covered the age range of five to eight years and thus provided no information on these children's progress and adjustment during adolescence and the early adult years. Even with these constraints, the outcomes reported by this independent research agency must be seen as encouraging. In addition to the Battelle study, a few other investigations have reported information on enrolled children upon entry into the public schools; for example, see Zeitlin (1981) and Weiss (1981).

Goodman, Cecil, and Barker (1984) recently compared the progress of thirty-five retarded children who attended a hospital-affiliated highly specialized program for an average of sixteen months with that of a contrast group of thirty-six children. The contrast children were selected to match the intervention group on diagnosis, age, SES, IQ, and social status. Most of these children attended community day care programs which "offered little or no individual work with parents or children . . ." (p. 49). Over an average of sixteen months, results from the Bayley Scales and Stanford-Binet found a mean gain of 8.1 IQ points for the treatment children and 0.8 points for the contrast group.

Summary

Conducting follow-up or longitudinal research is an arduous task as reflected by the paucity of studies in the literature. The methodological and design problems identified in the earlier summary sections also create barriers to the conduct of longitudinal research, and most likely these problems are compounded by the passage of time during which a complex array of variables may change and become realigned. Nonetheless, the few longitudinal studies that exist on organically impaired populations have provided an optimistic base for the generation of more carefully controlled investigation.

The literature contains other reviews of the efficacy of early intervention with at-risk and handicapped children. The interested reader is referred to Haskins, Finkelstein, & Stedman, 1978; Simeonsson, Cooper, & Scheiner, 1982; Dunst & Rheingrover, 1981; Odom & Fewell, 1983; Strain, 1984; and White, Mastropieri, & Casto, 1984.

PROGRAM IMPACT ON FAMILIES

The evaluation made of early-intervention programs has been primarily focused on addressing child outcome variables. Attempts to examine program impact on other social agents in the child's life have been sparse (Clarke-Stewart, 1981) largely because programs have lacked the necessary resources and tools to conduct such research. The family members' comfort with their at-risk or handicapped child as well as their ability to manage the child may often be more important to maintaining the child in the home and community than whether or not the child reaches specific developmental objectives. The program-impact information that has been collected on families can be conveniently categorized into three areas: (1) acquisition of instructional skills by parents, (2) interaction between the caregiver and child, and (3) quality-of-life changes in the families.

Acquisition of Instructional Skills

One of the most rigorous research investigations on the effects of training parents as interventionists was conducted by Baker and his colleagues (Baker & Heifetz, 1976; Baker, Heifetz, & Murphy, 1980). One-hundred-sixty families with mentally retarded children between the ages of three and fourteen participated in this study. The parents were divided into four groups, each having a different training format. A fifth group received delayed training and served as a control. The parents were assessed on a Behavioral Vignettes Test (Baker & Heifetz, 1976) before and after training. The training focus of each group was to assist parents in the acquisition of behavior modification techniques (e.g., use of systematic praise, planned ignoring). Four different approaches were used: (1) training manual; (2) training manual and biweekly phone calls; (3) training manual and group meetings; and (4) training manuals, group meetings, and home visits. All methods required the parents to teach specific skills to their children. The training lasted approximately twenty weeks and was completed by 87 percent of the families.

All the mothers involved in training demonstrated a significant improvement on the Behavioral Vignettes Test when compared to control mothers (Baker & Heifetz, 1976). The results for the fathers were related to the type of training they received. The children of trained parents improved significantly in skill acquisition over the control group, suggesting that the child change was directly related to the parents' acquisition of behavioral teaching skills.

As described earlier, the study conducted by Bidder, Bryant, and Gray (1975) with the mothers of Down syndrome infants reported findings similar to those of the Baker and Heifetz study. After training of the mothers, significant differences were found in favor of the treatment group on the language and performance scales of the Griffiths, and positive trends were found on the locomotor and eye-hand scales.

A small number of investigations with few subjects and using single-subject analyses report that parents have successfully learned to use specific intervention procedures such as task analysis (Filler & Kasari, 1981), shaping techniques (Adubato, Adams, & Budd, 1981), reinforcement strategies (Petrie, Kratochwill, Bergan, & Nicholson, 1981) and more appropriate antecedents (Cheseldine & McConkey, 1979). Each of these investigations reports that parents acquired the targeted behavioral teaching strategy and found that parents were able to employ the acquired skills to effectively instruct their disabled child.

Interactional Change

The Verbal Interactional Project was one of the first early-intervention projects to focus on interactional change (Levenstein, 1970; Madden, Levenstein, & Levenstein, 1976). The goal of the project was to improve low-income mothers' verbal interaction style with their high-risk children. The home visitor brought a toy or book and modeled verbal stimulation techniques. After a year, the experimental mothers demonstrated significantly greater use of these techniques than thirty-one control parents who received nine home visits with toys but no verbal modeling. The experimental children also had a significant increase in Binet IQ scores when compared to the controls.

The Carolina Abecedarian Project has reported that participation in this intervention program enhanced the mother-infant relationship in a population of rural poverty black families (Ramey, MacPhee, & Yeates, 1983). Likewise, the Milwaukee Project found that the mildly retarded urban poor mothers involved in the project changed the manner in which they interacted with their children by becoming more responsive and verbal (Garber & Heber, 1977). Similarly, Johnson (1975) described a project involving two-hundred Mexican-American families living in poverty. After the second year of intervention, the experimental mothers, when compared with a nonintervention control group, were found to be significantly warmer and less intrusive and to use more play materials with their infants. The experimental children also scored significantly higher than the control children on the Stanford-Binet.

Gordon and Kogan (1975) intervened with mothers of cerebral palsy children to change interactional patterns. After baseline interactional patterns were determined, parents were divided into an intervention group and a delayed intervention group. The delayed group received training eight weeks after the first group. The intervention included an interview discussing specific behavioral strategies and an interaction session between parent and child. After the intervention period, both groups of mothers improved their interactional style, and significantly more positive behaviors were displayed by both mothers and children. This study was replicated by Tyler and Kogan (1977), and again, the intervention was found to significantly reduce negative interactions between mothers and their children.

Christophersen and Sykes (1979) reported a study using three parent-child dyads. The preschool-age children were moderately retarded. A parent-child interactional code was used to measure the effectiveness of intervention. The parents were trained to reward appropriate behavior and to use time out or a verbal reprimand for inappropriate behaviors. All subjects showed (1) an increase in positive parent-child interactions, (2) a decrease in negative interactions for two subjects, (3) a decrease in parent nonattending, and (4) an increase in child compliance.

These few investigations that were focused on affecting the interactional dimensions of parent-child relationships and conducted with handicapped and environmentally at-risk children, taken in tandem with studies conducted on at-risk infants (Minde, Shosenberg, Marton, Thompson, Ripley, & Burns, 1980; Bromwich & Parmelee, 1979; Field, Widmayer, Stringer, & Ignaloff, 1980), have produced encouraging outcomes. Projects designed to enhance positive dimensions of parent-child relationship seem feasible and effective.

Quality-of-Life Changes

A comprehensive evaluation of the effects of early intervention on families was undertaken by Rescorla and Zigler (1981). Originally, eighteen children, age birth to three years, from low-income families participated in this study. Parents of the children were visited in the home twice a month for the first year of the project and monthly thereafter. The focus of the visit was the parents' social and economic needs. These parents were also given free medical care, and day care was provided. Child progress was assessed at periodic intervals for the experimental and matched comparison group. An evaluation of the program found that twelve of the seventeen mothers in the experimental group sought further education during the program and that eight of these mothers continued their education. There was a decline in the number of experimental parents seeking welfare. An analysis of the five-year follow-up data indicated a significant difference favoring the experimental group on socioeconomic status, number of children (fewer), employment, and general quality of life. The children in the experimental group also had significantly higher scores on the Peabody Picture Vocabulary Test than control children.

The Milwaukee Project collected data on quality-of-life changes in participating families (Heber & Garber, 1975). More mothers from the experimental group were employed, and of those who were working, there was an average difference of nearly forty dollars for weekly salary in favor of the experimental mothers. A significantly greater portion of experimental mothers were literate. Ramey and his colleagues (Ramey, MacPhee, & Yeates, 1983) also reported educational and employment changes in project parents. Though the groups were educationally equivalent at the time of the child's birth, the experimental mothers had acquired significantly more formal education by the time their children were fifty-four months old. As might be expected, more of the experimental mothers held semiskilled or skilled jobs than the control mothers.

Field (1981) compared the effects of two intervention approaches involving teenage mothers and their preterm infants. The mothers and infants of the control group were assessed every four months for a year, while the intervention groups participated in either a home-visit program for a year or a center-based nursery program for six months. The intervention groups received the same type of informational input; however, the center-participating mothers served as paid staff members in the nursery program and as such were expected to care for infants other than their own. Post-intervention results indicated that the infants attending the center-based program performed better on growth and developmental measures and that their mothers found employment more frequently than the mothers in the other groups. The incidence of repeat pregnancy was also lower among the center mothers.

The Carolina Abecedarian Project, the Milwaukee Project, and the project reported by Field (1981) reported favorable attitudinal changes in participating parents. However, two studies reporting attitudinal changes in parents of handicapped children are conflicting. Hetherington, Suttill, Holmlund, and Frey (1979) measured the attitudes of sixty parents of severely developmentally delayed children (mean age = 5.6 years). Thirty of these parents participated in an intervention project. After two years of intervention, participating parents had more "negative attitudes" toward the severely handicapped child than before intervention and than the control group. The authors suggest that the lack of progress by the children during intervention may have caused discouragement in the parents. On the other hand, Spiker (1982) reported that thirty-two mothers of Down syndrome children were positive about their experiences when participating in intervention programs.

Summary

The review of efficacy programs focused on parents leads to several conclusions:

1. Comparatively little empirical work determining program impact on parents has been reported.
2. The major thrust of the reported work has been on teaching parents behavior management skills. The results clearly indicate that parents can acquire specific management and teaching skills. However, what is less clear is the parents' ability to generalize these skills in functional ways.
3. The impact of programs on a number of important variables concerning quality of life has been studied infrequently and more research in this area is needed.

As will be discussed in Chapter 7, the involvement of parents in intervention programs has changed dramatically during the past decade. As partially reflected in the efficacy literature reviewed, researchers are shifting from measuring program impact exclusively on children to measuring program impact on parents. An additional change has been to expand the research focus from investigations of instructional/management skills to studying interactional and quality-of-life variables.

ISSUES ASSOCIATED WITH EFFICACY OUTCOMES

Two important issues are associated with determining the impact of early-intervention programs on young children: the longevity of program impact and expectancies. Each of these issues is discussed here.

Longevity of Program Impact

A serious criticism of early-intervention efforts is that the effects produced on enrolled children tend to disappear or "wash out" over time (Clarke & Clarke, 1977). The investment of resources in early-intervention programs is questioned when initial reported superiority of the experimental subjects is not maintained over time. Taken at face value, such criticism would seem valid; however, at least two factors need consideration.

I remember Sue Gray saying years ago that early intervention is not an inoculation against future educational practice, and she has reaffirmed this position recently (Gray, Ramsey, & Klaus, 1982). Yet critics seem to expect that early gains made by children should be maintained regardless of the child's future circumstances. Ample evidence exists that indicates that without subsequent proper environmental arrangements (e.g., reinforcement of a learned response), acquired behavior will not necessarily be maintained and/or new responses may not be developed as expected. The literature is replete with examples in which children have acquired behavior that does not generalize to other settings or is not maintained. Does this mean that the intervention should never have occurred? Or, rather, does it suggest that additional attention should be given to subsequent environments to ensure the generalization and maintenance of learned skills? Research from longitudinal intervention programs suggests that by continuing systematic educational intervention, gains made during the preschool period can be maintained into the elementary years (Ramey et al., 1983; Heber & Garber, 1975; Weiss, 1981; Horton, 1976).

A second dilemma that arises when studying the longevity of effect is the notion of continuity (see also Chapter 2 for a discussion of continuity). The controversy surrounding continuity of behavior has long been a favorite topic of developmental specialists (see, e.g., Kagan, Kearsley, & Zelazo, 1978). Some theorists argue that human behavior is continuous. That is, earlier behavior provides the foundation for subsequent development, and clear regularities in growth and development are apparent for individuals over time (Lewis & Starr, 1979). Others argue that there is little evidence of continuity for the human organism, as indicated by such factors as the poor predictive power of an infant's performance on a standardized test for later development (McCall, 1979).

The relationship between behavioral continuity and early intervention is important. If early behavioral repertoires are directly linked to future motor and conceptual development, logic would argue for the importance of early experience for the child's subsequent development. If, however, behavior is discontinuous, then early experience may be of less importance to the child's future, as Clarke and Clarke have suggested (1976). The continuity dilemma hinges, in part, on the length of time one would expect to be able to predict behavioral continuity. Further, some amount of the predictability would seem to be predicated on the relative continuity of the individual's environment. Even those strongly committed to the continuity position recognize that dramatic changes in an environment tend to produce significant changes in a child's behavior.

The continuity issue will no doubt remain a controversy for many years; however, for present purposes, a reasonable resolution might be to accept the notion of contiguous continuity. That is, current behavioral repertoires provide the foundation for the development of the next succeeding stage which, in turn, directly affects the next subsequent stage or level of development. This perspective was discussed in more detail in Chapter 2.

Whether behavior acquired earlier in the child's life is reflected much later is a moot point for now. What is obvious is the immediate impact of the child's current behavioral repertoire on the acquisition of subsequent new response forms. Perhaps the more reasonable hope should be to demonstrate successive impact over time rather than attempting to predict, based on the preschool years, much later behavior. It seems rather remarkable that investigations have been able to report long-term effects such as those described by Lazar et al. (1982). These outcomes suggest the importance of studying the environments of the children to determine what aspects have maintained the original gain or what changes have occurred to reduce or dilute the initial experimental and control differences.

The collection of such information will no doubt reflect the interactive nature of development, as has been proposed by a number of major theorists (Piaget, 1970; Uzgiris, 1981; Sameroff & Chandler, 1975; Lewis & Rosenblum, 1974). Development is systematically shaped by the transactions between the organism and the environment. An intricate web of reciprocal transactions occurs that leads to the transformation of the child's behavioral repertoire. Unless the child's biology and environment remain relatively constant, one would be correct to predict variable outcomes for individual children. When investigations report that experimental groups maintain their superiority over time, one might speculate that the early intervention has not only affected the child but influenced other important environmental factors as well.

What, then, is a reasonable expectation for the longevity of program impact? A simple answer seems unlikely. Rather, longevity of program impact is most likely determined by a number of variables. The length, quality, and content of an early-intervention effort will doubtless affect the longevity of the impact. The Early Training Project developed by Gray and Klaus (Gray, Ramsey, & Klaus, 1982) documented the change of the experimental and control children enrolled in this project over a period of eighteen years in tandem with attempting to examine economic and political changes in the environments of the children and their families. The outcomes of this investigation accurately reflect the issues raised in the preceding discussion. That is, one cannot reasonably hope to evaluate the long-term impact of early-intervention efforts in a vacuum. Rather, the subsequent environments experienced by the children and their families must be seen as the mediator of subsequent development and be responsible, in part, for subsequent outcomes. Early-intervention programs cannot protect at-risk or handicapped children from the future. Such programs may be able to enhance the child's development, but these enhancements are surely not automatically retained. Rather, the child's progress will depend upon his or her current repertoire and the transactions that occur between the child and subsequent environments.

The Expectancy: Normal Behavior?

Another philosophical issue facing early interventionists and those concerned with the enterprise is the selection of outcome goals. Said another way, what is, or should be, the expectancies for children participating in early-intervention programs? An immediate response is often to mention the paramount need for individualization of goals and objectives for children, thus requiring expectancies to be personalized as well. However, expectancies seem to acquire an added dimension when general program impact is examined. For groups of children, expectancies appear to drift toward normalcy. Readers may disagree that the expectation of normal functioning is a goal of early-intervention programs focused on handicapped children. Nevertheless, the majority of early-intervention programs previously reviewed employed measures that were standardized on normal children. Although such measures may be useful (Ramey, Campbell, & Wasik, 1982), their deployment suggests an implicit comparison with normal behavior. Establishing a target of normal functioning may be at times appropriate and sensible and may become troublesome only when programs which fail to reach that goal are devalued exclusively because of such comparisons.

Although decisions about program effectiveness tend to be based on whether the intervention produced differences found to be statistically significant, a corollary step is to establish the educational significance or worth of such differences. For example, Clunies-Ross (1979) reported that the Down syndrome infants who were enrolled earlier in an intervention program made the greater progress. The next question to ponder is that of the significance of such progress. Does an increase in the IQ render the quality of the child's or family's life better? I would venture to predict that if a program changed the enrolled children's IQ scores from 40 to 60, a less enthusiastic response by reviewers would be expected than if the IQ scores shifted from 70 to 90. The latter gain suggests that the children are functioning within normal limits, while the gain, from 40 to 60, does not. I do not believe that investigators, practitioners, and consumers consciously make such distinctions, but I strongly suspect that an inarticulated hope or expectancy for the handicapped child is for functioning within the realm of normalcy. When programs fall short of this expectancy, their worth may be questioned (Piper & Pless, 1980; Ferry, 1981; Gibson & Fields, 1984).

Given current technology and knowledge, programs often assist handicapped children in making only modest gains (Bricker & Dow, 1980; Hanson & Schwarz, 1978; Ludlow & Allen, 1979), giving rise to the question of whether the resource investment was "worth" the gain. Society appears to have agreed that assisting the handicapped individual to gain more independence is an acceptable goal toward which resources should be expended (e.g., P.L. 94–142). If so, then it seems important to tease from this commitment the often accompanying expectancy that intervention will render the child normal. Expectancies need to be tempered with the reality that less dramatic outcomes for impaired children are the rule rather than the exception. Although the goal of normal functioning may not be within reach of many children, this does not mean that efforts to assist the handicapped child should be diluted or reduced. Rather, expectancies should be changed to accept consistent progress toward independent and satisfactory functioning, even if there is no associated evidence of change on more traditional standardized measures. Such changes in expectancy require that other reliable and valid indices of child progress be developed, a problem addressed in a later section of this book.

SUMMARY

This chapter has presented a review of a variety of early-intervention programs designed to eliminate or attenuate deficits in populations of handicapped children or to keep deficits from occurring in populations of medically or environmentally at-risk children and to affect families in a positive manner. Although objective data on program impact were provided, the majority of these studies have serious methodological or design flaws which may lead critics to question the validity of such data in evaluating program effectiveness (see Dunst & Rheingrover, 1981; Odom & Fewell, 1983; Gibson & Fields, 1984).

Many of the method and design flaws result from conducting research on intervention programs primarily designed to meet the needs of participating children and families. For example, of the reviewed studies, few had matched controls. Establishing nonintervention controls is difficult because of federal and state mandates, not to mention ethical and humanitarian concerns for the provision of services to disabled children. Comparing approaches or models is often difficult because participating children and families may not necessarily be similar in terms of critical variables such as age, SES, or developmental level. Except in large metropolitan areas, problems stemming from low-incidence groups, attendance, and attrition cause serious problems for investigators attempting to examine change. Failure to specify the program philosophy, content, and instructional strategies also may render outcomes questionable. Without detailed knowledge of what and how material is presented, it is difficult to determine what reported gains by children and parents actually reflect in terms of programmatic input. Finally, instruments that reflect a program's emphasis and measure functional and useful change are lacking. These deficiencies present significant barriers to the intervention researcher.

Rather than to belittle past efforts at program evaluation, a more serviceable perspective is to use these investigations to provide guidance for developing a template for change. The analyses of available program evaluation data are an ideal base from which to develop future guidelines for investigators interested in documenting program impact. In particular, more attention must be given to developing or isolating relevant and appropriate outcome measures for children and families. Then more innovative strategies for measuring change on these variables will be required. Finally, alternative nontraditional but acceptable control procedures must be found for comparing program impacts.

References

Adelson, E., & Fraiberg, S. (1975). Gross motor development in infants blind from birth. In B. Friedlander, G. Sterritt, & G. Kirk (Eds.), *Exceptional infant* (Vol. 3). New York: Brunner/Mazel.

Adubato, S., Adams, M., & Budd, K. (1981). Teaching a parent to train a spouse in child management techniques. *Journal of Applied Behavior Analysis, 14,* 193–205.

Aronson, M., & Fallstrom, K. (1977). Immediate and long-term effects of developmental training in children with Down's syndrome. *Developmental Medicine and Child Neurology, 19,* 489–494.

Bagnato, S., & Neisworth, J. (1980). The intervention efficiency index: An approach to preschool program accountability. *Exceptional Children, 46,* 264–269.

Bailey, E., & Bricker, D. (1984). The efficacy of early intervention for severely handicapped infants and young children. *Topics in Early Childhood Special Education, 4*(3), 30–51.

Baker, B., & Heifetz, L. (1976). The Read Project: Teaching manuals for parents of retarded children. In T. Tjossem (Ed.), *Intervention strategies for high risk infants and young children.* Baltimore, MD: University Park Press.

Baker, B., Heifetz, L., & Murphy, D. (1980). Behavioral training for parents of mentally retarded children: One year follow-up. *American Journal of Mental Deficiency, 85,* 31–38.

Barrera, M., Routh, D., Parr, C., Johnson, N., Arendshorst, D., Goolsby, E., & Schroeder, S. (1976). Early intervention with biologically handicapped infants and young children: A preliminary study with each child as his own control. In T. Tjossem (Ed.), *Intervention strategies for high risk infants and young children.* Baltimore, MD: University Park Press.

Bayley, N. (1969). *Bayley Scales of Infant Development.* New York: The Psychological Corporation.

Beller, E. (1979). Early intervention programs. In J. Osofsky (Ed.), *Handbook of infant development.* New York: Wiley.

References

Berry, P., Gunn, V., & Andrews, R. (1984). Development of Down's syndrome children from birth to five years. *Perspectives and Progress in Mental Retardation, 1,* 167–177.

Bidder, R., Bryant, G., & Gray, O. (1975). Benefits of Down's syndrome children through training their mothers. *Archives of Disease in Childhood, 50,* 383–386.

Bricker, D. (1981, January). *A handicapped children's early education program: Rationale, program description, and impact.* Final report for the Division of Innovation and Development, Office of Special Education. Eugene, OR.

Bricker, D., Bailey, E., & McDonnell, A. (undated). *Early intervention program.* Final report submitted to the Handicapped Children's Early Education Programs, U.S. Department of Education. Eugene, OR.

Bricker, D., & Carlson, L. (1982). The relationship of object and prelinguistic social-communicative schemes to the acquisition of early linguistic skills in developmentally delayed infants. In G. Edgar, N. Haring, J. Jenkins, & C. Pious (Eds.), *Mentally handicapped children.* Baltimore, MD: University Park Press.

Bricker, D., Carlson, L., & Schwarz, R. (1981). A discussion of early intervention for infants with Down's syndrome. *Pediatrics, 67,* 45–46.

Bricker, D., & Dow, M. (1980). Early intervention with the young severely handicapped child. *Journal of the Association for the Severely Handicapped, 5,* 130–142.

Bricker, D., & Sheehan, R. (1981). Effectiveness of an early intervention program as indexed by child change. *Journal of the Division for Early Childhood, 4,* 11–27.

Bromwich, R., & Parmelee, A. (1979). An intervention program for preterm infants. In T. Field, A. Sostek, S. Goldberg, & H. Shuman (Eds.), *Infants born at risk.* Jamaica, NY: Spectrum Publications.

Bronfenbrenner, U. (1975). Is early intervention effective? In B. Friedlander, G. Sterritt, & G. Kirk (Eds.), *Exceptional infant: Assessment and intervention* (Vol. 3). New York: Brunner/Mazel.

Caldwell, B. (1978). *Home observation for measurement of the environment.* Syracuse, NY: Syracuse University Press.

Cheseldine, S., & McConkey, R. (1979). Parental speech to young Down's syndrome children: An intervention study. *American Journal of Mental Deficiency, 83,* 612–620.

Christophersen, E., & Sykes, B. (1979). An intensive, home based family training program for developmentally delayed children. In L. Hamerlynck (Ed.), *Behavioral systems for the developmentally disabled: I. School and family environments.* New York: Brunner/Mazel.

Cicchetti, D., & Sroufe, A. (1976). The relationship between affective and cognitive development in Down's syndrome infants. *Child Development, 47,* 920–929.

Clarke, A., & Clarke, A. (1976). *Early experience: Myth and evidence.* New York: The Free Press.

Clarke, A., & Clarke, A. (1977). Prospects for prevention and amelioration of mental retardation: A guest editorial. *American Journal of Mental Deficiency, 81,* 523–533.

Clarke-Stewart, K. (1981). Parent education in the 1970's. *Educational Evaluation and Policy Analysis, 3,* 47–58.

Clunies-Ross, G. (1979). Accelerating the development of Down's syndrome infants and young children. *The Journal of Special Education, 13,* 169–177.

Connolly, B., Morgan, S., Russell, F., & Richardson, B. (1980). Early intervention with Down syndrome children. *Physical Therapy, 60,* 1405–1408.

Dmitriev, V. (1979). Infant learning program for Down's syndrome. In B. Darby & M. May (Eds.), *Infant assessment: Issues and applications.* Seattle, WA: WESTAR.

Dunst, C., & Rheingrover, R. (1981). An analysis of the efficacy of infant intervention programs with organically handicapped children. *Evaluation and Program Planning, 4,* 287–323.

Ferry, P. (1981). On growing new neurons: Are early intervention programs effective? *Pediatrics, 67,* 38–41.

Field, T. (1981). Intervention for high-risk infants and their parents. *Educational Evaluation and Policy Analysis, 3,* 69–78.

Field, T., Widmayer, S., Stringer, S., & Ignaloff, E. (1980). Teenage, lower-class black mothers and their pre-term infants: An intervention and developmental follow up. *Child Development, 51,* 426–436.

Filler, J., & Kasari, C. (1981). Acquisition, maintenance and generalization of parent-taught skills with two severely handicapped infants. *The Journal of the Association for the Severely Handicapped, 6,* 30–38.

Folio, R., & DuBose, R. (1974). *Peabody developmental motor scales* (IMRID Behavioral Science Monograph, No. 25). Nashville, TN: Peabody College.

Fowler, W. (1975). A developmental learning approach to infant care in a group setting. In B. Friedlander, G. Sterritt, & G. Kirk (Eds.), *Exceptional infant* (Vol. 3). New York: Brunner/Mazel.

Fraiberg, S. (1975). Intervention in infancy: A program for blind infants. In B. Friedlander, G. Sterritt, & G. Kirk (Eds.), *Exceptional infant* (Vol. 3). New York: Brunner/Mazel.

Friedman, S., & Sigman, M. (Eds.) (1981). *Pre-term birth and psychological development.* New York: Academic Press.

Garber, H., & Heber, R. (1977). The Milwaukee project. In P. Mittler (Ed.),

Research to practice in mental retardation: I. Care and intervention. Baltimore, MD: University Park Press.

Gibson, D., & Fields, D. (1984). Early stimulation programs for Down's syndrome: An effectiveness inventory. In M. Wolraich & D. Routh (Eds.), *Advances in Developmental and Behavioral Pediatrics* (Vol. 5). Greenwich, CN: JAI Press.

Goodman, J., Cecil, H., & Barker, W. (1984). Early intervention with retarded children: Some encouraging results. *Developmental Medicine and Child Neurology, 26,* 47–55.

Gordon, N., & Kogan, K. (1975). A mother instruction program: Behavior changes with and without therapeutic intervention. *Child Psychiatry and Human Development, 6,* 89–105.

Gray, S., Ramsey, B., & Klaus, R. (1982). *From 3 to 20: The early training project.* Baltimore, MD: University Park Press.

Guralnick, M., & Bricker, D. (in press). The effectiveness of early intervention for children with cognitive and general developmental delays. In M. Guralnick & F. Bennett (Eds.), *The effectiveness of early intervention.* New York: Academic Press.

Hanson, M. (1976). Evaluation of training procedures used in a parent-implemented intervention program for Down's syndrome infants. *AAESPH Review, 1,* 36–52.

Hanson, M. (1977). *Teaching your Down's syndrome infant: A guide for parents.* Baltimore, MD: University Park Press.

Hanson, M., & Schwarz, R. (1978). Results of a longitudinal intervention program for Down's syndrome infants and their families. *Education and Training of the Mentally Retarded, 13,* 403–407.

Harris, S. (1981). Effects of neurodevelopmental therapy on motor performance of infants with Down's syndrome. *Developmental Medicine and Child Neurology, 23,* 477–483.

Haskins, R., Finkelstein, N., & Stedman, D. (1978). Infant stimulation programs and their effects. *Pediatric Annals, 7,* 123–144.

Hayden, A., & Beck, G. (1982). The epidemiology of high risk and handicapped infants. In C. Ramey & P. Trohanis (Eds.), *Finding and educating at-risk and handicapped infants.* Baltimore, MD: University Park Press.

Hayden, A., & Dmitriev, V. (1975). The multidisciplinary preschool program for Down's syndrome children at the University of Washington model preschool center. In B. Friedlander, G. Sterritt, & G. Kirk (Eds.), *Exceptional infant* (Vol. 3). New York: Brunner/Mazel.

Hayden, A., & Haring, N. (1976). Programs for Down's syndrome children at the University of Washington. In T. Tjossem (Ed.), *Intervention strategies for high risk infants and young children.* Baltimore, MD: University Park Press.

Hayden, A., & Haring, N. (1977). The acceleration and maintenance of developmental gains in Down's syndrome school-age children. In P. Mittler (Ed.), *Research to practice in mental retardation: I. Care and intervention.* Baltimore, MD: University Park Press.

Hayden, A., & McGinness, G. (1977). Bases for early intervention. In E. Sontag, J. Smith, & N. Certo (Eds.), *Educational programming for the severely and profoundly handicapped.* Reston, VA: Council for Exceptional Children.

Heber, R., & Garber, H. (1975). The Milwaukee project: A study of the use of family intervention to prevent cultural-familial mental retardation. In B. Friedlander, G. Sterritt, & G. Kirk (Eds.), *Exceptional infant* (Vol. 3). New York: Brunner/Mazel.

Hetherington, R., Suttill, J., Holmlund, C., & Frey, D. (1979). Evaluation of a regional resource center of multiply handicapped retarded children. *American Journal of Mental Deficiency, 83,* 367–379.

Horton, K. (1976). Early intervention for hearing-impaired infants and young children. In T. Tjossem (Ed.), *Intervention strategies for high risk infants and young children.* Baltimore, MD: University Park Press.

Hunt, J. (1980). Implications of plasticity and hierarchical achievements for the assessment of development and risk of mental retardation. In D. Sawin, R. Hawkins, L. Walker, & J. Penticuff (Eds.), *Exceptional infant: Vol. 4. Psychosocial risks in infant environment transactions.* New York: Brunner/Mazel.

Jensen, A. (1969). A theory of primary and secondary familial mental retardation. In N. Ellis (Ed.), *International review of research in mental retardation* (Vol. 4). New York: Academic Press.

Jew, W. (1974, May–June). Helping handicapped infants and their families. *Children Today,* 7–10.

Johnson, D. (1975). The development of a program for parent-child education among Mexican-Americans in Texas. In B. Friedlander, G. Sterritt, & G. Kirk (Eds.), *Exceptional infant: Assessment and intervention* (Vol. 3). New York: Brunner/Mazel.

Kagan, J., Kearsley, R., & Zelazo, P. (1978). *Infancy: Its place in human development.* Cambridge, MA: Harvard University Press.

Karnes, M., Schwedel, A., Lewis, G., Rats, D., & Esry, D. (1981). Impact of early programming for the handicapped: A follow-up study into the elementary school. *Journal of the Division for Early Childhood, 4,* 62–79.

Kysela, G., Hillyard, A., McDonald, L., & Ahlster-Taylor, J. (1981). Early intervention, design and evaluation. In R. Schiefelbusch & D. Bricker (Eds.), *Early language: Acquisition and intervention.* Baltimore, MD: University Park Press.

LaVeck, B., & Brehm, S. (1978). Individual variability among children with Down's syndrome. *Mental Retardation, 16,* 135–137.

References

Lazar, I., Darlington, R., Murray, H., Royce, J., & Snipper, A. (1982). Lasting effects of early education: A report from the consortium for longitudinal studies. *Monographs of the Society for Research in Child Development,* 47(Serial No. 195). Chicago: University of Chicago Press.

Leib, S., Benfield, G., & Guidabaldi, J. (1980). Effects of early intervention and stimulation on the preterm infant. *Pediatrics, 66,* 83-90.

Levenstein, P. (1970). Cognitive growth in preschoolers through verbal interaction with mothers. *American Journal of Orthopsychiatry, 40,* 426-432.

Lewis, M. (1976). What do we mean when we say "Infant intelligence scores?" A sociopolitical question. In M. Lewis (Ed.), *Origins of intelligence.* New York: Plenum Press.

Lewis, M., & Rosenblum, L. (1974). *The effect of the infant on its caregiver.* New York: Wiley.

Lewis, M., & Starr, M. (1979). Developmental continuity. In J. Osofsky (Ed.), *Handbook of infant development.* New York: Wiley.

Ludlow, J., & Allen, L. (1979). The effect of early intervention and preschool stimulus on the development of the Down's syndrome child. *Journal of Mental Deficiency Research, 23,* 29-44.

Madden, J., Levenstein, P., & Levenstein, S. (1976). Longitudinal IQ outcomes of the mother-child home program. *Child Development, 47,* 1015-1025.

McCall, R. (1979). The development of intellectual functioning in infancy and the prediction of later IQ. In J. Osofsky (Ed.), *Handbook of infant development.* New York: Wiley.

McCarthy, D. (1972). *McCarthy Scales of Children's Abilities.* New York: Psychological Corporation.

Minde, K., Shosenberg, N., Marton, P., Thompson, J., Ripley, J., & Burns, S. (1980). Self help groups in a premature nursery—A controlled evaluation. *The Journal of Pediatrics, 96,* 933-940.

Moore, M., Fredericks, H., & Baldwin, V. (1981). The long-range effects of early childhood education on a trainable mentally retarded population. *Journal of the Division for Early Childhood, 4,* 93-110.

Nielsen, G., Collins, S., Meisel, J., Lowry, M., Engh, H., & Johnson, D. (1975). An intervention program for atypical infants. In B. Friedlander, G. Sterritt, & G. Kirk (Eds.), *Exceptional infant* (Vol. 3). New York: Brunner/Mazel.

Odom, S., & Fewell, R. (1983). Program evaluation in early childhood special education: A meta-evaluation. *Educational Evaluation and Policy Analysis, 5,* 445-460.

Oregon State Mental Health Division (1977). *The Student Progress Record.* Salem, OR.

Petrie, P., Kratochwell, T., Bergan, J., & Nicholson, G. (1981). Teaching parents to teach their children: Applications in the pediatric setting. *Journal of Pediatric Psychology, 6,* 275-292.

Piaget, J. (1970). Piaget's theory. In P. Mussen (Ed.), *Carmichael's manual of child psychology* (Vol. 1). New York: Wiley.

Piper, M., & Pless, I. (1980). Early intervention for infants with Down's syndrome: A controlled trial. *Pediatrics, 65,* 463-468.

Ramey, C., & Campbell, F. (1979). Supplemental preschool education for disadvantaged children. *School Review, 82,* 171-189.

Ramey, C., Campbell, F., & Wasik, B. (1982). Use of standardized tests to evaluate early childhood special education programs. *Topics in Early Childhood Special Education, 1,* 51-60.

Ramey, C., Farran, D., & Campbell, F. (1979). Early intervention: From research to practice. In B. Darby & M. May, *Infant assessment: Issues and applications.* Seattle, WA: WESTAR.

Ramey, C., MacPhee, D., & Yeates, K. (1983). Preventing developmental retardation: A general systems model. In L. Bond & J. Joffe (Eds.), *Facilitating infant and early childhood development.* Hanover, NH: University Press of New England.

Rescorla, L., & Zigler, E. (1981). The Yale child welfare research program: Implications for social policy. *Education Evaluation and Policy Analysis, 3,* 5-14.

Revill, S., & Blunden, R. (1979). A home training service for preschool developmentally handicapped children. *Behavior Research and Therapy, 17,* 207-214.

Reynell, J. (1969). *Reynell developmental language scales.* Windsor, England: N.F.E.R. Publishing Co., Ltd.

Rogers, S., D'Eugenio, D., Brown, S., Donovan, C., & Lynch, E. (1977). *Early intervention developmental profile.* Ann Arbor, MI: University of Michigan Press.

Rosen-Morris, D., & Sitkei, E. (1981). Strategies for teaching severely/profoundly handicapped infants and young children. *Journal of the Division for Early Childhood, 4,* 79-93.

Rynders, J., & Horrobin, M. (1975). Project Edge: The University of Minnesota's communication stimulation program for Down's syndrome infants. In B. Friedlander, G. Sterritt, & G. Kirk (Eds.), *Exceptional infant* (Vol. 3). New York: Brunner/Mazel.

Rynders, J., & Horrobin, M. (1980). Educational provisions for young children with Down's syndrome. In J. Gottlieb (Ed.), *Educating mentally retarded persons in the mainstream.* Baltimore, MD: University Park Press.

Safford, P., Gregg, L., Schneider, G., & Sewell, T. (1976). A stimulation program for young sensory-impaired, multihandicapped children. *Education and Training of the Mentally Retarded, 11,* 12-17.

References

Sameroff, A. (1981). Longitudinal studies of preterm infants: A review of chapters 17–20. In S. Friedman & M. Sigman (Eds.), *Preterm birth and psychological development*. New York: Academic Press.

Sameroff, A., & Chandler, M. (1975). Reproductive risk and the continuum of caretaking casualty. In F. Horowitz, M. Hetherington, S. Scarr-Salapatek, & G. Siegel (Eds.), *Review of child development research* (Vol. 4). Chicago: University of Chicago Press.

Scarr-Salapatek, S., & Williams, M. (1973). The effects of early stimulation on low-birth-weight infants. *Child Development, 44,* 94–101.

Shapiro, L., Gordon, R., & Neiditch, C. (1977). Documenting change in young multiply handicapped children in a rehabilitation center. *The Journal of Special Education, 11,* 241–257.

Shearer, D., & Shearer, M. (1976). The Portage Project: A model for early childhood intervention. In T. Tjossem (Ed.), *Intervention strategies for high risk infants and young children*. Baltimore, MD: University Park Press.

Shearer, M., & Shearer, D. (1972). The Portage Project: A model for early childhood education. *Exceptional Children, 39,* 210–217.

Simeonsson, R., Cooper, D., & Scheiner, A. (1982). A review and analysis of the effectiveness of early intervention programs. *Pediatrics, 69,* 635–641.

Simmons-Martin, A. (1981). Efficacy report: Early education project. *Journal of the Division for Early Childhood, 4,* 5–10.

Skeels, H. (1966). Adult status of children with contrasting early life experiences. *Monographs of the Society for Research in Child Development, 31*(3, Serial No. 105). Chicago: University of Chicago Press.

Soboloff, H. (1981). Early intervention—Fact or fiction? *Developmental Medicine and Child Neurology, 23,* 261–266.

Spiker, D. (1982). Parent involvement in early intervention activities with their young children with Down's syndrome. *Education and Training of the Mentally Retarded, 17,* 24–29.

Stock, J., Wnek, L., Newborg, E., Schenck, J., Gabel, J., Spurgeon, M., & Ray, H. (1976). *Evaluation of handicapped children's early education program (HCEEP)*. Final report to Bureau of Education for the Handicapped, U.S. Department of Education. Columbus, OH: Battelle.

Strain, P. (1984). Efficacy research with young handicapped children: A critique of the status quo. *Journal of the Division for Early Childhood, 9,* 4–10.

Tyler, N., & Kogan, K. (1977). Reduction of stress between mothers and their handicapped children. *The American Journal of Occupational Therapy, 31,* 151–155.

Uzgiris, I. (1981). Experience in the social context. In R. Schiefelbusch & D. Bricker (Eds.), *Early language: Acquisition and intervention*. Baltimore, MD: University Park Press.

Uzgiris, I., & Hunt, J. McV. (1975). *Assessment in infancy: Ordinal scales of psychological development.* Urbana, IL: University of Illinois Press.

Weiss, R. (1981). INREAL intervention for language handicapped and bilingual children. *Journal of the Division for Early Childhood, 4,* 40–51.

White, K., Mastropieri, M., & Casto, G. (1984). An analysis of special education early childhood projects approved by the Joint Dissemination Review Panel. *Journal of the Division for Early Childhood, 9,* 11–26.

White, O., Edgar, E., Haring, N., Affleck, J., Hayden, A., & Bendersky, M. (1980). *UPAS: Uniform performance assessment system.* Columbus, OH: Charles E. Merrill.

Zeitlin, S. (1981). Learning through coping: An effective preschool program. *Journal of the Division for Early Childhood, 4,* 53–61.

Zigler, E., & Cascione, R. (1977). Head start has little to do with mental retardation: A reply to Clarke and Clarke. *American Journal of Mental Deficiency, 82,* 246–249.

CHAPTER 5

LEGAL AND LEGISLATIVE DECISIONS

Although numerous legal decisions and legislative enactments have affected education policy and services in the United States, the focus of this chapter will be those decisions and enactments that have had an impact on Early Childhood/Special Education. Further, no attempt will be made to provide extensive detail on particular cases or legislative enactments. Rather, the goal is to provide a general sense of the history that has led to contemporary perspectives, which will, in turn, serve as indicators for future decisions and policy.

This chapter begins with a discussion of the evolution of rights for minority and handicapped persons. This legal and legislative foundation has been essential to the development of programs and services for the child who has not yet entered the public education system. This legal and legislative foundation also has served to modify public schools to accommodate previously excluded preschool-age children. Given this background, federal policy that affects the handicapped infant and preschool-age child is reviewed. Information on the federal scene is complemented by information that governs state and local policy. A discussion of selected legal issues of particular pertinence to the birth-to-five population is then offered. Finally, issues that will face parents and professionals in the future are highlighted.

EVOLUTION OF RIGHTS FOR THE HANDICAPPED

Understanding current laws and policy that affect the handicapped infant and preschool-age child can be enhanced by a cursory examination of the historical development of rights for the handicapped in general.

Legal and Legislative Decisions

Civil Rights Movement

Many authorities believe that the development of the civil rights movement for minorities was the major impetus underlying the gradual acquisition of rights for the handicapped person. Often, those of us working with handicapped populations tend to forget that these persons compose a minority group whose rights have been historically violated in ways similar to those experienced by other minority groups. Whether a person is discriminated against because of his or her race or because of a physical disability makes little difference in the outcome—that is, that the person's rights have been diminished or entirely restricted. The civil rights movement of the early 1950s required that the nation face the active discriminatory acts perpetuated in training, hiring, housing, and the public schools for racial minorities, the poor, and the handicapped (Allen, 1984). The civil rights movement brought into sharp focus the rights of the individual and, in particular, the "rights of children not to be labeled, right of due process, and the right of a child to challenge a system that purports to be operating in his interest" (Cohen & DeYoung, 1973, p. 262).

Early Court Cases

Perhaps the most influential case for establishing rights for minority groups in the realm of public education was *Brown v. Board of Education* (1954). As most people know, this case addressed the separate-but-equal stance of the public schools. Previous to this supreme court decision, many local public school districts operated one school or schools for white children and separate schools for black children. Public school officials who maintained separate facilities argued that, although the schools were separate, they were equal. The supreme court disagreed and ruled that separate is inherently unequal. The intent of the supreme court decision was to assure an equal educational opportunity for all children attending public schools. Although *Brown v. Board of Education* provided the basis for the federal government to become enmeshed in the development of educational policy (Noel, Burke, & Valdivieso, 1985), many years elapsed before an equal education was assured for all minority groups. This has been particularly true for the handicapped child, who, well into the 1970s, was excluded from the "mainstream" of American education.

A second important early case was *Hobsen v. Hansen* (1967), in which the procedure of placing children in educational tracks based on test scores was challenged. The evidence indicated that children from poverty and minority circumstances were being labeled and assigned to "special education" tracks more frequently than nonminority children. The court ruled that the tracking system be abolished because the system represented "wrongful vestiges of the District's past history of segregation" (Burt, 1975, p. 315).

Two additional cases have had a significant impact on public school practice in relation to the testing and labeling of children. In both *Diana v.*

Board of Education (1970) and *Larry P. v. Riles* (1972), the inappropriate or incorrect labeling of children from minority groups was addressed. The decisions rendered by the courts in both cases radically changed the public school code in California by requiring that:

- children be tested in their primary language
- children from minority groups (e.g., black, Mexican, and Chinese) currently in classes for the mentally retarded be reevaluated
- the state develop and standardize IQ tests appropriate for minority groups (Abeson & Zettel, 1977)

Not only were the effects of these decisions felt in California but have, over time, rippled out to affect other states' statutes as well as affect federal policy and legislation (e.g., P.L. 94–142).

Litigation Directly Related to the Handicapped Individual

In the early 1970s, advocacy efforts of parents of handicapped children began to reap outcomes. Parents who had grown weary of battling public school teaching and administrative personnel took their grievances to court in an attempt to achieve educational equity for their handicapped children. In a series of landmark decisions, the court affirmed or reaffirmed a child's rights to:

- a free and appropriate education
- due process for grievances
- special education services without regard to arguments about lack of funds
- not be labeled handicapped or placed in a special education program without an adequate diagnosis (Gallagher, 1984)

Four important cases assisted in establishing these rights for handicapped children and their family: *PARC v. Commonwealth of Pennsylvania* (1971); *Mills v. Board of Education of Washington, D.C.* (1972); *Wyatt v. Stickney* (1971); and *New York ARC v. Rockefeller* (1972).

In *PARC v. Commonwealth of Pennsylvania,* the plaintiffs charged that because they were retarded they had been excluded or excused from attendance in public schools, had their admissions postponed, or in other ways been denied free access to public education (Cohen & DeYoung, 1973). After the arguments had been presented, the plaintiffs and the Commonwealth of Pennsylvania agreed to a consent decree, which specified that the state could not invoke any policy that would postpone, terminate, or deny children diagnosed as mentally retarded access to a publicly supported education. Further, the court decreed that the Commonwealth was to provide all retarded children between ages six to twenty-one with a publicly supported education by 1972 (Abeson & Zettel, 1977). For the first time, any school-age child, no matter how impaired, was eligible to receive a free, appropriate public education.

The parents of seven children residing in the District of Columbia brought a class action suit on behalf of all school-age handicapped children not currently being served in the District's public schools. In action similar to the PARC case, the court ruled that all school-age children, regardless of the severity of their handicap, were entitled to an appropriate, free education (Abeson & Zettel, 1977). Further, the public schools' arguments that adequate funds were unavailable for compliance with the court's ruling was explicitly addressed:

> If you have no special education funds, Judge Waddy (the presiding judge in the Mills case) replied, then reduce your expenditures on other educational programs, so that all children at least share equally in inadequate schooling. (Burt, 1975, p. 296)

Finally, both the PARC and Mills decisions required access to education in the most normalized environment and assured procedural due process when problems or disagreements with school officials were encountered (Gilhool & Stutman, 1978). For a more detailed discussion of the PARC and Mills cases, see Kirp, Kuriloff, and Buss (1975).

The PARC and Mills cases were focused on exclusion of handicapped children from the public schools. *Wyatt v. Stickney* and *New York ARC v. Rockefeller,* known as the Willowbrook case, addressed grievances brought by handicapped people incarcerated in large state residential facilities. In both cases, the plaintiffs argued that placement in such facilities required offering adequate treatment that is appropriate to their needs. In the Wyatt case, Judge Johnson ruled that institutionalized individuals have a constitutional right to appropriate treatment and that it be conducted in the least restrictive setting. While in the Willowbrook case, the court ruled that institutionalized retarded people had the constitutional right to be protected from harm.

These early court cases have affected the provision of educational services for handicapped children. However, the nature of the impact has not always been clear nor necessarily produced the most desired outcomes, for two reasons. First, as pointed out by Burt (1975), the courts have not always focused on the more critical issues. For example, Burt (1975) argues that the Wyatt court should have spent more effort in determining the community resources necessary to afford equal opportunities for institutionalized people rather than establishing detailed regulations for institutional living. In the PARC ruling, greater progress may have occurred if more effort had been directed toward emphasizing placement in least restrictive environments, rather than some of the other areas chosen for attention. So, too, in *Diana v. Board of Education,* the basic question should have been the merits of using only one test[1] to determine a child's intellectual capacity rather than using a culturally fair instrument (Burt, 1975).

The second reason for the unclear or undesired effects on the handicapped population of these and other related court decisions has been the court's inability to monitor or enforce implementation of judicial rulings. Kirp, Kuriloff, and Buss (1975) suggest five implementation difficulties faced by courts:

1. Changes in legal rulings do not automatically change the behavior of school personnel.
2. Some changes are extremely difficult to implement despite court rulings.
3. Some mandated changes are not pragmatically possible.
4. Some change may require the undertaking of prerequisite tasks not specified by the courts.
5. Mandated legal change is not always congruent with variations in children, settings, and other factors (e.g., parents may not want their child placed in a mainstream classroom; communities may not want group homes for retarded people located in residential areas).

These realities often produce unexpected or unwanted outcomes following legal rulings; however, taken as a whole, these early court cases have provided, in part, the basis for current rulings as well as the basis for federal and state policy concerning education of the handicapped child.

FEDERAL POLICY

Before a discussion of the specific federal policy that provides today's guidelines for education and treatment of handicapped populations, an understanding of the development of policy may be useful. Most often, federal policy is determined by legislation passed by the United States Congress. However, the interpretation of the legislation and, thus, the policy, often falls to the courts. In addition, the executive branch of government is largely responsible for the implementation of law passed by the Congress. Finally, concerned constituencies (e.g., public reaction, whether in general or from specific lobby or advocacy groups) can be instrumental in the determination

---

[1] Tests sample only aspects of the individual's behavioral repertoire, and most standardized tests were developed for nonhandicapped populations. Thus, to use only one such test to determine a disabled person's ability may produce a significantly biased and unrepresentative picture of the person's functioning.

Legal and Legislative Decisions

of federal policy. Thus, the content of legislation from which federal policy derives is determined by the slowly evolving political process of compromise and negotiation between legislative bodies, executive agencies, and concerned constituencies (Garwood, 1984; Noel, Burke, & Valdivieso, 1985). The schematic in Figure 5-1 reflects the impact of legislation and public reaction on the development of federal, state, and local policy.

As shown in Figure 5-1, the federal agency primarily responsible for the development of federal policy for the handicapped is the Office of Special Education and Rehabilitative Services (OSERS).[2] This agency is directed by relevant legislation passed by the U.S. Congress and is also responsive to public reaction. The policy evolved by the OSERS and other relevant federal

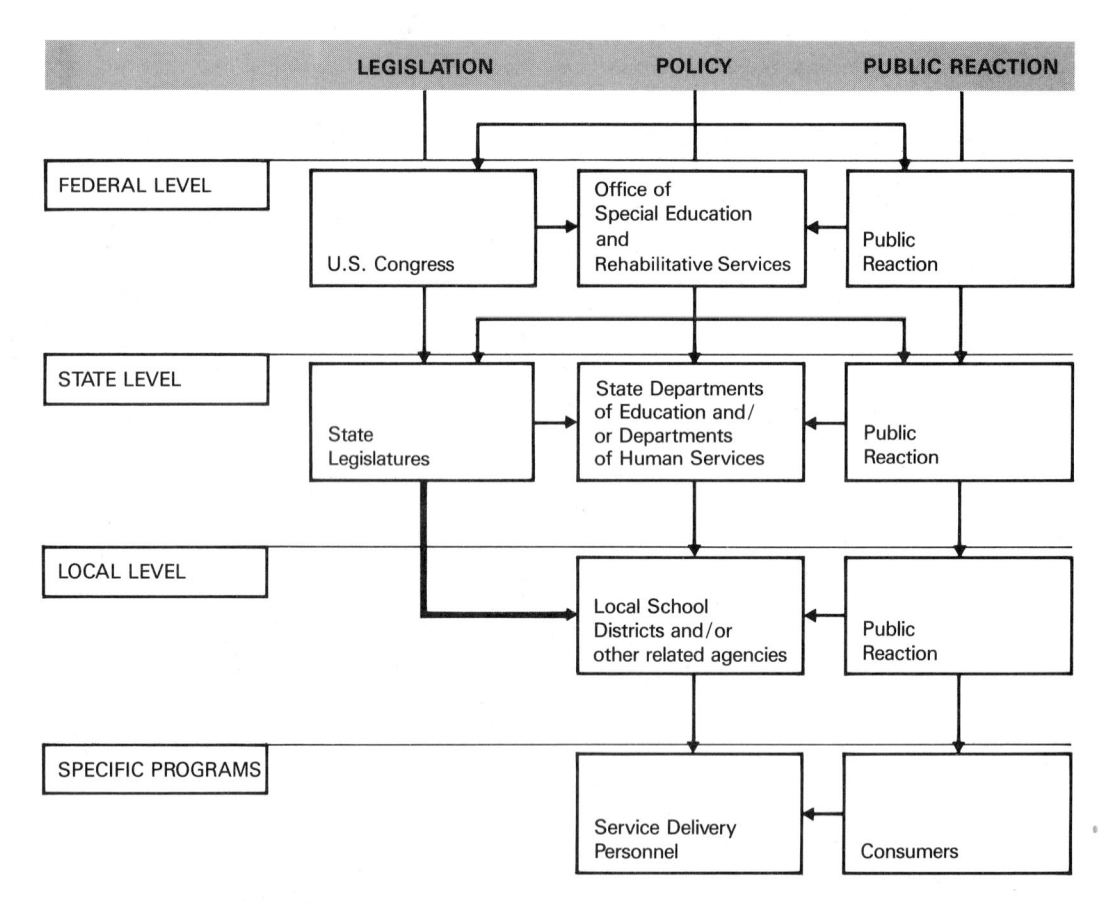

FIGURE 5-1. *Relationship of legislative bodies and public reaction to federal, state, and local administrative bodies responsible for policy development.*

[2]Other federal agencies, such as Maternal and Child Health, are also involved in the provision of services for at-risk and handicapped children.

108

agencies, in turn, affects the development of state policy by state departments of education or departments of human services. State or human services departments also are responsible for the development of state policy emanating from laws enacted by state legislatures. Local school districts and other relevant public agencies develop their policy based on laws passed by their state legislature and policy developed by their state department of education and/or human services. Service delivery personnel are the ultimate recipients of the federal and state policy that should provide the guidelines for their specific program. As indicated in Figure 5-1, public reaction can affect policy development and/or its implementation at the federal, state, and local levels.

FEDERAL LEGISLATION

Early Legislation

In the late 1950s, a rapid expansion in the development of federal policy for the handicapped began. According to Noel, Burke, and Valdivieso (1985), "The development of the federal policy base for special education is generally tied to the passage of two pieces of legislation"; these are P.L. 85-926 and the National Defense Education Act (NDEA). P.L. 85-926 provided support to institutions of higher education for training teachers to work with the mentally retarded population. NDEA authorized the use of federal funds to develop educational media for the mentally retarded and as such was the first major use of federal funds for educational purposes, thus providing the federal government an entry into the field of education of the handicapped.

From this modest beginning, the federal role in the determination of educational policy grew significantly during the Kennedy administration. In particular, several laws passed during this period established federal programs for training facilities construction, research, and direct service. According to Allen (1984), P.L. 88-164, which was passed in 1964, was:

> . . . the first major landmark for the participation of the federal government in service, training, and research activities focused specifically on mental retardation and related developmental problems. (p. 11)

This law was responsible for establishing the original thirty-six University Affiliated Facilities (UAF). The primary charge of the UAFs was multidisciplinary training of personnel from an array of disciplines to develop and implement diagnostic, service, and research programs to benefit the developmentally disabled person. In 1965, the passage of the Elementary and Secondary Education Act, or P.L. 89-10 and its amendments, established federal aid to education as a national policy; while P.L. 89-313 authorized federal assistance to state-supported schools and institutions and P.L. 89-750 provided the basis for federal involvement in special education (Noel, Burke, & Valdivieso, 1985).

In 1968, the U.S. Congress passed the first federal legislation specifically directed at young handicapped children. P.L. 90-538, or the Handicapped Children's Early Education Assistance Act, authorized the use of federal funds to establish a nationwide network of model demonstration programs designed to serve handicapped children. The intent of the federal legislation was to provide "seed" money for the development of model programs whose operation was to be assumed by the state or local district after thirty-six months. As discussed in Chapter 3, the Handicapped Children's Early Education Program (HCEEP) has met its original mission by establishing an influential network of early-education programs throughout the nation—the majority of which have been maintained by local efforts upon the termination of the federal support (Swan, 1980).

The Early and Periodic Screening, Diagnostic, and Treatment Program, or P.L. 90-248, was enacted in 1967 and was designed to promote early detection and/or prevention of developmental problems in young children. According to Allen (1984), passage of this law reflected congressional concern about variations in state law and policy focused on handicapped and chronically ill children. In 1972, P.L. 92-924, an amendment to the Economic Opportunity Act, required that the Head Start Program serve handicapped children. A further amendment, P.L. 93-644, passed in 1974, redefined the term *handicapped* to include more severely impaired children. In spite of the many federal enactments previously described, many handicapped persons continued to be excluded from public education programs or placed in programs of questionable value. This reality, heightened by parent advocacy, served to goad the U.S. Congress into passage of P.L. 93-112, P.L. 94-142, and, most recently, P.L. 98-199—perhaps the three most significant legislative acts passed for the handicapped person.

Section 504 of the Rehabilitation Act of 1973 (P.L. 93-112) was enacted to prevent discrimination on the basis of an individual's disability. Discrimination of a qualified handicapped person through architectural barriers and/or nonaccess to educational programs or services is explicitly prohibited by Section 504. Specifically for the young child, if a state offers programs to nonhandicapped children, these services must also be available to handicapped children. Failure to comply could result in withholding from the offending state all federal funds from the Department of Health and Human Services and the Department of Education (Ballard, 1977).

P.L. 94-142

Most authorities agree that the Education for All Handicapped Children Act (P.L. 94-142) is the single most important piece of legislation enacted to date for the handicapped child. According to Allen (1984):

A free, appropriate education in the least restrictive environment became, at long last, the right of every handicapped child. P.L. 94-142 also ensures the right of parents to procedural due process in decisions on classification and placement of their child, thus enabling parents to hold professional educators accountable. (p. 13)

Although the interpretation and implementation of some regulations stipulated in P.L. 94-142 have been varied, the laws appear to be clear in mandating:

- right to education—all handicapped children are to be provided with free appropriate public education
- right to nondiscriminatory evaluation
- right to IEP—clear statement of objectives for each child along with documentation of child's current and expected performance
- right to education in least restrictive environment
- right to due process
- right of parental participation (Gallagher, 1984)

Unless explicitly mandated by state law, P.L. 94-142 does not require the provision of educational programs for non–school-age children, although Part B of the Act does offer small incentive grants to encourage states to develop programs for handicapped children three to five years of age. However, some writers have suggested that this part of the law has resulted in a reduction in the number of preschool children served (Cohen, Semmes, & Guralnick, 1979; Insight, 1980). This may have occurred because the emphasis of P.L. 94-142 is on the school-age child. States may have diverted previously allocated funds for preschool-age children to develop expanded services for school-age children mandated by P.L. 94-142.

Although the law was heralded as landmark legislation for the handicapped, evaluative reports of the law's implementation suggest that complete compliance of many of the legislated mandates remains to be accomplished at state and local levels. For example, the second annual report to Congress on the implementation of P.L. 94-142 (1980) reported that a significant number of challenges remain to be met before P.L. 94-142 is fully implemented.

Such findings are probably responsible, in part, for the recent passage of P.L. 98-199 in December 1983. This act is known as the Education of the Handicapped Act Amendments of 1983 and was passed to revise and extend P.L. 94-142. Although a number of changes have been made, two are particularly pertinent to the handicapped infant and child. First, the preschool incentive grants program has been amended to include children birth to three years. In programs for handicapped children, the definition now

Legal and Legislative Decisions

explicitly "includes children from birth through eight years of age" and makes explicit that state plans must include "all handicapped children from birth through five years of age" (Section 623, P.L. 98-199). However, services for this population are still not mandatory by federal law. Second, P.L. 98-199 emphasizes the crucial role that parents have in the education of their handicapped child. According to Vencidos (no date), parents' roles should be expanded to:

1. provide training to parents and volunteers to assist them in becoming more effective when dealing with professionals
2. ensure that the majority of board members for private nonprofit programs be parents of handicapped children
3. ensure that private nonprofit organizations provide parent training and dissemination of information

Protection of Human Subjects

Children are frequently subjects in research, demonstrations, training, intervention, and evaluation activities. In order to protect the rights of these children as well as those of other human subjects, the federal government has enacted legislation for the protection of human subjects. In 1971, the Department of Health, Education and Welfare (DHEW) issued its first policy statement on the protection of human subjects. In these regulations, neither the definition of *subject* nor the definition of *at-risk* (for harm) indicated that children should be placed in a category receiving special safeguards.

In 1974, the Federal Register (Vol. 34, No. 105, May 30, 1974) indicated that the DHEW protection of human subject regulations were to become codified with some change. In the preamble to these new regulations, DHEW indicated that the agency is "developing policies dealing more specifically with research, development, and related activities involving the prisoner, the child, the fetus, the abortus, and the institutionalized individual with mental disability."

In July 1978, the National Research Act (P.L. 93-348) was signed into law, creating the National Commission for the Protection of Human Subjects of Biomedical and Behavioral Research. Among other charges, the commission was to study the nature of research involving children and how to protect the rights of children as subjects.

On January 26, 1981, the Department of Health and Human Services issued what it called the final regulations for the protection of human subjects. These regulations permit the exemption of certain types of research (e.g., studies likely to involve minimal risk to human subjects, such as research conducted in typical educational settings involving normal educational practices) from review by duly appointed review boards and indicated that other types of research (e.g., investigation requiring voice recordings, mild exercise, or study of existing data) could be expedited by not requiring a full review. These regulations made no mention of any additional or different protective procedures for children. However, revised regulations providing additional protection for children were issued in 1983. These regulations disallow the use of the exemption category for children and require assent by the child, if possible, in addition to parental consent.

Although federal regulation regarding the protection of human subjects was not specifically directed to at-risk or handicapped children, the rules have significance for researchers and interventionists. Specifically, those working with children are required to adhere to the general regulation as well as to those specifically directed to children. Most human-subject review boards require research protocols to contain detailed descriptions of the procedures, samples of informal consent and release forms, and information on how the privacy of the subject is to be protected.

It has taken twelve years to develop protection procedures directed specifically to children, and procedures specifically for at-risk or handicapped children are yet to be developed. Given recent court cases, such as Baby Jane Doe, specific federal regulations for the protection of at-risk and handicapped children appear imminent. In the interim, personnel working with these populations should become knowledgeable about existing human protection regulations and establish procedures to provide maximum protection for the children and families participating in their program.

An analysis of the federal legislation previously described suggests several trends in federal policy. Since the 1960s, the federal government has become increasingly involved in the development of policy for the education of the nation's young. In particular, mandates directed to ensuring equity for children of racial minorities or poverty and those with handicapping conditions have been passed. Gradually, the federal government has enacted laws to protect children whose rights have been violated. Federal law now requires placement in least restrictive settings and comparable programs for handicapped and nonhandicapped children. Another trend seen in federal policy has been the extending of services to the more severely handicapped, the handicapped infant/preschooler, and the older disabled youth. Passage of P.L. 98-199 makes clear the Congress's intent that states provide programs for the handicapped child under three years and for those at the secondary level as well as community transition programs. Finally, a clear trend emphasizing the family's participation in their handicapped child's education is apparent. Taken together, it appears that the U.S. Congress has accepted an increased responsibility both to protect and to enhance the lives of handicapped citizens.

FEDERAL AGENCIES

Within the Department of Education is an agency entitled the Office of Special Education and Rehabilitative Services (OSERS). This agency is primarily responsible for the development of programs for the handicapped person and is composed of three programs, as shown in Figure 5-2. Office of Special Education Programs (OSEP) is the principal agency for developing federal policy, programs, and projects relating to the education and training of the handicapped.[3] This agency deals primarily with state agencies of education and with institutions of higher learning that receive grants for research and model program development. In addition, OSEP provides funds and technical assistance for the development of more effective methods and materials and to disseminate this information to all state education agencies. OSEP has four divisions:

1. The Division of Innovation and Development, which supports research, demonstration, and evaluation activities. This Division supports the HCEEP network.
2. The Division of Personnel Preparation, which supports training programs for special education teachers, administrators, parents, and volunteers.
3. The Division of Assistance to States, which provides aid to state special education programs and for implementing P.L. 94-142.
4. The Division of Educational Services, which develops and disseminates educational media.

The National Institute of Handicapped Research was established in November 1978. The misssion of this agency is to provide a comprehensive

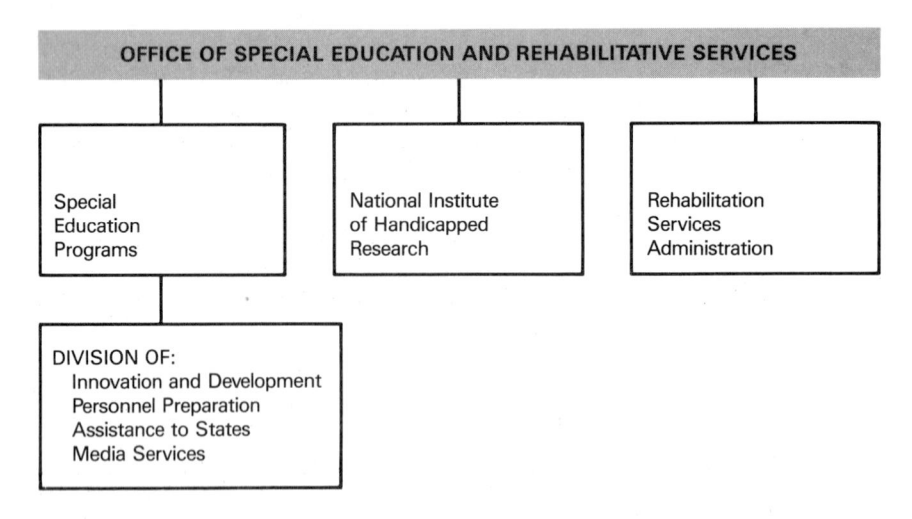

FIGURE 5-2. *Organizational structure for the Office of Special Education and Rehabilitative Services.*

[3]This information was taken from DHEW publications entitled Directory of National Information Sources on Handicapping Conditions and Related Services, August 1982.

and coordinated federal approach to all government funded research projects addressing handicapped populations. The Rehabilitation Services Administration provides services to disabled persons to assist them in becoming employable.

The ECH/SE area has historically been influenced most by the policy and program support coming from Office of Special Education Programs. In particular, the Division of Innovation and Development, which is responsible for the Handicapped Children's Early Education Program, and the Division of Personnel Preparation, which has been instrumental in supporting colleges and universities in training teachers, supervisors, and administrators to operate early-intervention programs.

STATE POLICY

One might assume that state educational policies closely reflect federal policy; however, Noel, Burke, and Valdivieso (1985) argue that state and local procedures often compromise the intent of federal policy. The implementation of federal policy at the state level is determined, in part, by the availability of necessary resources and by public opinion and interpretation of nonspecific federal mandates. Thus, differences in interpretation and implementation of federal policy do occur across states.

The U.S. Congress has never appropriated the necessary funds for states to completely implement the mandates of P.L. 94-142; thus, states have been required to provide much of the financial support for its implementation. So, as Noel, Burke, and Valdivieso (1985) note, "Differences in state educational policies largely reflect the general wealth of an individual state, the strength of its commitment to the handicapped, and its available resources" (p. 27). Further, in P.L. 94-142, educational services for the three-to-five age group were encouraged but not mandated, unless by state law, and the birth-to-three group was not mentioned. P.L. 98-199 has now extended the age to require state plans to "address the special education and related service needs of all handicapped children from birth through five years of age . . ." (P.L. 98-199, 97 stat. 1366). The federal government has gradually extended national policy to cover all handicapped children birth to twenty-one years; however, not all state policy has kept pace.

States that passed laws or instituted regulations for the handicapped preschool-age child have generally employed two strategies. Some states have chosen to lower the school age for its handicapped children, making preschool children eligible to receive services. The rules and regulations governing school-age children have been expanded to include the younger children. Other states have chosen to establish a new authority with rules and regulations specific to preschool-age handicapped populations (Smith, 1980). Even so, few states require that *all* handicapped children between birth to five years receive services. Rather, most states have statutes that mandate services only to identified subgroups of children (e.g., hearing impaired, visually impaired). Less than half of the states mandate services for all handicapped children three to five years, and far fewer states have any mandatory programs for the birth-to-three population (O'Connell, 1983; Smith, 1984).

Currently, both federal and state legislation addressing the birth-to-five population is in flux. Some states, like Oregon, have expanded their mandate for the handicapped infant and preschool child, while others, such as Idaho, have enacted new, more restrictive laws curtailing services to the birth-to-five population. Smith (1984) reports, "While several states have enacted laws over the past twenty years mandating early intervention, an almost equal number have repealed mandates" (p. 34).

In 1981, O'Connell (1983) conducted a survey of fifty states plus the District of Columbia to ascertain the mandated educational services for birth to five-year-old handicapped children. Table 5-1 presents the results of the O'Connell survey.

Not only is there extreme variation in the age and disability group served, but states also vary considerably in their definitions of preschool handicapped children, which are critical in determining who is eligible to receive services. The more restricted the definition, the more easily children can be denied services. Lessen and Rose (1980) report of the forty-four state consultants who responded to their survey:

- seven states had specific definitions
- fourteen states used existing categorical definitions
- four states used miscellaneous criteria
- nineteen states had no current guidelines

Likewise, state standards and regulations for certifying teachers of preschool handicapped children vary. O'Connell (1983) indicates that eighteen states have established certification standards, twelve states are developing standards, and twenty-one states report no specific standards.

TABLE 5-1 Number of states mandating services for handicapped children birth to five years of age

Number of states	Eligibility age for children	Disabilities served
8	0–5	All handicapped groups
12	3–5	All handicapped groups
4	0–3	Selected subgroups
7	3–5	Selected subgroups

NOTE: Data from fifty states plus the District of Columbia.
For more information, see O'Connell (1983).

The lack of certification or specific standards for personnel in this area can lead to two unfortunate outcomes. First, personnel may be poorly prepared in terms of content and strategies required to work effectively with handicapped infants or preschool children. Second, personnel prepared to work with school-age children may be inappropriately assigned to programs that serve preschool populations. The uniqueness of handicapped infants and young children and the necessary focus on the family as the intervention target require that personnel working with this group receive specialized training if intervention programs are to be effective.

Although the statistics reported previously may have changed somewhat in the ensuing years, it seems apparent that this nation lacks a consistent and comprehensive policy to provide guidance in establishing a consistent definition for the population; training and certification guidelines for personnel to work with the birth-to-five group; and mandated services to this population.

LOCAL POLICY

The lack of a comprehensive federal mandate for the birth-to-five age group and the reluctance and lack of resources at state levels to implement programs for this population have clearly affected service delivery at the local or community level. Several serious barriers exist to the implementation of programs for the birth-to-five population.

First, either because states do not provide guidelines or because the interpretation of the regulations is open, programs may be faced with considerable ambiguity concerning mandates or, worse, may have to adhere to inappropriate interpretation of state and federal law. On the state level, there may be disagreement about which agency is responsible for providing services, or two agencies may overlap in the provision of services, causing conflict or other problems at the local level. Interagency collaboration continues to be a serious problem for early-intervention programs and the families they serve.

Second, local programs are chronically underfunded if they depend entirely on state or local support, or both. This problem becomes particularly acute when local programs are not receiving adequate funds even to meet established state guidelines.

Third, often adequately trained personnel and instructional resources are not available. Programs may be staffed by individuals poorly prepared or trained to work with other age groups. In addition, resources for assisting in selecting evaluation and curricular materials may be unavailable at the local level, and states often cannot or do not provide adequate technical assistance.

Finally, programs for handicapped infants and young children are developed and maintained through a variety of agencies: (1) public schools with local district and state support; (2) other state-supported agencies, such as mental health, human services; (3) national nonprofit organizations, such

Legal and Legislative Decisions

as UCP; and (4) federally-supported programs, such as Head Start and the Handicapped Children's Early Education Program. Support and regulations for these programs can vary considerably along many dimensions, introducing one more source of inconsistency.

In spite of the problems facing the ECH/SE area, programs for infants and young children continue to grow. A network of programs has been established, and personnel are beginning to recognize the need for consistency in services and the need for adequate communication at the local, state, and federal levels.

Summary

This discussion of federal, state, and local policy should emphasize the need for further clarification, coordination, and extension of policy for the birth-to-five population. Wiegerink and Bartel (1981), among other authorities, believe that early-intervention programs are severely hampered because of

1. conflicting or ambiguous federal, state, and local legislation and regulations
2. poor or nonexistent interagency coordination
3. variation in definitions and eligibility requirements
4. confusion in leadership for the area

Recognition of such difficulties is a first step to their solution. The ensuing years will generate solutions to many of these current problems, resulting in a service delivery system that can effectively respond to the needs of all identified at-risk and handicapped infants and young children.

LEGAL ISSUES

> . . . recent Supreme Court interpretations of federal law governing educational rights of handicapped students make clear that school districts have significant procedural and substantive legal responsibilities to handicapped children. (Laski, 1985, p. 37)

This statement emphasizes the importance of past and future litigation for the handicapped child. The purpose of this section is to highlight four major legal issues that have had and will continue to have significant implications for all handicapped children. These issues include the right to appropriate education, to due process, to appropriate placement, and to treatment.

Legal Issues

Right to an Appropriate Education

Through earlier court action (e.g., *PARC v. Commonwealth of Pennsylvania, Mills v. District of Columbia*) and subsequent federal legislation, the foundation for access to public education was assured to even the most severely handicapped student. Although access to public education was granted, the quality of that education remains questionable. The result has been that the quality and appropriateness of the provided education has been a frequent issue in the courts.

Beginning with the PARC consent agreement, the courts have attempted to specify parameters of appropriate education for the handicapped student. The PARC decree stipulated the parameters of an appropriate program of education, including hours of instruction, pupil-teacher ratios, curriculum, and teacher qualification (Laski, 1985). However, subsequent scrutiny by the courts determined that the PARC decree did not result in many severely handicapped students receiving an "appropriate" education. Even with the advent of P.L. 94-142, which addresses the issue of an appropriate education through the mechanism of the IEP and multidisciplinary evaluation, many youngsters continued to be educated under regimes that were not designed to meet their educational needs.

In 1977, a petition for contempt and for enforcement of the PARC decree was brought to the U.S. District Court. In this action, the parents of two severely retarded boys alleged that the education their youngsters were receiving under the PARC decree was not appropriate. In 1982, the court ruled that the Philadelphia public schools must provide an appropriate education for their severely handicapped students, and the court has attempted to assure this through detailed specification of the school district's obligations.

In *Board of Education of Hendrick Hudson Central School District v. Rowley,* a deaf child's parents had requested that the child be provided with a sign-language interpreter. This request was denied by school officials. Through appeal, this case provided the Supreme Court with its first opportunity to interpret the provisions of P.L. 94-142. In 1982, the Supreme Court ruled that local schools must provide the necessary education and related services to permit the child to benefit from the instruction; however, "The majority further reasoned that it is not the role of courts to give substance to the term appropriate education" (McCarthy, 1983, p. 520). Thus, according to McCarthy (1983), the Supreme Court argued that the legal obligations imposed on states by P.L. 94-142 are primarily procedural and that determination of educational level or methods is the domain of state and local school officials.

A related court ruling occurred in *Campbell v. Talladega County Board of Education.* The court found that the instructional program provided to the plaintiff was inappropriate and ruled that the school district redesign the student's program to focus upon the acquisition of functional skills in four curricular areas: daily living activities, vocational activities, recreational activities, and social and community adjustment (Laski, 1985).

This brief review of selected legal action that has addressed the handicapped student's rights to an appropriate education leads to two observations. First, issues surrounding the determination of an appropriate education have been addressed by the courts, and thus, legal involvement specifying the parameters of an appropriate education is occurring. Second, the issue of appropriate education is far from resolved. Thus, the future should see continued legal activity directed toward further clarification of what constitutes an appropriate education for the handicapped population.

Appropriate Placement

The major issue surrounding the appropriate placement of handicapped students is their access to least restrictive environments. The clear intent of P.L. 94-142 is to place handicapped students in educational environments that provide them with maximal opportunity to interact with nonhandicapped students, *but* the intent also is that the students benefit educationally from placement. These two issues have produced considerable controversy and conflict within public schools. The goal is to place students in classes and programs that are as normalized as possible and yet still can provide the handicapped student an appropriate instructional program.

Gilhool and Stutman (1978) have argued that Section 504 and P.L. 94-142 were formed by the Congress to eliminate the historic segregation of handicapped individuals into institutions or isolated programs. Through this legislation, the congressional intent was to integrate handicapped children when possible into regular education programs and community settings. Gilhool and Stutman (1978) contend that "The integration imperative is thus crucial to all the purposes of the Acts [504 and P.L. 94-142]."

Many of the court decisions occurring in the 1970s are reflected in the Section 504 and P.L. 94-142 legislative intent for equal access and integration of the handicapped person into society. In particular, Gilhool and Stutman (1978) point out that the PARC decree states that placement in a regular class is preferred to placement in a special class and that placement in a special education class is preferable to placement in more isolated programs (e.g., special school, institutions). The Mills case encouraged placement in the most normalized settings, while the Wyatt ruling determined that even institutionalized persons have the right to be placed in the least restrictive setting necessary for effective training or education.

Although the courts clearly appear to support the integration of the handicapped person into the mainstream of life, these rulings have, to date, provided little guidance in how to assess the adequacy of specific placements. Establishing the criteria to be used to gauge a successful placement most

Legal Issues

appropriately falls to the group of professionals designing, implementing, and evaluating programs and *not* to the courts. The legal decisions and federal legislation have made the intent clear. The challenge remains to develop functional methods for placing and maintaining handicapped people in least restrictive environments.

Right to Due Process

> In years past, prior to clarification of the due process obligations of public schools, thousands of children were arbitrarily suspended, excluded, pushed out of school, or prevented from enrolling. (Abeson, Bolick, & Hass, 1975, p. 1)

After years of exclusion from schools and appropriate programming, parents of handicapped students began to seek assistance from the courts. In particular, the PARC and Mills cases provided court rulings pertinent to the establishment of due process procedures. According to Abeson, Bolick, and Hass (1975), the PARC decree set out a twenty-three step process for guaranteeing due process to parents or guardians of mentally retarded students. The Mills decision broadened the court ruling to include all handicapped students.

Federal legislation and pertinent court rulings have also ensured due process for concerns other than exclusion from the public schools. Inappropriate labeling and placement of children into special classes have been addressed in the courts (see, e.g., *Hobsen v. Hansen*) as have inappropriate evaluations (e.g., *Diana v. State Board of Education*) and inappropriate instructional programs (e.g., *Fialkowski v. Shapp*).

As a result of litigation and legislation, parents or guardians are assured the right of due process over a range of areas that concern their child's evaluation, placement, and education. Abeson, Bolick, and Hass (1975) indicate that the following procedures must be available to meet minimum due process standards:

1. Written notification before evaluation. In addition, parents always have the right to an interpreter/translator if their primary language is not English.
2. Written notification before change in [the child's] educational placement.
3. Periodic review of educational placement.
4. Opportunity for an impartial hearing . . .
5. Assignment of a surrogate parent for children when:
   The child's parent or guardian is not known.
   The child's parents are unavailable.
   The child is a ward of the state.
6. Access to educational records. (Abeson, Bolick, & Hass, 1975, pp. 20–21)

Legal and Legislative Decisions

These procedures permit parents or guardians to obtain relevant information about their child, to be informed of proposed changes for the child, and finally, to seek an impartially run meeting to discuss disagreements with action taken by school officials.

Smith (1981) reports a survey of state special education departments to determine the status of due process hearings. Data were obtained from forty-two states, although not all states responded to all questions. All respondents indicated that hearing officers were available, the majority being lawyers or representatives from higher education. The number of due process hearings held was reported to be 3,691, significant variability in numbers occurring across states. Mentally retarded children were the most frequent classification seeking a due process hearing, and the most prevalent issue raised by parents was their child's placement. Interestingly, although parents sought the hearing 96 percent of the time, rulings have occurred more often in favor of the schools.

The information obtained in this survey suggests that some parents are exercising their right to due process when they disagree with action taken by schools; however, this survey does not permit drawing conclusions about the number of parents, if any, who are not choosing to exercise their due process rights. In addition, because no federal mandate exists for the birth-to-five age range, due process remains in many states a future goal for parents of these children. Nevertheless, the legal and legislative base for due process has been laid. The remaining challenges are to educate parents on their rights and to develop procedures that benefit both schools and children.

Right to Medical Treatment

This intensely dramatic issue concerning the right of the handicapped to medical treatment looms on the legal horizon. The focus has been primarily on handicapped infants who have been born with life-threatening conditions that normally can be corrected through some form of medical intervention. The controversy has occurred because some parents have chosen to forego treatment and thus allow their infant to die. Two major considerations are associated with this controversy. The first is ethical, while the second is practical (Taft, 1983). The ethical issue concerns the rights of the handicapped infant to be accorded the same treatment as nonhandicapped infants. The practical issue concerns ensuring compliance and cost of treatment.

In 1982, a Down syndrome infant with an incomplete esophagus was born. The parents of this infant, who became known as "Baby Doe," refused to permit the necessary corrective surgery; and before timely legal action could be taken, the baby died of starvation. The public and the Reagan administration reacted, and in May 1982, the Secretary of Health and Human Services issued a statement that informed hospitals that were recipients of federal support that it was unlawful to withhold appropriate nutrition or medical treatment from handicapped infants (Nice, 1983).

Legal Issues

In 1983, a rule was published in the Federal Register that required all hospitals to post a notice to read: Discriminatory failure to feed and care for handicapped infants in this facility is prohibited by federal law. The notice also invited reporting of any questionable practice to the Department of Health and Human Services. The posting of this notice was challenged by several professional organizations and brought to court. The presiding judge struck down the rule as "arbitrary and capricious" (Nice, 1983). Subsequently, the Reagan administration has rewritten the rule, which is currently under review.

This controversy was again brought to the public's attention when parents of a seriously handicapped infant refused to permit corrective surgery for an open spinal lesion. In consultation with medical, legal, and religious advisers, the parents of "Baby Jane Doe" decided against corrective surgery. Citing violation of Section 504, the government brought the case to court. In this instance the court ruled in favor of the parents and did not require that the surgery be completed; nevertheless, the issue remains unsettled. As noted by the columnist George Will, "Today, government policy concerning such cases is unformed, evolving, tentative, and moderate" (1983, *The Washington Post*).

In addition to the ethical issues involved in withholding medical treatment from handicapped persons are practical matters, particularly in the area of enforcement and cost. The American Academy of Pediatrics has been opposed to government regulation in this area and recommends that decisions concerning medical treatment be made by a bioethics committee (Taft, 1983). For some, such a recommendation is appealing because it permits consideration of individual cases rather than forcing physicians and parents to adhere to a set of inflexible regulations.

A factor that often escapes attention is the significant cost associated with the maintenance of some handicapped infants. Medical costs continue to escalate, and families may be faced with financial ruin if an array of elaborate medical procedures are undertaken. If the family cannot shoulder the financial burden, then society becomes responsible. The question then becomes, As a society are we willing to spend considerable resources in the treatment of severely or profoundly impaired infants who may not survive or, if they do, will most likely not become contributing members of society?

In a recent document prepared by The Association for Persons with Severe Handicap's Critical Issues Subcommittee on Infant Concerns (Guess, Dussault, Brown, Mulligan, Orelove, Comegys, & Rues, 1984), the argument is put forth that when we operate from a philosophy that values all life, determining who lives and who dies by using a cost analysis is inappropriate and unethical. This report discusses in detail the legal, economic, psychological, and ethical variables that need consideration before decisions are made to withhold treatment, withdraw treatment, or withhold sustenance from an infant because the infant is severely handicapped. This report concludes with a policy statement issued by the Executive Board of this organization, which:

> ... reaffirms the right to equal medical treatment for all infants in accordance with the dignity and worth of these individuals, as protected by the Constitution and Bill of Rights of the United States of America. (Guess, et al., 1984, p. 30)

The legal issues raised by the right to treatment are complex and emotion laden; however, these issues need to be faced. As Powell and Hecimovic (1985) emphasize, both the professional and the lay community should begin working toward solutions that at least attempt to acknowledge the inherent complexities surrounding medical treatment of severely disabled infants. Society must face the dilemma posed by withholding medical or other treatment from infants, and the courts clearly will play a fundamental role in the policy that evolves.

SUMMARY

The intent of this chapter has been to review federal, state, and local policy and legal action as they relate directly or indirectly to Early Childhood/Special Education. The evaluation of mandates and regulations makes clear the general movement to provide more protection to the handicapped population and to assure, where possible, equal rights. Progress toward these goals has been substantial; however, the least satisfactory progress has generally occurred for the young child because often rulings and mandates have not extended to include the infant and preschool population.

As Lessen and Rose (1980) note:

> It is necessary for parents, professionals, and government representatives to join together in a concerted effort to produce a set of recommendations that would maximally benefit this under-served group of children. (p. 469)

These recommendations should focus on expanding services, clarifying policy, and reducing ambiguity in definitions, and on eligibility requirements. In particular, action should be taken to develop a comprehensive system of mandated services from birth in which interagency conflict and problems of jurisdiction are resolved. Definitions of eligible children should become more consistent and standardized, and those infants determined to be at-risk should be included.

References

Abeson, A., Bolick, N., & Hass, J. (1975). *A primer on due process.* Reston, VA: The Council for Exceptional Children.

Abeson, A., & Zettel, J. (1977). The end of the quiet revolution: The education for all handicapped children act of 1975. *Exceptional Children, 44*(2), 114–128.

Allen, K. (1984). Federal legislation and young handicapped children. *Topics in Early Childhood Special Education, 4*(1), 9–18.

Ballard, J. (1977). *Public Law 94-142 and Section 504—Understanding what they are and are not.* Reston, VA: Governmental Relations Unit, The Council for Exceptional Children.

Burt, R. (1975). Judicial action to aid the retarded. In N. Hobbs (Ed.), *Issues in the classification of children* (vol. 2). San Francisco: Jossey-Bass.

Cohen, J., & DeYoung, H. (1973). The role of litigation in the improvement of programming for the handicapped. In L. Mann & D. Sabatino (Eds.), *The first review of special education.* Philadelphia: JSE Press.

Cohen, S., Semmes, M., & Guralnick, M. (1979). Public law 94-142 and the education of preschool handicapped children. *Exceptional Children, 45,* 279–285.

Gallagher, J. (1984). Policy analysis and program implementation/P.L. 94-142. *Topics in Early Childhood Special Education, 4*(1), 43–53.

Garwood, S. (1984). Social policy and young handicapped children. *Topics in Early Childhood Special Education, 4*(1), 1–8.

Gilhool, T., & Stutman, E. (1978). Integration of severely handicapped students: Toward criteria for implementing and enforcing the integration imperative of P.L. 94-142 and Section 504. *Developing criteria for the evaluation of the least restrictive environment provision.* Washington, DC: U.S. Office of Education.

Guess, D., Dussault, B., Brown, F., Mulligan, M., Orelove, F., Comegys, A., & Rues, J. (1984). *Legal, economic, psychological, and moral considerations on the practice of withholding medical treatment from infants with congenital defects.* A report prepared by the Critical Issues Subcommittee on Infant Concerns. Seattle, WA: The Association for Persons with Severe Handicaps.

Insight (June 30, 1980). *Changes found in states' ages of eligibility.* The Council for Exceptional Children Government Report, Vol. 11, No. 6.

Kirp, D., Kuriloff, P., & Buss, W. (1975). Legal mandates and organizational change. In N. Hobbs (Ed.), *Issues in the classification of children* (Vol. 2). San Francisco: Jossey-Bass.

Laski, F. (1985). Judicial address of education for students with severe mental handicaps: From access to schools to state-of-the-art. In D. Bricker & J. Filler (Eds.), *The severely mentally retarded: Research to practice.* Reston, VA: The Council for Exceptional Children.

Lessen, E., & Rose, T. (1980). State definitions of preschool handicapped populations. *Exceptional Children, 46,* 467–469.

McCarthy, M. (1983). The Pennhurst and Rowley decisions: Issues and implications. *Exceptional Children, 49,* 517–522.

Nice, G. (1983). Federal government, state legislature respond to "Baby Doe" controversy. *Interface, 8*(Nos. 4 & 5).

Noel, M., Burke, P., & Valdivieso, C. (1985). Educational policy for the severely mentally retarded. In D. Bricker & J. Filler (Eds.), *The severely mentally retarded: Research to practice*. Reston, VA: The Council for Exceptional Children.

O'Connell, J. (1983). Education of handicapped preschoolers: A national survey of services and personnel requirements. *Exceptional Children, 49*(6), 538–543.

Powell, T., & Hecimovic, A. (1985). Baby Doe and the search for quality of life. *Exceptional Children, 51,* 315–323.

Smith, B. (1980, October). *Policy options related to the provisions of appropriate early intervention services for very young exceptional children and their families*. (Policy Options Project). Reston, VA: The Council for Exceptional Children.

Smith, B. (1984). Expanding the federal role in serving young special needs children. *Topics in Early Childhood Special Education, 4*(1), 33–42.

Smith, T. (1981). Status of due process hearings. *Exceptional Children, 48*(3), 232–236.

Swan, W. (1980). The handicapped children's early education program. *Exceptional Children, 47,* 12–16.

Taft, L. (1983). A doctor's view . . . *Interface, 8*(Nos. 4 & 5).

U.S. Department of Education (1980). *Second annual report to Congress on the implementation of Public Law 94-142: The education for all handicapped children act*. Washington, DC.

Vencidos, J. (no date). Education of the handicapped act amendments of 1983, Section 631. *Coalition Quarterly, 3*(No. 3).

Wiegerink, R., & Bartel, J. (1981). Early childhood services for the '80's: Executive summary. In R. Wiegerink (Ed.), *Review of early childhood services: A state of the art series*. Chapel Hill, NC: Frank Porter Graham Development Center.

CHAPTER 6

POPULATION DESCRIPTION

Labeling and classifying exceptional children have been continuing problems for professionals and parents. From the late 1960s to the early 1970s, the concern intensified and became a paramount issue in special education and other associated fields. To bring clarification to the labeling and classification of exceptional children, a project headed by Dr. Nicholas Hobbs to study the salient issues associated with labeling children was commissioned by Elliot Richardson, Secretary of the U.S. Department of Health, Education and Welfare (currently the Department of Education). An array of professionals representing a variety of disciplines (e.g., law, education, medicine, sociology) were asked to address aspects of labeling and classification, and each was asked to write a chapter based on his or her study and analysis. These chapters were compiled into two volumes and published in 1975. A third companion volume presented a synthesis of the information and opinion contained in Volumes 1 and 2 and offered a set of recommendations concerning the labeling and classification of children. These three volumes, entitled *Issues in the Classification of Children, Vol. 1* (Hobbs, 1975a), *Issues in the Classification of Children, Vol. 2* (Hobbs, 1975b), and *The Futures of Children* (Hobbs, 1975c), provide a rich source of information as well as comprehensive and useful perspectives about the need for labels and subsequent classification.

Although a message of concern about the misuse of labels and labeling is a prominent theme through the three volumes, a consensus about the need for effective classification systems exists. Hobbs (1975c) argues that persons who insist that labeling and classification of children is not required are not attending to the many demands of funding eligibility and practical management considerations. Methods for determining whether children are eligible for special services and methods for effectively grouping and managing children are essential elements for therapeutic and educational intervention. Thus, effective intervention programs require valid and reliable strategies for classifying children and acquiring the kind of resources that will maximize their chances for growth and development. Conversely, care should always be taken to assure that the labeling and classification of children does not serve to harm or hinder rather than assist.

The younger the child, the more concern professionals and parents have about assigning labels. Considerable caution should be exercised in labeling an infant or young child because, historically, our ability to predict subsequent outcomes based on earlier behavior has been poor in all but extreme cases (McCall, 1979). The eventual impact of early biological insults and environmental variables is often unknown and thus renders our knowledge of the development of many infants questionable. Such realities require that infants not be prematurely labeled as either normal or not normal.

Having made this brief introduction to labeling and classification, this chapter presents:

1. a description of early development as a basis for understanding deviations or atypical development
2. a discussion of factors that can interfere with normal development
3. a description of the population of at-risk and handicapped infants and young children
4. a discussion of problems associated with early diagnosis, labeling, and classification

EARLY DEVELOPMENT

Developmental Models

Many descriptions of early development begin by emphasizing the need to understand that normal or typical development can vary significantly. The study of developmental norms for most milestone behavior (e.g., see Cohen & Gross, 1979) emphasizes that skills can be acquired within a range of several months and youngsters still be considered normal. All children do not walk by twelve months, talk by fifteen months, or fear strangers at eight months. Rather, one infant may talk at ten months, while another may not utter his first words until sixteen months. Both infants may be developing appropriately. Nor do such discrepant onsets of specific behaviors mean that the "earlier" talker will retain his or, more likely, her headstart over the "later" talker. By age six years, the "late" talker may be significantly more verbal than the "early" talker.

A number of models have been proposed to account for variations in children's development. Lewis (1984) has characterized these models as the status or medical model, the environmental model, and the transactional or interactional model. The medical model argues that the relative status of the child remains more or less stable over time because the environment can do little to influence the basic biological integrity of the organism. The environmental model asserts that development is controlled primarily by environmental influences except where extremely damaged children are concerned. Finally, the transactional model posits that a child's development is continually affected by the interaction between the environment and the child's biological status. The transactional model accommodates change in children's status over time through variations in environment or variations in the organism's biology that continually interact to produce change in the child's repertoire.

Each of these models has generated a number of theories to explain deviation in development; however, one of the more satisfactory, in terms of explaining the range of development, is the theory proposed by Fischer (1980). Fischer suggests that cognitive and other domains of behavior are a composite of individual skills. Skill acquisition follows a developmental hierarchy that moves from the simple concrete level to the representational level to the level of abstraction. Initially, skill sequences develop relatively independently. However, once a certain level is attained, coordination between skills or clusters of skills occurs. The skills that develop and the speed with which they are acquired depend upon environmental emphasis and input. This position would predict differences in skill acquisition across children and variability in individual children's mastery of different skills.

Determining how much a child can deviate from the norms and still be considered developmentally appropriate remains a challenge. Clearly, the repertoires of some infants and young children are so developmentally deviant that labeling the child as atypical is not a problem; however, the majority of children showing deviations may fall into a gray range that makes their development suspect but not clearly atypical. Only with the passage of time can an appropriate diagnosis be made. This reality argues for caution in labeling infants and young children, for understanding that normal development tolerates significant deviations, and for awareness that the status of a youngster can vary significantly over time. With these caveats made, a brief discussion of early development follows.

Developmental Principles

Development can be conveniently divided into three major periods: prenatal, perinatal, and postnatal. Prenatal refers to the period from conception to the infant's birth, usually nine months in length. Because interventionists do not typically deal with parents during this period, prenatal development will not be discussed here. Perinatal refers to the period from birth to three to four weeks of extrauterine life. Although always considered important from a biological perspective, during the past ten years this period has become important also in terms of the infant's social-emotional behavior (Klaus & Kennell, 1976). The postnatal period refers to the child's development after the perinatal period and is often divided into infancy, early childhood, and later childhood.

Because many books address development in detail, this chapter will highlight only the molar changes that index developmental change. As a foundation for this discussion, a set of critical developmental principles are reviewed.

Michael Lewis (1984, p. 3) has suggested that there are five important principles that can be derived from the important tenets associated with early development:

1. the infant as a competent organism
2. the infant as a social organism
3. the infant as an active organism
4. the infant's development as proceeding from undifferentiated to differentiated abilities
5. the infant's development as an interactive process between the infant's status at any point in time and the environment in which the infant is immersed

An important change during the past decade has been the perception of the infant. A contemporary research thrust has focused on demonstrating the "competence" of the infant, in stark contrast to an earlier prevailing view of the infant as having limited perceptual, memory, and discriminatory abilities (Bricker, 1982; Kagan, Kearsley, & Zelazo, 1978). A number of studies done over the past decade have emphasized the competencies of the young human organism. See, for example, the volume edited by Minifie and Lloyd (1978). Many investigators have demonstrated that even neonates are capable of sophisticated visual and auditory discriminations. These findings have demonstrated the infant's ability to search for and process a variety of environmental information shortly after birth and most likely before birth. This reality requires reexamination of the early developmental periods as a learning time for infants and would seem to have particular relevance for those infants experiencing some problem or difficulty.

Increasing emphasis is being placed on recognition of the infant's social responsiveness. The infant who smiles, coos, babbles, and subsequently produces words not only is practicing a number of skills but also is initiating and eliciting social feedback. The almost singular concern with the development of intellectual abilities is being displaced by growing attention to the sociocultural context of the child's learning. Meaning is not derived exclusively from manipulation of physical entities but is also garnered by the infant from observing the caregiver's interpretation and actions. Thus, infants appear to need considerable social stimulation and feedback to become adequately adjusted as well as to learn about the social and physical world in which they live.

Most major theorists concerned with human learning have emphasized the need for the learner to be actively involved if new information and/or responses are to be acquired. Bruner (1966), Piaget (1970), and Skinner (1961) have all advanced the notion that the learner needs to be actively involved if efficient learning is to occur. Infants and young children appear to be highly motivated to explore their social and physical environments. Active exploration permits the child to acquire details about the physical properties of his or her tangible world. One can see the young child shake, bang, mouth, manipulate, and visually explore objects that are new or even discover new "means" to use familiar toys through active exploration. The infant appears equally active in the social realm by responding to and initiating vocal interactions, by watching, listening, and touching other humans in the environment. Infants who are lethargic, or unresponsive, are of concern to parents and interventionists. Children who are difficult to move into action may continue to learn slowly and inefficiently presumably because they are not actively involved in the process of acquiring new information and skills.

As many books on early development note, the young child's growth moves from undifferentiated to differentiated and more complex responses. In fact, an important aspect of Piaget's theory of development is the view that the infant gradually learns to discriminate between environmental conditions first through accident, then by trial and error, next by purposeful exploration, and finally through mental manipulations. This process directs the infant from using a few basic responses indiscriminately with all encountered stimuli to gradually learning to match his or her response to the object or situation. Thus, the infant gradually acquires an array of responses and learns to apply those responses in differentiated ways. At four months, an infant may bang a ball, doll, hammer, and book; but through experience and differential feedback the infant learns to bang the hammer, roll the ball, look at the book, and pat the doll. The infant also gradually learns to differentiate social responses. For example, the child learns to behave differentially with familiar and unfamiliar adults and learns to respond differently to "no" versus "that's fine."

Viewing the development of children as a series of circles as those shown in Figure 6-1 may be useful. The first circle represents the basic reflexive responses that the infant exercises during the first weeks of life. Through systematic interaction with the environment, the infant learns to emit a few poorly controlled motor responses, such as visually tracking objects, waving arms, and kicking legs. Once acquired, these primitive responses become more controlled and differentiated so that the infant learns to watch his or her hands, roll the body, vocalize when content or upon hearing an adult. Subsequently, these responses are expanded, modified, and combined to produce increasingly more differentiated behavior. For exam-

Population Description

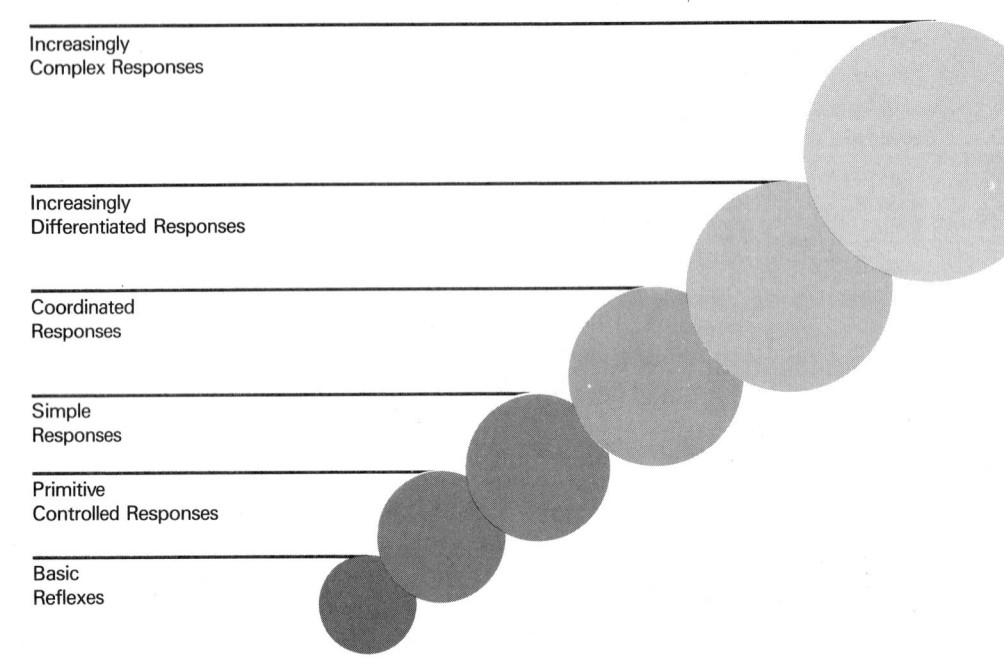

FIGURE 6-1. Developmental change from basic reflexive responses to gradually more differentiated and complex responses.

ple, the child can coordinate his or her eyes and limbs to reach, grasp, and return an object to the mouth; to balance the head and trunk in order to sit; and to babble speechlike sounds.

The final principle noted by Lewis (1984) is that development is determined by the continual interactions between the child and the environment. The transactional model was discussed in Chapter 3 and consequently will be only briefly reviewed here. Neither maturational nor environmental variables alone can account for development; rather, one must look to the interaction between the child and the environment. The healthy young infant comes equipped with organized reflexes, such as sucking, grasping, vocalizing, and looking. By interacting with the environment, the infant modifies these basic reflexive responses. Gradually shifting from involuntary to voluntary activation, the infant becomes capable of active exploration of the physical parameters of the world. Such modifications result in more complex behavior. Environmental interactions allow the infant to gradually build a more sophisticated knowledge of the world by selecting information and fitting it to his or her current organizational structure.

A similar interactive system exists between the child and the social environment. The interactional process between child and caregivers accounts for the shaping of socially acceptable affective response forms into the child's repertoire. Without appropriate feedback, the child may not develop socially appropriate smiling, eye contact, and gazing; or establish joint reference and joint actions, which appear to provide the basis for more advanced communicative exchanges. The importance of interactional or transactional processes for appropriate development should be underscored.

In addition to the five principles of Lewis (1984), one further concept is required to complete the list. The principle of disequilibrium suggests that development is predicated, in part, on the occurrence of events that produce conflict with the child's current level of understanding or organization. The important Piagetian principle of "moderate novelty," or a just tolerable disequilibrium, is critical in the process of development or adaptation (Kagan, Kearsley, & Zelazo, 1978). Adaptation occurs as a function of the assimilation of new environmental inputs which, in turn, permit accommodation of these inputs to existing schemes or structures. The effectiveness of learning appears to be influenced by the amount of discrepancy between the novel or more difficult environmental information to be acquired and the current schemes available to the child. If the discrepancy is too great, adaptation does not occur, possibly because of a paucity of external/internal cues pointing to a common linkage between the new circumstances and the existing schemes (Hunt, 1961). Similarly, if the discrepancy is too small, the child's interest is not maintained and the process of adapting to this environmental situation is terminated (Bricker, Bricker, Iacino, & Dennison, 1976).

Development is probably optimal if environmental demands create a balance between asking too much and asking too little from the child. Arranging the environment to create a just manageable discrepancy between the child's current skill level and the next level of acquisition involves the arousal of conflict or disequilibrium by the presentation of a problem just beyond the child's current developmental level.

Birth to Six Months

According to Piaget, infants arrive in the world with a set of reflexive behaviors that are automatically triggered by either internal states or environmental stimuli (1970). As infants exercise these reflexes, their form changes to simple controlled responses that are maintained by the environmental changes they produce. Through subsequent interaction with both people and objects, these simple responses or action schemes (i.e., tracking, reaching, mouthing) become modified and elaborated into more complex and coordinated schemes (i.e., eye-hand coordination).

The basis for development is described by Piaget (1970) as the inevitable succession of states of disequilibrium that are produced as a natural consequence of encountering new environmental objects and events (both physical and social) for which no repertoire is available. During the first few months of life, adjustments toward equilibrium form the basis for expanding the reflexive behavior of newborns in terms of the number and the characteristics of stimuli that evoke reflexive forms of behavior. When a particular reflexive behavior produces a consequence that is interesting to infants, the rate of that behavior will increase. Infants develop a number of different action schemes but do not use these schemes in a particularly differentiated manner. For example, an infant may attempt to suck any object placed in the mouth.

As a result of environmental interactions, infants begin to learn which objects (e.g., mobile ones) produce which consequences (e.g., moving) in response to specific forms of behavior (e.g., kicking). Thus, infants learn to discriminate among objects and events. The beginning of differential responding based on feedback from the environment forms the basis for infants' primitive knowledge about the social and physical environment.

Infants' first affective responses are rooted in attention to the human face and voice. Such responses can take many forms, such as quieting, becoming alert, or attempting to keep the face or voice in the visual field. In the early stages of development, infants may smile when presented with a pleasant situation (e.g., a caregiver's attention, observation of an interesting object) and may indicate stress through crying when exposed to an aversive or excessively novel stimulus. Emde, Kligman, Reich, and Wade (1978) suggest the organization of the central nervous system is such that around three months of age, three dimensions of emotional expression can be reliably discriminated in infants. These dimensions are:

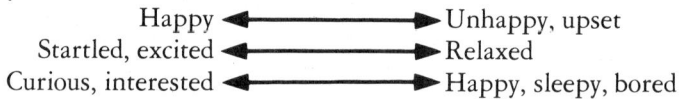

$$\text{Happy} \longleftrightarrow \text{Unhappy, upset}$$
$$\text{Startled, excited} \longleftrightarrow \text{Relaxed}$$
$$\text{Curious, interested} \longleftrightarrow \text{Happy, sleepy, bored}$$

As infants develop, they begin to discriminate social smiling and show affective anticipation of common events. Once they become facile at discriminating mother and familiar persons from others, wariness and fear of strangers or of different situations may emerge. The range of social responses and emotions that infants can produce is expanded; infants also become more adept at discriminating different social contexts. As infants learn both to discriminate and to produce a variety of social-emotional responses that depend upon both internal states and external conditions, they are also acquiring other social-affective behaviors of potential importance to the subsequent development of language.

During the first few months of life, the vocal behavior produced is not like speech but composed primarily of vowel-like sounds (Oller, 1981). Infants seem to be learning to operate the sound-production mechanism and at this stage can produce noises and sounds that adults have difficulty imitating. Early sound production indicates that infants have learned to differentiate vocal activity into pleasurable (i.e., cooing) and distressful (i.e., crying) sounds. At this early age, infants can discriminate or perceive differences between certain speech sounds and a number of nonspeech variables, such as duration, intensity, and pitch (Trehub, Bull & Schneider, 1981).

Infants learn to attend to objects in the environment and gaze at them for long periods of time. They learn to shift their gaze from object to object and turn their heads to locate an object. Around the fourth month, infants begin to vocalize when hearing sounds produced by the caregiver. Infants also learn to locate sound sources at this stage. An indication that infants are becoming aware of their social-communicative environment is their apparent attempt to synchronize their activities or engage in actions similar to the adults (Condon & Sander, 1974). For example, if an adult waves an arm, infants, if watching, will often move their arms (Uzgiris & Hunt, 1975).

In the first few months of life, infants learn to attend to speech and, in time, to wait before responding to utterances. By following mother's gaze, the infant is able to discover the mother's focus of attention and establish the same reference point. Likewise, the infant learns to direct the adult's gaze by visually focusing on objects to which the adult subsequently attends. Mothers often interpret their infant's intent by assigning meaning to the child's actions and vocal patterns.

During this period, infants are also gaining control of their motor system. Newborns' motor responses are jerky and uncoordinated. Moving or making contact appear to be accidental occurrences over which infants have little or no control. Continual use of arms, legs, trunk, head, fingers and other body parts produces increasing control, moving from the head to the extremities. Thus, infants first learn to move the eyes in a controlled manner then to stabilize and turn the head. Trunk control is evident when infants begin to roll and squirm. Sitting requires that infants be able to balance the head and trunk, initially with support, then independently. Infants become increasingly more adept at using their hands and feet to explore the environment, and by six months, they can retrieve a variety of objects within reach.

Six to Twelve Months

Between seven and ten months, most infants become facile at vocalizing the same speechlike sounds repeatedly. This form of vocal behavior is termed *babbling*. Around the tenth to eleventh month, infants' babbling has acquired many features of adult inflection. The force, quality, and pitch characteristics of vocal behavior are called prosodic features, and acquisition of early forms of prosodic features coincides developmentally with the acquisition of speech sounds.

Prior to nine months, infant vocalizations and primitive gestures appear as unconventionalized schemes, i.e., generally their form and purpose (or intent) are not mutually agreed upon by familiar persons. During this period, infants' communicative signals often seem oriented more toward direct goal attainment than primary social purposes. When the seven-month-old child plays with objects, action patterns tend to be directed solely toward the objects themselves (e.g., banging two blocks together and then dropping them into a container) or solely toward a person (e.g., vocalizing and reaching toward the adult). Instances in which a person and an object are involved in a social exchange are rare.

Around nine months, however, significant shifts are seen in infants' behavior as they start to coordinate actions with persons and objects. As their behavior becomes coordinated, infants are essentially demonstrating the capacity for social tool use, as in employing a person as a means for obtaining an unreachable desired object and using an object as a means for gaining adult attention. Infants can coordinate schemes to look and to point to a favorite toy beyond reach, shift their gaze to the mother, vocalize, and look back to the goal. If further social bidding is necessary, infants can tug at mother's clothing and then mark the toy with a vocal or hand gesture. Coordination is also apparent in the behavior of infants who hold toys up to mother, look at her, gesture, and vocalize. At the same time that coordination of objects and persons develops, important changes in the infants' communicative signals may be observed. Existing sound/gesture schemes gradually undergo conventionalization. The meaning previously conveyed through signals is made more explicit and takes a form that is more easily interpretable by others (e.g., pointing to desired objects, calling for attention). Thus, by the end of the first year, infants become increasingly capable of integrating social interactions with object schemes, using conventional gestures, and showing an interest in social interaction.

Affective behavior seems to be interrelated with cognitive systems. Kagan, Kearsley, and Zelazo (1978) have described the growth function of one aspect of affective behavior, separation distress. Studies of this phenomenon show that crying or inhibition of play after maternal departure is infrequent before eight months of age. From nine to eighteen months, infants characteristically show distress, and beginning soon after eighteen months, such behavior declines. Kagan et al. (1978) suggest that the upswing in distress observed between nine and eighteen months may be due to the infant's improved memory capacity. When mothers depart, ten-month-olds are capable of detecting the incongruence between the scheme for their mother and the now empty environment. The third trend of the growth function, in which distress accompanying maternal departure diminishes, seems to coincide with the infants' enhanced ability to retain structures of past experiences (e.g., mother will return) and concurrently generate anticipations of the future (e.g., wait for mother to return).

From six to twelve months, infants gain considerable control over their motor system. They learn to sit, first with support, then independently. Many infants can shift from sitting to other positions, such as being prone, being on the knees, or pulling to stand with support. Crawling, creeping, or some form of forward motion is generally acquired, permitting infants to access a considerably greater portion of their environment. The development of a precise pincer grasp occurs as does excellent control of hand and feet movement. The pinnacle of motor development during this period is the onset of independent walking or, at least, the acquisition of precursors to walking.

As the description of the acquisition of these responses suggests, there is a gradual sophistication of the motor system that culminates in the infant's anticipation of vertical mobility. In addition, infants have become adept at using their hands to acquire objects, hang on to adults, and manipulate most toys or objects in some way. By the first birthday, most children have acquired a vast array of skills that moves them from early infancy to the beginning of the toddler stage.

One to Two Years

During the second year, the development of more complex and coordinated systems occurs. For example, children may learn to push a chair around the room as one coordinated response and to climb up and down from the chair as another coordinated response. Thus, when a toddler pushes the chair to the table and then climbs onto it to get a cookie, the child has coordinated two schemes and is thereby beginning to separate means from goals.

The separation of means and goals also generally coincides with a differentiation of self from others. This stage occurs from about twelve to eighteen months of age and is the basis for exploratory behavior. As children increase the number of differentiated responses in their repertoires and coordination among such organization increases, they may tire of known events and may actively search for the unknown in order to test existing repertoires.

Children's receptive language skills become more overt toward the end of the first year. Children will stop and turn when their names are called, will cease activity when an adult says no, and will produce meaningful gestures upon a familiar request, such as "wave bye-bye." Although most children are able to produce a variety of sounds during their first year of life, it is during the second year that conventional words are produced. Studies of initial word acquisition suggest that these words serve two broad functions for the child: social-communicative and referential. Social-communicative functions incorporate requests, demands, greetings, and so forth, while referential language is used to name, classify, and comment on the world (Nelson, 1979).

The production of early words clearly shows the interrelatedness of early communicative processes. That is, when the child says "car," the function as well as the referential meaning must be interpreted by the listener. The sequence of early-word production suggests that young children tend to focus their linguistic attention on those aspects of the environment that hold the greatest saliency for them—that is, young children talk about what they want, see, and do. In the early productions of young children, both overextension and underextension of word meaning have been reported (Bowerman, 1976). However, no consistent pattern has been noted, suggesting that word-meaning acquisition may begin as a rather idiosyncratic undertaking by young children.

Between eighteen and twenty-four months, most toddlers begin sequencing words (Prutting, 1979). Producing two-word utterances is generally considered to be the initial stage of grammatical or syntactical development. Sequencing words presupposes that the child has developed a rudimentary organizational system that functions by using rules. These rules enable a child to convey intentions and be understood by members of the language community. Many of the two-word utterances produced by young children can be classified as representing a variety of semantic relations. Brown (1973) reports that for children whose mean length of utterance is between 1.0 and 2.0 words, the following semantic relations describe the majority of their utterances:

Semantic Relation	Example
Agent-action	Boy sit; kitty run
Action-object	Hit block; go car
Agent-object	Baby rattle; mama chair
Action-locative	Go there; eat here
Entity-locative	Ball there; dog here
Entity-attributive	Ball red; baby cold
Demonstrative-entity	That bed; this girl
Possessor-possession	Daddy pipe; dog bowl

During this period, most children learn to walk with ease, and some learn to move with surprising speed and coordination. Children have learned many sophisticated motor responses, but these responses are used less on a trial-and-error basis and more often with obvious internal problem solving occurring. The final stage of the sensorimotor period is often called *invention of new means through mental combinations*. This stage is exemplified by the ability of eighteen to twenty-four month old children to deal with practical "here and now" problems through the use of various schemes that have become differentiated as means to a variety of ends. Toddlers have developed a repertoire of movements and discriminated relationships that allows them to overcome barriers, to use sticks and strings to obtain objects that are out of reach, to open new containers through exploratory manipulations, and to use chairs to reach desired objects. The hallmark of this period is children's ability to anticipate events based on environmental cues and to regulate and organize their behavior based on predictions of successive happenings (Uzgiris, 1976). For example, if this happens, then that will occur. The baby crying for a drink sees mother open the refrigerator and stops crying because he or she "knows" a drink is coming.

Two to Three Years

At this stage, the period of infancy is completed and the repertoire has become more organized, differentiated, and complex in terms of both motor and cognitive-linguistic skills. Children are capable of mental manipulations (e.g., they do not have to directly manipulate an object to "know" what the object can do) and can solve problems through the use of primitive logic (e.g., if I pull this string, I can get the toy attached to it). During this age span, children move from the sensorimotor stage to the preoperational or preconceptual stage (Flavell, 1977).

> "Cognitive representation" at this level takes the form of the preconcept because the highest adaptive thought of which the child is capable in this phase of development still remains close to either imitative representation or symbolic play. The preconcepts which are superimposed on sensorimotor schemata as a function of the image and language lack both true generality . . . and true individuality in the sense of constancy of the object outside the immediate field of action. (Hunt, 1961, p. 197)

A hallmark of this age is children's increased facility with understanding and using language, not only with familiar adults and siblings but with other persons encountered in the environment. Specifically, children expand their knowledge and use of semantic relations to three- and four-unit (word) constructions. Children also learn to use articles, indicate possession, and use selected verb markings, such as attaching the "ing" suffix. Children can answer yes/no questions and pose questions through changes in intonation. The nonconventional (e.g., child will say "no want milk") use of negatives occurs as well. In addition to the verbal skills, children learn to construct models using blocks or similar toys, to complete puzzles, or to form boards. At this age, children are adept at pointing to named pictures of known objects, events, or people.

In the area of socialization, children are now able to recognize themselves and can provide their name upon request. Play is readily initiated, and they may be content to play alone or join with other children. Important self-help milestones are reached by most children during age two to three. Children acquire the skills to wash their hands and self-feed with both spoons and forks. Simple zippering and buttoning is done, and toilet training is accomplished by most children during this period. Finally, children at this age understand common dangers.

Three to Five Years

Children in this age range are capable of semilogical thinking. They use reasoning processes that are not always valid, but nonetheless show that they understand that the world operates in a predictable fashion. What is important, youngsters give evidence that they recognize invariants of identities (e.g., objects) even though the conditions of size, shape, placement, and other dimensions may change considerably. For example, a glass, though dropped and broken, is still the glass. They also recognize invariants of functions—

when placed on an incline, a ball will roll, and the steeper the incline, the faster the ball rolls. Understanding such invariants and regularities makes the world more understandable and predictable for children.

Language can now be used to manipulate information, and children at this age can learn from the communication of others. Extensive dialogues and discussion of topics that are not immediately happening or present can be managed. Linguistic productions become more elaborate as children's grammar expands and becomes more refined. Corrective feedback is sought by questioning or restatements, and children can comply with complex requests. Most four- and five-year-olds know their name and address.

During this age period, self-regulation, or self-control, begins to develop. Children have moved from an organism that responds to whims to one that has learned to wait or even to inhibit certain responses. The process of developing control appears to entail shifts in two dimensions. First, the regulation or inhibition shifts from others to the child; and, second, regulation shifts from verbal to nonverbal, and eventually most children are able to completely internalize the control.

Mastery of several preacademic skills occurs during the three-to-five age. Children acquire the concepts of matching and reproducing shapes, understand relative size, and are able to sequence, arrange, or classify using logical rules. Several basic premath concepts, such as simple counting and discrimination of groups of objects with "more" or "less," are also acquired.

Children become well coordinated during this time, so that they can avoid barriers while running, can climb ladders and trees, and can ride wheeled toys without problem. A number of self-help skills are learned. Children are able to brush their teeth, wash and dry face and hands, brush their hair, use a knife, fix simple snacks, and independently use the toilet. Although children can successfully complete such tasks, some supervision is still necessary. Most children during this stage learn to work and play independently, but they are also able to cooperate with other children and adults.

Summary

The early-childhood stage encompassing the birth-to-five age range is marked by enormous growth and change. Neonates' behavior is restricted, disorganized, uncoordinated, and undifferentiated. As infants use their simple actions schemes, the environment provides corrective feedback and information. The assimilation of new information provides infants the basis for elaboration of current schemes and the replacement of familiar responses with many more effective modes for interacting with the environment. As infants interact with their social and physical worlds, they "construct" more coordinated, differentiated response patterns. One can observe the infant's successful levels of cognitive organization leading from accidental interactions to undirected exploration to trial and error to systematic testing of

Early Development

strategies to finally being able to mentally manipulate images in order to solve problems or accomplish desired goals. Similar patterns in motor, communication, social, and self-help areas occur. Children's early responses are poorly directed and often ambiguous and require significant interpretation and help from caregivers. Gradually, children assume increasing direction and independence. By the end of the early-childhood period, a remarkable metamorphosis has been completed, and now children's behavior is characterized by organized strategies for dealing with environmental demands and self-initiated responses to acquire the elements necessary to meet the child's daily needs and desires.

This section has presented a brief overview of early development as a basis for understanding development that is either slowed or has gone astray, producing significant problems for the children and their families. More detailed descriptions of early development can be found in the following sources: Flavell, 1977; McCandless & Trotter, 1977; Bijou & Baer, 1978; Charlesworth, 1982; Mussen, Conger, & Kagan, 1980. In addition, Appendix A contains a list of the more important developmental skills and the approximate ages when they occur.

Factors That Disrupt or Interfere with Development

The brief overview of development that was provided should serve to set the general parameters of normal or, more comfortably, typical development. Most children follow—more or less—the general outlined sequences. Unfortunately, some children's development strays from the typical pattern enough to be of mild to profound concern.

The onset of a problem can occur any time during the three major developmental periods: prenatal, perinatal, and postnatal (Hayden & Beck, 1982). During the prenatal period, problems can arise because of mutant genes, radiation, toxic chemicals, harmful drugs, fetal malnutrition, maternal infection, blood incompatibility, placental insufficiency, and environmental factors such as maternal age, socioeconomic status, and family size. In the perinatal period, problems can arise as the result of difficulties or trauma during labor and/or delivery, neonatal medications, prematurity, anoxia, or low birth weight. Problems may occur in the postnatal period for a wide variety of reasons, including illness, chronic disease, accidents, late onset of central nervous system disorders, environmental toxins, and other environmental factors, such as poverty, abuse, and family dysfunction (Ramey, Trohanis, & Hostler, 1982).

The traditional categories used for exceptional children can be related to nine separate causes:

1. infections (e.g., encephalitis)
2. intoxication (e.g., poisoning)
3. trauma (e.g., blow to the head)

4. metabolic disorders (e.g., PKU, or phenylketonuria)
5. central nervous system disorders (e.g., tumors in the CNS)
6. chromosomal disorders (e.g., Down syndrome)
7. gestational disorders (e.g., prematurity)
8. psychosocial disorders (e.g., environmental deprivation)
9. unknown (e.g., no overt causal factor)

These factors are discussed in more detail and as they specifically relate to the various subgroups of the target population in the following section.

TARGET POPULATION

This book is addressed to interventionists interested in working with at-risk and handicapped infants and young children. It is therefore important to define the parameters of these two populations of children in functional ways.

Attempting to establish the number of children who are at-risk or handicapped is an unsatisfying endeavor. For school-age children, the estimate of children requiring some special service generally ranges from 12 to 15 percent. For non–school-age children, such percentages are more difficult to determine because of variations in definitions, eligibility guidelines, and services available across states. (Some of these problems were discussed in Chapter 5.) However, statistics do exist for some easy-to-identify conditions, such as Down syndrome. Even more elusive are data on children classified as at-risk because of variations in definitions, services, and follow-up procedures not only across but within states.

Given the elusiveness of numbers associated with at-risk and handicapped populations, it may be useful to conceptualize these populations as depicted in Figure 6–2. As shown in Figure 6–2, the largest proportion of children develop without problems that require some form of intervention, the next largest proportion have at some time been exposed to some factor (or factors) that places their development at-risk. Progressively smaller proportions of children are found to be mildly, moderately, and severely handicapped. It should be emphasized that the clear distinctions between categories shown in Figure 6–2 do not reflect the reality that children whose repertoires place them on the borders of categories (e.g., the slow child who manages well socially but cannot read at grade level) can and do shift from one category to the other. The onset or termination of pathology or inappropriate environmental conditions may shift the child to the adjacent category.

It is helpful to dismiss the idea that uncontaminated categories of children exist. Rather, classification systems should be viewed as a convenient professional shorthand. Classification or categorical systems are

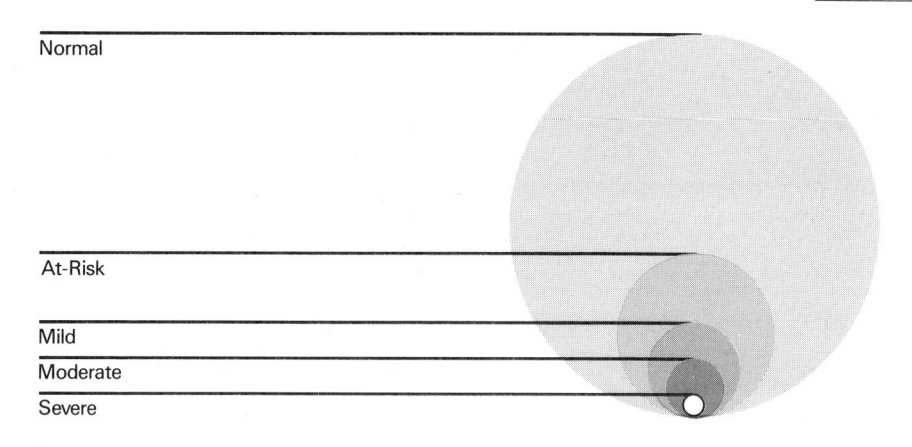

FIGURE 6-2. *Estimated proportion of children by classification of normal, at-risk, and mildly, moderately, and severely handicapped.*

necessary and can be helpful; however, the imprecision of such systems requires that they be used with flexibility and good sense.

At-Risk Infants and Young Children

Infants or children can be assigned to the at-risk category for either biological or environmental factors. Although some overlap exists, children whose risk factors are biological can be seen as distinct from those whose risk factors are environmental in origin. The concept of risk as applied to the classification of children indicates that presently the infant or child is functioning normally or is expected to catch up (e.g., premature infant) or is likely to recover (e.g., infant with respiratory distress syndrome), *but* the concept indicates that these factors or conditions place the child in greater jeopardy for failing to attain or maintain a subsequent normal rate or pattern of development than children who had not experienced such conditions.

The classification of biological risk is assigned to infants or children with a history during the prenatal, perinatal, neonatal, or early developmental period of a biological insult to the central nervous system or of a diagnosed medical disorder (Tjossem, 1976). Prematurity is the most frequent condition leading to the classification of biological risk. The more premature the infant, the greater the risk. Other biological risk factors include birth weight less than 1,500 grams—a condition often associated with prematurity; infection; seizures; the need for resuscitation; and maternal disorders (Denhoff, 1983).

Though infants suffering some biological or medical insult have a higher percentage of neurological and developmental problems than fullterm infants, the field has been continually frustrated in attempts to accurately predict subsequent developmental outcomes based on the biological/medical status of infants during the early developmental periods. As Sameroff (1981) has argued, the current best predictors are social factors such as maternal education and family income. Indeed, the largest number (not percentage) of children who will require intervention services are term babies who appear to be functioning well during the neonatal period. Nevertheless, studies have repeatedly found that 30 percent of the infants identified as biologically at-risk will require some form of intervention by age six (Scott & Masi, 1979). These findings suggest that many of the babies identified as at-risk are likely to have problems, and, therefore, this group continues to be of concern to early interventionists. A remaining challenge is to discover more cost-efficient and more accurate methods for determining which at-risk infants will need assistance and which will not (Bricker & Littman, 1985).

Environmentally at-risk infants or children are those for whom some factor(s) or condition(s) in the social or physical milieu, or both, has a high probability of interfering with the youngster's normal developmental pattern. These children most often reside in poverty stricken or abusive homes. Often infants who are at environmental risk may have experienced other biologically threatening conditions as well. For example, women who live in poverty often do not have access to or seek consistent prenatal care, or teenagers who become pregnant may have a diet sufficiently poor to affect fetal development. The conditions of poverty often produce both biological and environmental risk factors.

Handicapped Infants and Young Children

An enormous array of handicapping conditions and causes exist. For example, there are estimates of 500 different anomalies associated with mental retardation, over 4,000 separate causes of severely handicapping conditions, and over 220 recognizable patterns of malformations (Hayden & Beck, 1982). This multitude of conditions can be caused by biological or psychosocial factors or combinations of both. The classification of handicapped differs from that of at-risk because the infant or child shows significant structural or behavioral deviation that requires medical or educational intervention, or both. As with the classification of at-risk, handicapping conditions can be divided into those that result from biological or environmental factors. Causes of biological handicaps can be conveniently divided into genetic factors, neurological/physical factors, infections, teratogens, sensory factors, and developmental delays.

Biological Factors

Genetic and Chromosomal Disorders.
According to Crain (1984), 25 percent of the birth defects are due to gene disorders, and another 12 percent are due to chromosomal disorders. Genetic disorders occur because a gene or genes of one parent or both are abnormal, affecting the offspring.

Chromosomal disorders occur when chromosomes are rearranged or when part of a chromosome detaches from its normal location and reattaches to another chromosome pair (Crain, 1984).

The most common chromosomal disorder is Down syndrome, which is most often the result of an abnormal arrangement of the twenty-first chromosome. Estimates of the disorder range in the neighborhood of 1.5 per 1,000 live births (Hayden & Beck, 1982); however, this rate is affected by maternal age. Characteristics of these children generally include poor muscle tone, slanting eyes, folds of skin at the corners of the eyes, low-set ears, short neck, small oral cavity, and small hands, feet, and stature. In addition, heart defects are present in 40 percent of the children, hearing impairments are frequent, and intellectual impairment ranges from mild to severe (Garwood, 1983).

Other genetic disorders are:

- Turner's syndrome, resulting from a female infant having only one X chromosome
- Klinefelter's syndrome, resulting from the male infant having two X chromosomes
- Cri du chat syndrome, resulting from an incomplete fifth chromosome pair

A variety of genetic disorders produce serious metabolic disturbances in infants. These disorders produce biochemical imbalances that can have devastating effects on the infant. Perhaps the best known metabolic disorder is phenylketonuria (PKU). Infants with PKU have an enzyme deficiency that permits the buildup of phenylalanine to toxic levels that affect the brain. If the disorder is not treated, the result can be severe retardation. Another deficiency is known as Tay Sach's disease. The onset occurs during the first year and results from an enzymatic defect in the metabolism of certain lipids essential to brain development. This condition is fatal to the affected child. Galactosemia is a metabolic disorder in which the infant is unable to digest milk. If this disorder goes uncorrected, the child will fail to thrive and will develop progressive psychomotor retardation (Crain, 1984).

Many other genetic and chromosomal disorders have been identified, but their incidence is extremely low. For readers interested in more detail about chromosomal and genetic disorders, see Crain, 1984; Hayden and Beck, 1982.

Neurological and Physical Impairments. The large number of central nervous system (CNS) abnormalities that have been identified are generally associated with a prenatal onset. Hayden and Beck (1982) indicate that most CNS abnormalities are recognized at birth or shortly thereafter. However, in instances of mildly to moderately involved cerebral palsy infants, early accurate identification does not always occur. Within this category, the following more common disorders will be briefly discussed:

cerebral palsy, spina bifida, hydrocephalus, epilepsy, physical impairments, and other frequent health impairments.

Cerebral palsy is caused by damage to the brain's motor control system. It is estimated that three of every one thousand children born in the United States are affected by cerebral palsy. Cerebral palsy is generally characterized by paralysis, weakness, and poor coordination (Garwood, 1983). Involvement can range from slight, which causes the child few problems, to major, in which all muscle systems are involved. In this latter group, volitional control of muscle movements may be almost impossible—even the acts of breathing and swallowing may cause the child serious difficulty. As noted before, some instances of cerebral palsy in infants may be difficult to diagnose before six to nine months; however, early diagnostic signs include difficulty in sucking and feeding, weak cry, abnormal muscle tone, and continuation of reflexes past the time when they should become integrated into other response systems (Langley, 1983). Cerebral palsy is frequently accompanied by retardation, speech difficulties, and emotional problems (Garwood, 1983).

The onset of spina bifida occurs during the fetal development period and can take two forms, meningocele and myelomeningocele. During the development of the nervous system, some disruption interferes with the fusion of the vertebrae, producing an open lesion in the spinal column. The higher the lesion occurs on the spinal column, the more serious the child's impairments. Characteristics of spina bifida include mild to severe visual and perceptual-motor disorders, mild to moderate tone, strength, and muscle movement problems, and disorganized language and thought processes (Langley, 1983). A frequently encountered problem associated with myelomeningocele is lack of bladder and bowel control, which can lead to physical and emotional problems. It is estimated that one child in three-hundred to four-hundred births in the United States is born with spina bifida.

Hydrocephalus often occurs in conjunction with myelomeningocele. Generally, a structural defect obstructs the flow of cerebrospinal fluid and produces a buildup of fluid that causes progressive cranial distention and resulting damage (Langley, 1983). Characteristics include an enlarged head, thin scalp, upward retraction of the face skin, and in the more severe cases, generalized spasticity and poor motor control (Langley, 1983). Disorders in language and retardation often accompany hydrocephalus.

Epilepsy is caused by disturbances in electrical discharges of the brain, resulting in loss of control over specific muscle groups and observable seizures. There are three major types of epilepsy. Grand mal seizures are characterized by the child becoming unconscious and losing postural control. Muscles become rigid, and then jerking reactions take over, lasting from one to ten minutes. Petit mal seizures can occur as a variety of minimal muscle reactions and last only a few seconds. The number of seizures can vary, some children having as many as one-hundred seizures per day (Garwood, 1983). This form of epilepsy is generally accompanied by mental retardation. Psychomotor epilepsy is characterized by a sudden loss of muscle tone and involuntary contraction of limb and trunk muscles (Langley, 1983).

Physical impairments encompass neurologic, orthopedic, or health-related conditions that adversely affect the child's development and performance. Such conditions can include muscular dystrophy, osteogenesis imperfecta, rheumatoid arthritis, and spinal and bone deformities (for a discussion of these problems, see Langley, 1983, pp. 105–113). The extent of the impairment produced by these and other disorders varies and determines whether the child is mildly, moderately, or severely disabled.

Health impairments that affect the child's development or ability to cope with environmental demands can be acute (e.g., hepatitis, mononucleosis) or chronic (e.g., congenital heart defect, cystic fibrosis, diabetes, nephrosis). The severity of the condition often determines the impact on the child.

Infections. In utero infections of the fetus with syphilis, rubella, cytomegalovirus, toxoplasmosis, or herpes may result in spontaneous abortion or a variety of manifestations, depending upon the severity of infection and the gestational age when infection occurs (Crain, 1984, p. 34). Prevention of maternal infection is preferred because no effective treatment is yet available for many of these viral infections (for further discussion of prenatal infection, see Crain, 1984).

Teratogens. Environmental substances implicated in producing malformations in developing organisms are called teratogens. Well-known teratogens include certain drugs such as Thalidomide and alcohol, chemicals such as PCB, mercury, and lead, and radiation. The effect on the child is determined, in part, by the quantity of the substance ingested and the developmental period in which the substance is ingested. For example, the drug Thalidomide appears to be teratogenic only during the first trimester of pregnancy (see Crain, 1984, for further information).

Sensory Impairments. Hearing impairments can range from mild to severe. Forty to sixty percent of hearing impairments result from genetic or chromosomal abnormalities, while the remaining causes are disease related. Children whose hearing disability precludes auditory processing of spoken language are considered deaf, while children who can successfully understand speech, with or without an aid, are considered hard-of-hearing (Fewell, 1983). The severity and the age at which children become hearing impaired affect their facility with language. Congenital impairments tend to have the greatest impact.

Visual impairments can be divided into the categories of blind and partially sighted. Functionally, children who must read using Braille are classified as blind, while children who can read print using magnifying devices or large print are classified as partially sighted (Hallahan & Kauffman, 1978). Frequent causes of visual impairment are infectious disease, trauma, and exposure to harmful substances (e.g., an excess of oxygen during the perinatal period that produces retolental fibroplasia). Although marked delays may occur in early motor development, given adequate environmental compensation, most visually impaired children function within normal limits in important domains of behavior by age six.

Developmental Delays. Some children show a developmental delay or disorder in communication, cognition, motor development, or social development that appears to have no specific etiology or in which the cause is unclear. Many children exhibiting general delays are eventually labeled as mentally retarded. Within this classification, one can be severely, moderately, or mildly retarded. Psychosocial (environmental) and unknown factors account for the cause of approximately 75 percent of the mentally retarded population; however, causes of more severe retardation can often be pinpointed as genetic, teratogenic, infectious, or neurologic. Characteristics of retarded children vary, depending on the level of retardation and the effectiveness of the environmental intervention.

Language-delayed or disordered children are a second large group of children found under the classification of developmental delays. Some children in this group show abnormal patterns of speech and language development (e.g., disorders), while other children show typical patterns but ones that are significantly delayed in their emergence (e.g., delayed). Often language delays or disorders are associated with difficulty in problem solving and other academic functioning (Cole & Garwood, 1983).

Environmental Factors

Although the causal factors for many handicapping conditions are biological, there are significant numbers of children with deficiencies in behavioral repertoires but for which there is not obvious biological cause. However, the absence of a clearly specifiable biological factor does not necessarily rule out such factors. There are, without doubt, genetic and neurological deficits or dysfunctions that have yet to be identified. In the future, certain handicaps of currently unknown origin may become identified as a specific syndrome or the result of a certain biological problem.

The more severely handicapped the child, the more probable the cause can be identified as biological as opposed to environmental. As already indicated, the causes for 75 percent of the mentally retarded population are attributed to unknown or environmental factors. Many of the children served in Head Start programs or in classes for the educable mentally retarded come from poor homes that often fail to provide adequate stimulation or nutrition. Some are even abusive. Such conditions may adversely affect the child's rate or quality of learning. Without adequate early intervention, many children living in circumstances of poverty fall progressively behind their age mates (Ramey, MacPhee & Yeates, 1983) and eventually are assigned to programs for exceptional students.

During infancy, problems with a biological basis are more dramatic, more devastating, and thus more visible; however, as children reach school age, the effects of abusive or deficient environments produce an increasingly heavy toll on their behavioral repertoires.

PROBLEMS IN IDENTIFYING AND LABELING THE TARGET POPULATION

The previous discussion has defined the populations of at-risk and handicapped infants and young children that are the focus groups for the conceptual and practical intervention framework described in this volume. The ensuing discussions of the major prenatal, perinatal, and postnatal factors resulting in development that is at-risk or deviant should not be construed to mean that professionals are able to accurately identify and correctly label most infants and young children during the early developmental period who will eventually require intervention.

Throughout this chapter, problems in appropriately identifying infants and young children in need of assistance have been mentioned. For a variety of reasons, our ability to correctly identify those infants and young children who would benefit from some form of intervention is imperfect. A small percentage of infants can be identified as handicapped at birth; but for the majority of children, problems do not become clearly manifest until later in their lives. Further, some infants and young children have problems that are transitory. In particular, as many as 70 percent of the infants labeled as at-risk eventually are functioning within the normal range of development (Scott & Masi, 1979). There are two major problems associated with the appropriate diagnosing, labeling, and classification of infants and young children: the range of acceptable variations in development and longitudinal prediction based on early repertoires.

Variations in Development

In spite of the abundance of information on developmental norms and growth, as shown in Appendix A, for example, abnormal development in infants and young children is often difficult to identify with certainty for several reasons. Developmental norms are derived from large groups of children, and thus, application to the individual child must be done with caution. That is, the central tendency is reported, and often little indication of the variation around it is provided. Also, if one compares the reported onsets of specific skills, considerable variations can be found. These variations are probably the result of differences in the definitions and in the criteria for the normative performance.

Some children appear to stray significantly from the more typical path of development and yet eventually are found to function within normal limits. For example, many premature infants show considerable delays in the acquisition of developmental milestones; but by age two, most are developing without problem. Other children may show atypical patterns, for example, failure to crawl prior to walking, and yet learn to perform more advanced gross motor skills without difficulty. These deviations suggest that the human organism is capable of wide variations in development and still acquiring a normal behavioral repertoire. Some children's development deviates enough so that intervention in some form is required to assist the child in moving back toward societal norms. The problem is how to differentiate between the child's developmental deviations that are within the range of acceptability or will self-correct and deviations that will not self-correct and that will move the child beyond the range of appropriate and expected functioning.

Prognosis

The previous discussion provides insight into some of the problems associated with the prognosis of development in young populations. As the discussion in Chapter 2 indicates, in spite of the lack of empirical support, most of us are comfortable with the idea that there is continuity in development. The most frequent strategy employed to study the relationship between early performance and later development has been the use of intelligence tests. Infants are tested during the early years and then tested again as children or adults. The relationship between the individual's IQ scores is then examined. As reported by a number of investigators (see, e.g., Lewis, 1976; Honzik, 1976; McCall, 1979), infant intelligence scores obtained before age two have no relationship with later IQ scores. Although these findings call into question the notion of continuity in development, they should not be unexpected.

Attempting to establish a prognosis for many infants and young children is hampered by many factors. First, as already described, significant deviations exist in developmental rates and patterns. Second, a number of investigators have suggested that qualitative changes in mental functioning occur between infancy and childhood (Zelazo & Kearsley, 1980). If qualitative changes do occur, this would argue for discontinuity between infancy and early childhood and explain the inability to predict later performances from earlier performances. Third, it seems that a prognosis made on an infant's current level of performance does not take into account the impact of the environment. As discussed in Chapter 3, the transactional perspective argues that the quality of the child's repertoire is determined by the continuing interaction between children and their environment. Attempting to predict a child's future performance based on the current repertoire does not recognize the potential impact of the environment. Fourth, the accuracy and quality of information generated by infant assessment instruments is suspect (Bricker, 1978). Although significant advancements in testing the perceptual and mental processes of infants have occurred (see, e.g., Minifie & Lloyd, 1978), considerable concern still exists about the validity of the information obtained from early infant testing for prediction. Each of these reasons can hamper the field's ability to examine early developmental repertoires and to establish an accurate prognosis of children's subsequent problems.

Difficulties in Diagnosis, Labeling, and Classification

Reflection upon the problems in establishing the parameters of abnormal development and accurate prognosis makes obvious many of the difficulties with diagnosing, labeling, and classifying children by their performances during the early developmental periods. Infants and young children exhibit a wide range of behaviors and patterns of development that do not fit neatly into single diagnostic categories. Without accurate diagnostic procedures, establishing appropriate labels and subsequent classifications becomes guesswork. Dangers in misidentifying normal children and missing children with problems exist. Given this state of affairs, one might reasonably ask, Why label or classify? As indicated earlier in this chapter, the field must have systems for placement and obtaining support for children who require additional services, thus the need for labeling and classification. If at-risk and handicapped infants and children are to receive appropriate intervention services, they must be identified and, at the very least, labeled as needing some form of support services.

SUMMARY

A general overview of early development was offered to assist in establishing the parameters and definitions of at-risk and handicapped populations. Based on these definitions, discussions of the major factors or causes associated with these two populations were presented. Volumes have been written about early development and the factors that interfere with the acquisition of normal repertoires; the present discussions were able only to highlight selected critical pieces of information. The purpose was not to assist the reader in becoming fluent in these areas but to provide exposure to the general parameters of the at-risk and handicapped populations and what major factors might contribute to the infant or child being labeled and classified as either at-risk or handicapped.

References

Bijou, S., & Baer, D. (1978). *Behavior analysis of child development*. Englewood Cliffs, NJ: Prentice-Hall.

Bowerman, M. (1976). Semantic factors in the acquisition of rules for word use and sentence construction. In D. Morehead & A. Morehead (Eds.), *Normal and deficient child language*. Baltimore, MD: University Park Press.

Bricker, D. (1978). Early intervention: The criteria of success. *Allied Health and Behavioral Sciences Journal, 1,* 567–582.

Bricker, D. (Ed.) (1982). *Intervention with at-risk and handicapped infants.* Baltimore, MD: University Park Press.

Bricker, D., Bricker, W., Iacino, R., & Dennison, L. (1976). Intervention strategies for the severely and profoundly handicapped child. In N. Haring & L. Brown (Eds.), *Teaching the severely handicapped.* New York: Grune & Stratton.

Bricker, D., & Littman, D. (1985). Parental monitoring of infant development. In R. McMahon & R. Peters (Eds.), *Childhood disorders: Behavioral development approaches.* New York: Brunner/Mazel.

Brown, R. (1973). *A first language: The early stages.* Cambridge, MA: Harvard University Press.

Bruner, J. S. (1966). *Toward a theory of instruction.* Cambridge, MA: Harvard University Press.

Charlesworth, R. (1982). *Understanding child development.* Albany, NY: Delmar.

Cohen, M., & Gross, P. (1979). *The developmental resource: Behavioral sequences for assessment and program planning.* New York: Grune & Stratton.

Cole, K., & Garwood, S. (1983). Language development and language disorders in young children. In S. Garwood (Ed.), *Educating young handicapped children: A developmental approach.* Rockville, MD: Aspen Systems Corp.

Condon, W., & Sander, L. (1974). Synchrony demonstrated between movements of the neonate and adult speech. *Child Development, 45,* 456–462.

Crain, L. (1984). Prenatal causes of atypical development. In M. Hanson (Ed.), *Atypical infant development.* Baltimore, MD: University Park Press.

Denhoff, E. (1983). Intervention practices for developmentally disabled and high risk infants: Rationale and management. *The exceptional child, 30*(1), 67–75.

Emde, R., Kligman, D., Reich, J., & Wade, T. (1978). Emotional expression in infancy: I. Initial studies of social signaling and an emergent model. In M. Lewis & L. Rosenblum (Eds.), *Development of affect.* New York: Plenum Press.

Fewell, R. (1983). Working with sensorily impaired children. In S. Garwood (Ed.), *Educating young handicapped children: A developmental approach.* Rockville, MD: Aspen Systems Corp.

Fischer, K. (1980). A theory of cognitive development: The control and construction of hierarchies of skills. *Psychological Review, 87,* 477–531.

Flavell, J. (1977). *Cognitive development.* Englewood Cliffs, NJ: Prentice-Hall.

References

Garwood, S. (1983). Physical bases of handicapping conditions. In S. Garwood (Ed.), *Educating young handicapped children: A developmental approach.* Rockville, MD: Aspen Systems Corp.

Hallahan, D.P., & Kauffman, J.M. (1978). *Exceptional children: Introduction to special education.* Englewood Cliffs, NJ: Prentice-Hall.

Hayden, A., & Beck, G. (1982). The epidemiology of high-risk and handicapped infants. In C. Ramey & P. Trohanis, *Finding and educating high-risk and handicapped infants.* Baltimore, MD: University Park Press.

Hobbs, N. (Ed.) (1975a). *Issues in the classification of children* (Vol. 1). San Francisco: Jossey-Bass.

Hobbs, N. (Ed.) (1975b). *Issues in the classification of children* (Vol. 2). San Francisco: Jossey-Bass.

Hobbs, N. (1975c). *The futures of children.* San Francisco: Jossey-Bass.

Honzik, M. (1976). Value and limitations of infant tests: An overview. In M. Lewis (Ed.), *Origins of intelligence.* New York: Plenum Press.

Hunt, J. McV. (1961). *Intelligence and experience.* New York: Ronald Press Co.

Kagan, J., Kearsley, R., & Zelazo, P. (1978). *Infancy: Its place in human development.* Cambridge, MA: Harvard University Press.

Klaus, M., & Kennell, J. (Eds.) (1976). *Maternal-infant bonding.* St. Louis: Mosby.

Langley, M. (1983). The implications of physical impairments for early intervention strategies. In S. Garwood (Ed.), *Educating young handicapped children: A developmental approach.* Rockville, MD: Aspen Systems Corp.

Lewis, M. (1976). What do we mean when we say "infant intelligence scores"? A sociopolitical question. In M. Lewis (Ed.), *Origins of intelligence.* New York: Plenum Press.

Lewis, M. (1984). Developmental principles and their implications for at-risk and handicapped infants. In M. Hanson (Ed.), *Atypical infant development.* Baltimore, MD: University Park Press.

McCall, R. (1979). The development of intellectual functioning in infancy and the prediction of later IQ. In J. Osofsky (Ed.), *Handbook of infant development.* New York: Wiley & Sons.

McCandless, B., & Trotter, R. (1977). *Children behavior and development.* New York: Holt, Rinehart and Winston.

Minifie, F., & Lloyd, L. (1978). *Communicative and cognitive abilities—early behavior assessment.* Baltimore, MD: University Park Press.

Mussen, P., Conger, J., & Kagan, J. (1980). *Essentials of child development and personality.* Hagerstown, PA: Harper-Row.

Nelson, K. (1979). The role of language in infant development. In M.

Bornstein & W. Kessen (Eds.), *Psychological development from infancy: Image to intention.* Hillsdale, NJ: Lawrence Erlbaum Associates.

Oller, D. (1981). Infant vocalizations: Exploration and reflexivity. In R. Stark (Ed.), *Language behavior in infancy and early childhood.* New York: Elsevier.

Piaget, J. (1970). Piaget's theory. In P. Mussen (Ed.), *Carmichael's manual of child psychology* (Vol. 1). New York: Wiley.

Prutting, C. (1979). Process: The action of moving forward progressively from one point to another on the way to completion. *Journal of Speech and Hearing Research, 44,* 3–23.

Ramey, C., MacPhee, D., & Yeates, K. (1983). Preventing developmental retardation: A general systems model. In L. Bond & J. Joffe (Eds.), *Facilitating infant and early childhood development.* Hanover, NH: University Press of New England.

Ramey, C., Trohanis, P., Hostler, S. (1982). An introduction. In C. Ramey & P. Trohanis (Eds.), *Finding and educating high-risk and handicapped infants.* Baltimore, MD: University Park Press.

Sameroff, A. (1981). Longitudinal studies of preterm infants: A review of chapters 17–20. In S. Friedman & M. Sigman (Eds.), *Preterm birth and psychological development.* New York: Academic Press.

Scott, K., & Masi, W. (1979). The outcome from the utility of registers of risk. In T. Field, A. Sostek, S. Goldberg, & H. Schuman (Eds.), *Infants born at risk.* Jamaica, NY: Spectrum Publications.

Skinner, B. (1961, November). Teaching machines. *Scientific American* (reprint), 1–13.

Tjossem, T. (1976). Early intervention: Issues and approaches. In T. Tjossem (Ed.), *Intervention strategies for high risk infants and young children.* Baltimore, MD: University Park Press.

Trehub, S., Bull, D., & Schneider, B. (1981). Infant speech and nonspeech perception. In R. Schiefelbusch & D. Bricker (Eds.), *Early Language: Acquisition and intervention.* Baltimore, MD: University Park Press.

Uzgiris, I. (1976). Organization of sensorimotor intelligence. In M. Lewis (Ed.), *Origins of intelligence: Infancy and early childhood.* New York: Plenum Press.

Uzgiris, I., & Hunt, J. (1975). *Assessment in infancy: Ordinal scales of psychological development.* Urbana, IL: University of Illinois Press.

Zelazo, P., & Kearsley, R. (1980). The emergence of functional play in infants: Evidence for a major cognitive transition. *Journal of Applied Developmental Psychology, 1,* 95–117.

CHAPTER

7

PARENTS AND FAMILIES

Being an effective parent is an arduous endeavor demanding a commitment and understanding that few recognize before coming face to face with an infant shortly after birth. As the baby grows and his or her repertoire and needs become increasingly more complex, the realities of parental roles and responsibilities become apparent. Equally important are the concomitant expansion of parental expectations and ever increasing demands on the child to keep pace with peers by acquiring more complex behavior and becoming socialized. The foundation for a varied, intricate interaction has been established. Parents and children use a variety of mechanisms to balance the needs and demands of their complex interactive system; however, when the balance of this interactive system is upset, disruption in the child-parent relationship can occur. The birth of a handicapped infant often can be the beginning of a serious and long-term disruption in family functioning; therefore, it is essential that professionals working or preparing to work with handicapped children and their families acquire a "sense" for the impact that these children may have on the family constellation.

To disregard or to underestimate the potential impact of a handicapped child on the family may interfere with all aspects of the prescribed plan and delivery of services to that child. As Phil Roos (1978) suggests, a productive parent-professional partnership is constructed on mutual respect and understanding. One of the first steps in the professional's gaining respect and understanding is to attempt to grasp what many parents feel upon learning their child is handicapped. What is the impact of a handicapped infant on families?

> I did not choose to have a retarded child, nor do I feel glorified because of the experience. Our family simply accepted

Billy, along with his retardation, and did the best we could. However, the things we have learned in the process have helped other people. (Schultz, 1985, p. 19)

The birth of the blind baby was a disaster for each of the families we have known. The defective baby opened up old wounds in the femininity and masculinity of the young mother and father. Three of our fathers developed potency problems soon after the birth of the baby. There may have been others too shy to tell us. Unconscious revulsion in mother or father took the form of avoidance, of not touching the baby except when it was necessary. In several cases, babies were brought to us for consultation at six months, or ten months, or twelve months, with bald spots on the back of the head, which gave mute testimony to long hours spent supine in a crib. They were described as quiet babies who never complained. For most of their twenty-four hour day, these babies lived in a sensory desert. The unspeakable thought, "He would be better off dead," was translated, "as if he were dead." (Fraiberg, 1975, p. 43)

Because the family is forced to cope with the advent of a disabled infant, the professional needs to understand and appreciate the perceived lack of support available to many families. From whom can families seek help?

Most parents make it, given time. But they are generally ill prepared for the trauma, and the familiar ways of relieving grief are not available. It is not like having a death in the family, when people come together to grieve and draw comfort from the presence of friends and family. Learning that one's child is "not normal" is a lonely experience; having such a child tends to thrust the parents outside the mainstream of help, comfort, and advice. Uncommon problems cannot be shared with next-door neighbors. Friends and relatives feel, and often are, ill qualified to advise or assist. The usual sources of professional help, like one's physician, may seem inappropriate. The parent himself may feel some alienation from the "normal" world around him. (Gorham, DesJardins, Page, Pettis, & Scheiber, 1975, p. 156)

Professionals should try to gauge the trauma associated with the recognition that the child will never be normal. How do parents rationalize this reality?

I felt my ego had been wiped out. My superego with all its guilts had become the most prominent part of my personality and I had completely lost my self-esteem. I felt I was nobody. Any credits of self-worth that I could give myself from any of my personal endeavors meant nothing. Graduating from college and a first-rate medical school, surviving an internship, practicing medicine and having two beautiful sons and a good marriage counted for nil. All I knew at this point was that I was the mother of an abnormal and most likely retarded child. (Ziskin, 1978, p. 75)

Parenting is a significant responsibility made more complicated when the child has a handicap. What resources can families generate to cope with the added stress of having a handicapped child?

The fact of life for parents of handicapped children which is least understood by others is this: It is difficult and exhausting to live normally, and yet we must. To decide on the other route, to admit that having a disabled child makes us disabled persons, to say no to the ordinary requirements of daily living is to meet the second enemy—loneliness. It means drifting slowly out of the mainstream of adult life. In a very real sense, we are damned if we do make the extraordinary effort required to live normally, and damned if we don't. (Morton, 1978, pp. 144–145)

These questions and parental words are offered to assist in creating a heightened sensitivity to the realities and responsibilities facing families who have a handicapped member. Our effectiveness with families may be dependent, in part, upon our expertise in recognizing and respecting the variety of feelings and concerns found in the families seeking our help.

The purpose of this chapter is to provide information covering a broad range of topics related to family functioning when a disabled child is present. In particular, the discussion will focus on (1) the relationship between the young child and his or her family, (2) interactive effects of early experiences on infants, (3) potential disruptions of the family-child relationship, and (4) some general intervention strategies for involving families in their child's educational program. However, before these topics are addressed, a brief discussion of the historical evolution of parent involvement in special education programs will be presented.

PARENT INVOLVEMENT

Parental participation in programs for young handicapped or at-risk children seems commonplace today and is the expectation that most professionals hold. Reminding ourselves that parental involvement in early education previously was the exception rather than the rule may be useful. During the decade of the 1970s, there has been a dramatic and radical shift in both the philosophy and the practice of involving parents in their child's educational program.

Although in the early 1970s parent participation was encouraged in a few exemplary or model programs (see Tjossem, 1976), most programs and professionals did not seriously consider the inclusion of the parent until the advent of P.L. 94-142 in 1975. Turnbull, Turnbull, and Wheat (1982) argue that the United States Congress revolutionized special education by enacting P.L. 94-142 not only because this law mandated parental involvement, but because it also required nondiscriminatory evaluation, individualized education programs, and placement in least restrictive environments.

Although passage of Section 504 of the Rehabilitation Act in 1973 ensured a legal basis for nondiscriminatory practice against the handicapped as well as other minority groups, this legislative act did not ensure parental involvement in the handicapped child's education as discussed in Chapter 5. The passage of P.L. 94-142 stipulated parental participation and thus established a legal basis for the inclusion of the parent in the handicapped child's educational program. Since the passage of P.L. 94-142, a struggle to develop a reasonable and productive rapprochement between parents and the professional community has been underway. And, indeed, it has been a struggle.

Before the advent of P.L. 94-142 and, more recently, P.L. 98-199, parental participation was largely restricted to attending meetings during which the professional would explain the child's problems or progress. Occasionally, parents might be asked to attempt to reinforce the occurrence of specific behaviors within the home once those behaviors had been acquired under the tutelage of professional interventionists. During the early 1970s, and more obviously after the passage of P.L. 94-142, some parents developed into vocal advocates for their children's rights. Often, school personnel felt beleaguered by forced compliance with a set of regulations they felt poorly prepared to actualize, a situation compounded by the demands of angry, combative parents.

In hindsight, the legitimate implementation of P.L. 94-142 may have been seriously hindered by rash and defensive reactions by some parents and some members of the professional community. Neither group was probably entirely objective nor able to articulate an unbiased approach to implementing the spirit of the law. Some due process hearings may have served a useful purpose, but many did not yield results productive for the parent, child, or professional (Strickland, 1982). Angry and emotional attacks by parents, which may or may not have been justified, have served to drive some effective, dedicated interventionists from the field and to entrench less responsible professionals into positions that hinder effective communication and action. Then, too, continued inappropriate actions and attitudes on the part of program personnel have served to further embitter parents and build substantial obstacles to constructive parental involvement. Reactions from both parents and the professional community have served to seriously impede the participation of many parents in their child's educational program.

A second problem that has contributed to the subversion of the genuine intent of P.L. 94-142 has been a common, misguided professional philosophy about the manner in which parents should be involved in their child's education (Darling, 1983). Often well-meaning professionals fail to see the barriers they erect to effective parental involvement because they presume to specify for the parents the nature of their involvement in the child's program. For example, the teacher who developed a child's educational plan prior to the IEP meeting surely must have conveyed to the attending parents that their input in the development of goals and objectives for their child is not necessary. Program personnel who require that all parents perform the same function must be suspect in terms of their genuine interest and ability in determining the needs and values of individual parents. Morgan's (1982) analysis of IEP meeting data tends to indicate that while attendance is high for parents, contributions to the IEP for their children is low. That is, parents attend, but assume the role of listener during the meeting. As professionals, we need to ask ourselves why parents are reluctant to speak up. An equally important question to ask is why we have been so unsuccessful in involving those parents who tend to be less well educated and who come from less affluent environments.

An examination of the current status of parent involvement in early-intervention programs is optimistic. A trend toward professional awareness of the parent and other family members as legitimate members of the intervention team is occurring. Further, many early interventionists have become aware that much of the success of a child's programs hinges on how effectively the family is able to deal with the child. Thus, often the family, in addition to the child, should be the target of intervention. These new perspectives are laying the foundation for two major changes. The first is a reconceptualization by program personnel of their approach to, and inclusion of, family members in the child's program. The second is the recognition that the child is a part of a larger social milieu, the family, wherein change in any member can produce change in other members. Thus, intervention with children should be formulated in the context of the family's goals and designed to fit comfortably with the way the entire family functions. These two conceptual changes will require considerably more individualization and flexibility in our approach to involving parents in programs.

Changing Parental Roles

Early-intervention program personnel appear to have been more assertive and concerned about including parents in programs for young children than public school personnel, whose clientele is older. The enthusiasm and manner in which parents have been involved in early-intervention programs are, however, undergoing a steady and remarkable shift. Initially, parents were encouraged to participate by engaging in the structured formats designed by programs for parental involvement. Reading previously published program descriptions gives the impression that professionals conceived of parents as a homogeneous group able to contribute little to the understanding of their children's current behavioral repertoire and being in need of firm guidance from professionals. This guidance was most often offered in intervention packages developed a priori by the interventionists.

Many programs described in the literature have suggested that their parent programs have been successful in terms of both attendance and short-term changes in behavior (see e.g., Baker & Heifetz, 1976). However, more careful analysis, as well as information derived from informal exchanges, tends to suggest that parent programs are often successful with only a select group of parents. Most programs are able to successfully engage a certain percentage of parents, are partially successful with another group, and are unsuccessful with a third group. The percentage of parents that falls into each of these categories is probably largely dependent upon three intersecting sets of variables: characteristics of family members, program personnel expertise, and logistics, such as transportation that may affect the ability of the program to successfully reach all of the participating families.

Given the general approach adopted by many programs, the lack of success with specific groups of parents should not surprise us. The most prevalent approach appears to have been the devising of a parental involvement program composed of a combination of large group meetings and, as the need arose for a parent, individual meetings (see Bricker & Casuso, 1979). In the past, programs rarely reported systematic attempts to elicit interest or needs assessments from parents prior to the development of a parent program. Implicit in this approach is the attitude that the professional worker "knows" what the family needs and how best to present that information. Slowly, we are coming to recognize the fallacy of such thinking. If this attitude has been pervasive, it is perhaps not surprising that our programs have often missed the mark of meaningful family involvement across a range of diverse cultural, educational, and economic populations.

More recent descriptions of parent involvement programs (see, e.g., Vadasy, Fewell, Meyer, Schell, & Greenberg, 1984; Bailey & Bricker, 1984) indicate a changing attitude in how best to involve family members in their child's program. This changing attitude is reflected in two areas: (1) the growing professional interest in eliciting from the parents statements of needs and preferences for their child and themselves before the development of a set of goals and objectives; and (2) the professional's willingness to expand the parent's role.

A growing data base indicates that parents can accurately identify problems in their children, assess the nature of those problems, and intervene effectively when provided assistance by the professional community (Walker, Slentz, & Bricker, 1985). For example, Brooks-Gunn and Lewis (1979) report that parents often are the first to suspect their child has a problem and may actually have informally diagnosed the problem months before a professional does so. In a large study that examined the ability of parents to monitor the development of their at-risk infant at four-month intervals using a simple question format, parents were found to be in agreement with the results obtained by professional examiners using the

Gesell approximately 80 percent of the time (Bricker, Jusczyk, & Mounts, 1984). Finally, there is a rich literature on the ability of parents to acquire effective instructional strategies (Bruder, 1983). These data indicate that many of the roles and functions previously thought to be the exclusive domain of the professional need not be so. There is ample evidence that many parents can accurately assess, intervene, and evaluate their child (Walker, Slentz, & Bricker, 1985).

In addition to parent roles directly related to the child that Stoneman and Brody (1984) have characterized as "manager" and "teacher" roles, parents can fill a variety of other roles that may enhance their feelings of self value and satisfaction and their knowledge that they have much to contribute to their child's welfare. The key to expanding the role of parents is the professional's willingness to acknowledge that parents often know most accurately and adequately what their needs and interests are. We, as professionals, can no longer afford to presume that we can determine the goals and objectives for the child as well as the role the parents should assume in their child's education. Rather, we should be working toward the development of communications that convey the importance we attach to the parents' own desires for themselves and their child. The development of the child's IEP and the parental participation in a program should ideally be jointly determined by the parent and the professional.

Family Systems

The second major change pervading early childhood/special education in terms of parental involvement is the acknowledgment of the importance of examining the ecological context of the at-risk or handicapped child when formulating an intervention plan. Historically, the field has moved its focus from the child to the child-caregiver dyad to the child within the family and the family within the community. Increasingly, early interventionists are recognizing that for educational plans to be effective, they must be developed with a consideration of the many subsystems that affect the child and the parents (Parke & Tinsley, 1982).

Family system theorists such as Minuchin (1974) postulate four major types of subsystems within the nuclear family. These subsystems are parent-child (parental); parent-parent (executive); child-child (sibling); and family-extrafamily, which includes extended family, friends, neighbors, and the larger community. There are several important features to remember about the roles that family members play in these subsystems. First, the roles of individuals within the different subsystems may vary considerably across families. There are no static definitions of how family members behave within a subsystem. Therefore, the roles taken by Mr. and Mrs. Smith in the parent-parent subsystem may be remarkably different from the roles that Mrs. Jones and Mr. Jones play in their family's parent-parent subsystem. Second, roles differ for family members, depending upon the subsystem within which they are functioning. For example, in a parent-child subsystem, five-year-old Suzy may assume a dependent role and permit her mother to make decisions about her daily activities. While in the child-child subsystem, Suzy may take on the role of teacher with her three-year-old sister. A third way in which roles may vary occurs as conditions warrant change. If, for example, Mr. Smith becomes seriously disabled, Mrs. Smith may have to take on the role of family provider while Mr. Smith may accept the role of cook. As children mature, roles within the parent-child subsystem are expected to change along a developmental dimension to allow the child to assume more independence and terminate the parent's role as caregiver.

Finally, roles that individual family members take within each subsystem are dependent upon how functional or dysfunctional each family member is in a given role. For example, parents are described as having established a functional executive system within the family if they demonstrate effective control over family affairs, which include child management, and a dysfunctional system if they are not able to command control. Thus, the interventionist's effectiveness would be greatly enhanced if he or she understood the various roles that family members play within each of the subsystems and the dynamic nature of these roles over time and with changing conditions.

Using a family systems approach to working with families with a disabled member, Turnbull, Summers, and Brotherson (1983) describe a model based on four major assumptions:

1. Each family is unique, due to the infinite variations in personal characteristics and cultural and ideological styles.
2. The family is an interactional system whose component parts have constantly shifting boundaries and varying degrees of resistance to change.
3. Families must fulfill a variety of functions for each member, both collectively and individually, if each member is to grow and develop.
4. Families pass through developmental and nondevelopmental changes that produce varying amounts of stress affecting all members. (Turnbull, Summers, & Brotherson, 1983, pp. 2–3)

These assumptions emphasize the difference between a family systems approach and one that is focused primarily on the child or on the child and the primary caregiver. If one is comfortable with the assumption that the social context in which the young child resides has a major impact on the child's development, then the adoption of a family systems approach holds great appeal. In the future, intervention plans should be based on relevant goals and objectives for the child as before; but these goals and objectives should be derived through careful analysis of the young child's primary social context, the family. To understand and work effectively with an at-risk or handicapped child, it is helpful to understand the dynamics of the various nested subsystems within the child's family. Perhaps the subsystem that holds the potential for the greatest impact for most young children is that of the parent-child. The next section of this chapter discusses the at-risk or handicapped child's relationship with his or her family, in particular, the child-parent interaction.

THE RELATIONSHIP BETWEEN THE CHILD AND THE FAMILY: AN INTERACTIVE MODEL

Before understanding the impact of handicapped children on their environments, it is necessary to have an idea about the evolution of the feedback system, or the developing relationship between children and their caregivers.

Not too many years ago, the predominant theoretical position concerning parent-child interaction appeared to be unidirectional. That is, investigators looked primarily at the effect the caregiver or the environment had on the infant or young child and did not concern themselves with the child's effect on the caregiver. For example, in a series of influential investigations (e.g., Bowlby, 1973; Spitz, 1946), findings were reported that suggested the dramatically depressing effect of institutional environments on young children. The focus of this important body of research was unilateral because the investigators focused primarily on what they thought were the effects of inconsistent caregiving or mothering on the young child.[1] These investigators did not, however, look at the effect of the child on the child's environment. Of equal interest was another group of investigations that concerned themselves with more specific infant responses that could be controlled or manipulated by the caregiver. For example, Rheingold, Gewirtz, and Ross (1959) found that responses such as vocalizing are affected by social consequences provided by caregivers. These investigators found that providing pleasurable social consequences to babies increased the frequency of vocalization while neutral consequences reduced the frequency. Although such investigations were important in demonstrating that environmental manipulations can control affective behavior, again the focus of these investigations was unilateral because the investigators examined only the effect of the caregiver's behavior on the child's behavior.

Although an interactionist model has been a feature of many theories of cognitive development, Piaget perhaps being the most notable of interaction theorists, an interactionist position did not appear to have much influence on aspects of the child-parent relationship until the early 1970s. A number of investigators (see, e.g., Lewis & Rosenblum, 1974) were beginning to explore

---

[1] A number of investigators (e.g., White & Held, 1967; Dennis & Najarian, 1963) have suggested that the reactions of infants that Bowlby and his colleagues observed could have been attributed to the lack of any appropriate environmental stimulation rather than caused primarily by maternal deprivation.

the child-caregiver relationship as one in which both participants affected the behavior of the other. That is, there appeared to be a reciprocal exchange governed by each participant's response to the other. The caregiver responds to a baby's crying by comforting the infant, who, in turn, quiets and may coo to the adult, who, in turn, may smile at the infant, the smiling, in turn, eliciting a smile from the baby. One can begin to see a pattern of interaction that appears, in many instances, to be governed by the participants' responses to each other.

This circular feedback system could be viewed as a simple interaction model; however, Lewis and Lee-Painter (1974) have discussed in detail the problems associated with the position that the child-caregiver interaction is a simple interactive system. Rather, these investigators suggest a complex model in which both the child and caregiver are actively involved and "significantly influence each other."

A model of child-caregiver interactions shown in Figure 7–1 contains elements of the Lewis–Lee-Painter model (1974) but presents the dyadic interaction between child and caregiver in a more simplified manner. This model is composed of a number of elements. First, the large arrows at the interaction junctures between the child and the caregiver suggest an impact following behavioral exchanges that travels in at least three directions: The child affects the caregiver (point B); the caregiver affects the child (point A); and the nature of such interactions affect future interactions between the child and caregiver (point 1). The latter effect is indicated by the downward arrow. Subsequent interactions that occur, for example, interactions 2 and 3, are influenced by previous interactions. The caregiver continues to influence the child, as illustrated by arrows D and F; and likewise, the child affects the caregiver, as illustrated by arrows C and E.

A description of this model will clarify its interactional elements. A mother takes her young child to the grocery store and seats the child in the cart. The child sees a box of cookies and indicates to the mother "want cookie," which is the initiation of this interactive exchange. Mother says, "No cookies now, but you can have one later at home." This response produces a reaction (point A) in the child (e.g., denial of child's request produces anger) and a reaction (point B) in the mother (e.g., pleasure at being firm with the child for an inappropriate request), which leads to a second exchange (interaction 2). The child begins to cry and scream for a cookie (point C). The mother responds to the child (point D) by ignoring the child's crying and pointing to an interesting situation in the store, leading to the third interaction in the sequence. The child responds by looking toward the indicated activities and stops crying, then the mother smiles and talks to the child about the activity.

At each interaction point, the behavior of both the child and mother has the potential of being different based on their reactions to each other and their past experience in similar situations. For example, if the child had a history of obtaining cookies in the store by crying, the mother may have been

Relationship Between the Child and the Family: An Interactive Model

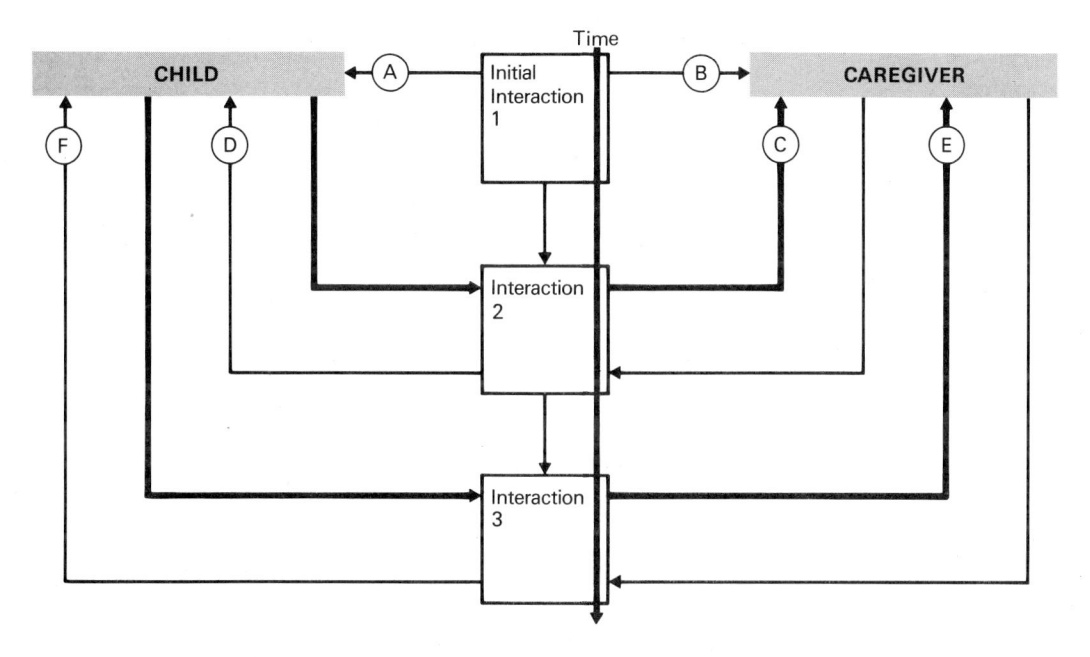

FIGURE 7-1. Model of child-caregiver interaction. Reprinted from Bricker & Carlson (1981), p. 492.

unsuccessful at her attempts to distract the youngster, and the third interaction might have been one of more crying by the child producing an angry response from the mother. Yet another scenario is possible. Had the mother responded affirmatively to the child's initial request for a cookie, the probabilities are high that the subsequent exchanges between the mother and child would have followed a different course of action.

Clearly, chains of interactions between the child and the parents are governed by multiple factors that must be appreciated if we are to develop mechanisms for influencing parent-child interactions.

> In summary, then, the parent-child system is a reciprocal relation involving two or more individuals who differ greatly in maturity although not in competence, in terms of ability to affect each other. The relationship involves much more and longer-range intention on the part of one participant than on the part of the other. There is a certain balance of controls, in that the greater intentional behavior of the parent is off-set by two features of the offspring's behavior: 1) the active short-range initiation of interactions, and 2) the organization of the behavior so that it is compelling and selectively reinforcing. Much of the modification of child behavior toward cultural norms occurs in the context of parental adjustments and accommodations to the initiations of the young. (Bell, 1974, p. 15)

Understanding the interaction between child and social environment is paramount to establishing a framework from which to view parenting and the child-parent relationship.

THE INTERACTIVE EFFECTS OF EARLY EXPERIENCE ON THE CHILD

There seems to be a consensus that both cognitive and affective developments are the result of an interactive system (Hunt, 1961; Decarie, 1978; Saarni, 1978). The environment affects the child and, of equal importance, the child affects the environment. Having established the interactiveness between the child and the environment, we can next examine early factors that tend to influence the child-parent relationship. However, as a foundation for evaluating these factors, let us briefly discuss early affective development.

According to Piaget, the infant arrives in the world with a set of reflexive behaviors that are automatically triggered by either internal states or environmental stimuli (1970). As the infant exercises these reflexes, the form changes to simple volitional responses that are maintained by the environmental changes they produce. Through subsequent interaction with both people and objects, these simple responses, or action schemes (e.g., tracking, reaching, mouthing), become modified and elaborated into more complex and coordinated schemes (e.g., hand-eye coordination). During the sensorimotor period, the behavioral repertoire of the infant continues to expand as the infant looks, touches, listens, and acts on the environment. Although the acquisition of cognitive or problem-solving behavior is of critical importance, so, too, is the infant's affective development.

For any number of reasons, studying affective behavior and its development has been a more elusive, difficult task than exploring the genesis of more cognitive forms of behavior. The affective domain of behavior refers to those responses that have to do with feelings or emotions that produce psychological change in the organism. In general, there are two basic models found in the literature to explain the development of affective behavior: the biological model and the socialization model (Lewis & Rosenblum, 1978). The biological model suggests that certain conditions produce specific emotional responses that are unlearned. That is, the approach of an unfamiliar adult may automatically trigger "fear" in an infant. Contrarily, the socialization model suggests that relationships between internal states (e.g., increased heart rate) and surface behavior (e.g., look of fear on the face) are learned behaviors. "Thus, the emotional state or experience is a consequence of the social environments' responses to the child's behavior in a specific context" (Lewis & Rosenblum, 1978, p. 8). It is likely that the development of affective behavior results from learned *and* unlearned behavior. There may be some basic unlearned, biologically based emotional responses (e.g., rocking, crying) to specific conditions (Harlow & Mears, 1978), but it is equally

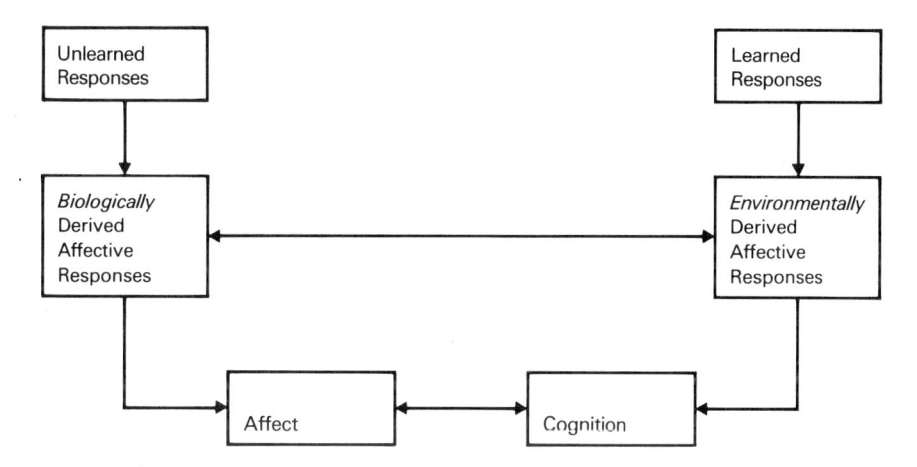

The Interactive Effects of Early Experience on the Child

FIGURE 7-2. Elements contributing to affective development.

probable that more complex meaning-laden affective behavior is learned through interaction with the social environment. Figure 7-2 presents a schematic representation of these elements.

Although some investigators feel that affective and cognitive behaviors are separate areas of development, attempts at separation are often futile and unsatisfactory—particularly in the case of the young child.

> From an ontogenetic standpoint, it appears impossible to study cognitive development in the absence of affective development. This follows because the behavioral performance that we observe and infer as being the result of cognitive functioning is equally a result of affective functioning (i.e., motivation, interest, expectancy). As Piaget contends (and I concur), without affect, there would be no intelligence, from either a competence or a performance point of view. (Saarni, 1978, p. 362)

If one accepts this position, then as Decarie (1978) suggests, it makes little sense to ask whether cognitive or affective behavior occurs first or which causes which. Rather, there is a reciprocal, interactive, ongoing relationship between cognitive and affective behavior.

Emde, Kligman, Reich, and Wade (1978) have proposed a preliminary model to explain the development of affective expressions in the infant. In their developmental model, they suggest:

> ... that the organization of the central nervous system is such that soon after three months of age, the three dimensions of emotional expression are apparent. In contrast, categories of emotional expression, characterized by discrete messages, undergo an epigenesis continuing through the first postnatal year and beyond. Cognitive development

plays an increasingly important role in this epigenesis, and the study of its integration with ongoing motoric components of expression offer an exciting challenge. (Emde, Kligman, Reich, & Wade, 1978, p. 145)

Using the elements of the Emde et al. model and the levels of cognitive organization suggested by Uzgiris (1976), a speculative account of the parallel development of the affective and cognitive systems and how they may reciprocally affect each other has been constructed. This speculative model of parallel development is shown in Table 7-1.

The purpose of the present section has been to provide a brief overview of how young children acquire cognitive and affective forms of behavior. The difficulty of attempting to separate the development of the cognitive from that of the affective systems in the young child has been emphasized. The parallel, yet intertwined nature of these two systems argues that early experience of a young child, no matter what its nature, will likely have a significant effect on both cognitive and affective development. It is important to view environmental input to the young handicapped child from this perspective; therefore, a healthy, productive parent-child interaction is essential to all aspects of growth and development of the young handicapped child.

THE IMPORTANCE OF THE PARENT-CHILD RELATIONSHIP

The quality of interaction in the parent-child relationship seems to be affected by two major variables: the timing and the topography of the responses made to the partner. The back-and-forth nature of parent-child interactions presupposes an underlying time-sequence frame. That is, one partner's response generally precedes the other's. The timing, or "synchrony," of the mother's or the caregiver's response to the baby appears to have the potential of seriously affecting the quality of their relationship even during the very early phases of development (Osofsky, 1976). Especially in the case of parent-child interactions, synchrony of responding refers to the parents' ability (and to a lesser extent, the child's capacity) to monitor the state, mood, or needs of the child and respond in a facilitating manner according to the child's needs. For example, if a baby is thrashing and crying vigorously, a synchronous move on the part of the parent might be to respond with behaviors that would be soothing to the infant; therefore, the parent might lift the child, rock him, and talk quietly in his ear. If the baby were in an awake, alert state, an appropriate response might be to offer some form of stimulation the baby might find interesting, for example, showing the baby a bright colorerd toy, tickling her toes, or returning her coos and gurgles.

Such synchronous responding to infants and young children would seem to take the form of "doing what comes naturally" to most parents.

Levels of Developmental Organization	Age	Affective System*	Sensorimotor System†
I	Neonate	Biologically based affective expressions of: pleasant–unpleasant high activation–low activation internal–external	Reflexes: e.g., rooting, sucking, startle
II	4–9 months	Regulation of categorical responses (fear, surprise, anger)	Simple undifferentiated actions (mouthing, looking, banging)
III	8–12 months		Differentiated actions (throw balls, pound with hammer)
IV	12–18 months		Regulation by differential feedback
V	18–24 months	Affective response in anticipation of event	Anticipatory regulation

*Emde et al. (1978), pp. 141–145.
†Uzgiris (1976), pp. 150–155.

TABLE 7-1 *Hypothetical Sequence of Affective and Sensorimotor Development*

Fortunately, most babies and their parents do arrive at a reasonably effective synchrony of their reciprocal responses. However, as noted by a number of investigators (Brazelton, Koslowski, & Main, 1974; Bell, 1974; Denenberg & Thoman, 1976), the needs of some babies apparently exceed the ability of their caregivers to cope or respond in a healthy, productive manner. The development of an asynchronous relationship may result from having a difficult-to-manage child (e.g., an autistic child) or from a caregiver with little sensitivity to the state or needs of the child. Child abuse or neglect, either psychological or physical, may result when the unfortunate combination of a difficult-to-manage child with an insensitive parent occurs; although as Sameroff and Chandler (1975) suggest, the causal factors for abuse are probably multiple and complex. In examining caregivers' sensitivity, Brazelton et al. (1974) report the differential effects produced by mothers on two similarly tense, overreactive infants. The mother who was able to modulate or synchronize her behavior to that of the infant apparently assisted the baby in becoming more responsive, while in the other case, the infant appeared to learn to escape his mother's increased stimulation by tuning her out.

These two parallel cases demonstrate that a mother's behavior "must not only be reinforcing and contingent upon the infant's behavior, but that it must meet more basic 'needs' of the infant in being aware of his capacity to receive and utilize stimuli" (Brazelton et al., 1974, p. 60).

Although the quality of the early parent-child interaction is probably more dependent upon the sensitivity of the adult, asynchrony in the relation-

Parents and Families

ship can be produced by the infant as well. Denenberg and Thoman (1976) discuss a case in which the infant's irritable and unresponsive behavior made it extremely difficult for a mother to respond appropriately. An investigation of the state or mood changes of this infant was revealing because this baby was found to shift states significantly more often than other infants of comparable age. Apparently, this baby's erratic behavior made it difficult for the mother to modulate her responses accordingly, and the amount of time this mother spent with her infant was observed to gradually decrease over time. Decreasing the amount of interaction between the child and parent may eventually lead to a progressively ineffectual relationship. Other investigators (e.g., Jones, 1977) have also reported asynchrony between mothers and their handicapped infants.

If, as we believe, synchrony of the interaction between the child and the parent is important, it will be useful for the purposes of this chapter to examine the possible disruptions of this relationship caused by the birth of a handicapped child. These disruptions could result from the psychological, physical, and/or behavioral differences in or surrounding the birth of a handicapped child.

POTENTIAL DISRUPTIONS IN THE PARENT-CHILD RELATIONSHIP

With the birth of an at-risk or handicapped child, at least two unusual events tend to occur: extended physical separation between parent and child and the psychological impact of being told that the infant is ill and/or handicapped. The birth of a handicapped or medically fragile child may necessitate a number of unusual and often dramatic maneuvers. In many cases, the hospital staff may have to perform a number of lifesaving medical procedures. The premature or sick infant is often placed in an isolette, and the parents' first view of their baby may be with the infant attached to a threatening array of tubes, wires, and machines. Seeing their child under such conditions must be frightening for parents, and their feelings of concern and apprehension may be heightened by being unable to hold or be close to the infant. The physical separation may interfere dramatically with the development of "normal" bonding or attachment between parents and child (Klaus & Kennell, 1976). The parent may not have the opportunity to touch, hold, or care for the infant for days, weeks, and in some cases, months. Such extended separation may produce significant barriers to the development of positive early interactions between the infant and the parents.

A second possible disruption is the shock of being told one's child is seriously ill or handicapped. Interviews with parents give credence to the apparent emotional upheaval produced by having a handicapped child. Following is a mother's account of her feelings shortly after the birth of her Down syndrome baby:

> And I looked at him again, and I said he just isn't right. I just knew he wasn't.... I just couldn't talk anymore after I said that, just couldn't say another word. I was maybe dumbfounded or shocked, and woke up in the recovery room and Walter was at my side crying and crying and very tan, and I said, "Oh, just look at his face, he just isn't right." And he just kept crying and crying and I thought, "Just get him out of here, just get him out of here."... I didn't want him. All I wanted to do was run away. ... I guess I just felt like this was the end of the world. (Klaus & Kennell, 1976, p. 183)

Such feelings on the part of the parents, along with the subsequent guilt and pain for having felt such emotions about one's own child, could have a serious impact on the future parent-child relationship.

The birth of a handicapped child tends to shatter not only the psychological but also the physical expectations of the parent. In many instances, the handicapped infant or child looks significantly different. The child may have a physical anomaly (e.g., open spine), motor impairment (e.g., cerebral palsy), sensory deficit (e.g., blindness), or atypical features (e.g., Down syndrome) that are clearly visible to the parent as well as to the rest of the world. Such overt physical differences may affect the parent's ability to interact with the child.

The general appearance alone of a handicapped or premature infant may elicit unusual responses from parents. Seeing an infant that is obviously distressed, ill, or both no doubt colors the parent's perception of the baby and his or her needs. Much of the "overprotection" demonstrated by parents of the at-risk or handicapped child may stem from their initial contact with the infant. Parents who have experienced periods during which the survival of the child was in question may acquire feelings about and reactions to the child that are counter to the development of independent, adaptive behaviors in the child (Gabel, McDowell, & Cerreto, 1983).

Behavioral as well as physical differences may affect parent-child interactions. Mothers seem to endow even the neonate with behavioral intentionality; and when the infant's behaviors are discrepant or do not meet the parent's expectations, then disruptions in the relationship may occur. For example, in comparing the smiling behavior of Down syndrome babies with that of normally developing babies, Emde, Katz, and Thorpe (1978) report observable differences. Although the onset of social smiling was somewhat delayed in the Down babies in these investigators' sample, the most significant differences seem to be more qualitative in nature; the corners of the mouth turn up less, less eye contact is made, the eyes are less bright, and there is less motoric activity. The end result is that the Down baby "seems less engaging" when smiling and therefore does not meet the general expectancy of the onlooker. In effect, the adults are disappointed because the baby does not meet their expectations for a smiling baby (Emde, Katz, & Thorpe, 1978). Cicchetti and Sroufe (1976) also report finding affective differences in the responding of Down syndrome infants when compared to nonhandicapped babies. Fraiberg (1975), too, has discussed the problems parents face when their baby does not meet their expectations. In particular, she notes that the result of smiling at a blind baby who does not return the smile "feels curiously like a snub." Each of us has certain expectancies in terms of others' behavior toward us, and those infants or children that cannot or do not meet the behavioral expectations of their parents run the risk of developing a less than satisfactory parent-child relationship.

Asynchronous interactions between the parent and at-risk or handicapped children are likely to occur for a number of reasons. The advent of a "different" infant demands that family members either expand existing skills or acquire new ones to cope with the disequilibrium produced by the aytpical infant. Thus, a major objective for most program personnel dealing with at-risk or handicapped infants is to assist family members in their adjustment to and subsequent ability to cope effectively with their atypical infant.

STRATEGIES FOR INTERVENTION

The beginning sections of this chapter have been devoted to a rather extensive description of the interactive system between parent and child. The most important aspect of the parent-child relationship is that the parents' behavior affects the child and, equally important, the child's behavior affects the parents. In such an interactive system, the quality and timing of each partner's response contributes substantially to the overall relationship.

Further, the early relationship established between parent and child will quite possibly affect the quality of the interaction over time. That is, the development of mutually reinforcing behaviors by the parent and child early in the child's life enhances the probability that mutual satisfaction will be maintained. The lack of a mutually reinforcing system between parent and child may lead to frustration, neglect, and even abuse (Klaus & Kennell, 1976; Denenberg & Thoman, 1976). The advent of an at-risk or handicapped child appears to produce, for most families, significant emotional trauma. The reaction of parents to their at-risk or handicapped offspring, as well as the often atypical physical appearance or behavioral discrepancies of the child, places an extraordinary strain on the development of a mutually reinforcing parent-child relationship. The potential jeopardy of this relationship, in concert with a number of other variables often associated with at-risk or handicapped children, argues strongly for two points. First, families should have access to support and intervention services to help them deal effectively with their at-risk or handicapped child. Second, such intervention/support services should be available before a destructive or nonreinforcing relationship develops between the infant and family members.

Rationale for Family Involvement Programs

Support/intervention services for families have been labeled Family Involvement Programs for a very specific purpose. Intervention offered to parents should not be prescriptions proffered by "experts"; nor should the "experts" be providing all the intervention or making all the moves in the child's program. Rather, our approach is to involve the parent or other family members at all levels of intervention, from deciding on the intervention goals to their subsequent implementation. Following are a number of points that form the rationale for family involvement in intervention programs for young at-risk or handicapped children.

Perhaps one of the strongest arguments for parental involvement has to do with time and contact. Except in unusual circumstances, parents spend more time with their preschool-age child (e.g., birth to six years) than does anyone else. It is hard to conceive of an effective intervention program without including those individuals who spend the most time with the child. For example, the initiation of a toilet training program without the inclusion of the home environment will be, at best, only partially successful. Without extending training into the home, it is doubtful that the toilet training success achieved elsewhere will transfer. In fact, it would, in most instances, make more sense to initiate a toilet training program in the home since that is the environment in which young children are apt to use the bathroom most often. Other important behaviors, such as expressive language, will, no doubt, be acquired more rapidly if training is implemented at home where the child generally spends more time. Work on any important training target should include participation of those individuals who spend considerable portions of the day with the child, for reasons of consistency as well as increased learning opportunities.

The second point in our rationale concerns factors of economics. The trend in public education and in agencies concerned with handicapped individuals (e.g., mental health agencies, developmental disabilities programs, etc.) seems to be the provision of extended services to more clients with fewer resources. Such demands do now and will continue to tax the ability of public agencies to provide quality services. Clearly, more efficient, economical strategies will be necessary to meet these demands. We are far short of trained personnel to provide programs for handicapped preschool children. Given the fiscal picture, it is doubtful that the number of professionals in early childhood/special education will expand significantly. Often, when dealing with infants or severely handicapped children, effective intervention approaches demand a high teacher-to-student ratio. Many profoundly retarded or severely motorically handicapped children are relatively helpless without extensive input by an adult. The child needs to be positioned correctly, to be provided with appropriate stimuli, to have diapers changed, and to be fed meals, which are but a few activities that require adult supervision and attention.

One obvious solution to the discrepancy between the number of handicapped children needing intervention and the number of available trained personnel is to enlist the parent. Most parents have a healthy investment (psychological as well as economic) in their children. They have more to lose and more to gain than anyone else associated with intervention. With the support and assistance of the professional staff, parents can become effective agents of long-term change with their children (Hanson, 1977). The use of parents either in serving as primary change agents or in working in conjunction with a teacher is an economically sound strategy for dealing with young at-risk and handicapped children and constitutes the second point in our rationale for family involvement.

A third reason for involving families rests with legal and legislative mandates. As most readers are no doubt aware, the Education for All Handicapped Children Act of 1975 (P.L. 94–142) specifies that parents are to be integrally involved in the development of their child's Individual Education Plan (IEP). The IEP is a document that states the long-term and short-term educational goals for the child. The plan or behavioral objectives are to be selected by the teacher, necessary support staff, parents, and the child, if possible. If parents are active, involved members of the intervention team, then their participation in the IEP process not only makes sense but will be fruitful. If parents are treated as outsiders, then their participation in the formulation of the IEP is apt to be vacuous and merely a facade to meet the letter, rather than the intent, of the law.

A number of court cases have been initiated by parents in behalf of their handicapped children, such as *PARC v. the Commonwealth of Pennsylvania* (see also Chapter 5). In many of these cases, parents are seeking appropriate care or education for their children. In general, the court rulings are in favor of the handicapped individual and his or her parents as advocates. In the due process procedures established by P.L. 94–142, parents may question the placement of their child and the appropriateness of their child's education. Such hearings, not to mention more formal litigation, are costly. One may ask if the more active involvement of parents in their handicapped child's programs might not reduce the need for such legal activity.

The federal government has established some stringent mandates concerning informed consent. That is, before children may participate in a wide variety of activities (e.g., research or the dissemination of materials), parents must agree. Prior to the agreement, the activity must be explained in detail to the parents. Also, parents must be apprised of any potential risk to their child. The parents are free to decide if they will allow their child to participate in the activity. Active involvement of the parents should mean that they are knowledgeable about the program's daily operation and their child's individual training goals and special events such as field trips, research, or evaluation activities. Informing parents becomes an integral, ongoing responsibility of the program. The inclusion of the parents in the intervention program responds to federal mandates and should reduce possible future conflicts between program personnel and the home.

Another source of information arguing for the inclusion of parents in the intervention process is more empirical. A number of investigators have reported that early-intervention programs that actively focus on the parent or include the parent as an important part of the intervention program produce gains in the children that are maintained longer (Bronfenbrenner, 1975; Karnes & Teska, 1975).

The final point in our rationale for family involvement is parental rights. Underlying the preceding arguments is the assumption that parents have the basic right to be included in the intervention and the planning-decision making process (Turnbull, Turnbull, & Wheat, 1982). As suggested earlier, no one has more to gain or more to lose in designing effective intervention procedures for the young at-risk or handicapped child than the child's parents. Responsibility for the child lies with the parent and, therefore, the parents should take an active role in determining the goals of intervention. Without substantial parental involvement in the program, it will be difficult if not impossible to establish intervention targets that are relevant for the child, satisfactory for the parent, and acceptable to the trained staff in terms of their professional judgment.

Principles Underlying Parental Involvement

In the preceding sections, we have examined the many reasons why the birth of an at-risk infant could have an adverse effect on the family. Others have pointed out the continued drain and trauma on families that have handicapped children (Roos, 1977; Turnbull & Turnbull, 1978). Therefore, the first underlying principle of family involvement is to begin intervention before destructive parent-child and/or child-family relationships develop. To intervene months or years after the development of an interaction that is punishing for family members and the child means that substantial amounts of time and energy must be devoted to eliminating ineffective or destructive interaction patterns. Time and energy could be more productively used to assist the family members in helping the child gain new appropriate social and cognitive behaviors. Although there are data that suggest that the negative effects of traumatic early experiences need not be permanent (Clarke & Clarke, 1976), there are other investigations that suggest that early experience can have profound negative effects (Thompson & Melzack, 1956) or positive effects (Weikart & Lambie, 1970). Most young children do not have time to waste in the task of becoming independent, productive adults. Allowing the development of undesirable behaviors or inappropriate interactional skills often means the serious loss of valuable training time. To avoid such losses, support services should be available to family members and children at the point a problem is detected.

A second principle of family involvement focuses on the need for an ecological approach to intervention to ensure maximum behavioral development in the young at-risk or handicapped child. As Bronfenbrenner (1975) has suggested, all elements of a child's environment need to be working in concert if maximum benefit from intervention are to be obtained. To provide an exceptionally fine preschool program can probably only partially offset the effects of a nonstimulating, inappropriate home environment. Gains made during the day at school may be neutralized by the hours spent with parents and family who do not respond appropriately to the child. There is a need to coordinate home and school expectations, which demands designing an intervention program that includes as many facets of the child's life as possible.

The need for individualization of approach is the third principle that should guide intervention efforts with families. As Beckman-Bell (1981) argues:

> The process of identifying specific characteristics that are both potentially stressful and amenable to intervention must be continued by identifying the individual needs of families and designing specific interventions directed at those individual needs. (p. 51)

Carefully designed individualized programs are necessary if interventionists hope to be effective with participating families. Implementing general approaches that fail to recognize the individuality of each family constellation is doomed to be as ineffective as general nondiscriminating approaches have been with children who have varying needs. Program personnel need to devise strategies for determining individual families' functioning patterns as well as determining parental goals for themselves and their children. These strategies need to take into account individual differences in parental interest, motivation, and abilities as factors that influence participation in programs. Individualization of intervention targets and strategies for family members is as important as individualization for children.

The fourth principle underlying family involvement concerns the delineation of parental and professional roles in the intervention process. Although it would be unwise to attempt a detailed specification of parent-professional roles, a general description may be appropriate and useful. Variations of the parental role are to be expected depending upon the child's problem and the type of intervention provided; however, in educational programs it is appropriate that the parent become one of the primary change agents. That is, the parent should be one of the child's primary teachers (Sullivan, 1976). Taking such a role seems both advisable and necessary because of the amount of time the young child is apt to spend with his or her parents. Depending upon the thrust of a program, the professional can fill the role of teacher, supporter, or both. The intervention program may be designed so that the professional staff (e.g., teacher, therapist, or parent interventionist) are expected to provide direct input to the child on a regular basis (e.g., center-based program). Equally possible is that the professional staff serve primarily as a support system to the parent (e.g., home-based program). In either situation, the parent must assume or share the role as primary change agent. Such role specification leads to establishing the parameters of the parent-professional partnership.

Professionals should avoid becoming "the experts" and telling the parent what to do and how to do it (Roos, 1977; Sullivan, 1976). Rather, it is more facilitative if the partners work toward a cooperative relationship in which each has valuable information and skills to contribute (Turnbull, 1983). A major responsibility of professionals should be, then, to assist parents in learning to become working partners. Becoming a member of the team has an associated responsibility that should be taken seriously by every parent. Unfortunately, the past exchanges between parent and professional have too often led to adversarial positions. Parents have had to fight to gain rights for their children. Some parents have continued to attack professionals even when unjustified. It is often easier to find fault than to evolve constructive solutions. Parents should continue to defend their rights without losing sight of the responsibilities associated with the acquisition of those rights. To push individuals and systems beyond their limits may result in losses for all involved. Concurrently, professionals should strive to avoid overly defensive reactions when challenged by distraught or critical parents.

Parent Involvement Strategies

Initial approaches to involve parents in early-intervention programs tended to focus on teaching parents specific intervention skills to assist them in becoming more effective change agents with their child. Although this still is a paramount goal, interventionists have learned that other family needs must often be met before parents are able to learn to apply educational intervention strategies to assist their at-risk or disabled child. As the major theme of this chapter suggests, family involvement should be comprehensive. For example, a mother's feeling of protectiveness may prevent her from dealing effectively with a problem of compliance in self-feeding. In other cases, a family's need for food stamps and financial assistance may supersede the implementation of a home training program for their child. It is often essential to provide families with social service assistance and counseling as well as educational information and skill training.

The family situation itself dictates where, when, how, and in what areas to begin intervention. As in child programming, one must assess the family situation, select objectives, intervene, and then evaluate progress toward the established objectives. An effort should be made to develop programs that allow parents to be teachers within their regular daily routine rather than at the expense of the parent-child relationship. Intervention targets should be based primarily on a family's needs and secondarily on information and skills that professionals believe a parent of a handicapped child should have.

It also seems necessary that parental involvement programs accommodate the significant need for individualization. As mentioned before, intervention targets should be based on an individual family's needs. Families participating in programs often have widely disparate cultural, socioeconomic, and educational backgrounds. Such divergence mandates program flexibility and individualization both in the content of intervention targets and in the method used to obtain those targets. The individualization and flexibility necessary may far exceed the expectations of many early interventionists. For example, as Winton and Turnbull (1981) point out, there is "... the very legitimate need that some parents have to *not* be formally involved at times" (p. 18). Such recognition may tax many structured parent training programs as well as confront philosophies held by the professionals who have developed such programs.

Service Delivery Approaches

Filler (1983) has categorized approaches to parent training as home-based, center-based, and a combination. Cartwright (1981) adds the category of media-based programs for those few programs that have employed the use of written materials in lieu of human instruction (e.g., Baker & Heifetz, 1976). Each of these approaches has some similarities and differences. The goals of most parent programs, regardless of the service delivery model, can be generally categorized as (1) to assist parents in becoming more effective teachers or managers with their children and (2) to assist the family in meeting other needs that will enhance family-child interaction. Although the goals are similar, the strategies adopted by program personnel to reach these goals are varied. For example, some programs use a group format to teach parents management and handling techniques, while others employ an individual approach, and some programs use both. Some programs have trained parents to act as interventionists with other parents; others have used spouses or family members as teachers. Some programs employ sophisticated video equipment, while others rely on feedback from human observers.

Home-based programs require access to the home on a regular basis. The professional, usually called a home visitor or parent trainer, visits the child at home and assists the primary caregiver in implementing training strategies with the infant or child. Most home visitors have a regular routine designed to maximize their impact with the caregiver and child. The specific approach employed is determined by the visitor and the family. That is, the home visitor attempts to approach the parent or caregiver in a manner that will build rapport and accomplish the intervention goals established for the child and the family. Most home visitors spend the first few minutes catching up on the families' happenings and feeling the parent-caregiver out in terms of problems. The second phase usually focuses on a specific discussion of the child's progress. Using feedback from the caregiver and available objective information, the home visitor encourages further work in an area or suggests an alternative. During the final phase, the home visitor may demonstrate or discuss the suggested changes.

There are many reasons to adopt a home-based approach. For example, parent participation is required, the home visitor has many opportunities to observe the caregiver-child interactions, and generalization of new skills may be enhanced. Conversely, drawbacks have been noted. Parents may feel isolated and lack opportunity to talk with other parents or receive respite from the child. In addition, special services such as physical therapy may be more difficult to access on a regular basis. An obvious solution to these difficulties is to offer a combination approach in which training occurs in the home but in which parents have regular opportunities to participate in programs outside the home.

Programs that serve the birth-to-three population often use a home-based approach, while programs servicing the three-to-five group often employ a center-based model. Most center-based models offer a structured classroom program for participating children usually three to five times per week. These programs tend to have a set format that combines large-group, small-group, and individual training activities. The instructional strategies and curricular focus are largely determined by the program personnel's philosophy and can range from experiential to direct instruction approaches (Harbin, 1979). Most programs have small child-to-staff ratios, and staff may be required to have some form of teacher certification. Many programs begin with a large-group activity in which all the children are expected to participate in some way. After the large-group exercise, children may be assigned to small-group or individual training activities. Many programs attempt to assist children in all essential developmental areas: social, self-help, communication, cognitive, gross motor, fine motor, and preacademic. To do this, the interventionists develop IEPs for each child and then have some procedures for monitoring each child's progress towards his or her individual training targets.

Although parents may be encouraged to participate in a center-based program, some parents never become involved, and some parents may decrease their involvement over time. Often, center-based approaches have relatively structured parent training programs that center on regular group meetings. A variety of topics may be covered during these meetings, and generally, topics that are of interest to parents are selected. In addition, the classroom personnel are available to parents at specific times should they wish to discuss their child's progress or other issues. Some programs encourage parents to participate in the classroom activities with their child (see Bricker, Bailey, & McDonnell, 1984); however, such participation is generally restricted to a few highly motivated parents that have available time.

The major drawback attributed to center-based approaches is the lack of consistent communication between home and school. Often, interventionists do not have adequate time to make regular home visits; thus, the parent must shoulder the responsibility of transferring the child's newly acquired skills into other environments. Parents may be poorly equipped to assist the child in generalization of skills, and consequently, progress in the application of useful skills by the child may occur less efficiently and effectively.

The positive aspects of center-based approaches are that they provide the child with more professional input, which can be effectively coordinated if professionals communicate with one another; they provide the child with the opportunity to interact with a variety of other children and to experience other environments; and they provide parents respite and the opportunity to meet each other.

As suggested for the home-based approaches, a home- and center-based combination seems to answer the major criticisms of the center-based approaches. As family involvement takes on importance, it is likely that more programs will adopt models that combine elements of the home- and center-based approaches. The problem with such omnibus programs will most likely be the cost associated with operating a center-based program while offering extensive home visitation. However, a number of investigators are exploring combination approaches in attempts to capture the essential elements of both approaches but to do so in a cost-accountable manner.

SUMMARY

Professionals' attitudes about parents have changed dramatically over the past ten years, and fortunately, changing attitudes often are accompanied by performance changes. Early interventionists have given "lip service" to the involvement of parents for many years, and yet, the outcomes of our efforts have been circumspect, indeed. However, the confluence of legal decisions, legislative enactments, advocacy by parents, and genuine change by many in the professional community has led to three important new perspectives. First, professionals are beginning to recognize that parents and other family members can assume many roles in the education of their at-risk and handicapped children. Second, the objectives and goals selected for the child as well as the family must be determined in concert with the parents. Third, for intervention efforts to be effective, they should be formulated from the perspective of the family as a system composed of many subsystems. Change produced in one family member may well induce change in others. If we do not acknowledge the interrelated functioning of a family's subsystems, formulated interventions may be less effective or even produce undesirable outcomes.

References

Bailey, E., & Bricker, D. (1984). The efficacy of early intervention for severely handicapped infants and young children. *Topics in Early Childhood Special Education, 4*(3), 30–51.

Baker, B., & Heifetz, L. (1976). The Read Project: Teaching manuals for parents of retarded children. In T. Tjossem (Ed.), *Intervention strategies for high risk infants and young children.* Baltimore, MD: University Park Press.

Beckman-Bell, P. (1981). Child-related stress in families of handicapped children. *Topics in Early Childhood Special Education, 1*(3), 45–53.

Bell, R. (1974). Contributions of human infants to caregiving and social interaction. In M. Lewis & L. Rosenblum (Eds.), *The effect of the infant on its caregiver.* New York: Wiley & Sons.

Bowlby, J. (1973). *Attachment and loss: Separation, anxiety, and anger.* New York: Basic Books.

Brazelton, B., Koslowski, B., & Main, M. (1974). The origins of reciprocity: The early mother-infant interaction. In M. Lewis & L. Rosenblum (Eds.), *The effect of the infant on its caregiver.* New York: Wiley & Sons.

Bricker, D., Bailey, E., & McDonnell, A. (1984). *Early intervention program.* Final report submitted to the Handicapped Children's Early Education Programs, U.S. Department of Education, Washington, DC.

Bricker, D., & Carlson, L. (1981). Issues in early language intervention. In R. Schiefelbusch & D. Bricker (Eds.), *Early language: Acquisition and intervention.* Baltimore, MD: University Park Press.

Bricker, D., & Casuso, V. (1979). Family involvement: A critical component of early intervention. *Exceptional Children,* 1979, *46,* 108–116.

Bricker, D., Jusczyk, A., & Mounts, L. (1984). *Development and evaluation of strategies for monitoring and intervening with handicapped and at-risk infants.* Final report prepared for The National Institute for Handicapped Research, U.S. Department of Education, Washington, DC.

Bronfenbrenner, U. (1975). Is early intervention effective? In B. Friedlander, G. Sterritt, & G. Kirk (Eds.), *Exceptional infant: Assessment & intervention* (Vol. 3). New York: Brunner/Mazel.

Brooks-Gunn, J., & Lewis, M. (1979, June). *Parents of handicapped infants: Their role in identification, assessment, and intervention.* Paper presented at the Ira Gordon Memorial Conference, Chapel Hill, NC.

Bruder, M. (1983). *Parents as interventionists for their children and other parents.* Unpublished doctoral dissertation, University of Oregon.

Cartwright, C. (1981). Effective programs for parents of young handicapped children. *Topics in Early Childhood Special Education, 1*(3), 1–9.

Cicchetti, D., & Sroufe, A. (1976). The relationship between affective and cognitive development in Down's syndrome infants. *Child Development, 47,* 920–929.

Clarke, A., & Clarke, A. (1976). *Early experience: Myth and evidence.* New York: The Free Press.

Decarie, T. (1978). Affect development and cognition in a Piagetian context. In M. Lewis & L. Rosenblum (Eds.), *The development of affect.* New York: Plenum Press.

Denenberg, V., & Thoman, E. (1976). From animal to infant research. In T. Tjossem (Ed.), *Intervention strategies for high risk infants and young children.* Baltimore, MD: University Park Press.

Dennis, W., & Najarian, P. (1963). Development under environmental handicap. In W. Dennis (Ed.), *Readings in child psychology.* Englewood Cliffs, NJ: Prentice-Hall.

Emde, R., Katz, E., & Thorpe, J. (1978). Emotional expression in infancy: II. Early deviations in Down's syndrome. In M. Lewis & L. Rosenblum (Eds.), *The development of affect.* New York: Plenum Press.

Emde, R., Kligman, D., Reich, J., & Wade, T. (1978). Emotional expression in infancy: I. Initial studies of social signaling and an emergent model. In M. Lewis & L. Rosenblum (Eds.), *The development of affect.* New York: Plenum Press.

Filler, J. (1983). Service models for handicapped infants. In G. Garwood & R. Fewell (Eds.), *Educating handicapped infants.* Rockville, MD: Aspen Publications.

Fraiberg, S. (1975). Intervention in infancy: A program for blind infants. In B. Friedlander, G. Sterritt, G. Kirk (Eds.), *Exceptional infant* (Vol. 3). New York: Brunner/Mazel.

Gabel, H., McDowell, J., & Cerreto, M. (1983). Family adaptation to the handicapped infant. In G. Garwood & R. Fewell (Eds.), *Educating handicapped infants.* Rockville, MD: Aspen Publications.

Gorham, K., DesJardins, C., Page, R., Pettis, E., & Scheiber, B. (1975). Effect on parents. In N. Hobbs (Ed.), *Issues in the classification of children* (Vol. 2). San Francisco: Jossey-Bass.

Hanson, M. (1977). *Teaching your Down's syndrome infant: A guide for parents.* Baltimore, MD: University Park Press.

Harbin, G. (1979). Mildly to moderately handicapped preschoolers: How do you select child assessment instruments? In T. Black (Ed.), *Perspectives on measurement: A collection of readings for educators of young handicapped children.* Chapel Hill, NC: TADS.

Harlow, H., & Mears, C. (1978). The nature of complex, unlearned responses. In M. Lewis & L. Rosenblum (Eds.), *The development of affect.* New York: Plenum Press.

References

Hunt, J. (1961). *Intelligence and experience.* New York: Ronald Press Co.

Jones, O. (1977). Mother-child communication with pre-linguistic Down's syndrome and normal infants. In H. Schaffer (Ed.), *Studies in mother-infant interaction.* New York: Academic Press.

Karnes, M., & Teska, J. (1975). Children's response to intervention programs. In J. Gallagher (Ed.), *The application of child development research to exceptional children.* Reston, VA: The Council for Exceptional Children.

Klaus, M., & Kennell, J. (Eds.) (1976). *Maternal-infant bonding.* St. Louis: Mosby.

Lewis, M., & Lee-Painter, S. (1974). An interactional approach to the mother-infant dyad. In M. Lewis & L. Rosenblum (Eds.), *The effect of the infant on its caregiver.* New York: Wiley & Sons.

Lewis, M., & Rosenblum, L. (Eds.) (1974). *The effect of the infant on its caregiver.* New York: Wiley & Sons.

Lewis, M., & Rosenblum, L. (1978). Introduction: Issues in affect development. In M. Lewis & L. Rosenblum (Eds.), *The development of affect.* New York: Plenum Press.

Minuchin, S. (1974). *Families and family therapy.* Cambridge, MA: Harvard University Press.

Morgan, D. (1982). Parent participation in the IEP process: Does it enhance appropriate education? *Exceptional Education Quarterly, 3,* 33–40.

Morton, K. (1978). Identifying the enemy—A parent's complaint. In A. Turnbull & H. Turnbull (Eds.), *Parents speak out.* Columbus, OH: Charles E. Merrill.

Osofsky, J. (1976). Neonatal characteristics and mother-infant interaction in two observational situations. *Child Development, 47,* 1138–1147.

Parke, R., & Tinsley, B. (1982). The early environment of the at-risk infant. In D. Bricker (Ed.), *Intervention with at-risk and handicapped infants.* Baltimore, MD: University Park Press.

Piaget, J. (1970). Piaget's theory. In P. Mussen (Ed.), *Carmichael's manual of child psychology* (Vol. 1). New York: Wiley & Sons.

Rheingold, H., Gewirtz, J., & Ross, H. (1959). Social conditioning of vocalizations in the infant. *Journal of Comparative Physiological Psychology, 52,* 68–73.

Roos, P. (1977). A parent's view of what public education should accomplish. In E. Sontag, J. Smith, & N. Certo (Eds), *Educational programming for the severely and profoundly handicapped.* Reston, VA: The Council for Exceptional Children.

Roos, P. (1978). Parents of mentally retarded children—Misunderstood and mistreated. In A. Turnbull & H. Turnbull (Eds.), *Parents speak out.* Columbus, OH: Charles E. Merrill.

Saarni, C. (1978). Cognitive and communicative features of emotional experience, or do you show what you think you feel? In M. Lewis & L. Rosenblum (Eds.), *The development of affect.* New York: Plenum Press.

Sameroff, A., & Chandler, M. (1975). Reproductive risk and the continuum of caretaking casualty. In F. Horowitz, M. Hetherington, S. Scarr-Salapatek, & G. Siegel (Eds.), *Review of child development research* (Vol. 4). Chicago: University of Chicago Press.

Schulz, J. (1985). Growing up together. In H. Turnbull & A. Turnbull (Eds.), *Parents speak out—Then and now.* Columbus, OH: Charles E. Merrill.

Spitz, R. (1946). Hospitalism: A follow-up report. *Psychoanalytic Study of the Child, 2,* 313–342.

Stoneman, Z., & Brody, G. (1984). Research with families of severely handicapped children: Theoretical and methodological considerations. In J. Blacher (Ed.), *Severely handicapped young children and their families: Research in review.* New York: Academic Press.

Strickland, B. (1982). Parental participation, school accountability, and due process. *Exceptional Education Quarterly, 3,* 41–49.

Sullivan, R. (1976). The role of the parent. In A. Thomas (Ed.), *Hey, don't forget about me!* Reston, VA: The Council for Exceptional Children.

Thompson, W., & Melzack, R. (1956, January). Early environment. *Scientific American* (reprint), 1–6.

Tjossem, T. (1976). *Intervention strategies for high risk infants and young children.* Baltimore, MD: University Park Press.

Turnbull, A. (1983). Parent professional interactions. In M. Snell (Ed.), *Systematic instruction of the moderately and severely handicapped.* Columbus, OH: Charles E. Merrill.

Turnbull, A., Summers, J., & Brotherson, M. (1983). *Working with families with disabled members: A family systems approach.* Lawrence, KS: University of Kansas Research and Training Center.

Turnbull, A., & Turnbull, R. (Eds.) (1978). *Parents speak out.* Columbus, OH: Charles E. Merrill.

Turnbull, H., Turnbull, H., & Wheat, M. (1982). Assumptions about parental participation: A legislative history. *Exceptional Education Quarterly, 3,* 1–8.

Uzgiris, I. (1976). Organization of sensorimotor intelligence. In M. Lewis (Ed.), *Origins of intelligence: Infancy and early childhood.* New York: Plenum Press.

Vadasy, P., Fewell, R., Meyer, D., Schell, G., & Greenberg, M. (1984). Involved parents: Characteristics and resources of fathers and mothers of young handicapped children. *Journal of the Division for Early Childhood, 8,* 13–25.

References

Walker, B., Slentz, K., & Bricker, D. (1985). *Parent involvement in early intervention.* Rehabilitation Research Review, National Rehabilitation Information Center, The Catholic University of America, Washington, DC.

Weikart, D., & Lambie, D. (1970). Early enrichment in infants. In V. Denenberg (Ed.), *Education of the infant and young child.* New York: Academic Press.

White, B., & Held, R. (1967). Experience in early human development: II. Plasticity of sensori-motor development in the human infant. In J. Hellmuth (Ed.), *Exceptional infant: Vol. 1. The normal infant.* Seattle, WA: Straub and Hellmuth.

Winton, P., & Turnbull, A. (1981). Parent involvement as viewed by parents of preschool handicapped children. *Topics in Early Childhood Special Education, 1*(3), 11-19.

Ziskin, L. (1978). The story of Jennie. In A. Turnbull & H. Turnbull (Eds.), *Parents speak out.* Columbus, OH: Charles E. Merrill.

CHAPTER

8

APPROACHES TO INTERVENTION AND COMMON ELEMENTS

Before the 1960s, predeterminism and genetics were considered crucial for predicting a child's future success. With the advent of the sixties came a resurgence of the environmental position. In particular, beliefs supported by evidence accumulated by investigators such as Hunt (1961) reinforced the idea of the importance of early experience. As discussed in Chapter 2, these beliefs were responsible, in part, for the development of compensatory education in this country and the gradual growth of intervention programs for young handicapped children.

Today, early-intervention programs can be found throughout this nation and in many other countries. Since 1968, the federal government has supported a network of projects developed under the aegis of the Handicapped Children's Early Education Program. As mentioned in Chapter 5, many states have mandatory services for preschool handicapped children, and some even require that services be provided for the under age three population. Such legislation has been responsible for the development of a network of publicly supported programs at state and local levels. In addition, programs are supported by private nonprofit organizations such as Easter Seal and United Cerebral Palsy.

The purpose of this chapter is to provide an overview of contemporary approaches to early intervention. The elements or components common to most programs will be discussed followed by brief descriptions of a number of representative programs.

Before discussing the various approaches to and elements of early-intervention programs for at-risk and handicapped infants and young children, it may be useful to note briefly why a single generic description of early-intervention programs will not suffice. First, programs serve children with a variety of ages, etiologies, behavioral repertoires, and family backgrounds. Thus, a singular approach given such population variability seems unwarranted. Second, personnel in programs come from an array of disciplines and training backgrounds, which produces variations in approaches and program emphases. Third, pragmatic and logistic concerns may produce substantial differences in program approaches. These circumstances have generated a range of approaches that share some commonalities but that also are significantly different. The ensuing discussion attempts to highlight both the consistencies and the variations in approaches.

CONTEMPORARY EARLY-INTERVENTION APPROACHES

Early-intervention programs serve children from birth through five years, and some programs may serve older, more severely impaired children. In addition, children ranging from those designated as at-risk to the most profoundly impaired child can be found participating in early-intervention programs. The backgrounds of the enrolled children vary as well. For example, some programs may be especially designed for teenagers with infants (Badger, 1977), while others may serve a range of families with different economic and educational backgrounds (Bricker & Sheehan, 1981).

To provide the reader with a sense of the program variability, a series of tables in Appendix B presents populations and program descriptions for a number of representative programs. For convenience, programs were classified as those serving primarily:

- heterogeneous groups of biologically impaired children (Table B-1)
- children with Down syndrome (Table B-2)
- medically at-risk children (Table B-3)
- environmentally at-risk children (Table B-4)
- parents of at-risk or handicapped children (Table B-5)

Within programs serving the biologically impaired population, a distinction can be made between programs that serve Down syndrome children exclusively and programs that serve children with a variety of etiologies (e.g., genetic, metabolic, motor, and neurological disorders). The at-risk population can be divided into those medically and those environmentally at-risk. However, as discussed in Chapter 6, many medically at-risk children are also environmentally at-risk, thus this distinction is often somewhat misleading.

Information provided in Tables B-1 through B-5 in Appendix B indicates the number of children or parents served by a program, the age of the children when intervention was begun, and whether the intervention target was the child, the parent, or both. Specifics about the program include length, program description, evaluation design, and instruments employed. The information in these tables is not intended to be comprehensive in the sense of providing either detailed program descriptions or coverage of all existing program approaches. Rather, this information is presented to give the reader an overview of the types of programs in operation.

Program Rationales

Rationales for contemporary early-intervention programs can be conveniently divided into direct impact, indirect impact, and societal benefits. Direct impact refers to program goals and objectives designed to alter the behavior of the child and the immediate family. Most programs see child change and family support as their primary objectives, and rationales are developed to reflect these foci. Indirect impact refers to changes in the child and in family members that permit maintenance of the child in the least restrictive educational setting. A second important indirect impact is the family or community's willingness to maintain the child in the home and community.

Finally, many programs suggest that their impact on the child and family produces benefits for society. In a state-of-the-art report compiled by Interact (Garland, Swanson, Stone, & Woodruff, 1981), it is argued that early intervention assists parents in maintaining their child at home, thus reducing the costs of institutionalization, which often the community must help bear. The maintaining of disabled children in the mainstream of regular education produces significant savings to the taxpayer as well (Bricker, Bruder, & Bailey, 1982). The more disabled the child, the more costly the programs; therefore, any early habilitative efforts that lead to the placement of the child in a less restrictive environment meet the legal requirements specified in P.L. 94–142 and in Section 504 of the Vocational Rehabilitation Act as well as potentially save finite educational resources.

Service Delivery Approaches

According to Filler (1983), three service delivery approaches are used by early-intervention programs: home-based, center-based, and a combination of home- and center-based. Cartwright (1981) has suggested a fourth approach, which she has labeled media-based programs.

Programs for infants often deliver services in the home (Hanson & Schwarz, 1978). The target in the home-based approach may be the parent or caregiver, who is helped to acquire effective intervention skills to use with the child. As implied in the name, the center-based model requires that the infant or child be brought to an educational setting on a regular basis. The setting may be a classroom or a more informal arrangement. The focal target in center-based models is usually the child; however, many center-based programs stress parental involvement (Hayden & Dmitriev, 1975) and may even provide structured training for the parent (Bricker, Seibert, & Casuso, 1980).

Some programs have adopted a combined approach in one of two ways. First, there are programs that stress that training occur both in the classroom and in the home (Bricker & Sheehan, 1981). Second, there are programs that serve the child initially in the home. After the child reaches a certain age or develops targeted skills, he or she is transferred to the center-based component of the program (Kysela, Hillyard, McDonald, & Ahlsten-Taylor, 1981).

Media-based approaches employ methods that do not require face-to-face instruction. Approaches such as videotapes or self-instruction manuals are examples (Cartwright, 1981).

The home-based, center-based, and combination approaches that make up the bulk of early-intervention programs are composed of a set of fundamental elements or components. Although the composition of most programs includes these fundamental elements, the programs vary in the ways they are operationalized.

PROGRAM ELEMENTS

A review of the literature and our experiential base suggest that effective early-intervention programs contain a number of elements or components. These elements include a well-articulated philosophical/curricular approach, use of instructional strategies based on behavioral principles of learning, family involvement, an appropriately trained and deployed staff, and a comprehensive assessment/evaluation system. Each of these five elements is discussed in the following sections.

Philosophical/Curricular Focus

Essential to the functioning of an effective early-intervention program is a clearly articulated philosophy. This philosophy provides the necessary structure for selection of program goals, curricular content, and individual education plans for the enrolled children and families. In addition, this structure provides the guidelines for selection of appropriate evaluation tools. Without a clearly articulated orientation, the program is apt to be inconsistent, overlook important intervention targets, and generally lack the cohesiveness of a smoothly operating system.

Perhaps one of the more important functions of a program's philosophical orientation is to provide guidelines for the selection of a curricular approach and the content to be targeted in the program. Two theoretical perspectives have influenced the major curricular efforts for at-risk and handicapped infants and young children. These perspectives are (1) developmental and (2) functional.

The developmental approach is based on the assumption that important developmental changes are both hierarchical and sequential. That is, developmental progress involves the integration and reorganization of earlier acquired behavioral schemes, and development occurs in a generally consistent sequential order. Age-related developmental milestones such as those identified by Arnold Gesell (Gesell & Armatruda, 1962) often make up the curricular content for this approach.

One frequently employed developmental approach is based on the work of Piaget (Piaget, 1970). With this approach, curricula for at-risk and handicapped infants and young children center on sensorimotor and initial preoperational skills. Personnel using this perspective focus training efforts on assisting children in acquiring developmental processes such as object permanence and means-ends through the adoption of progressively more complex skills.

The basic premise of the functional model is that development should be viewed as the acquisition of those skills that will immediately or in the future improve a child's ability to interact with the environment and to become more self-sufficient and independent. The content of such a curriculum consists of those skills that are or will be functional for the child.

According to Le Blanc, Etzel, and Domash (1978), the essential aspect of a functional curricular approach is establishing relevant curricular goals. The goals should then be analyzed in terms of their observable behaviors and the environmental conditions necessary to teach these behaviors. Thus, the instructional staff's primary roles are to assess the child's current behavioral repertoire, to operationalize the target responses, and to arrange the environment to assist the child in acquiring these responses. For a detailed description of a functional curricular approach, see Le Blanc, Etzel, and Domash (1978).

Although programs can and do operate using a variety of orientations, our preference is for the adoption of a flexible combination of the developmental and functional approaches. A developmental orientation assumes several underlying constructs about the nature and cause of growth and change. As mentioned before, this position assumes that important developmental changes are both hierarchical and sequential. Current developmental progress by a child involves the integration and reorganization of earlier acquired behavior, and development occurs in a generally consistent sequential order. In addition, this position assumes that many important developmental changes result from the resolution of disequilibrium between the child's current level of development and the demands of the environment. The problem posed by the environment must be neither too simple nor too difficult for the child's developmental level for change to result (Hunt, 1961). The task of the interventionist is to structure the environment in such a way as to place increasing demands on the child's current level of functioning. With these greater environmental demands that require that the child actively adapt, growth and change occur. The type and nature of the environmental demands should be tempered, in part, by knowledge of those skills that will assist the child in adapting to his or her present and future environments. Finally, the approach assumes that what is critical to development in some cases may be specific behaviors, and in other cases, broad conceptual targets tied to a class of behaviors rather than one specific behavior. These broad conceptual targets index changes in underlying structural organization as well as change in the behavioral topography.

The majority of programs providing services to at-risk or handicapped children tend to offer a comprehensive menu of educational targets. The comprehensive nature of these programs is appropriate because by definition, handicapped infants and young children tend to show deficits in many critical areas of functioning. There is often need to assist the child in gaining cognitive, communication, social, self-help, and motor skills, thus making mandatory a comprehensive curricular approach.

Chapter 13 provides a more detailed discussion of curricular issues and controversies. In addition, a general curricular approach is suggested.

Instructional Strategies

Instructional strategies adopted to present the curricular content rely on some form of environmental engineering. That is, the teaching staff arrange antecedent events to elicit and reinforce the occurrence of targeted behaviors by the children. However, the rigor and rigidity with which the behavioral technology is employed varies considerably across programs.

Harbin (1979) has suggested using a continuum that classifies curricula as experiential, Montessori, Piagetian, information processing, diagnostic-prescriptive, or behavioral. A fair generalization may be that those programs reflecting the more teacher-directed approaches are the programs that tend to begin training focused on specific targets using highly controlled presentation formats. As the child shows progress in the acquisition of the target response, the instructional presentation shifts to encourage generalization of the response to other settings and appropriate conditions. Those programs that are more child-directed tend to employ a more flexible application of behavioral principles. The child is encouraged to use a targeted response in a variety of settings and conditions with the primary goal of making the response functional. Once the response becomes functional, the use of artificial contingencies can be eliminated. Application of an instructional technology requires that staff be skilled behavior managers and programmers if children are to make adequate progress.

The application of operant technology has provided the most effective and useful set of instructional principles currently available. Initially, these principles to manage behavior and to instruct were often applied using extremely structured formats. Children were tutored one-on-one, and frequently, the educational targets were narrowly focused (e.g., teaching children specific imitative responses). Often, teachers or researchers failed to extend the training to assure generalization of responses across settings, people, and events. The early use of operant learning principles tended to minimize flexibility and adaptability because children were primarily reinforced for adherence to adult-imposed tasks.

As experience has been gained in the application of instructional and management strategies, important changes have occurred (Warren & Rogers-Warren, 1985). These changes reflect the need to assist children in developing more generalized and adaptive behavioral repertoires—for example, from learning discrete responses under the control of a specific cue to developing a variety of responses for problem solving or obtaining information from the social environment. Interest continues to grow in how to apply sound and empirically verifiable behavioral teaching principles to aid handicapped children in acquiring more functional and independent repertoires (Hart, 1985), and concern increases for assisting disabled individuals in learning to initiate and make choices based on self-determined needs (Guess & Siegel-Causey, 1985).

Contemporary views held by interventionists tend to favor instructional approaches that specify the goals and objectives for the child but leave the implementation to be decided, in part, according to events occurring in the environment and the interests of the child. For example, a training goal might be to assist the child in using more agent-action-object phrases. Rather than using a specific drill on a set number of predetermined phrases, the interventionist uses opportunities that arise during the day to target this activity. Looking at a book chosen by the child might provide the interventionist many opportunities to teach agent-action-object sequences. Using such an approach requires careful attention to the daily activities to assure that each child is receiving adequate training on selected objectives. Often, it is difficult to monitor the training of each objective, and successful employment of such a system requires systematic collection of data on the child's progress toward specified objectives.

Some programs focus on reinforcement of the desired response by using some form of tangible or verbal feedback. Often, this feedback is in the form of verbal comments such as "good boy," "that's right," "you did that well," and so on. If tasks are selected primarily by the adult, one may assume that motivation for the children may be a more consistent problem and therefore require the use of artificial contingencies. When children have more freedom to determine the activities in which the training exercises will be embedded, reinforcement is often inherent in the activity and thus is preferable (Mahoney & Weller, 1980). For example, searching for a desired toy promotes the concept of object permanence, and finding the toy provides the reinforcement and subsequent motivation for further searches. It is probably not necessary or useful to tell the child "good looking" when the child discovers the toy. Pouring juice into a cup provides practice in wrist rotation and self-help skills, and getting to drink the juice may be reward enough to continue to practice the behavior.

The goal then is to employ strategies that embed training objectives in daily/functional activities that are of interest to children. Designing an environment that elicits and reinforces appropriate responses should lead to the children's efficient acquisition of independent coping behaviors. More detail on instructional strategies is provided in Chapter 14.

Family Involvement

As argued in Chapter 7, there is an increasing awareness that intervention plans for children must be designed and implemented within the family context. From the development of the IEP and Family Program Agreement to their implementation, family members need to be consulted and involved in decision making and the education/therapeutic effort. Increasingly, programs are recognizing the legal as well as the training benefits to be accrued through active family involvement.

Family involvement in a program should begin as soon as parents feel that benefit for their child and themselves will occur. For different families, the time needed to adjust to the birth of a handicapped or even at-risk infant is variable. Some families appear to want immediate involvement in an intervention effort and to benefit from it, while other families need time to work out their feelings prior to beginning active involvement. Nevertheless, a goal should be to involve families before destructive parent-child and/or child-family relationships develop. To intervene after the development of interactions punishing for the parent, child, or more likely, both means substantial amounts of time and energy must be devoted to changing these patterns. Time and energy could be more productively used to assist parents in helping their handicapped child gain new appropriate social and cognitive behaviors.

A second principle of family involvement focuses on the need for an ecological approach to intervention (i.e., include family members in the intervention effort) to assure maximum behavioral development in the infant and young child. As Bronfenbrenner (1975) has suggested, elements of a child's environment need to be working cooperatively if maximum benefit from intervention is to occur. The provision of an exceptional preschool program can probably only partially offset the effects of a nonstimulating, inappropriate home environment. Gains made during the day at school may be neutralized by the hours spent with parents and family who do not respond appropriately to the child. There is a need to coordinate home and school expectations, which demands designing an intervention program that includes as many facets of the child's life as possible.

The family situation itself should dictate where, when, how, and in what areas to begin intervention. As in child programming, one must assess the family situation, select objectives, intervene, and then evaluate progress toward the established objectives. Our philosophy is that intervention targets should be based primarily on a family's needs and secondarily on information and skills we, as professionals, believe family members should have.

It is essential that the family involvement program accommodate the significant need for individualization. Families included in programs often have widely disparate cultural, socioeconomic, and educational backgrounds. Such divergence mandates program flexibility and individualization both in the content of intervention targets and in the method of reaching those targets.

Finally, we have found the need to approach family participation and education from a comprehensive base. Isolated skill training with parents often is not effective. For example, assisting a mother in working on the development of labeling skills without assisting her in developing strategies to manage the child may be counterproductive. In other cases, it is necessary to appreciate that a family's need for recreation should, at times, supplant the implementation of a home training program for their child. Often, the interventionist should see that families are accessing necessary social service assistance and counseling as well as educational information and skill training.

If professionals establish themselves as "the experts" telling the parent how to behave, change in parents may occur slowly or not at all (Roos, 1977; Sullivan, 1976). Rather, the goal should be the development of a cooperative relationship in which both the parent and the professional have valuable information and skills to contribute. Becoming a member of the team has associated responsibility that should be taken seriously by every parent and by every professional.

Training and Deployment of Staff

Program staff members are responsible for the shape and flavor of a program. The way in which the staff operate the program is influenced by at least two important variables: the quality of their training and the fidelity with which they adhere to established program goals and objectives. No doubt, other factors could be specified as well, but these two seem of overriding importance.

Many early-intervention programs are operated by staff members who have had minimal formal training in the area of early childhood/special education. Often, teachers "left over" because student enrollment has decreased in other areas are reassigned to become the teachers in the early-intervention program. Although this may be a political reality, the underlying assumption that a teacher who worked effectively with fourth-grade learning disabled children can work effectively with handicapped infants or preschoolers is unwarranted. Although overlap may exist in some educational strategies employed, obvious differences exist. Working effectively with infants and young children is somewhat dependent upon understanding the process and content of early-childhood development. With infants and children experiencing problems, what is the appropriate instructional content and the sequence of that content? What teaching techniques are effective? What type of data collection and measurement strategies are suited to the population? What of managing family involvement and parent education and counseling? Where is the available literature that suggests the ideas and methods that have been shown to be effective with young disabled children? What are the new and important directions being explored? One does not often hear of an electrical engineer being assigned to design a bridge, nor an industrial psychologist to conduct clinical intervention with psychotic individuals; it is perhaps no more reasonable to expect teachers of elementary-age children to be able to effectively cope with younger populations without additional training. Thus the acquisition of staff with appropriate preservice or inservice training is essential. To keep staff members current, on-going training should be provided.

Personnel working in early-intervention programs can be divided into two categories: direct service and support service. Direct-service personnel are those interventionists, teaching aides, parents, or others who interact with the child in a regular and consistent manner; for example, the classroom teacher in a center-based program or a parent trainer in a home-based approach. Early interventionists and other direct-service personnel are called on to fill a number of roles as developmental specialist, behavior manager, synthesizer, and evaluator. These roles are discussed in detail in Chapter 10.

Support personnel include specialists, such as physical therapists or communication specialists, who have been trained in a specific discipline. In addition, bus drivers, administrative personnel, and others who provide the intervention staff with services that are necessary for the operation of an effective program fall into the category of support personnel.

Prior to the initiation of a program, P.L. 94–192 requires an appropriate assessment be conducted on the child. To be appropriate, the participation of a physical therapist, occupational therapist, communication specialist, psychologist, medical personnel, and possibly other professionals may be required. Once the IEP is developed, if special services such as physical therapy are included, a physical therapist should be available to evaluate the child's progress, formulate the daily intervention plan, and teach and supervise the direct-intervention personnel in the delivery of the necessary therapeutic routines.

As indicated, contributions from a variety of professionals are essential to the delivery of quality services to at-risk and handicapped infants and young children. Because most programs cannot support a cadre of needed professionals full-time, specialists can be more effectively used by adopting a consulting model. In such a model, the specialist functions primarily as an evaluator and consultant who subsequently monitors the implementation of the developed program. The primary hands-on training of the child is provided by the direct-service personnel rather than by specialists.

The success of the consulting model is predicated on the willingness of the direct interventionists and the specialists to interact. In particular, there is an ongoing need to share information about specific children. In effect, the interventionist's attempt to acquire relevant information will be futile if the specialist does not support such a model. The specialist must be willing to explain, share, and assist in implementing appropriate programs. This willingness is predicated on the specialist's belief that the interventionist is capable of using specific input properly and that allowing the interventionist to function in such a role is an efficient, effective approach for habilitation of the child.

The consulting model has been adopted by many programs, in part because of financial exigencies; however, many staff, parents, and specialists have become convinced that, generally speaking, this model is more effective in producing desired change in the child. Established training or therapeutic regimes can be employed throughout the day rather than for only brief periods when the specialist is available to work directly with the child. Employing a consulting model increases the training time as well as enhances generalization across settings, people, and events (Bricker, 1976).

When first introduced, the consulting model met considerable resistance; however, observation of its use over time has convinced many direct-service and support-service personnel of its value. As the demands for services from early-intervention programs increase, a parallel growth in the popularity of the consulting model will occur. More detail on the consulting model is provided in Chapter 10.

Assessment and Evaluation

Evaluation of early-intervention programs has been generally focused on measuring child change (Bricker, Bailey, & Bruder, 1984). A few programs have measured training impact on parents, and even fewer have collected information on other relevant variables, such as changes in attitude, cost factors, or longitudinal effects (Ramey, MacPhee, & Yeates, 1983). Perhaps even more disturbing is that many programs described in the literature do not provide any objective evaluation information on program impact on child or family or on any other variables.

As argued in Chapter 15, the development of an assessment/evaluation plan and its implementation is essential for effective intervention. The assessment of individual change and programmatic impact requires that intervention methods and systems be undergirded with procedures that are appropriate for evaluating their efficacy. Evaluation should determine the program format and success of intervention for individual children and should assess the impact of programs on groups of children. Thus, evaluation serves three distinct but complementary functions: it guides development of individual programming, it provides feedback about success of individual programming, and it yields information for determining the impact of an intervention system on groups of infants, and children, and families.

The need for a comprehensive evaluation of the child requires that the assessment measures be carefully selected. The measures should tap the child's abilities across a wide range of domains, since the IEP will be constructed on the basis of the initial assessment information. Second, assessment instruments should be geared to the developmental age of the child. A test that is above or below the level of the child will provide practically no useful information for evaluation of either the individual child's progress or the program's impact on the child. Third, the instrument or format should be usable by available program personnel. Selection of a sophisticated instrument that cannot be administered appropriately by program personnel is of little value. Finally, at least some of the assessment/evaluation tools should yield information that can be used directly to formulate the child's IEP and specific program plans.

In addition to the more global assessments/evaluations that tend to be conducted episodically, programs should develop procedures for the collection of weekly probe data that indicate a child's progress toward established short-term training objectives. Thus, staff should collect systematic objective information weekly on child change.

Similar assessment/evaluation needs exist for family involvement. Upon the family's entry into a program, assessment of family functioning and needs is necessary if an effective family-program agreement is to be developed and implemented. Monitoring of progress toward selected family involvement targets is required to determine program success.

A useful assessment/evaluation system is essential to monitor the impact of program input. Without comprehensive evaluation plans, early interventionists can only guess at their impact. Chapter 15 provides an extensive description of a linked assessment-intervention-evaluation approach.

SUMMARY

The goal of this chapter has been to assist the reader in gaining some general knowledge about the nature of early intervention programs. A review of programs providing services to at-risk and handicapped infants and young children reveals considerable variability in the way in which intervention for this population is conceived, implemented, and evaluated. However, some consistencies do exist among programs. Most programs, for example, appear to operate from a rationale that argues that change can be made in the target children and families and that such change, in turn, may produce other, indirect positive outcomes. Although staffing patterns, family involvement, curricular content, instructional strategies, and evaluation systems differ along many dimensions, there exists a commonality of effort to enhance the repertoire of the child and family members.

A number of writers (Guralnick & Bricker, in press; Gentry & Olson, 1985) have indicated that successful programs contain certain elements. Those elements approved by the joint Dissemination and Review Panel of the U.S. Department of Education and National Institute of Education include (1) a philosophical basis on which a program is developed, (2) a clearly specified curriculum, (3) an appropriately trained staff, (4) parent and family involvement, and (5) a comprehensive program evaluation plan. In the present chapter, instructional strategies have been discussed as an element separate from curriculum, while the philosophical orientation and curricular approach have been combined. These alignments appear to reflect differences in how to group functions into elements as opposed to including or excluding specific elements. Thus, considerable agreement about necessary elements exists for early-intervention programs.

Progress has been made in serving infants and young children, yet significant needs remain. Future activities should be directed toward more complete descriptions of programs and enhanced evaluation efforts. Through the identification of critical program elements, progress toward the development of more cost-accountable programs can be made as well as the development of more effective programs.

Future Trends

Most likely, future trends in early intervention will be a continuation of the changes and advances in current practice that have evolved from the need to increase the quality of services. There exists a general trend in education toward cost-benefit accountability. This move for programs to become more accountable should lead to improvements in the areas of assessment, curricula, and instructional technologies. Because of the shortage of adequate, relevant program assessment/evaluation measures, there will be an increase in the development and use of assessment instruments specifically for the infant and young child. In the area of curriculum, Brinker (1985) suggests there will be a greater synthesis between behavioral, developmental, and ecological perspectives. Gentry and Olson (1985) further suggest that the new curricula and instructional strategies that are a result of the synthesis between perspectives will be incorporated into more "naturalistic," less structured models of intervention. There is a growing trend in early intervention in general toward greater parent and family involvement; this trend will continue to develop (Walker, Slentz, & Bricker, 1985). Although few states have special certification for teachers or personnel who work with this young population (O'Connell, 1983), recognition of the need for specialized training has led to a concern that special educators trained to work with school-age handicapped children are not adequately prepared to work with handicapped infants and preschoolers. As a result, there will continue to be an increase in the number of early childhood/special education training programs offered by universities and colleges and an increase in the number of states offering preschool teacher certification (Cohen, Semmes, & Guralnick, 1979).

A final future trend that seems certain is increased activity in determining the impact of early-education programs on at-risk and handicapped infants and children and their families. In particular, we believe an emphasis will be on research designed to determine what approaches produce the more significant outcomes, what program elements contribute substantially to child/family growth, and what is the comparative cost-outcome of specific intervention procedures.

References

Aronson, M., & Fallstrom, K. (1977). Immediate and long-term effects of developmental training in children with Down's syndrome. *Developmental Medicine and Child Neurology, 19,* 489–494.

Badger, E. (1977). The infant stimulation/mother training project. In B. Caldwell & D. Stedman (Eds.), *Infant education: A guide for helping handicapped children in the first three years.* New York: Walker & Company.

Badger, E., Burns, D., & DeBoer, M. (1982). An early demonstration of educational intervention beginning at birth. *Journal of the Division for Early Childhood, 5,* 19–30.

Bagnato, S., & Neisworth, J. (1980). The intervention efficiency index: An approach to preschool program accountability. *Exceptional Children, 46,* 264–269.

Baker, B., & Heifetz, L. (1976). The Read project: Teaching manuals for parents of retarded children. In T. Tjossem (Ed.), *Intervention strategies for high risk infants and young children.* Baltimore, MD: University Park Press.

Bidder, R., Bryant, G., & Gray, O. (1975). Benefits to Down's syndrome children through training their mothers. *Archives of Diseases in Childhood, 50*(5), 383–386.

Bradley, R., & Caldwell, B. (1976). The relation of infants' home environments to mental test performance at fifty-four months: A follow-up study. *Child Development, 47,* 1172–1174.

Brassell, W., & Dunst, C. (1978). Fostering the object construct: Large scale intervention with handicapped infants. *American Journal of Mental Deficiency, 82,* 507–510.

Bricker, D. (1976). Educational synthesizer. In M. Thomas (Ed.), *Hey, don't forget about me!* Reston, VA: The Council for Exceptional Children.

Bricker, D., Bailey, E., & Bruder, M. (1984). The efficacy of early intervention and the handicapped infant: A wise or wasted resource? *Advances in Developmental and Behavioral Pediatrics, 5,* 373–423.

Bricker, D., Bruder, M., & Bailey, E. (1982). Developmental integration of preschool children. *Analysis and Intervention in Developmental Disabilities, 2,* 207–222.

Bricker, D., & Dow, M. (1980). Early intervention with the young severely handicapped child. *Journal of the Association for the Severely Handicapped, 5,* 130–142.

Bricker, D., Seibert, J., & Casuso, V. (1980). Early intervention. In J. Hogg & P. Mittler (Eds.), *Advances in mental handicap research.* London: Wiley & Sons.

Bricker, D., & Sheehan, R. (1981). Effectiveness of an early intervention program as indexed by child change. *Journal of the Division for Early Childhood, 4,* 11–27.

Brinker, R. (1985). Curricula without recipes: A challenge to teachers and a promise to severely mentally retarded students. In D. Bricker & J. Filler (Eds.), *Severe mental retardation: From theory to practice.* Reston, VA: The Council for Exceptional Children.

Bromwich, R., & Parmelee, A. (1979). An intervention program for preterm infants. In T. Field, A. Sostek, S. Goldberg, & H. Shuman (Eds.), *Infants born at risk.* Jamaica, NY: Spectrum Publications.

Bronfenbrenner, U. (1975). Is early intervention effective? In B. Friedlander, G. Sterritt, & G. Kirk (Eds.), *Exceptional infant* (Vol. 3). New York: Brunner/Mazel.

Bruder, M.B. (1983). *Parents as interventionists for their children and other parents.* Unpublished doctoral dissertation, University of Oregon.

Cartwright, C. (1981). Effective programs for parents of young handicapped children. *Topics in Early Childhood Special Education, 1,* 1–9.

Cheseldine, S., & McConkey, R. (1979). Parental speech to young Down's syndrome children: An interaction study. *American Journal of Mental Deficiency, 83*(6), 612–620.

Christopherson, E., & Sykes, B. (1979). An intensive home-based family training program for developmentally-delayed children. In L. Hamerlynck (Ed.), *Behavioral systems for the developmentally disabled: (I). School and family environments.* New York: Brunner/Mazel.

Clunies-Ross, G. (1979). Accelerating the development of Down's syndrome infants and young children. *The Journal of Special Education, 13,* 169–177.

Cohen, S., Semmes, M., & Guralnick, M. (1979). Public Law 94–142 and the education of preschool handicapped children. *Exceptional Children, 45,* 279–285.

Connolly, B., Morgan, S., Russell, F., & Richardson, B. (1980). Early intervention with Down syndrome children. *Physical Therapy, 60,* 1405–1408.

Field, T., Dempsey, J., & Shuman, H. (1981). Developmental follow-up of pre- and post-term infants. In S. Friedman and M. Sigman (Eds.), *Preterm birth and psychological development.* New York: Academic Press.

Filler, J. (1983). Service models for handicapped infants. In G. Garwood &

R. Fewell (Eds.), *Educating handicapped infants*. Rockville, MD: Aspen Publications.

Filler, J., & Kasari, C. (1981). Acquisition, maintenance and generalization of parent-taught skills with two severely handicapped infants. *The Journal of the Association for the Severely Handicapped, 6,* 30–38.

Garland, C., Swanson, J., Stone, N., & Woodruff, G. (1981). *Early intervention for children with special needs and their families.* WESTAR Series paper No. 11. Seattle, WA.

Gentry, D., & Olson, J. (1985). Severely mentally retarded young children. In D. Bricker & J. Filler (Eds.), *The severely mentally retarded: From research to practice.* Reston, VA: The Council for Exceptional Children.

Gesell, A., & Armatruda, C.S. (1962). *Developmental diagnosis.* New York: Paul B. Hoeber.

Gray, S., Ramsey, B., & Klaus, R. (1982). *From 3 to 20: The early training project.* Baltimore, MD: University Park Press.

Guess, D., & Siegel-Causey, E. (1985). Behavioral control and education of severely handicapped students: Who's doing what to whom? And why? In D. Bricker & J. Filler (Eds.), *Severe mental retardation: From theory to practice.* Reston, VA: The Council for Exceptional Children.

Guralnick, M., & Bricker, D. (in press). The effectiveness of early intervention for children with cognitive and general developmental delays. In M. Guralnick & F. Bennett (Eds.), *The effectiveness of early intervention.* New York: Academic Press.

Hanson, M., & Schwarz, R. (1978). Results of a longitudinal intervention program for Down's syndrome infants and their families. *Education and Training of the Mentally Retarded, 13,* 403–407.

Harbin, G. (1979). Mildly to moderately handicapped preschoolers: How do you select child assessment instruments? In T. Black (Ed.), *Perspectives on measurement: A collection of readings for educators of young handicapped children.* Chapel Hill, NC: TADS.

Hart, B. (1985). Naturalistic language training techniques. In S. Warren & A. Rogers-Warren (Eds.), *Teaching functional language.* Baltimore, MD: University Park Press.

Harris, S. (1981). Effects of neurodevelopmental therapy on motor performance of infants with Down's syndrome. *Developmental Medicine and Child Neurology, 23,* 477–483.

Hayden, A., & Dmitriev, V. (1975). The multidisciplinary preschool program for Down's syndrome children at the University of Washington model preschool center. In B. Friedlander, G. Sterritt, & G. Kirk (Eds.), *Exceptional infant* (Vol. 3). New York: Brunner/Mazel.

Hayden, A., & Haring, N. (1977). The acceleration and maintenance of developmental gains in Down's syndrome school-age children. In P. Mittler

(Ed.), *Research to practice in mental retardation: I. Care and intervention.* Baltimore, MD: University Park Press.

Heber, R., & Garber, H. (1975). The Milwaukee project: A study of the use of family intervention to prevent cultural-familial mental retardation. In B. Friedlander, G. Sterritt, & G. Kirk (Eds.), *Exceptional infant: Vol. 3.* New York: Brunner/Mazel.

Hunt, J. (1961). *Intelligence and experience.* New York: Ronald Press Co.

Hunt, J. (1980). Implications of plasticity and hierarchical achievements for the assessment of development and risk of mental retardation. In D. Sawin, R. Hawkins, L. Walker, & Penticuff (Eds.), *Exceptional infant: Vol. 4. Psychosocial risks in infant-environment transactions.* New York: Brunner/Mazel.

Jew, W. (1974, May-June). Helping handicapped infants and their families. *Children Today,* 7–10.

Kogan, K. (1980). Interaction systems between preschool handicapped or developmentally delayed children and their parents. In T. Field, S. Goldberg, D. Stern, & A. Sostek (Eds.), *High-risk infants and children.* New York: Academic Press.

Kysela, G., Hillyard, A., McDonald, L., & Ahlsten-Taylor, J. (1981). Early intervention, design and evaluation. In R. Schiefelbusch & D. Bricker (Eds.), *Early language: Acquisition and intervention.* Baltimore, MD: University Park Press.

Le Blanc, J., Etzel, B., & Domash, M. (1978). A functional curriculum for early intervention. In K. Allen, V. Holmes, & R. Schiefelbusch (Eds.), *Early intervention—A team approach.* Baltimore, MD: University Park Press.

Leib, S., Benfield, G., & Guidubaldi, J. (1980). Effects of early intervention and stimulation on the preterm infant. *Pediatrics, 66,* 83–90.

Ludlow, J., & Allen, L. (1979). The effect of early intervention and preschool stimulus on the development of the Down's syndrome child. *Journal of Mental Deficiency Research, 23,* 29–44.

Mahoney, G., & Weller, E. (1980). An ecological approach to language intervention. In D. Bricker (Ed.), *A resource book on language intervention with children.* San Francisco: Jossey-Bass.

Marton, P., Minde, K., & Ogilvie, J. (1981). Mother-infant interactions in the premature nursery: A sequential analysis. In S. Friedman & M. Sigman (Eds.), *Preterm birth and psychological development.* New York: Academic Press.

Moxley-Haegert, L., & Serbin, L. (1983). Developmental education for parents of delayed infants: Effects on parental motivation and children's development. *Child Development, 54,* 1324–1331.

Nielsen, G., Collins, S., Meisel, J., Lowry, M., Engh, H., & Johnson, D. (1975). An intervention program for atypical infants. In B. Friedlander, G.

References

Sterritt, & G. Kirk (Eds.), *Exceptional infant: Vol. 3.* New York: Brunner/Mazel.

O'Connell, J. (1983). Education of handicapped preschoolers: A national survey of services and personnel requirements. *Exceptional Children, 49*(6), 538–543.

Piaget, J. (1970). Piaget's theory. In P. Mussen (Ed.), *Carmichael's manual of child psychology* (Vol. 1). New York: Wiley.

Piper, M., & Pless, I. (1980). Early intervention for infants with Down's syndrome: A controlled trial. *Pediatrics, 65,* 463–468.

Piper, M., & Ramsay, M. (1980). Effects of early home environment on the mental development of Down syndrome infants. *American Journal of Mental Deficiency, 85*(1), 39–44.

Ramey, C., MacPhee, D., & Yeates, K. (1983). Preventing developmental retardation: A general systems model. In L. Bond & J. Joffe (Eds.), *Facilitating infant and early childhood development.* Hanover, NH: University Press of New England.

Revill, S., & Blunden, R. (1979). A home training service for pre-school developmentally handicapped children. *Behavior Research and Therapy, 17,* 207–214.

Roos, P. (1977). A parent's view of what public education should accomplish. In E. Sontag, J. Smith, & N. Certo (Eds.), *Educational programming for the severely and profoundly handicapped.* Reston, VA: The Council for Exceptional Children.

Rosen-Morris, D., & Sitkei, E. (1981). Strategies for teaching severely/profoundly handicapped infants and young children. *Journal of the Division for Early Childhood, 4,* 79–93.

Rynders, J., & Horrobin, M. (1980). Educational provisions for young children with Down's syndrome. In J. Gottlieb (Ed.), *Educating mentally retarded persons in the mainstream.* Baltimore, MD: University Park Press.

Safford, P., Gregg, L., Schneider, G., & Sewell, J. (1976). A stimulation program for young sensory impaired, multihandicapped children. *Education and Training of the Mentally Retarded, 11,* 12–17.

Sandow, S., Clarke, A., Cox, M., & Stewart, F. (1981). Home intervention with parents of severely subnormal pre-school children: A final report. *Child: Care, Health, and Development, 7,* 135–144.

Scarr-Salapatek, S., & Williams, M. (1973). The effects of early stimulation on low-birth-weight infants. *Child Development, 44,* 94–101.

Shapiro, L., Gordon, R., & Neiditch, C. (1977). Documenting change in young multiply handicapped children in a rehabilitation center. *The Journal of Special Education, 11,* 241–257.

Shearer, D., & Shearer, M. (1976). The Portage Project: A model for early childhood intervention. In T. Tjossem (Ed.), *Intervention strategies for high risk infants and young children.* Baltimore, MD: University Park Press.

Springer, A., & Steele, M. (1980). Effects of physicians' early parental counseling on rearing of Down syndrome children. *American Journal of Mental Deficiency, 85*(1), 1–5.

Stock, J., Wnek, L., Newborg, E., Gabel, J., Spurgeon, M., & Ray, H. (1976). *Evaluation of handicapped children's early education program (HCEEP).* Final report to Bureau of Education for the Handicapped, U.S. Office of Education. Columbus, OH: Battelle.

Sullivan, R. (1976). The role of the parent. In A. Thomas (Ed.), *Hey, don't forget about me!* Reston, VA: The Council for Exceptional Children.

Walker, B., Slentz, K., & Bricker, D. (1985). *Parent involvement in early intervention.* Rehabilitation Research Review, National Rehabilitation Information Center. Washington, DC: The Catholic University of America.

Warren, S., & Rogers-Warren, A. (1985). Teaching functional language. In S. Warren & A. Rogers-Warren (Eds.), *Teaching functional language.* Baltimore, MD: University Park Press.

Weiss, R. (1981). Inreal intervention for language handicapped and bilingual children. *Journal of the Division for Early Childhood, 4,* 40–51.

PART TWO

PRACTICAL APPLICATION

CHAPTER 9

PROGRAM OVERVIEW AND OPERATION

As indicated in the overview chapter of this book, the intent of the first part of this volume is to acquaint the reader with the theory and conceptual framework that underlies the practice contained in Part 2 of this volume. Thus, based on the major current perspectives evident in the field of ECH/SE and on the already presented rationale for providing early-intervention services to at-risk and handicapped infants/children and their families, the following section describes the program philosophy that undergirds the practice presented in the following chapters.

PROGRAM PHILOSOPHY

A sound and effective educational program needs to be governed or regulated by a program philosophy or framework. Such a framework should provide cohesiveness and consistency to the program by directing the decision-making process at a number of levels, which include (1) the determination of program goals and objectives; (2) the selection of assessment targets and strategies; (3) the determination of individual child/family goals and objectives and the selection of curricular content and instructional strategies for facilitating acquisition of the established child/family objectives; and (4) the selection of appropriate evaluation instruments to monitor change and modify instructional programs. Figure 9–1 presents a schematic of how a program philosophy links to goal setting and decision-making at the four specified levels.

The program philosophy presented here is based on a developmental model in which the implementation of curricular content is governed by behavioral learning principles. Stated differently, the developmental literature provides the source for the content of instruction, while the behavioral learning literature provides information for selecting

Program Philosophy

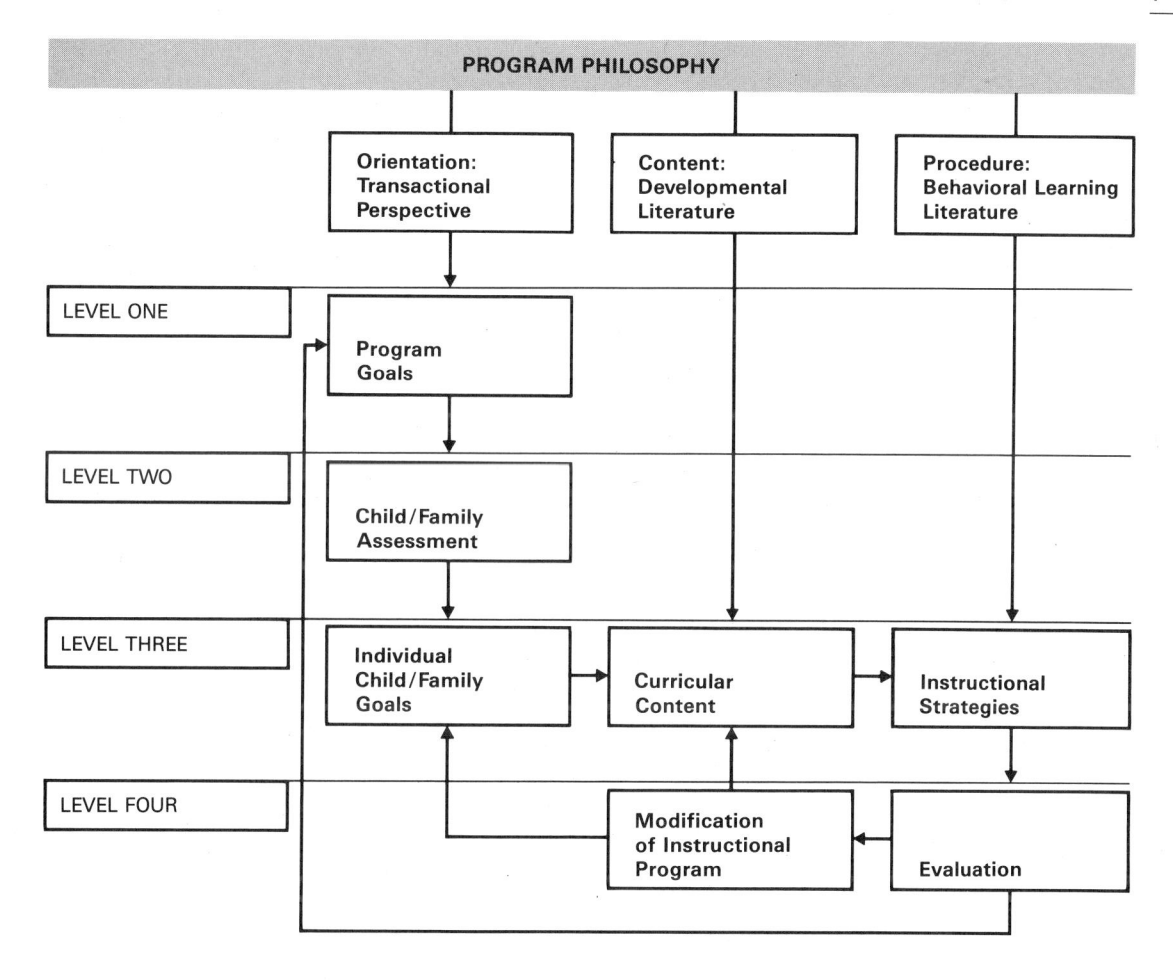

FIGURE 9-1. How a program philosophy directs, selects, and guides decision-making for program goals, assessment, child/family goals, and evaluation.

the instructional strategies used in the program. Finally, the transactional model provides the perspective from which to view the developing infant/child within the environment. As indicated before, a program philosophy should guide and direct the decision-making of the program personnel. The program philosophy and the four implementation levels presented in Figure 9-1 that evolve from the program philosophy are described in the following sections.

Orientation: Transactional Perspective

Piagetian theory has been instrumental in the growth of educational intervention for the infant and young child. In early programs for handicapped children, attempts to interpret and incorporate the basic premises of Piagetian theory to guide intervention efforts have been undertaken (Bricker, Seibert, & Casuso, 1980). Our early intervention efforts using Piagetian theory and a rich new literature on early development (see Schaffer, 1977; Osofsky, 1979) have led to expansions and new interpretations of developmental theory that may render intervention efforts more effective. In particular, more emphasis is being placed on the reciprocal nature of the child-environment interaction and the social context in which these interactions occur. This emphasis focuses attention on the families of at-risk and handicapped children in addition to the children themselves.

The Piagetian position suggests that development is the result of a complex interactional process between an organism (organismic structure) and environmental input. Interactional process between structure and environment refers to the progressive and continuous adaptations that the infant must make to develop into a mature organism. Neither maturational nor environmental variables alone can account for development. Rather, one must look to the interaction between the child and the environment. The healthy neonate's repertoire consists of organized reflexes such as sucking, grasping, vocalizing, and looking. By interacting with a demanding environment, the infant modifies this basic reflex structure and gradually shifts from involuntary to voluntary action. Such modifications result in more flexible and generalizable responses that in time are reorganized into more complex structures.

The organism-environment interactions allow infants to gradually build a sophisticated knowledge of the physical and social world by selecting information and fitting it to their current structured organization or understanding. These two processes, the modification of structures and the acquisition of information, Piaget has called accommodation and assimilation, respectively. This position tends to place the emphasis on the child as explorer of the physical environment and tends to underrate the social aspects of the environment (Uzgiris, 1981). That is, Piaget's focus is on the child and what the youngster is able to glean from first watching events occur, then exploring for the source of actions, and finally learning to efficiently produce a consequence. How the environment may aid or deter that progress is given little attention.

Environmental responsiveness may be of minimal concern for the child who is biologically intact but takes on increased importance for those infants or children who have significant impairments. Uzgiris (1981) has also pointed out that Piagetian theory tends to minimize the importance of the social context in a child's development. Uzgiris (1981) favors, as do we, the increased recognition of the importance of the sociocultural context for the child's interpretation of incoming social and nonsocial stimuli. Meaning is not derived solely from manipulation of physical entities (e.g., objects), but is also garnered from the caregivers' interpretations and actions.

The transactional (Sameroff & Chandler, 1975) or interactional (Lewis & Lee-Painter, 1974) model is focused upon the social responsiveness of the environment and interactive nature of the child-environment exchange. The child's growth and development are the sum of the actions to and reactions from the environment over time (Sameroff, 1981). Consequently, concern must extend to environments and their impacts on children as well as the reverse. The transactional perspective is represented in the simple schematic here, which was designed to indicate the cyclical and reciprocal nature of the child-environment interaction.

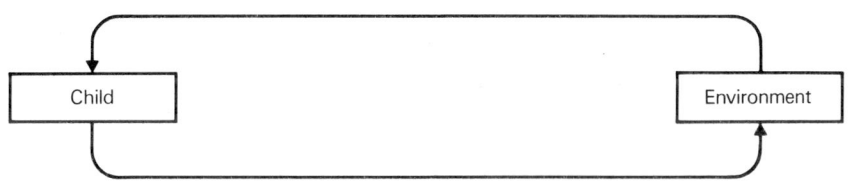

```
┌──────────────────────────────────────┐
│                                      ↓
[ Child ]                      [ Environment ]
↑                                      │
└──────────────────────────────────────┘
```

In addition to an emphasis on the reciprocity between child and environment, the transactional model reinforces the importance of the infant/child's social environment. The infant's earliest experiences with the physical environment are largely mediated by the primary caregivers. This social mediation is of significant importance and should be a focal point for interventionists interested in facilitating the development of handicapped infants and young children.

The importance of the transactional perspective as the primary orientation from which to derive a context of intervention is emphasized by four additional points. First, infants possess a wealth of organized behaviors. Infants have the ability to discriminate and to show preferences among stimuli (Fagan, 1978), to take the roles of initiators and responders in social interaction, and to actively organize, integrate, and adapt to experiences (Bruner, 1975). Infants' characteristics and behaviors elicit and influence the quality of caregiving they receive (Massie, 1980). Second, problems arising from prenatal and perinatal difficulties may be attenuated or intensified by the conditions of the environment. Third, increased understanding of mutual adaptations made by infants and families would make professional intervention more effective. Fourth, critically important social-communicative behaviors evolve during the period of infancy from reciprocal exchanges between caregivers and infants. For example, analyses of "communicative" interaction between mothers and infants show it to be based on a turn-taking structure. Turn-taking seems to be both a force and a result of early socialization. The alternating interchange allows the mother or caregiver to model or provide corrective feedback at a time when the child's attention is focused. These early vocal interactions seem to lay the groundwork for later communicative interactions (Bricker & Carlson, 1981).

Intervention personnel should be trained to facilitate activities that will enhance transactions between the child and the environment. Mutual stimulation should be arranged for the caregiver and infant in a recurring daily context (usually during caretaking and play). A context of shared experiences increases the likelihood that each partner stimulates the responses of the other and should develop patterns that are frequent and sustained. Adults should respond directly to infants' initiations so that infants may learn the direct effects of their social-communicative behavior. Adults should model and prompt responses to sustain and accelerate infants' social communication. The initial goal for intervention should not be to teach infants specific responses but to enhance the infants' reciprocal social-communicative acts that are fundamental to the development of more complex skills.

The basis for social-communicative exchanges is the partners' responsiveness to one another. Strategies for molding these exchanges may differ greatly if the child is handicapped. For impaired infants, programs of visual, tactile, kinesthetic, and auditory stimulation should be undertaken as soon as the caregiver is able to comfortably interact with the infant. Both the child's expressive and receptive capabilities should be enhanced by these transactional experiences. Early and continuous stimulation may do much to remediate developmental delays and maximize an infant's possibilities of acquiring a functional behavioral repertoire.

Not only are transactions between the infant and the primary caregivers vital but the field is becoming increasingly aware of the importance of the transactions among all family members. The quality of intervention for the target child seems directly related to the comfort and support provided to family members and garnered by each other and by external support systems (Parke & Tinsley, 1982). A mother may be unable to effectively initiate and maintain a home intervention routine with her handicapped infant if the father is hostile to the procedure or if other children make excessive demands on her time. Without consideration of the transactions that occur among parents, siblings, and family and community agents, the usefulness and effectiveness of proposed intervention regimes may be seriously compromised.

Too often, the transactional perspective has been restricted to examining and formulating interventions for infants and their mothers. In the present approach, the transactional perspective is applied to the entire family constellation. Consequently, the formulation of intervention plans must include the parents and must attend to needs expressed by parents, siblings, and other significant others (e.g., grandparents, babysitters) as opposed to myopically focusing on the needs of the target child.

Content: Developmental Theory and Literature

We have drawn heavily on developmental literature to provide a framework by which to formulate program content. Developmental theory and, in particular, Piagetian theory provide a useful description of normal development during infancy and early childhood.

A critical premise of Piagetian theory that provides an appropriate theoretical basis for educational intervention is that development is the result of a complex interactional process between organism (organismic structure) and environmental input. This interactional process between structure and environment refers to the adaptations that the infant must make to develop into a mature organism. Neither maturational nor environmental variables alone can account for that development; rather, one must look to the interaction between children and their environment.

A second critical premise of Piaget's theory asserts that the general sequence of development is both universal and invariant; although, contrary to common misconceptions, the theory is not maturational. Rather, it asserts that the hierarchy and sequence of development are determined by the logic of the interactional process, i.e., that certain levels of understanding must logically precede higher, more complex levels of understanding. Piaget's assertion that the general sequence of development is both universal and invariant has resulted in criticism of adopting Piagetian theory for use with populations of handicapped infants (Brinker & Bricker, 1980). Often, the interventionist working with handicapped populations finds that the children do not appear to follow the predicted patterns either in terms of content or sequence. That is, the premise underlying stage theory is not met (Brown & DesForges, 1977). This criticism is indeed accurate and has caused us difficulty, both from a programming perspective and at a conceptual level.

An answer to the criticisms of the Piagetian approach has been developed by Fischer (1980), who has proposed an approach termed *skill theory*. Fischer suggests that cognitive and other domains of behavior are a composite of individual skills. Skill acquisition follows a developmental hierarchy that moves from the simple concrete level to the representational level to the level of abstraction. A skill sequence develops relatively independently of certain levels, at which time coordinations between skills or clusters of skills occur. The skills that develop and the speed with which they are acquired are dependent upon environmental emphasis and input. This position would predict differences in skill acquisition across children and variability in the individual child's mastering of different skills. A home that encouraged running and ball playing might well produce a child with running and ball throwing skills that, for a time, exceed reading and writing skills. This picture represents more closely the reality of observed behavior, particularly with handicapped populations as opposed to children moving consistently and uniformly forward in the mastery of all skills.

We believe the application of general developmental theory is enhanced by the skills theory perspective. Developmental theory provides general maps of emerging behavior. These maps are based on data that suggest typical patterns of development for the young child in the motor, sensorimotor, communication, social, and self-help domains. The resultant developmental hierarchies should be viewed as composites of sequentially

Program Overview and Operation

acquired skills that constitute the most appropriate focus of most educational intervention. Such a framework specifies terminal objectives and also suggests programming sequences. However, these sequences only provide *general* guidelines, and interventionists must expect that many handicapped children will *deviate* from the typical pattern as well as show variation in acquisition rates across skill areas.

Attention to developmental prerequisites can also suggest what the immediate intervention priorities should be. Sensitivity to relationships among domains of behavior can help the interventionist select targets that are appropriate both within and across domains. For example, many early social and self-help skills require a level of understanding of objects in terms of their social functions (e.g., a spoon is for eating, shoes are to wear). To understand these functions, children must have passed the stage at which objects are only sucked, banged, or dropped. Children must have begun to attend to the unique physical properties of objects before they can begin to understand their social significance. Likewise, children must have an understanding of means-ends relationships in order to use a spoon as a tool to bring food to their mouths. Self-feeding, of course, may be a good context in which to stimulate development of the understanding of such means-ends relationships. Nevertheless, ultimate success in training self-feeding with a spoon will depend on the infants' understanding of the spoon as a tool or means to the end of getting food to the mouth.

In the area of gross motor development, observations of blind infants have demonstrated the role of sensorimotor development in the emergence of crawling. Fraiberg and her colleagues (Fraiberg, 1975; Adelson & Fraiberg, 1975) observed that blind infants do not begin to crawl until they learn that sounds signal the presence of objects or of persons to crawl toward. Apparently, crawling must be considered not only as a gross motor development but as a goal-directed behavior within the context of sensorimotor development (e.g., to retrieve an object or seek proximity to the caregiver).

The developmental framework indicates strategies of intervention to foster development toward the chosen program objectives. Beyond suggesting a task analysis, the information available from the developmental-interactive framework suggests strategies that should, if applied correctly, produce more functional and generalizable response forms. For example, the interventionist operating within this framework will not focus exclusively on verbal expression when working on communication but will also target important sensorimotor and conceptual skills that research suggests underlie early language acquisition. The interventionist operating from this framework will also make use of strategies that provide experiences that conflict with children's current level of understanding or development. Such conflicts produce disequilibrium that should assist children in acquiring new levels of cognitive organization.

The developmental framework provides a basis for selecting evaluation instruments that specify reasonable developmental sequences. Such sequences should provide a framework for selecting objectives according to the processes that probably underlie the target areas and suggest, as well, the interrelationships among target areas. These sequences, once translated into valid and reliable procedures, provide the means for assessing progress toward the acquisition of both long-range goals and training objectives. Perhaps equally important for assessment, the developmental-interactive framework assists the interventionist in classifying responses into those that are critical training targets themselves (e.g., head control, sitting) and those that serve only as indices of underlying structures or understanding (e.g., pulling covers off hidden objects or using sticks as tools). Generally, traditional measures such as frequency counts can be used to monitor critical targets, while monitoring responses that serve as indices may necessitate the adoption of assessment strategies that consider intentionality as well as generalizability.

Finally, the developmental framework can direct the modifications and adaptations of curricular materials for individual children as well as guide the construction of new materials. For example, in attempting to train a child with cerebral palsy in the concept of object permanence, the teacher may find it necessary to substitute rigid cardboard screens for the more traditionally used soft clothes. The stiffness of the screens allows the child with only gross motor movements to push or move the screens from the hidden object. Programs focusing on severely to profoundly handicapped young children should be prepared to make many modifications in instructional strategies and training content. Interventionists should have an adequate grasp of the major underlying training targets to successfully reconstitute the surface response or specific training activities to accommodate the varying deficits of the severely handicapped child.

The job of early interventionists can be facilitated by the adoption of a consistent theoretical framework. The alternative with most current appeal is the developmental approach because it aids in determining objectives and priorities, selecting intervention strategies, choosing appropriate assessment and progress monitoring systems, and adapting or constructing curricular materials. More detail on curricular issues and materials is provided in Chapter 13.

Procedures: Behavioral Learning Principles

Developmental theory and skill theory provide the content and general structure for the systematic selection of curricula content and its most likely sequence of presentation. However, these theories provide little assistance in the delivery of that educational content. Currently, the most effective instructional strategies available rely on the behavioral technology that has evolved from the experimental analysis of behavior. Because this technology has been described in detail elsewhere (see, e.g., Alberto & Troutman, 1982; O'Leary & O'Leary, 1977; Axelrod, 1977; Sulzer-Azaroff & Mayer, 1977), the focus here will be on its application within the present approach. In particular, the context and manner in which these principles are implemented are discussed.

Whenever possible, training should be woven into the child's on-going activities. For example, rather than establishing special sessions for teaching specific responses, teaching should be conducted in the context of a relevant activity. In this way, the training is most likely to become salient for the child. In addition, such integration of training targets into the child's daily activities eliminates motivational problems often found when the infant or young child is forced to engage in a tutorial session. When embedding training in child-selected activities, contingent events often are naturally reinforcing. For example, when the child requests a toy, the payoff is receiving the requested object, and it should not be necessary to introduce an artificial reward. Further, this approach assists in keeping training objectives functional and relevant for the child. Each acquired skill should be useful and aid the child in adjusting to and coping with environmental demands. Although monitoring a child's change is more difficult with ecologically relevant instructional strategies, the outcomes warrant the additional effort.

Training that is embedded in the infant/child's daily routines and activities can be called an activity-based approach. Effectively meeting a child's educational objectives with such an approach requires considerable understanding and finesse from interventionists. A formal structure to guide the selection of daily training activities is essential to ensure the right types and quality of activities for enhancing the acquisition and maintenance of targeted behaviors. The interventionist needs to be able to operationalize behavioral learning principles across a variety of settings and within a range of activities. For example, consequences should be designed to co-occur with the activity or be introduced in a manner that enhances rather than detracts from the child's participation. Finally, interventionists should be tuned to capitalize upon the many daily unplanned opportunities that can be used to assist the child in acquiring targeted skills and using those skills in more functional and independent ways. The activity-based approach is described in detail in Chapter 14.

Level One: Program Goals

As can be seen in Figure 9–1, the first level at which the program's philosophy guides and directs a program is establishing the overall goals. Early-intervention programs should have a set of formal goals that assist the staff in planning, organizing, and implementing an intervention program with the target population. The program's goals evolve directly from the program philosophy that has also dictated the orientation, content, and procedures. For example, if the orientation chosen is the transactional perspective, this approach should be reflected in the program goals by the inclusion of the parents or other caregivers as primary recipients of training. A set of program goals generated by the program philosophy previously discussed is as follows:

1. To maximize the infant/child's progress toward independent functioning in the self-help, social, cognitive, gross motor, fine motor, and communication areas. Developmental literature is used to select individual child objectives and the sequence in which those objectives *might* be taught.
2. To maintain the infant/child in the family context by assisting the parents/family in gaining information and developing skills to maximize their adjustment to the infant/child and to one another. To intervene, when possible, the focus being child-family transactions.
3. To employ instructional strategies based on behavioral learning principles and to do so in an ecologically relevant manner.

Level Two: Assessment

Initial assessments are conducted on the child and other family members, consistent with the program's transactional orientation. Further, the program goal of (1) maximizing the child's progress in the motor, cognitive, social, communication, and self-help areas dictates the general parameters of the child assessment, and the goal of (2) assisting the family in gaining information and acquiring skills dictates the general parameters of the assessments to be conducted with the family. Finally, the reliance on behavioral learning principles requires that the instruments or procedures chosen be restricted to collecting data on behaviors that can be objectively observed and reliably measured.

Assessment of the child's behavioral repertoire should be comprehensive to reflect program goals and to provide interventionists with information on how the child functions in cognitive, communication, motor, social, and self-help areas. Consequently, instruments or procedures that cover these areas are needed. Most likely, the intervention staff will have to select a variety of assessment strategies to obtain useful information on the infant or child's ability to function in each of these important areas.

Assessment of the family addresses three interrelated areas. First, an effort is made to determine the parent or family's needs and concerns and what they wish to obtain from participation in the program. Second, strategies to determine the family's understanding of the child's problems and appropriate intervention strategies to address these problems are necessary. Third, determining the parent's or caregivers' instructional skills is essential to determine if training in how to manage and instruct their child is necessary. The intervention staff will most likely be required to select several different assessment tools or strategies to obtain the information necessary to formulate sound intervention plans for parents and families.

Level Three: Individual Child and Family Goals

The selection of goals for individual children and families is guided by the program goals and more specifically by the information collected on the child and family during the initial assessments. Program staff develop individual educational plans for the child and the family. Although the program goals set the general guidelines for the selection of these child and family goals, the specific data collected during the initial assessment procedures provide the specific information that permits the establishment of appropriate goals for the child and the family. At least three types of long-range goals are considered.

The first type of long-range goals includes those that address the child's deficits or behavioral areas that need attention. For example, a child with cerebral palsy may need assistance in developing better control of the motor system and work on cognitive and communication skills. The second type of long-range goals focuses on the parent or family. For example, an overburdened mother may need some respite from caregiving activities. The third type of goals addresses the interactions or transactions between the child and other family members. For example, parents may need assistance in learning how to manage the child's negative and uncooperative behavior.

Once the long-range goals are selected by the intervention staff together with the family, the curricular content is determined. Again, there is a direct relationship between the individual child/family goals and the content of intervention. If the child's ability to communicate is poor and work on this area is selected as an individual goal, then a communicative intervention program needs to be developed that is appropriate both for the child and for reaching the established goal. After a specific goal has been selected, as shown in Figure 9-1, the curricular content is determined in large part by examining information provided by the developmental literature—although, as indicated before, significant deviations are often necessary, especially for the more severely disabled child.

The final component of level three is the determination of the instructional strategies used to present curricular materials in such a way that they meet the individual goals. Selection of the instructional strategies, as indicated in Figure 9-1, is guided by the program philosophy and by the individual goals established for the child and the family. For example, if it has been determined that the vocal exchanges between parents and a hearing impaired infant are too infrequent, the parents could be assisted in increasing the frequency by using a variety of strategies based on behavioral learning principles. When the infant vocalizes, the parent could be instructed to vocalize in return and nuzzle the infant. The parent could hold the infant and vocalize in front of a mirror. The parent could show the infant a desired object and wait for the baby to reach and vocalize before giving the object to the baby.

Level Four: Evaluation and Modification

The fourth level at which a program philosophy has impact is the selection of evaluation strategies. Program goals and individual child/family goals exert a direct influence on the selection of evaluation strategies. These strategies include the measurement of general program impact by examining group progress toward the established program goals and the measurement of progress by infants and families toward specific individual goals. The selection of instruments reflects the program philosophy, the program goals, and the individual child/family goals.

In addition, as shown in Figure 9-1, the evaluation procedures provide the necessary feedback for modifying individual child/family goals, curricular content, and instructional strategies. Evaluation of a child's progress toward developmental objectives assists the staff and parents in determining if the intervention plan is being effective or if some modification in the goal, content, or instruction is required. The same form of feedback is provided at the level of program goals. More detail on program assessment and evaluation is provided in Chapter 15.

Summary

The approach to intervention with at-risk or handicapped infants, young children, and their families advocated in this book directly links the program philosophy to the goals and operational procedures of the program. Such a linked system enhances the organization and cohesiveness of the program. Program staff, parents, and others can discern the common threads that provide the substance and structure of the program.

A clearly articulated philosophy provides the basis for developing program goals and individual child/family goals. The determination of goals, in turn, influences the selection of curricular content and instructional strategies. Further, the selection of curricular content and instructional strategies is dictated by the program philosophy. In effect, a matrix exists that emphasizes the need for coordination and consistency among the various levels of program operation. The specification and linkage between these levels specified in Figure 9-1 are essential to the delivery of effective services to at-risk and handicapped infants, young children, and their families.

PROGRAM COMPONENTS

The program approach being advocated is composed of an educational component for infants and children and a second, interdependent family-involvement component. Unless located in a large metropolitan area, most early-intervention programs must face the reality of providing adequate services to children and their families who vary widely across a number of important variables and characteristics. Thus, programs should be formulated to permit flexibility in service delivery to accommodate, when possible, the variability found in children and families. Even programs that use stringent criteria for admission—for example, only Down syndrome children—are faced with considerable child and family variability. The assumption that the same etiology produces similar behavioral manifestations is rarely supported by empirical findings (see, e.g., LaVeck & Brehm, 1978).

The present approach is applicable for children (1) who range in age from birth to six years; (2) who have a variety of etiologies, conditions, or problems; and (3) who have behavioral repertoires that range from on-target to severely deficient or inappropriate. Families may represent a range on socioeconomic, occupational, and educational parameters. To effectively accommodate such variability, this program has acquired the hallmark of individualization for both children and families. No program can successfully meet the needs of all children and families. Children's needs may be so specialized (e.g., those of autistic children) that they cannot be managed effectively by programs designed to accommodate a range of children. Then, too, some families may have members so disturbed or deviant that highly specialized assistance is required.

Because of such limitations, most early-intervention programs are advised to offer maximum flexibility in their service-delivery format. Thus, in the present program, families can select from a continuum of services from maximum to minimum involvement. Maximum involvement includes participation in the center-based unit, with associated home visits and regular attendance at parent meetings. Minimum involvement is participation in the intake interview, IEP meetings, and periodic home visits. The extent of child and family involvement depends on several variables, including the child's problem and age; the family's available time and transportation and child-care resources; and the family's expressed needs for support and child management. In this program, individual child/family involvement is determined by weighing these and other relevant factors to determine the type and extent of participation. As child/family needs change, different arrangements for children and family members are negotiated.

Educational Program Component

Based on the information acquired during the intake process, which is described in Chapter 11, an assignment of the child and family is made to the home-based unit, center-based unit, or a combination of both.

Home-Based Unit   After enrollment in the program and development of the IEP and Family Program Agreement (FPA), the family is contacted by a home interventionist to establish a time for the home visits. When initiated, most home programs are designed to see the child/family weekly, although variations exist. Home visits are divided into four phases. Upon arrival, the home interventionist spends time talking with the caregiver about the success of the home programming undertaken the previous week. During the second phase, the home visitor observes the caregiver and child working on current training objectives. The home interventionist provides feedback and encouragement to the caregiver and suggests and models alternative teaching strategies. During the third phase, new training objectives are introduced if the child and caregiver have demonstrated adequate competence on previous targets. The final phase is a wrap-up, when the home interventionist reviews the session with the caregiver.

Variations on this format are frequently made to address individual child and family needs. If the home visitor arrives and finds the infant ill, the session may be used to discuss management problems the mother may be having with the older siblings. If on another occasion the caregiver is particularly disturbed by a recent incident, then part or all of the session may be beneficially used to discuss the incident. Periodic variations in the home interventionist's plans are tolerated and even encouraged at times. Only when sessions routinely stray from the decided upon training targets is concern raised and corrective action taken.

The majority of children served in the home-based unit fall into four categories: infants less than fifteen months of age; severely impaired infants or children whose conditions (e.g., on respirators) suggest home treatment rather than traveling to a center; families who live significant distances from the center; and families who do not have the resources to transport the child to and from the center.

Center-Based Unit The center-based unit is composed of classrooms for children whose developmental levels range from fifteen to thirty-six months and classrooms for children whose developmental levels range from thirty-six to sixty months. Each classroom has several nonhandicapped children, and often these children are the siblings of an at-risk or handicapped child enrolled in the program. The classrooms operate four days per week from 9:00 to 12:00 A.M. The fifth day is used for staff meetings, home visits, and recordkeeping. This schedule permits the operation of additional classes in the afternoon, should a program have the need and adequate resources to run a double shift. Upon completion of the intake procedure, children are enrolled in the classroom appropriate to their developmental level. Their parents are encouraged to become involved in the classroom in a variety of ways.

The classrooms operate using an activity-based approach in which children's individualized training objectives are embedded in small- and large-group activities. The curricular focus is comprehensive and includes activities designed to teach information and skill acquisition in the fine motor, gross motor, self-help, social, cognitive, and communication domains.

Specific schedules for classroom activities are described in Chapter 12, but in general the classrooms have similar schedules. Upon arrival, children and parents are greeted and may engage in self-selected activities until all children arrive. Parents often take this opportunity to talk with the interventionist or chat with one another. The first formal activity is a large-group one in which the focus is on assisting children in generalizing learned skills, developing social skills, using acquired information, and having fun. The next portion of the day is divided into a variety of small-group activities. The children participate in several successive group activities designed to provide training opportunities for their individual training objectives. Between 10:00 and 10:30, snacks are prepared and consumed followed by outside activities. When the children return to the classroom, the small-group activity sessions are replicated. The day concludes with another large-group activity.

Home-Center Combinations Some families participate with their child in a combination home-center program. This combination program offers the family the advantage of receiving assistance within the home setting and also permits the child/caregiver to attend a center-based activity group. Although variation exists, in general the caregiver brings the child to the center for one or two sessions per week and receives a home visit every one or two weeks. This option has been selected most often by families with infants between the ages of eight and eighteen months. Often these infants are unable to cope adequately with a four-days-per week classroom program but benefit from more limited exposure to other settings and children provided by the less formal activity group. These so-called baby groups begin with a large-group activity followed by small-group and individual work. Each child's caregiver must attend to help arrange and execute the specified training regimes with the child. During the sessions, caregivers have an opportunity to talk with one another about their children and related concerns.

The combined home-center option is particularly appealing to caregivers who want assistance in the home but feel isolated if not provided the opportunity to participate in activities outside the home. Many parents apparently benefit significantly from the chance to meet other parents and to share and discuss common concerns and problems about their children and families.

Family-Involvement Component

The family-involvement program can be conveniently divided into three areas: education, social service, and advocacy. Participation in each of these areas is dictated by the Family Program Agreement (FPA). The FPA, which is described in detail in Chapter 11, contains a set of parent/family objectives agreed upon by parents and staff. These objectives direct the parent/family involvement with the program.

The educational area covers three types of activities: individual instruction, small-group participation, and large-group participation. Individual instruction is provided to family members by the classroom interventionist, the home interventionist, or the support staff. The type of individual instruction and the appropriate provider is determined by the caregiver's need. The major thrust of the home-intervention component follows this individual-instruction-to-caregiver approach, but often caregivers of children in classroom programs also request individual attention.

In addition to individual instruction, small-group instruction is provided on a regular basis by specific staff members. The topics for small-group instruction are determined by the caregivers' need. A questionnaire is distributed quarterly, and then groups are formed on the basis of the needs specified on the questionnaire by caregivers. The objective of the groups is to assist caregivers in acquiring more effective child-management and instructional skills. Small-group meeting topics include behavior management, Individual Education Programs (IEPs), available community resources, and the development of instructional skills in the communication, social, cognitive, fine motor, gross motor, and self-care areas.

Two types of large-group meetings occur regularly. Parents meet one morning a week to discuss mutual concerns and problems, to make announcements, and to share their feelings about their children. A counselor serves as the facilitator for the Parent Concerns Group. A wide variety of professionals (e.g., educators, physicians, legislators) are invited to address the group on specifically selected topics. Spin-off parent groups also meet on a regular basis with advocacy efforts as their central concern. These advocacy efforts are primarily directed at lobbying for mandated services for young handicapped children.

The social service areas encompass a broad range of activities to assist parents in meeting some environmental or psychological need. The social service needs of our families range from transportation to marital counseling. Parents with the latter problem or other serious problems are referred to appropriate community mental health professionals. The role of the project in these cases is one of referral, liaison, and follow-up, as appropriate.

The type of family involvement in the program is determined by the parents in negotiation with the intervention staff and is specified in the FPA. The involvement varies from that of mothers and fathers who participate in the classroom daily and attend all parent meetings to that of caregivers who attend only the IEP meeting once a quarter.

PROGRAM OPERATION

The organizational and administrative structure of a program can facilitate or undermine the effectiveness of intervention efforts. Advanced planning and the development of procedural guidelines assist the staff in using their time more efficiently and ensure consistency among interventionists. A

Program Overview and Operation

Scheduling	Personnel	Physical Environment	Instructional Program	Intake Assessment Evaluation	Administration	Operational Policies
1. Home Program: Appointments Activities	1. Intervention Staff Responsibilities and Roles	1. Home: Remove obstacles Encourage exploration	1. Curricular Content	1. Schedule Activities: Daily Weekly Yearly	1. Budget	1. Absenteeism
2. Classroom Program: Daily/weekly/ yearly activities Routine activities Transition	2. Support Staff Responsibilities and Roles	2. Classroom: Arrange furniture and equipment Repair and replace	2. Instructional Strategies	2. Data Collection and Display Procedures	2. Feedback to Parent Agency	2. Consent Forms
	3. Staff Training		3. Behavior Management Strategies		3. Personnel: Hiring Firing Vacation Evaluation	3. Emergencies
3. Conferences/ Meetings	4. Staff Coordination		4. Materials: Order Repair	3. Tests: Order Maintain		
	5. Family Members Responsibilities and Roles					

TABLE 9-1 *Activities requiring organization and management*

variety of organizational and management issues confront intervention programs. Table 9-1 provides an overview of some of the more prominent activities that benefit from attention to their organization and management. These activities have been divided into several somewhat arbitrary categories, including scheduling, personnel, environment, instructional program, intake-assessment-evaluation, administration, and operational policies.

Scheduling

The smooth functioning of an intervention program is somewhat dependent upon the efficiency with which personnel and other resources are deployed. Appropriate scheduling of activities can help attain the goal of efficient program operation.

For home programming, scheduling is developed in conjunction with the caregiver and therefore tends to be idiosyncratic to each family's specific needs. The determined schedule of activities is followed by the home interventionist to ensure that objectives are met during each visit.

The classroom program requires more formal and systematic scheduling. General schedules are developed for daily, weekly, and yearly activities. In addition, schedules for routine activities, such as arrival, departure, and snack time, are formulated. Transitions between activities are also scheduled, to eliminate wasted time in moving the children to new activities and locations.

A management problem of some significance is the scheduling of staff meetings and parent conferences. Again, effective scheduling can reduce wasted effort. IEP conferences are scheduled routinely at the beginning of each term for participating families. In addition, specific times are available for parent meetings that are needed in the interim. Regular times are set for weekly staff meetings. A consistently scheduled time for staff meetings and family conferences enhances the chances of people attending and being prepared.

Personnel

A number of organizational and management issues surround the responsibilities and roles of the intervention and support staff. Deploying the intervention and support staff effectively is dependent, in part, upon how their available time is scheduled. Each staff member is responsible for designing daily activities to maximize the probability of meeting the educational goals established for participating children and families. Coordination of staff members' various schedules is required as well.

Scheduling inservice training efforts is designed to coincide with program and personnel needs. A survey of staff and program needs is conducted each year. These needs are compiled and prioritized. Inservice training sessions are then scheduled in response to the established priorities.

Environment

Effective organization of the physical environment and management of physical resources is essential to ensuring maximum impact by intervention personnel. Although interventionists have little control over a child's home environment, caregivers are often responsive to suggestions that do not require major rearrangements of their home. For example, parents are encouraged to remove dangerous or breakable objects to allow the child more freedom to explore.

Within classrooms, staff try to arrange inside and outside activity areas, furniture, and equipment to best meet program goals. Areas are made inviting and accessible to the children. Management strategies for purchasing, repairing, and periodically rearranging furniture, play apparatus, and smaller toys are necessary.

Instructional Program

The curricular content and delivery of that content require organization. Training targets are sequenced from easier to more difficult. Thus, the interventionists begin working on those behaviors that appear to be the most appropriate next target for the child. Instructional strategies can be organized from least to most intrusive. Interventionists begin with the strategy, usually verbal cues, that requires the most independent response from the child. If the child is unable to perform the target response, then a more controlling, structured strategy is invoked.

Prior to intervention, policies for managing child behavior are designed by staff and shared with parents. Again, these strategies are arranged in order of invasiveness. Initially, the least invasive strategy is selected. If this procedure does not yield the desired outcome, then more controlling procedures are employed.

The ordering and purchasing of curricular materials require an organizational scheme. The materials selected are determined through careful consideration of program goals and according to the needs of participating children and families and the staff's background. Once materials are available, management of their use is required. Replacement and repair need consideration as well.

Intake, Assessment, and Evaluation

As indicated in Table 9-1, a number of activities in this category require organization and management. Scheduling of intake, assessment, and evaluation activities is done by the staff. Organization of the initial and final assessment-evaluation procedures is particularly essential if information on children and families is to be gathered within a specified time frame.

Organized procedures for collecting weekly, quarterly, and annual data are necessary to permit timely gathering of the appropriate information. Systems for obtaining raw data and for compiling and displaying data are designed and then employed by the staff. The same general procedures are employed across enrolled children and families.

Management of the test materials is required. The program's standardized and criterion-referenced tests are used by several staff members, thus systems for scheduling the use of these tests are necessary as well as strategies to indicate when test materials need repair or replacement.

Administration

A number of activities are assigned to the administration category. Budgets are organized to indicate what expenditures have been made and what fiscal resources remain for the year. Untimely feedback on the program's fiscal status may lead to premature expenditure of funds or having a significant surplus.

Most programs must provide reports and feedback to their parent agency; for example, information often sought is the number and type of children served by programs during the year. Without adequate recordkeeping, the staff will be unable to provide such information.

All but the smallest of programs will have need for personnel policies to cover staff evaluation, hiring, firing, vacations, and other similar areas that require established policy.

Operational Policies

Most programs will have a number of areas that require the development of specific policies if the situations are to be handled efficiently and fairly, for example, child absenteeism from the program. Families who cancel three consecutive home visits without adequate cause are warned that their participation in the program is in jeopardy. So, too, children who have more than four unexcused absences in a month in the center-based program are warned. Failure to rectify the unexplained absenteeism results in dismissal from the program.

Consent forms are necessary, thus, strategies for their distribution and return are necessary. Before the child enters the program, the parent is required to have completed all forms. This policy has eliminated children attending the program without the proper release, consent, and medical forms being completed.

Development of policies for emergencies is also necessary. To minimize the disruption that an emergency situation produces, procedures for handling accidents are posted in the classrooms for immediate referral by staff. Procedures for handling the child as well as procedures for covering for missing staff are specified.

Many other areas or situations exist that can benefit from systematic organization and management. The areas and examples presented in Table 9-1 are more illustrative than comprehensive. Attention to the development of efficient organization and management systems yields consistent rewards for staff, children, and families.

SUMMARY

The detailed articulation of a program's philosophy provides a cohesive framework from which to evolve the program orientation, program components, and general operational framework. The program's philosophy should guide the determination of program and individual child/family goals. These goals, in turn, govern the selection of assessment-evaluation tools, curricular focus, and instructional strategies.

The program philosophy adopted for the present approach emphasizes the linkage between assessment-intervention-evaluation. The service-delivery format is flexible to meet a range of child and family needs. Finally, attention to the organizational and management aspects of program elements leads to more efficient and effective deployment of program resources.

References

Adelson, E., & Fraiberg, S. (1975). Gross motor development in infants blind from birth. In B. Friedlander, G. Sterritt, & G. Kirk (Eds.), *Exceptional infant* (Vol. 3). New York: Brunner/Mazel.

Alberto, P., & Troutman, A. (1982). *Applied behavior analysis for teachers.* Columbus, OH: Charles E. Merrill.

Axelrod, S. (1977). *Behavior modification for the classroom teacher.* New York: McGraw-Hill.

Bricker, D., & Carlson, L. (1981). Issues in early language intervention. In R. Schiefelbusch & D. Bricker (Eds.), *Early language: Acquisition and intervention.* Baltimore, MD: University Park Press.

Bricker, D., Seibert, J., & Casuso, V. (1980). Early intervention. In J. Hogg & P. Mittler (Eds.), *Advances in mental handicap research.* London: Wiley & Sons.

Brinker, R., & Bricker, D. (1980). Teaching a first language: Building complex structures from simpler components. In J. Hogg & P. Mittler (Eds.), *Advances in mental handicap research.* London: Wiley & Sons.

Brown, G., & DesForges, C. (1977). Piagetian psychology and education: Time for revision. *British Journal of Educational Psychology, 47,* 7–17.

Bruner, J. (1975). The ontogenesis of speech acts. *Journal of Child Language, 2,* 1–19.

Fagan, J. (1978). Infant recognition memory and early cognitive ability: Empirical, theoretical, and remedial considerations. In F. Minifie & L. Lloyd (Eds.), *Communicative and cognitive abilities—Early behavioral assessment.* Baltimore, MD: University Park Press.

Fischer, K. (1980). A theory of cognitive development: The control and construction of hierarchies of skills. *Psychological Review, 87*(6), 477–531.

Fraiberg, S. (1975). Intervention in infancy: A program for blind infants. In B. Friedlander, G. Sterritt, & G. Kirk (Eds.), *Exceptional infant* (Vol. 3). New York: Brunner/Mazel.

LaVeck, B., & Brehm, S. (1978). Individual variability among children with Down's syndrome. *Mental retardation, 16,* 135–137.

Lewis, M., & Lee-Painter, S. (1974). An interactional approach to the mother-infant dyad. In M. Lewis & L. Rosenblum (Eds.), *The effect of the infant on its caregiver.* New York: Wiley & Sons.

Massie, H. (1980). Pathological interactions in infancy. In T. Field (Ed.), *High-risk infants and children.* New York: Academic Press.

O'Leary, K., & O'Leary, S. (1977). *Classroom management.* New York: Pergamon Press.

Osofsky, J. (1979). *Handbook of infant development.* New York: John Wiley.

Parke, R., & Tinsley, B. (1982). The early environment of the at-risk infant. In D. Bricker (Ed.), *Intervention with at-risk and handicapped infants.* Baltimore, MD: University Park Press.

Sameroff, A. (1981). Longitudinal studies of preterm infants: A review of chapters 17–20. In S. Friedman & M. Sigman (Eds.), *Preterm birth and psychological development.* New York: Academic Press.

Sameroff, A., & Chandler, M. (1975). Reproductive risk and the continuum of caretaking casualty. In F. Horowitz, M. Hetherington, S. Scarr-Salapatek, & G. Siegel (Eds.), *Review of child development research* (Vol. 4). Chicago: University of Chicago Press.

Schaffer, H. (Ed.). (1977). *Studies in mother-infant interaction.* New York: Academic Press.

Sulzer-Azaroff, B., & Mayer, R. (1977). *Applying behavior-analysis procedures with children and youth.* New York: Holt, Rinehart & Winston.

Uzgiris, I. (1981). Experience in the social context. In R. Schiefelbusch & D. Bricker (Eds.), *Early language: Acquisition and intervention.* Baltimore, MD: University Park Press.

CHAPTER 10

DEPLOYMENT AND TRAINING OF PROGRAM PERSONNEL AND FAMILY MEMBERS

Although a number of dimensions contribute to the quality of a program, one of the more important elements is the personnel who operate the program. The best designed curricula, instructional strategies, and evaluation plans, are effective only when executed properly. Conversely, the effectiveness of even the most qualified personnel may be severely curtailed if a program lacks cohesiveness, structure, and organization. The goal of this chapter is to discuss the roles and responsibilities of the direct interventionists, support personnel, and family members who participate in this program. The model used to deploy personnel is also described in some detail. Finally, the plan for initial and continuing training of staff members and participating family members is presented.

PERSONNEL ROLES AND RESPONSIBILITIES

Staff roles and responsibilities in an early-intervention program should reflect the program's philosophy and structure. To facilitate the program's effectiveness, roles, responsibilities and policies should be defined and understood by the staff, parents, and volunteers.

The program coordinator's responsibilities include monitoring the quality of intervention and ensuring that procedures for intake, assessment–evaluation, IEP and Family Program Agreement (FPA) development, activity-based instructional programming, and data collection be systematically implemented. Additional responsibilities include providing feedback to the staff, organizing and providing inservice training for staff, serving as facilitator–resource person for parent education groups, coordinating evaluation efforts, serving as a liaison with outside agencies, and conducting general administrative tasks.

Each educational unit (e.g., home and classroom components) is headed by an interventionist certified in special education. This interventionist's responsibilities encompass training and supervising involved personnel, assisting in conducting initial assessment procedures, developing and implementing IEP and FPA goals and objectives for enrolled children and families, monitoring appropriate data collection procedures, implementing quarterly and annual evaluation procedures, and providing systematic feedback to parents of enrolled children.

The classroom units also have an assistant whose role is structured by the interventionist. In general, the assistant is responsible for ensuring that the classroom activities occur smoothly and as scheduled. The assistant also assumes the responsibilities of the interventionists when the need arises (e.g., if the interventionist is absent or meeting with parents).

Roles of the Home and Classroom Interventionists

The home and classroom interventionists are expected to fill five major roles: conceptualizer, synthesizer, instructor, evaluator, and counselor. A conceptualizer approaches teaching from a broad conceptual base. A synthesizer seeks and coordinates input from a variety of professionals. An instructor provides information and models instructional approaches for parents and paraprofessionals. An evaluator designs and implements strategies for determining program impact. A counselor listens and provides appropriate feedback to parents. Each of these roles is described in more detail in the following sections.

Conceptualizer

The multiplicity of conditions and their presenting manifestations and the variability of functioning levels both within and across children labeled as at-risk and handicapped are too great for any single instructional procedure, any single material, or any single prescribed curriculum to be applicable across the entire population. Interventionists who are trained to use "cookbook" approaches that emphasize the acquisition of situation-specific responses by following "frozen" curricular sequences are limited in their effectiveness. Rather, interventionists are well-advised to approach the educational problems of the young at-risk and handicapped population from a broad conceptual base. A conceptual base should provide the basis for the selection of optimal content and the sequence of instruction within any given domain (as would be specified by our most up-to-date empirical information on development and learning). It should also permit flexibility in the presentation of training opportunities required by individual differences in children.

Only if interventionists have an adequate grasp of the content of instruction covered by a particular educational domain and of the probable sequence of acquisition can they effectively "develop" a program of creative activities relevant for a specific child in a particular learning situation. For example, an interventionist might develop a training sequence to teach a child the concept of tool use. Awareness of how tool-use skills fit into an overall developmental progression for a child (e.g., as a component of more complex means-end sensorimotor tasks) should be the first concern. This awareness provides a perspective on how the development of tool use fits into the large scheme of general development. In addition, the interventionist needs to become familiar with the content and the sequence of that content for the development of tool-use skills. Having knowledge of the parameters of tool-use skills should allow for greater flexibility in generating training activities and routines that are child-appropriate throughout the day. Rather than having only specific training times when the child is presented with activities that necessitate using an extension of the arm to gain a desired goal, the interventionist would remain alert to using activities that occur naturally throughout the day and that can be used to engineer the shaping or practice of more sophisticated skills. For example, when the child is attempting to grasp a desired toy that is out of reach, the interventionist should use this opportunity to help the child problem solve by obtaining a stick to push the toy into reach. Using such opportunities maximizes the child's own motivation—the child wants the toy and so may actively use his or her skills to find a tool to solve the problem.

The integration of training activities into the child's daily routine should also facilitate the generalization of the target responses across settings and stimuli. With an adequate understanding of the content of instruction (behavioral targets) and some idea of effective sequences (developmental hierarchies or task analysis), interventionists can generate, both on a preplanned and on a spontaneous basis, specific instructional activities that have a high probability of being effective in the various intervention situations that constitute a comprehensive and individualized educational program.

At least two bodies of information are important in helping an interventionist build a knowledge base for the development of conceptual skills: knowledge of developmental processes and familiarity with the broad content of curricular domains. For too long we have made the mistake in special education teacher training of creating relatively sophisticated pathologists who can talk at length on various handicapping conditions and their manifestation and incidence but who are unable to describe the language of a typical two-year-old. (For example, a review of major textbooks in special education reveals no attention to an explanation of normal development.) Surely, if the interventionist is to fill the role of a normalization agent as specified by many of our current concepts of "least restrictive environment," then that interventionist needs to be conversant with the target—normal development. Background knowledge of normal developmental behaviors and progressions can serve as a prerequisite to the effective use of developmental assessments and curricula. Without knowledge of sequential skill development, it is difficult to assess a child's present functioning level and to determine the next appropriate developmental target.

An objection often raised to adopting a developmental approach concerns the validity of the assumption that handicapped children do progress through typical sequences of development (Sailor & Haring, 1977). Exact alterations in developmental patterns associated with various handicapping conditions have not yet been determined. When a handicapped child is observed to deviate from typical developmental progressions of behaviors, the modifications may be adaptations to topographically more convenient responses rather than basic alterations of underlying organizational structure. For example, a visually impaired infant obviously cannot display those behaviors relating to object constancy that require visual tracking or searching; such typical behaviors are simply not part of the possible repertoire. But to conclude that the child does not follow typical developmental progression may be inaccurate. Alternative behaviors, such as tactile or auditory tracking and searching, may be present and be substituted for gaining environmental input that would facilitate the more basic development of the object concept (Fraiberg, 1975).

This example of a response form modification is relatively straightforward, but perhaps a little simplistic. Many other more complex modifications in response form that are far less obvious may be the mechanism by which the handicapped child progresses through developmental levels despite the handicap and the greatly reduced rate of progress. For example, rather than just learning to babble and then produce labels, a motorically impaired child may learn to scan the environment and then eye point. Until more definitive data become available, it would seem that the developmental approach can provide a theoretical framework from which to program long-range goals and training objectives for at-risk and handicapped children even though major modifications in topographical structure may be necessary.

The selection of appropriate developmental pinpoints for programming across various domains lays the basis for a comprehensive approach to educational programming. With a developmental orientation, an interventionist is less likely to devise a program for a child that unwittingly emphasizes motoric development at the expense of cognitive programming. Moreover, since such targets can be developmentally ordered, more information can be obtained on prerequisite behaviors that are often necessary for the building of the targeted skills. For example, programming for more complex language activities for a child who does not demonstrate mastery of sensorimotor skills thought to be prerequisite for representational thought (Carlson & Bricker, 1982) is less likely to occur if the interventionist is aware of the connection between early cognitive and communicative development.

The second major focus of the interventionist as a conceptualizer is a knowledge of curricular domains. As discussed previously, the effective interventionist must be opportunistic; that is, naturally occurring environmental situations should be seized to assist the child in practicing or building a targeted skill (Brinker & Lewis, 1982). The interventionist working with at-risk or handicapped children may not have adequate curricular guides available to develop the necessary instructional programs for all enrolled children. Rather, the interventionist needs to have a working knowledge of curricular domains and the hierarchical sequences for major behaviors in order to effectively program for children and be able to use opportune environmental happenings, sometimes referred to as incidental teaching (Halle, Alpert, & Anderson, 1984).

Curricular content is important, but so is the process of curriculum development. Although new curricular materials are becoming increasingly available, many of these new materials have distinct problems. First, at-risk and handicapped children exhibit a wide variety of individual differences. A curricular activity may be completely appropriate for a severely intellectually impaired child but totally irrelevant to a severely motorically impaired child who is functioning cognitively within normal limits. Even curricula that have activities appropriate for specified developmental ages may be of little interest to differing chronological ages. Educational materials and suggestions for their use may be different for a four-year-old child than for an eighteen-year-old child (both of whom could easily be developmentally at the same level). In order to deal with this type of curricula selection and implementation problem, interventionists should be prepared to modify existing curricula and to develop their own materials and methods (Baldwin, 1976).

Synthesizer

The interactive effects of children's physical and mental health, nutrition, and social environment on their developmental progress make it imperative that program staff actively seek, evaluate, and use information from a wide range of professionals. To act as a synthesizer, the interventionist must engage in three activities: (1) to seek input from appropriate specialists, (2) to coordinate input from specialists into a cohesive program for the child, and (3) to devise an effective service delivery program.

Prior to or during the IEP-FPA meeting, the relevant and appropriate specialist should be contacted to participate in the development of the child's IEP. If the necessary support personnel are not on staff, then the interventionist must seek their input as appropriate for individual children and families. Since the advent of P.L. 94–142, completing this goal is not difficult. Most specialists are alert to and supportive of the need to evaluate a child's needs in specific areas in order to develop an appropriate intervention plan.

The second activity is the coordination of various specialized inputs into a consistent, comprehensive, and realistic educational program. A nutritionist's advice on food types and textures should be coordinated with the occupational therapist's input on feeding techniques. Positioning recommendations from the physical therapist need to be translated into classroom activities to maximize cognitive stimulation as well as provide muscular strengthening practice. To maximize the impact of intervention efforts, the recommendations made by one specialist should be consistent with suggestions made by another specialist. Often the home or classroom interventionist is responsible for ensuring that specialists' recommendations do not conflict with but rather blend into a cohesive intervention approach.

Another task of the synthesizer involves encouraging specialists to accept and utilize the valuable information that classroom personnel have acquired about the child. Every specialist runs the risk of diagnosing or recommending a program change based on insufficient data. Information derived from a brief assessment or evaluation session conducted in surroundings unfamiliar to a child may result in an inaccurate picture of the child's typical behavior. The program staff and parents, however, may be able to offer more reliable information on a child's typical performance levels. By recognizing the value of interventionists and parent observations, pediatricians could compile valuable medical information, physical therapists could compile more detailed information on range of motion in various settings and positions, and communication specialists could learn about vocalizations or alternative communication systems used daily. Careful documentation is essential to offering such information. Readiness with accurate, well-documented information may encourage specialists to continue to seek staff and parental input.

The final activity of the synthesizer is to determine how "special" interventions will be delivered to children. The more traditional model has been that the specialist provides the special therapy or recommended procedures. Except in unusually well-funded programs, this approach means that the child receives the special treatment once or twice per week. If the remedial effect of these helping professions is to make a significant impact, specialists should be willing to actively share their expertise. Rather than always providing direct therapy to each child, specialists must adopt the role of a resource person using the program staff and parents as the primary implementers of the rehabilitative program (Sternat, Nietupski, Messina, Lyon, & Brown, 1977).

Personnel preparation programs should be oriented toward facilitating acceptance of such a consulting model. This can be done by ensuring that interventionists are provided with general background information upon which various therapists and other specialists can rely for a basic level of understanding and communication. The level of information across various specialty areas is not sufficient to provide the skills to develop a program independently but could provide some common terminology and a basic framework that should facilitate understanding and correct implementation of programs discussed by the specialist. For example, physical therapists may have a much easier time implementing a program to inhibit an asymmetrical tonic neck reflex in a child if they could communicate with a teacher who had some general information on reflex development and positioning. Obviously, some activities will remain in the province of a highly trained clinician, but it is becoming apparent that many forms of therapy may be effectively conducted by program staff, parents, or both. Sufficient numbers of trained personnel in most specialties are not available to meet the demand for their services; consequently, alternative approaches need to be employed.

Instructor

The first and most obvious instructional target for the interventionist is the at-risk and handicapped children enrolled in the program. To be an effective instructor, a working knowledge and the ability to effectively apply behavioral learning principles are deemed essential since this technology functions as a basic tool for producing behavioral change. What is being advocated, however, is a sensitive and discriminating application of this technology both to the individual child and to a specific instructional task. Interventionists must wrestle with the difficult task of structuring educational situations that provide adequate environmental cues to elicit the desired behavior (antecedent event manipulation), that facilitate the gradual approximation toward the desired target behavior (response event management), and that provide appropriate environmental feedback on the effect of such behaviors (consequence tactics). This program recommends modification in the more traditional application of this technology.

First, the use of appropriate forms of consequence is recommended. Gratefully, the heyday of M&M popping is past. What, unfortunately, may not be so archaic in typical practice (but which should be considered archaic) is the routine dispensing of "socially" positive feedback (e.g., "good walking," "good sitting"). These so-called reinforcers are rarely evaluated by the only appropriate test of a reinforcer: the impact on behavior. The careful application of traditional consequence tactics is also in order because of indications from studies that some potentially undesirable effects of using artificial consequence or prolonged programs of contingency management may be occurring (Guess & Siegel-Causey, 1985; Brinker & Bricker, 1980).

Interventionists need to create educational situations in which the production of the targeted behavior is functionally reinforcing for the child. Creating situations in which aspects of the training activity are designed to be inherently interesting to the child and which capitalize on that interest should be a goal. In some cases, this may be as simple as placing interesting toys on low tables for children who need practice in pulling to a standing position. In other cases, development of functional reinforcers may require considerable thought and preparation.

The second instructional target group includes parents or other primary caregivers. Just as interventionists must actively solicit and receive the informational support of other trained professionals, they must, in turn, be willing to extend that type of partnership to parents. Inclusion of parents or other caregivers in educational programming for their children is important because federal policy specifies the right of parents to be informed of and participate in educational decision-making for their child at every level, from classroom placement to short-term program targets. P.L. 94-142 and P.L. 98-199 clearly indicate the necessity for educational planners to consult and be guided by parental desires in program preparation.

The actual number of intervention hours required for a child to make significant developmental gains certainly exceeds the amount of time the child spends with the program staff. Consistent programming should be carried out across settings (not just home, but also grocery stores, buses, restaurants, etc.) so that the effect of intervention efforts will not be greatly diminished or even neutralized. Implementing a toilet training program without follow-through in the home poses a difficult challenge, indeed.

In addition to increasing the amount and consistency of intervention time, inclusion of parents in the child's educational program makes sense for other pragmatic reasons. Parents often have valuable information about a child's ability to respond that may take many weeks for a teacher to discover (Roos, 1977). In many cases, it will be more efficient to ask parents what they think the potential effect of a particular program, consequence, or situation may be for their child. Additionally, parents often are more effective than interventionists in providing consequences for their child. They often have both a greater number of and more powerful consequences available to them than does the interventionist: meal times, leisure activities, mild punishers. Parents and other family members also have had a longer time to become reinforcing agents for their children. Even the most skillful interventionist may never acquire as many reinforcing properties as relatively consistent parents. Program follow-through by caregivers also provides a crucially needed method for training the child to generalize a skill. To assume that the handicapped child will generalize learning across situations and personnel without specific training is often erroneous.

While the advantages of parent participation in the intervention process are real, it would be naive to expect that all parents will immediately adopt this new partnership role. The interventionist should develop skills to encourage and maintain appropriate and realistic parental involvement (Turnbull, 1983). This encouragement may take the form of sitting down with the parents and indicating the advantages of their follow-through at home, or it may take the form of training parents in specific skills that will be necessary for such follow-through. Many parents may not recognize their potential role in some specific area without careful instruction. If such parent-teacher partnerships are going to be built and maintained, then strategies for including the home-based caregivers in the implementation of the intervention plan must be used.

The third group requiring instruction by interventionists are others who may be working in the program, for example, teaching aides, volunteers, or personnel such as bus drivers. Assisting these ancillary personnel in acquiring effective intervention skills may be beneficial to the children and their families as well as assisting in a more smoothly operating program.

Evaluator

The initial evaluation task is assessment of a child's and family's current level of functioning and needs. The purpose of such assessment is the determination of appropriate training targets. Those types of assessment activities that merely define a child as a member of a particular group or rank the child in relation to other children, while appropriate for other purposes, have little utility for the classroom program. Generating appropriate training targets is a more important purpose for the initial assessment effort. Once such targets are derived, there needs to be some system of prioritizing the targets. For many children, there may be more acceleration and deceleration targets than can be covered in daily programming. The systems used to set priorities (e.g., parent concerns, required curricula guides, prerequisites to other programming, life support, etc.) may vary, but it is essential that some effort be exerted to assign weights to the various potential interventions. Once targets have been established and prioritized, intervention strategies can be developed. An integral part of programming is having an objective system to monitor progress. Regardless of the strategy for monitoring change, to be worthwhile the data collected must be translated into useful information for making program decisions.

To adequately fulfill these evaluation requirements, the interventionist is faced with several tasks: developing evaluation objectives that are congruent with program goals, selecting measurement tools or procedures that reflect the evaluation objectives, establishing procedures for implementing the evaluation plan, and monitoring the specific evaluation activities. For successful completion of these tasks, the interventionist needs to have specific skills and information including knowledge of appropriate tests or measurement procedures, skills to accurately administer or train others to administer the selected procedures, and finally, skills to interpret and use the outcomes to adjust the program.

Implementing a complete evaluation plan provides interventionists with direct and continuous indication of the effects (or lack of them) of their programs. A certain aspect of programming requires educated and creative guessing. Even knowing that some intervention strategies and materials are more likely to be effective does not mean they will be with a specific child. In a sense, any preplanned program is a hypothetical statement to be tested. Only by building an adequate evaluation system into the program will the feedback necessary to make decisions on the efficacy of the proposed strategy be ensured.

Another crucially important, yet occasionally unacknowledged, benefit from careful evaluation is reinforcement for program staff. Significant efforts are expended by interventionists and specialists to produce changes in the behavior of enrolled children and family members. To maintain the interventionists' motivation, some mechanism by which they can derive a sense of accomplishment is necessary. A sensitive, thorough evaluation system can demonstrate to the interventionist and parents the beneficial effects of their effort. Without such evidence of their successes, interventionists may not maintain enthusiasm for their jobs.

Counselor

As our understanding of the importance of including parents and other family members in the intervention process has grown, a fifth role as counselor has evolved for the interventionist. This role should not be construed as the interventionist engaging in psychotherapy but rather developing and using skills that enhance listening, question asking, and assisting parents in problem solving.

From time to time, most family members experience problems with one another. There have been suggestions in the literature (see, e.g., Gabel, McDowell, & Cerreto, 1983) that families with handicapped members are under more stress than families without handicapped members. Although this may be an inaccurate generalization, there are families with young children, handicapped or not, who experience a range of difficulties. When these difficulties are associated with the child, the interventionist may become involved in the family's concern.

To fill the counselor role, the interventionist needs to develop three types of skills: listening, evaluating, and problem solving. Accurate listening is essential for evaluating and problem solving. The interventionist needs to be able to listen nondefensively and separate fact from perception as well as to try to determine the nature of the problem. A young mother may say she is unable to manage the child at meal time. Such statements taken at face value may be misleading. The mother may be saying she cannot manage her other children. Asking a few pertinent questions may assist in clarifying the problem. If the siblings are misbehaving, designing a management program exclusively for the handicapped child may exacerbate the mother's difficulty.

A second important skill is to evaluate and determine whether the problem exceeds the bounds of the program or the expertise of the personnel. Parents may be having marital difficulties that affect the child; if so, the parents should be encouraged to seek assistance from other professionals particularly trained to handle relationship problems. Thus, the interventionist must learn to listen to the problem and then determine what type of assistance should be sought.

Finally, in the counselor's role, the interventionist should be prepared to suggest problem-solving strategies. Although listening may be essential and helpful in and of itself, most problems of any consequence cannot be resolved without additional action. Interventionists should be able to assist parents in finding problem-solving strategies that produce desired outcomes. For example, if a family needs medical assistance for the child, the interventionist can assist the parents in locating several potential sources who could make appropriate referrals.

One problem often confronted by well-meaning but naive interventionists is to assume too much responsibility in solving families' problems. Rather than help a family find an appropriate medical resource, the interventionist finds the resource. Assuming too much responsibility is inappropriate for two reasons. First, the parents or other family members do not learn to handle or solve their own problems. Instead, they become dependent upon others to derive solutions for them. Second, problem solving is time-consuming, and interventionists may find that they are spending valuable instructional time engaged in noninstructional activities *or* that their personal time is being spent on problems of participating families.

Viewing the family as the context for the child makes every member integral to the success of the program. Family members may require assistance and feedback in numerous areas. Listening and providing appropriate constructive feedback are skills to be learned and used by interventionists.

Roles of Specialists

Contributions from a variety of professionals are essential to the delivery of quality services to at-risk and handicapped infants and young children. Many programs have access to the services of physical therapists, psychologists, speech pathologists, and counselors.

The program described in this book employs a consulting model that requires the specialist to fill three roles: assessor, program consultant, and evaluator. Some children with extensive or particularly difficult problems may require direct intervention by a specialist. Once the training for these children becomes specifiable, then the specialist relinquishes the role of direct interventionist.

The child who has a specific problem that requires some form of specialized treatment should be recognized prior to the IEP-FPA meeting. Once a problem has been identified, the appropriate specialist is called in to undertake the necessary specialized assessment. In this role, the specialist must select and administer the appropriate assessments to determine the necessary programming information.

The second role for the specialist is that of program consultant. In this role, armed with the assessment results, the specialist can assist in developing an appropriate IEP for the child. Those domains and subsequent long-range goals affected by the child's particular problem or disability should receive detailed input from the specialist. For example, a hearing-impaired child should be assessed by a communication specialist who then assists in developing the long-range goals and training objectives for the communication domain. The second aspect of program consultant is to provide guidance to the interventionist staff and parents in the implementation of the instructional program. For the motorically disabled child, the motor specialist should instruct parents and staff in positioning, handling, and other pertinent aspects of the motor program.

The final role for the specialist is that of evaluator. The specialist is responsible for monitoring the fidelity with which specific procedures are used and the impact of those procedures on the child. For example, if signing is used with a child, do the staff and parents use it consistently, and, if so, is the child learning to communicate?

Family Members' Responsibilities and Roles

Family members, most often parent or other primary caregiver (e.g., grandparents, foster parents, baby-sitters), have three major areas of responsibility. First, they should assure that the child receives the services specified in the IEP. In the case of the home-based program, caregivers are responsible for setting appointments at convenient and appropriate times (e.g., not during the child's nap period). For center-based services, the caregiver is responsible for ensuring that the child is transported to and from the center.

The second area entails following through on agreed upon intervention strategies for the child or themselves. Programs are to be implemented as specified in the IEP and FPA. The final area of responsibility is to carry through on other agreed upon program relevant activities. Thus, if a mother has agreed to assist in the classroom three days per week, she is expected to fulfill that responsibility. If another parent has accepted a liaison role with a community agency, it is his or her obligation to act in this capacity.

THE MODEL FOR DEPLOYING PERSONNEL

Traditionally, physical therapy, occupational therapy, and speech-language therapy have been offered using an "isolated therapy model," in which the designed intervention is provided in a treatment room apart from the living and working environment two or three times per week. The problems associated with the use of the isolated-therapy model have been discussed by Nietupski, Scheutz, and Ockwood (1980). These authors suggest that one problem is the episodic nature of the intervention when deploying an isolated-therapy model. Services provided for one-half hour, two or three times per week, have not generally been found to be effective. Episodic training is particularly ineffective and unappealing when the intervention target is the development of functional communication skills (Bricker & Schiefelbusch, 1984). For most disabled children, more frequent and long-term intervention is required.

A second problem often found in the application of the isolated-therapy model is the lack of systematic communication between the specialist and the primary caregiver or instructor. When the handicapped child is removed from the home or school to receive therapy, the "significant others" in those environments generally are not free to participate in or observe the therapy session. Given this situation, it becomes essential for the specialist to arrange a time to meet and discuss the therapy activities with caregivers, teachers, other specialists, and individuals who interact on a regular basis with the handicapped child. Often because of heavy time demands and scheduling problems, adequate numbers of meetings are not arranged, are cancelled, or are limited to brief exchanges in passing. This limited exchange of information may result in nonsystematic intervention approaches, or worse, conflicting content or strategies. For example, it is highly likely that uninformed caregivers or instructors may unintentionally inhibit the child's use of communication skills by persisting in using old patterns of social interaction (Mahoney & Weller, 1980; Lewis, 1978; Brinker & Lewis, 1982).

Thirdly, generalization becomes a concern when using an isolated-therapy model. As indicated before, it has been well documented that children with problems often do not spontaneously demonstrate a transfer of skills from one learning environment to another or often from one task or activity to another (Bricker & Bricker, 1974). Generalization of behaviors can be facilitated by systematically varying the instructional materials, persons, verbal cues, and training settings. For example, Bricker and Carlson (1980) and Mahoney and Weller (1980) suggest that providing training within the environments in which the handicapped person must ultimately use newly acquired communication skills permits access to a variety of persons who can provide meaningful social interactions. In addition, the acquired communication skills can be used to identify salient objects and events as well as provide a means for discussing predictable routines and interesting topics that occur. Such meaningful experiences can stimulate active learning and more spontaneous use of communication skills.

When an isolated-therapy model is deployed to teach communication or language, a fourth problem arises. Communication is a social behavior; the desire to share information with another human being, or to make your needs or desires known by responding with verbal or gestural signals, must be established if intentional communication is to occur (Bates, 1976). Labeling pictures of animals or household items and practicing rote phrases or isolated words or gestures in simulated activities does not create the same level of interest or learning that "real life" situations appear to provide for children. The routine and familiarity of real conversations and real social activities allow children to anticipate the positive consequences of their behavior and, therefore, may functionally reward the development and use of more adequate communicative behaviors. The use of small groups or the inclusion of significant others in the isolated-therapy activities may increase the realism of the communicative drills, but the effort to organize such gatherings seems senseless when real social groups and situations already exist (Nietupski et al., 1980).

One final and important problem inherent in the isolated-therapy model requires attention. In most states, personnel and resources for providing services to all those handicapped persons needing services are limited. State and federal legislation backed by recent court decisions (Laski, 1985) mandates that all disabled children who demonstrate a need for support services, such as physical therapy or speech-language therapy, must be provided those services as specified in their IEP. The delivery of such support services using a traditional isolated-therapy model in which the specialist delivers the direct service is extremely costly from two perspectives. First, the instructor-to-client ratio (in this case, the specialist) must be high, requiring that programs either allocate significant amounts of money to hire specialists *or* do not provide all clients with adequate services. This latter alternative is, of course, no longer a legal option. Thus, schools and centers must find ways to develop more cost-efficient strategies to provide appropriate support services.

The second cost factor to be considered is the effectiveness of the isolated-therapy model. The problems discussed previously may lead to the conclusion that such an approach is inefficient in terms of assisting the child in generalizing acquired skills from training to other environments. If training were conducted within the individual's daily environments, it would seem logical that generalization might occur more readily and thus training time significantly reduced. A reduction in training time would mean that finite resources were being used in more cost-effective ways.

The problems with the isolated-therapy model argue strongly for the use of other approaches. One alternative approach requires change in the roles and responsibilities of the direct interventionist and the specialist and is described in the next section.

Interventionist as Synthesizer—Specialist as Consultant

Because many programs cannot support the cadre of needed professionals on a full-time basis, a model termed *the educational synthesizer* (Bricker, 1976) was developed. In this model, the specialist functions primarily as an evaluator and consultant who subsequently monitors the implementation of the developed program. In such a model, the primary hands-on training of the child is provided by the classroom or home visitation staff and parents rather than by specialists. In this approach, the interventionist must organize the input from other disciplines into an integrated, developmentally sound approach.

The success of the synthesizer model is based on the willingness of the direct interventionist and the specialist to interact. In particular, there is an ongoing need to share information about specific children. In effect, the interventionist's attempt to acquire relevant information will be futile if the specialist does not support such a model. The specialist must be willing to explain, share, and assist in implementing appropriate programs. That willingness is based on the specialist's belief that the interventionist is capable of using specific input properly and that allowing the interventionist to function in such a role is an efficient, effective approach for habilitation of the child.

The synthesizer approach has been adopted, in part, because of financial exigencies, but also because staff, parents, and specialists have become convinced that, generally speaking, this model is more effective in producing desired change in the child.

An educational synthesizer is any interventionist who:

1. Seeks appropriate information or techniques from specialists in other disciplines,
2. Applies such information or techniques to develop effective intervention strategies, and
3. Implements such strategies to remediate problems (e.g., ensuring special diets for children with allergies, monitoring seizure activity) or to facilitate the acquisition of new skills (e.g., implementing muscle relaxing activities or special language training procedures).

The educational synthesizer needs skills to organize the inputs from disciplines that either are not or cannot be included as daily, integral parts of an intervention program. The educational synthesizer becomes the pivotal force in the overall educational program by seeking and coordinating the necessary resources to produce growth and change in the child. When the interventionist takes on the role as the synthesizer or case manager, the specialist operates in a consulting capacity rather than as a direct intervention agent. For this approach to succeed, both the specialist and the interventionist must be willing to modify their roles. For example, rather than providing a child with a brief period of therapy each week, the physical therapist trains the teacher how to lift, carry, position, and exercise the child. In this way, the child receives the benefit of continuous appropriate muscle movement, which should enhance the acquisition of motoric functioning and control.

The development of an educational synthesizer model demands that two basic goals be pursued. First, the interventionist must be helped to gain those skills necessary for the successful synthesis of material from other disciplines. Second, for successful implementation, the specialist's role must be reshaped. That is, the specialist needs to develop skills that will allow productive interactions with interventionists and parents. The interventionist needs to seek or encourage inputs from other disciplines, while the specialist needs to provide relevant information. Not only are eliciting and giving information important, but the form and content of such material becomes critical. For example, the physical therapist who tells the interventionist to exercise the child's deep tendon reflexes may be of little assistance unless the interventionist knows what deep tendon reflexes are and how to exercise them. Conveying useful information is not solely the responsibility of the specialist; interventionists must consider the development of a functional relationship their responsibility as well.

Several underlying principles or general strategies are necessary for developing a productive interaction between the interventionist and the specialist; these include attitude, accessibility, communication, and transmittal of selected information. Any on-going functional interaction is probably dependent upon the willingness of both parties to interact; in this instance, a willingness to seek and share information. In effect, the attempt to acquire relevant information will be nonproductive if the specialist is not supportive of such a model. The specialist needs to explain, share, and assist in implementation. That willingness is probably predicated on the specialist's belief that the interventionist is capable of using specific inputs properly and that the interventionist's functioning in such a role is an efficient, effective approach to intervention. Without such an attitude, the specialist may be reluctant or even unwilling to share information. Equally vital is the interventionist's attitude toward the inclusion of other disciplines in educational intervention strategies.

A second underlying principle necessary for the successful interaction is accessibility. An interventionist cannot become a synthesizer if there is no external resource providing information. Ideally, regular contact with a nutritionist, physical therapist, occupational therapist, communication specialist and with medical personnel should be possible. The interventionist should be readily accessible to the specialist. In some settings, accessibility to specialists may be limited and the interventionist may have to rely on secondary sources (e.g., books) or infrequent visits from consultants. Although less ideal, the interventionist must be helped to manage with infrequent contact or secondary sources, until a more satisfactory arrangement can be established. Existing in close proximity does not automatically result in a productive interaction, but, generally speaking, it is a condition one would seek in order to facilitate the exchange between interventionists and specialists.

A third condition that may facilitate a productive interaction is the attempt to enhance communication by the reduction of professional jargon. We have all probably experienced lectures in which the speaker from another discipline fails to properly explain terms or jargon and leaves you wondering what was said. Not only should nonessential jargon be reduced, but interventionists should be willing to ask for explanations of unfamiliar language. In describing a child, the speech pathologist can say that the child has difficulty coordinating tongue, lips, and mouth movements rather than saying that the child is dysarthric. Concurrently, educators should feel some obligation to increase their vocabulary as well as their understanding of other fields. A solution to communication problems can be developed by employing behavioral descriptions whenever possible and using objective outcomes to support statements about children, families, and program impact.

A final strategy that may prove important in developing a functional interaction between the interventionist and the specialist could be called selective informational transferral. Specialists and interventionists have spent many years acquiring information pertinent to their particular area of expertise. Specialists should not try to convey all the information they have gained during their professional lives; rather, they should pinpoint relevant and helpful information. Discussing material that is technical and specific to the specialist's discipline has the potential of interfering with efficient decision making and program implementation. For instance, in planning a special diet for an allergic child, the teacher does not need to understand the body's reaction to certain substances. What is essential is that the teacher become aware that the child should not ingest foods containing lactose and aware of which foods contain this substance.

Establishing the basis for a productive interaction between the teacher and the specialist is vital. The synthesizer approach encourages the interventionist and specialist to exchange information necessary to develop a comprehensive instructional program appropriate to the children's and the families' needs.

STAFF TRAINING, COORDINATION, AND MEETINGS

The interventionist working with at-risk children and children with a wide range of handicapping conditions must engage in activities that extend beyond traditional teaching roles. Therefore, training and development should be viewed as a critical element in providing better services to children and their families.

Staff training is divided into two phases: initial training and ongoing training. The purpose of the initial staff inservice training is to familiarize the staff with aspects of the program philosophy, assessment strategies, IEP-FPA process, program curriculum, data collecting procedures, and classroom organizational procedures. To continue to build staff skills, inservice training remains a priority even after the program is underway. Topics for inservice training are determined by conducting a needs assessment of the staff at the beginning and throughout the year.

Staff meetings provide a channel for communicating within the system. Regular meetings provide a mechanism for the coordination of activities, personnel, and events that occur daily, weekly, or quarterly.

The staff regularly participate in a variety of meetings. Program staff meetings are held twice a month. During these meetings, general topics of concern, program-wide modifications, and discussions of ensuing activities are targeted. These meetings are also used as inservice training vehicles throughout the year. Weekly meetings between interventionists and the coordinator are held, also. At these meetings the interventionists and coordinator are able to share problems and discuss strategies for solving difficulties as well as share information about successful ventures with children and families. The third type of regular meeting occurs within individual classrooms. Classroom intervention personnel convene weekly to discuss problems relevant to their particular groups of children. These regularly scheduled classroom meetings include all staff and parents working in the classroom. Meeting agendas include general classroom business and organizational issues and group problem-solving sessions. In addition, the programming for an individual child is reviewed in detail to solicit ideas from the group on needed changes and to emphasize priorities and specialized techniques for that child. Outcomes, timelines, and responsibilities are recorded on the meeting agenda next to the corresponding agenda item.

PARENT EDUCATION

Experience has suggested that early-intervention projects should offer parents and family members at least three types of educational or training opportunities: group, individual, and parent-to-parent. The structure and content of these training formats are described here.

Group Instruction

Two types of group educational or training vehicles are offered. Once a week, parents or other caregivers can join a group focused on discussing problems and concerns, or a group primarily addressing the acquisition of management and instructional skills for use with their child, or both. The parent support and concern group—so labeled by participating parents—meets weekly to address topics introduced by participating caregivers. The group is largely self-motivated and self-directed, although a trained counselor serves as facilitator and monitor to see that discussions do not stray into unproductive areas. The goals for this group are to permit caregivers a regular time to share feelings and concerns, to provide constructive feedback to participants, and to acquire communication and problem-solving skills that may enhance the families' well being.

The second type of group meeting occurs infrequently throughout the year for special purposes. A group meeting is held at the beginning of the school year to provide general information to participating families. Subsequently, large group meetings are held to provide a forum for an invited speaker or for a social activity that may be of interest to most caregivers.

Individual Training

Individual training sessions are held for parents or other family members if requested by parents or by staff. For a parent who is having difficulty applying the management skills presented in the group format, some individual instruction may be helpful. Thus, an appropriate staff member may provide the caregiver with additional training in the home, classroom, or both until the caregiver is able to generalize the management skills across settings and other relevant conditions. Individual educational sessions with caregivers are also in order when a specific problem is detected, such as chronic absenteeism, lack of child progress, or inappropriate child nutrition. At such meetings, areas may be uncovered for which specialized instruction may assist in eliminating the problem.

Parent-To-Parent Education

Personnel associated with early-intervention programs have discovered the many advantages of having parents and other family members involved in the child's intervention program. A new and equally promising strategy is the use of selected parents to assist other parents. Once parents or other caregivers demonstrate adequate knowledge and skills in an area, they are encouraged to offer instruction to other caregivers. At present there are parents who are prepared to offer instruction to other parents who wish to participate in the classroom programs.

Having a parent instruct other caregivers serves three functions. First, it does not drain the resources or use excessively the time of the intervention staff. Second, the caregiver most likely receives more instructional time. Third, the parent-instructor continues to enhance his or her skills. Parents also provide individual instruction to other caregivers apart from the classroom program. This approach has been successful in terms of parents learning targeted skills and saving professional resources (Bruder, 1983). Finally, some parents serve in a program liaison capacity. In this role, they provide information to the public as well as other professionals interested in the program.

SUMMARY

The roles and responsibilities of personnel and family members associated with this program have been described. Although most programs will have idiosyncratic personnel needs, there appear to be three requisites for efficient functioning: delineation of roles, establishment of responsibility and activities for specified roles, and adequate training to ensure that roles are properly executed.

Roles and their associated activities have been specified for the interventionists, support staff, and parents. The roles vary, and yet interdependence is the rule. In particular, an approach is detailed that permits the use of support staff in an efficient and effective manner. The classroom or home interventionist acts as the "generalist" who coordinates and integrates the variety of information obtained from the "specialist" into a cohesive intervention program.

Philosophical changes toward parent involvement have served as an impetus to reevaluate how caregivers are expected to function in programs. Rather than being passive recipients of information, they are being encouraged to design their own educational agendas. Once competent in a specific area, they are being asked to share their knowledge and skills with other parents. As the attitudes of professionals and parents change, a foundation is being laid for more effective involvement of family members in their child's education. If such involvement is maintained, the impact on the public education system may be dramatic.

References

Baldwin, V. (1976). An evaluation of curriculum for the severely/profoundly handicapped. In A. Thomas (Ed.), *Hey, don't forget about me: Education's investment in the severely, profoundly, and multiply handicapped.* Reston, VA: The Council for Exceptional Children.

Bates, E. (1976). *Language and context: The acquisition of pragmatics.* New York: Academic Press.

Bricker, D. (1976). Educational synthesizer. In A. Thomas (Ed.), *Hey, don't forget about me: Education's investment in the severely, profoundly, and multiply handicapped.* Reston, VA: The Council for Exceptional Children.

Bricker, W., & Bricker, D. (1974). An early language training strategy. In R. Schiefelbusch & L. Lloyd (Eds.), *Language perspectives: Acquisition, retardation, and intervention.* Baltimore, MD: University Park Press.

Bricker, D., & Carlson, L. (1980). An intervention approach for communicatively handicapped infants and young children. In D. Bricker (Ed.), *Language resource book.* New York: Jossey-Bass.

Bricker, D., & Schiefelbusch, R. (1984). Infants at risk. In L. McCormick & R. Schiefelbusch (Eds.), *Early language intervention.* Columbus, OH: Charles E. Merrill.

Brinker, R., & Bricker, D. (1980). Teaching a first language: Building complex structures from simpler components. In J. Hogg & P. Mittler (Eds.), *Advances in mental handicap research.* London: John Wiley.

Brinker, R., & Lewis, M. (1982). Contingency intervention. In J. Anderson (Ed.), *Curricula for high-risk and handicapped infants.* Chapel Hill, NC: TADS.

Bruder, M. (1983). *Parents as interventionists for their children and other parents.* Unpublished doctoral dissertation. Eugene, OR: University of Oregon.

Carlson, L., & Bricker, D. (1982). Dyadic and contingent aspects of early communicative intervention. In D. Bricker (Ed.), *Intervention with at-risk and handicapped infants.* Baltimore, MD: University Park Press.

Fraiberg, S. (1975). Intervention in infancy: A program for blind infants. In B. Friedlander, G. Sterritt, & G. Kirk (Eds.), *Exceptional infant: Vol. 3. Assessment and intervention.* New York: Brunner/Mazel.

Gabel, H., McDowell, J., & Cerreto, M. (1983). Family adaptation to the handicapped infant. In G. Garwood & R. Fewell (Eds.), *Educating handicapped infants*. Rockville, MD: Aspen Publications.

Guess, D., & Siegel-Causey, E. (1985). Behavioral control and education of severely handicapped students: Who's doing what to whom? And why? In D. Bricker & J. Filler (Eds.), *Severe mental retardation: From theory to practice*. Reston, VA: The Council for Exceptional Children.

Halle, J., Alpert, C., & Anderson, S. (1984). Natural environment language assessment and intervention with severely impaired preschoolers. *Topics in Early Childhood Special Education, 4*(2), 36–56.

Laski, F. (1985). Judicial address of education for students with severe mental handicaps: From access to schools to state-of-the-art. In D. Bricker & J. Filler (Eds.), *Severe mental retardation: From theory to practice*. Reston, VA: The Council for Exceptional Children.

Lewis, M. (1978). The infant and its caregiver: The role of contingency. *Allied Health and Behavioral Sciences Journal, 1*, 469–492.

Mahoney, G., & Weller, E. (1980). An ecological approach to language intervention. In D. Bricker (Ed.), *A resource book on language intervention with children*. San Francisco: Jossey-Bass.

Nietupski, J., Scheutz, G., & Ockwood, L. (1980). The delivery of communication therapy services to severely handicapped students: A plan for change. *Journal of the Association for the Severely Handicapped, 5*(1), 13–23.

Roos, P. (1977). A parent's view of what public education should accomplish. In E. Sontag, J. Smith, & N. Certo (Eds.), *Educational programming for the severely and profoundly handicapped*. Reston, VA: The Council for Exceptional Children.

Sailor, W., & Haring, N. (1977). Some current directions in education of the severely/multiply handicapped. *AAESPH Review, 2*, 3–23.

Sternat, J., Nietupski, J., Messina, R., Lyon, S., & Brown, L. (1977). Occupational and physical therapy services for severely handicapped students: Toward a naturalized public school service delivery model. In E. Sontag, J. Smith, & N. Certo (Eds.), *Educational programming for the severely and profoundly handicapped*. Reston, VA: The Council for Exceptional Children.

Turnbull, A. (1983). Parent-professional interactions. In M. Snell (Ed.), *Systematic instruction of the moderately and severely handicapped*. Columbus, OH: Charles E. Merrill.

CHAPTER 1

PROGRAM PRELIMINARIES: INTAKE PROCEDURES AND DEVELOPMENT OF INDIVIDUAL EDUCATION PLAN AND FAMILY PROGRAM AGREEMENT

To effectively integrate the educational intervention and parent involvement components of this program, the staff developed a detailed set of procedures for the various phases of the intervention process. These procedures reflect the program philosophy and are used to maximize staff effectiveness in meeting the project objectives. Included are descriptions of procedures for:

1. Intake and program orientation
2. Initial assessment
3. IEP and Family Program Agreement (FPA) procedures

INTAKE PROCEDURES AND PROGRAM ORIENTATION

Locating and identifying eligible children in need of services are important functions of any educational agency. Under P.L. 94-142, local educational agencies are held legally responsible for identifying children within their jurisdiction who are eligible for special education services. Although the legal mandate does not apply to discretionary service providers, such as many early-intervention programs, an ethical responsibility still exists. The development of an effective and comprehensive system for notifying appropriate medical and community agencies of available early-intervention/family involvement services and for rapidly following up on incoming referrals is an important step in the design of a service-delivery system. The overall process can be divided into several facets:

1. Coordination with referral sources
2. Screening of referrals for eligibility
3. Enrollment procedures
4. Family orientation to intervention program

General objectives exist for each of these facets. Optimal design or procedures to meet these objectives vary considerably, depending on the constraints and resources of local and regional service-delivery systems.

Coordination with Referral Sources

Parents of handicapped children are most likely to learn of the existence of early-intervention services through another community agency or their pediatrician. To ensure that parents of eligible children have the best chance of accessing services, it is important to keep those community agencies most likely to serve as intermediate referral sources updated on relevant information about the early-intervention services. This information should include contact person, phone number and address, what type of services are provided, who is eligible for services, and whether openings for children exist. Community agencies to contact include three basic categories: medical agencies (e.g., newborn follow-up clinics); educational agencies (e.g., local school districts, private schools providing special education, university or college departments in related fields); and social service or advocacy agencies (e.g., Association for Retarded Citizens, Children's Services Division, information switchboards, and community referral agencies).

A specific staff member should be identified to receive all incoming referrals, regardless of the source of the referral or what program representative is originally contacted. This minimizes the confusion of duplicate referral and/or waiting lists and facilitates prompt and consistent responses to all inquiries. Any inquiries made to other staff are immediately referred to the intake coordinator.

Screening for Eligibility

As soon as a referral is received, an initial screening is conducted by the intake coordinator to determine if the child is eligible for services. The initial screening is conducted on the phone with the child's parents and obtains the following information: the child's age, the child's problem, and whether the family is interested in having the child enrolled in an early-intervention program. Any child who is clearly ineligible (e.g., is too old) for the program is referred to a more appropriate service provider. If the child appears to be eligible but no openings currently exist, the family is notified of any alternative services that may be available to the child while the family is on a waiting list.

Eligibility for program services is primarily determined by age. Any child with identified developmental delays or handicaps is eligible if the child is between birth and sixty months of age at the time services are initiated. Parental willingness to arrange transportation for attending the center-based component or to carry out home programming for the home-based component is an additional factor. A completed referral form provides the

Intake Procedures and Program Orientation

Child's name:	Birthdate:
Diagnosis:	Referred by:
Agency:	Date referred:
Parent's name:	Phone number:

Address:

School district:

What agency conducted the diagnostic evaluation:

Is there a case manager?

Has this child received any services from other agencies in the community?
If so, please list them:

If this child is placed in the center-based program, will the family be able to provide transportation? yes ☐ no ☐

Briefly list the child's problems and recommendations:

Problems	Recommendations

Parent preference:

Home-based component:

Center-based component:

Center-based parent-child/group component:

Projected date of enrollment:

Component:

TABLE 11-1 *Program's Referral Form*

intake coordinator with adequate information to make an initial eligibility decision on referrals. A copy of such a form is found in Table 11-1. This form also provides information on how to contact the family to initiate the enrollment procedures and on which program component parents prefer.

Enrollment Procedures

Enrollment procedures are designed to efficiently collect information and parental consent prior to a child beginning in the intervention program. Once eligibility is determined, enrollment procedures are initiated unless no openings exist. In this case, enrollment procedures are delayed until the child is admitted to the program. As part of the enrollment procedures, an evaluation of the child's current developmental status is completed and parents or guardians are required to complete relevant forms prior to program admission.

The Revised Gesell Developmental Schedules (Knobloch, Stevens, & Malone, 1980) are used to evaluate the child's current developmental status prior to enrollment. The Gesell is a standardized assessment instrument developed for use with children between the ages of four weeks and four years. Test results provide developmental quotients and a maturity age score for general development, adaptive behavior, and gross motor, fine motor, language, and personal-social areas. The intake coordinator schedules a time with the parents for administering the Gesell. Gesell results serve as a final screening of the child's eligibility for intervention services. Gesell scores are also used as part of the overall evaluation of program effectiveness.

The number of forms required for program admission is kept to a minimum. To make completion of the forms less cumbersome, parents are given all forms in one packet. Consent forms for testing and acquiring confidential information from other educational or medical agencies are included as are medical authorization and immunization records.

As part of the enrollment process, the intake coordinator has parents complete a packet of forms when they bring their child in for the Gesell test. Table 11–2 contains a checklist of all forms to be completed. Copies of these forms are found in Appendix C, and each is briefly described here.

The *Educational and Psychological Testing Consent Form* has three purposes: to alert parents that their child will be tested at periodic intervals while participating in the program; to indicate that all test results are confidential; and to seek parental permission for the proposed testing. The purposes of the *Consent Form to Photograph, Videotape and Audiotape* are similar to those of the testing consent form: to provide parents information and obtain their permission for conducting these various procedures.

The *Medical Authorization Form* is primarily to obtain information to be used should an emergency arise with the child and to obtain permission from parents to carry out appropriate emergency procedures should the need arise. The *Medical Report and Immunization Record Form* provides health information about the child, specifically, a record of diseases or conditions, immunization summary, and the results of a recent medical examination. Completion of this form is important to protect the safety of all participating children.

Form	Obtained and Completed
1. Consent form to evaluate with educational and psychological tests	☐
2. Consent form to photograph, videotape, audiotape	☐
3. Medical authorization form	☐
4. Medical report and immunization record form	☐
5. Demographic form	☐
6. Authorization to request confidential information form	☐
7. Program description (given to parent to retain)	☐

All forms must be completed and signed before child can be admitted to intervention program!

TABLE 11-2 Checklist of Program's Intake Forms

The *Demographic Form* is designed to collect information on the child and the family. This particular form is designed so that the information can be easily transferred to a computer file. The purpose of the *Authorization to Request Confidential Information Form* is to provide the program with permission to obtain any information that may assist program personnel in developing more effective programs for enrolled children and their families.

The purpose for using each form is briefly described to the parents, and they are given an opportunity to ask questions. At this time, a brief written description of the program is given to parents.

Family Orientation to Intervention Program

Initial contacts with a family are important in setting the tone for future interactions. Parents of young handicapped children may only recently have been informed about their child's disabilities, so that sensitive and well-planned interactions become particularly important. In addition, many families will be having contact with an educational service provider for the first time, and it is desirable to take advantage of this opportunity to establish cooperative partnership roles rather than adversarial or competitive ones. Objectives for the parent orientation to the intervention program include:

1. Providing parents with basic information about the program
2. Providing parents with a brief introduction to program philosophy and objectives
3. Establishing rapport with parents and providing a brief description of parent involvement in the educational process

Frequently, the most pressing questions for parents at the time of enrollment focus on what program participation means in terms of day-today planning. What hours and days their child attends, what to bring with their child, how snack and toileting/diapering routines are handled, and what to do when their child is ill are frequent concerns. Having these questions answered allows parents to focus their attention on some of the more rewarding aspects of program participation.

After enrollment procedures are completed, families meet with the assigned intervention staff. During this introductory meeting, parents are given a parent handbook. This handbook is designed to answer frequently asked questions. It has the advantage of giving parents a written resource for referral as questions arise. Parents are also provided with a copy of the classroom schedule so they will know what to expect on the first day.

Parents should have a basic understanding of the program's philosophy and operational structure. While any intervention program should be flexible enough to accommodate a wide variety of family needs and beliefs, some common philosophical ground is likely to be necessary for effective family-staff cooperation. Frequently, a brief introductory explanation helps parents understand procedures that may otherwise seem mysterious or contradictory to recommendations they have read or received from other professionals.

During the introductory meeting, parents receive a brief overview of the program philosophy and structure. Specifically, the rationale for activity-based instruction is discussed, along with an explanation of how children's individual instructional objectives are incorporated into group activities. Professional terminology is a frequent stumbling block to good family-staff communication, so the various developmental domains are introduced with a definition of the domain and examples of included skills. For example, the staff explains that the gross motor area covers large muscle development and includes such skills as sitting and crawling.

A subjective goal for program orientation is to establish a cooperative and supportive relationship between the parents and intervention program personnel. For this reason, the program orientation is structured as a dialogue rather than an opportunity to "talk at" parents. Parents are encouraged to ask questions and provide input and to express any special concerns about their child or the needs of the family.

During the introductory meeting with parents, the importance of their role is emphasized. A brief description of the amount and types of parent involvement included in the program is provided. Parents are also introduced to the IEP and the Family Program Agreement (FPA) process, and their roles in these processes are discussed. More detailed information and training about the IEP-FPA process are provided to parents at a later date.

At the start of a new year, a group orientation meeting is needed in addition to meeting with individual families. An evening meeting for family members near the start of the school year provides an opportunity for parents and staff to meet one another, allows parents who work during the day to attend, and prevents the need for staff to repeat some types of information.

INITIAL ASSESSMENT

Assessment is essential for effective intervention. The assessment of individual change and programmatic impact requires that intervention methods and systems be undergirded with procedures that are appropriate for assessing and evaluating their efficacy. Evaluation should determine the format and success of intervention for individual children and assess the impact of programs on groups of children. Thus, assessment-evaluation serves three distinct but complementary functions: it guides the development of individual programming; it provides feedback about the success of individual programming; and it yields information for determining the value of an intervention system designed to benefit groups of children (Bricker & Littman, 1982). Without appropriate assessment information, evaluation is not possible.

Obtaining comprehensive information on the child requires that the assessment battery be carefully constructed. This battery should tap the child's abilities across a range of domains since the IEP will be constructed on the basis of the initial assessment information. In addition, assessments should be geared to the developmental age of the child. Three major types of assessment data are collected:

1. Demographic information
2. Child change measures
3. Family impact measures

Demographic Information

The demographic form (see Appendix C) used by the program contains items that have been constructed to yield quantifiable responses. The areas covered include identification and description of the child and family, prenatal data, and information regarding children's handicapping conditions. As already indicated, the demographic form is completed for each child and the family as part of the enrollment procedure. Information on this form is updated at the beginning of each school year and when children leave the program.

Child Change Measures

Table 11-3 presents the assessment focus, measures, frequency of administration, and expected outcomes for the standardized and program-relevant tests used to monitor child change.

Standardized tests. There are no ideal or completely appropriate standardized instruments available for use with populations of handicapped infants and preschoolers. In recognition of this, interventionists must make

Assessment Focus	Measure	Frequency of Administration	Expected Outcomes
Child	*Standardized Tests:*		
General development	Revised Gesell Developmental Schedules (Knobloch, Stevens, & Malone, 1980)	Entry into program; updated beginning of each year and at six-month intervals thereafter	Developmental quotients, mental maturity age scores
	Program-relevant Tests:		
Specification of behavioral repertoire	Evaluation and Programming System: For Infants and Young Children (Bricker & Gentry, 1985)	Entry into program; updated beginning of each year and at quarterly intervals	Percent of items passed; information to develop IEP
	Uniform Performance Assessment System (White, Edgar, Haring, Affleck, Hayden & Bendersky, 1980)	Entry into program; updated beginning of each year and at quarterly intervals	Percent of items passed; information to develop IEP
	Evaluation and Programming System: For Infants and Young Children—Parent Form (Bricker & Gentry, 1985)	Entry into program; end of year	Percent of items passed; information to develop IEP
Family			
Determination of family needs	Family Interest Checklist	Entry into program	Information to develop Family Program Agreement
Involvement in program	Family Participation and Activity Record	Weekly summary	Information to monitor family involvement
Effectiveness of parent support group	Parent Self-Evaluation Record	Entry and exit from program	Information to determine impact of support group
Satisfaction with program	Family Satisfaction Questionnaire	End of school year; exit from program	Information to determine satisfaction with program

TABLE 11-3 *Program's Child and Family Change Measures*

compromises in selecting the norm-referenced instrument to be used. Although of limited utility in the development of individual programming, standardized tests have some advantages for evaluating an intervention program's success with groups of children (Ramey, Campbell, & Wasik, 1982). For this reason, the Revised Gesell Developmental Scales (Knobloch, Stevens, & Malone, 1980) are included in the assessment battery. The Gesell was developed for use with infants and young children and provides norms based on a nonhandicapped population. It was designed to be used by a trained administrator. Test results yield developmental quotients and maturity age scores in the adaptive behavior, gross motor, fine motor, language, and personal-social development areas. The Gesell test results are used as part of the overall program evaluation.

The Gesell is given to all children upon enrollment. The test is readministered at periodic intervals for as long as children remain in the program.

Program-relevant tests. The Evaluation and Programming System (EPS) For Infants and Young Children (Bricker & Gentry, 1985) is an experimental instrument.[1] This criterion-referenced test reflects the educational objectives of the program and thus is program relevant in terms of intervention emphasis. The EPS was developed for use with handicapped infants and children whose developmental range covers birth to thirty-six months. The preferred method of assessment is through observation of the child in a familiar environment; however, direct testing and parent report are permitted. This test is composed of six domains: gross motor, fine motor, communication, cognitive, self-help, and social. The EPS differs from norm-referenced instruments in three important ways. First, each domain is composed of many items that are hierarchically arranged from simple to increasingly complex. Second, each item is a potentially relevant training objective, making the link between assessment and intervention direct and relevant. Third, modifications or adaptations of the items for sensory and motorically impaired children are permitted.

Each of the six domains is composed of a series of strands that represent major response clusters or conceptual classes in a domain. Each strand is divided into a series of long-range goals that encompass a series of hierarchically arranged training objectives. The objectives are arranged in steps, beginning with the highest order response form and moving to progressively easier items. Failed training objectives are selected as IEP training objectives, and failed long-range goals are selected as long-range IEP goals as appropriate for individual children.

The EPS was designed to be used by interventionists. Each training target is accompanied by a detailed description of the assessment procedures, the necessary equipment, and the criteria for indicating successful performance of the item. Each item is scored either plus or minus, and the number of correct responses is tallied per domain. This raw score can be converted to a percentage-correct score. The EPS is administered at quarterly intervals to monitor the child's progress toward selected IEP goals and objectives.

In addition to the EPS form completed by the professional staff, a parent form is completed. This measure, referred to as the EPS-P (parent form), reflects the EPS content. The EPS-P was developed by taking each of the EPS long-range goals and rewriting them in wording thought to be easier for parents to understand.[2] The EPS-P long-range goals are arranged on the

---

[1] However, while still being field tested, this instrument has more data on its validity and reliability than most available criterion-referenced tests. See Bailey, 1983.

[2] The EPS-P is being field-tested as well. This test has been used with a number of parents and has undergone change based on their feedback. See Gumerlock, 1984.

recording form in a developmental sequence and divided into skills most likely to emerge during normal development spans of 0–12 months, 12–24 months, and 24–36 months, although age spans are not indicated on the forms. Each long-range goal is followed by the corresponding EPS code number for the convenience of the interventionist.

Parents are asked to indicate for each long-range goal whether their child does perform the skill, does not perform the skill yet, or does so only occasionally. The scoring system matches that of the EPS. Parents are also asked to star the highest priority long-range goals for their child. A cover sheet provides directions for completion of the EPS-P. Parents are asked to complete an EPS-P prior to the IEP-FPA meeting. Parents complete the EPS-P again at the end of the school year.

For children whose developmental level exceeds that of thirty-six months, the Uniform Performance Assessment System, or UPAS (White, Edgar, Haring, Affleck, Hayden, & Bendersky, 1980), is used. This criterion-referenced measure also reflects the educational objectives of the program. The Uniform Performance Assessment System is composed of fine motor/preacademic, gross motor, communication, self-help/social, and behavior management scales. Each scale is composed of developmentally sequenced items accompanied by extensive administration guidelines. Each item has a detailed description of the testing procedure, the necessary equipment, and the criteria for successful performance of the item. Scores can be derived for each domain and combined into an overall score.

Other assessment procedures. Recent research in child development points to certain areas that are important to child growth and are related to intellectual progress. Some of these areas are not comprehensively measured by norm- and criterion-referenced tests. These include such areas as child affect and parent-infant interaction. Consequently, for certain children, other assessment procedures are employed to provide supplemental information.

Family-Impact Measures

Table 11–3 presents the assessment focus, measure, frequency of administration, and expected outcomes for the family-impact measures. The four measures used are described here.

All participating parents complete the *Family Interest Checklist*. This checklist was developed by program personnel and is designed to find out what services or resources the family is interested in obtaining from the program and what services the family could contribute to the program. Parents complete the questionnaire independently or with assistance from staff by checking those items of interest or concern. This information is used in developing the Family Program Agreement. A copy of this form is found in Appendix D.

Individual Education Plans and Family Program Agreements

The program is interested in finding out how parents and other family members tend to spend their time when interfacing with the program. To acquire these data, the staff completes the *Family Participation and Activity Record* weekly. Using this form, staff members indicate the type of activity, week, date, and time for each participating family. Activities can include participating in (1) a parent education group, (2) a classroom program, (3) observing the child, (4) a conference with staff, (5) an IEP-FPA conference, (6) a parent support group, (7) social activity, (8) a group parent meeting, (9) training other parents, (10) supporting other parents, and (11) child training and management. A copy of this form is in Appendix D.

Parents who participate in the Parent Support Group, which meets weekly to discuss their concerns, complete the *Parent Self Evaluation Record* upon entry into and exit from the program (see Appendix D). This scale contains twenty-one items that were designed to measure parents' perception of how well they can handle issues concerning their handicapped child. A goal of the Parent Support Group is to have parents develop improved feelings about their ability to seek information, problem solve, and manage their lives.

The final measure is the *Family Satisfaction Questionnaire* designed to determine satisfaction with the program. This questionnaire is composed of questions that are designed to elicit from parents and other family members what they found positive and negative about the program. This questionnaire is completed at the end of the school year. A copy is found in Appendix D.

INDIVIDUAL EDUCATION PLANS AND FAMILY PROGRAM AGREEMENTS

Since the passage of P.L. 94-142, the Individualized Education Program (IEP) has become an integral part of special education services. The federal regulations governing the development and content of an IEP mandate many of the practices characteristic of quality education services, including individualized selection of instructional objectives and procedures based on a child's current functioning level, parental involvement in the educational planning process, use of objective evaluation procedures to monitor the child's progress, and educational placement based on the child's needs rather than on a label of handicapping condition or administrative convenience (see Chapter 5). Procedures that help in the optimal development of IEPs are needed. This section describes a set of procedures that may be helpful in developing a comprehensive and efficient IEP-FPA process. This IEP-FPA process consists of three major facets:

1. Parent-teacher preparation for the IEP-FPA meeting
2. IEP-FPA meeting
3. IEP-FPA implementation and follow-up

Preparation for IEP and FPA Development

Parent preparation. IEP-FPA meetings are frequently conducted on the educational agency's "turf" with an array of specialists present who are familiar with the IEP-FPA process. Many parents walking into this situation are uncomfortable, and their participation is limited to signing-off on IEP objectives recommended by the special education team. The importance of parents' involvement in their child's education, particularly for the infant and young child, cannot be overemphasized. Therefore, it is important to use an IEP-FPA process that generates meaningful parent and family involvement. Some ways of encouraging active parent involvement are to provide parents with an understanding of the IEP-FPA process before the IEP-FPA meeting is actually conducted and to develop strategies to assist parents in selecting and prioritizing appropriate goals for their children and their family.

To begin, parents should be provided information on the legal rights of their child and an overview of the IEP-FPA process. Written descriptions are helpful because the amount of information can be overwhelming. A number of pamphlets have been developed by school districts and other educational agencies that explain P.L. 94–142 and the IEP process in terms generally understandable to parents. Parent inservices or individual conferences can also be useful in familiarizing parents with any local variations in or additions to the basic IEP process.

A strategy for enhancing active parental involvement in the IEP-FPA process is to provide information to help parents select relevant educational goals for their child and their family. The EPS-P has been developed for this purpose. The long-range goals on the EPS-P are directly related to the EPS long-range goals. The direct relationship connecting the program assessment instrument, the EPS, the EPS-P, and the development of the IEP provides an important link between assessment and educational programming. Parents are given the EPS-P and asked to complete it prior to the IEP-FPA meeting. In addition to completing the EPS-P, parents are given and asked to review a list of potential family goals that could be used to develop the Family Program Agreement at the IEP-FPA meeting. These goals can be classified into three broad areas: (1) having the child fit comfortably into the family, (2) learning how to effectively care for the child's specific needs, and (3) becoming an effective teacher for the child. A copy of this list of potential family goals and objectives is found in Table 11–4. Parents are encouraged to select goals and objectives that reflect their priorities and interests.

Parents of at-risk and handicapped children receive numerous papers and handouts concerning their child over the course of a year. This information is more likely to be used by parents if they have a strategy for collecting and organizing it so specific information is readily retrievable. As part of the parents' preparation for the IEP-FPA meeting, parents are given a parent

Goals	Objectives
Have the child fit comfortably into the family.	1. Understand the child's handicapping condition 2. Parents enjoy the child 3. Siblings enjoy the child 4. Learn about community resources
Learn how to effectively care for the child's special needs.	1. Learn how to identify a problem 2. Learn how to combine special therapy routines into daily activities
Become an effective teacher for the child.	1. Learn how to describe the child's current behaviors and skills 2. Learn how to select toys, materials and activities that are appropriate to the child's level of development 3. Learn how to elicit skills that the child has learned in one setting in other places 4. Learn how to generalize new responses to other people, objects, settings

TABLE 11-4 Potential Family Goals and Objectives

notebook, a looseleaf binder with tabbed dividers for organizing information. Parents are encouraged to use these notebooks throughout the year to save relevant information.

Staff preparation. In addition to helping parents prepare for the IEP-FPA meeting, the staff have a series of activities to complete in preparation for the meeting and that include:

1. Scheduling of the IEP-FPA meeting
2. Obtaining input from relevant support staff
3. Summarizing assessment results
4. Developing tentative recommendations
5. Planning the IEP-FPA meeting agenda
6. Preparing forms

A convenient time and place for the IEP-FPA meeting is arranged with the child's parents, and relevant staff members are notified. Every effort is made to keep the number of individuals attending the meeting small so that parents feel comfortable. Some parents want to have the various specialists who work with their child participate in the meeting. If so, every effort is made to accommodate their wishes. Input is also obtained from support staff prior to the actual meeting. Specialists may provide valuable input on the child's current level of functioning or selection of long-range goals and instructional techniques. The interventionists are prepared to provide parents with a summary of assessment results. Particular attention is paid to domains in which instructional programming is required. Although parents sometimes want an overall "score," the main emphasis is on providing

Program Preliminaries: Intake Procedures and Development of IEP and FPA

parents with information on the presence and absence of specific skills that contribute to and detract from the child's independence.

The meetings are begun by reviewing what the child is able to do followed by what remains to be learned. The selection of the IEP goals and objectives is a compromise between well-prepared and concerned individuals—parents and staff. It is in the child's best interest if both parental preference and professional judgment enter into the selection of goals. Long-range goals selected for inclusion on the child's IEP are taken directly from the EPS and EPS-P or UPAS. This procedure provides continuity between interventionists and parents and directly relates the assessment outcomes to the intervention program.

Having a standard agenda to follow during IEP-FPA meetings is helpful. Information and issues relevant to a particular family can be added before the meeting. Use of a standard agenda speeds up preparation for meetings and makes forgetting important steps less likely. The standard agenda used is presented later in this chapter.

IEP forms. The IEP forms used by the program staff include an *Individual Education Plan Cover Form,* shown in Table 11-5, and an *Individual Long-Range Goal Form,* in Table 11-6. On the IEP cover sheet, the child's name, birthdate, parents, address, phone, interventionist, date of meeting, date IEP is to be initiated, duration of IEP, and persons attending the meeting are recorded. A place for the parent's signature is provided. The cover sheet also provides space to indicate specific services to be delivered to the child.

The IEP Individual Long-Range Goal Form contained in Table 11-6 lists the child's name, the domain, persons responsible for implementation, current functioning level, long-range goals, and training objectives. Space for describing parental involvement is also provided. Columns are provided to indicate the dates training objectives are initiated, the projected completion date for training objectives, and a quarterly progress report. An Individual Long-Range Goal Form is completed for each long-range goal and its associated training objectives. Guidelines for completion of each section of the Individual Long-Range Goal Form include the following:

1. *Current level of functioning.* Assessments in each domain are completed and summarized as the current level of functioning on the form. Percent of items passed or other scores may be included, but several specific skills that the child is and is not able to do are to be included to provide an immediate picture of the child's functioning level without referring to test results.
2. *Long-range goals.* Long-range goals appropriate to each domain are selected from the EPS and EPS-P and worded in general terms.
3. *Training objectives.* Identification of training objectives is completed after the child's long-range goals are specified. A brief specification of the antecedent conditions, the behavior to be performed, and the

Individual Education Plans and Family Program Agreements

Name _____   Birthdate _____
    Last   First

Parents or Guardians _____

Address _____   Phone _____

Interventionist _____

Date of Meeting _____   Date IEP Initiated _____

Anticipated Duration of IEP _____

Persons attending IEP meeting (specify role): _____

Services:

Description of Service	Frequency of Service	Date of Initiation	Duration	Who Will Be Responsible

See attached pages for statement of current level of educational functioning, long-range goals, training objectives, and person(s) responsible.

Directions:

Long-Range Goals: Long-range goals should be selected from domains in which child is showing delays.

Training Objectives: Every objective must include a performance statement including antecedent conditions, criteria, and method of evaluation.

I/we have participated in the development of the IEP and approve the educational plan.

_____   _____
Parent/Guardian/Surrogate Parent Signature(s)   Date

TABLE 11-5 Program's Individual Education Plan Cover Form

criterion and evaluation for mastery of the skill is done for each training objective. Any training objective initially taught in a classroom setting also includes targeting of functional performance of the skill in the home or other relevant environments. Attention is given to performance of the skill in response to naturally occurring antecedents and with naturally occurring consequences that will maintain the behavior.

Training objectives are taken from the EPS or UPAS. The interventionist uses these to formulate IEP training objectives, adding specific information as needed for individual children.

4. *Reporting columns.* The first column, date initiated, indicates the projected date the IEP goal is to be initiated. The projected completion is estimated for each training objective. At the first quarterly reporting

Program Preliminaries: Intake Procedures and Development of IEP and FPA

Name _____ Domain _____

Person Responsible _____

Current Functioning Level _____

Long-Range Goal	Training Objective(s)	Date Initiated	Projected Completion	Progress* 1st Q	2nd Q	3rd Q	Comments
Parent Involvement:							

*C = completed; IP = in progress

TABLE 11-6 *Program's Individual Long-Range Goal Form*

period, the interventionist records "C" in the first Q column if the training objective is completed and "IP" for targets for which the child has not reached mastery. This reporting procedure is repeated at each quarter.

5. *Comments.* Space is available on the IEP for comments pertaining to specific training objectives.

Individual Education Plans and Family Program Agreements

Child's Name: T.L. Parent's Signature: *Mr. and Mrs. L.* Date: 11/4/85
Interventionist's Signature: *Ms. S. Jones* Date: 11.4.85

Objectives	Priority	Activities	Resources Needed	Date Started	Evaluation Method	Date Ended
1. Acquire skills to elicit verbal skills T.L. has learned at school	1	Incorporate specific language program steps into daily routine at home	Input from staff regarding appropriate ways to elicit and reinforce language usage at home Classroom instructional programs	11/9/85	Weekly verbal report to interventionist; data taken from Family Participation and Activity Record	6/1/86
2. Acquire information to permit accurate description of child's current behavioral repertoire	2	Record weekly new words/word approximations T.L. uses	Appropriate recording form	11/15/85	Share list with interventionist weekly	6/1/86
3. Learn how to select toys, materials, and activities appropriate to T.L.'s level of development	3	Look at books with T.L. for at least 15 minutes daily: name pictures, actions, etc., and have T.L. imitate; ask T.L. questions about pictures	Variety of picture books (checked out from program's library)	11/15/85	Verbal report to interventionist; comparison of type and frequency of book selection during the quarter	6/1/86

TABLE 11-7 *Completed Copy of the Program's Family Program Agreement Form*

8. *Parental involvement.* The parental involvement section is used to specify the role of the parent in carrying out the training objectives for a particular long-range goal. The type of parental involvement is stated in specific terms so that both parents and program staff understand the parent's role. The progress-reporting column is used to indicate when the parent begins each type of involvement, how long it is expected to continue, and the status at the quarterly review. Changes in the parent role are dated and noted in the comments section.

Family Program Agreements. The IEP equivalent for families for determining goals is the Family Program Agreement (FPA). The FPA is used to record the objectives the parents and other family members select for themselves prior to or during the IEP-FPA meeting. Each objective is divided into a series of activities that the interventionist and parent feel will facilitate the parent's meeting the objective. Resources needed to conduct these activities are listed as well as the method by which the effectiveness of the activities is to be evaluated. The dates each activity are started and ended are also indicated. Objectives are prioritized so that the interventionist and parents know where their efforts are to be concentrated. A copy of a completed Family Program Agreement is found in Table 11-7.

The IEP-FPA Meeting

Unlike in IEP meetings in school districts, educational placement is seldom a major decision to be made in early-intervention program IEP-FPA meetings. The major functions of the IEP-FPA meeting are:

1. Selection of goals and objectives for the child and family
2. Prioritization of goals and objectives
3. Specification of responsibilities

Careful attention to the IEP-FPA meeting functions can be accomplished through use of a standardized agenda and by following some basic guidelines. Table 11-8 shows the standard agenda used by program staff. A brief description of various items on the agenda follows. Giving parents a copy of the standard agenda before the meeting is helpful.

1. *Introductions.* All individuals attending the meeting are introduced and their roles briefly explained.
2. *Review of purpose and process of IEP-FPA meeting.* The major objectives for the IEP-FPA meeting (selection and prioritization of goals/objectives and specification of responsibilities) are stated. A brief look at the process for meeting those objectives is accomplished through a review of the agenda.
3. *Specification of current functioning level.* Parents and staff share results for each developmental domain. Parents present what they have recorded on the EPS-P form and the staff present results of the EPS or UPAS assessment. Priority is given to domains in which the child is showing developmental delays. The focus is on presence and absence of skills rather than scores.
4. *Selection of child objectives.* Child objectives are selected from the long-range goals on the EPS and EPS-P or UPAS. Parents' priorities are given first consideration, additional input coming from the staff or support personnel attending the meeting. Attention is given to selecting goals that establish a comprehensive but manageable educational program for the child.
5. *Selection of family objectives.* Family objectives are selected from the list of potential family goals shown in Table 11-4; however, families can select

Individual Education Plans and Family Program Agreements

1. Introductions
2. Brief review of
   a. purpose of IEP-FPA meeting
   b. process to be followed
3. Specification of child's current functioning level
   a. parent—EPS-P
   b. staff—EPS and other applicable tests
   c. domains
      1) communication
      2) fine motor
      3) gross motor
      4) self care
      5) cognitive
      6) social
4. Selection of child objectives
   a. parent input
   b. staff input, other(s) when applicable
      NOTE: Long-range goals should be recorded on IEP forms at this time.
5. Selection of family objectives
   a. parent input
   b. staff input, other(s) when applicable
6. Prioritization of goals and objectives
   a. child goals/objectives
   b. parent goals/objectives
7. Specification of responsibilities (family and program staff)
   a. child objectives
      1) discussion of training objectives
      2) specification of parent involvement for child objectives
         NOTE: Parent involvement should be recorded on IEP forms
   b. Family objectives
      1) discussion of objectives
      2) specification of responsibilities for parent objectives
8. Summarization of decisions and completion of IEP cover sheet and FPA form

TABLE 11-8 Program's Standardized IEP Meeting Agenda

goals that are not listed. Family priorities are again given first consideration, but the staff may recommend additional objectives based on observed needs.

6. *Prioritization of goals and objectives.* Child goals and family objectives are prioritized so that parents and staff know where intervention efforts should be most heavily concentrated. It is usually helpful to prioritize within domains and then across domains.

7. *Specification of responsibilities.* The respective parent and program responsibilities for working toward objectives are formalized as part of the IEP-FPA meeting. For child objectives, it is useful to briefly discuss with the parent what programming strategies are included in the training objectives. Although the actual training objectives are written later, this is an appropriate opportunity to seek parental input. Minor changes in training objectives or parental involvement are made if necessary when the interventionist and parents meet to review the training objectives.

A process parallel to that used for child objectives is followed with family objectives. First, objectives are discussed, then the respective responsibilities of intervention program staff and parents are specified.

8. *Summarization of decisions and completion of IEP cover sheet and FPA*

form. To close the meeting, the joint decisions made by the staff and parents about selection of goals and assignment of responsibilities are summarized. This is followed by parents signing the IEP cover sheet and FPA form that indicates participation in the development and approval of the plan.

IEP-FPA Implementation and Follow-Up

Effective use of the IEP is accomplished through implementation of the following procedures: developing specific training objectives, reviewing these training objectives with parents, implementing intervention as prescribed by the training objectives, and summarizing progress toward training objectives and long-range goals at the year's end. Each of these procedures is described in the following sections.

Development of training objectives. Once long-range goals are jointly determined by the staff and parents during the IEP-FPA meeting, the next step is to write quarterly training objectives. Training objectives are written to reflect the specific programming needs of the child. These objectives specifically define strategies that should enable the child to independently perform the long-range goal in response to daily antecedents and consequences.

The first training objective should require slightly more complex or independent responding than the child's current level of functioning. For example, if the assessment summary indicates that a child is walking with total physical assistance from an adult, the first training objective might be for the child to walk with less physical assistance (e.g., one finger guidance from an adult). The guidelines used by the interventionists for writing training objectives are included on the IEP cover sheet. Training objectives are modified at any time deemed necessary during program implementation. When a new training objective is initiated, the date is indicated in the appropriate progress reporting column on the Individual Long-Range Goal Form (Table 11-6).

Although programming strategies are reviewed with parents as part of the IEP-FPA meeting, the interventionist meets subsequently with parents to review the training objectives and parent and program responsibilities. This is an ideal time to clear up any confusions and to make modifications in goals and objectives if necessary. The parents receive copies of the IEP and FPA to keep in their parent notebook. Copies are also placed in the child's file.

Implementation of IEP. Intervention and data-collection procedures and individual instructional program plans are designed to match those specified in the IEP training objectives. When careful implementation of the training objectives as written indicates that the objective is not appropriate, then changes are made in the instructional program plan *and* in the IEP so that the match is preserved. Individual program plan development and monitoring procedures are described in Chapter 12.

Every three to four months, the staff reviews progress made toward training objectives. This is done by recording the appropriate symbol in the progress-reporting column for the quarter on the Individual Long-Range Goal Form (Table 11-6). A "C" is recorded for completed objectives and an "IP" for those in progress. The staff use quarterly IEP reviews as a method of evaluating the effectiveness of intervention. If children are not matching expected rates of progress, intervention strategies are examined to see where improvements can be made. A staff-parent conference is arranged to go over the results of the quarterly review. If changes in long-range goals or training objectives are made, the parents' copy of the IEP is updated.

Year-end evaluation. The year-end evaluation is designed to provide a summary of the child's progress throughout the academic year and to assist in the transition to the upcoming year, especially in the instance of a transfer to a new program or a new interventionist. A copy of the form used is shown in Table 11-9. The following information is required:

CHILD'S NAME:

INTERVENTIONIST'S NAME:

DATE: Date year-end evaluation was written.

ATTENDANCE: Percent of days present each month.

SUMMARY OF BEHAVIOR: According to the data provided by teaching staff, Gesell, EPS or UPAS, and parents, the abilities and behaviors the child exhibited when entering the program and at the end of the year are summarized (e.g., general affect, behavioral problems, increase in expressive language).

GENERAL RECOMMENDATIONS FOR THE COMING YEAR: This section should include any ideas or strategies thought to be helpful for the child during the next year.

LONG RANGE GOALS: Goals selected during the IEP process.

GOALS MET YES/NO: Indicate the long range goals accomplished.

CURRENT LEVEL OF FUNCTIONING: Specify where the child is functioning in terms of each goal.

COMMENTS: Any additional information that may be useful.

SUMMARY

This chapter was designed to offer the reader a structure for and detailed information on intake procedures, initial assessment strategies, and the development of an IEP and FPA. Every early-intervention program is faced

Program Preliminaries: Intake Procedures and Development of IEP and FPA

Child's Name: _____ Interventionist(s): _____ Date: _____

ATTENDANCE: (%)   OCT   NOV   DEC   JAN   FEB   MAR   APR   MAY   JUN

SUMMARY OF BEHAVIORS:

Beginning of year: _____
_____
_____

End of year: _____
_____
_____

General recommendations: _____
_____
_____

Long-Range Goal	Long-Range Goal Met? Yes	Long-Range Goal Met? Not Yet	Current Level of Functioning	Comments
Gross Motor				
1. _____				
2. _____				
3. _____				
4. _____				
Fine Motor				
1. _____				
2. _____				
3. _____				
4. _____				
Social				
1. _____				
2. _____				
3. _____				
4. _____				

Summary

Long-Range Goal	Long-Range Goal Met? Yes	Long-Range Goal Met? Not Yet	Current Level of Functioning	Comments
Cognitive				
1.				
2.				
3.				
4.				
Self Care				
1.				
2.				
3.				
4.				
Communication				
1.				
2.				
3.				
4.				

TABLE 11-9 Program's Individual Education Plan Yearly Report Form

with finding, enrolling, and developing an educational plan for participating children. A cohesive, well-designed approach can help ensure that such routine, but important, processes are conducted efficiently and that outcomes are genuinely useful. Too often, program staff are faced with information that is irrelevant or vague, requiring that they repeat procedures. Such redundancies are wasteful to programs and to parents.

The heart of any effective intervention program is the IEP developed for participating children. Time spent on developing an accurate and useful IEP is never wasted. More likely, hastily constructed IEPs will result in poorly conceived goals that will require reformulation. Strategies that ensure the development of comprehensive and appropriate IEPs will consistently pay off for the staff and the children.

Although many programs indicate that parental involvement is essential, few have specific procedures that help ensure meaningful participation of parents. The use of the EPS-P provides a mechanism for the parent to become involved with the development of the child's IEP. The parents' first attempt to complete the EPS-P may not be accurate. However, we have found that over time, most parents can learn to become accurate assessors of their child's repertoire. In addition, the use of the FPA conveys to families the staff's interest and concern about their feelings and what objectives they see as important. These formalized procedures, once understood by parents, can assist significantly in enhancing their meaningful involvement in the program.

References

Bailey, E. (1983). *Psychometric evaluation of the early comprehensive evaluation and programming system.* Unpublished doctoral dissertation. Eugene, OR: University of Oregon.

Bricker, D., & Gentry, D. (1985). *Evaluation and programming system: For infants and young children.* Eugene, OR: University of Oregon.

Bricker, D., & Littman, D. (1982). Intervention and evaluation: The inseparable mix. *Topics in Early Childhood Special Education, 1,* 23–33.

Gumerlock, S. (1984). *Psychometric evaluation of the parent rating form.* Unpublished master's thesis. Eugene, OR: University of Oregon.

Knobloch, H., Stevens, F., & Malone, A. (1980). *Manual of developmental diagnosis: The administration and interpretation of the revised Gesell and Armatruda developmental and neurologic examination.* Hagerstown, MD: Harper & Row.

Ramey, C., Campbell, F., & Wasik, B. (1982). Use of standardized tests to evaluate early childhood special education programs. *Topics in Early Childhood Special Education, 1,* 51–60.

White, O., Edgar, E., Haring, N., Affleck, J., Hayden, A., & Bendersky, M. (1980). *UPAS: Uniform performance assessment system.* Columbus, OH: Charles H. Merrill.

CHAPTER 12

THE INTERVENTION PROCESS

Previous chapters have specified the roles and responsibilities of staff and parents, the intake process, and the procedures for the development of the IEP and FPA. The present chapter describes the intervention process for participating children and families.

PROGRAM START-UP AND MAINTENANCE

Beginning the program in an efficient and effective manner provides an important professional atmosphere for the remainder of the year and uses the initial start-up time wisely. An effective beginning requires planning and organization. The yearly start-up schedule for the program helps ensure efficient use of staff and parents' time.

Week 1

Staff inservice training

Intake of children and families

Week 2

IEP and FPA assessment begin

Classroom setup and organization completed

Week 3

Home visits begin

Classroom program begins

IEP-FPA meetings begin

Week 4

IEP-FPA meetings completed

Program plans written

Week 5

Activity plans written

Programming for children and families begins

Data collection begins

273

Week 6 to final week
Individual programs for children and families executed
Final week
Quarterly evaluations completed

To maintain program efficiency, the staff regularly participate in a variety of meetings. Full program staff meetings are held twice a month. During these meetings, general topics of concern, program-wide modifications, and ensuing activities are targeted for discussion. These meetings are also used as inservice training vehicles throughout the year. In addition, weekly meetings are held for the interventionists and the coordinator. At this time, problems are shared and strategies discussed for solving difficulties, as well as sharing information about successful ventures.

The third type of regular meeting occurs within units. Intervention personnel for a specific unit (e.g., classroom) convene weekly to discuss problems relevant to their particular group of children and families. These regularly scheduled meetings include all appropriate staff. During these meetings, the programming for individual children is reviewed in detail to solicit ideas on needed changes and to emphasize priorities and specialized techniques for that child. Outcomes, timelines, and responsibilities are recorded on the meeting agenda next to the corresponding agenda items.

Scheduling

Scheduling for home-based intervention is dependent upon the needs of the children and families. However, in general, home visits can be divided into four phases:

1. Arrival—Caregiver and child are greeted.
2. Review of previous week's programming—Discussion and examination of data collected by caregiver are completed.
3. Introduction of new training objectives or modifications of existing program—Depending on the caregiver's feedback and nature of the data, the program plan is continued as is or revised, or new training objectives are established.
4. Wrap up—Session is reviewed and plans for coming week recapitulated.

The activity-based nature of the program and the age of the children served require that schedules change as the school year progresses; however, initially, the classrooms follow the schedule presented here:

9:00–9:20	Arrival and free play
9:20–9:30	Opening circle
9:30–9:50	Instructional activity group 1

Program Start-Up and Maintenance

Time	Monday	Tuesday	Wednesday	Thursday
9:00–9:30	Arrival and free play	→	→	→
	Opening circle	→	→	→
9:30–9:50	Instructional Activity Groups — Group 1: Cognitive, Communication	→	→	→
9:50–10:10	Group 2: Motor, Social	→	→	→
10:10–10:30	Outside play	→	→	→
10:30–10:50	Toileting	→	→	→
10:50–11:10	Snack and storytime	→	→	→
11:10–11:30	Instructional Activity Groups — Group 3: Motor, Sensorimotor	→	→	→
11:30–11:50	Group 4: Art, Communication	→	→	→
11:50–12:00	Closing circle	→	→	→

NOTE: The children attend four days per week. Friday is used for inservice and planning by staff.

TABLE 12-1   Daily Classroom Schedule

    9:50–10:10   Instructional activity group 2
    10:10–10:30   Outside play
    10:30–10:50   Toileting
    10:50–11:10   Snack and story time
    11:10–11:30   Instructional activity group 3
    11:30–11:50   Instructional activity group 4
    11:50–12:00   Closing circle

The children's instructional programming is primarily conducted during the four instructional activity groups. Some children also participate in individual instructional sessions that may be scheduled during any group activity except opening or closing circle. Opening and closing circle, outside play, and snack time are large-group activities with all children included. The instructional activity groups are composed of two to four children with one to two adults, depending on the children's developmental level and behavioral control. Each activity group has an assigned adult activity leader who is responsible for managing the activities for the forty-minute period. During this forty-minute session, two successive groups of children rotate to the activity. Activity groups occur before and after the mid-morning snack and the outdoor play period. Table 12-1 includes a copy of the daily classroom

The Intervention Process

Activity	Assignment for Major Responsibility
Opening circle	Anne
Instructional activity groups 1 and 2	
Cognitive	Katie
Communication	Frank
Motor	Anne
Social	Joe
Outside play	Katie and Anne
Toileting	All staff
Snack	All staff
Story time	Frank
Instructional activity groups 3 and 4	
Motor	Anne
Sensorimotor	Katie
Art	Joe
Communication	Frank
Closing circle	Joe

TABLE 12-2 *Staff and Parent Assignments for Daily Activities*

schedule. In addition to the daily classroom schedule, each classroom interventionist provides a schedule of assigned responsibilities for each staff member and parent assigned to the interventionist's classroom, as shown in Table 12-2.

A more detailed description of a typical classroom day is presented here:

> *9:00-9:20* Arrival of children and parents—Children are assisted by parents in removing and hanging up coats and putting personal belongings in individual cubbies. Any early toileting is done by parents. Staff are prepared for groups so that they can greet children and parents. Parents take their children into a free play area and assist them in locating an activity. Parents may then leave.
>
> *9:20* Opening circle—Large-group activities such as singing.
>
> *9:30* Instructional activity group 1—Children are assigned to one of four groups. Each group of children is then assigned to one of the four concurrently run instructional activity groups depending upon their priority IEP goals and quarterly training objectives. Four instructional activity group options exist: those with a cognitive, communication, motor, or social emphasis. The emphasis is obtained through the selection of activities. For example, for a motor group, the activities might require systematic use of large muscles, such as ball throwing, while the communication group might select an activity such as watching fish in an aquarium.

Staff and parents encourage the development and use of any appropriate target skill within a group activity.

9:50 Instructional activity group 2—Children rotate to second group for twenty minutes.

10:10 Outside play—Unstructured time, although appropriate use of equipment and appropriate peer interaction is encouraged.

10:30 Toileting—Children are toileted or diapered then assisted in washing their hands.

10:50 Snack and storytime—Children are seated; the adult presents snacks upon appropriate requests by children. Snack time is used to encourage language and social skills. After finishing snack, children are encouraged to clean up and quietly move to the reading area where they may look at a book independently or listen to a story read by an adult.

11:10 Instructional activity group 3—A replication of early activity groups, the groups having the following emphasis: sensorimotor, motor, art, and communication.

11:30 Instructional activity group 4—Children rotate to second group for twenty minutes.

11:50 Closing circle—Large-group activities, generally with parents present.

During each of the general activities, all children have specific goals that are incorporated. Inclusion of language goals are part of every activity.

Organization of Materials and Environment

The utilization of space and arrangement of equipment and materials is an integral part of planning. Ample room should be available for varied activities to occur simultaneously. Examples of classroom areas used to promote learning and interaction among children include.

1. Housekeeping area—dress up clothes, play kitchen and utensils, dolls and doll furniture
2. Block building area—varied types of building materials (e.g., wooden blocks, Legos), small dolls, and animal figures to use with constructions
3. Arts and crafts area—variety of paints, paper, crayons, felt pens, scissors, paste, and other small materials (e.g., yarn, sponge pieces)
4. Manipulative area—puzzles, nested cups and boxes, pegs and pegboards, beads, and other materials requiring fine motor control
5. Quiet area—pillows, selection of books

6. Large-group area—rug or floor space large enough for children to sit in a large circle
7. Gross motor area—variety of climbing apparatus (e.g., stairs, jungle gyms), tunnels to crawl through, mats, balls, slides, scooter boards
8. Outdoor play area—variety of tricycles, small riding toys, balls, push toys, rocking horses, and playground equipment available for self-selection by children
9. Snack area—appropriate sized tables and chairs, seating arranged to promote interaction among children
10. Theme toys area—small sections of room for certain types of toys (e.g., barn with animals, cars and trucks, airport and airplanes)
11. Sandbox or water play area—sandbox or pool of water with a variety of containers and small toys to fill and dump, sink/bury, and retrieve

The types of materials included in the program are important, because some materials lend themselves to a greater likelihood of interactive play (Quiltich, Christopherson, & Risley, 1977). Safety and durability of the materials are always considered.

Inclusion of Nondelayed Children and Their Parents

The Education of All Handicapped Children Act of 1975 specifies that handicapped children should receive a free and appropriate education in the least restrictive environment. The early years seem to be an ideal time to begin "mainstreaming."

Integrating handicapped and nonhandicapped children can be advantageous for both groups (Bricker, Bruder, & Bailey, 1982). Nonhandicapped children can play a critical role in promoting learning in handicapped children by providing a model for normal behaviors. It is also likely that nonhandicapped children who have had the opportunity to interact with handicapped children will grow into adulthood with a greater tolerance and understanding of individuals with disabilities (Bricker & Sandall, 1979).

A group of nondelayed children are included in the classroom programs. Preference is given to children classified as at-risk and nonhandicapped siblings of handicapped children. All parent-involvement options, classroom activities, and supplementary services for parents are available to families of enrolled nonhandicapped children; however, development of IEPs and individual instructional programs is not routinely done for the nonhandicapped children.

Classroom Behavior Management Procedures

Because of the many individuals who often participate in the classrooms, it is important to develop a set of consistent behavior management strategies.

Exceptions or additions to these general guidelines are needed for some children. When these occur, the specific information is kept on the child's clipboard. The general classroom behavior management guidelines are given here:

Compliance.   Minimize the use of commands when possible by:

1. pointedly reinforcing the desired behavior in other children,
2. offering several appropriate choices to the child, *or*
3. providing less directive prompts for the desired behavior.
   - If you are not offering the child a choice, do not phrase it as one (e.g., "Let's . . ." *not* "Do you want . . . ?").
   - When telling children to do something, use a positive and enthusiastic tone of voice and sound confident that they will comply.
   - If a child does not move to comply within 5–10 seconds of a request, physically help the child to comply. Do not verbally reprimand; just see that the child does what was asked. Consistently and calmly follow through *every* time this situation arises. Ignore any whining or crying. Acknowledge appropriate participation.

Transitions among activities.   Be sure that any child leaving a group activity "arrives" at another activity and is not aimlessly wandering around or playing unsupervised.

Clean-up.   A child should put away toys and materials before getting out additional ones. The child may need help or a reminder to do this.

- A child should help clean up any spills or messes for which he or she is responsible (e.g., juice spilled at snack time).

Group management.   Appropriate behavior (e.g., attending, interacting with peers or materials) is rewarded by providing logical consequences to the behavior, including an enjoyed activity and materials, and through specific, social praise.

- Ignore inappropriate behavior (e.g., whining, crying, nonattending) that does not threaten the safety of the child or others and does not disrupt the activity.
- If a child is using materials inappropriately (e.g., writing on a table), briefly remove the materials with an explanation. Give the child another chance in about a minute.
- A child should remain in a structured activity until it is completed. If the child tries to leave the activity early, indicate that he or she can leave when the activity is completed.

The Intervention Process

- Avoid physical restraint for keeping a child in groups. Develop and implement a consistent management program for a child who regularly disrupts or leaves groups (e.g., a child who is new to the school setting or who remains outside the periphery of the activity).

Free play. During "free play," or child-initiated activities, children may choose with whom and what they want to play and how, as long as they are appropriately engaged in an activity.

- A child must remain in the supervised free-play area.
- Do not allow a child to engage in self-stimulation. Interrupt this behavior and redirect child to appropriate play activities.
- If a child is sitting unoccupied, acknowledge children who are playing appropriately. If an unoccupied child still has not initiated an appropriate play activity, encourage him or her to engage in an activity.

Aggressive or destructive behavior. When a child hits, bites, kicks, or scratches another child, is destructive to toys or other materials, or does something that endangers his or her own safety, do the following: Tell the child what behavior is unacceptable, then remove the child from the activity. Have the child sit and watch until he or she is calm for one minute; then return the child to the activity with a positively stated reminder of appropriate behavior. Be sure to emphasize the specific behavior (e.g., "No hitting") rather than labeling characteristics of the child (e.g., "You're too mean to stay in group"). For a child who has serious behavior management or compliance problems, program personnel should develop a set of techniques to be considered prior to initiation of an aversive behavior management procedure.

To break the downward "no-win" spiral in which punishment provides attention that reinforces negative behavior, it is essential to focus on positive interactions. Staff should plan ways of handling the child's behavior in a preventive rather than in a reactive manner. Following are some of the strategies that emphasize positive methods of managing children's behaviors. These approaches should be employed before adopting negative or aversive management techniques.

- Provide positive consequences for incompatible responses.
- Interrupt established behavior chains.
- Rearrange the environment.
- Redirect child's activity.
- Develop competing behaviors (training sequences to develop com-

peting behaviors should begin as soon as an inappropriate behavior is identified as requiring staff attention).

In the interest of promoting a positive management atmosphere in the classrooms, a set of generic classroom rules are posted in each class. The rules are simply and positively stated. The few rules reflect the behavioral expectations of a well-managed classroom.

The purpose of establishing classroom rules is threefold. First, they provide a consistent basis for managing children. Having rules to govern behavior forces discussion (and sometimes compromise) among staff on expected classroom behaviors, provides consistency for the children, and can help to depersonalize corrective adult-child interactions when rules are broken. A second reason for having stated rules is to sensitize staff to the types of desirable classroom behavior rather than focusing attention primarily on undesirable behaviors. All children can then be reinforced for following the general rules, in addition to more specific, individualized incompatible behaviors. Having the rules visible can serve to remind adults in the classroom to "notice when children are using appropriate behaviors." An important third reason for having a set of management rules is to set standards that guide the development of management programs for individual children. When staff agree that a child is persistently breaking one or more rules, it is a signal to discuss and agree upon a more structured approach to manage the child's behavior.

DEVELOPMENT AND MONITORING OF INSTRUCTIONAL PROGRAMS

All of the information necessary for implementation of a child's IEP needs to be collected and organized into a system that facilitates acquisition of the selected educational goals. Within the program, this organization is accomplished through the use of clipboards. The clipboards are hung on the classroom wall so that they are easily accessible to staff and parents for instructional and monitoring purposes. For home programs, clipboards are kept in accessible locations. Each child's clipboard contains the following information:

1. *Program plan overview:* For each curricular domain, the training objectives are briefly stated. A copy of this form is found in Table 12-3.
2. *Child information:* The parents' home and work phone numbers, who to contact in case of emergency, medical information, and behavior management information are provided. A copy of this form is found in Table 12-4.
3. *Instructional program plans:* Each training objective has at least one accompanying instructional program. Each instructional program

The Intervention Process

Name _____	Intervention Unit _____
Domain	**Training Objectives**
Gross Motor	
Fine Motor	
Communication	
Cognitive	
Social	
Self-Help	

TABLE 12-3 Program Plan Overview Form

Name _____ Birthdate _____ Interventionist _____

Parent's Name(s) _____ Home Phone _____ Work Phone _____

In case of emergency contact _____ Phone _____

Medical Information

Allergies _____ Medication _____

Positioning _____

_____

Other _____

Behavior Management

Behavior Problems   Consequences

Other Comments

TABLE 12-4 Program's Child Information Form

282

Development and Monitoring of Instructional Programs

Name Susie   Interventionist Parent   Date Started 10/1/   Date Completed
Domain Self-Care   Type of Data Trial-by-trial   Days Data Collected M T W Th
Type of Instructional Setting   ☐ Group Activity   ☐ Individual Instruction   ☒ Home Program

Long-Range Goal Spoon feeds independently with minimal spilling

Training Objective Given spoon, bowl and food, C* will spoon feed independently

Criterion Scoops food from bowl and moves to mouth with minimal spilling on 80% of the trials for 5 consecutive days

Materials Spoon, food, bowl, bib

PROGRAM STEPS
1. I† physically assists C to grasp spoon, scoop the food, bring spoon to mouth, and return spoon to bowl.
2. I physically assists C to grasp spoon, scoop food, bring food in front of mouth, and C independently inserts spoon in mouth, physical assist to return spoon to bowl.
3. I assists C until spoon is at neck level; C inserts spoon in mouth and I assists to return spoon to bowl.
4. I assists C until spoon is at chest level; C inserts spoon in mouth and I assists to return spoon to bowl.
5. C grasps spoon, I assists with scooping, C inserts spoon in mouth and I assists to return spoon to bowl.
6. C grasps spoon, I assists with scooping, and C inserts spoon in mouth and returns it to the bowl.
7. C grasps spoon, scoops food, inserts spoon in mouth, and returns spoon to bowl.

TEACHING PROCEDURES

Antecedents	Response	Consequences	Decision Rule
1–4. Given spoon and food, I will provide physical assistance for grasping and scooping.	1–4. C inserts spoon in mouth from specified level and receives assistance to return spoon to bowl.		After 3 training sessions per program-step, C's progress will be reviewed. If C's performance has not improved by 50%, the instructional program and/or consequence will be examined to determine if a change is indicated. If after 6 training sessions C's performance has not improved by 50%, a change in the instructional program is mandated.
5. I presents materials.	5. C grasps spoon; receives assistance for scooping; C inserts spoon in mouth and receives assistance for returning spoon to bowl.	*Correct:* C receives food, verbal praise. *Incorrect:* Provide assistance at previously mastered level. Repeat antecedent.	
6. I presents materials.	6. C grasps spoon; receives assistance for scooping; and C inserts spoon and returns it to bowl.		
7. I presents materials.	7. C feeds independently.		

* C = Child
† I = Interventionist

TABLE 12-5   *Program's Instructional Program Plan Form*

includes the data-collection procedures, the materials to be used, the program steps, and the teaching procedures specified in an antecedent-response-consequence format. Table 12-5 shows a completed program plan form.

4. *Summary graphs:* Graphs that summarized the data collected for individual instructional programs are included behind the instructional program plans.

5. *Domain dividers:* Tabbed dividers are used to divide the clipboard into the various curricular areas for which the child has IEP goals.

Developing Program Plans

Each quarterly training objective on a child's IEP is developed into an educational program plan and written on an Instructional Program Plan Form. As can be seen in Table 12-5, the program plan contains the following items:

- Identification information
- Date started and completed
- Domain of target intervention and interventionist
- Type of data and when to be collected
- Instructional setting
- Long-range goal
- Quarterly training objective
- Criterion
- Materials
- Program steps
- Teaching procedures specified in an A-R-C plan
- Decision rules

Figure 12-1 provides a schematic of a systematic implementation plan from long-term goals to specific program steps and the associated evaluation plan.

Data-Collection Procedures

Systematic instructional intervention should be accompanied by objective data-collection and recording procedures if the impact of the educational intervention is to be accurately assessed. Data collection for individual program steps and/or individual children can be handled with ease. However, when one attempts to assess the impact of instruction using a group format with the training activities embedded in the on-going activities, the process becomes considerably more complex. A number of strategies have been tried,

Development and Monitoring of Instructional Programs

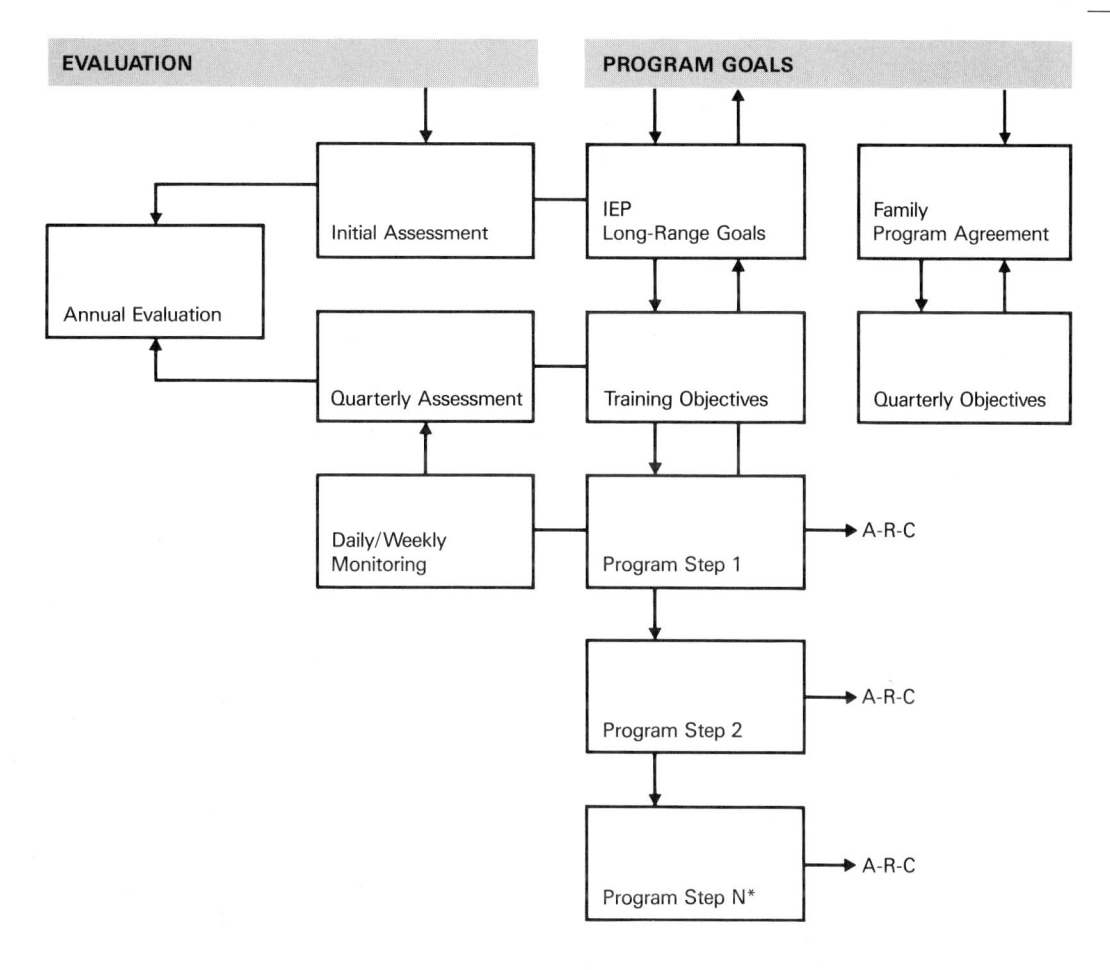

FIGURE 12-1. Systematic implementation plan from long-range goals to specific program steps and the associated evaluation plan. A = antecedent; R = response; C = consequence.

and the strategy found to be consistently most useful involves the use of data-collection grids.

The data-collection grid is a flexible format that allows the interventionist to target several diverse skills for each child during each activity group. As shown in Table 12-6, the grid format can accommodate individualization of antecedents, responses and consequences; type and frequency of data collection and dispersion of instruction; and data collection across settings and instructors. The A-R-Cs on the data grids are an abbreviated version taken from the instructional program plans. The grid is also used to collect data while running a group activity, thus enabling the acquisition of direct performance information. The grids are covered with acetate page protectors, and data are recorded directly on the acetate covering the grids.

The Intervention Process

Domain	Child 1	Child 2	Child 3	Child 4	Child 5
Expressive Language	A: Give verbal model, e.g., "paper" R: c says CV word approximation C: c receives object; adult expands child utterance CP: Repeat trial with exaggerated model	A: Ask c "What do you want?" R: c uses sign for object C: Receives object CP: Model sign for desired object; repeat trial	A: Varied context of activity group R: Uses 2+ word phrase spontaneously C: Expansion, interpretation Tally No. of spontaneous 2+ word phrases	A: Give verbal model, i.e., "Who wants paper?" R: c uses 2-word phrase C: c receives objects, verbal expansion of phrase CP: Repeat question; provide model	*
Trials	1 2 3 4 5	1 2 3 4 5	1 2 3 4 5	1 2 3 4 5	
Receptive Language	*	A: Give 2-part command R: c follows 2-part command C: Inherent in activity CP: Assist child through command	A: Present object with 1 distractor R: c picks/points to object C: Receives object CP: Point to correct object	*	A: Give verbal cue, e.g., "Where's the paint?" R: Child locates named common object in context C: c uses object CP: Point to object
Trials		1 2 3 4 5	1 2 3 4 5		1 2 3 4 5
Fine Motor	A: Present c with jar and lid with paste inside R: c uses wrist rotation to open jar C: c uses paste CP: Give minimal physical assistance, e.g., untighten lid	*	A: Present c with small objects R: Picks up object using pincer grasp C: c uses object in functional manner CP: Model grasp, repeat trial	*	*
Trials	1 2 3 4 5		1 2 3 4 5		

TABLE 12-6   Sample Data-Collection Grid Used for Monitoring Five Children's Progress During a Group Activity

For example, a common strategy is to conduct five probe trials for a specific objective during an activity group. The symbols for correct/incorrect responses are recorded over the numbers 1–5 for each child for each target objective on the grid. Other types of data (e.g., levels of assistance, frequency counts) can be recorded in a similar manner. These data are then transferred to each child's individual multiband-graphs as described in the next section. Small Post-It notes are used for the individual objective sections within the data grids. This allows changes to be made in one of a child's objectives without rewriting or copying the rest of the grid.

Summarizing Results

The plotting of data aids in making interventionists conscious of a child's performance over time. Often, interventionists can recognize trends visually

Development and Monitoring of Instructional Programs

Domain	Child 1	Child 2	Child 3	Child 4	Child 5
Gross Motor	A: Give verbal cue, e.g., "It's time for painting" R: c climbs into chair independently C: c begins activity CP: Give c physical prompt	*	*	A: Give verbal cue, e.g., "It's time for painting" R: c walks to activity using crutches C: c participates in activity CP: Give minimal physical assistance	*
Trials	1 2 3 4 5			1 2 3 4 5	
Cognitive	*	A: Give verbal cue, e.g., "It's time for our paintings to dry" R: c puts object in its usual location C: Verbal praise CP: Point to location	*	*	A: Present c with object (e.g., paintbrush) R: c uses object in functional manner C: Reinforcement inherent CP: Model functional use of object, physical prompt
Trials		1 2 3 4 5			1 2 3 4 5

*No specific data collection procedure for this child during this activity
Abbreviations: A = antecedent; R = response; C = consequence; c = child; CP = correction procedure.

TABLE 12-6   continued

from a graph, while data trends depicted on tabular or other forms are not as apparent.

Data are collected according to the specifications detailed in the child's Program Plan; however, a minimum requirement is the collection of probe data at least once a week. The data collected on each program step described on the instructional program plans are summarized daily and transferred to multiband-graph paper. (Figure 12-2 contains a sample of a summary graph.) Each single graph band was used to chart the child's progress for each selected quarterly training objective over time.

Listed here are the guidelines used when charting data on the multiband-graph paper for establishing criteria for objectives and for making data-based programming decisions.

Multiband-Graph Paper

Multiband-graph paper is designed to allow practitioners to chart a child's daily progress for an entire quarter and to obtain a visual representation of:

287

The Intervention Process

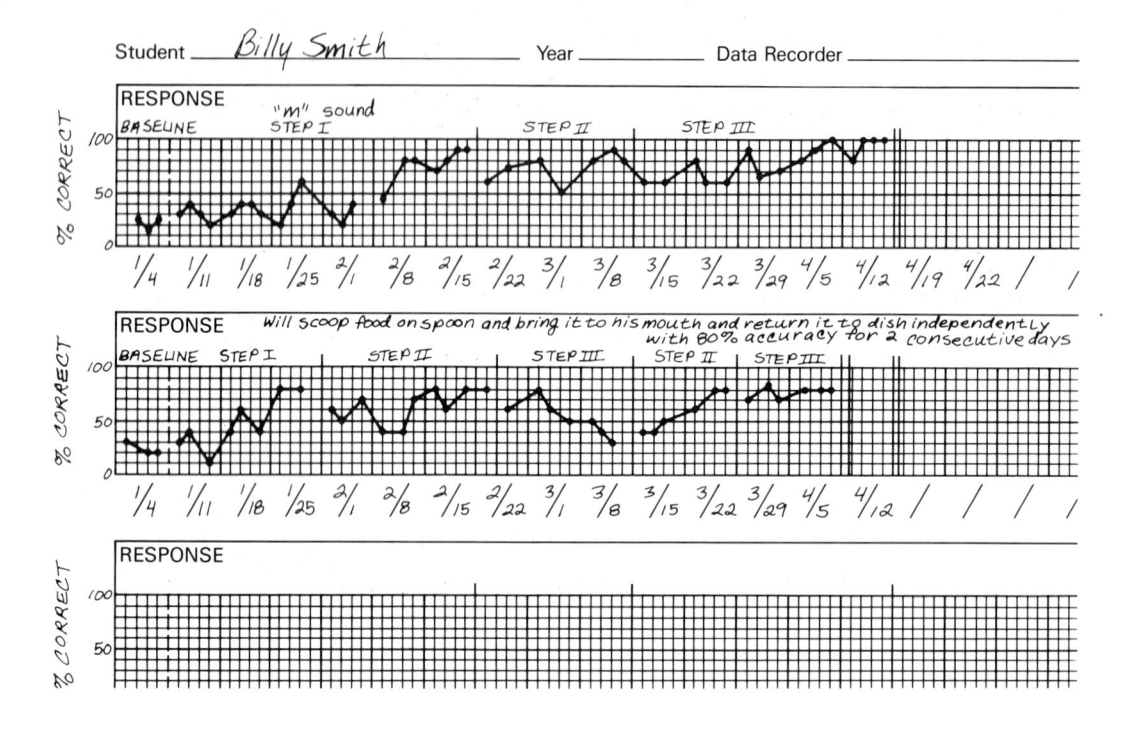

FIGURE 12-2. Sample summary graphs.

- child progress through one program with multiple steps, e.g., performance of increasingly larger portions of a backward chaining task;
- child performance on up to four separate programs, e.g., different behavior management objectives or coordinated skills;
- child performance on a single objective across different sessions, activities, instructors, consequences, etc.; or
- the performance of two to four students on a single program.

Each band is divided into 25 units, each unit representing one week of school. Two graphs cover an entire school year. A graph should be synchronized with the school year, i.e., charting of data should coincide with the first week of the fall quarter. Record the month and day for each week that the program is in effect by filling in the bar below the corresponding unit. For example, Monday, September 1, is encoded 9/1.

If a session is cancelled, no data are entered for that day, and the next data points are not connected to the previous point. On days when the session is not conducted, note the date and the reason for cancellation on the back of the graph. When several sessions (over five school days) are missed because of vacation or illness, enclose that period in dotted lines and briefly note the reason for cancellation.

If data are collected on a probe basis (e.g., M–F or T–Th), then points may be connected across calendar days: all consecutive data days are to be connected. If, however, a child is absent on a scheduled probe day, treat it as any other absence and do not connect to the previous day. If the child is absent on days when data collection is not planned, it is not necessary to record those absences.

To the left of the band (the ordinate of the graph), the horizontal lines on the grid are numbered using the appropriate response unit (e.g., 10, 20, 30 for percent correct or 1, 2, 3 for frequency counts). In the space to the left of the band that runs parallel to the vertical axis of the grid, the type of data are indicated (e.g., percent correct responses, frequency of tantrums).

In the panel labeled "Response" above each band, briefly define the specific training target. For instructional programs, responses should be referenced to program steps indicated on the Instructional Program Plan. A solid line should be drawn to separate the steps. The identity of the step should be noted on the graph as, for example, Step 1 or Step 6. Separate training objectives are charted on successive bands.

The collected data measure progress toward the IEP long-range goals and training objectives. In establishing criteria for these goals and objectives, keep in mind the level of behavior considered functional by the general public. For instance, high accuracy alone (e.g., proper use of utensils at meal time) might not be functional if fluency is still abnormally low (e.g., taking two hours to finish a meal). Also, avoid criteria that require 100 percent correct responding.

- The desired performance should occur across several days.
- If only one trial per day is measured (such as toothbrushing at school), the criterion should be more stringent (such as four or five days consecutively).
- For two to five trials per day, the criterion should be specified in terms of the average over a three-day period.
- For more than five trials per day, the criterion can "skip" a day, as in, "Four out of five consecutive days, Johnny will . . ."

Decision Rules

Since the purpose of collecting formative data is to provide information for making intervention decisions about children, "data decision rules" that facilitate such decisions are necessary. When data are collected without such rules, the use of the data will tend to be inefficient and/or inappropriate. In general, the rule is simple: if the child's progress is satisfactory, do not change the program; if it is not, change the program.

The Intervention Process

To determine whether progress is satisfactory, compare expected progress with actual progress. A prediction line of minimal acceptable performance (based on IEP objectives, the starting date, and the target date) is drawn. If a prediction cannot be made, then the minimum acceptable performance should be established. Other general guidelines for deciding whether or not to change a program include:

- Run a program five to seven days to determine its effectiveness before initiating program change.
- If performance fails to meet the prediction line for three straight days, or if performance does not improve over three days, change the program.
- If no progress is apparent from one week to the next, change the program.
- Do not change a program when correct responses are increasing and are more frequent than incorrect responses.

Many options are available for deciding to change the intervention program. These options include (1) returning to the previous program step; (2) changing antecedents (e.g., prompts and cues); (3) creating a new step in the program between the previous step and the present step; (4) changing consequences; (5) changing the setting; and (6) reconsidering the program and/or its objectives.

Many other factors may require consideration when developing decision rules. Unless the program is totally ineffective and/or the interventionist has a strong hunch about necessary changes to produce improvement, only one variable should be changed at a time. Make changes in antecedent conditions when correct responses are low, errors are high, and performance is not improving. Make changes in consequences when correct responses are relatively high and are not increasing and when errors are low. Consider slicing back in the program when correct responses are near zero or at chance level and errors are increasing. Consider creating a new mid-step when the child scores almost all correct on one program and then scores almost all incorrect on the next program step. Finally, remember that regressing to an easier step is rarely as effective as improving the instructional strategies for teaching the present step in the program.

ACTIVITY-BASED INSTRUCTION

The initial instructional technology used in early-intervention programs for handicapped preschool populations evolved from the application of operant learning principles to more deviant and generally institutionalized populations (Bricker & Carlson, 1980; 1981). To manage these populations who often lived in atypical and unreinforcing environments, it was necessary to carefully design structured approaches that relied heavily on the use of primary reinforcers. This technology was adopted by the majority of early-intervention personnel for younger handicapped children living at home.

Although such structure and approaches produced changes in the target population, the nature of the change and the generalizability of acquired responses was often unsatisfactory. Because the approach to training was rigidly structured, the responses learned were often discrete and could be elicited only under the specific training conditions. Children failed to develop generative repertoires that enhanced their adjustment and adaptability across environments. To counter this effect, interventionists have searched for alternative strategies that still incorporate the principles of operant learning but do so in a way that assists the child in developing generative repertoires that enhance adjustment and adaptability in a variety of settings and under changing conditions.

A second set of problems that occurs when employing the operant technology in a tutorial manner—that is, one-to-one instruction under carefully controlled conditions—concerns overlooking other environmental/teaching resources. A tutorial approach weighs heavily on the adult-instructor as the primary change agent and tends to obviate the natural and useful teaching that can occur through arrangement of the physical environment and the social communicative learning that may occur when children are encouraged to interact with one another. This problem becomes particularly relevant for programs that have heterogeneous groups of at-risk and handicapped infants and young children who may provide effective training models for each other.

To deal with the realities of community-based programs for at-risk and handicapped infants and young children, this program uses an activity-based instructional format. This approach teaches skills by embedding the training regimes into functional daily activities that are of interest to the participating children.

One important advantage of activity-based instruction is that the skills are taught as functional behaviors. For example, if a pincer grasp is the target skill, the child should be required during snack time to use this grasp with a raisin, apple slice, or cheese wedge or during an art activity for picking up pieces of tape. This is in opposition to seating a child at a table and conducting a series of structured trials with no apparent functional outcome (e.g., putting pegs in a board on command).

Incorporated into teaching functional skills in the child's natural environment is the notion of providing relevant antecedents and consequences within an activity. When the antecedent and consequences are relevant or part of an activity, motivational and attentional problems tend to occur less frequently.

Activity-based instruction also addresses the issue of generalization and maintenance. Teaching a particular skill is not limited to only one activity but rather can be taught by a variety of instructors across a variety of materials and settings.

Selection of Activities

Planning an activity that will incorporate and provide experience to meet many different individual goals for a group of diverse young children can be challenging. Many of the goals of activity-based instruction can be met if the activities chosen have more than one purpose. For example, crunching paper, tissue, or cellophane during an art activity also focuses on fine motor skills such as reaching and grasping, transferring, voluntarily releasing, and placing. This same activity can have a language component if the child is encouraged to gesture or vocalize for more tissue; a cognitive component, if the tissue is out of reach and the child has to retrieve it; and a social component, if the child observes another child doing similar activities and attempts to interact with a peer.

The following are additional considerations that may aid in developing interesting and motivating activities that can incorporate individual child goals. Activities are selected that

- Allow for grouping similar objectives of different children into one activity
- Allow for grouping different goals of the same child into one activity
- Are adaptable for varying ages and skill levels
- Minimize the need for adult direction and assistance
- Are child initiated, when possible, to enhance motivation

Guidelines for Implementing Activities

The program staff use the following guidelines for enhancing effective and efficient use of instructional time within the activity-based format:

1. Plan the classroom activities in advance to allow for the incorporation of as many individual training objectives as possible.
2. Physically arrange the group in such a way that (a) physical assistance can be provided when necessary; (b) children can interact not only with the adults but with one another; (c) potentially disruptive children are positioned for optimal management; and (d) instructional and data-collection materials are easily accessible without being obtrusive.
3. Involve the children in antecedent and consequent events. Involvement in the delivery of antecedent events may be as simple as the interventionist handing an object to one child who in turn hands it to another child. By including peers in the antecedent-response-consequence (A-R-C) paradigm, children may learn to respond to different people who

present antecedents for their behavior, thus facilitating generalization across persons. Just as involving children in the delivery of antecedent events provides opportunities for peer interaction, so does allowing students to deliver consequent events to each other.

4. Follow established behavior-management procedures. For example, reinforce appropriate behavior and attending. Make sure to distribute attention to all children.
5. Have back-up activities planned. Be sensitive to when children have lost interest and move on to another activity.

Classroom Activity Plan

Once an activity is selected for an activity group, it is described on a group activity plan. This form provides a systematic means for recording the following information:

1. Description of the group activity
2. Materials needed
3. General objectives of the activity
4. Examples of ways to present the activity, expected child responses, and reinforcement and error-correction procedures (A-R-C format)

An example of a Classroom Activity Plan Form is found in Table 12-7. Activity plans are posted prior to their implementation and for review by classroom staff and parents.

Since at-risk and handicapped populations tend to be heterogeneous, it is sometimes necessary to supplement the activity-based approach with individual instruction. Consideration for supplementing children's programs with additional individual training is undertaken when (1) children are not making satisfactory progress and the antecedents and consequences have been systematically modified or (2) children are severely delayed in one or more areas and clearly need more structure and practice to meet their training objectives.

TRANSITION TO OTHER PROGRAMS

One of the priorities at the end of every school year is the transition of children into the next educational service setting. Children often exit into public school kindergartens or special education settings. Because of the range of options available to parents under different administrative structures, the program has a policy of providing parents with information about other possible placements available to their child within the financial and time resources available to the family.

The Intervention Process

DESCRIPTION OF ACTIVITY: Cornmeal Table—Children have cookie trays of cornmeal, cups, spoons, water (to spray, pour, shake), food colors (and anything else you like) to mix and manipulate (and make a mess).
MATERIALS: cornmeal, bowls, cookie sheets, spoons, cups, spray bottle, shaker-top bottle, food colors

Activity Objectives:

	Children's Level of Functioning		
Fine Motor	Pouring (w/ assist), shaking food color	Pouring (w/ assist) if needed), shaking food color	Independent pouring, pincer squeeze for food color
Gross Motor	N/A	N/A	N/A
Self-Care	Cleaning self, hands (w/ assist); allowing paint shirt to be put on	Cleaning self, hands; helping to put paint shirt on (arm out)	Cleaning self, hands; independently putting on paint shirt
Cognitive	Visual & auditory attention, manipulation of objects, functional & creative use	Visual & auditory attention, imitation of motor movements, physical manipulation of objects	Visual & auditory attention, imitation of motor sequences, physical manipulation of objects
Communication	Following simple commands, request with reach or vocalization, auditory attention	Following multiple commands, requesting, labeling, auditory attention	Following multiple commands, requesting, labeling, auditory attention
Social	Playing proximally to peers, watching peers	Sharing materials with prompt, interacting with adults and peers	Sharing materials with prompt, interacting with adults and peers

ARC Procedures:

	Children's Level of Functioning		
Antecedent (Ways to Present Activity)	Model pouring (other actions) and verbal instructions	Model (as above), give 1- to 2-step commands	Model (as above), multiple commands, encourage sharing, interactions
Response (What Child Does)	Requests with reach or vocalization, interacts with materials	Imitates, interacts with materials, requests with word approximation, follows commands	Imitates, interacts with materials and peers, requests with labels, follows commands
Consequence	Give materials, label action/object	Social, praise, give objects	Social, praise, give objects
Error Correction	Verbal prompt w/or assist	Verbal prompt w/or assist	Verbal prompt w/or assist

TABLE 12-7 *Program's Classroom Activity Plan Form*

Steps in Transition Process

The staff coordinate with three different agencies/individuals in implementing the transition process: (1) the child's parent(s), (2) the school district in which the child resides, and (3) the child's next educational service setting if it has been identified. A list of the steps to be completed in coordinating the transition with these three groups has been outlined in Table 12-8. The staff monitors progress on completing the transition process with the parent.

Inservices are held for parents in the spring to acquaint them with the range of service options available for their children. The process for selecting an educational placement and getting their children enrolled is also discussed.

Transition to Other Programs

Step	Action
1	Provide parents with information about service delivery options.
2	Assist parents in selecting preferred placement; if child's eligibility is questionable, identify alternative placements.
3	If appropriate, identify the school district in which the child is eligible for a school program.
4	Parents visit possible placement sites.
5	Staff identifies skills child is expected to have upon entry into future placement.
6	Provide parents information on enrollment process.
7	Verify if intake/enrollment completed, or if parents have not made decision or have not completed enrollment process, send letter summarizing process to this point, what remains to be done.
8	Discuss with parents notification of school district or next placement and their role in transition, final FPA meeting.
9	Obtain signed consent to exchange confidential information with school district or next placement unless parents object.
10	Invite personnel from future placement to visit program to observe child and to participate in May/June IEP-FPA meeting.
11	Send copy of child's file to new placement at end of year.
12	Contact personnel to ascertain status of child's progress in new program.

TABLE 12-8   Steps in Transition Process

End-of-the-Year IEP Meeting

Part of the process of transitioning a child to the next educational setting is to invite representatives from that next placement to the IEP-FPA meeting held at the end of the year. These meetings have two major purposes: (1) to review the child's progress for the year and to determine current functioning level, and (2) to finalize or to review plans for the child for the summer and/or for the following school year. During this meeting, the following topics are addressed:

1. Brief overview of meeting agenda
2. Specification of child's current functioning level
3. Review of year-end report, including child's and family's progress made on IEP-FPA goals
4. Review of program placement plans for next year: School district and/or next placement representative answer parents' questions, and/or ask staff or parents questions about child
5. Discussion of summer plans for child and recommendations for future placement

SUMMARY

The heart of the intervention process is the development and implementation of the IEP for the child and the FPA for families. This chapter has been concerned with describing a structure that permits efficient implementation of developed IEPs and FPAs.

Procedures for organizing and scheduling program activities and personnel were presented. The procedures and forms used to develop individual program plans and activity plans were discussed in detail. The intent is not to encourage wholesale adoption of these procedures by other program personnel. Rather, the purpose is to provide a description of a model that has worked with the intent that others select those elements that are relevant and feasible for their setting, philosophy, staff, and children or families.

References

Bricker, D., Bruder, M., & Bailey, E. (1982). Developmental integration of preschool children. *Analysis and Intervention in Developmental Disabilities, 2,* 207–222.

Bricker, D., & Carlson, L. (1980). An intervention approach for communicatively handicapped infants and young children. In D. Bricker (Ed.), *Language resource book.* New York: Jossey-Bass.

Bricker, D., & Carlson, L. (1981). Issues in early language intervention. In R. Schiefelbusch & D. Bricker (Eds.), *Early language: Acquisition and intervention.* Baltimore, MD: University Park Press.

Bricker, D., & Sandall, S. (1979). The integration of handicapped and nonhandicapped preschoolers: Why and how to do it. *Education Unlimited, 1,* 25–29.

Quiltich, H., Christopherson, E., & Risley, T. (1977). The evaluation of children's play materials. *Journal of Applied Behavior Analysis, 10,* 501–502.

CHAPTER

13

CURRICULAR APPROACHES AND CONTENT

The curricular content chosen for a program is of importance to the children, families, and staff. Selection of an appropriate curricular approach requires time and effort. Knowledge of the major differences to be found in various approaches seems essential to adopting curricular materials that are consonant with program goals and individual child objectives. The necessity for meshing a program's rationale, content, instructional strategies, and assessment and evaluation procedures has already been discussed in detail in Chapter 9.

Curriculum has been defined as programmatic goals or targets for instruction, as the content of education, or as a planned arrangement of learning experiences (Mori & Neisworth, 1983). Each of these definitions makes clear that curriculum should be thought of as synonymous with program content. Although many different curricular approaches are available, each appears to share some important elements: planned activities, systematic presentation sequence, specified educational objectives, and a guiding orientation or theoretical perspective.

As already indicated, formal curricula are composed of planned activities to be conducted by an interventionist or arranged through environmental engineering. The activities that constitute a curriculum are generally sequenced in some systematic fashion from simple to increasingly more complex. Most curricula contain a number of areas or domains in which activities are hierarchically sequenced within each domain. Most curricular activities have been designed to assist a child in attaining a specific objective or generalized goal. Finally, the content and the nature of the presentation in the curriculum generally reflects the underlying orientation or theoretical persuasion of the curricular approach.

CURRICULAR ISSUES

The historical roots of early-intervention programs for handicapped children lie in programs designed for older children and adults. These early programs employed principles derived from the experimental analysis of behavior. Much of the early work was focused on devising educational programs for seriously handicapped children residing in institutional settings (Bricker & Bricker, 1975).

Residential populations often required rigorous application of behavior modification techniques in order to gain control over the child's behavior before any attempt could be made to introduce an educational program for the acquisition of new skills. The work and technology derived from focusing on such deviant populations was then transferred to programs for children who were younger and were living at home (Bricker & Carlson, 1981). The application of the operant technology was found effective—that is, we were able to control the children's behavior and assist them in acquiring a variety of skills.

Although the importance of this work should not be underestimated, researchers with more cognitive orientations began wondering about the utility and generalizability of the skills being taught to children under such rigorously controlled and structured regimes. These regimes minimized flexibility and adaptability because children were reinforced for careful adherence to the adult-imposed structure. Variations from specified routines were openly discouraged. Also, the technology affected the curricular content. Specific responses were targeted using task analytic approaches. Little attention was given to how content might overlap across domains or how the child might be assisted in developing generative repertoires that would lead to more complex problem-solving abilities and greater independent functioning. The problem was, of course, not in the behavioral technology but rather the manner in which interventionists applied it.

In large measure, Piaget, his American interpreters, and some psycholinguists (see, e.g., the volume edited by Schiefelbusch & Lloyd, 1974) provided the impetus for early interventionists to reconsider the impact of their intervention efforts with at-risk and handicapped infants and children. These theorists and investigators argued that rather than using individual skill acquisition, the educational enterprise might be aided by adopting a theoretical framework that would help shape the nature and content of early-intervention curricular efforts. The initial efforts in undertaking such a process were perhaps predictable because many interventionists, as behavioral engineers, operationalized early sensorimotor and communicative behavior into a set of independent skills to be acquired response by response under structured conditions. Again, the child was viewed as a passive receptacle who contributed little to the training enterprise, even though Piaget (1970) had argued, as had Dewey, for the child's active involvement in discovering the physical and social environment.

Contemporary views held by interventionists have further moderated or changed curricular approaches. Unfortunately, however, recently proposed changes are often formulated as a dichotomy that pits the behaviorist against the developmentalist (see, e.g., Guess, Sailor, & Baer, 1977). This dichotomy is unfortunate and does not accurately represent the nature of the disagreement between various curricular approaches (Brinker & Bricker, 1980). The polarization of behavioral and developmental positions has not assisted in clarifying issues.

What, then, are the differences between programs that follow carefully specified arrangements of specific antecedents-responses-consequences and programs that rely more on freely occurring events and arrangements of the environment to provide the necessary antecedents and consequences for effective instruction? The former programs usually can be identified by their carefully structured lesson plan format in which the interventionist's behavior as well as the child's response is specified. Often, it is assumed that programs that do not follow carefully specified sequences are less objective and precise. This, of course, is not necessarily accurate. The objectivity and precision of an instructional program are determined by its implementation. In addition, many assume that less direct instructional approaches do not employ behavioral teaching principles. Again, this is not necessarily accurate. All intervention programs use behavioral technology; it is the manner and precision of implementation that are at issue. For a more thorough discussion of this topic, see Brinker and Bricker, 1980; Brinker, 1985; and Chapter 14 of this book.

Controversy about the implementation of behavioral technology touches several areas that affect curricular approaches, such as child versus adult-imposed control, delivery of consequences, generalization procedures, instructional content, and functionality of educational targets. These differences are discussed in the following sections.

CHILD VERSUS ADULT CONTROL

In curricular approaches in which the daily lesson plans are predetermined, the child has little opportunity to affect the content of the daily lesson plans. Other approaches may specify the goals and objectives for the child but leave the implementation to be decided, in part, by events occurring in the environment and the interests of the child. For example, a training goal might be to assist the child in using more agent-action-object phrases rather than specific drill on a set number of predetermined phrases. The interventionist then uses opportunities that arise during the day to work on this objective. Looking at a book chosen by the child might provide the parent or interventionist many opportunities to teach agent-action-object sequences.

Considerable work is underway in this area. For example, a recently edited volume describes a number of useful approaches for designing functional communication program (Warren & Rogers-Warren, 1985). Using these approaches requires careful attention to the daily activities to ensure that each child is receiving adequate training on selected objectives. Often, it is difficult to monitor the training given to each objective, and successful employment of such a system requires systematic collection of data on the child's progress toward specific objectives. Programs that employ a specific lesson plan format can use other times of the day to allow the child to select activities or enhance generalization of specific responses, as done in the Early Education Project (Kysela, Hillyard, McDonald, & Ahlsten-Taylor, 1981). The reverse is also true because programs that generally do not employ specific lessons can use planned instruction when and if desirable. Unfortunately, it seems that program staff tend to adopt one curricula approach to the exclusion of others.

INHERENT VERSUS EXTERNAL CONSEQUENCES

Another difference found in curricular approaches is in the administration of consequences. Some programs focus on reinforcement of the desired response using some form of obvious feedback. Often, this feedback is in the form of verbal comments such as "good boy," "that's right," "you did that well," and so on.

If tasks are primarily selected by the adult, the children's motivation may be a consistent problem, and, therefore, artificial contingencies may be needed. In programs in which the child has more freedom to determine the activities in which the training exercises are embedded, reinforcement is often inherent in the activity (Mahoney & Weller, 1980). For example, searching for a desired toy promotes the concept of object permanence, and finding the toy may provide the reinforcement and subsequent motivation for further searches. It is probably not necessary or useful to tell the child "good looking" when the child discovers the toy. Pouring juice into a cup provides practice in wrist rotation and self-help skills, and getting to drink the juice may be reward enough to continue to practice the behavior. Conversely, turning uninteresting objects to practice wrist rotation may require the delivery of some form of verbal praise to keep the child engaged in the training activity. All of us engage in activities and responses that are maintained through artificial contingencies, but much of our behavior is determined by events integrally linked to the activity. If movement toward independence is a major objective, might some curricular approaches develop an overreliance on artificial or nonfunctional consequences?

GENERATIVE REPERTOIRES

Another dimension along which curricula differ is their approach to generalization. Some approaches place an emphasis first on establishing an antecedent-response relationship that is specific and discrete. Once this single-cue-single-response association is developed, the next step becomes generalization of the response to other appropriate exemplars of the class or antecedent events. In such approaches, establishing control over the child's behavior may inadvertently reduce the child's chance for generalization or development of a generative problem-solving strategy. By use of rigid programming, sources of unsystematic variation are reduced, and the child acquires a response as predetermined. Such procedures eliminate or greatly reduce the infusion of variability in the acquisition of new skills and concepts that might significantly enhance generalization of the action or concept. Of course, some individuals are so impaired that the acquisition of simple contingencies is a reasonable expectation; however, for most handicapped children, the future is far more optimistic, and thus the need to rethink approaches to assist children in acquiring concepts and responses that lead to dynamic and generative repertoires.

PREACADEMIC VERSUS SOCIAL-COMMUNICATION EMPHASIS

Recently, some significant changes in the content focus of early-intervention curricula have occurred; historically, the emphasis has been on acquiring self-help, motor, and "academic" skills (Kirk & Johnson, 1951). The presumption is that growth in the more academic areas would be the most useful for the child in successive placements. An examination of both curricular and measurement tools used by programs suggests the importance placed on preacademic skills (see, e.g., *Inventory of Early Development* by Brigance, 1978). Indeed, the instructional format followed by many programs emphasizes an academic focus. That is, little children are required to sit in small groups around tables and work on selected school-like activities. Activities such as "free play" are viewed as fillers between training activities rather than as educational opportunities.

In spite of Piaget's declarations on the importance of play for the young child, it has taken some relatively recent research to convince many early interventionists of the importance of play for children (Chance, 1979). A growing body of work suggests that play is the work of little children and that during periods of play, children acquire a number of important behaviors, such as appropriate role playing, interactional skills, and how to successfully engage the physical environment. It seems that play allows the young child the freedom to explore, vary, and rearrange without undue restriction or direction from the social environment.

Another area of curricular neglect has been social-communicative or pragmatic development. As we have argued elsewhere (Bricker & Carlson, 1981; Bricker & Schiefelbusch, 1984), early social-communicative exchanges between children and their social environment may serve as an important foundation for the conceptual and more advanced pragmatic structure of later language usage. The importance of acquiring nonacademic, social, and communicative skills to be successful both in school and in later life is often underestimated. As MacMillan (1977) and Zigler (1984) report, the reasons that retarded populations fail to adjust to social and vocational environments are often noncognitive factors, such as social skills and personality variables.

FUNCTIONAL VERSUS NONFUNCTIONAL TRAINING

The final curricular issue to be discussed is the usefulness, or functionality, of selected training objectives for the at-risk or handicapped child. It is unclear whether early interventionists have consciously or unconsciously avoided the issue of the functionality of teaching targets. For whatever reason, ignoring the usefulness of training objectives should no longer be tolerated. The usefulness of learned responses for the child underlies other issues of child versus adult-imposed activities, motivation, generalization, and content. If the responses selected for teaching are functional for the child—that is, functional in that they lead to greater independence and adaptability—then acquiring such responses may be largely child directed and reinforcing. Children appear to strive to master behavior and information that offers means for greater control over their environment.

The functionality of responses should be a major criterion in determining the content of the intervention program. For example, teaching the child to use a pincer grasp can be done in a variety of activities. Often, interventionists appear to choose having the child pick up small pegs and place them in containers. This might be the activity of choice if, for some reason, this response/activity is functional for the child. On the other hand, practicing the pincer grasp for picking up cereal, raisins, or small beads for stringing or for turning on light switches, and so on, may be more functional for the child because such responses produce a practical and desirable outcome that more likely enhances the child's independence and adaptability.

One further point needs to be made about curricular approaches. One senses that many interventionists feel a program cannot be valid *if* the children enjoy themselves. Rather, going to "school" should be primarily hard work and fun activities sprinkled in only occasionally throughout the day. The older the children, the more prevalent this attitude. The joy of exploration, invention, and innovation is largely eliminated from the curriculum, and children are required to engage in predetermined activities that may or may not be of interest to them. How unfortunate for young children that highly controlling programs are seen by many as programs of excellence and that those programs that permit flexibility, choice, and even some disorganization are harshly criticized. Such judgments require the careful examination of program objectives. What are or should be the outcomes for children who participate in early-intervention programs? Is the acquisition of specific skills paramount to all else? As Guess and Siegel-Causey (1985) ask: Should not children have the right of choice?

We are not arguing for approaches that have no structure or that permit children free rein. Rather, we are suggesting that program personnel find mechanisms that allow a balance between requirements and choice. It is possible to design a curriculum that capitalizes on the children's motivation. The knowledgeable interventionists can often allow a child to set the pace and the direction and find ways to weave the child's selected educational targets into the activities. Is it not possible to assist children in enhancing their conceptual and behavioral repertoires and still permit them to enjoy the process?

THE PRESENT APPROACH

Our experience as well as that of others (see, e.g., Filler, Robinson, Smith, Vincent-Smith, Bricker, & Bricker, 1975) dictates the adoption of a developmental framework that focuses on building generative response classes that lead to independent functioning and adaptable problem-solving abilities.

> Developmental theory leads to the position that the rules by which actions and entities are organized in infancy are more useful keys to development than the specific actions and entities observed. (Brinker & Lewis, 1982, p. 37)

The curricular approach used in this program is based on developmental theory and suggests that:

1. Early developmental processes are so intimately related as to render them often inseparable for educational or training purposes;
2. The child and the environment are engaged in ongoing reciprocal activities that continually influence intervention efforts;
3. Behavior changes from simple to complex forms following general but consistent guidelines that provide a set of behavioral targets for intervention; and
4. Disequilibrium produced by changing environmental demands is necessary for building new adaptive responses.

The selection of content for the curriculum is based on multiple considerations, including developmental theory, research, and behavioral task analyses. The approach for content selection is developmental because theorists such as Piaget were used to establish the overall domains of behavior to be included. The developmental model was also used to establish, in a general sense, a hierarchy of relatively predictable steps (e.g., most children learn to sit up, creep, scoot, or crawl before acquiring mobility in an upright position). However, there is divergence from many developmental approaches because there is no requirement that all children must necessarily acquire the same specific skills (even at the molar level) to become adaptive adults (e.g., a deaf child may adequately communicate using signs rather than speech). In addition, there are special skills or behaviors that are essential for handicapped children to acquire but do not necessarily appear in the repertoires of normally developing youngsters. This requires that some nondevelopmental items be included and that all curricular content be adaptable.

In addition to determining the general demarcation of domains and establishment of general hierarchies, developmental theory is instrumental in the creation of long-range goals for the cognitive and communication domains that compose the curricular materials for this project. In other domains, such as gross motor, fine motor, and self-help, task analytic procedures were employed with attention to general hierarchical sequences in which component skills are typically acquired. Finally, the social domain content was derived from a synthesis of theory appearing in the literature. No single theory or approach was found completely satisfactory, and, consequently, a synthesis was necessary.

Content generated by developmental theorists, taken in tandem with our collective knowledge of young handicapped children, led to the selection of six content domains for inclusion in the curriculum. These domains are (1) fine motor, (2) gross motor, (3) cognitive, (4) self-care, (5) social, and (6) communication. Once a domain was selected, the following activities were undertaken: (1) determining the parameters of that domain; (2) organizing the domain into systematic, logical groups of hierarchical behaviors called *strands;* (3) generating long-range goals; (4) developing training objectives; (5) developing a set of program steps; and (6) suggesting some possible "adaptations" for training objectives for children who would be unable to execute the response in the typical or expected manner.

Within domains, different subgroups of behavior or content areas were specified. These groups of behaviors are referred to as strands and are composed of behaviors thought to be functionally uniform or conceptually related behaviors. This means that either the essential function or the form of the behaviors is the same throughout the strand. However, the individual long-range goals may include different levels of development of that essential function or behavior.

Each strand is composed of several long-range goals arranged in a hierarchical or developmental sequence. Figure 13-1 presents each domain, its associated strands and long-range goals (LRG). The developmental hierarchies of strands are composed of a sequence of long-range goals, beginning with the most primitive or simplest response and progressing in stages to the most difficult response. Each LRG has a set of associated training objectives (TO), which are hierarchically arranged from simple to more difficult. The TOs, in turn, have a set of programming steps that suggest training strategies and activities for assisting the child in acquiring

The Present Approach

Domains	Strands	Long Range Goals
Fine Motor	Reach, grasp, and release	1. Reaches across midline to obtain an object with the left and the right hands. 2. Brings two objects together at or near midline. 3. Activates levers with the right hand and the left hand using the tip of the first finger and thumb. 4. Grasps a hand-sized object with either hand using ends of thumb, index, and 2nd fingers. 5. Places and releases an object balanced on top of another object with one hand.
	Functional use of fine motor skills	1. Rotates wrist on horizontal plane with the left hand and the right hand. 2. Assembles or manipulates toys or games that require putting pieces together. 3. Pushes buttons with an extended finger.
Gross Motor	Movement and locomotion in supine/prone position	1. Creeps forward using alternating arm and leg movements. 2. Rolls by turning segmentally from stomach to back and from back to stomach. 3. Turns head, moves arms and kicks legs independently of each other.
	Balance in sitting	1. Independently assumes sitting position on floor. 2. Independently climbs into and out of child-sized chair.
	Balance and mobility in standing/walking	1. Walks avoiding obstacles. 2. Stoops and recovers without support. 3. Walks up and down stairs independently.
	Coordinated action in movement	1. Jumps forward with both feet together. 2. Pedals and steers tricycle. 3. Runs avoiding obstacles. 4. Catches ball or other similar object with two hands.
Cognitive	Sensory stimuli	1. Orients to tactile, visual, and auditory events.
	Object permanence	1. Visually follows object/person to point of disappearance. 2. Searches for object/person which is no longer visually apparent.
	Causality	1. Correctly manipulates simple toy. 2. Correctly activates mechanical toy to produce effects which are not directly apparent. 3. Reproduces part of interactive game/action in order to continue game/action
	Imitation	1. Imitates words not currently present in vocabulary. 2. Imitates motor actions that child cannot see herself/himself doing and are not currently in use.
	Problem solving	1. Uses a variety of objects to obtain desired object. 2. Transports more than two objects. 3. Uses a variety of strategies to solve a range of common problems. 4. Navigates objects around barriers. 5. Arranges objects in horizontal and vertical order—and into containers.
	Preacademic skills	1. Demonstrates functional use of one-to-one correspondence. 2. Groups/classifies objects according to broad-based category.
	Interaction with objects	1. Uses imaginary objects in play.

Curricular Approaches and Content

Domains	Strands	Long Range Goals
Self-Care	Feeding	1. Uses tongue and lips to take in and swallow solids and liquids. 2. Uses jaw and teeth or gums to bite through and chew hard, chewy foods. 3. Independently finger feeds self large pieces of hard and soft food. 4. Independently uses a cup/glass for drinking. 5. Independently uses fork and spoon when self-feeding. 6. Transfers food and liquid from one container to another.
	Personal hygiene	1. Completes toileting routine independently. 2. Independently washes and dries face. 3. Completes tooth-brushing routine.
	Dressing and undressing	1. Independently dresses and undresses self. 2. Independently unfastens garment. 3. Independently fastens garment.
Social	Interaction with adults	1. Initiates reciprocal interaction with *familiar* adults. 2. Initiates affection with familiar adults. 3. Responds appropriately to negative affect from familiar adults. 4. Initiates communication with familiar adults.
	Anticipation of routine events	1. Initiates behaviors associated with routine events. 2. Responds to changes in normal routines.
	Interaction with peers	1. Plays in group of two or three children. 2. Initiates reciprocal play with peers. 3. Initiates communication with peers.
Communication	Social communicative interactions	1. Attends to or turns to speech while person is within three feet of the child. 2. Follows gaze of another person to establish joint attention. 3. Engages in reciprocal vocal exchanges with others. 4. Uses vocal and gestural communicative signals to gain person's attention and refer to objects.
	Comprehension of words and sentences	1. Upon request locates named common objects, events, or persons in pictures. 2. Follows two-step directions *without* contextual cues.
	Production of signals, words, and sentences	1. Uses consistent word approximations. 2. Uses a vocabulary of 60 words. 3. Uses 10 different two-word utterances conveying the meaning of agent-action, action-object, and agent-object. 4. Uses 3 different relational words with 5 or more object labels. 5. Uses three-word utterances.

FIGURE 13-1. Curricular domains with associated strands and long-range go

the TO. Definitions and examples of the curricular content presented in Figure 13-1 are shown in Figure 13-2.

Developing curricular activities using the format offered in Figure 13-2 permits the interventionist to see the hierarchical development from program steps to the LRG. Having such an organization system permits training to move systematically to increasingly more difficult concepts or skills in a cohesive and coordinated manner. In addition, this format is directly related to the IEP developed for each child.

Generally, the educational objectives within a strand are considered to be a progression from simple to complex, or from an early to an advanced stage of learning. However, targets within certain strands are equivalent rather than hierarchical.

One essential feature pervades the curricular content shown in Figure 13-1. An attempt has been made to formulate the LRGs and training objectives (TOs) in the form of conceptual or response classes rather than as singular, specific responses. That is, the form of the LRG and the TO is generic rather than specific. This generic formulation is based on the belief that most essential behaviors can and should be generalized conceptual or response classes that are both elicited by and performed across a variety of settings and conditions. For example, the demonstration of means-ends behavior should occur whenever the child is faced with a problem that necessitates the use of a person or object as a tool to obtain a desired end, such as pulling a napkin to obtain a cookie, tugging on a string attached to a desired toy, turning a faucet to obtain water, or vocalizing and pointing for the adult to retrieve a dropped toy. Although the infant's response differs, the effect is the same—the use of some tool (broadly defined) to obtain a desired end. The specific form is important only as an index of the infant's general problem-solving scheme as shown in the diagram.

Curricular Format	General Description	Example
Domain	Behavioral Area	Gross Motor
Strand	Group of related behaviors within an area	Balance in sitting
Long Range Goal	Generic Educational Goal	Independently assumes sitting position on floor
Training Objective	Specific Educational Objective	Assumes a hands-and-knees position from sitting using rotation
Program Step	Specific Training Activity	Assumes a hands-and-knees position from sitting using rotation when given physical prompt while playing a game

FIGURE 13-2. *Curricular format with a description of each level and an example.*

Antecedent	Response	Effect
Desired ends not directly obtainable	Pull Tug Turn Vocalize	Achieve desired end

In terms of conceptual classes, a similar situation exists for the infant or child in the sense that generally the desired outcome is the appropriate response to the indicated salient feature across stimuli rather than the establishment of one-to-one correspondences. For example, to have a functional concept, children must identify a wide array of phenomena as cars. The child must be able to extract the salient features of "carness" in order to produce and understand the word appropriately under a seemingly infinite set of changing conditions. The extraction of the essential features builds for the infant a conceptual class as indicated in the diagram.

Antecedent	Response	Effect
Picture of a car Red toy car Real car Green toy car	Car	Accurate communication

The concern has been to develop assessment targets that are formulated from the perspective of response and conceptual classes; therefore, a TO that is focusing on prehension is written as:

The child places and releases an object in a controlled fashion:

1. onto a flat surface
2. into a container
3. balanced on top of another object

This form is used rather than "The child puts pegs into the peg board" or "Builds a tower of 2 cubes."

The form of the curricular items should allow for maximum flexibility to take advantage of environmental variability and motivational parameters. In addition, the generic formulation of the LRGs and TOs as response classes lends itself to the subsequent development of essential programming targets with specific goals, for example, the pincer grasp, not the placement of pegs into a board.

CRITICAL BEHAVIORS AND CRITICAL FUNCTIONS

Variations in the presentation format and the expected child response are not often addressed in curricular materials. A standard presentation format is appropriate for a nonhandicapped population but clearly presents major problems when dealing with a handicapped population. Generally, the more severely impaired the population, the more difficulty is encountered with a standardized presentation. Thus, the introduction of the concepts of critical behaviors and critical functions is appropriate. Essentially, a critical behavior is one that is important because either (1) it is used to accomplish many skills (e.g., hands to midline) or (2) it is a necessary component in building more complex skills (e.g., balancing the trunk). The nature of critical behaviors renders them nonmodifiable or nonadaptable. In general, the fine and gross motor domains are composed of critical behaviors.

The second category of LRGs and TOs refers to skills that are defined in terms of what function is accomplished rather than in terms of specific behaviors and, therefore, can be modified or adapted. For example, locomotion is a critical function, since it may be accomplished using a variety of behaviors (e.g., walking, crawling, use of wheelchair). The use of symbols to request an object is another example of a critical function, since the response may be verbal, manual, or graphic. With the critical function, the focus is on determining whether the child has *any* means of demonstrating the targeted objective, regardless of how it is done. The Cognitive, Communication, and Social Domains are comprised of critical functions. The distinction between critical responses and critical functions becomes important because there can be no modification in procedures when testing for critical behaviors, but wide latitude exists when testing for critical functions. Modifications or adaptations in assessment procedures are acceptable when testing for critical functions, but not for critical behaviors.

Critical behaviors are by definition those responses essential to the completion of LRGs or TOs and, therefore, are not subject to adaptations. For example, the princer grasp is a critical behavior for obvious reasons and cannot be adapted; however, moving objects from place to place (e.g., cracker from the plate to one's mouth) is a critical function, and any number of strategies could be appropriately used. In an instance in which a child with cerebral palsy is unable to execute the pincer grasp, he or she would receive no training on that training target; however, the child would be trained to move objects from place to place (e.g., with the mouth or feet).

ADAPTATIONS

A major point of departure between the curricular approach described here and other approaches is the definition of LRGs and TOs as critical functions and the associated concept of adaptation. Underlying the concept of critical functions is the attendant notion of adaptations, in the sense that an effect (function) can be obtained through any number of strategies. The adaptations of procedures that are made for an individual child should be a reflection of his or her particular handicapping conditions. While this may appear to lead to an unwieldy number of potential adaptations, the number is most likely limited.

Adaptations are changes in the curricular material to accommodate a child's particular handicapping condition. Adaptations are not intended to change the difficulty of the target being taught. Functional equivalence, however, may not always be the same as developmental equivalence or equivalence in task difficulty. If the child must receive information through an alternative rather than the preferred sensory modality or use an alternative response system, the problem posed to him or her may be functionally more demanding or difficult in its adapted form.

There are three general classes of possible adaptations. First, there can be changes in the *stimulus presentation* for children whose handicapping condition interferes with the reception of the standard target's directions or cues. An example of such adaptation is the presentation of an object-permanence task to a blind child. The stimulus presentation for this child may involve the use of auditory and tactile cues in place of visual ones. This is also an instance in which the adaptation maintains functional equivalence (success is still defined in terms of retrieval of a perceptually absent object) but in which the tasks are not developmentally equivalent.

A second class of adaptations involves variation in the *acceptable response* for children whose handicapping condition interferes with production of the preferred response. An example of a situation that requires this kind of adaptation occurs in a child whose handicap includes oral-motor movement. The child's handicap precludes ordinary speech production, so manual signing may become an acceptable response.

The third kind of adaptation is simply a *combination* of the two previous classes. Both stimulus presentation and acceptable response must be modified because the child's handicap or handicaps interfere with reception and production. An example of a situation requiring this dual adaptation occurs with a deaf child who must be presented linguistic information visually (e.g., with signs) and may only be able to respond manually. This third class of adaptation is in many cases the most difficult to make, since neither stimulus presentation nor response occur in the standard format.

SUMMARY

The curricular approach described in this chapter is comprehensive in that instructional targets and activities are available across six essential domains of behavior. The format is organized to link directly with the assessment/evaluation activities and IEP development for participating children. To assist the staff in developing a cohesive and organized intervention plan, the curricular format moves systematically from specific training content, called program steps, to increasingly more generic response classes, called LRGs. In addition, each LRG has an associated set of TOs organized from simple to complex. The content and its systematic arrangement helps ensure that

Summary

PURCHASING INFORMATION		INTENDED USE	
Curriculum/Author(s)	Publisher/Address	Type/Purpose	Audience/Population
Brigance Diagnostic Inventory of Early Development *Brigance, A.*	Curriculum Associates 5 Esquire Road North Billerica, MA 01862	Includes 98 skill sequences in the following areas: psychomotor, self-help, speech and language, general knowledge and comprehension, and early academic skills. May be used as an assessment instrument, an instructional guide, a record-keeping tracking system, a resource for training professionals and parents in child growth and development.	Designed to be used by professionals and paraprofessionals working with infants and children who have not reached the developmental age of 7 years.
High/Scope Cognitively Oriented Curriculum *Weikart, D., Rogers, L., Adcock, C., & McClelland, D.*	High/Scope Educational Research Foundation 600 N. River Street Ypsilanti, MI 48197	Organized framework of defined key experiences within the areas of cognitive development with suggested learning activities for each experience. Child initiative and active learning are the main focus.	Designed to be used by early childhood educators using group experiences for three- and four-year-old children and other children who are functioning at Piaget's "preoperational" level (18 months–6 years).
Portage Project *Bluma, S., Shearer, M., Frohman, A., & Hilliard, J.*	Portage Guide to Early Education The Portage Project Cooperative Educational Service Agency 12 412 East Slifer Street Portage, WI 53901	Six developmental domain areas are covered: infant stimulation, socialization, language, self-help, motor, cognitive. Three major components include: the Portage Guide Kit, the Portage Parent Form, and the Parent Guide to Early Intervention. Focuses on the child's home setting with parents as the main change agents.	Designed to be used with handicapped preschoolers and their parents originally, currently it encompasses a wider population including developmentally normal children. Implementation can be readily carried by a certified teacher; a series of training workshops are suggested for paraprofessionals and parents.
Developmental Programming for Infants and Young Children *Schafer, D., Moersch, M. (Eds.), with Rogers, S., D'Eugenio, D., Brown, S., Donovan, C., & Lynch, E.*	The Early Intervention Project for Handicapped Infants and Young Children Institute for the Study of Mental Retardation and Related Disabilities The University of Michigan Press P.O. Box 1104 Ann Arbor, MI 48106	Three volumes to be used by multidisciplinary teams with combined skills in motor, language, and cognitive development. Parents included as part of treatment team. Major goal is to link assessment and programming.	Parts 1 and 2 intended for early-intervention specialists; Part 3 is intended primarily for professionals and paraprofessionals working with infants and young children (birth–36 months) and secondarily for parents.

PURCHASING INFORMATION		INTENDED USE	
Curriculum/Author(s)	Publisher/Address	Type/Purpose	Audience/Population
Hawaii Early Learning Profile Activity Guide (HELP) *Furuno, S., O'Reilly, C., Hosaka, C., Inatsuka, T., Allman, T., & Zeisloft, B.*	VORT Corporation P.O. Box 11757 Palo Alto, CA 94306	Two parts to be used in obtaining an overall profile of the child. The Chart Assessment is a developmental sequence divided into one-month increments in 6 developmental domains: cognitive, expressive language, gross motor, fine motor, self-help, socioemotional. The Activity Guide provides activities and strategies intended to facilitate development.	Early-childhood educators and special educators working with infants and children who are under the developmental age of 3.
Carolina Curriculum for Handicapped Infants *Martin-Johnson, N., Jens, K., & Attermeier, S.*	Paul Brookes Baltimore, MD	Nineteen developmental areas are identified with logical sequencing of teaching steps designed to enhance the child's strengths and remediate weaknesses.	Designed to be used by professionals and paraprofessionals in both center-based and home-based settings. Parents can incorporate curriculum materials into daily routines. Appropriately used with handicapped infants/children functioning in the birth-to-12-month developmental age range.
Learning Accomplishment Profile (LAP) *Sanford, A.*	KAPLAN 600 Jonestown Road Winston-Salem, NC 27103	Seven components to be used by early childhood personnel responsible for implementing specific objectives and activities. Individual objectives are hierarchically arranged under 6 specific domains: gross motor, fine motor, social, self-help, cognitive, language.	Designed to be used in infant centers, child development centers, Head Start classes, preschools and mainstreamed kindergartens, and parent involvement programs with "normal" and developmentally delayed children from birth to 5 years.
COMP Curriculum *Forsberg, S., Neisworth, J., & Laub, K.*	The HICOMP Outreach Project Division of Special Education and Communication Disorders 327 CEDAR Bldg. Pennsylvania State University University Park, PA 16802	Covers 4 major domains: communication, own-care, motor, and problem solving. Each domain is subdivided into subdomains and lists specific hierarchical developmental behaviors. Record-keeping method is efficiently designed to provide more time to work with individuals or groups.	Designed to be used by early-childhood educators, paraprofessionals, and parents of "normal" and developmentally delayed children from birth through 5 years of age.

TABLE 13-1   *Selected curricular programs for at-risk and handicapped children*

appropriate educational sequences are selected and followed as dictated by child progress over time.

In addition to the curricular approach outlined in this chapter, a number of other useful approaches and materials are available. A brief description of selected curricular materials and names and addresses for obtaining them are found in Table 13-1. In addition, two excellent compendiums are available:

Robinson, C., Davey, K., & Esterling, L. *A Review and Catalog of Early Childhood Special Education Resources.* Omaha, NE: Meyers Children's Rehabilitation Institute, University of Nebraska Medical Center, 1982.

Bagnato, S., & Neisworth, J. *Linking Developmental Assessment and Curricula.* Rockville, MD: Aspen, 1981.

References

Bricker, D., & Carlson, L. (1981). Issues in early language intervention. In R. Schiefelbusch & D. Bricker (Eds.), *Early language: Acquisition and intervention.* Baltimore, MD: University Park Press.

Bricker, W., & Bricker, D. (1975). Mental retardation and complex human behavior. In J. Kauffman & J. Payne (Eds.), *Mental retardation: Introduction and personal perspectives.* Columbus, OH: Charles E. Merrill.

Bricker, D., & Schiefelbusch, R. (1984). Infants at risk. In L. McCormick & R. Schiefelbusch (Eds.), *Early language intervention.* Columbus, OH: Charles E. Merrill.

Brigance, A. (1978). *Inventory of early development.* North Billerica, MA: Curriculum Associates.

Brinker, R. (1985). Curricula without recipes: A challenge to teachers and a promise to severely mentally retarded students. In D. Bricker & J. Filler (Eds.), *Severe mental retardation: From theory to practice.* Reston, VA: The Council for Exceptional Children.

Brinker, R., & Bricker, D. (1980). Teaching a first language: Building complex structures from simpler components. In J. Hogg & P. Mittler (Eds.), *Advances in mental handicap research.* London: John Wiley.

Brinker, R., & Lewis, M. (1982). Contingency intervention. In J. Anderson (Ed.), *Curricula for high-risk and handicapped infants.* Chapel Hill, NC: TADS.

Chance, P. (1979). *Learning through play.* New York: Gardner Press.

Filler, J., Robinson, C., Smith, R., Vincent-Smith, L., Bricker, D., & Bricker, W. (1975). Mental retardation. In N. Hobbs (Ed.), *Issues in the classification of children. Vol. 1: A sourcebook on categories, labels, and their consequences.* San Francisco: Jossey-Bass.

Guess, D., Sailor, W., & Baer, D. (1977). A behavioral-remedial approach to language training for the severely handicapped. In E. Sontag (Ed.), *Educational programming for the severely and profoundly handicapped*. Reston, VA: Council for Exceptional Children..

Guess, D., & Siegel-Causey, E. (1985). Behavioral control and education of severely handicapped students: Who's doing what to whom? And why? In D. Bricker & J. Filler (Eds.), *Severe mental retardation: From theory to practice*. Reston, VA: The Council for Exceptional Children.

Kirk, S., & Johnson, G. (1951). *Educating the retarded child*. Cambridge, MA: Houghton-Mifflin.

Kysela, G., Hillyard, A., McDonald, L., & Taylor, J. (1981). Early intervention, design and evaluation. In R. Schiefelbusch & D. Bricker (Eds.), *Early language: Acquisition and intervention*. Baltimore, MD: University Park Press.

MacMillan, D. (1977). *Mental retardation in school and society*. Boston: Little, Brown & Co.

Mahoney, G., & Weller, E. (1980). An ecological approach to language intervention. In D. Bricker (Ed.), *A resource book on language intervention with children*. San Francisco: Jossey-Bass.

Mori, A., & Neisworth, J. (1983). Curricula in early childhood education: Some generic and special considerations. *Topics in Early Childhood Special Education, 2*(4), 1–8.

Piaget, J. (1970). Piaget's theory. In P. Mussen (Ed.), *Carmichael's manual of child psychology* (Vol. 1). New York: Wiley & Sons.

Schiefelbusch, R., & Lloyd, L. (Eds.) (1974). *Language perspectives: Acquisition, retardation and intervention*. Baltimore, MD: University Park Press.

Warren, S., & Rogers-Warren, A. (Eds.) (1985). *Teaching functional language*. Baltimore, MD: University Park Press.

Zigler, E. (1984). A developmental theory on mental retardation. In B. Blatt & R. Morris (Eds.), *Perspectives in special education: Personal orientations*. Glenview, IL: Scott, Foresman and Co.

CHAPTER

14

ENVIRONMENTAL ENGINEERING

While the focus of Chapter 13 is the content of instruction, this chapter is aimed at suggesting how to arrange and deploy elements of the physical and social environment to enhance learning. As such, it may be useful to view this chapter as the reciprocal of Chapter 13. Instructional content and the strategies employed to present that content should be complementary. So that this chapter is not restricted to a discussion of instructional techniques, the larger context of environmental engineering will be adopted.

In the present context, environmental engineering refers to the management of the environment's physical and social attributes to efficiently assist children in acquiring and using targeted skills and information. In particular, the following areas are addressed: use of physical space and equipment, management of staff, implementation of instructional strategies, and use of other children as educational change agents.

As a number of writers have noted (e.g., Rogers-Warren, 1982), little empirical work has been conducted to determine the environmental elements that are essential for effective learning or how to deploy those elements with at-risk or handicapped populations less than five years of age. State and federal regulations specify health and safety features of environments that house young children, but rarely do such regulations describe the elements that are appropriate or useful in providing enriching contexts for children to play and learn. Most personnel who provide services for at-risk and handicapped children are forced to resort to their experiential backgrounds or anecdotal reports from colleagues as to what approaches or strategies have been successful. Thus, it may not be surprising that current home and center-based programs pay little, if any, attention to the arrangement of the physical and social environments to assist in the intervention effort. The field of ECH/SE is in need of well-controlled investigations to determine the impact of various environmental elements.

Before discussing how to manage physical and social elements of the environment, we should observe three caveats. First, it is unlikely that the "goodness" or "badness" of environmental arrangements can be determined with an absolute scale. Rather, the appropriateness is determined within the context of the educational targets established for individual children and families. Program resources and other relevant variables (e.g., facilities) may also need consideration. Consequently, suggestions for environmental engineering strategies are offered as general guidelines that require individualization prior to their application.

A second caveat is that the environment should be seen as a dynamic interrelationship of social and physical elements. Changes in one set of elements may require adjustment in other elements. Remembering the dynamic nature of the environment should assist in instigating and accommodating change and adjustment.

Third, programs should be conducted in locations reasonably free from confusion, disorganization, and intense, uncontrolled stimulation. Experience suggests that infants and young children can become distressed when the noise and confusion exceed their ability to filter out extraneous incoming stimulation. Observation of the general arousal state of children should determine whether the environmental stimulation is too intense (e.g., high levels of noise and movement by children and adults). Of course, it is also possible for the environment to become too muted and static, which also may be counterproductive. The young handicapped child should learn to adapt to more "typical" settings, which often are laced with "reasonable" noise and confusion. Learning to cope with such environments is necessary if the child is to have the opportunity to experience a broad range of settings and activities. Maintaining a training setting that is overly quiet, isolated, or unchanging may not enhance the child's ability to cope with a broad range of alternative environments.

As indicated, the location of the training environment can be the home, classroom, or playground, as long as the surroundings are arranged to consistently demand more from the child. Thus, the environmental engineering strategies suggested in the following sections should be seen as relevant to all of the child's surroundings. Change in the social and physical environment in the home may be as vital as it is in the classroom.

USE OF PHYSICAL SPACE AND EQUIPMENT

Preschool environments for handicapped preschool-age children have often been described as cold, barren, and uninteresting (Olds, 1979). In fact, a study reported by Bailey, Clifford, and Harms (1982) suggests that programs for handicapped preschool children do differ from programs for nonhandicapped preschoolers. The nature of the reported differences suggests that a less "rich" environmental context is generally provided for handicapped children. Because handicapped children often have attention and learning problems, interventionists may believe that less stimulating environments—in the sense of fewer distractions—are preferred.

Focusing solely on the richness or stimulating value of the physical environment is a somewhat misguided evaluation strategy. The most important analysis should be based on the needs of the children and families that can be met within the context of program resources. Determination of the number of pictures, the variety of colors, or the placement of toys should not be done apart from the established program goals and IEP/FPA goals for individual children and families.

Physical Space

Systematic observation of classroom programs and home environments—particularly areas where children play—strongly suggests that too little thought is given to the physical arrangement of furniture and pieces of equipment that constitute the infant's or child's world. Observation of classroom programs and homes often indicates no apparent planning of the physical environment or organization from the perspectives of efficiency, functionality, accessibility, and promotion of independence.

Efficiency. Environmental arrangements that enhance efficiency are often more pertinent for the parent or interventionist than for the child. Efficiency suggests that the physical space is arranged to make completion of tasks and activities smooth, easy, and quick. If art materials are stored some distance from where art activities are conducted, the interventionist may have to make many trips back and forth between storage and activity areas. Time spent bringing materials to the table lessens instructional time with the children. A mother who must retrieve a dry diaper from a cabinet located away from the changing area or bathroom may expend valuable time moving back and forth between areas and run the risk of the child becoming injured during the absence. A study of the physical set-up can generate valuable information for arranging the environment to permit maximum efficiency in conducting the daily activities in which parents and interventionists engage.

Accessibility. Accessibility may often be an inherent aspect of efficiency; however, in some cases, the parent or interventionist may need to consider accessibility to equipment, materials, and the physical environment separately. A piece of equipment may be strategically located, yet inaccessible. For example, if small toys are dumped into a toy box rather than placed side by side on a shelf, the accessibility may be limited for a young child. The adult may also have to spend needless time searching through the jumbled toy box to locate specific items. Cubbies for children may be appropriately located beside the door to the outside but may be too high for use by small children. Lack of access may require that the adult retrieve the children's coats for each outdoor excursion. Requiring the adult to retrieve coats reduces the child's opportunity to learn and practice important self-help skills and uses valuable adult time in a nonproductive manner.

Functionality. Functionality of environment refers to using space and equipment in a manner that is useful for the child. For example, having a rocking horse available that physically impaired children cannot negotiate is not functional. Providing foam mats—although perhaps not as attractive as the rocking horse—for the physically disabled child may permit the child freedom of movement not otherwise possible. Picture books that lack haptic variety may not be particularly functional for visually impaired children, and toys that produce quiet sounds may not be functional for hearing impaired children. Toys with many small pieces that require considerable hand-eye coordination are generally not functional or safe for infants. Objects that are easy to grasp and maneuver are more functional and appropriate for infants who are developing grasping and manipulative skills.

Independence. The final general consideration in arranging the physical environment is whether the arrangement assists in promoting independent functioning. If most objects and toys are not within a child's reach, the child must depend on adults or older children to obtain a desired object. Independent hand washing and toileting can be enhanced by placement of a sturdy stool that permits the child access to the sink or toilet without assistance. Materials placed at the child's level encourage self-selection and also allow the child to put materials away. Any arrangement that promotes independent functioning, even for the most severely handicapped child, should be encouraged.

Equipment

Equipment is the second aspect of the physical environment to be considered. Considerations should focus on safety, durability, flexibility, functionality, and the equipment's usefulness in arousing active participation from children. Selection of equipment should be determined by the nature of the population being served. The importance of safety and durability is self-evident; however, flexibility and functionality need further explanation. As a rule, the greater the number of different activities that a piece of equipment can be used for, the more satisfactory it is. Perhaps that is why so many classrooms have balls that bounce, roll, float and can be chewed, squeezed, or placed in containers. Learning to do a variety of activities with the same object promotes testing and exploratory behavior in young children—skills to be encouraged. Functionality refers to the equipment's capacity to assist

Use of Physical Space and Equipment

the child in acquiring responses that will be useful in other environments, for example, use of a real telephone.

Equipment that elicits continued active participation by the child is clearly preferable to items that merely require activation and watching. Piaget (1970) contends that young children acquire their knowledge of the environment through active manipulation. When possible, children should be actively engaged in their surroundings.

Equipment can be either general or specialized. General refers to items such as tables, chairs, small manipulables, climbing apparatus, and the like, that are found in most programs for young children. Specialized equipment refers to specific items essential to encourage more effective functioning of individual children. Often, the addition of some special equipment will make it possible for a child to execute a skill he or she could not otherwise perform (Campbell, Green, & Carlson, 1977). For example, the addition of a small wooden peg to the tray of his high chair allowed one young spastic child the stability to learn to feed himself. The child would grasp the peg with the left hand, pulling him forward which allowed a flexed position that provided his upper torso with the additional stability required to feed himself with the right hand (Banerdt & Bricker, 1978). For more specific information on how toys and equipment can influence children's behavior, see Ross, 1982; Quiltich and Risley, 1973; and Day, 1983.

Arranging the Space and Equipment

The introductory section of this chapter was intended to provide some general guidelines to consider for arranging the physical and social environment. These guidelines are meant to serve as a foundation for the development of a systematic strategy to organize the environment to facilitate children's growth and development and to assist family members in acquiring targeted skills. The strategy suggested to organize and use physical space and equipment is composed of four steps: (1) develop goals, (2) devise a plan to meet the goals, (3) implement the plan, and (4) evaluate its effectiveness in meeting the established goals.

Develop Goals. A consistent theme throughout this volume has been the need to develop goals and objectives for the program and participating children and families. The effective use of space and equipment also requires the development of goals and objectives.

These goals should lead naturally from and be consistent with the program goals and the individual IEP and FPA goals developed for participating children and families. If a program goal is to enhance communicative development in participating children, then the physical environment should be arranged to engage the children in communicative behavior. The equipment should also be purchased and deployed to encourage communication. Thus, the personnel operating a center-based program should give careful consideration to program and individual child goals when arranging the environment. Likewise, home interventionists should assist parents in arranging the environment, whenever possible, to assist in meeting the IEP goals established for their child.

Devise a Plan. Given a set of operationalized goals and objectives, parents and interventionists are ready to devise a plan that will organize the physical space and available equipment to facilitate the achievement of established goals. In devising a plan, personnel should remember the general features of efficiency, accessibility, functionality, and promoting independence. Space should be arranged to ensure these features are an integral part of the environmental arrangements. If a program goal is to enhance independent mobility for severely motorically impaired preschool children, then a plan should be devised that is responsive to that goal. Adequate space should be available for children to practice their mobility skills, and support should be available for those youngsters who require assistance in moving about the classroom. If a goal for an infant in a home program is to enhance his or her concept of means-ends and object permanence, the parents should be encouraged to place toys and other desired objects out of their child's reach. The child can be then encouraged to develop skills to search for and obtain out-of-reach items.

Implement the Plan. If an interventionist invests time in developing goals and devising plans for reaching established goals, the manner in which space and equipment are arranged will be done with cohesiveness and purpose. The arrangement of space shown in Figure 14–1 illustrates a design that takes into account the need for efficiency, accessibility, functionality, and independence and is consistent with program and individual child goals.

In this classroom design, the children's cubbies are located next to the entry door. Upon entry, children can immediately remove their wraps and stow their possessions in the appropriate cubby. Adjacent to the cubbies, but separated by low shelves appropriate to the height of the children, is an area designated for free play. Children are free to access this area and play with toys located in this space. The shelves act as boundaries that help protect the children from those choosing to engage in activities appropriate to the large muscle activity area. On the other side of the free play area, separated by low shelves, is a designated quiet area. Children can look at books or engage in quiet activities in this area. Rugs and pillows are available in this area. Next to the quiet area is an area used for large-group activities. A blackboard and record player are kept in this area. Adjacent to the large-group area is a section where small-group or individual instructional activities can be conducted. This area is separated by medium-height cloth barriers that help protect the children from outside distractions but still enable the interventionist to see the rest of the classroom. There is a specific area for snacks that contains tables with appropriately sized chairs. The snack area is next to the bathroom.

Use of Physical Space and Equipment

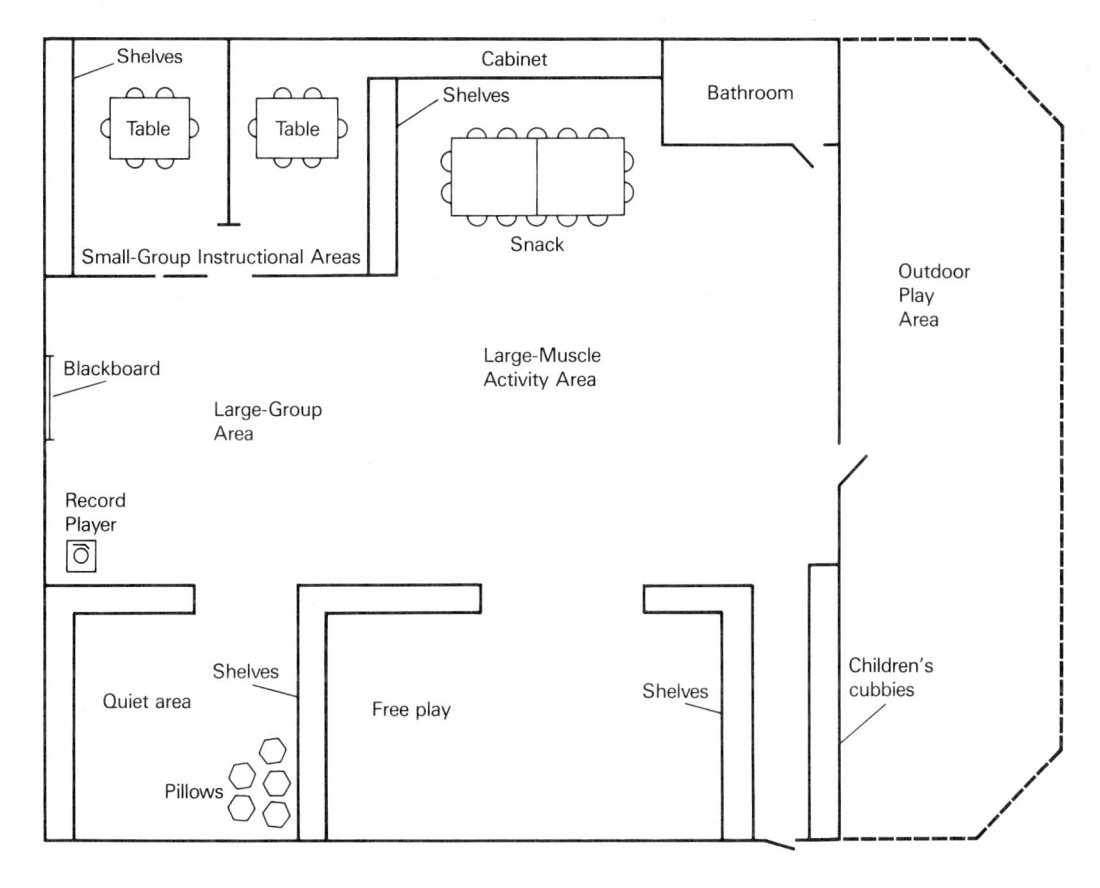

FIGURE 14-1. *Classroom floor plan.*

Although the arrangement shown in Figure 14-1 may not be suitable for some programs, it does represent a well-designed classroom for the following reasons. It is efficiently arranged in that each area has adequate shelf space to store relevant and needed materials so that they are accessible. It is efficient also because the cubbies are situated close to the entry and exit ways, and the bathroom is near the snack area. This layout is arranged so that all areas are accessible to the staff and the children, and the cubbies and storage shelves are accessible to the children. In addition, the layout is functional because it permits easy movement from area to area, the staff can monitor children's activities throughout the room because no visual barriers exist, and the physical boundaries (e.g., shelves) help the children make discriminations about the match between activities and areas. This design fosters independence because the spacial arrangement provides the children with adequate structure for conducting activities in the appropriate areas. Finally, the accessibility of equipment and materials enhances the children's ability to engage in independent activities as appropriate.

Evaluation. As with instructional programs, the determination of the effectiveness of environmental arrangements should be accomplished through objective evaluation procedures. Collecting in-depth information on the effectiveness of the use of space and equipment across extended periods may exceed the resources of most intervention programs. However, most interventionists should be able to design a simple strategy for determining if the arrangement of space and equipment is producing the desired outcomes. It may be useful to have a staff member or parent observe certain child behaviors to ascertain if the arrangement is having the desired impact. For example, if a goal is communication between handicapped and nonhandicapped children, observation of the number of contacts occurring after changing some aspects of the physical environment may be in order. The staff may choose to undertake some other systematic changes to see which physical arrangement produces greater interaction between the two groups of children.

Personnel delivering services within the child's home may have more restrictions in arranging space and equipment; however, families may be agreeable to some change, if such change makes caring for the child easier and the child's progress is enhanced. Interventionists working in home-based programs should be as concerned about environmental engineering as are interventionists involved in center-based programs.

Summary

There are those who believe "the environment is the curriculum" (Olds, 1979). The position advocated in this section of the chapter is that the arrangement of space and the type of available equipment are important elements of an instructional program. These elements can be used in a planned and purposeful manner to enhance learning in children, or they can be disregarded. Doing the latter eliminates a powerful set of factors capable of aiding the instructionial staff as well as the learners.

To maximize the impact of the physical environment, a plan should be devised and implemented that is consistent with program and individualized child/family goals. A plan promotes the effective arrangement of space and equipment that can optimize teaching and learning opportunities. For additional information on classroom designs, see Olds, 1979; Bailey and Wolery, 1984; and Rogers-Warren, 1982.

MANAGEMENT OF STAFF

"A teacher's primary responsibility is to teach" (Hart, 1982), and the child's primary responsibility is to learn. Thus, a paramount goal is to arrange the instructional environment, whether home or elsewhere, to maximize the interventionist's teaching opportunities and the child's and family's learning opportunities. The more appropriate opportunities to instruct and learn that are available, the more likely the child and other family members will progress toward established goals. An important requisite to developing the necessary instructional opportunities is to systematically deploy the staff to maximize their effectiveness.

Having a staff well-trained in the content of instruction and the use of effective instructional strategies is necessary but not sufficient for effective intervention. Much of a staff's expertise can be wasted if systems are not devised and executed for the utilization of that expertise in ways that benefit the participating children and their families. Time spent in designing a plan for staff deployment is essential to a well-run and effective intervention program.

Classroom Programs

A plan for the use of classroom personnel should contain three elements: daily schedules for staff for instructional activities, daily schedules for transition periods, and contingency plans for unexpected events.

Instructional Activities Schedule. By daily schedule, it is not meant that a staff member is assigned to opening group from 9:00 to 9:15 and to an instructional group from 9:15 to 9:45. Rather, each staff member should have a daily assignment schedule that indicates his or her role and responsibilities in the various program activities. For example, during opening group, John's assignment is to lead the group in singing songs and in other relevant group activities. Inherent in this assignment are organizing the opening-group activities to include the children, parents, and staff; ensuring that each staff member understands and executes his or her assigned responsibility; selecting appropriate activities; assembling the necessary equipment and ensuring that it functions properly; monitoring the children's participation; evaluating the activity; and adjusting the activity based on evaluative feedback.

After the opening group, John is responsible for children assigned to a small instructional group focused on enhancing communication and problem solving. Responsibilities for this activity would include selecting activities that appropriately target the communicative and problem-solving goals of the participating children; assembling the necessary equipment and materials and having them accessible to the children; selecting appealing strategies for presentation of the materials; ensuring that all children participate in ways that permit them to gain new skills and/or practice acquired responses; managing the children's behavior so that the activities can occur without disruption; evaluating the effectiveness of the activities and the children's progress; and adjusting activities as indicated by the evaluative feedback. If each staff member carefully designs his or her activities throughout the day with an eye toward comprehensive organization and responsibility, then the probability exists that the impact of the instructional day is maximized. To properly execute the selected activities with the children requires preplanning and systematic presentation that takes into account all relevant variables.

In assigning activities to staff members, at least two options are available. Staff members can be assigned a specific group of children for whom they are responsible. Using such a system means the staff member moves with the children as they change activities throughout the day. This approach permits maximum familiarity with the children and their respective IEP goals and may allow the interventionist to use many opportunities throughout the day to build and expand the children's repertoires. The major drawback may be children's more limited access to others. Interacting with a variety of people can help children generalize skills and learn to cope with variability.

An alternative strategy is to assign staff members a particular part of the room, of the activity, or of both. This plan permits the children more chance to interact with a variety of staff members. It may provide the staff members more variety as well. However, the staff members are required to be familiar with the goals of many more children and thus may not be as attuned to individual children's needs. The plan chosen should reflect the goals and resources of the program. Often, trying both procedures will result in a final plan that incorporates aspects of each approach.

Transition Schedules. In addition to designing a schedule for the various instructional activities, it is essential to plan for transition points during the day. Often, when children are required to move from one activity to another, instructional time is lost and considerable confusion occurs. Children may wander away, remove toys from designated areas, or engage in nonproductive activities, and other confusion may result. Problems arise during transitions because program personnel do not spend adequate time in planning for efficient, effective, and functional movement of children from activity to activity. Again, staff should be assigned specific responsibilities and develop strategies (e.g., cues to alert children that it is time to change activities) to ensure that transition times become effective instructional times.

Unexpected Events. The advent of unexpected events requires staff to develop contingency plans for such occurrences. At least three types of contingency plans should be developed. First, there are plans to cover times when an activity for a child or a group of children is being particularly effective and the interventionist would like to continue the activity. In such cases, staff members should have developed some means to communicate with one another and implement an alternative plan for other, noninvolved children until the activity is completed. Second, the reverse may occur, a selected activity being unsuccessful for some reason. Thus, staff members should have an alternative plan available to replace the planned activity for that day. Finally, emergencies may occur that require the temporary absence of a staff member. Plans developed for such occurrences should be familiar to all staff members.

Home Programs

The need for plans to deploy a home interventionist may appear less necessary, but it is the illusion of the relaxed, informal "visit" that most jeopardizes effectiveness. Without consideration of the interventionist's time during the home visit, goals and objectives may not be attended to from visit to visit. Thus, the interventionist should carefully plan the activities to be conducted, assemble the necessary materials and equipment, and develop procedures for implementation and evaluation. In most cases, the parent is involved, which requires that the interventionist plan the parental involvement as well as strategies to accomplish that involvement. The interventionist needs to have alternative plans to allow for situations in which the original activity is unacceptable to the parents or child, or some unforeseen circumstance interferes with the execution of the original plan (e.g., the primary caregiver is ill and another family member participates).

Summary

In deploying staff in either center-based or home programs, two considerations are important. First, a balance should be struck between change and routine. Neither too little nor too much change is facilitative for staff, parents, or children. Programs that change schedules too frequently can cause confusion and waste staff time and effort in learning new routines. Programs that rarely change may drift into routines that are uninteresting and unrewarding to children, families, and staff. Programs should be continually evaluated and change undertaken when feedback suggests that goals are not being met or not reached within expected time frames.

A second consideration is the need for communication among staff members and between staff members and parents. Each member of the direct intervention staff and the support team needs to be knowledgeable about each other's activities. Without consistent sharing of information, problems will occur. Each staff and family member should be working in concert to assist the child if expected progress is to be maintained toward established goals. Functional communication will not occur without recognition of its importance and without formal mechanisms to ensure its occurrence.

IMPLEMENTATION OF INSTRUCTIONAL STRATEGIES

Since the advent of behaviorism, there have been disagreements about its appropriateness for explaining and modifying human behavior (Evans, 1971). Some have argued that the principles espoused by the behaviorist are inappropriately applied to the human organism, except, perhaps, to more seriously impaired individuals. Behaviorists' discussions of the control and manipulation of human behavior have often polarized people into camps of believers and critics. Believers tend to disregard concepts such as free will and argue that most forms of human behavior can be manipulated through environmental arrangement of antecedent and consequent events. Nonbelievers argue for the need to appreciate nonobservable variables from which human motivation, choice, and direction are derived. For interventionists, this polarization has tended to force people into unilateral, defensive positions that have been nonproductive and often destructive. Debates and energy often have focused on areas that have yielded little of relevance for problems confronting interventionists.

Whether one likes or dislikes the term *behaviorist* is secondary to the recognition that we are all behaviorists. Overt responses of individuals, whether motoric or verbal, provide the only data available from which to derive information and generate hypotheses. In addition to the recognition that the behavior of the individual is our primary data source, there is the need to understand and apply principles of operant learning for instructional purposes.

Considerable misunderstanding and ignorance of operant learning principles exists. This problem is, at least in part, the result of the polarization between behavioral and developmental or cognitively oriented approaches. All interventionists arrange antecedent events to elicit responses, and provide some consequence (even ignoring is a consequence). The question is whether these arrangements are conducted in an unplanned, haphazard fashion or in a logical, cohesive manner. Again, we all employ operant principles of learning; the issue is how effectively the principles are used. The psychotherapist who nods as a client discusses a problem is employing the same principle as an interventionist who hugs a child following the successful completion of a task.

Since most interventionists use observable behavior as a primary source of information, and since they also apply operant learning principles, what are the primary differences between philosophies and programs? The important differences between those programs that use an operant learning perspective versus those more focused on cognitive and motivational variables are (1) the level of inference the intervention staff is willing to accept and (2) the rigor with which the operant principles are applied.

Inferences

The level of inference refers to how removed explanations of cause and effect are from observable behavior. Behavior analysts observe behavior and record events objectively and as faithfully as possible. For example, while observing an interaction between a child and his mother, the observer might record that Billy hit his mother on the arm with a toy car as she bent toward him. A more cognitively oriented person might observe the same scene and add that Billy was angry with his mother, his anger causing him to strike her with the car. The determination that Billy was angry is an inference based on the child's behavior. Both descriptions use observable events; the difference lies in the level of inference drawn from the observable events.

Drawing inferences is a legitimate activity and one that most people use frequently. If we could not draw inferences, the world would be far less interesting. However, when operating in the professional realm, it is essential to recognize when inferences are made and the basis for drawing the inference. Too often, inferences are taken as fact, which can result in misguided intervention efforts. For example, a teacher's observations of Suzy's noncooperative behavior during large-group time leads to the inference that the child is obstinate. The interventionist designs a program to encourage cooperative behavior from Suzy. Implementation of the program leads to little change in Suzy's behavior because, unknown to the interventionist, the child is hearing impaired and is unable to respond appropriately to verbal directions provided during group time. If the interventionist recognizes his or her inference about Suzy's behavior, then a suitable change in the program may occur in an efficient manner. If the interventionist treats the inference about Suzy as fact, then relevant program changes may be long in coming.

Rather than casting people into opposing camps, it is more useful to recognize that as interventionists, we all use behavioral principles in our assessment, intervention, and evaluation strategies. The primary difference lies in the degree of inference one is willing to make from observable events. Drawing inferences is appropriate as long as one is able to discriminate between the inference and the observable events that serve as the basis for the inference.

Operant Principles of Learning

Operant principles of learning have been developed into the most effective instructional technology currently available. No matter what one's theoretical orientation, it is important that ECH/SE personnel be knowledgeable about and competent users of this technology. Interventionists have the choice of understanding and applying these principles in a purposeful and organized manner or allowing events to occur in ways that may or may not serve the interests of children, families, and interventionists. The choice is easy.

Basic Paradigm

The basic formulation that serves as a foundation for the instructional technology advocated here is:

$$A(antecedent) \longrightarrow R(response) \longrightarrow C(consequence).$$

Antecedent refers to any event that serves to set up and call forth the targeted response. Consequences are the events that follow the occurrence of the target response. These three elements—antecedents, responses, and consequences) work in tandem, and therein lies the strength of the technology. Interventionists should think in terms of ARC units rather than of individual elements (e.g., consequences) when developing intervention programs.

It is important to understand the broad and generalized application of the ARC equation. Too often, ARC units are understood and conceptualized as one-to-one correspondences, such as the example illustrated here:

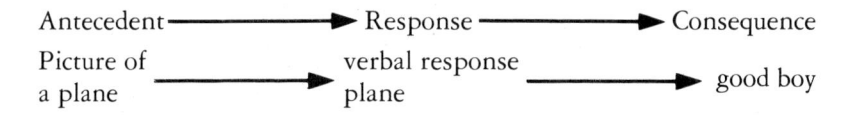

Antecedent ⟶ Response ⟶ Consequence
Picture of a plane ⟶ verbal response plane ⟶ good boy

Using ARC units only to formulate specific and structured contingencies is an overly narrow application of the technology. Rather, the interventionist should be working to have the child respond appropriately across a range of appropriate and relevant antecedent events, such as different pictures of planes, toy planes of various sizes, colors and shapes, and real planes. Each of these antecedent events should be capable of eliciting the verbal label *plane*. Maintaining the word in the child's repertoire is accomplished through the use of a variety of consequences, such as receiving affirmation, acquiring a toy, or initiating a conversation.

Although the initial training may focus on establishing a one-to-one correspondence between a specific antecedent and a response, for most children, it is essential to quickly vary the antecedent events and to tolerate variability in the response topography (e.g., "plane", "airplane"). Consequences should vary and be functionally related to the response whenever possible.

Employing the Technology

Employing the technology has been addressed in a number of helpful books. The purpose of the present section is not to replicate the information provided in these books but to suggest a general plan of operation that sometimes does not accompany the more detailed accounts of how to employ the technology.

Following is listed a set of general steps that provides a framework for selecting target responses, arranging program elements, and collecting outcome data.

Step 1: Write behavioral objectives
Step 2: Measure occurrence of response

Step 3: Implement program
Step 4: Collect and graph data
Step 5: Modify program as necessary

The objective of Step 1 is to define the response or behavior of interest in a particular domain. Having a relevant assessment instrument can be helpful in determining which training objective (TO) should be targeted. The approach to initial assessment described in Chapter 15 yields a series of Long Range Goals (LRG) and TOs. Each TO should be further divided into a series of program steps. Each program step should be written as a behavioral objective. According to Halle and Sindelar (1982), behavioral objectives should be written in terms of observable components, the context in which they occur, and the criterion level. For example:

> For eight consecutive days, Paul will independently indicate wants during snack time by saying, "more juice" and "more cracker." The production of words will be intelligible and produced at least once each day to receive a snack.

Once defined, the second step requires measuring the occurrence of the response. During the observation, the interventionist should note those antecedent and consequence events that appear to affect the occurrence or nonoccurrence of the targeted response. Measurement can yield a permanent or nonpermanent result. For example, a permanent outcome might be a polaroid picture of the curve of the child's spine, while a nonpermanent record might be the number of times a child hits another child.

In most instances, the response will be measured using event recording, duration recording, or interval recording (e.g., time sampling). Event recording refers to systematically counting the number of times or the frequency that a response occurs. Using the example given, the observer would record the number of times Paul requests juice and crackers by independently saying "more juice, more cracker" during snack time. Placing checks on a recording form each time Mary cries is another example of event recording. In event recording, it may be important to note the length of the observation period.

Duration recording refers to noting the length of time a response occurs. For example, noting the frequency that a child has tantrums—if they occur infrequently—may be less useful than recording the duration of the tantrum. Interval recording refers to systematically selecting periods of time to note the occurrence of a response. Generally, a time period is pre-designated (ten minutes), and at the end of the interval, the recorder checks to see whether or not the target response is being exhibited. For more detail on data recording systems, see Alberto and Troutman, 1982; Axelrod, 1977; and Hall, 1971.

Step 3 is implementation of the program to meet the child's behavioral objectives. Content for behavioral objectives and learning activities was described in Chapter 13. This step focuses on applying learning principles to assist the child in acquiring the content (behavioral objective). Relevant learning principles can be divided into strategies for arranging antecedents, promoting responses, and providing consequences.

Effective management of antecedent events entails selection of events that help elicit the target response. Two aspects need consideration: the sequence and the format in which events are presented. After a well-designed curricular sequence, a set of program steps, or task analysis, generally ensures that the sequence of events will be appropriately ordered from least to most difficult. Training should generally begin with the easiest response and move progressively toward the more difficult level of responding. More options are generally available for selecting the presentation format. The interventionist needs to consider the available options, such as activities and types of material, and select the format most appropriate for the child, setting, and behavioral objectives.

Promoting the occurrence of the target response can be done using a variety of instructional techniques including shaping, various modeling and prompting strategies, and chaining. Shaping is the differential reinforcement of successive approximations to a target behavior. If the target behavior is walking using alternate steps, a successive approximation might be cruising using side steps. Prompts refer to additional aids that increase the likelihood that a response will occur. Physical prompts can include various levels of physical assistance and modeling. Verbal prompts can be cues or full descriptions of the desired response. Chaining refers to sequences of linked behaviors. For example, shoe-tying is composed of a series of discrete responses that culminates in shoes being tied. Often, it is helpful to teach a more complex response through the use of backward or forward chaining. A large number of helpful resources exist that explain in detail the use of these and other instructional strategies. The effective interventionist needs to be fluent in the application of these strategies.

Consequences can be classified as positive or punishing. Positive reinforcement increases the probability that a response will occur, while punishers inhibit or decrease the occurrence of a response. In most cases, interventionists should use punishing events infrequently. Positive consequences should not be construed to be only artificial contingencies, such as receiving candy or verbal praise. Rather, positive reinforcement consequences can and should be, when possible, an integral part of the activity. For example, saying "juice" should produce juice for the child and serve as sufficient reinforcement.

The discussion of instructional strategies offered here provides only cursory information that should be supplemented through other sources. There are a number of books designed specifically for interventionists that discuss these techniques. See, for example, Alberto and Troutman, 1982;

Axelrod, 1977; Sulzer-Azaroff and Mayer, 1977; and Bailey and Wolery, 1984.

OTHER CHILDREN AS EDUCATIONAL CHANGE AGENTS

Other children can serve as valuable instructional resources. Unfortunately, this resource is often disregarded by adult interventionists. As argued earlier in this book, development of more complex repertoires is largely a function of progressive environmental demands. Consequently, programs should be designed to stimulate and demand progressively more sophisticated responses from participating children. Overly solicitous adults who respond for children, or arrange conditions so children do not have to change, are counterproductive to children's growth and development. Having handicapped children surrounded by children who have similar problems or deficits may not provide a maximally demanding environment. In addition, there is evidence that handicapped children as a group are less socially capable (Guralnick, in press). If other children can be effective change agents, then it would seem wise to include children that are socially adept and can serve as effective models for less competent children.

Integrating handicapped and nonhandicapped children has the potential to create a more demanding environment for the at-risk and handicapped child—an environment that may assist in the continued development of the child's behavioral repertoire. It is possible that when young impaired and nonimpaired children are grouped together, interventionists and parents may develop more realistic expectations about what handicapped children should be attempting to do. Furthermore, such an environment is likely to be more demanding. Not only may the physical environment be filled with more interesting objects, as indicated by the research reported by Bailey, Clifford, and Harms (1982), but the nonhandicapped peers may expect and encourage behavior that could produce significant changes in the handicapped children.

It seems clear that children can learn through imitation (Bandura, 1971), but the willingness of children to imitate others is affected by a range of motivational and reinforcement variables. Programs that include nonhandicapped youngsters may enhance the possibility of imitation learning by the handicapped youngster for several reasons. First, in order for children to acquire new responses by observing and modeling other children's behavior, the opportunity for watching and imitating more complex behavior must be available. Isolation of young handicapped children from nonhandicapped peers may reduce an important avenue of stimulation and subsequent learning. For example, it seems unlikely that hearing impaired children benefit linguistically from exclusive associations with other hearing impaired children. Being exposed to appropriate language models should assist the hearing impaired child in developing better communication skills.

Second, active participation appears to enhance imitation learning, a finding that argues for programs that provide contact between handicapped and nonhandicapped children. Third, there are indications that children model selectively. That is, children tend to imitate the behavior of more competent individuals who are more skillful (Strichart, 1974).

Other children, particularly more competent children, can fill valuable instructional roles. Thus, program personnel should explore means for inclusion of nonhandicapped children in programs that serve at-risk and handicapped children. However, it is questionable that merely placing nonhandicapped children in a program will ensure interaction between the two groups or that at-risk or handicapped children will observe and imitate the actions of the more competent children (O'Connell, 1984). Rather, the interventionists must plan and organize activities to encourage interaction between the groups of children. For descriptions of programs and procedures for integrating handicapped and nonhandicapped children, see Guralnick, 1978; Vincent, Brown, and Getz-Sheftel, 1981; Allen, 1981; O'Connell, 1984; and Guralnick, 1981.

SUMMARY

This chapter has discussed four constellations of factors that can be arranged or engineered to facilitate learning in at-risk and handicapped children. A major theme has been the numerous options available to assist children in acquiring targeted behaviors. Too often, instruction is viewed from an inordinately narrow perspective that dictates that learning occurs under specific conditions. The position advocated here is that myriads of options are available for assisting children in the learning process.

The physical arrangement of space and equipment can serve as a teaching vehicle and/or enhance instructional activities, or can deter the process through inappropriate and nonfunctional arrangements. The manner in which staff are deployed can also add or detract from the intervention process. Systems for the smooth and efficient use of the instructional staff can enhance learning opportunities. An equally important perspective is the use of other children as instructional resources. A vertical teaching model in which more competent children assist those less competent holds great appeal both from the point of view of husbanding resources and as an effective teaching method for the child-teacher and the child-learner.

Finally, a variety of carefully developed instructional strategies is available for use. Interventionists have the choice of understanding and employing these procedures in efficient, effective ways or using these valuable strategies in less effective ways. The better the interventionist understands these principles of learning, the more flexibly these principles can be applied, the greater becomes the potential benefit to participating children and their families.

References

Alberto, P., & Troutman, A. (1981). *Applied behavior analysis for teachers.* Columbus, OH: Charles E. Merrill.

Allen, K. (1981). Curriculum models for successful mainstreaming. *Topics in Early Childhood Special Education, 1,* 45-55.

Axelrod, S. (1977). *Behavior modification for the classroom teacher.* New York: McGraw-Hill.

Bailey, D., Clifford, R., & Harms, T. (1982). Comparison of preschool environments for handicapped and nonhandicapped children. *Topics in Early Childhood Special Education, 2*(1), 9-20.

Bailey, D., & Wolery, M. (1984). *Tracking infants and preschoolers with handicaps.* Columbus, OH: Charles E. Merrill.

Bandura, A. (1971). Influence of models' reinforcement contingencies on the acquisition of imitative responses. In E. McGinnies & C. Ferster (Eds.), *The reinforcement of social behavior.* Boston: Houghton Mifflin Co., pp. 75-81.

Banerdt, B., & Bricker, D. (1978). A training program for selected self-feeding skills for the motorically impaired. *AAESPH Review, 3,* 222-229.

Campbell, P., Green, K., & Carlson, L. (1977). Approximating the norm through environmental and child-centered prosthetics and adaptive equipment. In E. Sontag, J. Smith, & N. Certo (Eds.), *Educational programming for the severely and profoundly handicapped.* Reston, VA: The Council for Exceptional Children.

Day, D. (1983). *Early childhood education.* Glenview, IL: Scott, Foresman & Company.

Evans, R. (1971). Aversive versus positive control of behavior (Interview with B. F. Skinner). In E. McGinnies & C. Ferster (Eds.), *The reinforcement of social behavior.* New York: Houghton Mifflin Co.

Guralnick, M. (1978). Integrated preschools as educational and therapeutic environments. In M. Guralnick (Ed.), *Early intervention and the integration of handicapped and nonhandicapped children.* Baltimore, MD: University Park Press.

Guralnick, M. (1981). The efficacy of integrating handicapped children in early education settings: Research implications. *Topics in Early Childhood Special Education, 1*(1), 57-72.

Guralnick, M. (in press). The peer relations of young handicapped and nonhandicapped children. In P. Strain, M. Guralnick, & H. Walker (Eds.),

Children's social behavior: Development, assessment, and modification. New York: Academic Press.

Hall, R. (1971). *Managing behavior* (5 vols.). Lawrence, KS: H. & H. Enterprises, Inc.

Halle, J., & Sindelar, P. (1982). Behavioral observation methodologies for early childhood education. *Topics in Early Childhood Special Education, 2*(1), 43–54.

Hart, B. (1982). So that teachers can teach: Assigning roles and responsibilities. *Topics in Early Childhood Special Education, 2*(1), 1–8.

O'Connell, J. (1984). Preschool integration and its effects on the social interactions of handicapped and nonhandicapped children: A review. *Journal of the Division for Early Childhood, 8,* 38–48.

Olds, A. (1979). Designing developmentally optimal classrooms for children with special needs. In S. Meisels (Ed.), *Special education and development.* Baltimore, MD: University Park Press.

Piaget, J. (1970). Piaget's theory. In P. Mussen (Ed.), *Carmichael's manual of child psychology* (Vol. 1). New York: Wiley.

Quiltich, M., & Risley, T. (1973). The effects of play materials on social play. *Journal of Applied Behavior Analysis, 6,* 573–578.

Rogers-Warren, A. (1982). Behavioral ecology in classrooms for young, handicapped children. *Topics in Early Childhood Special Education, 2*(1), 21–32.

Ross, D. (1982). Selecting materials for mainstreamed preschools. *Topics in Early Childhood Special Education, 2*(1), 33–42.

Strichart, S. (1974). Effects of competence and nurturance on imitation of nonretarded peers by retarded adolescents. *American Journal of Mental Deficiency, 78,* 665–673.

Sulzer-Azaroff, B., & Mayer, R. (1977). *Applying behavior-analysis procedures with children and youth.* New York: Holt, Rinehart & Winston.

Vincent, L., Brown, L., & Getz-Sheftel, M. (1981). Integrating handicapped and typical children during the preschool years: The definition of best educational practice. *Topics in Early Childhood Special Education, 1*(1), 17–24.

CHAPTER

15

A LINKED ASSESSMENT-INTERVENTION-EVALUATION APPROACH

The generation of systematic objective evidence of program effectiveness has been a continuing problem for interveners who work with young handicapped children. Early childhood special educators must contend with all of the problems faced by evaluators of educational programs for older, nonhandicapped children, complicated by the particular problems related to handicapping conditions in young children. Yet program survival depends upon the adequacy of objective data, as funding agencies increasingly require evidence of program impact. (Sheehan & Keogh, 1982, p. 81)

In addition to accountability, assessment and evaluation are essential for effective intervention. The assessment and evaluation of individual change and programmatic impact requires that intervention methods and systems be based on procedures that are appropriate for evaluating their efficacy. Assessment and evaluation should determine the format and success of intervention for individual children and determine the impact of programs on groups of children. These objectives require that assessment and evaluation procedures serve three distinct but complementary functions: (1) guidance for the development of individual and family program plans, (2) feedback about the success of individual programming for children and families, and (3) a means for determining the value of an intervention program for groups or subgroups of program participants. Underlying these three functions is the important concept that these separate assessment/evaluation objectives be linked into a unified approach.

For a number of reasons a strong relationship between program goals, assessment procedures, curricular content, and subsequent evaluation of individual and group

A Linked Assessment-Intervention-Evaluation Approach

```
Program Goals → Assessment → Intervention → Evaluation
      ↑_____|
```

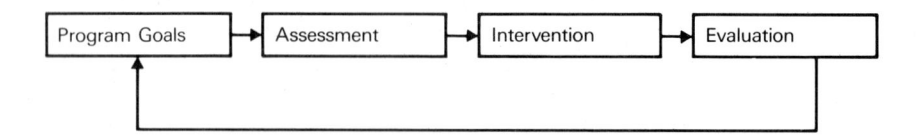

FIGURE 15-1. *Relationship among program goals, assessment, intervention, and evaluation.*

progress should exist. This linked system is graphically represented in Figure 15-1. If the assessment procedures used do not yield information necessary to develop effective long-range goals and training objectives, then one might ask, why use them? The generation of data that do not lend themselves to the development of relevant IEPs are of questionable value. Rather, the assessment procedures employed should produce data that can be used directly to formulate individual child and family goals and objectives. Further, these goals and objectives should be related directly to the curricular content and emphasis employed by a program. Ensuring these direct relationships requires a strong link between the assessment procedures, the development of IEPs, and the subsequent curricular materials used to meet the selected IEP objectives.

The assessment-intervention linkage should be extended to include evaluation. To appropriately determine the impact of the selected intervention content and procedures, it is necessary to employ methods of comparison that take into account the child's behavior prior to and following intervention. If the purpose is to determine the impact of an intervention program, then it is only sensible that the content of the intervention be reflected in the evaluation procedures. This reality requires a strong and continuing linkage from assessment to IEP development to curricular emphasis to evaluation. Interestingly, such approaches are seldom found in intervention programs. As Bagnato and Neisworth (1981) suggest, often little relationship appears to exist between the assessment, curricular focus, and evaluation that programs employ. The use of assessment and evaluation procedures that do not reflect program emphasis explains, in part, one major difficulty in the generation of useful efficacy data for early-intervention programs (Bricker, Bailey, & Bruder, 1984).

One might logically ask why more programs do not employ linked assessment-intervention-evaluation systems. Two reasons are apparent. First, many personnel who operate early-intervention programs did not receive preservice or inservice training on methods for linking assessment-intervention-evaluation. In fact, many received little training on the topics of assessment and evaluation, and thus, must struggle to establish any form of accountability. Thus, less than adequate linkage systems often reflect the program personnel's lack of training and information in the areas of assessment and evaluation.

A second reason one finds few operationally linked assessment-intervention-evaluation systems is that descriptions of such approaches are seldom found in the literature. Most frequently, descriptions focus on one element such as assessment and fail to extend the descriptions to other program elements. Other descriptions, which may be more relevant, remain at the theoretical level and fail to provide interventionists with strategies for implementing the type of linked system being advocated. The book by Bagnato and Neisworth (1981) is an exception and provides both a model and extensive description of how to implement a linked assessment-curricular system.

The organizational framework for a linked assessment-intervention-evaluation system proposed in this chapter includes the three functions of assessment/evaluation already described. In particular, the focus is on using the initial assessment data to develop appropriate intervention objectives and as a baseline for evaluation of progress and program effectiveness at the group or aggregate level. Before this linked approach to assessment, intervention, and evaluation is discussed, definitions and examples of screening, norm-referenced, and criterion-referenced tests are presented. In addition, the major assessment and evaluation dilemmas facing early interventionists are described.

MEASUREMENT: SCREENING, ASSESSMENT AND EVALUATION

An examination of the assessment/evaluation procedures employed by many early-intervention programs reveals discrepancies even in terminology. Verbal and written descriptions suggest that discriminations between the processes of screening, diagnosis, educational assessment, and evaluation often fail to occur. Thus, a brief delineation of these four processes may be useful.

As indicated in Figure 15-2, these processes are separate but can be and often are related. Screening generally occurs first, and during this process, which can be formal or informal, a binary decision is reached as to whether the child is developing with or without problems. Diagnosis is the process of determining the problem and is generally conducted by a multidisciplinary team of professionals. If a problem is identified, the child is labeled and referred to an appropriate program. When the child enters a program, assessment measures are administered to determine what specific intervention goals and objectives should be established for the child and the family. Assessment and evaluation differ in that the assessment process provides baseline information but no comparison. The process of evaluation requires a comparison—most frequently, comparing the child's performance before and after intervention, as indicated by arrows in Figure 15-2.

A Linked Assessment-Intervention-Evaluation Approach

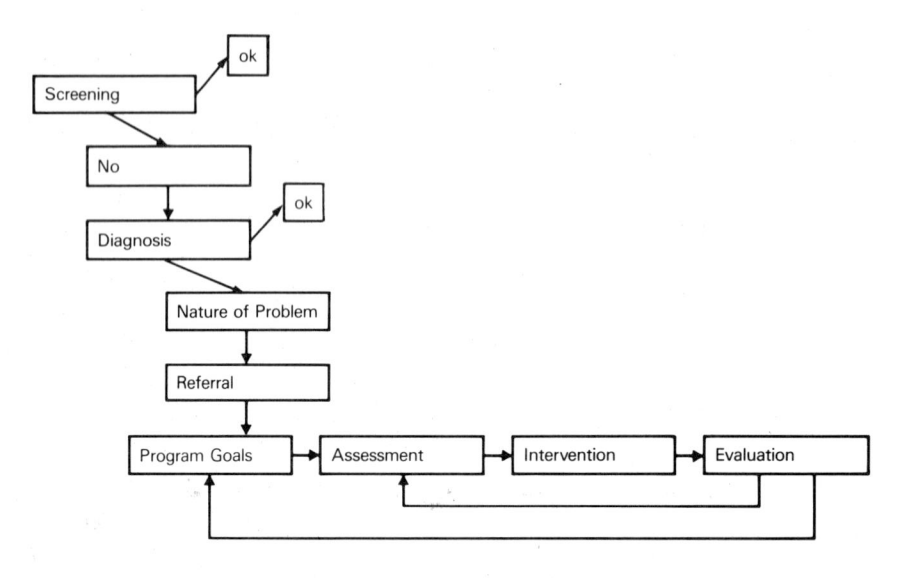

FIGURE 15-2. Relationship among the measurement processes of screening, diagnosis, assessment, and evaluation.

Screening Tests

> Screening is defined as the presumptive identification of unrecognized disease or defects by the application of tests, examinations or other procedures which can be applied rapidly. (Kemper & Frankenburg, 1979, p. 12)

Table 15-1 contains a list of screening instruments frequently used with infants and young children. This table contains the name of the test, the population for whom it is intended, the age range, the purpose, domains covered, availability of psychometric data, and type of test outcomes.

Norm-Referenced Tests

According to Salvia and Ysseldyke (1978), norm-referenced tests:

> ... allow the tester to discriminate among the performances of a number of individuals and to interpret how one person's performance compares to that of other individuals with similar characteristics. In norm-referenced testing, a person's performance on a test is measured relative to or in reference to the performances of others who are presumably like that person. Norm-referenced tests are standardized on groups of individuals and typical performances for students of certain ages or in certain grades are obtained. (p. 28)

Measurement: Screening, Assessment, and Evaluation

Test Name	Target Population and Age Range/Purpose	Domains Covered	Psychometric Data Available	Outcomes
The TARC Assessment System (Sailor & Mix, 1975)	Retarded or severely handicapped children Overview of current level of functioning; assessment	Self-Help Motor Communication Social	Yes	Profile; standard score per domain
The Preschool Attainment Record (PAR) (Doll, 1966)	Sensory impaired infants and preschoolers birth–7 years Screening measure (parent interview)	Physical Social Intellectual	Yes	Attainment age scores; "attainment quotients"
Denver Developmental Screening Test (DDST) (Frankenburg & Dodds, 1970)	Infants and children birth–6 years Screening; detecting developmental delays	Gross Motor Language Fine Motor- Adaptive Personal-Social	Yes	Age level
The Perceptions of Developmental Skills Profile (PODS) (Bagnato & Neisworth, 1977)	Handicapped preschoolers 2–8 years Screening measure (subjective ratings of significant adults)	Communication Own-Care Motor Problem-solving	Preliminary Data	Profile
Developmental Activities Screening Inventory (DASI) (Dubose & Langley, 1977)	Sensory impaired preschoolers 6–60 months "Interim" screening measure between identification of developmental problems and diagnostic assessment	Fine Motor Causality- Means/Ends Number concepts Size Discrimination Seriation	Yes, but limited validity data	Skill inventory

TABLE 15–1 Selected Screening Instruments

Table 15–2 contains a list of the norm-referenced tests frequently used with infants and young children. This table contains the test's name, target population, purpose, domains covered, availability of psychometric data, and type of test outcomes.

Criterion-Referenced Tests

According to U.S. Office of Education validation guidelines (Tallmadge & Horst, 1976):

> The dominant characteristic of tests that are labeled "criterion-referenced" is that their content is clearly defined in terms of some performance dimension or interest. This relationship permits direct interpretation of individual scores in ways which have immediate practical implications. (p. 55)

A Linked Assessment-Intervention-Evaluation Approach

Test Name	Target Population and Age Range/ Purpose	Domains Covered	Psychometric Data Available	Outcomes
The Kent Infant Development (KIDS) Scale (Katoff, Reuter, & Dunn, 1978)	Infants and young handicapped children Evaluating the developmental status; assessment	Cognitive Motor Social Language Self-Help	Yes	Developmental age and profile of skills
Bayley Scales of Infant Development (BSID) (Bayley, 1969)	Infants 2–30 months Comprehensive analysis of infant development skills	Mental Psychomotor	Yes	Developmental quotient, developmental age
The Gesell Developmental Schedules (Knobloch, Stevens, & Malone, 1980)	Infants 1–72 months Functional assessment of infant's/preschooler's range of developmental skills	Communication Gross Motor Fine Motor Adaptive Personal-Social	Yes	Developmental quotient, maturity age
Marianne Frostig Developmental Test of Visual Perception (DTVP) (Frostig, 1966)	Children 3–8 years Measure visual perception and eye-motor coordination	Visual/ perceptual	Yes	Age level; scale; perceptual quotient
Illinois Test of Psycholinguistic Abilities (ITPA) (Kirk, McCarthy & Kirk, 1968)	Children 2–10 years Assess expressive and receptive language	Communication	Limited	Age level score
Peabody Picture Vocabulary Test– Revised (PPVT–R) (Dunn & Dunn, 1981)	Children and adults 2½–adult Assess receptive vocabulary	Receptive	Yes	Age level
Sequenced Inventory of Communication Development (SICD) (Hedrick & Tobin, 1975)	Children 4 months–4 years Evaluate development of verbal and nonverbal communication	Receptive and expressive communication	Yes	Age level
Stanford-Binet Intelligence Scale (Thorndike, Hagen & Sattler, 1985)	Children 2 years–adult Measure general intellectual ability	General intelligence	Yes	Mental age; IQ
McCarthy Scales of Children's Abilities (McCarthy, 1972)	Children 2½–8½ years Measure intelligence and identify children with possible learning disabilities	Verbal Perceptual Quantitative Cognitive Memory Motor	Yes, but limited validity data	Scale index, general cognitive index
The Developmental Profile II (Rev. ed.) (Alpern & Shearer, 1980)	Children birth–9 years Assess development for placement or educational programming	Physical Self-help Social Academic Communication	Yes	Inventory of skills; profile of functional developmental-age level

TABLE 15–2 Selected Norm-Referenced Assessment/Evaluation Instruments

Assessment/Evaluation Dilemmas

Table 15-3 contains a list of selected criterion-referenced tests used with infants and young children. This table contains information about target population, purpose, domains covered, availability of psychometric data, and type of test outcomes.

ASSESSMENT/EVALUATION DILEMMAS

Substantial problems exist in accurately, and perhaps more important, usefully assessing baseline behavior and monitoring subsequent change in populations of at-risk and handicapped infants and children (Bricker, 1978). In-depth discussions of these problems exist elsewhere (e.g., see Simeonsson, Huntington, & Parse, 1980; DuBose, 1981; Sheehan & Keogh, 1982; Bricker, Sheehan, & Littman, 1981); consequently, they will only be highlighted here. The nature of these problems can be conveniently categorized as:

1. Target population
2. Instruments
3. Assessment/evaluation models
4. Relationship of assessment to programming

Target Population

An immense problem that pervades the field of early intervention is the heterogeneity of the target population. As indicated in Chapter 6, the population of handicapped children has disabilities that range from mild to profound. Programs must serve children with sensory impairments, motoric disabilities, cognitive deficits, communication disorders, and general behavioral disturbances. Often, children have a combination of problems or have a disability so significant that it pervades all aspects of the child's behavioral repertoire. For example, infants, toddlers, and young children may be unable to understand directions or unwilling to perform certain tasks. Young children are often wary and uncommunicative until they come to know the adult and the setting. In addition, programs have recently begun to include populations of infants labeled at-risk for developing a problem in the future (Swanson, 1979). This further increases the variability in populations confronted by service-delivery programs. Other factors include socioeconomic background, which is associated with considerable variability in families' educational levels, and general parental perceptions of and expectations for children. Diversity of ethnic background of families requires that assessment and evaluation strategies take into account the different mores and customs of each particular culture (Casuso, 1978). All of these factors conspire to produce a diverse group of infants, toddlers, and young children, making the

A Linked Assessment-Intervention-Evaluation Approach

Test Name	Target Population and Age Range/ Purpose	Domains Covered	Psychometric Data Available	Outcomes
The Learning Accomplishment Profile-Diagnostic Edition (revised) (LAP-D) (LeMay, Griffin & Sanford, 1978)	Infants and preschoolers birth–5½ years Developmental task-analysis diagnostic	Language Cognitive Gross Motor Self-help Social Fine Motor	Yes	Diagnostic profile; initial developmental task analysis
The Brigance Diagnostic Inventory of Early Development (Brigance, 1978)	Handicapped infants and preschoolers birth–6 years Developmental assessment measure	Motor Speech/ Language Preacademic	None	Performance level and developmental age level
The Stages of Sensorimotor Intelligence in the Child from Birth to 2 Years (Casati & Lezine, 1968)	Infants birth–2 years Assess sensorimotor stages of development	Exploration Visual pursuit Object constancy Use of intermediaries Combination of objects	None	Profile of skill level
Albert Einstein Scales of Sensorimotor Development (Corman & Escalona, 1967)	Infants 2–25 months Assess sensorimotor stages of development	Object permanence Prehension Spatial relations	Limited	Profile of response pattern
The Hawaii Early Learning Profile (HELP) (Furuno, O'Reilly, Hosaka, Inatsuka, Allman, & Zeisloft, 1979)	Handicapped infants System for assessing development and planning educational programs	Cognitive Language Gross Motor Fine Motor Social-Emotional Self-help	Limited	Profile of skill level; approximate age levels
The Home Observation for Measurement of the Environment (HOME Inventory) (Caldwell, 1978)	Young children birth–6 years Sample aspects of the quantity and quality of social, emotional, and cognitive support available to the child in the home	Home environment	Yes	Inventory of support available to the child in the home
Sewall Early Education Developmental Profiles (S.E.E.D.) (Herst, Wolfe, Jorgensen & Pallan, 1976)	Young children birth–4 years Detailed assessment to be used in informal evaluation	Social-Emotional Gross Motor Fine Motor Adaptive Language Feeding Self-help	No	Profile of abilities
The Memphis Comprehensive Developmental Scale (MCDS) (Quick, Little, & Campbell, 1974)	Handicapped preschoolers 3–60 months Programming measure	Personal-Social Gross Motor Fine Motor Language Percepto-cognitive	None	Profile for individual programming
Ordinal Scales of Infant Development (Uzgiris & Hunt, 1975)	Infants birth–2 years Assess development	Object permanence Means-ends Imitation Causality Object relations Object schemes	Yes	Performance on scales

Assessment/Evaluation Dilemmas

Test Name	Target Population and Age Range/ Purpose	Domains Covered	Psychometric Data Available	Outcomes
The Evaluation and Programming System: For Infants and Young Children (EPS) (Bricker, Bailey, & Gentry, 1985)	Infants birth–36 months Comprehensive system for assessment, evaluation, and intervention	Gross Motor Fine Motor Communication Cognitive Social Self-Help	Yes	Profile of skill level
The Callier-Azusa Scale (Stillman, 1974)	Multihandicapped children birth–9 years Assessment of level of functioning; selection of instructional goals	Motor Perceptual Language Daily Living Social	None	Diagnostic profile of level of functioning
Uniform Performance Assessment System (UPAS) (White, Edgar, Haring, Affleck, Hayden, & Bendersky, 1980)	Children birth–6 years Monitor progress of skills	Preacademic/Fine Motor Communication Social/Self-Help Gross Motor Behavior Management	Yes	Profile of skill level
Vulpe Assessment Battery (Vulpe, 1977)	Children with atypical development birth–6 years Assess developmental competencies and prepare educational programs	Basic Senses Gross Motor Fine Motor Language Cognitive Organizational Daily Living Environment	Limited reliability studies	Performance analysis

TABLE 15-3 Selected Criterion-Referenced Assessment/Evaluation Instruments

accurate assessment and evaluation of individual children a difficult exercise and the evaluation of group performances extremely vulnerable to invalid outcomes (Bricker & Sheehan, 1981).

Instruments

A remarkably large number of screening, norm-referenced and criterion-referenced tests, checklists, and other types of tests are available. Unfortunately, few meet the necessary requirements for a linked assessment-intervention-evaluation system. Existing instruments can be deficient in assessing and evaluating program impact for at-risk and handicapped infants and young children for a variety of reasons.

Most norm-referenced tests were developed using populations of normally developing children. Many of the available instruments have little or no normative data reflecting an at-risk or handicapped population's performance on the measure. Although many of these instruments can be used for purposes of identification and diagnosis, they are not appropriate to chart the progress of at-risk or handicapped infants or children because no norms or benchmarks exist for these groups of infants and children (Johnson, 1982;

White & Haring, 1978). The further children's performances differ from normal development, the less applicable are such instruments for establishing baseline behavior and monitoring subsequent progress. Adequate documentation of progress for the more impaired child requires instruments that can reflect small changes in behavior.

Often, the content found in norm-referenced instruments may not be useful in developing IEPs for children. For example, Bayley Scale items, "Manipulates table edge actively" or "Discriminates strangers" or "Playful response to mirror," do not lend themselves to development of useful IEP goals. Items may be found that are inappropriate teaching targets. In addition, significant gaps between items may preclude systematic programming unless the interventionist is extremely knowledgeable about developmental sequences.

A further obstacle to using many existing measures is the population variability discussed earlier. Standardized tests require that items be presented precisely as specified. If test protocols are not followed, the results are invalid. Equally troublesome is the specification of the form of the response, which generally permits little latitude; for example, the child with limited hand use would be penalized on items that require execution of fine motor response within a given time period. The limitations and diversity within populations of handicapped infants and children require a basic reformulation of the approach to assessment and monitoring (Gratch, 1982; Robinson, 1982).

This is not to imply that norm-referencing or standardization of testing procedures is undesirable. Rather, the intent and the content of the currently existing norm-referenced instruments are generally inappropriate for assessing the impact of intervention procedures on handicapped infants or children. The majority of presently available norm-referenced tests were constructed to reflect the degree to which children approximate the behavior typical of their chronological peers. Whether "normal" behavior and developmental patterns represent relevant standards for the assessment of progress in handicapped infants and children is a matter of some debate (Scott, 1978).

Criterion-referenced tests avoid many of the problems associated with standardized tests but often have other difficulties. A review of Table 15–3 suggests that many criterion-referenced tests have little psychometric data; thus, the data they generate on individual child performances are suspect in terms of validity and reliability. If a test indicates the child has made progress from September to June, should the data be considered an accurate reflection of change in the child or the result of test error?

A second problem associated with criterion-referenced tests is that the content may not reflect the program emphasis. Thus, a child's performance may not show change because the instrument is focused on areas not taught in the intervention program. This common problem has, in the past, lead many interventionists to develop "homemade" tests. Although such tests may better represent the content of a program, this approach is somewhat shortsighted. Most homemade instruments are not used with an adequate sample size to collect adequate psychometric data; one is again faced with resulting information about change in children that is suspect.

These dilemmas often complicate the choice of an instrument. The interventionist may be faced with a choice between a psychometrically sound instrument that does not reflect the program's goals and a criterion-referenced instrument that reflects program goals but whose psychometric properties are unknown. Finally, many norm-referenced or criterion-referenced tests do not lend themselves to the development of a linked assessment-intervention-evaluation system.

Assessment-Evaluation Models

Over the past decade, educational services have been developed and extended to large segments of the handicapped population for whom meaningful educational programs did not previously exist. Initially, the major impact of those new programs was measured simply by indicating the number of children who were for the first time being provided *some* educational service. Now, as the evolution of program refinement begins, the need for more precise and meaningful program evaluation systems has increased. In recognition of that need, legislation has become increasingly specific in its requirements for program evaluation (e.g., Public Law 93-380, Public Law 94-142). U.S. Office of Education–sponsored evaluation guidelines have been developed (e.g., Horst, Tallmadge, & Wood, 1975), and panels of experts have convened to review and approve the evaluation procedures and results of federally funded education programs (e.g., the Joint Dissemination Review Panel). Still, efforts to assess and evaluate at-risk and handicapped populations have fallen short of providing adequate information.

There are several issues inherent in the assessment of an educational program's worth, but two questions are of major concern: (1) Are the children and families who are involved in the program making "acceptable" progress, and, if so, (2) is there reasonable evidence to indicate that observed progress is greater than if the children and families had been in alternative programs? In order to answer these questions, meaningful standards for "acceptable" progress must be established, and it must be possible to estimate what progress *would* have been if the family had *not* been associated with the program in question.

Inherent in making estimations is the need for a set of relevant benchmarks or expectancies against which child and family progress can be measured. Unfortunately, no agreed-upon set of standards exists that permits universal comparison of children and families to determine progress; there is no operationally defined prototype that is generally acceptable (Bricker, 1978). For example, agreement might be forthcoming that children should do well in school; however, attempts to operationally define "do well in school" highlight the necessity for qualifiers. Benchmarks are established or defined in relation to personal, family, and subcultural values and by the individual's personal resources, environmental, biological, or both. It is apparent that the standards of progress for a biologically normal child would be different from those for a youngster with Down syndrome or possibly those for a child from a background of poverty. These examples clarify the need for establishing agreed-upon and useful reference points (e.g., content areas, intervention targets) for measuring progress if meaningful analyses are to be conducted.

In the absence of functionally-derived and empirically-verified expectancies for handicapped infants and children, a normal developmental model has often been adopted. Many educators have reasoned that while handicapped children may never master all of the skills normal children are capable of performing, the skills that they learn should be acquired in essentially the same order as that of the normal skills and brought to at least a reasonable approximation of the normative response. To assess the degree and significance of handicapped children's progress, it should be necessary only to note how far along the normal developmental sequence the children have moved. Unlike items in a norm-referenced test, scale items would not be chosen simply for their ability to discriminate between children but would be chosen because they represent an ordered series of significant milestones along a continuum of normal growth and learning. Also, it would not be necessary for children to actually *reach* normal levels of performance before some change in children's performances was noted; sequential progress toward goals could be recorded.

Up until the age of at least two years, the sequence of normal human development *is* surprisingly consistent (Cohen & Gross, 1979). The actual time when certain skills appear will vary, but the order of their emergence is governed for the most part by apparent physiological interdependencies (e.g., before children are able to sit for long periods without support, they must be able to lift their heads). Between the years of two and six, the picture is a little less certain, primarily because of the increasing impact of experience upon development. Beyond the age of six, developmental patterns begin to vary even more, becoming increasingly dependent upon arbitrary curricula, instructional emphases, and many other variables in the child's environment (Fischer, 1980; McCall, 1981).

Such increasing variance from normal patterns of development has several implications. First, it underlines the importance of avoiding assessment devices that place total reliance on what is "normal." Such approaches may be insensitive to the significant and functional progress a child can still make when deviating from the norm becomes necessary. Second, attention is focused on the need to become more precise in the differentiation between what is "necessary" or "functional" and what is simply "usual." Certain motor development *is* necessary for walking, but this developmental sequence is not necessary for locomotion per se. Obviously, whenever a child

Assessment/Evaluation Dilemmas

can be taught skills that approximate the norm, an attempt should be made to achieve those aims. However, failure to move toward normality must not be equated with failure to develop functionally useful skills or to progress in any meaningful way.

The previous statements should not be interpreted as a disavowal of the usefulness of developmental theory or models. Rather, they caution against the wholesale adaptation of normal developmental models as the only or most appropriate sources to establish benchmarks or reasonable expectancies for at-risk or handicapped infants and children. Nevertheless, because few other useful models currently exist, normal developmental sequences used as a general reference are often the best available resource for establishing expectancies. However, interventionists should be prepared for children who will deviate significantly from established norms and have strategies for ensuring that such deviation becomes as functional as possible.

Relationship of Assessment to Intervention

The final problem associated with existing assessment/evaluation systems is the lack of continuity between assessment/evaluation and subsequent intervention efforts. This problem can be of two types: (1) assessment/evaluation items have no relationship to program objectives, or (2) the intervals between assessment/evaluation items are too great to reflect change in the target populations.

An examination of many existing tests reveals significant inadequacies when considered from the perspective of targets for educational programs. Bricker and Sheehan (1981) have argued elsewhere there should be a direct relationship between program objectives and the assessment instrument. Many currently available instruments seem, at best, remotely to reflect relevant and useful program goals and objectives.

A related issue of significant concern, particularly for the more severely impaired populations, is the usefulness/functionality of items in terms of enhancing children's repertoires. Many special educators are becoming increasingly attentive to the formulation of curricular materials from a programmatic perspective. The responses that will be of most use to the individual or build toward repertoires of independent functioning are becoming the focus. Rather than working on specific toy skills, such as skills with puzzles, peg boards, or other similar toys, many interventionists are directing training efforts toward functional skills and behaviors, such as turning switches and knobs, labeling essential objects or events, and communicating needs (e.g., thirst). Assessment/evaluation instruments should closely reflect program objectives.

A second problem area in relating the instrument to intervention efforts concerns the increments of change between items. Although substantial item intervals may be appropriate for children developing within normal limits, or even populations of mildly delayed children, problems arise when working with more severely handicapped infants and children. For example, severely handicapped preschool children involved in intensive intervention over a period of several months may show negligible change on standardized instruments but may show clear improvement on measures with more fine-grained item intervals. A need exists for instruments that have relatively small intervals between items to assist the interventionist in programming and also to reflect changes in the entire target population.

Summary

Educational services for populations of at-risk and handicapped infants and children have expanded dramatically in the last decade (Bricker, 1980). With the expansion of services has come the need to develop evaluation mechanisms to assess the incoming behavioral repertoires of these target populations and to monitor subsequent program impact on both individuals and groups. Subsequent progress has been made in both areas. Because of new assessment-programming-evaluation models, early-intervention personnel are increasingly able to conduct effective assessments, generate relevant IEPs, and complete useful individual and group evaluations. A description of one such model follows.

LINKING ASSESSMENT, INTERVENTION, AND EVALUATION

The evaluation plans and strategies undertaken by many early-intervention programs appear to lack a guiding theoretical rationale or focus. That is, there seems to be no articulated plan as to what type of data to collect or analysis to be conducted. The need for a well-structured plan becomes clear when one considers the implications of following a nontheoretical documentation process in which measures are selected and analysis conducted because they "might show something." Under such a regime, program personnel can be overwhelmed.

Figure 15-3 offers an organizational framework for the three functions of assessment and evaluation necessary to ensure effective intervention efforts. Though not all service-delivery programs will be able to allocate sufficient resources at each level, the field as a whole must consider each level of evaluation if progress is to be made in refining theory, content, and technology for early-intervention efforts across diverse populations of handicapped and at-risk infants and children. The proposed plan reflected in Figure 15-3 suggests that assessment-intervention-evaluation systems may be divided into several phases:

- initial assessment and formulation of individual education plans (IEP) and family program agreements (FPA);

Linking Assessment, Intervention, and Evaluation

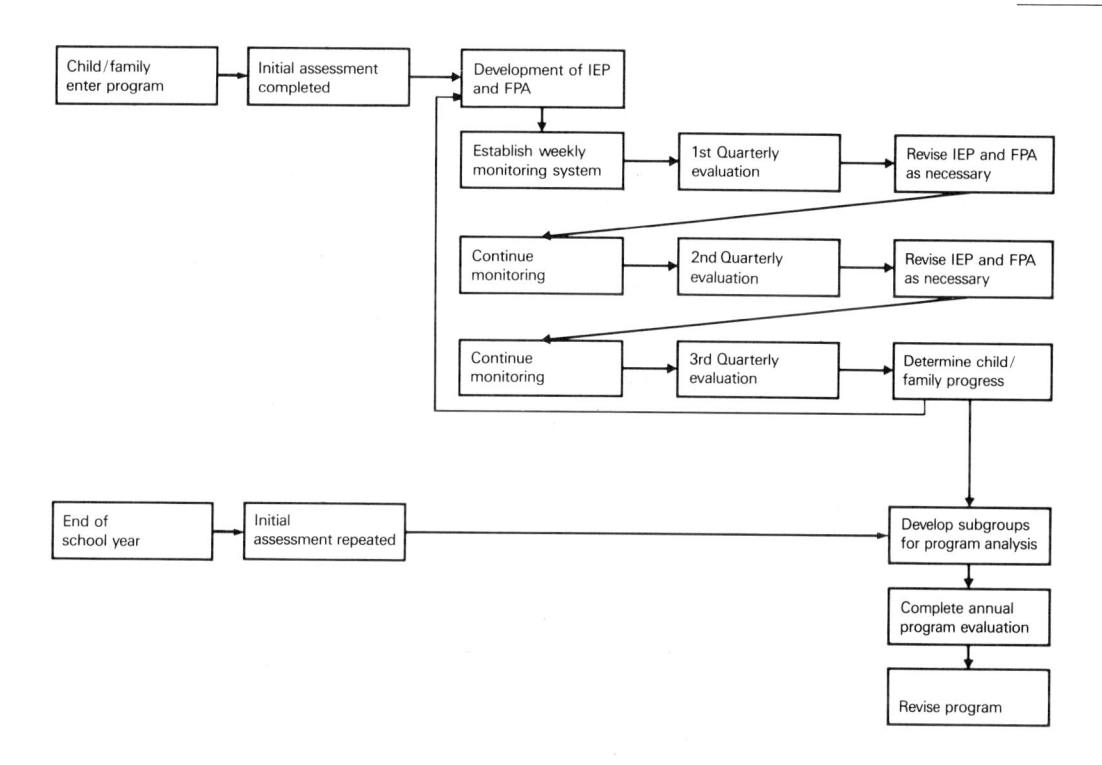

FIGURE 15-3. *Framework for an assessment-intervention-evaluation system.*

- weekly monitoring for immediate feedback about ongoing individual intervention procedures;
- quarterly evaluation of individual children and families; and
- annual evaluation of individual child/family progress and program effectiveness for subgroups of children and families.

The schematic presented in Figure 15-3 was designed to emphasize the direct and continuing linkage between assessment, intervention, and evaluation. An initial assessment is conducted on the child and family when they enter the program. The data generated from this assessment are used to develop an individual education plan (IEP) and family program agreement (FPA). A weekly monitoring system directly related to the IEP and FPA is established, and the data yielded from this monitoring are used for quarterly evaluations. Quarterly evaluations also require that program personnel

349

readminister the initial assessment tests. Based on the child's and family's charted progress, modifications of the IEP and FPA are made as necessary. The child and family continue to cycle through this system until the end of the school year or until they exit from the program. The annual evaluation is completed by readministering the initial assessments. The data are compared to initial and quarterly performances to establish program impact for individual children and families and for subgroups of children and families. This system ensures continuity from the initial assessment to the annual evaluation and should assist in obtaining maximum impact from program involvement.

Initial Assessments

The link between assessment, intervention, and evaluation begins with the entry of the child into a service program. Initial assessments can influence the delivery of services in three ways. First, determining the appropriateness of the program for children and families can be addressed. Second, determining the match between the program's goals and those of the family must be assessed to lay the groundwork for development of a family program agreement (FPA) that outlines the family's involvement in the program. Third, an appropriate individual educational plan (IEP) can be formulated for the child.

Programs are frequently oriented toward children with particular deficits. Every program cannot serve the needs of every child. Programs treating hearing-impaired children, for example, may be inappropriate for children with physical disabilities. Although diagnostic and evaluation services may assist in placing children in appropriate intervention programs, errors are made, and service-delivery agencies should verify that appropriate services can be provided for the child. This in-house assessment may enhance annual outcome data because data on children who should not be in the program and who may not improve as a result of inappropriate placement will not skew the evaluations of children who are appropriately placed.

The second objective of initial assessment should be the specification of the program's philosophy and approach for the parent. If program goals meet parental expectations, effective family program agreements (FPA) can be drawn up. Although the FPA need not contain a full specification of the child's IEP, it should be consistent with the goals of the IEP. The general goals of the child's program should be described in enough detail so that parents and staff understand and agree on areas of separate and joint responsibility. Specification of the family's role helps eliminate misunderstandings and frustration. Equally important, the parents are helped to understand that they are essential members of the intervention team.

The third major objective of initial assessment is the formulation of a realistic and appropriate IEP that has an accompanying individual evaluation plan. The initial assessment should (1) provide a picture of the historical, social, and medical factors that may be relevant to the delivery of services to the child and (2) determine the child's beginning skill level so that an intervention plan directed toward improving areas in which the child is deficient can be developed.

An effective IEP is the heart of an intervention program. The content of the IEP, along with that of the FPA, provides the road map for getting from the child's beginning skill repertoire to the skills specified as terminal or annual goals in the IEP. The development of the IEP goals epitomizes the inseparable mix of assessment and intervention. Poor initial assessment will lead to inappropriate or unrealistic IEPs, which will in turn lead to a failure to show improvement. The formulation of an IEP is as crucially dependent on appropriate assessment as the weaving of the best cloth is on the selection of the finest fibers.

The IEP should be based primarily on information accumulated during the initial assessment period, though this first testing should be validated at the first quarterly evaluation. The initial information should be used to develop a plan for action for the interventionists and to identify the specific content areas that the IEP will address. An IEP should contain long-range goals, training objectives, behavioral prescriptions, and a time-frame for meeting those goals. The operationalization of the IEP should be straightforward so that it can be used as a guide for the interventionist working with the child and as a criterion against which the success of intervention may be evaluated in quantitative terms.

Daily/Weekly Monitoring of the Child

A useful IEP specifies both the tasks to be carried out and the manner in which the success of the program will be evaluated. An inadequate IEP training goal might state, "Language will be targeted." A more useful IEP goal might state:

> "John's use of nouns in structured group settings will be targeted. He will be rewarded for each use of a noun in a group. The number of times he uses nouns in groups will be plotted every other day. Each week the average number of noun use will be determined. If the noun use has not increased twenty-five percent by the end of two weeks, the instructional strategy will be reevaluated."

This IEP goal is specific in two important ways. First, the goal clearly states the targets and the data to be collected. Second, and equally important, the goal incorporates the IEP into the feedback system. The results of weekly monitoring should have an impact on the IEP and on the delivery of services to the child. Failure to use weekly data to revise methods and instructional content will almost surely lead to poor progress at quarterly and annual evaluations.

The amount and type of data collected should be determined by the severity of the child's disability and the resources of the program. A project designed to demonstrate the effectiveness of a systematic program must devote extensive resources to monitoring and evaluation; a project primarily concerned with the delivery of services to large numbers of youngsters must of necessity balance data collection with timely delivery of services to all the children.

With appropriate planning, the collection of information on child progress gradually can be done in conjunction with service delivery. That is, the interventionist usually can monitor child behavior and prompt or shape a new response at the same time. Interventionists may collect trial-by-trial data or administer brief probes before and after training activities. In some situations, collecting data may be difficult, though with some ingenuity, it is possible. For example, an interventionist may use a wrist counter to record the number of communication gestures produced by the child during the training period each day. These daily data may then be used to monitor weekly progress as well as quarterly progress.

A variety of strategies may be used for weekly monitoring of children. The strategies selected should balance the resources of the program, the intervention efforts, and the necessity to use weekly monitoring as a source of feedback to keep the intervention effort on track. Weekly data should be viewed by the interventionist as a source of information rather than as a burden. Just as physicians are expected to make the best use of medical information in determining whether surgery or some other form of treatment is succeeding, interventionists should consider the collection of data to be part of their responsibility to children and their families. In addition to the benefits weekly monitoring has for the child, adjustments in the program resulting from these data may enhance the prospects of demonstrating individual improvement and program efficacy at quarterly and annual evaluations.

Quarterly Evaluation

Quarterly evaluation should focus on determining the effect of intervention efforts on quarterly objectives specified in the IEP and FPA. This can be done by using the initial assessment measures in conjunction with the weekly data. Quarterly evaluation should be used to compare the child's and family's progress with some standard or expectation. Without assigning an expected date of completion to objectives, interventionists may not be able to determine whether the progress made by the child and family is acceptable.

For example, quarterly IEP objectives should have automatic timelines; the child is expected to reach criterion on quarterly objectives within three months. Projections as shown in Figure 15–4 enhance intervention-

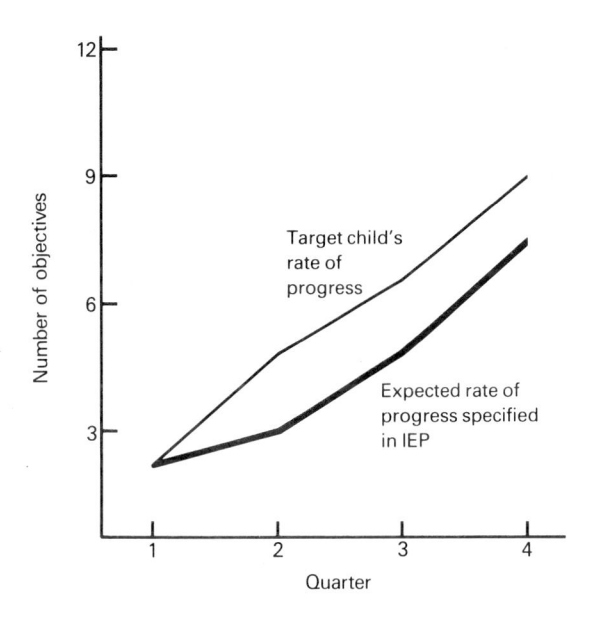

FIGURE 15-4. Comparing expected and actual child progress across quarters during one year.

evaluation efforts by comparing the expected rate of progress with the child's actual rate of progress. Through frequent plotting of the child's progress toward the established quarterly objectives, interventionists can establish more realistic objectives. In addition, comparisons between expected and attained outcomes will generate information that may eventually allow the establishment of relevant norms for subgroups of at-risk and handicapped children.

Quarterly evaluations provide information for revising the IEP and the FPA program. If all children fail to reach their established quarterly objectives in the motor domain, the program may not be providing enough training time in this area, or the training time may be used ineffectively. In either case the quarterly evaluation may suggest that a modification of the program is in order. Information from the quarterly evaluations provides feedback about child and family progress and about needed modifications or revisions in the IEP or FPA.

Annual Evaluation of Program Impact

Annual evaluations can be used to evaluate the progress of individual children and families and the generic impact of the program (e.g., subgroup analysis). That is, annual evaluation addresses both the impact of the program on individual children and families and the effectiveness of the program on subgroups. Without the latter comparisons, it is difficult to improve the development and implementation of effective intervention strategies with subpopulations of children. Methodological design and measurement problems facing the field of early intervention make subgroup evaluations difficult. However, conducting analyses on subgroups yields important findings on generalization of impact for certain constellations of children (e.g., all Down syndrome children) and families (e.g., parents with different educational levels).

Annual evaluation is the point of maximum intersection between evaluation of individual children and evaluation of programmatic effectiveness.

IMPLEMENTATION MODEL FOR DETERMINING CHILD AND FAMILY PROGRESS

Content of Progress

An effective strategy for establishing the content areas for measuring child and family progress is through the use of a framework composed of three independent, yet interrelated, levels of evaluation. Figure 15-5 provides a schematic of this approach. The greater the consistency among the three levels, the more efficient, appropriate, and useful will be the selected areas for measuring child/family change and program impact. The selection of program goals for children and families should be predicated upon the underlying philosophy or rationale that sets the general structure and atmosphere for the program. A frequent rationale for early intervention is that it facilitates (1) growth and development in important behavioral areas and (2) acceptance and enjoyment of the handicapped child by the family. Based on this rationale, a set of related program goals might include enhancing (1) children's acquisition and use of sensorimotor skills, (2) children's acquisition and use of social skills, (3) children's acquisition and use of communication skills, (4) children's acquisition and use of motor skills, (5) positive family interaction, and (6) parents' attitudes about their children. Such program goals (Level 3), in conjunction with initial assessment information, provide the professional staff and parents with a content framework from which to select and develop the individual child's and family's long-range goals and training objectives (Level 2). For a specific child, such related objectives based on program goals might be:

1. *Long-range goal.* The child will appropriately use social-communicative signals to indicate labels, requests, and greetings and to gain attention.

    Training objective (which is based on the long-range goal). The child will look at adult, point to objects, and vocalize to gain desired objects, actions, or events.

Implementation Model for Determining Child and Family Progress

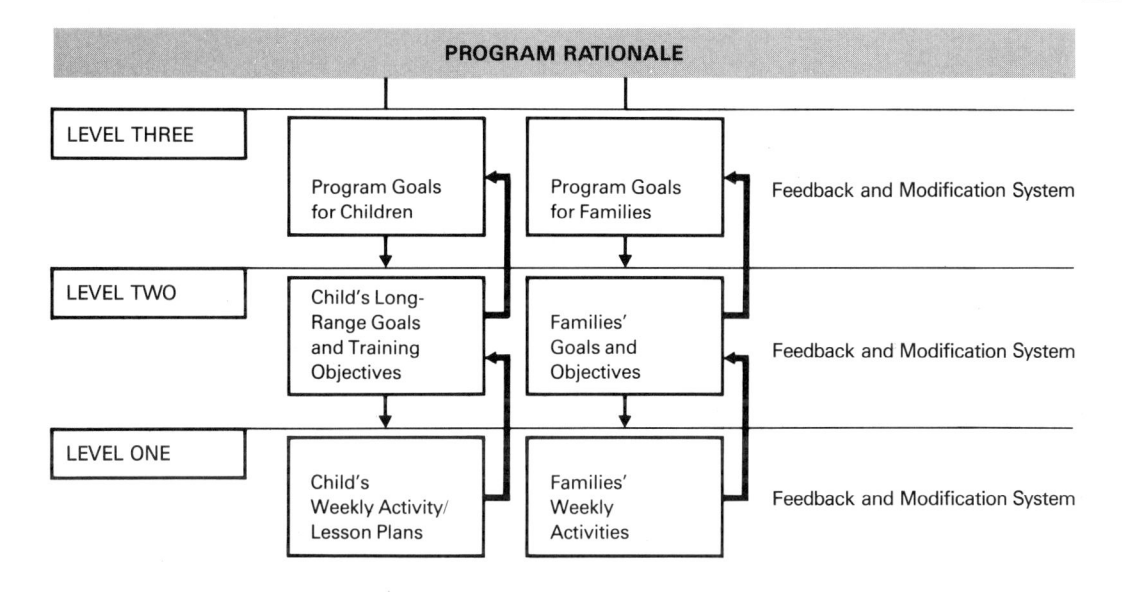

FIGURE 15-5. *Three interrelated levels of program evaluation.*

2. *Long-range goal.* The child will initiate appropriate interactions with peers.

    Training objective. The child will respond appropriately to interactions initiated toward him or her by peers.

The long-range goals and training objectives (Level 2) developed for each participating child and family provide the basis for the development of the child's individual weekly activity/lesson plan and the family's weekly activities (Level 1). Weekly activity plans for the child's training objectives might be:

1. During opening and closing group time, a desired object or event will be withheld while the child is prompted to look at adult, point, and vocalize.
2. During snack time, juice and crackers will be placed out of the child's reach and the child will be prompted to make eye contact, reach, and vocalize.
3. During small-group activities, peers will be prompted to initiate toward the child (e.g., share a crayon, throw a ball to), and the child will be prompted to reciprocate the action (e.g., give peer his or her crayon, roll the ball back).
4. During any program activity, the child will be immediately reinforced (e.g., given desired object, event, person) when he or she spontaneously makes eye contact, reaches, and vocalizes.

5. During any program activity, the child will be immediately reinforced (e.g., praised, given another turn) for responding appropriately to a peer's actions.

These examples reflect a nested series of training targets that evolve from global goals at Level 3 to increasingly more specific targets at Level 2 and Level 1. Such an organized nest of progressively more global training objectives provides a useful system for selecting the content to measure child progress at each of the three levels of evaluation. The measurement strategy and the comprehensiveness of the measurement target may change at these three levels, but the basic content remains the same. This content consistency provides a set of guidelines that directs measurement of child and family change and program impact.

Measurement of Progress

To evaluate child/family change, comparison with previous performances may be sufficient. However, to evaluate progress toward program goals, comparisons such as a standardized test, a set of norms, or a statistical analysis of change may need to be employed. The three-level framework offered in Figure 15-5 can also provide a useful system for measuring child/family change and program impact. Figure 15-6 parallels Figure 15-5 and suggests appropriate procedures and/or instruments for measuring progress at each of the three levels.

Level 1: Measuring Progress Toward Weekly Training Targets

The measurement of the child's and family's acquisition and use of specific training targets will, in most cases, have to be conducted without the benefit of a standardized, or criterion-referenced, instrument. To measure child/family change at this level, most interventionists will need to devise or adapt a specific data collection format (e.g., trial by trial, probes, observational sample) appropriate to training targets. Measurement approaches will vary across training objectives. For example, data collected on the child's use of vocalizations and gestures or on social interactions might be monitored through a weekly observation of the child at play. On the other hand, monitoring a mother's acquisition of a specific training skill might be accomplished by conducting weekly ten-trial probes.

The amount and type of data collected should be determined by the severity of the problem, the specific training objective, and program resources. Planning the collection of information on progress can be done in conjunction with the instructional program. That is, the interventionist can usually record the behavior and instruct a new response simultaneously if the data collection system has been properly devised. One useful strategy

Implementation Model for Determining Child and Family Progress

```
LEVEL THREE          Program Impact
                     Norm-referenced and/or
                     criterion-referenced tests
                              ▲
                              |
LEVEL TWO            Quarterly Child/Family Progress
                     Measures progress toward LRG & TO of
                     the children and families
                     (e.g., criterion-referenced tests)
                              ▲
                              |
LEVEL ONE            Weekly Child/Family Progress
                     Specific data collection
                     system (e.g., trial by trial,
                     probes, observational samples)
```

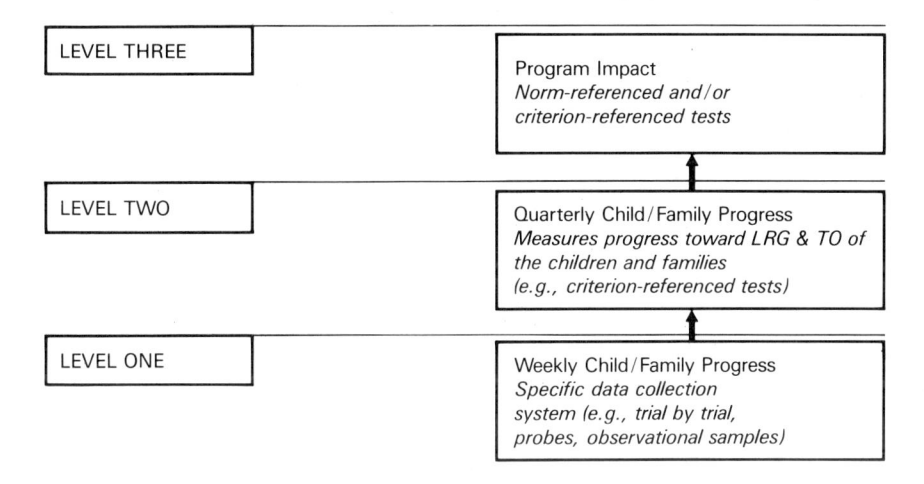

FIGURE 15-6. A three-level framework to direct selection of instruments for measuring progress.

involves the use of a grid format to record data. This system attempts to assess the impact of intervention using a group format with the training activities/lesson plans integrated into daily, on-going activities. The data-collection grid is a flexible format that allows the intervener to target several different skills for each child across activity groups, as shown in Figure 15-7. The grid format accommodates individualization of antecedents, responses, and consequence/error corrections; type and frequency of data collection and dispersion of instruction; and data collection across settings, adults, and peer groups. The antecedent-response-consequence written on the data grids are a shortened version taken from the individual child's program plan such as the one in Figure 15-8. The grid format also can be used for a series of training objectives for individual children or family members.

Level 2: Measuring Progress Toward Long-Range Goals and Training Objectives

The data acquired on specific targets for child and family change are essential to the formulation and implementation of a sound intervention program. The data collected on child and family progress toward more global long-range goals and training objectives can be employed to measure change as well. These data can also be used to evaluate program impact if the outcomes can be aggregated for total or subgroup analyses. For measuring progress toward long-range goals and training objectives, published instruments with norms and/or reliability and validity information may be useful. The instrument selected should be the same used during the initial assessment phase that provides the information used to formulate the IEP and FPA. Selection of an instrument should be based on several factors:

A Linked Assessment-Intervention-Evaluation Approach

DOMAIN	Teresa	Michael	Stephen

Communication	A: wants, needs, ideas
	R: sign and/or vocalize
	C: + receive object, praise
	   − repeat model
	   (physical assistance to sign)
	1　2　3　4　5
		A: desired object
		R: vocalize
		C: + receive object
		   − model
		1　2　3　4　5
			A: teacher model of word
			R: word approximation
			C: + praise
			   − repeat model
			ball　1　2　3　4　5
			book　1　2　3　4　5
			dog　1　2　3　4　5

Social	A: peer offers toy
	   (prompted by teacher)
	R: looks at peer and takes object
	C: + praise from peer
	   − physical assistance
	1　2　3　4　5		

Cognitive		A: verbal direction R: follow appropriately C: + praise − physical assistance "come here"　1　2　3 "sit down"　　1　2　3	
Gross Motor			A: bell ringing; time to transition to next group R: pulls to standing & walks with one hand held to next group C: + plays with objects at next group − physical assistance 1　2　3　4　5

KEY: A = antecedent
   R = response
   C = consequence (error correction)
   1–5 = number of trials

FIGURE 15-7.　Sample data grid.

1. The test will likely reflect the long-range goals and training objectives selected for participating children and families.
2. The test reflects the program's goals.
3. The test can be administered and scored by staff without undue difficulty.
4. The test's results are interpretable and useful.

For example, the Revised Gesell Developmental Schedules (Knobloch, Stevens, & Malone, 1980) may be appropriate for measuring achievement for a program with a developmental philosophy in which program staff intervene across adaptive behavior, gross motor, fine motor, language, and

Implementation Model for Determining Child and Family Progress

---

PROGRAM PLAN

CLIENT/CHILD Teresa   **TEACHER**
DOMAIN Communication
Decision Rule less than 50% for two days (change plan)
Type: Group ☒   Individual ☐   Home ☐

Long Range Goal Teresa will increase over baseline her spontaneous and appropriate use of signs accompanied with vocalizations to communicate her wants, needs and ideas.

---

1 Training Objective Teresa will imitate an adult model of a sign with vocalization with 90% accuracy over 2 consecutive days.

Program Steps   Antecedent: adult verbal and gestural model.
                Response: Teresa signs and vocalizes.
                Consequence: + give requested item and social praise.
                               − repeat model with physical assistance to sign.

2 Training Objective

Program Steps

FIGURE 15-8.   Sample program plan.

personal-social areas. However, a program concentrating on the inclusion of parents in the assessment process and without the resources to hire a psychologist or a qualified developmental specialist may find the Developmental Profile II (Alpern & Shearer, 1980) more appropriate for its needs. If an instrument is available that meets these program-relevant criteria, or with some modification meets the criteria, serious consideration should be given to the adoption of this test for a number of reasons. First, a published or broadly disseminated instrument may have norms or psychometric information not available for most "homemade" instruments. Second, more widely used instruments may have been developed with more care contributing to their face validity and usefulness. Third, such instruments may permit meaningful comparisons across children, groups, and/or programs.

Level 3: Measuring Progress Toward Program Goals

Assessing attainment of program goals can be used to monitor child/family change but is generally more useful for assessing the more generic impact of the program on participating children. The generic nature of this level of assessing progress and impact makes the adoption of a norm-referenced and/or standardized test generally the most desirable choice. The interventionist must decide the type(s) of child-progress goals for all children or subgroups of children. These goals may be (1) normal development in all areas, (2) normal development in several areas, (3) any development in all areas, or (4) any development in some areas (Sheehan, 1979). If the program goal is normality in the sensorimotor domain, then the Bayley Scales of Infant Development (Bayley, 1969) may be an appropriate instrument to select to measure progress toward that program goal. Standardized tests are a wise choice when evaluating program outcomes because of their long-term summative nature (Green, Ginsberg, & Hyman, 1974). However, programmatic evaluation using norm-referenced tests poses problems similar to those of individual assessment. These problems include population variability, suitability of existing instruments, and design/analytic strategies (Bricker & Littman, 1982). Interventionists should be aware of the limitations of norm-referenced tests and appropriately qualify their results (see Garwood, 1982; Ramey, Campbell, & Wasik, 1982).

It is important to establish criteria for selecting a test to measure attainment of program goals. Again, the test generally should have the following features:

1. appropriateness for the population, although the population on which the test was normed may be different;
2. administration and interpretation of the test within the resources of the program; and
3. results usable for program evaluation.

The first criterion suggests that the measure selected should be sensitive enough to detect change in children's performance and should also have reasonable agreement with program goals and objectives (Hamilton & Swan, 1981). The third criterion does not mean that the outcomes are necessarily useful for developing individual intervention procedures, but rather that they may offer general information on changes in the group or subgroups of children served by the program.

Analysis of Progress

Again, it is useful to use the three-level evaluation framework found in Figure 15-5 to discuss appropriate designs and analytical procedures. Designs and analyses should vary depending upon the purpose, content, and level at which progress is being monitored or program impact is being assessed.

Level 1: Analysis of Daily/Weekly Progress

At this level, progress toward the acquisition and use of specific training targets is of primary interest. Some form of weekly information should be collected and then systematic comparisons made between these data and those collected previously. Such comparisons require some consistent system for acquiring these data if comparison is to be valid. A number of different strategies can be employed. For example, the number of objectives reached within a given time period and/or length of time to reach criteria can be indicated. Data can be plotted on individual graphs to illustrate percent, proportion, frequency, or rate change over time. The most appropriate design for this level is probably single subject analysis. If possible, programs should attempt to demonstrate functional relationships between the instructional programs and changes in responses and/or patterns of behavior. However, some programs may not have the necessary resources to effectively carry out reversal or multiple baseline procedures. Program personnel should select a pragmatic and useful way to examine and display their weekly data to monitor progress and to make sound educational decisions.

Level 2: Analysis of Progress Toward Long-Range Goals and Training Objectives

This level of analysis can be conducted in much the same way as that described in Level 1 for individual children and family members. Use of a group design approach would be equally appropriate if the children and families can be meaningfully assigned to subgroups. Program staff have at least two general options available. The first procedure involves the statistical comparison of predicted progress with actual progress. The predicted progress can be derived in several ways, including reference to existing norms, correlation between performance on pretest and that on posttest, and correlations between posttest of one year and posttest of the next year. An alternative to a statistical comparison is to establish expectancies or timelines for which children/family members will reach criteria on training objectives and long-range goals. Then the actual progress can be plotted against the pretest timelines for each long-range goal and training objective. Problems with these approaches include assumptions of linear growth and stable estimates of progress.

The second alternative requires the comparison of one intervention program with other programs. This design also has problems, which include (1) ensuring the comparability of children and families across programs, (2) variability in critical program dimensions (e.g., staff), and (3) assessments that favor one group over another (e.g., communication assessment that requires only an oral response may unduly penalize children in programs where alternative communication strategies are encouraged).

The previous problems make it apparent that currently no perfect strategy exists for measuring progress (Bricker & Sheehan, 1981). Programs must evaluate their goals and resources and then select the design that offers the best compromise for their populations.

Level 3: Analysis of Progress Toward Program Goals

The analytic designs discussed for Level 2 are equally appropriate for this level of determining progress and/or program impact. At this level, some form of comparison seems mandatory if program impact is to be implied. As with Level 2, a number of serious barriers exist in evaluating progress toward program goals. These problems, discussed earlier, are population variability, suitability of available measures, lack of appropriate assessment models, and the relationship of assessment to programming.

The populations served by early-intervention programs range from at-risk to profoundly impaired, and the impairments are extremely diverse. In addition, great variability may be found in educational and socioeconomic backgrounds of families involved in programs. Often, this diversity creates extremely small numbers of children and families who can be meaningfully grouped. This heterogeneity affects the measures and designs that are applicable for examining program impact (Lewis & Wehren, 1982).

Existing instruments often fail populations of at-risk and handicapped children in at least two ways. First, selected items may be completely inappropriate for children with certain disabilities, and, second, for more severely impaired children, the developmental space between items may preclude reflecting any change or growth by this group of handicapped children. Other problems include inability to randomly assign children or families to experimental and control groups. Further, nonintervention controls are generally not possible for ethical reasons (e.g., services cannot be withheld from handicapped children). As discussed before, the design options suggested also have problems (Bricker, Sheehan, & Littman, 1981).

The barriers facing interventionists in documenting program impact are significant and are underlined with another pervasive difficulty. The majority of early-intervention programs do not have adequate resources to permit the conduct of elaborate and controlled comparisons of program impact. This reality should not provide a cover that allows interventionists to eliminate attempts at documenting program impact, nor should this reality condone poorly conceived and executed measurement plans. Rather, limited resources should require (1) thoughtful compromise, (2) extensive planning in order to use limited resources most effectively, and (3) dedication to searching for acceptable alternatives to present designs and analytical problems.

SUMMARY

This chapter has presented an approach to the evaluation of child and family progress that is based upon the conceptual position that assessment, intervention, and evaluation are inseparably linked. This interrelated system directly employs the information produced by the initial assessment to develop IEPs and FPAs. Data generated by quarterly evaluation of progress toward the IEP and FPA objectives are used to modify training targets and revise IEPs and FPAs as necessary. Annual evaluations entail comparisons with the child's/families' entry behavior and quarterly progress. The assessment, intervention, and evaluation phases are dependent on and directly linked to one another.

Although linked assessment-intervention-evaluation approaches assist significantly in the field's attempt to document progress and impact, there can be little doubt that the evaluation problems still to be overcome are enormous. Currently, the best we can do is to adopt compromise strategies that produce the greatest benefits. Limitations continue to exist in measuring child and family change and the impact of early-intervention programs. As noted by Bailey and Bricker (1984), the field of early childhood/special education has made significant progress during its short life. We have moved from wondering if we could intervene with a preschool population to developing systems that enhance our efforts and accountability. Continued work will yield assessment/evaluation measures, designs, and analytical techniques that will improve our ability to determine program impact on children and families.

References

Alpern, G., & Shearer, M. (1980). *The developmental profile II* (rev. ed.). Aspen, CO: Psychological Development Publications.

Bagnato, S., & Neisworth, J. (1981). *Linking developmental assessment and curricula.* Rockville, MD: Aspen Publications.

Bagnato, S., Neisworth, J., & Eaves, R. (1977). *The perceptions of developmental skills (PODS) profile.* University Park, PA: The Pennsylvania State University, HICOMP Preschool Project.

Bailey, E., & Bricker, D. (1984). The efficacy of early intervention for severely handicapped infants and young children. *Topics in Early Childhood Special Education, 4*(3), 30-51.

Bayley, N. (1969). *Manual for the Bayley scales of infant development.* New York: The Psychological Corporation.

Bricker, D. (1978). Early intervention: The criteria of success. *Allied Health and Behavioral Sciences Journal, 1,* 567-582.

Bricker, D., Bailey, E., & Bruder, M. (1984). The efficacy of early intervention and the handicapped infant: A wise or wasted resource? *Advances in Developmental and Behavioral Pediatrics, Vol. 5.* Greenwich, CT: JAI Press.

Bricker, D., Gentry, D., & Bailey, E. (1985). *The Comprehensive Early Evaluation and Programming System.* Eugene, OR: University of Oregon.

Bricker, D., & Littman, D. (1982). Intervention and evaluation: The inseparable mix. *Topics in Early Childhood Special Education, 1,* 23-33.

Bricker, D., & Sheehan, R. (1981). Effectiveness of an early intervention program as indexed by child change. *Journal of the Division For Early Childhood, 4,* 11-27.

Bricker, D., Sheehan, R., & Littman, D. (1981). *Early intervention: A plan for evaluating program impact.* Seattle, WA: WESTAR Publication.

Brigance, A. (1978). *Brigance diagnostic inventory of early development.* Worcester, MA: Curriculum Associates, Inc.

Caldwell, B. (1978). *Home observation for measurement of the environment.* Syracuse, NY: Syracuse University Press.

Casati, I., & Lezine, I. (1968). *The stages of sensorimotor intelligence in the child from birth-2 years.* (trans. E. V. Ristow). Paris: Center of Applied Psychology.

Casuso, V. (1978). Working with families of the preschool handicapped child in Spanish-speaking communities. In P. Trohanis (Ed.), *Early education in Spanish-speaking communities.* New York: Walker & Co.

Cohen, M., & Gross, P. (1979). *The developmental resource: Behavioral sequences for assessment and program planning.* New York: Grune & Stratton.

References

Corman, H., & Escalona, S. (1967). *Albert Einstein scales of sensorimotor development.* Rose F. Kennedy Center for Research in Mental Retardation and Human Development.

Doll, E. (1966). *Preschool attainment record.* Circle Pines, MN: American Guidance Service.

DuBose, R. (1981). Assessment of severely impaired young children: Problems and recommendations. *Topics in Early Childhood Education, 1,* 9–21.

Dubose, R., & Langley, M. (1977). *The developmental activities screening inventory.* New York: Teaching Resources.

Dunn, L., & Dunn, L. (1981). *Peabody picture vocabulary test-revised (PPVT-R).* Circle Pines, MN: American Guidance Service, Inc.

Fischer, K. (1980). A theory of cognitive development: The control and construction of hierarchies of skills. *Psychological Review, 87,* 477–531.

Frankenburg, W., & Dodds, J. (1970). *Denver developmental screening test (DDST).* Denver, CO: Ladoca Project and Publishing Foundation, Inc.

Frostig, M. (1966). *Marianne Frostig developmental test of visual perception (DTVP).* (rev. ed.). Palo Alto, CA: Consulting Psychologists Press, Inc.

Furuno, S., O'Reilly, C., Hosaka, C., Inatsuka, T., Allman, T., & Zeisloft, B. (1979). *HELP: Hawaii early learning profile activity guide.* Palo Alto, CA: VORT Corporation.

Garwood, G. (1982). Early childhood intervention: Is it time to change outcome variables? *Topics in Early Childhood Special Education, 1,* ix–xi.

Gratch, G. (1982). Piaget, the notion of action, and assessing intelligence in handicapped infants. In D. Bricker (Ed.), *Intervention with at-risk and handicapped infants: From research to application.* Baltimore, MD: University Park Press.

Green, D., Ginsberg, N., & Hyman, H. (1974). *The nature and uses of criterion and norm-referenced achievement tests.* Monterey: McGraw-Hill.

Hamilton, J., & Swan, W. (1981). Measurement references in the assessment of preschool handicapped children. *Topics in Early Childhood Special Education, 1*(2), 41–48.

Hedrick, E., & Tobin, A. (1975). *Sequenced inventory of communication development (SICD).* Seattle, WA: University of Washington Press.

Herst, J., Wolfe, S., Jorgensen, G., & Pallan, S. (1976). *S.E.E.D. developmental profiles* (Sewall early education development profiles). Denver, CO: Sewall Rehabilitation Center.

Horst, D., Tallmadge, K., & Wood, C. (1975). *A practical guide to measuring project impact on student achievement* (Stock No. 017-080-01460). Washington, DC: U.S. Department of Health, Education, and Welfare, U.S. Office of Education. U.S. Government Printing Office.

Johnson, N. (1982). An interventionist's perspective. In D. Bricker (Ed.), *Intervention with at-risk and handicapped infants: From research to application.* Baltimore, MD: University Park Press.

Katoff, L., Reuter, J., & Dunn, V. (1978). *The Kent infant development scale.* Kent, OH: Kent State University.

Kemper, M., & Frankenburg, W. (1979). Screening, diagnosis, and assessment: How do these types of measurement differ? In T. Black (Ed.), *Perspectives on measurement: A collection of readings for educators of young handicapped children.* Chapel Hill, NC: Technical Assistance Development System (TADS).

Kirk, S., McCarthy, J., & Kirk, W. (1968). *Illinois test of psycholinguistic abilities (ITPA)* (rev. ed.). Urbana, IL: University of Illinois Press.

Knobloch, H., & Pasamanick, B. (1974). *Gesell and Armatruda's developmental diagnosis* (3rd ed.). New York: Harper & Row.

Knobloch, H., Stevens, F., & Malone, A. (1980). *Manual of developmental diagnosis: The administration and interpretation of the revised Gesell and Armatruda developmental and neurologic examination.* Hagerstown, MD: Harper & Row.

LeMay, D., Griffin, P., & Sanford, A. (1978). *Learning accomplishment profile: Diagnostic edition* (rev. ed.). Winston-Salem, NC: Kaplan School Supply.

Lewis, M., & Wehren, A. (1982). The central tendency in study of the handicapped child. In D. Bricker (Ed.), *Intervention with at-risk and handicapped infants: From research to application.* Baltimore, MD: University Park Press.

McCall, R. (1981). Nature-nurture and the two realms of development: A proposed integration with respect to mental development. *Child Development, 52*(1), 1–12.

McCarthy, D. (1972). *McCarthy scales of children's abilities.* New York: The Psychological Corporation.

Quick, A., Little, T., & Campbell, A. (1974). *Memphis comprehensive developmental schedules.* Belmont, CA: Fearon Publishers.

Ramey, C., Campbell, F., & Wasik, B. (1982). Use of standardized tests to evaluate early childhood special education programs. *Topics in Early Childhood Special Education, 1,* 51–60.

Robinson, C. (1982). Questions regarding the effects of neuromotor problems on sensorimotor development. In D. Bricker (Ed.), *Intervention with at-risk and handicapped infants: From research to application.* Baltimore, MD: University Park Press.

Sailor, W., & Mix, B. (1975). *The TARC assessment system.* Lawrence, KS: H & H Enterprises, Inc.

Salvia, J., & Ysseldyke, J. (1978). *Assessment in special and remedial education.* Dallas: Houghton Mifflin.

Scott, K. G. (1978). Learning theory, intelligence, and mental development. *American Journal of Mental Deficiency, 82*(4), 325–336.

Sheehan, R. (1979). Measuring child progress: Large group design and norm-referenced alternatives. In M. May (Ed.), *Evaluating handicapped children's early education program.* Seattle, WA: WESTAR.

Sheehan, R., & Keogh, B. (1982). Design and analysis in the evaluation of early childhood special education programs. *Topics in Early Childhood Special Education, 1,* 81–88.

Simeonsson, R., Huntington, G., & Parse, S. (1980). Assessment of children with severe handicaps: Multiple problems—Multivariate goals. *Journal of the Association for the Severely Handicapped, 5,* 55–72.

Stillman, R. (1974). *The Callier-Azusa scale: Assessment of deaf-blind children.* Reston, VA: Council for Exceptional Children.

Swanson, J. (1979). Principles of infant assessment. In B. Darby & M. May (Eds.), *Infant assessment: Issues and applications.* Seattle, WA: WESTAR.

Tallmadge, G., & Horst, D. (1976). *A procedural guide for validating achievement gains in educational projects.* Washington, DC: U.S. Department of Health, Education, and Welfare, U.S. Office of Education. U.S. Government Printing Office.

Thorndike, R., Hagen, E., & Sattler, J. (1985). *Stanford-Binet intelligence scale,* ed. 4. Chicago: Riverside Publishing.

Uzgiris, I., & Hunt, J. (1975). *Assessment in infancy: Ordinal scales of psychological development.* Urbana, IL: University of Illinois Press.

Vulpe, S. (1977). *Vulpe assessment battery.* Canada: National Institute on Mental Retardation.

White, O., Edgar, E., Haring, N., Affleck, J., & Hayden, A. (1980). *Uniform performance assessment system.* Columbus, OH: Charles E. Merrill.

White, O., & Haring, N. (1978). Evaluating educational programs serving the severely and profoundly handicapped. In N. Haring & D. Bricker (Eds.), *Teaching the severely handicapped* (Vol. 3). Columbus, OH: Special Press

CHAPTER 16

MAJOR THEMES AND FUTURE DIRECTIONS

The writing of this book was prompted by an examination of textbooks addressing the field of early childhood special education. Currently available books have not blended a conceptual understanding of the field with implementation strategies. Therefore, the goal of this volume has been to provide a conceptual/organizational framework from which is developed an applied approach. The book's first part addresses the historical underpinnings of the ECH/SE field; the rationale for providing early intervention to populations of at-risk and handicapped children; the data on program impact; and legal/legislative precedents and current regulations that offer guidance for the provision of services to young children and their families. Chapters in the first part also define the population, discuss the rationale for including families in the intervention process, and provide descriptions of the major service delivery options used by early interventionists.

The second part of the book offers a detailed description of an intervention approach based on the conceptual and organizational framework presented in the first part. The second part begins with a discussion of the organizational system that guides the approach, subsequent chapters addressing staff and parent training and management, the intake and IEP process, the curricular approach, environmental arrangements, and evaluation of program impact. These chapters were formulated to offer interventionists sufficient information to design and deliver quality services to at-risk and handicapped children and their families. Thus, a unique aspect to this book is its attempt to provide the reader with the conceptual foundation that underlies the advocated intervention approach.

MAJOR THEMES

Throughout this book, a number of important themes have emerged. The more important of these themes are the need for (1) a professional approach to intervention; (2) the development and implementation of programs using goals and objectives; (3) organized systems to manage staff, curricular materials, physical environment, and evaluation; (4) a longitudinal perspective; (5) the inclusion of salient environmental and social elements in the intervention process; and (6) objective decision making.

A Professional Approach

For many people, the need for a profession of early-childhood specialists and formal intervention programs for children younger than school-age may seem questionable. Given adequate attention and nourishment, many people believe, infants and young children grow "naturally" into older children and ultimately into competent adults. Although it is generally acknowledged that caregivers significantly influence the development of their young children, much of what parents do for their young appears to occur appropriately without specific instruction or direction. Therefore, an appreciation of the importance of the early periods is held by most people, but that appreciation is not generally accompanied by a feeling that information and direction can enhance a child's outcome during the birth-to-five-year period.

The need for explicit instruction for children who are developing without problems is not obvious. In fact, it has only been during the past ten years that child development specialists have recognized the significant amount of informal instruction provided by parents to their infants and young children. Observation of interactional patterns between infants and their caregivers during the first year reveals parental use of systematic informal instructional routines. For example, mothers consistently label objects for their infants in ways that encourage the baby's understanding and use of words (Chapman, 1981). While doing this, most parents are unaware that they are actually instructing their infant; however, observations of parent-child interactions substantiate a significant effort by parents to informally teach the child about the world (Schaffer, 1977). Interestingly, a long-time noted difference between middle-income, better educated mothers and low-income, less well educated mothers is the former group's attention to providing adequate instructional information to their children (Hess & Shipman, 1965). For example, middle-income mothers tend to answer their children's questions with explanations geared to assist the child in understanding the phenomena of interest (e.g., "that is a special truck made to move rocks") or the rule being invoked (e.g., "you cannot touch the stove because it is hot and you will burn your finger"). Explanations provided by lower-income, more poorly educated mothers tend to be less helpful to the child from a sense of understanding the phenomena (e.g., "that's a truck") and more directive (e.g., "because I said so").

The amount and type of instruction required by nonhandicapped children to develop adequately may be considerably less than that needed by children with problems. In addition, the techniques and strategies generally employed by parents to deal with their children may be inadequate to manage the problems presented by at-risk or handicapped children. The inability of families to cope with the many needs of handicapped children requires support and direction from individuals specifically trained to address the needs of at-risk and handicapped children and their families.

Understanding and deriving solutions to the problems of young at-risk and handicapped populations and their families requires a cadre of mature, experienced, and appropriately trained professionals. Within the last ten years, early childhood/special education has grown into a legitimate field that combines information and expertise from special education, early-childhood education, and psychology. We have come to realize that early-intervention programs must be staffed with individuals specifically educated to address the unique problems of young children and their families.

Early childhood/special educators have left the era of providing respite baby-sitting services and have moved into an era of professionalism. This professionalism requires that ECH/SE personnel be specifically trained and provided with the appropriate certification or licensure. To maintain professional standards, programs should be thoughtfully developed using sound conceptual foundations that permit the delivery of quality services to children and their families.

The Need for Goals and Objectives

A consistent theme throughout this book has been the need for interventionists' activities to be directed by established goals and objectives. In order to ensure a systematic, cohesive approach, intervention efforts should be organized around a set of program goals. These goals should dictate the program's target population, focus, content, instructional strategies, and evaluation efforts. Each level of subsequent program implementation should be guided by program and individual child/family objectives consistent with and complementary to program goals.

Observation of programs suggests many of them lack systematic goals to direct the activities of their personnel. Then, too, programs that have developed a set of goals may have other problems. For example, program personnel appear to function as if the goals do not exist or in ways that suggest the program is controlled by other, nonspecified goals. In some cases there appears to be little relationship between program goals and individual child/family objectives, curricular content, instructional strategies, and evaluation efforts. Goals are written, but they provide only a facade rather than serving as a functional set of organizational guidelines.

The use of goals and objectives to guide and direct program activities is a requirement of a professional approach to intervention. Personnel who do not develop relevant and accountable IEPs for children are disregarding the law as well as sound educational practice. To efficiently intervene, the intervention staff must have a firm sense of the educational targets for participating children. Intervening without the necessary direction provided by individual educational objectives will result in a chaotic, ineffective approach.

Organized Management Systems

The development of program goals and individual child/family objectives is a necessary but not sufficient element for an effective intervention approach. Once appropriate goals and objectives are developed, established systems for managing program resources are necessary. The development and implementation of management systems should reflect the goals and objectives by generating functional strategies for reaching them by the effective arrangement and management of program resources. Without such organized systems, program resources are used inefficiently or perhaps even wasted.

Thought should be given to the development of logical and functional plans that permit the effective use of program personnel and of instructional and evaluation activities. For example, upon arriving at work, program personnel should be aware of the planned daily activities and what their respective responsibilities are to individual children and groups of children. Time for planning and preparing should be available prior to the appearance of the children and their families.

Consideration given to organizing all essential elements of a program enhances the use of the physical and social environment. Attention to the organization of the program resource yields savings of time and effort for staff and greater quality of services for children and families.

Longitudinal Perspective

ECH/SE personnel are responsible for developing and implementing programs for infant and preschool populations. This focus on the young in their early stages of development may lead to the development of shortsighted perspectives in terms of program and individual child/family goals. The ultimate goal for children is to become independent, self-sufficient, and happy adults. It may be difficult for parents and interventionists alike to maintain a long-term or longitudinal perspective when the child is still in diapers and barely able to toddle.

If one began with the expectation that the child will grow into an independently functioning adult, the chance of reaching such a goal is enhanced. If no such expectation exists, then it may be less likely that this goal will be attained by the child. Without the existence of such a goal, interventionists and parents may be content to dabble in instructional activities that are irrelevant and nonproductive for children. Maintaining a longitudinal perspective may discourage the use of activities that foster the development of fragmented and nonfunctional skills and may encourage training focused on more relevant and functional activities, such as generic problem-solving skills, communication with the social environment, and behaviors that will make the child more acceptable to the larger social community.

Two points about adopting a longitudinal perspective require further explanation. The first is clarification of what is meant by an independently functioning adult. This goal does not imply that the child will become "normal" but rather will have acquired as many skills as possible to enhance his or her ability for daily functioning with minimal support from the environment. For some children, this may mean becoming an adult who must use a wheelchair but who can ride public transportation, hold a responsible job, and engage in social activities of his or her choice. For other children, it may mean residing in a group home where support and guidance are provided but also the ability of the individual to work and enjoy social activities provided by the community. Parents must be helped to understand that even though their child may never be considered normal, he or she can become a participating member of the community. That goal should be paramount, beginning with the first intervention efforts.

The second point requiring clarification is the recognition that some infants or children may have impairments so serious that any form of independent functioning appears remote. In such cases, the interventionist still should assist parents in developing a long-term focus even though the goals may be somewhat different. For example, a goal for the severely motorically handicapped child might be to develop motor responses for the operation of sophisticated electronic equipment that will enhance the handicapped person's ability to control his or her life as well as assist caregivers. For profoundly retarded youngsters, goals may be focused on developing simple self-care skills that serve to enhance the person's dignity as well as assist caregivers. Equally important are goals that target helping retarded children develop skills that permit personal enjoyment. These individuals are often faced with significant periods of leisure time and yet have no strategies for using this time. Assisting such individuals in developing skills for occupying their free time is of great importance.

Our ability to predict children's progress is poor, and, consequently, interventionists are often faced with planning programs for children in which the ultimate level of independence is unknown. The task becomes one of striking a balance between long-term expectations that are not too modest and those not too ambitious. Interventionists are responsible for assisting parents in developing a perspective that enhances the child's growth. To carry out the first step in this process, the interventionist must adopt a longitudinal perspective for each child and share this perspective with the parent with the objective of having the parent develop a similar perspective.

Major Themes

Inclusion of Salient Physical and Social Environmental Elements

Another recurring theme found in this book is the need for interventionists to conceptualize environmental elements as potential teaching vehicles for infants and young children. Traditionally, educators and therapists have assumed that learning occurred only when the "teacher" was instructing and only in "instructional" settings such as the classroom. Gradually, we have begun to realize that such a perspective is narrow and obviates a plethora of resources that can be effectively managed to assist children in acquiring new skills. In particular, interventionists should acknowledge the potential usefulness of parents and other caregivers, arrangements of the environment's physical elements, and peers, or more competent children, as effective change agents.

Parents and other family members have finally acquired a status that encourages their inclusion as integral members of their child's intervention team. Professionals have come to acknowledge that family members can be effective change agents who spend considerable time with the child. If properly managed, this time can be used to promote the child's acquisition of important skills.

Elements of the physical environment can be used to encourage the development of new skills or generalization of already acquired skills. Too frequently, interventionists do not take advantage of the physical environment as an effective teaching vehicle. The organization and arrangement of the physical environment can promote the development of independence and functional skills. Furthermore, interventionists need to consider how instructional objectives can be addressed throughout the child's day, in the home and the classroom. For example, opportunities occurring during the day can be pinpointed to encourage the child's communication skills.

An instructional element often overlooked by interventionists is other children. Children can learn from other children (Guralnick, in press), as well as from adults. Yet most interventionists tend to overlook this valuable instructional resource as they plan their intervention efforts in the home, classroom, and elsewhere. The availability of older, more competent children in the home or classroom provides the interventionist and parent with a variety of potential opportunities for assisting children with problems to acquire a more sophisticated behavioral repertoire. Conversely, interventionists should not forget the potential value to handicapped children of becoming a "helper" to assist a younger or less competent playmate.

The social and physical environments are rich in varied instructional opportunities. Interventionists should recognize and use these various instructional elements in order to maximize the daily training opportunities that can be accessed to move children toward the goals of independence and happiness.

Objective Decision Making

The final theme stressed throughout this volume is the need for decision making based on objective findings. Again, this theme is closely related to issues of professionalism in the field of ECH/SE. It is unacceptable to offer intervention services without an accompanying strategy to measure the impact of the intervention. To observe informally that children are making progress is no longer—nor was it ever—adequate. The onus is on interventionists to devise usable evaluation plans that provide information about the progress children are making toward established educational objectives.

Unfortunately, available assessment and evaluation methods have many deficiencies. Current strategies produce a number of dilemmas for interventionists. Strategies that can be undertaken in a reasonable time frame generally do not provide comprehensive or accurate information on children's abilities, while strategies that are comprehensive may take inordinate amounts of administration time. Instruments with adequate psychometric data often are inappropriate for use with populations of at-risk and handicapped children. Some available instruments focus on content that does not lend itself to the development of useful or even appropriate educational targets for handicapped children.

These dilemmas require that interventionists select among imperfect strategies and recognize that whatever approach is selected has serious deficiencies. Even in the face of these dilemmas and deficiencies, the more serious offense is to employ no means for an objective evaluation of child progress and program impact. In the interim during which better assessment and evaluation tools are being developed, interventionists must maintain their commitment to objective decision making and employ those strategies that currently offer the best information on child progress and program impact.

FUTURE DIRECTIONS

Any field experiencing growth and change is confronted with problems created by the expansion. The field of ECH/SE is faced with problems from within as well as ones external to the enterprise. A number of important issues concerning the quality of services delivered to children and their families require study and the formation of acceptable solutions, but these solutions need to be developed with an appreciation for the larger ecological context of which they are a part. Pieces of the educational enterprise cannot be usefully viewed apart from the larger political, social, and economic contexts in which they reside. To overlook these contexts may mean that solutions derived to solve internal problems will not be effective because of limitations imposed by the larger context. Just as it is a mistake to view at-risk and handicapped children in isolation from the family, it is a mistake to view ECH/SE apart from the larger educational system or the educational system apart from its political niche in society.

Service Delivery

The position articulated here suggests a bias toward the movement of early-intervention programs into the domain of public education—a view not shared by everyone. However, a number of sound reasons exist for expanding public school systems to accommodate education for at-risk and handicapped children:

1. The public schools are the only social-political institutions suitably equipped to assimilate educational programs for young children.
2. Waste is inevitable if parallel educational intervention systems are to be maintained for infants and preschool children.
3. One system should enhance the continuity of delivering services in a more normalized setting.

If the majority of consumers and professionals accept the need for early intervention for handicapped and at-risk children either on philosophical or on empirical grounds, attention should be given to how these programs can be effectively integrated into established public school programs with the intelligent sharing of facilities, administration, and other resources. The current crazy-quilt pattern of program support, location, and administration dramatically reflects the need for leadership at the federal and the state level. An organizational framework within the rubric of public education will lead to the most sensible system of service delivery for at-risk and handicapped children and their families (Hobbs, 1975).

Curricular Focus

The move has already begun to shift the curricular focus from preacademics to include behaviors more social and functional. This shift should increase as infants and younger children are included in programs. Hopefully, this pendulum swing will not dilute the systematic use of behavioral technology. The behavioral technology that has evolved from operant conditioning is the most effective instructional strategy available. A shift in curriculum emphasis should not mean elimination of the systematic arrangement of antecedent events, operationalization of responses, consequation of behaviors, and use of teaching/shaping strategies. If anything, behavioral technology becomes more essential when the content and format are less controlled by the adult. Arrangement of antecedent events needs to be woven into the daily activities experienced by the young child and consequences made inherent in the activities whenever possible. Such approaches require care and thought in managing the environment, operationalizing the response in more detail, and understanding how to integrate consequences into the selected activity. The collection of data to monitor child change with these approaches is admittedly more difficult.

The previous description does not preclude the need for working with children on selected targets in a contrived setting. Systematic drilling on isolated skill sequences (e.g., using pincer grasp, labeling objects, pulling objects with strings, and rolling balls) may be necessary, *but* the use of such formats should be tempered by following the child's lead when possible and working toward general independence and problem-solving abilities.

Assessment and Evaluation Strategies

Without more sensitive, ecologically valid evaluation strategies, documentation of program impact will remain a challenge rather than a reality. Most contributors to the field recognize this problem, and efforts are underway to develop alternatives. Although recent work in the area of measurement is encouraging, the enormous effort to develop assessment-evaluation alternatives suggests a several-year interim before satisfactory solutions become widely available.

During this interim, the most useful solution may be to use a combination of assessment-evaluation tools. The pairing of standardized measures that have known psychometric properties with experimental instruments that are more program relevant may yield valuable information about the target population and about the new instrument simultaneously.

In particular, work is needed on instruments that (1) provide information from which to develop individual intervention programs and (2) assess aspects of programs previously ignored. Interventionists need tools that are practical to administer and that yield useful data on children and families. The nature of these data should be such that relevant long-term goals, training objectives, and specific program steps can be formulated (Bricker & Littman, 1982). Furthermore, tools, when used periodically, should provide systematic feedback on the child's progress toward the selected training targets.

Equally important is the need to assess other program features. Tools are needed to evaluate the effectiveness of programs with parents, which may range from support, counseling, and education to parent-child interactions. Cost analyses are woefully lacking, limiting knowledge about cost-effective parameters of programs. Lack of evaluation efforts in these areas may be related to the complexity of developing adequate tools to assess these critical variables. Nonetheless, we must move ahead, for only through exploration can alternative assessment-evaluation strategies be developed.

Personnel Preparation

With the growth of early-intervention programs comes the associated need for appropriately trained personnel. Program developers should consider the larger context as a basis for developing a philosophy and training regime for early-intervention personnel. Critical to personnel-preparation programs are decisions concerning the service-delivery system chosen for early-intervention programs. Current requirements for personnel vary across and within states. Many states do not offer a credential in early childhood/special education. If public schools assume the responsibility for at-risk and handicapped infants and children, associated certification will be necessary and will impact on personnel-preparation programs.

Personnel-preparation programs need to plan for the eventuality that an organized system of service delivery for early-intervention programs becomes a reality. Work should begin on locating and/or developing appropriate practicum sites. Programs of studies that reflect the current knowledge base should be designed, and faculties must begin to adjust their thinking about where early childhood/special education fits into the broader areas of special education and general education.

It seems unlikely that all institutions of higher education will initiate personnel preparation programs for early childhood/special education, and it also seems undesirable. Rather, considered decisions about which institutions should expand or shift their program offerings should be made at the state level. With adequate federal and state planning and support, a network of quality training programs should be established to produce an adequate number of qualified interventionists to meet the future needs of at-risk and handicapped children and their families.

Parents

Although progress has been made in changing attitudes about roles for parents, the goals of parents as diagnosticians, assessors, and intervenors specified by Brooks-Gunn and Lewis (1979) are not being met in most programs. Careful questioning of program staff generally reveals that only about 20 to 40 percent of the parents are genuinely involved (e.g., consistently work with their child, attend meetings, spend time with staff on a regular basis). For many programs, reports of parent involvement mean little more than infrequent attendance at meetings and verbal assurances to staff that training regimes are being implemented at home. In addition, it appears that most often those parents who are actively involved represent a biased sample of better educated, middle-income families. Those families who may require the greatest assistance may be those most reluctant to become active participants with their child or other aspects of the program.

Multiple causes exist for the lack of meaningful parent involvement. For example, there are staff attitudes, parent/family problems apart from the child, and economic conditions (e.g., both parents are employed). The purpose is not to allocate blame or responsibility but rather to recognize that for many families, efforts at involvement have been unsuccessful.

Just as interventionists are discovering there are many ways to work effectively with at-risk and handicapped children, interventionists need to understand that effective intervention with parents requires individualization. Successful programs are more likely to be those that attempt systematic assessment of family needs and then assist the family in meeting those needs even if the parental goals do not match the goals set by the professional intervention team.

SUMMARY

The primary goal of ECH/SE is to assist children in developing a repertoire of adaptive and success-producing behaviors for subsequent environments. A secondary goal is to maximize the family's adjustment to its handicapped member. The goal of this book has been to present a conceptual framework and an associated applied approach developed from that framework that is designed to meet these goals of ECH/SE. The approach presented in this book is designed to maximize the interventionist's possibility of devising and delivering quality services to at-risk and handicapped infants and young children and their families.

References

Bricker, D., & Littman, D. (1982). Intervention and evaluation: The inseparable mix. *Topics in Early Childhood Special Education, 1,* 23–33.

Brooks-Gunn, J., & Lewis, M. (1979, June). *Parents of handicapped infants: Their role in identification, assessment, and intervention.* Paper presented at the Ira Gordon Memorial Conference, Chapel Hill, NC.

Chapman, R. (1981). Mother-child interaction in the second year of life: Its role in language development. In R. Schiefelbusch & D. Bricker (Eds.), *Early language intervention.* Baltimore, MD: University Park Press.

Guralnick, M. (in press). The peer relations of young handicapped and non-handicapped children. In P. Strain, M. Guralnick, & H. Walker (Eds.), *Children's social behavior: Development, assessment, and modification.* New York: Academic Press.

Hess, R., & Shipman, V. (1965). Early experience and the socialization of cognitive modes in children. *Child Development, 36,* 869–886.

Hobbs, N. (1975). *The futures of children.* San Francisco: Jossey-Bass.

Schaffer, H. (Ed.) (1977). *Studies in mother-infant interaction.* New York: Academic Press.

APPENDIX

A

APPROXIMATE AGE RANGE FOR SELECTED DEVELOPMENTAL SKILLS

For further reference, see Cohen and Gross (1979).

Appendix A

DEVELOPMENTAL SKILLS

DOMAIN: Fine Motor
Approximate Age Range

Age	Skill	Description
birth–1 mo.	Reach	Random arm movements
	Release	Drops object placed in hand
	Grasp	Hand fisted
	Visual	Regards objects momentarily
1 mo.–4 mo.	Grasp	Successful palmer grasp
	Reach	Midline activity
	Visual	Alternating glance; hand to objects follows visually
4 mo.–6 mo.	Reach	Transfers object hand to hand
	Grasp	Attempts to secure pellet
	Visual	Turns to look for noisily falling object
6 mo.–12 mo.	Reach	Brings objects together at midline
	Grasp	Precisely picks up pellet
	Release	Purposefully releases objects
	Visual	Moves eyes toward adult movement across room
12 mo.–18 mo.	Visual	Eye-hand coordination
18 mo.–24 mo.	Grasp	Uses tools (crayons) with dexterity and control
	Visual	Imitates horizontal line
24 mo.–36 mo.	Visual	Copies +
	Grasp	Pours from a container
36 mo.–48 mo.	Grasp	Cuts with scissors
	Visual	Copies circles

Appendix A

DEVELOPMENTAL SKILLS

DOMAIN: Gross Motor
Approximate Age Range

Age	Skill	Description
birth–1 mo.	Reaching	Asymmetrical tonic neck reflex
	Standing	Planter grasp
	Balancing	Moro reflex
	Head righting	Marked head lag; turns to sides
1 mo.–4 mo.	Rolling	Nonsegmental roll from back to side
	Reaching	Hands to midline
	Sitting	Holds head steady
	Kicking	Hands play with feet
4 mo.–6 mo.	Support weight	Maintains weight on extended arms
	Head righting	No head lag, lifts head
	Reaching	Well-directed with overshoot
	Rolling	Rolls with rotation
6 mo.–8 mo.	Standing	Briefly with full weight
	Crawling	Progressive: right arm and left leg move together, followed by left arm, right leg
8 mo.–10 mo.	Cruising	Lifts one foot with full weight on other
	Balancing	Protective extension
	Standing	Pulls self to standing
10 mo.–12 mo.	Cruising	Takes steps with both hands held
	Balancing	Begins to climb
	Reaching	Well-directed with accuracy
12 mo.–18 mo.	Walking	Independently takes several steps
18 mo.–24 mo.	Sitting	Seats self in small chair
	Kicking	Kicks forward
	Walking	On tiptoes and unaided up stairs
24 mo.–36 mo.	Walking	Alternates feet on stairs
	Running	Whole foot, starts and stops
	Throwing	Throws with stiff arm and catches
36 mo.–48 mo.	Running	Avoids obstacles
	Throwing	Shifts body weight
48 mo.–60 mo.	Hopping	Either foot
	Jumping	Both feet together

381

Appendix A

DEVELOPMENTAL SKILLS

DOMAIN: Preacademic
Approximate Age Range

18 mo.–24 mo. Reading —— Chooses tactile books; listens to short rhymes with interesting sounds
  Writing —— Uses hands with definite preference; makes spontaneous scribbles
  Math —— Groups objects functionally

24 mo.–36 mo. Reading —— Knows 27% of alphabet by sight
  Writing —— Holds crayon with fingers; makes vertical and horizontal lines
  Math —— Forms graphic collections when presented with objects

36 mo.–48 mo. Reading —— Likes to look at books and may "read" to others or explain pictures
  Writing —— Forms a cross, a square, a circle; prints a few letters
  Math —— Understands "big" and "little"; matches numerals; counts objects

48 mo.–60 mo. Reading —— "Reads" by way of pictures; knows 38% of alphabet
  Writing —— Prints simple words, names letter or number
  Math —— Sorts according to color and form; shows understanding of ordinal correspondence; says numbers in order

Appendix A

DEVELOPMENTAL SKILLS

DOMAIN: Self-Help
Approximate Age Range

birth–4 mo.	Eating	Suck-swallow reflex
	Dressing	Tugs at clothes
4 mo.–8 mo.	Eating	Takes solids; holds bottle
	Dressing	Cooperates in dressing
8 mo.–12 mo.	Eating	Drinks from cup when assisted; rotary chewing; grasps with thumb and finger
	Dressing	Pulls off shoes and socks
12 mo.–18 mo.	Toileting	Controls bowels on a schedule
	Eating	Gives up bottle
18 mo.–22 mo.	Toileting	Controls bladder on a schedule
	Eating	Uses spoon to scoop
	Dressing	Unzips zipper
22 mo.–24 mo.	Eating	Begins using fork
	Dressing	Removes coat
24 mo.–36 mo.	Toileting	Self-initiates toileting
	Eating	Pours unassisted; uses straw
	Dressing	Puts on coat and shoes
	Grooming	Washes and dries hands
	Safety	Avoids simple hazards
36 mo.–60 mo.	Toileting	Cares for self at toilet unassisted
	Eating	Uses napkin and drinking fountain
	Dressing	Dresses and undresses except for tying
	Grooming	Washes face; brushes teeth

Appendix A

DEVELOPMENTAL SKILLS

DOMAIN: Social
Approximate Age Range

Neonate	Signaling responses	Shows consolability; makes vegetative sounds
2 wk.–4 wk.	Signaling responses	Smiles; produces comfort and distress sounds
	Differential social responses	Stares at faces; fixates eyes
2 mo.–4 mo.	Signaling responses	Smiles at "peek-a-boo" (cloth over infant's face)
	Differential social responses	Visually recognizes mother
	Establishes self-identity	Smiles at own mirror image
	Cooperative play	Enjoys play, games, socializing
4 mo.–6 mo.	Signaling responses	Stops crying when talked to; vocalizes to initiate socializing
	Differential social responses	Attends to faces; smiles at, reaches out to pat strange children
	Establishes self-identity	Turns when name is called
6 mo.–9 mo.	Signaling responses	Vocalizes to gain attention
	Differential social responses	Distinguishes strangers from familiars
	Establishes self-identity	Perceives mother as separate person
	Cooperative play	Plays pat-a-cake, so-big, bye-bye, and ball games
9 mo.–12 mo.	Signaling responses	Cries more frequently when mother is near
	Differential social responses	Cries when strangers confronted
	Establishes self-identity	Plays with mirror image
	Parallel play	Plays parallel to another child
	Cooperative play	Seeks approval; avoids disapproval

Appendix A

DEVELOPMENTAL SKILLS (continued)

Age	Skill	Description
12 mo.–18 mo.	Responsiveness	Demands attention; reacts to separation from mother
	Isolated play	Occupies self happily and contentedly; investigates objects
	Cooperative play	Shows shift in activity emphasis from objects to other children; shows increased negativism
18 mo.–24 mo.	Differential social responses	Demands proximity of familiar adult
	Establishes independent activities	Goes about house, yard
	Isolated play	Searches for objects to "go with" other things
	Cooperative play	Cooperates with playmates
24 mo.–36 mo.	Establishes self-identity	Recognizes self in photographs
	Isolated play	Initiates own play activities
	Cooperative play	Observes and joins other children at play
36 mo.–48 mo.	Differential social responses	Separates from mother without crying
	Cooperative play	Plays spontaneously with other children; shares play things
48 mo.–60 mo.	Establishes independent activities	Goes outside prescribed bounds
	Cooperative play	Needs other children to play with; names emotions

Appendix A

DEVELOPMENTAL SKILLS

DOMAIN: Sensorimotor/Cognitive
Approximate Age Range

Age	Category	Skill
birth–1 mo.	Visual	Orients to light and sound
	Means-end	Repeats reflexes
1 mo.–4 mo.	Visual	Follows slow-moving object
	Object permanence	Coordinates grasp-suck schemes; mouths some objects
	Means-end	Grasps toy; immediately repeats behaviors producing interesting results
4 mo.–8 mo.	Visual	Looks at point where moving object should reappear
	Object permanence	Searches for partially hidden object
	Means-end	Uses behaviors such as waving to cause events
8 mo.–12 mo.	Visual	Finds hidden objects
	Object permanence	Searches more persistently
	Means-end	Intentional goal-directed behavior; anticipates occurrences of routine events
12 mo.–18 mo.	Visual	Puts pellets in and out of bottle
	Object permanence	Searches systematically
	Means-end	Experiments and demonstrates interest in novelty
18 mo.–24 mo.	Visual	Matches color; uses simple form board
	Means-end	Mental problem-solving; shows foresightful behavior

DEVELOPMENTAL SKILLS

DOMAIN: Language
Approximate Age Range

Age	Category	Skill
birth–1 mo.	Production	Vegetative sounds
	Comprehension	Responds to sound
1 mo.–4 mo.	Production	Vowel sounds
	Comprehension	Orients to sound source
4 mo.–6 mo.	Production	Marginal babbling
6 mo.–12 mo.	Production	Babbles; uses gestures to communicate
	Comprehension	Responds to words used in context
12 mo.–14 mo.	Production	First word
12 mo.–16 mo.	Comprehension	Begins to find familiar objects out of view
	Comprehension/ relational meaning	Responds to commands having relational meanings
16 mo.–24 mo.	Production	Frequently uses functional words
	Production/ relational meaning	Successive single-word utterances; two-word combinations
	Comprehension/ relational meaning	Responds to commands
24 mo.–30 mo.	Production/ relational meaning	Uses three- and four-term semantic relations
	Production/ grammatical form	Marks verbs; uses negatives; asks questions

Appendix A

Appendix A

DEVELOPMENTAL SKILLS (continued)

30 mo.–42 mo. Production/
grammatical form ——————— Uses prepositional phrases and possessives

Comprehension/
grammatical form ——————— Understands some gender contrasts

42 mo.–60 mo. Production/
grammatical form ——————— Uses grammatical inflection "ed."

Comprehension/
grammatical form ——————— Understands modifiers; answers questions

APPENDIX B

EARLY-INTERVENTION PROGRAMS

For references in Appendix B see reference list in Chapter 8.

Appendix B

Investigators	Number	Age	Target	Length	Program Description	Evaluation Design	Instruments
Bagnato & Neisworth (1980)	16	Range, 16 to 60 mos.	*Child:* Multiple handicaps *Parent:* No reference to parental responsibilities	4 Mos. 2 yrs.	Center-based program concentrating on 4 developmental domains of language, motor, personal-social and problem-solving	Compared child progress using the Intervention Efficiency Index	1. Gesell Developmental Schedules 2. Preschool Attainment Record 3. COMP-Curriculum 4. Parental and teacher judgments
Brassell & Dunst (1978)	24 Experimental 67 Control	Mean, 21 mos.	*Child:* Ranged from nonhandicapped to profoundly retarded *Parent:* Carry out treatment procedures within context of play	4 to 5 Mos.	Multidisciplinary instructional approach with interdisciplinary team recommendations used to implement programs. Home-based, sequential experiences program intended to foster development of object concepts	Compared experimental group change on object concepts with control group	Ordinal Scales of Psychological Development
Bricker, Bruder, & Bailey (1982)	41	Range, 1 to 6 yrs.	*Child:* Ranged from normal to severely handicapped *Parent:* Voluntary classroom participation and extended home involvement. Voluntary attendance at parent meetings.	9 Mos. for 3 consecutive yrs.	Interdisciplinary, center-based program. Large- and small-group instruction with individual instruction when necessary. Emphasis on gross/fine motor, social/self-help skills, communication, and pre-academic areas. Parent involvement in training efforts	Compared child progress over time	1. Uniform Performance Assessment System 2. Student Progress Record 3. Bayley Scales of Infant Development 4. McCarthy Scales of Children's Abilities
Bricker & Dow (1980)	50	Range, 7 to 54 mos.	*Child:* Severely handicapped *Parent:* Involvement covered educational training, social services, counseling; completed needs assessment	1 Yr.	Interdisciplinary, center-based program composed of 5 components: classroom or direct intervention; parent involvement; support services; instructional content and procedures; and evaluation	Compared child progress over time	Uniform Performance Assessment System

TABLE B-1 Selected early-intervention programs serving heterogeneous groups of biologically impaired children

Appendix B

Investigators	Number	Age	Target	Length	Program Description	Evaluation Design	Instruments
Bricker & Sheehan (1981)	81	Range, 5 mos. to 7 yrs.	*Child:* Ranged from normal to severely handicapped *Parent:* To develop skills to become effective change agents	9 Mos.	Interdisciplinary, center- and home-based program with large- and small-group instruction, individual intervention when necessary	Compared child progress over time	1. Uniform Performance Assessment System 2. Student Progress Record 3. Bayley Scales of Infant Development 4. McCarthy Scales of Children's Abilities
Jew (1974)	36	Not specified	*Child:* Range of handicaps *Parent:* Stimulate and interact with children, work as staff members, participate in parent-to-parent discussions	3 Yrs.	Interdisciplinary, school and home-based program. Focused on promotion of growth in fine motor, gross motor, language development, and self-help skills	Compared intervention group with 2 non-intervention groups	1. Denver Developmental Screening Test 2. Parental Attitude Scales
Nielsen, Collins, Meisel, Lowry, Engh, & Johnson (1975)	19	Range, 0 to 3 yrs.	*Child:* Range of handicaps including Down's syndrome, microcephaly, Golden Hars syndrome *Parent:* Primary change agent	12 Mos.	Transdisciplinary home-based program to assist parents in care and management of child. Interdisciplinary, center-based program focused on separating child and mother gradually	Compared child progress over time	1. Bayley Scales of Infant Development 2. Denver Developmental Screening Test
Rosen-Morris & Sitkei (1981)	30	Range, 18 mos. to 6 yrs.	*Child:* Severely handicapped *Parent:* No parent involvement described	9 Mos.	Naturalistic strategies used in center-based program. Curriculum focused on fine motor tasks to promote spontaneous interaction with objects	Compared child progress over time	1. Bayley Scales of Infant Development 2. Student Progress Record 3. Preschool Attainment Record
Safford, Gregg, Schneider, & Sewell (1976)	6	Range, 26 to 51 mos.	*Child:* Range of handicaps, including cerebral palsy, retardation, and neurofibromatatosis *Parent:* Facilitate carry-over activities	6 Mos.	Interdisciplinary, center-based program with a one-to-one staff/child relationship focusing on appropriate sensory experiences	Pre-post comparison of child progress through observational procedures, standard-	1. Cattell Infant Intelligence Scale 2. Houston Test of Language Development

TABLE B-1 (continued)

Appendix B

Investigators	Number	Age	Target	Length	Program Description	Evaluation Design	Instruments
Safford, Gregg, Schneider, & Sewell (1976) (cont.)						ized measures, and parental interviews	
Shapiro, Gordon, & Neiditch (1977)	60	Range, 18 to 36 mos.	*Child:* Range of handicaps including cerebral palsy, spina bifida, developmental delay *Parent:* Required 1 full day per week in active participation at center	3 Mos.	Developmental-interactional, center-based program located at rehabilitation center as an inpatient, intensive educational program	Pre-post comparison of anecdotal records kept on child progress	1. Coding the records into hierarchical sequences 2. Correlational with clinical judgments
Shearer & Shearer (1976)	150	Range, birth to 6 yrs.	*Child:* Range of handicaps from mild to severe *Parent:* Main change agent. Collected data and participated in selection of target behaviors	Unspecified	Interdisciplinary, home-based program following precision teaching model. Emphasis on motor, self-help, socialization, cognitive, and language development	Compared child progress pre-post with controls	1. Cattell Infant Intelligence Scale 2. Stanford-Binet Intelligence Scale 3. Alpern-Boll Developmental Profile 4. Gesell Developmental Schedules 5. Number of program objectives
Stock, Wnek, Newborg, Gabel, Spurgeon, & Ray (1976)	160	Range, less than 1 yr. to 7 yrs.	*Child:* Range of handicaps including mental retardation, learning disabilities, emotional disturbances *Parent:* Ranged from major change agent to attendance at staff meetings	Not applicable	Evaluation of children in HCEEP to determine their effectiveness in meeting the educational needs of young handicapped children and to develop a monitoring and reporting system to facilitate the evaluation of HCEEP effectiveness on a continuing basis	Children selected from 32 HCEEP for external evaluation	Children's Early Education Developmental Inventory
Weiss (1981)	114	Range, 3 to 5 yrs.	*Child:* Language disorder *Parent:* No reference to parent responsibilities	9 Mos.	Center-based program designed to improve language and related learning skills. Also, redefined instruc-	Intervention group compared to control group	Fluharty Inreal Preschool Screening Test

TABLE B-1   (continued)

Appendix B

Investigators	Number	Age	Target	Length	Program Description	Evaluation Design	Instruments
Weiss (1981) (cont.)					tional role of speech-language pathologist as a classroom specialist		

TABLE B-1 (continued)

Investigators	Number	Age	Target	Length	Program Description	Evaluation Design	Instruments
Aronson & Fallstrom (1977)	16	Range, 21 to 69 mos.	*Child:* Down syndrome; all lived in nursing home *Parent:* Nursing home provided preschool training	1½ Yrs.	Institution-based program implemented by psychologist. Individualized training formulated to stimulate mental functions along normal developmental sequences	Pre-post comparison of trained groups with no-training groups	Griffiths Mental Development Scales
Clunies-Ross (1979)	36	Range, 3 to 37 mos.	*Child:* Down syndrome: 35 trisomy, 1 translocation *Parent:* Provide generalization and consolidation of center-based program	4 Mos. to 2 yrs.	Interdisciplinary center-based team instruction with home-based parental instruction	Compared 3 successive groups of enrolled children on pre-post test scores	Early Intervention Development Profile
Connolly, Morgan, Russell, & Richardson (1980)	20 Experimental, 53 control	Range, birth to 2.5 yrs.	*Child:* Down syndrome *Parent:* Primary change agent; counseling provided	20 Wks. to 3 yrs.	Interdisciplinary, center-based with professional teaching child and demonstrating for parent. General developmental model emphasizing intensive motor and sensory stimulation. Home-based to carry out center programs	Conducted follow-up comparison of an intervention with a nonintervention group	1. Stanford-Binet Intelligence Scale 2. Cattell Infant Intelligence Scale 3. Vineland Social Maturity Scale
Hanson & Schwarz (1978)	12	Range, 4 wks. to 6 mos.	*Child:* Down syndrome: 11 trisomy, 1 mosaic *Parent:* Primary change	24 Mos.	Home-based program with staff visiting homes to evaluate child's developmental status and estab-	Compared intervention group with reported milestones	Developmental Milestones

TABLE B-2 Selected early-intervention programs primarily serving Down Syndrome children

Appendix B

Investigators	Number	Age	Target	Length	Program Description	Evaluation Design	Instruments
Hanson & Schwarz (1978) (cont.)			agent		lish goals in conjunction with parents. Behaviorally-based teaching procedures used to carry out detailed educational programs		
Harris (1981)	20	Range, 2.7 to 21.5 mos.	*Child:* Down syndrome: 2 serious heart defects, all with varying degrees of hypotonia *Parent:* Encouraged observation, no direct instruction unless specifically requested	9 Wks.	Home-based with neurodevelopmental treatment approach emphasizing minimal decline in motor and mental development. Treatment performed by pediatric physical therapists	Compared child progress after neurodevelopmental treatment	1. Bayley Scales of Infant Development 2. Peabody Developmental Motor Scales 3. Attainment of treatment objectives
Hayden & Haring (1977)	94	Range, 20 mos. to 13.5 yrs.	*Child:* Down syndrome: 95% trisomy 21, 3% mosaic, 2% translocations *Parent:* Provide information on early major developmental milestones	Variable	Interdisciplinary center-based model preschool and public school programs. Focus on examining the relationship between age and developmental level across children of different ages	Compared progress of model preschool with control group who attended different programs	1. Down Syndrome Inventory 2. Peabody Picture Vocabulary Test 3. Stanford-Binet Intelligence Scale 4. Denver Developmental Screening Test 5. Vineland Social Maturity Scale
Kysela, Hillyard, McDonald, & Ahlsten-Taylor (1981)	22	Range, birth to 2.5 yrs.	*Child:* 19 Down syndrome; 3 undiagnosed *Parent:* Primary change agent; collected data, provided opportunities for generalization	Unspecified but program intervals ranged from 6–8 mos. for some children to 12–14 mos. for others	Home-based used direct and incidental teaching models. School-based used direct teaching format emphasizing language and group activities	Compared child progress over time	1. Bayley Scales of Infant Development 2. Stanford-Binet Intelligence Scale 3. Reynell Developmental Language Scale 4. Training Targets

TABLE B–2 *(continued)*

Appendix B

Investigators	Number	Age	Target	Length	Program Description	Evaluation Design	Instruments
Ludlow & Allen (1979)	72	Range, birth to 10 yrs.	*Child:* Down syndrome *Parent:* Participate in every area, support other parents, keep progress reports for home programs	Unspecified; 10-yr. follow-up	Interdisciplinary center-based team instruction with home-based program to continue center-based stimulation. Playground-base used to further independence and social acceptability	Compared pre-post test scores of 3 groups: (1) preschool experience, (2) no preschool experience, (3) residential placement center	1. Stanford-Binet Intelligence Scale 2. Griffiths Mental Development Scales
Piper & Pless (1980)	37	Range, 3 mos. to 3 yrs.	*Child:* Down syndrome *Parent:* Provide additional and on-going activities at home	6 Mos.	Interdisciplinary, center-based program for primary therapy. Home-based intervention between center sessions	Compared intervention group with control group on pre-post scores	1. Griffiths Mental Development Scales 2. Home Observation for Measurement of the Environment Inventory
Rynders & Horrobin (1980)	35	Range, 1 to 12 mos.	*Child:* Down syndrome: all trisomy 21 *Parent:* Change agent, collected data, modified center lessons and developed new lessons	5 Yrs.	Center-based for testing and provision of curricular materials. Home-based for program implementation focused on concept utilization and communication stimulation	Compared intervention groups with non-intervention groups over time	1. Bohem Test of Basic Concepts 2. Stanford-Binet Intelligence Scale 3. Bruinik-Oseretsky 4. Language Samples

TABLE B-2 *(continued)*

Investigators	Number	Age	Target	Length	Program Description	Evaluation Design	Instruments
Badger, Burns, & DeBoer (1982)	86	Newborn	*Child:* Premature, low birthweight *Parent:* Low socialeconomic status	1 Yr.	Center-based program focused on training nurses and parents in the NICU to implement a series of infant-stimulation techniques in conjunction with weekly classes to	Correlated mental scores with physical scores and maternal characteristics	1. Hobel Risk Scores 2. Brazelton Neonatal Behavioral Assessment Scale 3. Ordinal Scales of Psychological Development

TABLE B-3 *Selected early-intervention programs primarily serving medically at-risk children*

Appendix B

Investigators	Number	Age	Target	Length	Program Description	Evaluation Design	Instruments
Badger, Burns, & DeBoer (1982) (cont.)					meet the multiple needs of the families. Home-based program focused on development of IEPs		4. Bayley Scales of Infant Development 5. Maternal Risk Score
Bromwich & Parmelee (1979)	30	Newborn	*Child:* Premature infants	2 Yrs.	Home-based program focused on affecting parents' behavior so as to have indirect impact on infant's development	Compared intervention group with non-intervention group	1. Parent Behavior Progression 2. Play Interaction Measure 3. Staff judgments 4. Home Observation for Measurement of the Environment Inventory
Field, Dempsey, & Shuman (1981)	151	2 Yrs.	*Child:* Preterm with respiratory distress syndrome; postterm; normal term	2-Yr. follow-up	Center-based program focused on determining differences in current functioning level of the three groups of infants	Compared each of the three groups across multiple measures	1. Pediatric Complications Scale 2. Bayley Scales of Infant Development 3. Behavior Problems Checklist 4. Vineland Social Maturity Scale 5. Mother-Infant Play Interaction Form
Leib, Benfield, & Guidubaldi (1980)	28	Newborn	*Child:* High-risk preterm infants *Parent:* See, touch, feed, and hold infants if desired	16 Mos. total; intervention occurred before discharge with a six-mo. follow-up assessment	Multimodal sensory enrichment program, within a regional neonatal intensive care unit	Compared treatment group with control group	1. Bayley Scales of Infant Development 2. Neonatal Behavior Assessment Scale 3. Apgar Scores 4. Pediatric physical examinations and growth assessments
Marton, Minde, & Ogilvie (1981)	32	Newborn	*Child:* Premature	3 Mos.	Center- and home-based program both focused on	Performed an analysis of interactions and	Categorized Behavior Interaction Forms

TABLE B-3 (continued)

Investi-gators	Number	Age	Target	Length	Program Description	Evaluation Design	Instruments
Marton, Minde, & Ogilvie (1981) (cont.)					observation of mother/infant interaction	compared interaction patterns of NICU visits with later home visits	
Scarr-Salapatek & Williams (1973)	30	New-born	*Child:* Low birth-weight (1,800); low SES *Parent:* Implement home program	1 Yr.	Nursery-based program focused on visual, tactile, and kinesthetic stimulation. Home-based program focused on weekly visits to improve maternal care	Compared treatment group with control group	1. Apgar Scores 2. Cattell Infant Intelligence Scale 3. Brazelton Cambridge Newborn Scales

TABLE B-3 (continued)

Investi-gators	Number	Age	Target	Length	Program Description	Evaluation Design	Instruments
Bradley & Caldwell (1976)	49	3 Yrs.	*Child:* Environmentally at-risk	Un-spec-ified	Follow-up study focused on the relationship between the home environ-ment and mental test performance	Correlated HOME scores with Stanford-Binet scores	1. Home Observation for the Measure-ment of the Environment Inventory 2. Stanford-Binet Intelligence Scale
Gray, Ramsey, & Klaus (1982)	88	Vari-able	*Child:* Socially and economically deprived	4 Yrs. and follow-up	Center-based program focused on developing characteristics to promote school success. Home-based goal focused on con-tinuation of center-based program	Compared: (1) two ex-perimental groups, (2) experimen-tal groups with local control group, (3) experimen-tal groups with distal control group, (4) local con-trol group with distal control group	1. Stanford-Binet Intelligence Scale 2. Peabody Picture Vocabulary Test 3. Illinois Test of Psycho-linguistic Ability 4. Kagan's Matching Familiar Figures Test 5. Adapted Piers-Harris Self-Concept Test 6. Metropolitan Readiness Test 7. Metropolitan

TABLE B-4 Selected early-intervention programs primarily serving environmentally at-risk children

Appendix B

Investigators	Number	Age	Target	Length	Program Description	Evaluation Design	Instruments
Gray, Ramsey, & Klaus (1982) (cont.)							Achievement Test 8. Wechsler Intelligence Scale for Children 9. Parent interview
Heber & Garber (1975)	40	Range, 3 mos. to 6 yrs.	*Child:* Infants of low SES mothers with borderline intelligence	6 Yrs.	*Two phases:* 1. Maternal intervention on-site (nursing home) training to improve home-making skills and child-rearing skills 2. Infant intervention home- and center-based focused on cognitive-language, social-emotional, and perceptual-motor development	Compared intervention group with control group	1. Gesell Developmental Schedules 2. Illinois Test of Psycholinguistic Ability 3. Cattell Infant Intelligence Scale 4. Stanford-Binet Intelligence Scale 5. Wechsler Preschool and Primary Scale of Intelligence 6. Wechsler Adult Intelligence Scale
Hunt (1980)	66	Range, birth to 3 yrs.	*Child:* Foundlings without detectable pathology	Variable: up to 3 yrs.	Center-based (orphanage) program focused on changing and measuring a series of interventions on children	Compared treatment groups to control groups	Piaget's seven ordinal scales
Ramey, MacPhee, & Yeates (1983)	112	Range, 6 wks. to 3 mos.	*Child:* High-risk for school and psychosocial retardation	5 Yrs.	Center-based program focused on fostering language development and adaptive social behavior	Compared intervention groups with control groups	1. Wechsler Adult Intelligence Scale 2. Bayley Scales of Infant Development 3. Home Observation for the Measurement of the Environment Inventory 4. Dyadic Interactions (mother/child) 5. Stanford-Binet Intelligence Scale

TABLE B-4 (continued)

Investigators	Number	Age	Target	Length	Program Description	Evaluation Design	Instruments
Ramey, MacPhee, & Yeates (1983) (cont.)							6. Wechsler Preschool and Primary Scale of Intelligence

TABLE B-4 *(continued)*

Investigators	Number	Age	Target	Length	Program Description	Evaluation Design	Instruments
Badger (1977)	48	Range, 3 wks. to 18 mos.	*Parent:* Socially disadvantaged teenage mothers	Variable: up to 18 mos.	Center-based and home-based programs both focused on stimulating infant development by extending mother's role as primary teacher	Compared center treatment group with home-visited group	1. Ordinal Scales of Psychological Development 2. Bayley Scales of Infant Development
Baker & Heifetz (1976)	160	Range, 3 to 14 yrs.	*Parent:* all had children with varying levels of mental retardation	20 Wks.	Home-based program taught through 10 self-contained instructional manuals focusing on providing a parent's training package that would approximate the child's current educational needs	4 Training groups compared with a control group	1. Behavioral Vignettes Test 2. Behavioral Assessment Manual
Bidder, Bryant, & Gray (1975)	16	Range, 12 to 33 mos.	*Parent:* All had Down syndrome children	6 Mos.	Center-based program focused on teaching mothers behavior modification techniques and sessions to discuss personal problems and family involvement	Compared intervention group of trained mothers with controls	1. Griffiths Mental Development Scales 2. Mother's written statements
Bruder (1983)	9	Range, 10 to 26 mos.	*Parent:* Children considered to be at-risk for developmental delays	Dependent on time to reach criterion	Center-based program focused on (1) training parents to use four intervention techniques when teaching their	Examined effects of parental teaching on children and other parents	1. Gesell Developmental Schedules 2. Multiple baseline on specific training targets

TABLE B-5 Selected early-intervention programs focused on parents of at-risk or handicapped children

Appendix B

Investigators	Number	Age	Target	Length	Program Description	Evaluation Design	Instruments
Bruder (1983) (cont.)					children new behaviors, (2) training parents to instruct other parents		3. Fidelity of treatment
Cheseldine & McConkey (1979)	7	Mean, 62 mos.	*Parent:* All had Down syndrome children	2 Wks.	Home-based program focused on producing greater improvements in use of target words	Examined effects of parental teaching on language skills	Specific training targets
Christopherson & Sykes (1979)	3	Range, 3 to 5 yrs.	*Parent:* All had moderately mentally retarded children	Unspecified	Home-based program focused on increasing the number of appropriate parent-child interactions and reducing the number of inappropriate interactions	Compared mother/child interactions	Behavior observation
Filler & Kasari (1981)	2	4 and 14 mos.	*Parent:* All had severely handicapped children	Unspecified	Direct instruction procedure used to teach mothers to train their children specific skills through task analysis	Taught mothers teaching skills	Multiple baseline
Kogan (1980)	20	Range, 21 to 61 mos.	*Parent:* All had children with cerebral palsy	1 Yr.	Center-based play sessions were videotaped to observe dyadic interactions	Comparison of the frequency of occurrence of a single behavior checklist item at three points in time with each mother-child dyad being its own control	1. Washington Symptom Checklist 2. Interpersonal Behavior Constructs 3. Behavior frequency tabulations
Moxley-Haegert & Serbin (1983)	39	Range, 4 to 36 mos.	*Parent:* All had delayed infants	1 Mo.	Home-based program focused on teaching caregivers to administer treatment programs in 5 skill-building areas. In addition, experi-	Compared parent education group with parent no-education control group	1. Bayley Scales of Infant Development 2. Home Observation for Measurement of the Environment

TABLE B-5 (continued)

Appendix B

Investigators	Number	Age	Target	Program Length	Program Description	Evaluation Design	Instruments
Moxley-Haegert & Serbin (1983) (cont.)					mental group parents received a brief course in developmental education		Inventory
Piper & Ramsay (1980)	37	Range, 2.8 to 23.8 mos.	*Parent:* All had children with Down syndrome	6 Mos.	Changes in mental development were assessed in the home	Compared child progress over time	1. Griffiths Mental Development Scales 2. Home Observation for Measurement of the Environment Inventory
Revill & Blunden (1979)	19	Range, 8 mos. to 4 yrs.	*Parent:* All had developmentally handicapped children	8 Mos.	Home-based program focused on developing and evaluating a home training service for developmentally handicapped preschoolers	Compared child and parent progress over time	1. Griffiths Mental Development Scales 2. Portage Project Checklist 3. Activity Charts
Sandow, Clarke, Cox, & Stewart (1981)	32	Range, 17 to 42 mos.	*Parent:* All had severely subnormal preschool children	3 Yrs.	Home-based program focused on a series of educative and supportive visits	Compared two experimental groups with a third distal contrast group	1. Cattell Infant Intelligence Scale 2. Vineland Social Maturity Scale 3. Progress Assessment Charts 4. Portage Project Checklist
Springer & Steele (1980)	37 Couples	School age	*Parent:* All had Down syndrome children born since 1970	Unspecified	One or two 30- to 90-minute telephone interviews were conducted to identify the effects of physicians' early counseling on rearing Down syndrome child	Survey via telephone interviews	Telephone interview

TABLE B-5 (continued)

APPENDIX

C

INTAKE FORMS

Appendix C

EDUCATIONAL AND PSYCHOLOGICAL TESTING CONSENT FORM

Dear Parent,

For purposes of developing a useful intervention program for your child, it is necessary for the program staff to evaluate your child using special tests. These tests will measure your child's ability to: talk and understand words; perform a variety of motor activities such as sitting, walking, running, grasping and manipulating objects; solve simple problems such as finding objects and completing puzzles; play with other children; and carry out self-help skills such as feeding, dressing, and toileting. Unless this type of information is acquired, the program staff cannot develop an appropriate intervention program for your child; therefore, the administration of these tests is of great importance to you and your child.

Because the information is obtained by watching your child or asking the child to perform simple activities (e.g., stacking blocks), the testing procedures present no risk. The specific information provided by these tests is kept in your child's folder located in locked files. To protect your privacy, access to this information is restricted to the program staff, professional consultants, and yourself. Should you desire, a staff member will discuss the results of the tests with you.

Even though your child's participation in the program is voluntary, failure to complete the testing would not allow us to develop a program for your child.

I, _____, give my permission for the program staff to administer the appropriate educational and psychological tests to my child, _____ .

_____   _____
Parent's signature   Date

_____
Witness's signature

Appendix C

PHOTOGRAPHY, VIDEOTAPE, AND AUDIOTAPE CONSENT FORM

I give my consent for program staff members to photograph, videotape, and audiotape my child, _____, while participating in the program. These photos and tapes will be used for educational purposes only and not for publication. If possible, I will be permitted to review the pictures or tapes prior to their being shown. I understand signing this consent form is voluntary and will not affect my child's participation in the program.

_____   _____
Parent's signature   Date

_____
Witness's signature

MEDICAL AUTHORIZATION FORM

Child's name: Birthdate:
Mother's name: Home phone:
                                                 Business phone:
Father's name: Home phone:
                                                 Business phone:

Names of friends or relatives to contact in case of emergency if you cannot be reached:

1.   Phone: or
2.   Phone: or

Name of physician to be called in an emergency:

1.
2.

Medication (if any):

In the case that I cannot be reached, I authorize the program staff to take whatever emergency medical measures are necessary, in their judgment, for the protection of my child while he/she is in their care. I understand that this authorization includes calling the physician named above (or another physician if he/she is unavailable), implementing his/her instructions, and transporting my child to a hospital or clinic *without* first obtaining my consent. I further understand that staff will notify me of any injury or emergency at the first reasonable opportunity.

_____   _____
Parent's signature   Date

_____
Witness's signature

Appendix C

MEDICAL REPORT AND IMMUNIZATION RECORD FORM

Child's name _____ Birth _____ Sex _____
                Last   First   Mo.   Day   Year

Address _____ Phone _____

Check the following information about your child:

1. Past concussions — Yes ____ No ____ Year ____
   Past skull fractures — Yes ____ No ____ Year ____
2. Neck injury — Yes ____ No ____ Year ____
3. History of muscle, bone or joint disease — Yes ____ No ____ Year ____
4. Glasses or contact lenses for athletics — Yes ____ No ____ Year ____
   Loss or seriously impaired vision in one eye? — Yes ____ No ____ Year ____
5. Hearing problem — Yes ____ No ____ Year ____
6. Pneumonia — Yes ____ No ____ Year ____
7. Hernia — Yes ____ No ____ Year ____
8. Diabetes — Yes ____ No ____ Year ____
9. Rheumatic fever — Yes ____ No ____ Year ____
10. Kidney disease — Yes ____ No ____ Year ____
11. Fainting spells — Yes ____ No ____ Year ____
12. Epilepsy or other convulsive disorders or seizures — Yes ____ No ____ Year ____
13. Communicable diseases:
    German measles (3 day) — Yes ____ No ____ Year ____
    Red measles — Yes ____ No ____ Year ____
    Mumps — Yes ____ No ____ Year ____
    Chickenpox — Yes ____ No ____ Year ____
    Whooping cough — Yes ____ No ____ Year ____
    Scarlet fever — Yes ____ No ____ Year ____
    Other — Yes ____ No ____ Year ____
14. Allergies:
    Asthma — Yes ____ No ____ Year ____
    Insects/Bee sting — Yes ____ No ____ Year ____
    Hay fever — Yes ____ No ____ Year ____
    Poison oak — Yes ____ No ____ Year ____
    Other — Yes ____ No ____ Year ____
15. Tonsils Adenoids removed — Yes ____ No ____ Year ____
16. Currently taking medication or shots — Yes ____ No ____ Year ____
17. Premature birth — Yes ____ No ____ Year ____
18. Any other serious defects or operations — Yes ____ No ____ Year ____

Parent's Comment on "Yes": _____

_____

IMMUNIZATION SUMMARY:

	Initial series	1st Booster	Given Booster today	
Diphtheria	19 ____	19 ____	19 ____	____
Whooping cough	19 ____	19 ____	19 ____	____
Tetanus	19 ____	19 ____	19 ____	____
Smallpox	19 ____	19 ____	19 ____	____
Polio	19 ____	19 ____	19 ____	____
Sabin-Oral	19 ____	19 ____	19 ____	____

TESTS:

	Results	Given Today
Tuberculin	19 ____	____
Chest X-ray	19 ____	____
Other test	19 ____	____
Measles (vaccine)	19 ____	____
Mumps (vaccine)	19 ____	____
Rubella (vaccine)	19 ____	____

Parent's comments regarding behavior and any physical or emotional problems:

Appendix C

MEDICAL REPORT AND IMMUNIZATION RECORD FORM (continued)

PHYSICAL EXAMINATION:

Height _____
Weight _____
Blood pressure _____
Significant illnesses or injuries

Vision with glasses _____
Vision without glasses _____
R 20/ _____ L 20/ _____

Examination	Satisfactory	Unsatisfactory
Teeth		
Hearing		
Cardiovascular		
Respiratory		
Liver, spleen, kidney hernia, genitals		

Examination	Satisfactory	Unsatisfactory
Extremities		
Orthopedic/Posture		
Neurological		
Skin		
Indicated lab tests		
Urinalysis negative for sugar		

Comments on unsatisfactory conditions:

_____   _____
Physician's signature   **Date**

407

Appendix C

DEMOGRAPHIC FORM

Name: _____ Date form completed: _____

IDENTIFICATION INFORMATION
1. ID NUMBER: ☐☐☐☐☐☐ (1-6) ☐☐☐ (8-10)
2. NAME:
       Last, First
3. ADDRESS:
       Number, Street

       Town/City

       County

       Zip Code   Telephone

ADMISSION INFORMATION
4. Date of birth: month, day, year   ☐☐ (12-13)   ☐☐ (15-16)   ☐☐ (18-19)
5. Sex: (male = 1, female = 2)   ☐ (20)
6. Date of admission:
       month, day, year   ☐☐ (22-23)   ☐☐ (24-25)   ☐☐ (26-27)

FAMILY INFORMATION
7. Type of family (see code sheet)   ☐ (28)
8. Total number of other children in household   ☐☐ (29-30)
9. Birth order of child in intervention   ☐ (31)
10. Total number of adults in household   ☐ (32)
11. Head of household/main wage earner (see coding instructions)   ☐ (33)
    _____

12. Occupation of head of household/main wage earner   ☐ (34)
    (see coding instructions)
    _____

13. Occupation of mother (see coding instructions)   ☐ (35)
    _____

14. Education of main wage earner/head of household   ☐ (36)
    (see coding instructions)
15. Education of mother (see coding instructions)   ☐ (37)
16. Annual family income (see coding instructions)   ☐ (38)

Appendix C

DEMOGRAPHIC FORM (continued)

ETHNIC RACIAL GROUP
17. Caucasian = 1 ☐ (39)
    Black = 2
    Oriental = 3
    Biracial = 4
    Native American = 5
    Spanish surname = 6
    Other _____ = 7

TIME OF DELIVERY
18. Full term (37–42 weeks) = 1 ☐ (40)
    Premature (before 37 weeks) = 2
    Postmature (42 weeks or more) = 3
    Unknown = 4

IDENTIFIED CONDITIONS
19. Down syndrome = 1 ☐ (41)
    Cerebral palsy/Motor disorder = 2
    Myelomeningocele = 3
    Seizure disorder = 4
    Developmental delay = 5
    Sensory impairment = 6
    Other _____ = 7

LEVEL OF IMPAIRMENT
20. Non-Handicapped = 1 ☐ (42)
    At-Risk = 2
    Mild = 3
    Moderate = 4
    Severe = 5

Comments:

Appendix C

DEMOGRAPHIC FORM CODING INSTRUCTIONS

FAMILY INFORMATION

Family type
1 = single parent
2 = partnership
3 = extended family in same household

Main wage earner/head of
household relationship to infant
1 = mother
2 = father
3 = grandparent
4 = relative
5 = other
6 = mother and father (equal wages earned)

Occupational index
1 = higher executive, proprietor of large concern, major professional
2 = business manager of large concern, proprietor of medium-sized business, lesser professional
3 = administrative personnel, owner of small business, minor professional, owner of large farm
4 = clerical or sales worker, technician, owner of small business, minor professional, owner of large farm
5 = skilled manual employee
6 = machine operator, semi-skilled employee
7 = unskilled employee, unemployed, housewife (if no previous occupation)
8 = student (Hollingshead will be computed using 7)

Educational index
1 = completed graduate professional training
2 = standard college or university
3 = partial college training
4 = high school graduate
5 = partial high school (10–11 grades)
6 = junior high school (7–9 grades)
7 = under 7 years of schooling

Appendix C

DEMOGRAPHIC FORM CODING INSTRUCTIONS (continued)

Annual family income
1 = 0–5,000
2 = 5,001–10,000
3 = 10,001–15,000
4 = 15,001–20,000
5 = 20,001–25,000
6 = 25,000+

Class (Use the Hollingshead Index)
1 = 11–17
2 = 18–27
3 = 28–43
4 = 44–60
5 = 61–77

Appendix C

AUTHORIZATION TO REQUEST CONFIDENTIAL INFORMATION FORM

Name: Date of birth:
Parent or legal guardian: Phone:
Address:
          Street   City   State   Zip

Please list agencies, schools, doctors, or others that we are hereby authorized to contact and/or share information that could help us better assist your child.

Name   Address

_____   _____
_____   _____
_____   _____
_____   _____
_____   _____
_____   _____
_____   _____
_____   _____
_____   _____
_____   _____

_____   _____
Parent's signature   Date

_____
Witness's signature

APPENDIX D

FAMILY IMPACT MEASURES

Appendix D

FAMILY INTEREST CHECKLIST

Name: Date:

INSTRUCTIONS:

I. Listed below are the services we provide for families and other services you may be able to provide for us. Please check the box to the left of all areas that are of interest to you. Add explanatory comments on the right.

                                                        Comments

A. Would you like to participate:
- ☐ 1. in a small group with other parents?
- ☐ 2. individually with a professional?
- ☐ 3. in small parent-child work/play groups?

B. Would you prefer:
- ☐ 1. to attend a weekly group with other parents at the Center?
- ☐ 2. to have a professional visit your home?

C. Would you like the opportunity to:
- ☐ 1. discuss your child, how s/he relates to your family, his/her future, the public and private impact of the child on your life?
- ☐ 2. learn to improve the way you relate to your child, your partner, your family, professionals?
- ☐ 3. learn to teach your child within your daily routine?
- ☐ 4. teach other parents effective teaching and/or relationship skills?
- ☐ 5. learn to control your child's disruptive behavior?

D. Would you like to learn more about child development:
- ☐ 1. motor/physical development?
- ☐ 2. language development?
- ☐ 3. social and play skills?
- ☐ 4. cognitive/learning development?
- ☐ 5. self-care skills?

FAMILY INTEREST CHECKLIST (continued)

Comments

E. Would you like information about:
- ☐ 1. handicapping conditions/labels?
- ☐ 2. laws relating to special education?
- ☐ 3. advocacy and guardianship?

F. Are you interested in understanding tests and testing procedures:
- ☐ 1. reasons for testing?
- ☐ 2. interpretation and use of test results?
- ☐ 3. how tests affect your child?

G. Would you like to know the roles of other professionals:
- ☐ 1. physical therapist?
- ☐ 2. occupational therapist?
- ☐ 3. speech therapist?
- ☐ 4. evaluation teams?
- ☐ 5. caseworker?

H. Would you be able to:
- ☐ 1. provide transportation for others?
- ☐ 2. provide respite care?
- ☐ 3. have parent meetings at your home?
- ☐ 4. help other families with advocacy?

II. The following are some additional areas about which you may have questions or concerns. Our program(s) may not be able to assist you directly in these areas, but we will give you information and referrals to the appropriate programs or services. Please check each area of interest and add comments, as above, to describe your particular concern.

Comments

- ☐ 1. Physicians
- ☐ 2. Physical therapists
- ☐ 3. Speech/hearing therapists
- ☐ 4. Vision testing
- ☐ 5. Orthopedics
- ☐ 6. Public health care
- ☐ 7. Genetic counseling
- ☐ 8. Dental health
- ☐ 9. First aid procedures

Appendix D

FAMILY INTEREST CHECKLIST (continued)

Comments

- ☐ 10. Respite care
- ☐ 11. Transportation
- ☐ 12. Supplemental security income
- ☐ 13. Recreation
- ☐ 14. Aid to dependent children
- ☐ 15. Day care
- ☐ 16. Babysitting
- ☐ 17. Food stamps
- ☐ 18. Housing
- ☐ 19. Legal aid
- ☐ 20. Health insurance
- ☐ 21. Financial information
- ☐ 22. Availability of preschool programs for your child
- ☐ 23. Availability of religious instruction for your chlid
- ☐ 24. Availability of summer school programs for your child
- ☐ 25. Opportunity to attend a parent community support group, such as Association for Retarded Citizens
- ☐ 26. Opportunity to help in a classroom
- ☐ 27. Opportunity to speak to groups
- ☐ 28. Opportunity to work with local chapters of national organizations
- ☐ 29. Opportunity to work to influence legislative bodies

OTHERS

Appendix D

FAMILY PARTICIPATION AND ACTIVITY RECORD

Name:
Year: Quarter: 1st   2nd   3rd   Summer

I. *Required activities*

Week	Date	Activity	Explained absence	Recorder/ interviewer
Pre-enrollment		Intake interview		
1		Orientation meeting		
3–4		IEP meeting		

II. *Optional activities*

Week	Date	Activity	Hours	Explained absence	Recorder
1					
2					
3					
4					
5					
6					
7					
8					
9					
10					

Appendix D

PARENT SELF-EVALUATION RECORD

Name: Date:

Check the answer which most accurately describes your needs in each area, using the following scale:

1. I need little or no help in this area.
2. I need to know more in this area.
3. I need to know a lot more in this area.

AREA	SCALE			
	No need	Some need	Strong need	Does not apply to me
1. Know and can recognize normal developmental progress.	1	2	3	4
2. Can use everyday activities as learning opportunities for my child.	1	2	3	4
3. Can set goals for my child which are realistic for the child's abilities.	1	2	3	4
4. Can give my child a stable home life.	1	2	3	4
5. Can set rules and limits for my child's behavior and consistently enforce them.	1	2	3	4
6. Can build my child's self-concept.	1	2	3	4
7. Can find help or special services for my child.	1	2	3	4
8. Can accept my child as a unique and valuable individual.	1	2	3	4
9. Understand the disability and special needs resulting from my child's handicapping condition.	1	2	3	4
10. Can get other family members involved in the care and education of my child.	1	2	3	4
11. Can teach my child skills in daily living, such as dressing, eating, toilet training, and grooming.	1	2	3	4

PARENT SELF-EVALUATION RECORD (continued)

AREA	No need	Some need	Strong need	Does not apply to me
12. Can give my child good health care, including a balanced diet, home safety, cleanliness, and medical attention.	1	2	3	4
13. Can make plans for the future of my child.	1	2	3	4
14. Am aware of my own feelings about my child and the child's handicapping condition.	1	2	3	4
15. Can get professionals to understand my concerns about my child's health and/or development.	1	2	3	4
16. Can work out solutions to most problems concerning the family's responsibilities for my child's needs.	1	2	3	4
17. Can see to it that other family members have the time they need for their own activities.	1	2	3	4
18. Am able to get others (friends and relatives) to interact comfortably with or to care for my child.	1	2	3	4
19. Feel comfortable talking about difficulties in managing my child's behavior and care.	1	2	3	4
20. Feel comfortable seeking information or help from professionals.	1	2	3	4
21. Feel comfortable seeking information from others (other parents, friends, relatives, etc.).	1	2	3	4

Appendix D

FAMILY SATISFACTION QUESTIONNAIRE

Month child started in program:
My/our child is: (check one)
_____ handicapped or has developmental delays
_____ nonhandicapped

PART I: Involvement Activities

1. The types of activities participated in include: (check all that apply)
   _____ observing classroom instruction and testing
   _____ jointly planning my/our educational programming with intervention staff
   _____ working with my/our child in the classroom
   _____ working with other children in the classroom
   _____ running activity groups in the classroom
   _____ working on one or more of my/our child's goals at home
   _____ parent concerns group
   _____ providing transportation
   _____ helping other with advocacy (e.g., telephoning, writing letters, attending hearings)
2. Of the activities checked above, the *two* found most useful were:
   1.
   2.

PART II: Benefits for Families

Please rate each of the choices below on the 5-point scale by circling the appropriate number.

	Strongly disagree	Disagree	Neutral	Agree	Strongly agree
1. As a result of participation in the program, my *knowledge of development* has improved in the following areas:					
a. receptive language (how well child understands communication)	1	2	3	4	5
b. expressive language (how child communicates to others)	1	2	3	4	5
c. social development (how well child gets along with adults and other children)	1	2	3	4	5

Appendix D

FAMILY SATISFACTION QUESTIONNAIRE (continued)

	Strongly disagree	Disagree	Neutral	Agree	Strongly agree
d. gross motor skills (skills using large muscles, e.g., walking)	1	2	3	4	5
e. fine motor skills (skills involving small-muscle control; manipulating objects)	1	2	3	4	5
f. cognitive skills (problem solving and "thinking" skills)	1	2	3	4	5
g. self-help skills (e.g., eating and drinking, toileting, grooming, dressing and undressing)	1	2	3	4	5

2. Participation in the program has:

	Strongly disagree	Disagree	Neutral	Agree	Strongly agree
a. changed some of my/our expectations for my/our child	1	2	3	4	5
b. changed some of the ways I/we interact with my/our child	1	2	3	4	5
c. helped me/us understand my/our ability to improve my/our child's development/learning	1	2	3	4	5
d. increased my/our knowledge about community resources that are available (e.g., medical and dental care, physical and speech therapy, counseling)	1	2	3	4	5
e. increased my/our knowledge about support services (e.g., financial aid, babysitting, community support groups)	1	2	3	4	5
f. increased my/our knowledge about testing and evaluation (e.g., reasons for testing, results of tests, how tests affect my/our child)	1	2	3	4	5

Appendix D

FAMILY SATISFACTION QUESTIONNAIRE (continued)

PART III: Benefits for Children

	Strongly disagree	Disagree	Neutral	Agree	Strongly agree
3. As a result of participation in the program my/our child has shown improvements in the following areas:					
a. receptive language (how well child understands communication)	1	2	3	4	5
b. expressive language (how well child communicates to others)	1	2	3	4	5
c. social development (how well child gets along with adults and other children)	1	2	3	4	5
d. gross motor skills (skills using large muscles, e.g., walking)	1	2	3	4	5
e. fine motor skills (skills involving small-muscle control; manipulating objects)	1	2	3	4	5
f. cognitive skills (problem solving and "thinking" skills)	1	2	3	4	5
g. self-help skills (e.g., eating and drinking, toileting, grooming, dressing and undressing)	1	2	3	4	5

PART IV: Overall Program Effectiveness

4. I feel the overall quality of services provided by the program is (check one):
   _____ Excellent _____ Very good _____ Average _____ Below average _____ Poor
5. What are some of the best features of the program?

6. How would you improve the program?

Name Index

Abeson, A., 105, 106, 121, 124
Ackerman, P., 39, 47, 55
Adams, M., 86, 94
Adcock, C., 310
Addams, J., 35
Adelson, E., 79, 94, 212, 225
Adubato, S., 86, 94
Affleck, J., 74, 102, 256, 258, 272, 343, 367
Ahlster-Taylor, J., 70, 98, 189, 202
Alberto, P., 213, 225, 329, 330, 333
Allen, K., 104, 109, 110, 125, 202, 332, 333
Allen, L., 24, 28, 32, 66, 67, 92, 99, 202
Allman, T., 311, 342, 365
Alper, T., 23, 30
Alpern, G., 340, 360, 364
Alpert, C., 231, 248
Anderson, J., 19, 20, 30, 247, 313
Anderson, S., 231, 248
Andrews, R., 72, 73, 95
Arendshorst, D., 94
Armatruda, C. S., 190, 201
Aronson, M., 67, 94, 199
Attermeier, S., 311
Axelrod, S., 213, 226, 329, 331, 333

Badger, E., 45, 55, 187, 199
Baer, D., 141, 151, 299, 313
Bagnato, S., 76, 94, 199, 313, 336, 337, 339, 364
Bailey, D., 316, 322, 331, 333
Bailey, E., 51, 56, 73, 75, 79, 95, 160, 179, 181, 188, 196, 199, 257, 272, 278, 296, 336, 363, 364
Baker, B., 85, 86, 94, 160, 178, 181, 199
Baker-Ward, L., 18, 22, 26, 33
Baldwin, V., 93, 99, 231, 247
Ball, T. A., 46, 55
Ballard, J., 110, 125
Bandura, A., 331, 333
Banerdt, B., 319, 333
Barker, W., 84, 97

Barnard, K., 43, 56
Barnes, M., 53, 59
Barrand, N., 42, 56
Barrera, M., 77, 94
Bartel, J., 118, 126
Bates, E., 240, 247
Baumeister, A., 11, 13, 50, 56
Bayley, N., 70, 94, 340, 360, 364
Beck, G., 64, 97, 141, 144, 145, 153
Beckman, P., 52, 57
Beckman-Bell, P., 176, 181
Behrns, C., 46, 59
Bell, R., 7, 13, 51, 56, 165, 169, 181
Beller, E., 36, 40, 56, 81, 83, 94
Bendersky, M., 74, 102, 256, 258, 272
Benfield, G., 80, 99, 202
Bennett, F., 97, 201
Bergan, J., 86, 99
Berry, P., 72, 73, 95
Bertenthal, B., 31
Bidder, R., 73, 86, 95, 199
Bijou, S., 141, 151
Binet, A., 45, 46
Blacher, T., 184
Black, T., 182, 201, 366
Blatt, B., 26, 31, 39, 56, 314
Bloom, B., 36, 56
Bluma, S., 310
Blunden, R., 77, 100, 203
Bolick, N., 121, 124
Bond, L., 100, 154, 203
Boring, E., 23, 30
Bornstein, M., 154
Bowerman, M., 137, 151
Bowlby, J., 7, 14, 36, 56, 163, 181
Bradley, R., 199
Brassell, W., 199
Bray, D., 23, 31
Brazelton, B., 51, 56, 169, 181
Brehm, S., 65, 98, 218, 226
Bricker, D., 6, 14, 15, 24, 31, 33, 49, 51, 56, 59, 65, 70, 73, 74, 75, 76, 79, 92, 94, 95, 97, 98, 101, 125, 126, 130, 133, 144, 150, 152, 154, 160, 161, 165, 179, 181, 183, 185, 187, 188, 189, 196, 197, 198, 199, 200, 201, 202, 204, 208, 209, 211, 226, 227, 231, 234, 239, 240, 241, 247, 248, 255, 256, 257, 272, 278, 290, 296, 298, 299, 301, 303, 313, 314, 319, 333, 336, 341, 343, 345, 347, 348, 360, 362, 363, 364, 365, 367, 376, 378
Bricker, W., 6, 14, 24, 31, 133, 152, 240, 247, 298, 303, 313
Brigance, A., 301, 310, 313, 342, 364
Brinker, R., 200, 211, 226, 231, 234, 240, 247, 299, 303, 313
Brody, G., 161, 184
Bromwich, R., 45, 56, 87, 95, 200
Bronfenbrenner, U., 26, 31, 41, 56, 81, 95, 175, 176, 181, 193, 200
Brooks-Gunn, J., 160, 181, 377, 378
Brotherson, M., 184
Brown, C., 60
Brown, F., 123, 125
Brown, G., 211, 226
Brown, L., 152, 233, 248, 332, 334
Brown, R., 138, 152
Brown, S., 68, 100, 310
Bruder, M., 51, 56, 161, 181, 188, 196, 199, 200, 246, 247, 278, 296, 336, 364
Bruner, J. S., 131, 152, 209, 226
Bryant, G., 72, 86, 95, 199
Budd, K., 86, 94
Budetti, P., 42, 56
Bull, D., 134, 154
Burke, P., 104, 108, 109, 110, 115, 126
Burns, S., 87, 99, 199
Burt, R., 104, 106, 107, 125
Buss, W., 106, 107, 125
Butterfield, E., 11, 14

Caldwell, B., 55, 70, 95, 199, 342, 364
Campbell, A., 342, 366
Campbell, F., 81, 83, 92, 100, 256, 272, 360, 366
Campbell, P., 319, 333
Campos, J., 31, 58
Campos, R., 31
Caputo, D., 44, 56, 82
Carlson, L., 65, 70, 95, 165, 181,

423

Name Index

209, 226, 231, 240, 247, 290, 296, 298, 301, 313, 319, 333
Cartwright, C., 178, 181, 188, 189, 200
Casati, I., 342, 364
Cascione, R., 24, 33, 38, 39, 60, 63, 102
Casto, G., 85, 102
Casuso, V., 14, 49, 56, 160, 181, 188, 200, 208, 226, 341, 364
Cecil, H., 84, 97
Cerreto, M., 52, 57, 171, 182, 237, 248
Certo, N., 98, 183, 203, 248, 333
Chance, P., 10, 14, 301, 313
Chandler, M., 6, 15, 29, 33, 43, 49, 60, 63, 91, 101, 169, 184, 209, 227
Chapman, R., 369, 378
Charlesworth, R., 141, 152
Cheseldine, S 86, 94, 200
Christophersen, E., 87, 95, 200, 278, 296
Cicchetti, D., 65, 95, 171, 182
Cicerelli, V., 39, 56
Clarke, A., 20, 22, 25, 26, 27, 31, 33, 39, 50, 57, 58, 60, 63, 89, 90, 96, 102, 175, 182, 203
Clarke-Stewart, K., 85, 96
Clifford, R., 316, 331, 333
Clunies-Ross, G., 68, 69, 70, 92, 96, 200
Cohen, J., 104, 105, 125
Cohen, M., 128, 152, 346, 364
Cohen, S., 42, 44, 60, 82, 111, 125, 198, 200
Cole, J., 44, 57
Cole, K., 148, 152
Collins, S., 99, 202
Comegys, A., 123, 125
Condon, W., 135, 152
Conger, J., 141, 153
Connolly, B., 72, 96, 200
Cooper, D., 51, 60, 85, 101
Corman, H., 342, 365
Cornell, E., 42, 43, 44, 57
Corrigan, R., 14
Corsiri, R., 31
Cox, M., 203
Crain, L., 144, 145, 152
Cross, A., 52, 57
Cross, L., 58
Cuellar, I., 53, 59

Darby, B., 96, 100, 367
Darling, 159
Darlington, R., 29, 32, 40, 59, 83, 99
Davey, K., 313
Day, D., 333
DeBoer, M., 199
DeCarie, T., 166, 167, 182
Dempsey, J., 44, 57, 82, 200
Denenberg, V., 32, 51, 57, 169, 170, 177, 182, 185
Denhoff, E., 143, 152
Dennis, M., 31, 57
Dennis, W., 7, 14, 22, 23, 25, 30, 31, 32, 36, 37, 163, 182
Dennison, L., 133, 152
DesForges, C., 211, 226
DesJardins, C., 156, 182
Deutsch, 83
Dewey, J., 298
DeYoung, H., 104, 105, 125
Dmitriev, V., 65, 96, 97, 188, 201
Dodds, J., 339, 365
Doll, E., 339, 365
Domash, M., 190, 202
Donovan, C., 68, 100, 310
Dow, M., 74, 75, 76, 92, 95, 200
Downs, M., 11, 15
DuBose, R., 70, 96, 339, 341, 365
Dunn, L., 340, 365
Dunn, V., 340, 366
Dunst, C., 85, 93, 96, 199
Dussault, B., 123, 125

Eaves, R., 364
Edgar, E., 74, 95, 102, 256, 258, 272, 343, 367
Eichorn, D. H., 47, 60
Eilers, R., 11, 14
Ellis, N., 56, 58, 98
Emde, R., 134, 152, 167, 168, 169, 171, 182
Engh, H., 99, 202
Escalona, S., 342, 365
Esry, D., 58, 98
Esterling, L., 313
Etzel, B., 190, 202
Evans, J., 39, 56
Evans, R., 325, 333

Fagan, J., 12, 14, 209, 226
Fallstrom, K., 67, 94, 199
Farran, D., 81, 100
Ferry, P., 92, 96
Ferster, C., 333
Fewell, R., 14, 50, 57, 85, 93, 99, 147, 152, 160, 182, 184, 200, 248
Field, T., 44, 45, 57, 82, 87, 88, 95, 96, 154, 200, 202, 226
Fields, D., 44, 57, 63, 92, 93, 97
Filler, J., 14, 86, 96, 125, 126, 178, 182, 188, 200, 201, 248, 303, 313, 314
Finkelstein, N., 85, 97
Fischer, K., 14, 129, 152, 211, 226, 346, 365
Flavell, J., 139, 141, 152
Folio, R., 70, 96
Forehand, R., 50, 56
Forness, S., 34, 58
Forsberg, S., 311
Forsythe, A., 42, 44, 60, 82
Foster, P., 60
Fowler, W., 81, 96
Fraiberg, S., 79, 94, 96, 156, 172, 182, 212, 225, 226, 231, 247
Frankenburg, W., 338, 339, 365, 366
Fredericks, H., 83, 99
Freud, S., 17, 19, 31
Frey, D., 88, 98
Friedlander, B., 31, 48, 56, 57, 94, 95, 96, 97, 98, 99, 100, 181, 182, 200, 201, 202, 225, 226, 247
Friedman, S., 56, 57, 58, 59, 60, 61, 82, 96, 101, 154, 200, 202, 226
Frobel, F., 35
Frohreich, L., 53, 59
Frostig, M., 340, 365
Furuno, S., 311, 342, 365

Gabel, H., 52, 57, 171, 182, 237, 248
Gabel, J., 84, 101, 204
Gallagher, J., 52, 57, 105, 111, 125, 183
Galton, F., 18, 31
Garber, H., 81, 83, 87, 88, 90, 96, 98, 202

Name Index

Garfunkel, E., 26, 31, 39, 56
Garland, C., 188, 201
Garwood, S. G., 14, 57, 108, 125, 145, 146, 148, 152, 153, 182, 200, 248, 360, 365
Gentry, D., 197, 198, 201, 256, 257, 272, 343, 364
Gerwirtz, J., 8, 15
Gesell, A., 190, 201
Getz-Sheftel, M., 332, 334
Gewirtz, J., 163, 183
Gibson, D., 44, 57, 63, 92, 93, 97
Gilhool, T., 106, 120, 125
Gilkerson, L., 44, 57
Ginsberg, N., 360, 365
Ginzberg, A., 23, 31
Gladwin, T., 32
Goldberg, S., 45, 57, 95, 154, 200, 202
Goldstein, K., 44, 56, 82
Gooch, B., 46, 59
Goodenough, F., 37, 58
Goodman, J., 84, 97
Goolsby, E., 94
Gordon, N., 87, 97
Gordon, R., 77, 83, 101, 203
Gorham, K., 156, 182
Gottfried, A., 42, 43, 44, 57
Gottleib, J., 100, 203
Gratch, G., 344, 365
Gray, O., 72, 86, 95, 199
Gray, S., 29, 31, 39, 40, 58, 81, 83, 89, 90, 91, 97, 201
Green, D., 360, 365
Green, K., 319, 333
Greenberg, M., 160, 184
Gregg, L., 77, 100, 203
Griffin, P., 342, 366
Gross, P., 128, 152, 346, 364
Guess, D., 123, 125, 192, 201, 234, 248, 299, 302, 313, 314
Guidabaldi, J., 80, 99, 202
Gumerlock, S., 257, 272
Gunn, V., 72, 73, 95
Guralnick, M., 73, 79, 97, 111, 125, 197, 198, 200, 201, 331, 332, 333, 373, 378

Haith, M., 58
Hale, J., 53, 59
Hall, R., 329, 334
Hallahan, D. P., 147, 153

Halle, J., 231, 248, 329, 334
Hamerlynck, L., 95, 200
Hamilton, J., 361, 365
Hanson, M., 68, 69, 70, 92, 97, 152, 153, 174, 182, 188, 201
Harbin, G., 179, 182, 190, 201
Haring, N., 58, 65, 74, 95, 97, 98, 102, 201, 231, 248, 256, 258, 272, 343, 344, 367
Harlow, H., 21, 25, 31, 166, 182
Harlow, M., 21, 25, 31
Harms, T., 316, 331, 333
Harris, S., 65, 70, 97, 201
Hart, B., 192, 201, 322, 334
Haskins, R., 85, 97
Hass, J., 121, 124
Hawkins, R., 98, 202
Hayden, A., 12, 14, 45, 58, 63, 64, 65, 74, 97, 98, 102, 141, 144, 145, 153, 188, 201, 256, 258, 272, 343, 367
Hebb, D., 22, 31
Heber, R., 81, 83, 87, 88, 90, 96, 98, 202
Hecimovic, A., 124, 126
Hedrick, E., 340, 365
Heifetz, L., 85, 86, 94, 160, 178, 181, 199
Heinen, L., 42, 56
Held, R., 21, 31, 185
Hellmuth, J., 185
Herst, J., 342, 365
Hess, R., 369, 378
Hetherington, M., 15, 33, 60, 88, 98, 101, 184, 227
Hewett, F., 34, 58
Hilliard, J., 310
Hillyard, A., 70, 98, 189, 202, 300, 314
Ho, E., 53, 59
Hobbs, N., 125, 127, 153, 182, 313, 375, 378
Hogg, J., 14, 56, 200, 226, 247, 313
Holmes, V., 202
Holmlund, C., 88, 98
Honzik, M., 24, 28, 32, 150, 153
Horowitz, F., 15, 17, 33, 60, 101, 184, 227
Horrobin, M., 71, 72, 100, 203
Horst, D., 339, 345, 365, 367
Horton, K., 51, 53, 54, 58, 78, 79, 90, 98

Hosaka, C., 311, 342, 365
Hostler, S., 141, 154
Hunt, J., 36, 44, 58, 81, 82, 98, 135, 154, 166, 183, 186, 190, 202, 342, 367
Hunt, J. McV., 18, 20, 22, 32, 49, 58, 101, 133, 139, 153
Hunter, R., 43, 59
Huntington, G., 341, 367
Hyman, H., 360, 365

Iacino, R., 133, 152
Ignaloff, E., 87, 96
Inatsuka, T., 311, 342, 365
Itard, 46

Jenkins, J., 18, 30, 31, 58, 95
Jens, K., 311
Jensen, A., 63, 98
Jew, W., 77, 98
Joffe, J., 100, 154, 203
Johnson, D., 87, 98, 99, 202
Johnson, G., 301, 314
Johnson, L. B., 38
Johnson, N., 94, 311, 343, 366
Jones, O., 170, 183
Jorgensen, G., 342, 365
Jusczyk, A., 161, 181

Kagan, J., 4, 14, 16, 19, 25, 26, 32, 90, 98, 130, 133, 136, 141, 153
Karnes, M., 40, 58, 81, 83, 98, 175, 183
Kasari, C., 86, 96, 201
Katoff, L., 340, 366
Katz, E., 171, 182
Kauffman, J., 31, 147, 153, 313
Kearsley, R., 4, 14, 19, 32, 90, 98, 130, 133, 136, 150, 153, 154
Kemper, M., 338, 366
Kennell, J., 20, 32, 43, 58, 130, 153, 170, 171, 172, 182
Keogh, B., 335, 341, 367
Kessen, W., 154
Kirk, G., 31, 48, 56, 57, 94, 95, 96, 97, 98, 99, 100, 181, 182, 200, 201, 202, 203, 225, 226, 247
Kirk, S., 22, 26, 32, 37, 45, 46, 58, 301, 314, 340, 366
Kirk, W., 340, 366

425

Name Index

Kirp, D., 106, 107, 125
Klaus, M., 20, 32, 43, 58, 130, 153, 170, 171, 172, 183
Klaus, R., 29, 31, 39, 40, 81, 90, 91, 97, 201
Klein, R., 16, 25, 32
Kligman, D., 134, 152, 167, 182
Knobloch, H., 252, 256, 272, 340, 358, 366
Kogan, K., 11, 15, 87, 97, 101, 202
Kopp, C., 14, 41, 43, 44, 45, 58
Koslowski, B., 51, 56, 169, 181
Kratochwill, T., 86, 99
Kugel, R., 33, 60
Kuriloff, P., 106, 107, 125
Kysela, G., 70, 71, 98, 189, 202, 300, 314

Lambie, D., 175, 185
Langley, M., 146, 147, 153, 339, 365
Laski, F., 118, 119, 120, 125, 240, 248
Laub, K., 311
LaVeck, B., 65, 98, 218, 226
Lazar, I., 29, 32, 40, 41, 59, 83, 84, 91, 99
Lazerson, M., 35, 59
LeBlanc, J., 190, 202
Lee-Painter, S., 8, 15, 164, 183, 209, 226
Leib, S., 80, 99, 202
LeMay, D., 342, 366
Lessen, E., 116, 124, 125
Levenstein, P., 81, 83, 86, 99
Levenstein, S., 81, 83, 86, 99
Lewis, G., 58, 98
Lewis, M., 8, 13, 14, 15, 27, 29, 32, 56, 90, 91, 99, 128, 130, 132, 133, 150, 152, 153, 154, 160, 163, 164, 166, 181, 182, 183, 184, 209, 226, 231, 240, 247, 248, 303, 313, 362, 366, 377, 378
Lezine, I., 342, 364
Liberman, A., 53, 59
Little, T., 53, 59, 342, 366
Littlejohn, R., 47, 48, 59
Littman, D., 144, 152, 255, 272, 341, 360, 363, 364, 376, 378
Lloyd, L., 14, 33, 130, 150, 153, 247, 298, 314
Locke, J., 19

Lowry, M., 99
Ludlow, J., 28, 32, 66, 67, 92, 99, 202
Lynch, E., 68, 100, 310
Lyon, S., 233, 248

Mabry, J., 59
MacFarlane, J., 24, 32
MacMillan, D., 302, 314
MacPhee, D., 81, 86, 88, 100, 148, 154, 196, 203
Madden, J., 81, 86, 99
Mahoney, G., 192, 202, 240, 248, 300, 314
Main, M., 51, 56, 169, 181
Malone, A., 252, 256, 272, 340, 358, 366
Mann, L., 125
Marton, P., 87, 99, 202
Masi, W., 144, 149, 154
Masland, R., 23, 24, 32
Mason, M., 20, 21, 25, 32
Mason, W., 20, 21, 32
Massie, H., 209, 226
Mastropieri, M., 85, 102
Maurer, K., 37, 58
Maxim, G., 35, 36, 38, 59
May, M., 96, 100, 367
Mayer, R., 213, 227, 331, 334
McCall, R., 25, 26, 29, 32, 90, 99, 128, 150, 153, 346, 366
McCandless, B., 141, 153
McCarthy, D., 75, 99, 340, 366
McCarthy, J., 340, 366
McCarthy, M., 119, 125
McClelland, D., 310
McConkey, R., 86, 95, 200
McCormick, L., 313
McDonald, L., 70, 98, 189, 202, 300, 314
McDonnell, A., 75, 95, 179, 181
McDowell, J., 52, 57, 171, 182, 237, 248
McGinnies, E., 333
McGinnis, G., 63, 98
McHale, S., 10, 15
McMahon, R., 152
McManus, P., 42, 56
McMillan, M., 35
Mears, C., 166, 182
Meisel, J., 99, 202
Meisels, S., 334
Melzack, R., 21, 33, 175, 184
Merrill, M., 340, 367

Messina, R., 233, 248
Metzger, R., 46, 59
Meyer, D., 160, 184
Minde, K., 87, 99, 202
Minifie, F., 14, 33, 130, 150, 153, 226
Minuchin, S., 161, 183
Mittler, P., 14, 56, 96, 98, 200, 201, 226, 247, 313
Mix, B., 339, 366
Moersch, M., 310
Montessori, M., 35, 191
Moore, J., 11, 14, 47
Moore, M., 39, 55, 83, 99
Morehead, A., 151
Morehead, D., 151
Morgan, D., 159, 183
Morgan, S., 72, 96, 200
Mori, A., 297, 314
Morris, B., 314
Morton, K., 157, 183
Mounts, L., 161, 181
Moxley-Haegert, L., 202
Mulligan, M., 123, 125
Murphy, D., 85, 94
Murray, H., 29, 32, 40, 59, 83, 99
Mussen, P., 32, 58, 59, 100, 141, 153, 154, 183, 203, 314, 334

Najarian, P., 25, 31, 163, 182
Neiditch, C., 77, 101, 203
Neisworth, J., 76, 94, 199, 297, 311, 314, 336, 337, 339, 364
Nelson, K., 137, 153
Newborg, E., 84, 101, 204
Nice, G., 122, 123, 126
Nicholson, G., 86, 99
Nielsen, G., 77, 99, 202
Nietupski, J., 233, 239, 240, 248
Noel, M., 104, 108, 109, 110, 115, 126
Northern, J., 11, 15

Ockwood, L., 239, 248
O'Connell, J., 116, 126, 198, 203, 332, 334
Odom, S., 85, 93, 99
Ogilvie, J., 202
Olds, A., 315, 322, 333, 334
O'Leary, K., 213, 226
O'Leary, S., 213, 226
Oller, D., 134, 154
Olley, G., 10, 15

426

Name Index

Olson, J., 197, 198, 201
O'Reilly, C., 311, 342, 365
Orelove, F., 123, 125
Osofsky, J., 32, 50, 56, 58, 94, 99, 153, 168, 183, 208, 226
Owen, R., 35

Page, R., 156, 182
Pallan, S., 342, 365
Palmer, 83
Parke, R., 9, 15, 161, 183, 210, 226
Parmelee, A., 87, 95, 200
Parr, C., 94
Parse, S., 341, 367
Pasamanick, B., 366
Paterson, D., 18, 30, 58
Payne, J., 31, 313
Penticuff, J., 98, 202
Peters, R., 152
Peterson, D., 31
Petrie, P., 86, 99
Pettis, R., 156
Piaget, J., 29, 32, 49, 59, 91, 100, 131, 133, 154, 163, 166, 167, 183, 190, 203, 208, 211, 298, 301, 303, 310, 314, 319, 334, 365
Pick, A., 17, 26, 33
Pious, C., 95
Piper, M., 69, 70, 92, 100, 203
Pless, I., 69, 70, 92, 100, 203
Powell, T., 124, 126
Prutting, C., 137, 154

Quick, A., 342, 366
Quiltich, H., 278, 296, 319, 334

Ramey, C., 18, 22, 26, 33, 43, 81, 83, 86, 88, 92, 97, 100, 141, 148, 153, 154, 196, 203, 256, 272, 360, 366
Ramsay, M., 203
Ramsey, B., 29, 31, 40, 58, 59, 81, 90, 91, 97, 201
Ratts, D., 58, 98
Ray, H., 84, 101, 204
Reich, J., 134, 152, 167, 168, 182
Rescorla, L., 87, 100
Rettis, R., 182
Reuter, J., 340, 366
Revill, S., 77, 100, 203

Reynell, J., 71, 100
Rheingold, H., 8, 15, 163, 183
Rheingrover, R., 85, 93, 96
Rhodes, L., 46, 47, 59
Richardson, B., 72, 96, 200
Richardson, E., 127
Ripley, J., 87, 99
Risely, T., 50, 59, 278, 296, 319, 334
Ristow, E. V., 364
Robinson, C., 303, 313, 344, 366
Rogers, L., 310
Rogers, S., 68, 100, 310
Rogers-Warren, A., 192, 201, 204, 300, 314, 315, 322, 334
Roos, P., 52, 59, 155, 175, 177, 183, 194, 203, 235, 248
Rose, T., 116, 124, 125
Rosenblum, L., 13, 15, 29, 32, 56, 91, 99, 152, 163, 166, 181, 182, 183, 184, 226
Rosen-Morris, D., 75, 100, 203
Ross, D., 319, 334
Ross, H., 8, 15, 163, 183
Rossmiller, R., 53, 59
Routh, D., 94, 97
Royce, J., 29, 32, 40, 59, 83, 99
Rues, J., 123, 125
Russell, F., 72, 96, 200
Rynders, J., 71, 72, 100, 203

Saarni, C., 166, 167, 184
Sabatino, D., 125
Safford, P., 77, 100, 203
Sailor, W., 231, 248, 299, 313, 339, 366
Salvia, J., 338, 367
Sameroff, A., 6, 8, 15, 29, 33, 43, 44, 49, 59, 60, 63, 82, 91, 101, 143, 154, 169, 184, 209, 226, 227
Sandall, S., 278, 296
Sander, L., 135, 152
Sandow, S., 203
Sanford, A., 311, 342, 366
Sarason, S., 23, 32
Sawin, D., 98, 202
Scarr-Salapatek, S., 15, 33, 60, 80, 101, 184, 203, 227
Schafer, D., 310
Schaffer, H., 36, 60, 183, 208, 227, 369, 378
Scheiber, B., 156, 182
Scheiner, A., 51, 60, 85, 101

Schell, G., 8, 15, 160, 184
Schenk, J., 84, 101
Scheutz, G., 239, 248
Schiefelbusch, R., 33, 98, 101, 181, 202, 226, 227, 239, 247, 296, 298, 301, 313, 314, 378
Schiller, J., 39, 56
Schneider, B., 134, 154
Schneider, G., 77, 100, 203
Schroeder, S., 94
Schultz, J., 156, 184
Schwarz, R., 69, 70, 92, 95, 97, 188, 201
Schwedel, A., 58, 98
Schweinhart, L., 54, 60
Scott, K. G., 144, 149, 154, 344, 367
Seibert, J., 14, 49, 56, 188, 200, 208, 226
Semmes, M., 111, 125, 198, 200
Serbin, L., 202
Sewell, T., 77, 100, 203
Shapiro, L., 77, 101, 203
Shearer, D., 76, 77, 101, 203
Shearer, M., 76, 77, 101, 203, 310, 340, 360, 364
Sheehan, R., 65, 74, 95, 187, 189, 200, 335, 341, 343, 347, 360, 362, 363, 364, 367
Shepherd, P., 12, 14
Shipman, V., 369, 378
Shosenberg, N., 87, 99
Shuman, H., 44, 45, 57, 82, 95, 154, 200
Siegel, G., 15, 33, 60, 101, 184, 227
Siegelman, E., 46, 59
Siegel-Causey, E., 192, 201, 234, 248, 302, 314
Sigman, M., 42, 44, 56, 57, 58, 59, 60, 61, 82, 96, 101, 154, 200, 202, 226
Simeonsson, R., 51, 60, 85, 101, 341, 367
Simmons-Martin, A., 78, 101
Sindelar, P., 329, 334
Sitkei, E., 75, 100, 203
Skeels, H. M., 37, 46, 60, 83, 101
Skinner, B., 131, 154, 333
Slentz, K., 160, 161, 185, 198, 204
Smith, B., 115, 116, 126
Smith, J., 98, 183, 203, 248, 333

Name Index

Smith, R., 303, 313
Smith, T., 122, 126
Snell, M., 184, 248
Snipper, A., 29, 32, 40, 59, 83, 99
Soboloff, H., 77, 78, 101
Sontag, E., 98, 183, 203, 248, 333
Sostek, A., 45, 57, 95, 154, 200, 202
Spiker, D., 89, 101
Spitz, R., 20, 36, 60, 163, 184
Springer, A., 204
Spurgeon, M., 84, 101, 204
Sroufe, A., 65, 95, 171, 182
Stachnick, T., 59
Stark, R., 154
Starr, M., 27, 32, 90, 99
Stedman, D. J., 47, 55, 60, 85, 97, 199
Steele, M., 204
Stern, D., 202
Sternat, J., 233, 248
Sterritt, G., 31, 48, 56, 57, 94, 95, 96, 97, 98, 99, 100, 181, 182, 200, 201, 202, 203, 225, 226, 247
Stevens, F., 252, 256, 272, 340, 358, 366
Stewart, F., 203
Stillman, R., 343, 367
Stock, J., 84, 101, 204
Stone, N., 188, 201
Stoneman, Z., 161, 184
Strain, P., 85, 101, 333, 378
Strichart, S., 332, 334
Strickland, B., 158, 184
Stringer, S., 87, 96
Stutman, E., 106, 120, 125
Sullivan, R., 176, 177, 184, 194, 204
Sulzer-Azaroff, B., 213, 227, 331, 334
Summers, J., 162, 184
Suttill, J., 88, 98
Svejda, M., 31
Swan, W., 47, 60, 110, 126, 361, 365
Swanson, J., 188, 201, 341, 367
Sweet, N., 44, 60
Sykes, B., 87, 95, 200

Taft, L., 14, 44, 60, 122, 123, 126

Tallmadge, G., 339, 345, 365, 367
Taub, H., 44, 56, 82
Taylor, J., 300, 314
Terman, L., 340, 367
Teska, J., 175, 183
Thoman, E., 51, 57, 169, 170, 172, 182
Thomas, A., 184, 204, 247
Thomas, M., 199
Thompson, J., 87, 99
Thompson, W., 21, 33, 175, 184
Thorpe, J., 171, 182
Tinsley, B., 9, 15, 161, 183, 210, 226
Tjossem, T., 45, 48, 55, 56, 57, 58, 60, 94, 97, 98, 101, 143, 154, 157, 181, 184, 199, 204
Tobin, A., 340, 365
Trehub, S., 134, 154
Trohanis, P., 97, 141, 153, 154, 364
Trotter, R., 141, 153
Troutman, A., 213, 226, 329, 330, 333
Turnbull, A., 52, 59, 158, 162, 175, 177, 178, 183, 184, 185, 235, 248
Turnbull, H., 52, 59, 60, 158, 175, 183, 184, 185
Tyler, N., 11, 15, 87, 101

Ulrich, R., 59
Uzgiris, I., 29, 33, 81, 91, 101, 102, 135, 138, 154, 168, 169, 184, 208, 227, 342, 367

Vadasy, P., 160, 184
Valdivieso, C., 104, 108, 109, 110, 115, 126
Vencidos, J., 112, 126
Victor, 46
Vincent, L., 332, 334
Vincent-Smith, L., 303, 313
Voos, D., 20, 32
Vulpe, S., 343, 367

Wade, T., 134, 152, 167, 168, 182
Waldstein, A., 57, 60
Walker, B., 161, 169, 185, 198, 204

Walker, H., 333, 378
Walker, L., 98, 202
Warren, S., 192, 201, 204, 300, 314
Wasik, B., 92, 100, 256, 272, 360, 366
Weber, C., 60
Weberman, 54
Wehren, A., 362, 366
Weikart, D., 54, 60, 83, 175, 185, 310
Weiss, R., 84, 90, 102, 204
Weller, E., 192, 202, 240, 248, 300, 314
Werthmann, M., 41, 60
Wheat, M., 158, 175, 184
White, B., 163, 185
White, K., 85, 102
White, O., 74, 75, 102, 256, 258, 272, 343, 344, 367
Widmayer, S., 87, 96
Wiegerink, R., 118, 126
Wiggin, K., 35
Will, G., 123
Williams, M., 80, 101, 203
Wilson, W., 11, 14
Winton, P., 178, 185
Wnek, L., 84, 101, 204
Wolery, M., 322, 331, 333
Wolf, M., 50, 59
Wolfe, S., 342, 365
Wolfensberger, W., 19, 33, 34, 60
Wolraich, M., 57, 97
Wood, C., 345, 365
Woodruff, G., 188, 201
Woods, R., 35
Woolman, 83

Yeates, K., 81, 86, 88, 100, 148, 154, 196, 203
Ysseldyke, J., 338, 367

Zeisloft, B., 311, 342, 365
Zeitlin, S., 84, 102
Zelazo, P., 4, 14, 19, 32, 90, 98, 130, 133, 136, 150, 153, 154
Zeskind, P., 43, 59
Zettel, J., 105, 106, 124
Zigler, E., 24, 33, 39, 60, 63, 83, 87, 100, 102, 302, 314
Ziskin, L., 157, 185

Subject Index

Accessibility
  of equipment, in classrooms, 317–18, 320
  of specialists, 243
Accommodation, 208
Activity-based instruction, 290–93
  and classroom plan, 293
  guidelines for implementing, 292–93
  selecting activities, 292
  scheduling activities, 323
Activity groups, scheduling, 275–77
Advocacy, need for, 62
Affective development, 166–68, 169 *tab*.
  biological model of, 166
  socialization model of, 166
Age. *See also* Development
  and eligibility for services, 250
  and importance of care in labeling, 128
Aggressive behavior, managing, in classroom, 280–81
Albert Einstein Scales of Sensorimotor Development, 342
Alpern-Boll Developmental Profile, 76, 77
American Academy of Pediatrics, 123
Ancillary personnel, as target group for instruction, 235
Animal research, 20–22
Antecedents, 305
  in ARC equation, 328
  managing, 330
ARC equations, 328
Army General Classification Test, 23
Asphyxia, at birth, 7
Assessment, 196–97, 215, 350–52. *See also* Screening
  consulting model for, 195–96
  daily/weekly monitoring, 351–52
  and IEPs, 336, 350–51
  initial, 255–59, 350–51
  and intervention, 347–48
  managing, 224
Assessment-evaluation. *See also* Evaluation
  compared, 337
  function of, 335
  future of strategies for, 376
  and heterogeneity of target population, 341, 343
  importance of, 335
  models for, 345–47
  and problems with tests for, 343–45
Assessment-intervention-evaluation system, 336–54. *See also* Evaluation
  annual evaluation, 353–54
  daily/weekly monitoring, 351–52
  importance of linking, 336–37
  initial assessments, 350–51
  organization framework for, 348–50
  quarterly evaluation, 352–53
Assimilation, 208
Associative functioning, 22
The Association for Persons with Severe Handicap's Critical Issues Subcommittee on Infant Concerns, 123
At-risk children. *See* Environmentally at-risk children; Medically at-risk children; Handicapped children
Attachment. *See* Bonding
Auditory discrimination, in infants, 130, 134
Authorization to Request Confidential Information Form, 253

Babbling, 135
Baby Jane Doe, 113
Baby Doe, 122
Battelle Study, 84
Bayley Scales of Infant Development (BSID), 70, 71, 72, 74, 76, 81, 84, 340, 344
Behavior, and level of inference, 326–27
Behavioral development, 28–29
Behavioral learning principles, 213–14
  importance of knowledge of, 234
Behavioral objectives, 329. *See also* Training objectives
Behavioral vs. developmental approaches, 299
Behavioral Vignettes Test, 85, 86
Behaviorism, and instructional strategy, 325–26
Behavior management procedures, 278–81
Behavior modification techniques, 298
Biological factors, in handicaps, 144–48
Biologically at-risk children, 143–44
  assisting parents of, 45
  and bonding, 43
  preterm infants, 41–43
  programs for, 41–45
Biologically impaired children, programs for, 74–79. *See also* Down Syndrome, programs for children with
  Bagnato and Neisworth, 76
  Barrera, 77
  Bricker, Bailey and McDonnell, 75
  Bricker and Dow, 74, 75
  Bricker and Sheehan, 74–75
  Fraiberg, 79
  Horton, 78, 79
  Jew, 77
  Nielsen, 77
  Portage Project, 77
  Rosen-Morris and Sitkei, 75 76
  Safford, 77
  Shapiro, 77
  Simmons-Martin, 78
  Soboloff, 77–78
Biological model, of affective development, 166
Birthweight, 41, 143
Blind infants, study of, 79
Blindness, 147
Board of Education of Hendrick Hudson Central School District v. Rowley, 119

429

Subject Index

Boehm Test of Basic Concepts, 72
Bonding, 20, 43
   affect of separation on, 170
Brazelton Scales, 80
Brigance Diagnostic Inventory of Early Development, 310, 342
Brown v. Board of Education, 104
Bruininks-Oseretsky Motor Test, 72

The Callier-Azusa Scale, 343
Campbell v. Talladega County Board of Education, 119
Caregiver. *See also* Families; Family involvement; Parental involvement; Parents
   and family, 8, 9
Caregiver-infant interaction, enhancing, 209–10
Caregiver risk, 7–8
Caregiving environment, quality of, 6–7
Carolina Abecedarian Project, 86, 87, 88
Carolina Curriculum for Handicapped Infants, 311
Cattell Infant Intelligence Scale, 76, 80
Center-based educational unit, 219–20
Center-based programs, 188–89. *See also* Home-center based program
   with biologically impaired children, 77
   with multiply-handicapped children, 76
   and parental involvement, 178–80
   with severely/profoundly retarded, 74
   studies on, with Down Syndrome children, 69–70, 71
Cerebral palsy, 145–46
   and changing mother-child interaction, 87
   study on, 77–78
Certification, state policies on, 116–17

Chaining, 330
Child Development Units Program, 53
Child Information Form, 282 *fig.*
Children, as educational agents, 331–32, 373
Children's Early Education Developmental Inventory, 84
Civil rights movement
   and evolution of rights for the handicapped, 104
Classroom. *See also* Environmental engineering
   behavior management in, 278–81
   in center-based education, 219
   organization of, 277–78
Classroom Activity Plan, 293
Classroom Activity Plan Form, 294 *fig.*
Classroom design, 320–21, 321 *fig.*
Classroom programs, with biologically impaired children, 74, 75
Classroom schedules, 275–77. *See also* Scheduling
CNS development
   abnormalities, 145
   in infants, 134
Cognitive development, 166–68, 169 *tab.*
Cognitive representation, in toddlers, 139
Cognitive skills, in developmental curriculum, 306, 309
Communication
   between researchers and practitioners, 11–12
   and early infant-mother interaction, 209
   lack of, in isolated therapy model, 239–40
Communication, early developmental sequence of, 3–4, 4 *fig.*
   studies on, 6
Communication skills, in developmental curriculum,

307, 309
COMP Curriculum, 311
Comprehensive Early Evaluation and Programming System, 75
"Competence," of infants, 130
Consent Form to Photograph, Videotape, and Audiotape, 252
Consequences
   administration of, 300
   in ARC equation, 328
   classifying, 330
Consortium follow-up study, 40, 40n
Consulting model, 195–96, 233
Continuity
   developmental concept of, 27
   factors affecting, 26–27
   importance of, 17
   issue of, 90–91
   questions about, 27
Cost. *See also* Economic factors
   and isolated therapy model, 241
   of medical treatment for handicapped infants, 123
   of special education, 52–54
Counselor, interventionist's role as, 237–38
Crawling, development of, in blind infants, 212
Creche, study of, 36–37
Cru du chat syndrome, 145
Criterion-referenced tests, 339, 342–43, 344–45
Critical behaviors, 308–309
Cultural factors, 25. *See also* Sociocultural factors
   and at-risk infants, 44
   importance of, 82
Curriculum, 229–32, 297–303. *See also* Individual Education Plan
   adaptations in, 309, 312
   child vs. adult control in, 299–300
   conceptualizing, 229–32
   consequences in, 300
   content of, 231–32
   critical behaviors, 308–309
   developmental approach to, 231, 303–308

Subject Index

defined, 297
functional vs. nonfunctional training, 302–303
and generalization issues, 300–301
issues and views on, 298–99
organizing, 223–24
preacademic emphasis, 301–302
as program element, 189–91
selected programs for, 310–11 *tab.*
social-communication emphasis, 301–302
trends in focus of, 375–76

Data collection, in monitoring IEP, 284–86
Data grid, for measuring progress, 358 *fig.*
Day-care programs, and WW II, 35–36
Deaf children, study on program with, 78
Decision making, need for objective, 374
Demographic Form, 253
Demographic information, and assessment, 255
Denver Developmental Screening Test (DDST), 339
Department of Health and Human Services, 112
Department of Health, Education, and Welfare (DHEW), 112
Deprivation
animal studies, 21
recovery from, 25–26
Destructive behavior, managing, in classroom, 280–81
Development, 128–42. *See also* Affective development
birth–six months, 133–35
continuity of, 27
delays in, 148
factors that interfere with, 141–42
and differentiation, 131
models of, 128–29
one–two years, 137–38
periods of, 129–30

Piaget on, 131–32
principles of, 129–33
six–twelve months, 135–37
three–five years, 139–40
two–three years, 138–39
variations in, 128, 149–50, 346–47
Development, normal, importance of knowledge of, 230–31
Developmental Activities Screening Inventory (DASI), 339
Developmental approach
vs. behavioral approach, 299
in conceptualizing a program, 231
to curriculum, 189–90
Developmental curriculum, 303–308
content domains in, 304, 306–307 *tab.*
format for, 308
LRGs in, 304–305, 308
TOs in, 304–305, 308
Developmental curves, 28
Developmental hierarchies, 3–6
criticism of, 5–6
value of, 6
Developmental issues, and history of early-childhood education, 35
Developmental organization, of affective and sensorimotor systems, 169 *tab.*
Developmental perspective, 3–6
The Developmental Profile II (Rev. ed.), 340
Developmental Programming for Infants and Young Children, 310
Developmental status, appraising, and intake, 252
Developmental theory
and Piagetian theory, 211
of program philosophy, 210–13
and skill theory, 211
Diagnosis. *See also* Assessment; Labeling
defined, 337
difficulties in, 151
Diana v. Board of Education, 104–105, 106, 121

Differentiation, 131
Direct impact, 188
Discrimination, against handicapped children, 45
Disequilibrium, developmental principle of, 133
Down Syndrome, 7, 145
developmental curve of, 28
and smiling behavior, 171
variables within, 64–65
Down Syndrome children, home-reared *vs.* institutionalized, 47
Down Syndrome, programs for children with, 64–73
Aronson and Fallstrom, 67–68
Berry, Gunn and Andrews, 72–73
Bidder, Bryant and Gray, 72
Clunies-Ross, 68, 69 *fig.*
Hanson, 68–69
Harris, 70
Hayden and Haring, 65, 66 *fig.*
Kysela, 70–71
Ludlow and Allen, 66–67, 67 *fig.*
Model Preschool Project, 65
Piper and Pless, 69–70
Rynders and Horrobin, 71–72
Down Syndrome Performance Inventory, 65
Due Process, right to, 121–22
Duration recording, 329

Early and Periodic Screening, Diagnostic, and Treatment Program, 110
Early childhood education, history of, 35–36
Early Education Project, 300
Early experience, 16–30
animal research on, 20–22
contemporary views on, 19–24
and continuity, 17, 26–30
environmental influence, 19
historical perspective on, 18–19
human research on, 22–24
and psychoanalysis, 19–20

431

Subject Index

reinterpretation of primacy of, 24–26
Early Experience: Myth and Evidence, 25
Early intervention, 16, 26–30, 34–55. *See also* Programs, for early intervention
   advocacy for, 62
   with at-risk infants, 44–45
   and cost effectiveness, 52–53
   effectiveness of, 63
   family support/instruction, 51–52
   future considerations, 374–78
   history of program development, 34–49
   longevity of effect of, 90
   maximizing developmental outcomes, 49–50
   preventing secondary disabilities, 50–51
   and public schools, 375
   rational for, 49–55
Early-intervention approaches, 187–89
   contemporary, 187–89
   elements in, 189–97
   future trends in, 198–99
Early Intervention Development Profile, 68
Early Training Project, 29, 39–40, 91
Economic factors, in parental involvement, 173
Education. *See also* Instructional strategies; Learning; Parent Education
   defined, 9–10
   of mothers, 369
   right to, 119–20
Educational and Psychological Testing Consent Form, 252
Educational perspective, 9–10
Educational synthesizer model, 241–44
Education of all Handicapped Children Act of 1975, 110–12, 278. *See also* P.L. 94–142
Education of the Handicapped Act Amendments of 1983, 111–12. *See also* P.L. 98–199
Efficiency, in arranging classroom space, 317, 320
Elementary and Secondary Education Act, 109, 110
Eligibility, screening for, 250–51
Emotional expression, in infants, 134
Enrollment procedures, 252–53
Environment. *See also* Caregiving environment; Cultural factors; Sociocultural factors; Institutionalization
   -child interaction, 7–8
   influence of, 19, 20, 22–24, 36
   importance of studying, 91, 373
   and predeterminism, 18
Environmental engineering, 315–32
   avoiding uncontrolled stimulation, 316
   defined, 315
   and developing goals, 319–20
   and devising a plan, 320
   environment as dynamic, 316
   evaluating effectiveness of, 322
   general guidelines, 316
   implementing a plan for, 320–21
   and management of staff, 322–25
   sample design, 320–21, 321 *fig.*
   and use of physical space, 316–18
Environmental factors, in handicaps, 148–49
Environmentally at-risk infants and children, 144, programs for, 38–41
Environmental model, of development, 129
Environmental responsiveness, 208
Epilepsy, 146
Equipment, 318–19
   general or specialized, 319
   importance of accessibility of, 317–18
   placement of, and independence, 318
Evaluation, 196–97, 244. *See also* Assessment-evaluation; Assessment-intervention-evaluation system
   annual, 269, 353–54
   of effectiveness of environmental engineering, 322
   legislation on, 345
   and program philosophy, 217
   as task of interventionist, 236–37
   quarterly, 352–53
Evaluation and Programming System: For Infants and Young Children (EPS), 256, 257, 343
Evaluation and Programming System: For Infants and Young Children—Parent Form, 256
Event recording, 329
Expectancy, issue of, 92–93

Families. *See also* Parents
   assessment of, 215
   need for support, 210
   roles and responsibilities of, 239
   setting goals for, 216
Families, impact of programs on, 85–93
   interactional change, 86–87
   with instructional skills, 85–86
   quality of life changes, 87–89
   training parents of retarded children, 85–86
Family-center intervention, study on, with Down Syndrome children, 71–72
Family-child programs, with biologically impaired, 74, 75

Subject Index

Family impact measures, 258-59
Family Interest Checklist, 256, 258
Family involvement, 220-21. *See also* Parental involvement
   in program development, 193-94
   rationale for, 173-75
Family orientation, 253-54
Family Participation and Activity Record, 256, 259
Family Program Agreement (FPA), 259-62, 265-66
   forms for, 265-66
   implementation and follow-up, 268-69
   introducing parents to, 254
   meeting, 266-68
   parent preparation for, 260
   staff preparation for, 261-62
Family Satisfaction Questionnaire, 256, 259
Family systems
   four subsystems in, 161-62
   and parental involvement, 161-63
   roles within, 161-62
Family systems perspective, 8-9
Federal policy, 107-109. *See also* Legislation
   agencies, 113-15
   and local policy, 117-18
   and state policy, 115-17
Feedback system, 163-65
   of child-caregiver relationship, 8
   consequences in, 300
   example of, 164-65
   as instructional strategy, 192
   and parent-child interaction, 163-64
Fialkowski v. Shapp, 121
Follow-up studies, 82-85. *See also* Longitudinal perspective
Format, of antecedent events, 330
Forms. *See individual entries*
Free-play time, in classroom, 280
Functional behaviors, skills taught as, 291
Functional approach
   to curriculum, 189-90
   in engineering classroom environment, 318, 320
Functional training, 302-303
Future considerations, 374-78
The Futures of Children, 127

Galactosemia, 145
Generalization
   in activity-based instruction, 291-92
   as curriculum issue, 300-301
   problem of, in isolated therapy, 240
Genetic or chromosomal disorders, 144-45. *See also* Down Syndrome; Predeterminism; Reproductive risk
The Gesell Developmental Schedules, 75, 76, 340. *See also* Revised Gesell Developmental Schedules
Goals. *See also* Long Range Goals; Program goals; Training Objectives
   developing, and environmental engineering, 319-30
   establishing, for individual child and family, 214-16
   and instructional strategy, 192
   need for, 370-71
   program, 354-63
Government. *See* Federal Policy; Legislation; Head Start
Graphs, in monitoring IEPs, 286-89, 358
Great Depression, and history of nursery schools, 35
Griffiths Scales, 66, 67 *fig.*, 68, 70, 72, 77, 86
Group instruction, in parent education, 245
Group management, in classroom, 279-80

Handicapped children
   discrimination against, 45
   history of programs for, 47-48
   Littlejohn report on projects for, 47-48
Handicapped Children's Early Education Act, 110
Handicapped Children's Early Education Program (HCEEP), 47, 48, 84, 110
Handicaps, causes of, 144-48
   developmental delays, 148
   environmental factors, 148-49
   genetic and chromosomal disorders, 144-45
   infections, 147
   neurological and physical impairments, 145-47
   sensory impairment, 147-48
   teratogens, 147
Hawaii Early Learning Profile (HELP), 311, 342
Head Start, 24, 26, 38-39, 110
Hearing impairments, 147
   program for, at Mama Lere Home, 78, 79
High/Scope Cognitively Oriented Curriculum, 310
Historical perspective
   on early experience, 18-24
   on early-intervention programs, 34-49
Hobsen v. Hansen, 104, 121
Home, and impact of early intervention, 39
Home-based educational unit, 218-19
Home-based programs, 188-89
   with biologically impaired children, 76-77
   with Down Syndrome children, 70, 71
   and environmental engineering, 322
   and parental involvement, 178-80
   scheduling, 274, 325
   and staff management, 325
Home-center based programs, 188-89, 220
   with biologically impaired children, 77
Home Observation for Measurement of the Environment Inventory, 70, 342

433

Subject Index

Human subjects, protection of, 112–13
Hydrocephalus, 146

Illinois Test of Psycholinguistic Abilities, 340
Imitation, learning by, 331–32
Independence, arranging classroom to promote, 318, 320
Indirect impact, 188
Individual Educational Plan (IEP), 259–65. *See also* Curriculum
   data collection, 284–86
   daily/weekly monitoring, 351–52
   developing and monitoring, 281–90
   decision rules, 289–90
   end-of-year meetings, 295
   forms for, 262–65, 270–71, 282, 283, 294
   implementation and follow-up, 268–69
   importance of assessments to, 336
   introducing parents to, 254
   meeting, 266–68
   multiband-graph paper, 287–89
   parental involvement, 159, 174
   parent preparation for, 260
   specialist's input, 238
   staff preparation for, 261–62
   stating goals in, 351
   summarizing results, 286–87
   use of clipboard in monitoring, 281–82
   yearly report form, 270–71
Individualization
   need for, 6
   and parental involvement, 176, 178
Infant-caregiver relationship, 43
Infant-environment interaction, 208–209
   enhancing, 209–10
Infant mortality rate, 41
Infant research, and history of early education, 36
Infants
   abilities of, 209

changes in perception of, 130
development of, 133–35, 135–37
Infections, in utero, 147
Inferences, and analyzing behavior, 327
Informed consent, mandates on, 174
INREAL Program, 54
Institutionalization, 7, 37
   cost of, 53–54, 188
   study on, 22–23
Instructional Program Plan Form, 283 *fig.*
Instructional strategy, 191–93, 325–30
   and behaviorism, 325–26
   framework for, 328–30
   and inferences from behavior, 326–27
   and operant learning, 326, 327–28
   other children as educational agents, 331–32
Intake procedures, 249–54
   enrollment, 252–53
   family orientation, 253–54
   and referral sources, 250
   screening, 250–51
Integration, of handicapped and nonhandicapped children, 278, 331
Intelligence and Experience, 22, 49
I.Q.
   change in views on, 16, 18
   studies on, 22–24, 37
Interactional model, 209. *See also* Transactional model
Interactive model, of parent-child relationship, 163–66
Interventionists, 229–38. *See also* Personnel; Staff
   and conceptualizer, 229–32
   as counselor, 237–38
   as evaluator, 235–37
   as instructor, 234–35
   and parent participation, 234–35
   skills needed by, 237
   and specialists, 239, 241, 243–44
   as synthesizer, 232–34, 241–43
"Isolated Therapy Model," 239–41
Isolation, in animal studies, 21
Issues in the Classification of Children, Vol. 1, Vol. 2, 127

Jargon, importance of reducing, 243
Journal of the Division of Early Childhood, 12

Kent Infant Development Scale (KIDS), 340
Kindergartens, history of development of, 35
Klinefelter's syndrome, 145

Labeling, 127–28, 142–51. *See also* Assessment
   biologically at-risk children, 143–44
   and developmental variations, 149–50
   environmentally at-risk children, 144
   handicapped, 144–48
   problems in, 127–28, 142, 149–51
   and prognosis, 150–51
   project to study, 127
   target population, 142–49
Language development, 4 *fig.,* 4–5. *See also* Auditory discrimination
   one-two years, 137–38
   problems with, in isolated therapy model, 240
   three-five years, 140
   two-three years, 139
Larry P. v. Riles, 105
Learning, and need for active involvement, 131
Learning Accomplishment Profile, 311
Learning Accomplishment Profile—Diagnostic Edition (revised) (LAP-D), 342
Legal issues, 118–24
   appropriate education, 119–20
   appropriate placement, 120–21

Subject Index

due process, 121–22
medical treatment, 122–24
Legislation, 109–13. *See also*
P.L. 94-142
early, 109–10
on protection of human subjects, 112–13
Litigation, 103, 105–107
Littlejohn report, 47–48
Local Policy, 117–18
Longevity, of effect, issue of, 89–91
Longitudinal perspective, need for, 371–72. *See also* Follow-up studies
Long Range Goals (LRG)
and analysis of progress, 361–62
as critical functions, 309
in developmental curriculum, 304–305, 308
in instructional strategy, 329–30
and measuring progress, 354–55, 357–60

McCarthy Scales for Children's Abilities, 75, 340
Mama Lere Home, 53, 78, 79
Management, need for organized system of, 371. *See also* Staff, management of
Marianne Frostig Developmental Test of Visual Perception (DTVP), 340
Media-based programs, 188, 189
Medical Authorization Form, 252
Medical model, of development, 129
Medical Report and Immunization Record Form, 252
Medical treatment, right to, 122–24
Meetings
FPA, 266–68
IEP, 266–68, 295
parent conferences, 222–23
staff, 244, 274
The Memphis Comprehensive Developmental Scale (MCDS), 342
Merrill-Palmer Scale, 72
Metropolitan Achievement Test, 79
Mills v. Board of Education of Washington, D.C., 105, 119, 120, 121
Milwaukee Project, 86, 87, 88
Model Preschool Project, 65
Mothering, psychoanalytic views on, 20
Mothers. *See also* Parents; Parent-child relationship
and bonding, 43
educational level of, 369
and separation distress, 43, 136, 170
Motor development
in infants, 135, 136
in preschoolers, 140
in toddlers, 137, 138

National Commission for the Protection of Human Subjects of Biomedical and Behavioral Research, 112
National Defense Education Act (NDEA), 109
National Institute of Handicapped Research, 114
National Research Act, 112
Nature *vs.* Nurture, 19, 24
Neonatal intensive care units, 41–42, 44
and bonding, 43
Neurological research, 22
Newborns, development of, 133–35. *See also* Infant entries
New York ARC v. Rockefeller, 105, 106
Nonhandicapped children, as educational agents, 331–32
Normalcy, as expected behavior, 92–93
Norm-referenced tests, 338–39, 340, 343–44
Nursery schools, history of development of, 35–36

Office of Economic Opportunity, 38
Office of Special Education and Rehabilitative Services (OSERS), 108–109, 113–14
Office of Special Education Programs, 114, 115 (OSEP)
Operant learning principles, 191–92, 290–93, 327–28
misunderstanding of, 326
problems with, 291
Operation Head Start. *See* Head Start
Ordinal Scales of Infant Development, 342
Orphanage, study on children in, 81

PARC v. Commonwealth of Pennsylvania, 105, 106, 119, 120, 121
and parental involvement, 174
Parental feelings
about having handicapped children, 155–57, 170–71, 172
need to be sensitive to, 157
Parental involvement, 157–63, 173–75, 175–80, 377–78. *See also* Family involvement
and availability of personnel, 174
and center-based approaches, 178–80
and consistency, 235
current status of, 159
economic reasons for, 173
and family systems, 161–63
family systems model for, 162–63
and home-based approaches, 178–80
to insure maximum development, 176
legal basis for, 158, 174, 235
and need for individualization, 176
and parental rights, 175
and parent-professional roles, 176–77
and parental roles, 161
to prevent development of destructive relationships, 175

435

Subject Index

problems with, 158–59
strategies for, 177–78
success of programs for, 160
time as reason for, 173
variables involved in, 160
Parental rights, 175
Parent-child relationship, 163–66
and affective and cognitive development, 166–68
disruptions in, 170–72
and feedback system, 163–65
importance of synchrony in, 50–51, 168–70, 172
preventing destructive, 174
Parent Concern Groups, 221
Parent conferences, scheduling, 222–23
Parent education, 245–46
Parent-professional relationship, 155, 194
and parental involvement, 176–77
and understanding parental feelings, 155–57
Parents. *See also* Parental Involvement
assisting, of at-risk infants, 45
and preparation of IEPs and FPAs, 260
programs for training, 85–86, 86–87
as target group for instructors, 234–35
Parent Self-Evaluation Record, 256, 259
Parent-to-Parent education, 246
Parent training, study on, with Down Syndrome mothers, 72
Partially sighted, 147
Peabody Developmental Motor Scales, 70
Peabody Picture Vocabulary Test, 88
Peabody Picture Vocabulary Test—Revised (PPVT-R), 340
Perceptions of Developmental Skills Profile (PODS), 339
Perinatal period, problems arising in, 141

Personnel. *See also* Interventionists; Staff
ancillary, 235
assistants, 229
availability of, 174
and certification policies, 116–17
considerations in preparation of, 377
deployment of, 239–44
direct service, 195
interventionists, 229–38
limited, 240–41
managing, 223
and parent education, 245–46
program coordinator, 228
roles and responsibilities of, 228–39
specialists, 232–33, 238–39, 241, 243–44
support service, 195
training problems, 117
training, coordination, and meetings, 244–245
Perry Preschool Project, 54
Philosophy, 189–91
Piagetian theory, 207–208, 210–11
PKU, 145
Plan Overview Form, 282 *fig.*
Play, importance of, 10
Portage Project, 76–77, 310
Postnatal period, problems arising in, 141
Poverty. *See also* Sociocultural factors
and history of preschool programs, 34–35, 36
and programs for interactional change, 86–87
studies on programs for children of, 80, 81
Practitioners, active role of, 11–12
Preacademic emphasis, in curriculum, 301–302
Preconceptual stage, 139
Predeterminism, 16, 18–19
Prematurity, as risk factor, 143. *See also* Preterm infants
Prenatal period, problems arising in, 141

Preoperational stage, 139
Preschool Attainment Record (PAR), 76, 339
Preschool programs, history of, 34, 35
Preterm infants, 41, 143
and bonding problems, 43
cost of care for, 42
and cultural environment, 44
and quality-of-life project, 88
studies on programs for, 80, 81
Professionalism, importance of, 369–70
Professionals, role of, 194. *See also* Parent-professional relationship
and parental involvement, 176–77
Prognosis, problems with, 150–51
Program components, 217–21
center-based unit, 219–20
family involvement, 220–21
flexibility of, 218
home-based unit, 218–19
home-center combinations, 220
Program coordinator, responsibilities of, 228
Program goals. *See also* Long Range Goals
analysis of progress toward, 362–63
determining progress toward, 354–63
measuring progress toward, 360–61
Program operation, 221–25. *See also* main entries for Curriculum; Assessment, Evaluation; Intake; Environmental engineering; Personnel; Scheduling
administration, 224
curriculum, 223–24
development of policies, 225
intake, assessment, and evaluation, 224
personnel, 223
organizing the environment, 223
scheduling, 222–23

436

Subject Index

Program philosophy, 206–17
  and assessments, 215
  behavioral learning principles in, 213–14
  child and family goals, 216
  developmental model for, 206–207
  developmental theory and, 210–13
  establishing goals, 214–15
  evaluation and modification, 217
  need for, 206
  transactional perspective of, 207–10
Program Plan, 359 *fig.*
Programs, 34–39
  for at-risk children, 80–82
  for biologically impaired children, 41–45, 74–79
  day care, 35–36
  for Down Syndrome children, 64–73
  elements of, 189–97
  for environmentally at-risk children, 38–41
  follow-up studies of, 82–85
  for handicapped children, 45–48
  future trends in, 198–99
  Head Start, 38–39
  impact on families, 85–93
  kindergarten, 35
  longevity and continuity of, 89–91
  nursery school, 35
  preschool, 34
  outcome goals for, 92–93
  rationales for, 188
  transition to other, 293–95
  variability of, 187
Program start-up, 273–81
  behavior management procedures, 278–81
  including nondelayed children, 278
  organization of materials and environment, 277–78
  scheduling, 274–77
  start-up schedule, 273–74
Progress, 352–63. *See also* Assessment; Evaluation
  analysis of, 361–63
  content of, 354–56

monitoring, 352–53
  toward LRGs and TOs, 354–55, 357–60
  toward program goals, 360–61
  toward weekly targets, 356–57
Prompts, 330
Psychoanalysis, influence of, 19–20
Public Education, and early intervention programs, 375
P.L. 85-926, 109
P.L. 88-164, 109
P.L. 89-10, 109
P.L. 89-313, 109
P.L. 89-750, 109
P.L. 90-248, 110
P.L. 90-538, 110
P.L. 92-924, 110
P.L. 93-112, 110
P.L. 93-348, 112
P.L. 93-644, 110
P.L. 94-142, 34, 110–12, 188
  and assessments, 195
  funds for, and state policy, 115
  and IEPs, 259
  and parental involvement, 158, 174, 235
  rights protected by, 119, 120
P.L. 94-149, 249
P.L. 98-199, 110, 111–12, 113, 115
  and parental involvement, 158, 235

Quality-of-life, projects to change, 87–89

Referral form, 251 *fig.*
Referral sources, coordination with, 250
Reflexive behaviors, 166
Reform, early childhood education as means of, 35
Rehabilitation Act of 1973, 110, 158
Rehabilitation Services Administration, 115
Reproductive risk, 7–8
Research, 10–13
  animal, 20–22
  need to be aware of, 10–11

and protection of human subjects, 112–13
Residential treatment, study of Down Syndrome children in, 67
Response, 305
  in ARC equation, 328
Revised Gesell Developmental Schedules, 252, 256, 358
Reynell Developmental Language Scales, 71
Rights, for the handicapped, 103–105, 118–24. *See also* Legislation
  to appropriate education, 119–20
  to appropriate placement, 120–21
  and civil rights movement, 104
  to due process, 121–22
  and early court cases, 104–105
  evolution of, 103–105
  to medical treatment, 122–24
  guaranteed by P.L. 94-142, 111

Scales of Early Communication Skills, 78
Scheduling, 222–23, 274–77
  of instructional activities, 323–24
  of transition points, 324
  for unexpected events, 324–25
Screening, 250–51, 337–45
  criterion-referenced tests, 339, 342–43, 344–45
  defined, 337
  norm-referenced tests, 338–39, 340, 343–44
Secondary disabilities, prevention of, 50–51
Self-care, in developmental curriculum, 307
Self-control, development of, 140
Sensorimotor period, 139, 166
Separation issues, 43, 136, 170
Sequenced Inventory of Communication Development (SICD), 340

437

Subject Index

Severely/profoundly retarded, study on program with, 74
Sewall Early Education Developmental Profiles (SEED), 342
Shaping, 330
Skill acquisition, 129
Skill theory, 211
Smiling behavior, in Down Syndrome babies, 171–72
Social change, and early childhood education, 35
Social-communication emphasis, in curriculum, 301–302
Social development
 and communication, 137
 in infants, 134
 in toddlers, 139
Social environment
 importance of considering, 373
 infant interaction with, 132
Socialization model, of affective development, 166
Social responsiveness, of infants, 130
Social skills, in developmental curriculum, 307, 308
Societal benefits, 188
Sociocultural factors. *See also* Cultural factors; Environment
 importance of, 130
 and organism-environment interaction, 208
Space, use of, in engineering the classroom, 316–18
Specialists
 roles of, 238–39, 241, 243–44
 seeking and coordinating input from, 232–33
Spina bifida, 146
Staff, management of, 322–25
 and classroom schedules, 323–24
 and handling unexpected events, 324–25
 and home-based programs, 325
 preparation for IEP and FPA meetings, 261–62
 training and deployment of, 194–96
 and transition schedules, 324

Staff meetings, 244, 274
 scheduling, 222–23
Stages of sensorimotor intelligence in the child from birth to two years, 342
Standardized tests. *See* Norm-referenced tests
Stanford-Binet Intelligence Scale, 66, 67 *fig.*, 71, 72, 76, 77, 81, 84, 87, 340
Start-up. *See* Program start-up
State policy, 115–17
 and local policy, 117–18
Structured intervention, study of, with Down Syndrome children, 68–69
Student Progress Record, 75, 76, 83
Synchrony, 50–51, 168–70
Synthesizer approach, 232–34, 241–44

TARC Assessment System, 339
Target populations, 142–49
 assessment of, 341, 343
Tay Sach's disease, 145
Teenage mothers, in quality-of-life project, 88
Teratogens, 147
Tests, 255–59
 family-impact, 258–59
 program relevant, 257–58
 standardized, 255–56, 256 *tab.*
 for screening, 338–45
Thalidomide, 147
Thought processes, development of, 139, 140
Timing. *See* Synchrony
Toddlers, development of, 137–39
Topics in Early Childhood Special Education, 12
Toys. *See* Equipment
Tracking systems, court ruling on, 104
Training, of personnel and staff, 194–95, 244–45, 377
Training, of children, 214, 230
Training Objectives (TO)
 and analysis of progress, 361–62
 as critical functions, 309
 in developmental curriculum, 304–305, 308

 in IEP-FPA, 262–63
 in instructional strategy, 329–30
 and measuring progress, 354–55, 357–60
Transactional model, of development, 129, 132
Transactional perspective, 6–8, 9 *fig.*, 207–10
 extended to whole family, 210
 of program philosophy, 207–10, 209 *fig.*
Transitions
 managing, in classroom, 279
 to other programs, 293–95
 scheduling, in classroom, 324
Translators, need for, of research and clinical findings, 12
Trauma, of having handicapped child, 155–57, 170–71, 172
Turner's syndrome, 145

Uniform Performance Assessment System (UPAS), 74, 75, 256, 258, 343
University Affiliated Facilities (UAF), 109

Verbal interaction, programs to improve, 86–87
Verbal Interactional Project, 86
Visual discrimination, in infants, 130, 134
Visual impairments, 147
Visually reinforced infant speech discrimination (VRISD), 11–12
Vocal behavior, in infants, 134–35, 135–36
Vocational Rehabilitation Act, 188
Vulpe Assessment Battery, 343

Wash out, 25, 46, 89
The War on Poverty, 36
Wechsler Preschool Scale, 81
Willowbrook case, 105, 106
Word-object association, in developmental study, 6
WW II, and history of nursery schools, 35
Wyatt v. Stickney, 105, 106, 120

JUL 21 1992

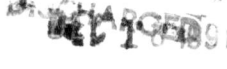

AUG 2 0 1993